Fifth Edition

Infants & Toddlers
Curriculum and Teaching

Dedication

Michael A. Watson

The fifth edition of *Infants & Toddlers Curriculum and Teaching* is dedicated to the memory of my husband, Dr. Michael A. Watson, who died after injuries sustained in an auto accident in South Africa, December 28, 2001.

Michael was his work. His professional influence was like ripples on water. Years of training in both educational and clinical psychology allowed him to create the National Parenting Scales, Focal Attention Training programs, Instructional Press and Institute, Parenting Web sites, Professional Forensic Group, Disease Prevention Services, and, of course, DouWat Enterprises.

Michael loved babies and never underestimated them. Children of all ages were a major part of his private practice. He was a man of many names—one six-year-old affectionately called him "Watty." Only one short year ago, Michael wrote to the family of a dear friend and colleague who had passed away, "The only thing I can figure is that God needed a good shrink." Well, Mike, the only thing we can figure is that Dori needed help.

So to Mickey, Son, Mash, Mikey, Daddy Mike, Dad, Dr. Mike, Hey Doc, Professor, Dear Friend, and Mike, with much sadness we continue to talk to you and say "keep the bench warm." We who loved you know you will stay in our hearts forever!

With much love and affection,
Linda, Marcus, Mindy, and Michele

Join us on the web at
EarlyChildEd.delmar.com

Fifth Edition

Infants & Toddlers
Curriculum and Teaching

Based on the CDA Competency Standards

Linda Douville-Watson, R.N., M.S.

Dr. Michael A. Watson, Ed.D.

LaVisa Cam Wilson

THOMSON

* **DELMAR LEARNING**™

Australia   Canada   Mexico   Singapore   Spain   United Kingdom   United States

THOMSON

———✦———™

DELMAR LEARNING

Infants & Toddlers: Curriculum and Teaching, 5e
Linda Douville-Watson, Michael A. Watson, and LaVisa Cam Wilson

Business Unit Executive Director:
Susan L. Simpfenderfer

Acquisitions Editor:
Erin O'Connor

Developmental Editor:
Melissa Riveglia

Executive Production Manager:
Wendy A. Troeger

Production Editor:
Joy Kocsis

Technology Project Manager:
Joseph Saba

Executive Marketing Manager:
Donna J. Lewis

Channel Manager:
Nigar Hale

Cover Design:
Kristina Almquist

Composition:
Publishers' Design and Production Services, Inc.

For permission to use material from this text or product, contact us by
Tel (800) 730-2214
Fax (800) 730-2215
www.thomsonrights.com

Library of Congress Cataloging-in-Publication Data
Douville-Watson, Linda.
    Infants & toddlers : curriculum and teaching. — 5th ed. / Linda Douville-Watson, Michael A. Watson.
        p. cm.
"Based on the CDA competency standards."
Includes bibliographical references and index.
ISBN 0-7668-4284-3
    1. Child care—United States. 2. Infants—United States.
3. Toddlers—United States. 5. Family day care—United States.
I. Title: Infants and toddlers. II. Watson, Michael A. III. Title.

HQ778.63. D68 2002
362.71'071—dc21   2002019284

NOTICE TO THE READER

Publisher does not warrant or guarantee any of the products described herein or perform any independent analysis in connection with any of the product information contained herein. Publisher does not assume, and expressly disclaims, any obligation to obtain and include information other than that provided to it by the manufacturer.

The reader is expressly warned to consider and adopt all safety precautions that might be indicated by the activities described herein and to avoid all potential hazards. By following the instructions contained herein, the reader willingly assumes all risks in connection with such instructions.

The publisher makes no representation or warranties of any kind, including but not limited to, the warranties of fitness for particular purpose or merchantability, nor are any such representations implied with respect to the material set forth herein, and the publisher takes no responsibility with respect to such material. The publisher shall not be liable for any special, consequential, or exemplary damages resulting, in whole or part, from the readers' use of, or reliance upon, this material.

Contents

PART III   MATCHING CAREGIVER STRATEGIES AND CHILD DEVELOPMENT   287

Preface

This book is intended to guide the reader through the skills necessary to provide high-quality care for infants and toddlers in any child care setting. Standards based on current research and knowledge for Infant/Toddler Caregivers are used throughout the book. Appropriate individual techniques and activities are provided for each child. Child care specialists, administrators, and parents will find practical information that can be put to immediate use to promote the highest-quality child care possible for all children.

Text Organization

We have maintained the same basic structure that previous readers have found helpful of presenting material as it relates to current CDA Goals and Objectives. Red CDA symbols are listed to the left of the text to guide the reader according to national standards for caregiving. The book is divided into three parts.

■ **Part I.** *Infant and Toddler Development and Caregiver Preparation.*

This section presents an overview of the history, theories, and strategies in the fields of child development and care to prepare the reader for certification and for the skills necessary to competently care for infants and toddlers. *Chapter 1* provides both historical and current overviews of environmental, social, cultural, and governmental influences in child care. *Chapter 2* ideal caregiving sets a standard of care and presents theories and definitions of development, learning, and teaching, as well as how these can be applied to enhance the development and care of infants and toddlers. *Chapter 3*, a new chapter, creates a framework for growth and development in five major areas from birth to preschool. *Chapter 4* presents the Master Tools of caregiving: Attention, Approval, and Affection as a model of conscious caregiving, combining practical principles and techniques from current theories and research in the field. *Chapter 5*, another new chapter, delineates specific functional tools the caregiver needs to enhance development and learning and establishes the structure for providing helpful activities and experiences to children.

■ **Part II.** *Establishing a Positive Learning Environment.*

Four chapters provide the reader with definitions, knowledge, and skills necessary to competently care for infants and toddlers in the home, school, or child care setting. *Chapter 6* provides specific applications of the skills necessary to effectively communicate with children, parents, and staff and gives specific examples of the skills necessary, including working with teenage parents. *Chapter 7* is devoted to creating and using space for conducting care in a variety of child care settings. *Chapter 8* covers all the standards and principles necessary to ensure safe and effective indoor and outdoor settings for children and presents the most common safety issues for children. *Chapter 9* presents practical techniques for designing curriculum and planning, structuring, and implementing a program of care that enhances the development of all children in care, including children with special needs.

■ **Part III.** *Matching Caregiver Strategies with Developmental Levels.*

Seven developmental levels are defined, ranging from birth through 36 months of age, and tasks, materials, and specific activities to enhance development are provided in *Chapters 10 through 16*. Developmental Profiles and Prescriptions are provided to establish the structure within which specific activities are accomplished, so that the caregiver has constant awareness of goals and growth in the major areas of development. This practical section provides specific techniques, activities, and solutions to most of the common problems confronted in the growth and development of infants and toddlers.

Major Revisions in the Fifth Edition

New chapters on specific developmental patterns (Chapter 3), the master tools the caregiver uses for conscious care (Chapter 4), and effective tools for child care and development (Chapter 5) have added a new "heart and soul" to this edition, which makes it a more functional, how-to text of child care. We have included hundreds of new Web sites from the recent explosion of information in human learning and development. With the advent of the Internet and availability of worldwide research and information, selecting the best information in child care, parenting, and child development was a major challenge in writing this edition. We have presented the most representative and practical information on topics, with the goal of giving the reader functional information and techniques to use in actual care settings. Since writing the Fourth Edition, social policy, cultural diversity in child care and development, and parental assessment and education have become major areas of importance. New sections have been added to inform the reader on these important topics. Major content revisions in this edition also include the following.

■ Chapter 1 includes changes in environment, social policies, and governmental factors that affect child care, such as poverty, HIV, and health care.

■ Major developmental and learning theorists and their practical contributions have been added to Chapter 2.

■ Chapter 3 provides specific developmental patterns in young children.

■ Chapter 4 defines caregiver self-health and powerful tools for positive interactions with children.

■ Issues related to cultural diversity are enlarged on, and specific strategies and activities for appreciating and celebrating cultural identities and differences are included. A Celebration of Life Calendar is provided in Chapter 9 and Appendix D to help children experience holidays from many cultures.

■ Sections have been added to help caregivers provide care to infants and toddlers with special needs.

■ Definitions of the terms curriculum and teaching are provided as guides.

Instructional Features

- Chapter overviews, behavioral objectives, and a specific chapter outline are provided for each chapter.
- New Key Terms used in each chapter are listed for easy reference, and important terms are presented in color within chapters.
- New case studies present real-life examples of concepts and principles discussed in each chapter.
- Helpful Web sites are provided for every chapter.
- The Glossary has been enlarged to cover definitions of terms as they apply to child care and development.
- References, student activities, and questions for review are provided at the end of each chapter.
- Sample Developmental Profiles and Prescriptions are provided for each age from birth to 36 months, and behavioral descriptions explaining Prescriptions accompany each.
- Numerous pictures and illustrations are included throughout to illustrate the concepts and materials presented.
- A comprehensive Developmental Prescription of behavioral expectations for children from birth to 36 months for each of the five major areas of development is provided to assist the caregiver in establishing Developmental Profiles and Developmental Prescriptions for each child in care.
- Complete current CDA Competency Standards for Infant/Toddler Caregivers in Center-Based Programs is provided to assist caregivers in awareness and preparation for CDA certification.
- The text is comprehensive so that professionals can use it to teach the teacher all essential skills necessary to function at nationally accepted standards of quality.
- The level of the language used is easy to follow and offers practical examples for self-study by new caregivers in training.

I would welcome questions or discussions on any of the topics that are covered in the book.

Linda Douville-Watson
energynurse1@yahoo.com

Ancillaries

Instructor's Manual

The instructor's manual includes activities, test questions, and class outlines for instructors of classes on infant and toddler care and development.

Computerized Test Bank

The computerized test bank is comprised of true/false, multiple choice, short answer, and completion questions for each chapter. Instructors can use the computerized test bank software to create sample quizzes for students. Refer to the CTB User's Guide for more information on how to create and post quizzes to your school's Internet or Intranet server. Students may also access sample quizzes from the Online Resources™ to accompany this fifth edition of *Infants & Toddlers: Curriculum and Teaching*.

Online Resources™

The Online Resources™ to accompany the fifth edition of *Infants & Toddlers: Curriculum and Teaching* is your link to early childhood education on the Internet. The Online Resources™ contain many features to help focus your understanding of infants and toddlers.

The Online Resources™ icon appears at the end of each chapter to prompt you to go on-line and take advantage of the many features provided.

You can find Online Resources™ at www.earlychilded.delmar.com

Acknowledgments

This fifth edition has been the most challenging revision yet because of the explosion of information available and the task of culling through it. We gratefully thank the following people for their support.

Michele, Milinda, and Marcus, who have given us back love and treasured life experiences a hundredfold for the caregiving we have provided them.

Erin O'Connor, our Acquisitions Editor, Melissa Riveglia, Developmental Editor, and Gail Farrar, for their understanding, patience, and opportunity to provide this fifth edition.

Geraldine Linton, for her special guidance.

Dr. Pamela Gallagher, for her work with cleft palate children and her insights.

Cecilia McCarton, for her continued work with special children and families.

Eileen Enriquez, for her reliable support and assistance in typing.

All of our reviewers, whose valued comments added insights.

Davia Allen, PhD, Western Carolina University, Cullowhee, North Carolina

Nancy Carlson, MA, Orange County Community College, Middletown, New York

Teresa Frazier, Thomas Nelson Community College, Suffolk, Virginia

Marsha Hawley, MEd, Erikson Institute, Chicago, Illinois

Judith Lindman, MEd, Rochester Community and Technical Colleges, Rochester, Minnesota

Margaret McGuire, EdD, Sam Houston State University, Huntsville, Texas

Amy Page, BS, Moultrie Technical College, Moultrie, Georgia

Becky Reid, SUNY Cobleskill, Cobleskill, New York

Jill Uhlenberg, PhD, University of Northern Iowa, Cedar Falls, Iowa

Linda Douville-Watson
Dr. Mike Watson

The CDA Competency Standards for Infant/Toddler Child Development Specialists

Competency Standards for child development specialists who specialize in infant/toddler development and care have been established by Child Development Associates (CDA), an association that uses six behavioral Goals and thirteen Objectives to evaluate child development specialist performance. A nationally recognized CDA Credential is awarded child development specialists who successfully complete a rigorous assessment based on these standards.

Whether you as the reader are a child development specialist in education, an early childhood educator, parent, or class instructor, it is essential to familiarize yourself with the CDA Goals and Objectives listed on the following page, and with the complete CDA Standards in Appendix C before proceeding with the text.

This book guides the reader through the national standards for competent caregiving by listing specific goals and objectives in shaded oval symbols to the left of related text. For example, the text on theories of child development relates to CDA GOAL VI. (Commitment to Professionalism)–13 (Professionalism).

Once the reader is familiar with the CDA Goals and Objectives, the text will serve as a guide to learn and practice the skills necessary to function according to national standards as a competent child development specialist for infants and toddlers.

Instructors will also find the Goals and Objectives a useful instructional tool for formal child development specialist preparation. Specific text related to the goals and objectives can provide the instructor with a structure for discussion, organization, and assessment of the skills and information necessary for competent caregiving.

CDA COMPETENCY GOALS AND DEFINITIONS REFERENCE GUIDE

I.   **To establish and maintain a safe, healthy learning environment**
  1. **Safe:** Candidate provides a safe environment to prevent and reduce injuries.
  2. **Healthy:** Candidate promotes good health and nutrition and provides an environment that contributes to the prevention of illness.
  3. **Learning Environment:** Candidate uses space, relationships, materials, and routines as resources for constructing an interesting, secure, and enjoyable environment that encourages play, exploration, and learning.

II.   **To advance physical and intellectual competence.**
  4. **Physical:** Candidate provides a variety of equipment, activities, and opportunities to promote the physical development of children.

5. **Cognitive:** Candidate provides activities and opportunities that encourage curiosity, exploration, and problem-solving appropriate to the developmental levels and learning styles of children.
6. **Communication:** Candidate actively communicates with children and provides opportunities and support for children to understand, acquire, and use verbal and nonverbal means of communicating thoughts and feelings.
7. **Creative:** Candidate provides opportunities that stimulate children to play with sound, rhythm, language, materials, space, and ideas in individual ways and to express their creative abilities.

III. **To support social and emotional development and provide positive guidance.**

8. **Self:** Candidate provides physical and emotional security for each child and helps each child to know, accept, and take pride in himself or herself and to develop a sense of independence.
9. **Social:** Candidate helps each child feel accepted in the group, helps children learn to communicate and get along with others, and encourages feelings of empathy and mutual respect among children and adults.
10. **Guidance:** Candidate provides a supportive environment in which children can begin to learn and practice appropriate and acceptable behaviors as individuals and as a group.

IV. **To establish positive and productive relationships with families.**

11. **Families:** Candidate maintains an open, friendly, and cooperative relationship with each child's family, encourages their involvement in the program, and supports the child's relationship with his or her family.

V. **To ensure a well-run, purposeful program responsive to particular needs.**

12. **Program Management:** Candidate is a manager who uses all available resources to ensure an effective operation. The Candidate is a competent organizer, planner, record keeper, communicator, and a cooperative coworker.

VI. **To maintain a commitment to professionalism.**

13. **Professionalism:** Candidate makes decisions based on knowledge of early childhood theories and practices. Candidate promotes quality in child care services. Candidate takes advantage of opportunities to improve competence, both for personal and professional growth for the benefit of children and families.

These competency goals form a foundation for a solid developmental curriculum. This book elaborates each functional area into a comprehensive curriculum for preparation as a child care professional.

About the Authors

Linda Douville-Watson is a Master's level nurse with 30 years of medical and child development and care experience. She is a trained CDA Representative. She has an appropriate practical approach, as well as respect for the child as an individual. She is author of the third edition of *Family Actualization through Research and Education (F.A.R.E.)*, and a comprehensive parent training program, *The 3A's of Childcare*. She is past president of Workplace Childcare, Inc. and is responsible for designing and implementing award winning turn-key operational corporate child care centers and staff development in New York and Maryland. She is presently an adjunct professor of psychology at Nassau Community College.

Michael A. Watson was a Clinical Child Psychologist who specialized in learning and development for 30 years. Dr. Watson taught and was a school psychologist in child care centers, preschools, district-wide special education programs, and elementary and high schools. A professor of psychology at St. John's University and Hofstra University doctoral programs, he published numerous research papers and articles on development and learning and a nationally standardized test (the WALDO Developmental Learning Skills Tests. Dr. Watson co-authored *The National Parenting Scales: A Comprehensive Measure of Parent Skills Using the CDA Standards*. He and his wife Linda co-authored many materials for Disease Prevention Services, Inc.

LaVisa Cam Wilson taught in child care centers, kindergarten, and first grade. She was a professor of Early Childhood Education at Auburn University and served as a Child Development Training Project Director. Dr. Wilson served on the Board of the Day Care Council of America, and on the Board of Directors of the National Child Care Association for Childhood Education.

PART I

Infant and Toddler Development and Caregiver Preparation

Since publication of the previous edition, an information explosion in child development and caregiving has continued. As a result, caregivers-in-training need to learn more theories, principles, and skills to keep pace with the growing status of their profession.

The CDA Standards require that caregivers learn to take good care of themselves, as well as children, and to be aware of the needs of the child, the care setting, the family, the community, and society as a whole. This section provides the history and current trends in care, theories and principles of child development, and a structure and model of caregiving that helps prepare the caregiver for the challenging and rewarding profession of child care.

This edition includes a new Chapter 3, on developmental patterns during early childhood. It should be used in conjunction with Chapter 4, which covers effective tools for the care and development of children. By completing assessments using Developmental Profiles and Prescriptions, the child care specialist will possess a powerful structure to use in caring for children.

When you finish this section, you will have the knowledge and principles necessary to effectively care for, and enhance the development of, each child through your direct interactions with them. The following sections build on this base of knowledge to give you all the specific skills, techniques, tools, and activities needed to confidently function as a professional.

History and Trends in Infant and Toddler Care and Development

1

Objectives

After reading this chapter, you should be able to:

- Define the terms *mobile infant, young infant, toddler, preschooler, curriculum, teaching,* and *guide.*
- Describe theories of child development, including the Ecological Systems Theory.
- Describe Bronfenbrenner's theory as it relates to current child care trends.
- Explain the use of mentors in current child care training.
- Outline the major historical and current trends in child care.

Chapter Outline

INTRODUCTION

To understand the history and current trends in child care and development we must define some of the basic terms used in the field. Definitions of the terms used in the title of this book give us a start in understanding child development and care.

Infants and **toddlers** are children from birth through 36 months of age. Three general age groups within this range are commonly used: children from birth to eight months old are called **young infants**; those age 9 through 17 months are called **mobile infants**; and children 18 through 36 months of age are called **toddlers** (CDA Standards, Appendix C).

Curricula, for the purposes of this text, are structured activities and experiences provided to infants and toddlers for the purposes of stimulating and enhancing growth and development. The standards for determining specific activities and experiences ranging from simple to complex are the behaviors provided in the Developmental Prescriptions listed in Appendix A.

Teaching is used to mean planned presentation of activities and experiences with the goal of motivating infants and toddlers to learn and develop in five major Developmental Areas.

Guide means to direct toward some desirable end. This book is intended to direct the reader in learning skills and information necessary to effectively and efficiently care for infants and toddlers in ways that enhance the growth and development of each child in care.

Caregiver and **Early Childhood Educator** are used interchangeably to refer to professionals who specialize in the direct care for, development of, or research with young children. Because the field is growing so rapidly, other terms also used in the literature to describe professionals include Early Childcare (or Childhood) Specialist, Child Development Associate (CDA), Childcare Worker, and Child Development Specialist (or Researcher).

With these terms in mind, we now turn our attention to the history and current trends in infant and toddler care and development.

HISTORICAL PERSPECTIVES ON DEVELOPMENT AND CARE

Past Theories and Views

Before the Reformation in Sixteenth-Century Europe, little importance was placed on children or child care. Children were considered little adults cared for by the females in the family. With the Reformation and the Puritan belief in **original sin** came harsh, restrictive child-rearing practices and the idea that the depraved child needed to be tamed (Shahar, 1990).

The Seventeenth-Century Enlightenment brought new theories of human dignity and respect. Young children were viewed much more humanely. For example, John Locke, a British philosopher, advanced the theory that a child is a **tabula rasa**, or blank slate. According to his theory, children were not basically evil but were completely molded and formed by their early experiences with the adults around them (Locke, 1690/1892).

Another important philosopher of the Eighteenth Century, Jean-Jacques Rousseau, viewed young children as **noble savages** who are naturally born with a sense of right and wrong and an innate ability for orderly, healthy growth (1955). His theory was the first child-centered approach, and it advanced two important concepts still accepted today: the idea of **stages** of child development and **maturation**, which means a naturally unfolding course of growth and development.

During the late 1800s Charles Darwin's theories of **natural selection** and **survival of the fittest** strongly influenced ideas on child development and care (1936/1859). Darwin's research on many animal species led him to hypothesize that all animals were descendants of a few common ancestors. He believed that the development of children followed the same general plan as the evolution of the species. While this concept was later proven inaccurate, his careful observations of child behaviors resulted in the birth of the science of child study.

At the turn of the Twentieth Century, G. Stanley Hall was inspired by Darwin. Hall worked with one of Darwin's students, Arnold Gesell, to advance the **evolutionary theory** that child development is genetically determined and happens automatically. Hall and Gesell are considered founders of the child study movement because of their **normative approach** of observing large numbers of children to establish average or normal expectations (Berk, 1997). At the same time in France, Alfred Binet was establishing the first operational definition of intelligence by using the normative approach to standardize his intelligence test, which is still sometimes used with young children (Siegler, 1992).

It was not until Sigmund Freud postulated his **Psychoanalytic Theory** of personality development in the early 1900s that child development and care became a legitimate discipline (1938). For the first time, Freud explained that infants and toddlers are unique individuals, whose earliest experiences and relationships form the foundation for self-concept, self-esteem, and personality, and why we experience life as adults the way that we do.

A proponent of Freud, Erik Erikson, expanded Freud's concepts into what became known as the **Psychosocial Theory** of child development. Erikson's theory, which is still used in child care today, predicted several stages of development, including the development of trust, autonomy, identity, and intimacy. How these stages are dealt with by child development specialists determines individual capacity to contribute to society and experience a happy, successful life (1950). Erikson's stages are presented in Chapter 2.

While Freud and his disciples greatly influenced the fields of child development and care, a parallel approach was being studied, called **behaviorism**. John Watson, who is considered the father of behaviorism, was influenced by a Russian physiologist named Ivan Pavlov and his scientific observations of animal **responses** to various environmental **stimuli** (Horowitz, 1992). In a historic experiment, Watson taught an 11-month-old named Albert to fear a neutral stimulus (a soft white rat) by presenting the rat several times accompanied by loud noises. Watson and his followers used experiments in **classical conditioning** to promote the idea that the environment is the primary factor determining the growth and development of children.

B. F. Skinner and coauthor Belmont expanded Watson's theories of classical conditioning to include his **operant conditioning theory** (1993). Skinner clearly demonstrated that child behaviors can be increased or decreased by applying **positive reinforcers** (rewards), such as food and praise, and **negative reinforcers** (punishment), such as criticism and withdrawal of attention.

During the 1950s, **social learning theories** became popular. Proponents of these theories, led by Albert Bandura, accepted the principles of behaviorism and enlarged on conditioning to include social influences such as **modeling limitation** and **observational learning** to explain how children develop (Grusec, 1992).

The theorist who has influenced the modern fields of child development and care more than any other is Jean Piaget. Piaget's **cognitive-developmental theory** predicts that children construct knowledge and awareness through manipulation and exploration of the environment, and that cognitive development occurs through observable stages (Beilin, 1992). Piaget's stages of cognitive development have stimulated more research on children than any other theory, and his influences have helped child development specialists view young children as active participants in their own growth and development. Piaget's contributions are clear and practical applications. However, recent research in **information processing theory** have brought some of his ideas into question.

Past Needs and Trends

Whereas cultural and social expectations for child care roughly follow historical theories and views of child development, specific social and cultural influences, including religion, governmental policy, war, and economic demands, have also affected the settings and approaches to child development and care.

Throughout history, the care and development of infants and toddlers has been the responsibility of the primary family unit and extended family, which often included members of the local community as well as blood relatives (Figure 1–1). Even

Figure 1–1 A grandparent can share in caring for an infant.

in cultures where governmental or religious needs required older children to be taken away from the family for training or education, infants and toddlers remained with the women and girls of the home and community.

Before the Reformation, child care was primarily the responsibility of the women in the family unit. However, since social groups were small (for example, tribe, village, hamlet), children were often cared for by all the women of the community, and it was common practice for one family to take over care of another family's children whose parents had died.

With increases in world population and the emphasis on religious education brought about by the Reformation, the Church established orphanages and schools so that young children were cared for in institutional settings outside the family for the first time. In cultures in which the population remained small or in which religious training was not a major influence, the family remained responsible for early child development and care.

Until the beginning of the Twentieth Century, the only exceptions to family care were extreme situations such as war, famine, or epidemics, at which times infants and toddlers had to be cared for in groups because a large number of people had died.

The industrialization of the major world cultures created a change in the social belief that only mothers should provide total care for young children. In the early Twentieth Century in the United States, fewer mothers of infants and toddlers were in the workforce than there are today. Mothers who worked in jobs to which they could not take their babies counted on older children, female relatives, or neighbors to care for their young. Professional child care settings as we know them today did not exist.

One factor that affected the number of working mothers was the prevalence of stereotyped male and female roles. The social norm was that the husband provided for the family's financial needs and the wife assumed all domestic responsibilities, including cooking, sewing, housework, and child care. Women who worked outside the home were often considered "out of place."

Another influence on the number of working mothers with infants and toddlers was the prevailing belief that only the mother could provide proper care for young children. A sibling or relative was thought to be an acceptable substitute for the mother, but the belief generally was that another person could not meet the needs of infants or toddlers for very long. The mother-child attachment was thought to be crucial, and it would be weakened if the infant was cared for primarily by someone else. The idea was that only the mother bonded well enough with her infant or toddler to meet the child's emotional needs. The two world wars brought more mothers into the workplace and changed the stereotype that only mothers could adequately care for young children.

Early research on child care was partly responsible for the social belief that only mothers could adequately care for young children. Institutionalized infants and toddlers provided the most easily accessible population for child study, so early research tended to concentrate on the effects of infant care by people other than the mother in hospitals and long-term care facilities. The results of this type of research generally found that the mother-child attachment was weakened in the situations studied (Bowlby, 1951; Goldfarb, 1943; Spitz, 1945).

CURRENT PERSPECTIVES ON DEVELOPMENT AND CARE

Current Theories and Views

New theories, research, and effective approaches to enhance the growth and development of young children are still being discovered. Among these exciting developments are information processing theories, ethnology, ecological systems theory, and sociocultural theory.

A recent approach, resulting from developments during the 1970s in human learning research and technology from computer design, is information processing theory. This approach involves the analysis of **sensory input**, the organization of information through **discrimination** and **association**, storage of information through memory, and the output of information through **verbal and motor responses** (Watson, 1972). Information processing theories can be viewed as symbol manipulating systems through which information flows (Klahr, 1992). Michael A. Watson's information processing theory is presented in detail in Chapter 2 as a basis of understanding the essential Developmental Learning Skills that young children use to perceive the world.

Another approach that has gained more acceptance in child care is called **ethnology**. It was developed by two zoologists, Konrad Lorenz and Niko Tinbergen (Dewsbury, 1992). *Ethnology* refers to behavior patterns that promote survival, thereby following Darwin's theories. Two major concepts from ethnology that have been applied to early childhood are imprinting and critical periods of development. Through their studies of animal behavior, Lorenz and Tinbergen found that baby birds closely follow their mother (or mother substitute) and imitate her movements. Because this imprinting behavior occurs during a specific, limited period, the concept of "critical periods" for the development of skills and abilities has been applied to early childhood development with limited value.

A recent theory of child development is the **ecological systems theory** developed by Urie Bronfenbrenner, an American psychologist (1995). Bronfenbrenner has expanded the view of influences on young children by hypothesizing four nested structures that affect development. At the innermost level is the **microsystem**, comprised of patterns of interactions within the immediate surroundings of the child. This system includes parents, child development specialists, direct influences on the child, and the child's influence on the immediate environment. The **mesosystem** is the next level of influence and includes school, day care, neighborhood, and local culture and community. The **exosystem** includes influences with which the child is not directly involved that affect development and care, such as parent education, parent workplace, and health and social services. The **macrosystem** consists of the values, laws, resources, and customs of the general culture in which a child is raised. This theory has wide applications in understanding and categorizing the factors that affect child care.

A final theory that is finding application as the world becomes a cross-cultural community is the **sociocultural theory**. A Russian psychologist, Lev Semenovich Vygotsky, hypothesized that culture, meaning the values, beliefs, and customs of a social group, is passed on to the next generation through social interactions between children and their elders (1986). Cross-cultural research has supported this theory through findings that young children from various cultures develop unique skills and abilities that are not present in other cultures (Berk, 1997).

It must be kept in mind that the United States is the world leader in the fields of child development and care, and we cannot assume that research findings on developmental skills and abilities from primarily Caucasian American children directly apply to other cultures outside, or subcultures within, the United States. Only through taking a world view of child care based on universal aspects of development will we be able to determine the skills, abilities, and practices that optimally enhance the growth and development of infants and toddlers all over the world.

Current Needs and Trends

Current child care trends are discussed within the framework of the Ecological System of Urie Bronfenbrenner: microsystem, mesosystem, exosystem, and macrosystem (1995). In this system, human relationships are described as bidirectional and reciprocal. *Relating* is the act of being with someone and sharing the same space and setting, expressing needs and accepting responsibility for interacting with each other.

Respecting children as equals is also expressed by other authorities in child development; such as Magda Gerber, who feels that one of the most important aspects of relating to infants is a child development specialist's respect for the child as an individual. Linda Douville-Watson's theory also emphasizes the child development specialist's self-health, awareness of self, and consciousness of care, which allows him or her to be mindful of positive intentions toward the child and reflects clear thought and good planning, resulting in positive outcomes for both.

Trends in the microsystem involve effects that adults and children have on each other. For example, an adult who consciously uses attention, approval, and affection with children elicits a positive response from children. Any third party who is present may also be affected. How this person is affected is determined by whether or not the reciprocal relationship is positive or negative. If the people interacting are supportive, the quality of the relationship is enhanced. An example of how a child development specialist can enhance an interaction as a third party is explained in detail later in the text under positive perspective.

The microsystem is the closest system to the child. It contains the child, the immediate nuclear family, and others directly relating to the child. Additionally, there are more children in subsidized care in the United States with many vastly different backgrounds than ever before. Between 1988 and 1993, the number of children in child care increased nearly 1.5 million to a total of more than 10 million (Casper, 1996). These children represent widespread cultural differences in customs and parenting styles. Many come from families who are learning to define their own traditions. Some families depend on the early child care setting to introduce them to their own rich heritages. Respectful, mindful child care specialists and teachers are necessary in all child care settings to promote interest, acceptance, and pride with children and parents.

The mesosystem includes child care settings. In the past, it was thought that the immediate family (microsystem) reflected the greatest single impact on a child's life. However, with so many more people entering the workforce today, the need for child care is so great that this is no longer true. Many young children spend more waking hours with child development specialists than they do with their primary families, which is of great concern to many child care experts.

Magda Gerber and Dr. Ron Lally voiced the concern that "rapid turnover in caregivers due to burnout, inconsistency, instability, including elementary schools, are not meeting children's individual needs as well as parental needs for support" (Hand, 1994). Magda Gerber is a national leader in infant care, and Dr. Ron Lally is a national expert in training. They suggested that "babies and young children need to be in the smallest groups possible." This is thought necessary because young children need consistency and a sense of permanence. Many people feel that public schools could do more to support their communities' young families. The following model is an example of a school program that demonstrates Bronfenbrenner's second level of Ecological System Theory, which states that the mesosystem fosters children's development by encompassing connections between home, school, child care center, and neighborhood.

Dr. Elliott Landon, Superintendent of Schools for Long Beach, New York, was responsible for establishing a model child care program within the public school system. Dr. Landon said, "We have a partnership between the community and parents." Dr. Landon's commitment demonstrates how the "parent-child and child development specialist-child relationships are likely to support development when there are links, in the form of an exchange of information, between home and day care settings" (Figure 1–2) (Berk, 1997).

Another current trend at the mesosystem level is the use of mentors. A mentor is described in *Webster's Dictionary* as an "experienced and prudent advisor." Mentors have been around for years, and are considered the best in their field. These kindhearted coworkers have been on the job for a long time, are committed to their profession, and help newcomers learn the ropes (Figure 1–3). They usually did all this without any additional compensation or recognition. The time they put into the job actually far exceeded their expected hours, and the extra work they performed was often excessive. In the child care field, workers were expected to work hard and extend themselves on behalf of the children. Such expert help, when available, was highly valued by coworkers.

Figure 1–2 School-based child care offers a familiar place in which to grow up.

In the 1980s, in response to the shortage of funds, isolated districts, and lack of trained personnel, the professional mentor became a creative answer for extending child care resources. Highly trained, experienced teacher-consultants were officially introduced as professionals to facilitate child care specialists with in-service and hands-on training and support.

Mentors are the cream of the crop: experienced, well-trained, and eager to share, teach, console, and broaden the horizons of newly appointed child development specialists. Mentors help with the frustration of adjusting to the integration of learned skills. They are different from supervisors in that they are normally not paid by the same source as teachers and are not bound by the same responsibilities as a supervisor, including promoting, hiring, and firing. Mentors are revered for their successful outcomes. Their confidential assessments do not involve their own continued employment, so they can help their proteges strive to reach their greatest potential as child development specialists, teachers, and decision makers without fear.

The mentor helps establish mutual goals and expectations without involvement with the employer (this is acceptable as long as none of the practices jeopardize the well-being of children, which would obligate the teacher-trainer to report to the proper authorities). This relationship of trust can be a support system that results in a win-win situation.

Mentor programs create a new step in the early childhood career progression by allowing staff members to advance professionally while continuing to educate and teach children directly. By creating a step in the career path that acknowledges the specialized skill of teaching others to care for and educate young children, and by combining this step with financial reward, mentor programs challenge the perception of child care as unskilled work (Whitebook & Bellm, 1996).

In 1996, mentor programs existed in more than 40 communities across the country, according to the advisory committee on Head Start Quality and Expansion. Head Start and the United States Army Child Development Services have established mentor programs for their preschool personnel. This progressive trend utilizes all the best

Figure 1–3 Mentors help newcomers learn the ropes.

child care resources available by the intelligent use of these experts. It is a way to touch many with few hands.

As Kathy Thornburg, President of the National Association for the Education of Young Children (NAEYC) has said, "Mentoring is now a buzzword in our literature. However, it means more than directing an academic program. It means finding people who will *improve* on what you have tried to do with your life. It means supporting their dreams, helping them reach their goals, and helping them become what they want to be. We must support students and young professionals, tutor them, advise them, and give them an anchor. Most of all, though, *we must be good role models and encourage them to think for themselves*" (Thornburg, 2001).

Another trend in the mesosystem of child care bears mentioning. With the advent of many highly publicized violent acts by school-age children against peers, there has been renewed interest in violence among children throughout the United States. This can be a positive trend because social pressure to understand and stop the causes of violence among young children can result in better parenting and child care practices. Many movements against violence are aimed at the care of preschool-age children. For example, NAEYC has established "ACT: (Adults and Children Together) Against Violence, a campaign in conjunction with the American Psychological Association and the Ad Council to teach young children positive, nonviolent ways to respond to conflict, anger, and frustration" (NAEYC, 2001). Teaching young children to become more emotionally intelligent instead of merely cognitively intelligent is one of the most important trends in child development and care today and will become even more so as people live closer together.

The mesosystem is clearly demonstrated by the development of professional mentor programs. The reader should note that the mesosystem operates best when there are supportive and consistent communication links between parent, child development specialist, and school director.

The exosystem refers to social settings that do not contain the child but still directly affect the child's development, such as community health services and other public agencies. This structure can best be demonstrated by grassroots groups who lobby and advocate for child care services.

In March 1997 on Long Island, New York, Ms. Gerry Linton, Director of Women's Services and Vice President in charge of Programming for the Long Island Coalition for Full Employment, co-chaired an open forum for child care advocates. Ms. Linton stated that "this forum centered on all interested in the welfare of children to advocate for quality, affordability, and accessibility in child care" (Linton, 1997).

Similar social activists worked in other states to ensure quality child care. Margaret Crawley, of the Michigan Coordinated Child Care Association, credits the increase in the number of the CDA-credentialed providers to strong legislative backing, training efforts, and collegiate support (1997).

Bibi Lobo Somyak (1997), Deputy Director at the Corporate Fund for Children in Texas, states that several factors account for this training trend:

1. The use of CDAs is advocated by individuals and communities.
2. CDA candidates are recruited publicly.
3. CDA training is paid for in part by coalition funds.

These and other local and regional organizations stress child care advocacy that sets higher standards of care and affects each child in the community.

Other social policies also are affected by the availability, affordability, and quality of care for very young children. The following current issues in development and care are discussed in depth in later chapters.

- Child abuse and neglect
- Homelessness
- Divorce and its impact on the family
- Needs for special children
- AIDS: impact on the community
- Adverse environmental factors
- Birth problems
- Education of the child development specialist

Now, we turn to trends within the macrosystem, which is the most general of Bronfenbrenner's Ecological Systems Theory. The child is ultimately affected by decisions made at this level because the macrosystem consists of the laws, customs, and general policies of the social system (government). This is where the availability of resources (money) is determined. The macrosystem structure of the United States went through a remarkable change in the late 1990s. This can be understood best by explaining the changes in Welfare Reform Legislation.

In the late 1980s and early 1990s child care needs increased significantly in the United States. In response to this need, providers expanded existing centers and opened new ones. This expansion increased the need for new curricula, materials, teachers, and directors. Training programs centered their efforts on the quality of services offered to families and children to continue to raise the standard of child care from the standpoint of federal support. In 1996, that standpoint was to change.

The Personal Responsibility and Work Opportunity Reconciliation Act was signed by President Clinton in 1996. The new law was designed to break the cycle of poverty by moving people from welfare into the workforce. This bill gave state governments the power to regulate funds and set parameters for child care training. It also allowed people to provide unpaid child care as a way to meet the work requirement. This provision set off an instant alarm to child care advocates everywhere.

> "To care for their children many mothers will rely on relatives and friends, some of whom will be loving and attentive and some of whom will not. . . . A recent study found that 40 percent of day care centers for infants and toddlers gave less than the minimal standard of care."

One out of every 10 children three years old and younger lives in extreme poverty at or below 50 percent of the federal poverty level. The 1994 report by the Carnegie Corporation, called Starting Points, identified a "quiet crisis" in the lives of our youngest children. Hillary Clinton also spoke on the importance of a child's earliest years (Collins, 1997).

The new welfare law allows states to exempt new mothers from work requirements for a year. Some states, such as Wisconsin, require new mothers to start looking for work when their babies are 12 weeks old. In 1996, the budget for Early Head Start was $146 million, and Health and Human Services awarded grants to 143 sites. The money is used to provide a variety of services to poor families with children under the age of four and to poor pregnant women.

Vermont has a "Success by Six" Program, and North Carolina has instituted a flexible county program called "Smart Start." In this program teachers, parents, doctors, nurses, child care providers, ministers, and businesspeople form partnerships to help young children and their families. Several states are trying to help educate parents about parenting; home visits by social workers or nurses are among the most successful.

Because of the emphasis on work, welfare reform placed significant stress on the existing system of early childhood services and caused broad ramifications for the quality, accessibility, and affordability of services for poor and working families. M. Theresa Gnezda stated, "Early childhood advocates must remind state and local policy makers that true welfare reform requires making sure that child care is much more than custodial care" (1996).

The new century has brought growing concern about quality in child care; the ability to compensate teachers, directors, and child development specialists; and the need for high-quality programs and support in responding to the family's changing roles. Richard Clifford, President of the NAEYC, asked in 1996, "Will the new pressures brought on by Welfare Reform continue to keep us from addressing our basic concerns about the quality of services offered to the youngest citizens of our country? . . . Will reform force a reduction in the standards of care provided all children to accommodate larger numbers of children?" The rendering of "unpaid child care" positions as a viable alternative to employment did two things: first, it recognized that nonparents and substitutes, such as grandparents, family members, neighbors, and child care professionals, were primary caregivers; and second, it did not mandate that everyone caring for children at any level be educated.

As a result, most professional who had been working diligently to improve the standards of training for child care demanded that their local governments raise training and care standards. This became necessary because many of the federally supported departments that funded and guaranteed these standards were no longer in existence. Good affordable day care is not a luxury or fringe benefit for welfare mothers and working parents but essential brain food for the next generation.

CULTURAL DIVERSITY PROGRAMS
AND ANTITERRORISM PROCEDURES

A current trend in child care is the development of programs emphasizing cultural diversity in child care settings. It is important for the child development specialist to accept the challenge to develop a cross-cultural curriculum that involves both parents and children because many young families are just exploring their own cultural backgrounds.

Cross-cultural curriculum development fits into Vygotsky's theory. He viewed "cognitive development as a socially mediated process . . . as dependent on the support that adults and more mature peers provide as children try new tasks" (Berk, 1997). A culturally rich curriculum encourages the recognition of cultural differences and helps young families connect with the traditions of their own heritage and culture.

Working with children, parents, and the community on cultural differences has become an essential child care component as the result of increased terrorist activities all over the world. We need to understand each other and work together to protect our children and community from people who are committed to the destruction of our society and way of life. Antiterrorist procedures must be established in the child care setting as well as within the community and government. These procedures fall into two general categories: increased security procedures and a disaster plan.

Security procedures begin with providing safe physical and personal environments. Children should never be expected to use a public restroom unless they are accompanied by an adult. Tips for security issues with children from the Department of Defense Education Activity (DoDEA) include ensuring children always carry some form of identification and know their home address and phone number. With preverbal children, this might take the form of identification attached to the babies' clothing. Child identification packets can also be made, including a photograph, fingerprints, and identification tag. A secret code word should be used by trusted adults to pick up a child and children taught to report anything that makes them afraid or uncomfortable (DoDEA, 2001).

A disaster plan should be established that details procedures necessary in the event of natural disaster, violence (such as bombing), and bioterrorist agents. Steps to be taken should be provided to all parents and be clearly posted in the care setting. Rehearsal for these events should be practiced so all are familiar with their roles.

It is important to recognize that another great challenge for child development specialists is to present a progressive cross-cultural curriculum that involves parents and children alike. In a section called the "Celebration of Life" in Chapter 9, a sampling of cross-cultural curricula is discussed. Two excellent examples for center-based care are featured. The curricula of the International Preschool Child Care Facility associated with the United Nations and the award-winning American Institute of Physics Child Care Centers are presented, along with suggested references and a reading list. Specific references for materials such as puppets, toys, stuffed animals, and simple age-appropriate objects that represent diversity also are explored. Appendix D presents an intercultural calendar that includes significant occasions for several cultures. Children, parents, and child care specialists can use this calendar to celebrate the unique contributions of each child's culture to the group and the entire child care program.

Bronfenbrenner's ecological systems theory assumes the interconnectedness of each person to others and the ways in which one system affects another. It implies the importance of respecting each individual's uniqueness and considers carefully the decisions made at every level that affect us all.′

Transactional Theories view care from the perspective of how the child interacts with and affects the environment (Sameroff et al., 1993). These theories help us understand that children are not passive recipients of whatever the environment provides but are very involved in affecting the environment and aiding their own development. It is important for the child care specialist to understand that even newborns have a part in their growth and development, and their wants, needs, and desires must be respected.

To summarize, current trends in child care involve the bidirectional and reciprocal relationship between the child and his or her environment. More children with a wide diversity of backgrounds are in care. As a result, there is an increased need for provider education; parent education, including proper selection of care settings; innovative and flexible care programs; effective use of resources, including professional mentors; social and political advocacy for quality, affordable, and accessible care; and use of culturally diverse materials in child care curricula.

It is our individual responsibility to be aware of the power of our actions and their future impact on children. Through understanding that the child development specialist also directly influences the family, community, and culture, one can truly understand the old African saying, " It takes a village to raise a child."

Key Terms

association	natural selection
behaviorism	negative reinforcers
caregiver	noble savages
classical conditioning	normative approach
Cognitive-Developmental Theory	observational learning
curricula	operant conditioning theory
discrimination	original sin
Early Childhood Educator	positive reinforcers
Ecological Systems Theory	Psychoanalytic Theory
ethnology	Psychosocial Theory
Evolutionary Theory	responses
exosystem	sensory input
guide	social learning theories
imitation	Sociocultural Theory
infants	stages
Information Processing Theory	stimuli
macrosystem	survival of the fittest
maturation	tabula rasa
mesosystem	teaching
microsystem	toddlers
mobile infants	verbal and motor responses
modeling	young infants

Student Activities

1. Describe the four levels of Bronfenbrenner's Ecological Systems Theory and tell how each relates to current child care issues.
2. Write a short paragraph on how school districts can respond to the needs of preschool children using current trends in the field.
3. List three ways you can support the need for more education in child care.
4. Name three developmental theorists who have contributed to early development, and describe the contributions of each.

Chapter Review

1. What is the historical setting for care of young children before the Twentieth Century?
2. What theorist is thought to have contributed the most to child development and care?
3. What are four current trends in child care and development?
4. How is the microsystem different from the mesosystem?

CASE STUDY   Caregiver-in-Training

Trisha is a caregiver-in-training at the Little Folks Child Care Center. When she started her course work at the local junior college toward her certification as a CDA, she was surprised to find that the 8-week to 17-month-old children she works with fall into different child care categories. She found that Ecological Systems Theory helped her understand the influences on her "little ones," and she became more active in the mesosystem as a result. Her head teacher and director used the information she gained in her coursework to establish a formal mentoring system at the child care center.

In addition to dealing with issues of child abuse and neglect in her setting, Trisha became actively involved in new security measures resulting from terrorism activities. She helped conduct a security assessment of the center, procedures for escaping disasters, and new health and safety plans for protection from bioterrorism. Children were issued photo IDs, and all adults entering the center are now required to present a photo ID on request.

Because her population of children is culturally diverse, Trisha works with parents, staff, and children on cross-cultural issues and uses a holiday calendar to celebrate all the cultures represented in her center and community. She also developed activities that teach values and child-rearing practices for different cultures and uses these activities with her children for an entire day each week.

Trisha is quickly learning the CDA Goals and Objectives as she works with children, parents, and staff. She attends classes, professional workshops, and conferences on child care and development. Trisha is enthusiastic and dedicated to her new and exciting profession as a Child Development and Care Specialist.

1. What child care categories do Trisha's children fall into?
2. In what other systems, besides the mesosystem, does Trisha work?
3. List four things you would do to prepare for a bioterrorist attack.

References

Beilin, H. (1992). Piaget's enduring contribution to developmental psychology. *Developmental Psychology, 28*, 191–204.

Berk, L. E. (1997). *Child development* (4th ed.). Boston: Allyn and Bacon.

Bowlby, J. (1951). *Maternal care and mental health.* Geneva: World Health Organization.

Bronfenbrenner, U. (1995). The bioecological model from a life course perspective: Reflections of a participant observer. In P. Moen, G. H. Elder, Jr., & K. Luscher (Eds.), *Examining lives in context* (pp. 599–618). Washington, DC: American Psychological Association.

Clifford, R. M. (1996). Partnerships with children. *Young Children, 52*(1), 2.

Collins, J. (February 1997). The day care crisis. *Time* Special Report.

Crawley, M. (1997). *States' efforts lead to increase in number of CDAs: Michigan.* Washington, DC: Council News & Views, CDA.

Darwin, C. (1936). *On the origin of species by means of natural selection.* New York: Modern Library (Original published 1859).

Department of Defense Education Activity (DoDEA) *Safety Program* (March 2001) Arlington, VA (1–15).

Dewsbury, D. A. (1992). Comparative psychology and ethology: A reassessment. *American Psychologist, 47*, 208–215.

Erikson, E. H. (1950). *Childhood and society*. New York: Norton.

Freud, S. (1973). *An outline of psychoanalysis*. London: Hogarth (Original published 1938).

Goldfarb, W. (1943). The effects of early institutional care on adolescent personality. *Journal of Experimental Education, 12*, 106–129.

Gnezda, M. T. (1996). Welfare reform: Personal responsibilities and opportunities for early childhood advocates. *Young Children 52*(1), 55–58.

Grusec, J. E. (1992). Social learning theory and developmental psychology: The legacies of Robert Sears and Albert Bandura. *Developmental Psychology, 28*, 776–786.

Hand, G. (1994). At risk stories for editors: Child and family studies. *Knight-Ridder/Tribune News Service*, June 28, 1994.

Horowitz, F. D. (1992). John B. Watson's legacy: Learning and environment. *Developmental Psychology, 28*, 360–367.

Klahr, D. (1992). Information processing approaches to cognitive development. In M. H. Bornstein & M. E. Lamb (Eds.), *Developmental psychology: An advanced textbook* (3rd ed.), (pp. 273–335). Hillsdale, NY: Erlbaum.

Linton, G. (1997). Open Forum for Childcare: A Panel Discussion. Long Island Coalition for Full Employment (Unpublished discussion).

Locke, J. (1892). Some thoughts concerning education. In R. J. Quick, (Ed.), *Locke on education* (pp. 1–236). Cambridge, London: Cambridge University Press (Original published 1690).

National Association for the Education of Young Children. (2001). ACT (Adults and Children Together) Against Violence. *Young Children, 5*, 55.

Rousseau, J. J. (1955). *Emile*. New York: Dutton. (Original published 1762).

Sameroff, A. J., Seifer, R., Baldwin, A., & Baldwin, C. (1993). Stability of intelligence from preschool to adolescence: The influence of social and family risk factors. *Child Development, 64*, 80–97.

Shahar, S. (1990). *Childhood in the Middle Ages*. London: Routledge & Kegan Paul.

Siegler, R. S. (1992). The other Alfred Binet. *Developmental Psychology, 28*, 179–190.

Skinner, E. A., & Belmont, M. J. (1993). Motivation in the classroom: Reciprocal effects of teacher behavior and student engagement across the school year. *Journal of Educational Psychology, 85*, 571–581.

Somyak, B. L. (1997). States' efforts lead to increase in number of CDAs: Texas. Washington, DC: News & Views; CDA, p. 5.

Spitz, T. (1945). Hospitalism: An inquiry into the genesis of psychiatric conditions in early childhood. *Psychoanalytic Study of the Child, 1*, 53–74.

Thornburg, K. R. (2001). The gift of mentoring. *Young Children, 5*, 4–5.

Vygotsky, L. S. (1986/1934). *Thought and language*. (A. Kozulin, trans.) Cambridge, MA: MIT Press.

Watson, M. A. (1972). *The Waldo Program of Developmental Learning Skills*. New York: Educational Activities.

Whitebook, M., & Bellm, D. (1996). Mentoring for early childhood teachers and providers: Building upon and extending tradition. *Young Children, 52*, 1, 59–64.

Additional Resources

Advisory Committee on Head Start Quality and Expansion. (1993). *Creating a 21st Century Head Start, Final report*. Washington, DC: Head Start Bureau, Administration Children, Youth, and Families.

Douville-Watson, L. (1983). *Three A's of infant development; Lecture Series 2*. Bayville, NY: Instructional Press.

Douville-Watson, L., & Watson, M. A. (1988). *Family actualization through research and education: FARE* (3rd ed.). New York: Instructional Press.

Gerber, M. (1989). *Educaring: Resources for infant educarers*. Los Angeles: Resources for Infant Educarers.

Grolnich, W. S., & Slowiacvek, M. L. (1994). Parents' involvement in children's schooling: A multi-dimensional conceptualization and motivational model. *Child Development, 65*, 237–252.

Lally, J. R. (Ed.). (1992). *Language development and communication: A guide*. San Francisco: Far West Lab.

Landon, E. (1997). Open Forum for Childcare: A Panel Discussion. Long Island Coalition for Full Employment (Unpublished discussion).

Nash, J. (1997). Fertile minds. *Time* Special Report.

Helpful Web Sites

Association for Childhood Education International Supports child-centered whole curriculum education from infancy through early adolescence. http://www.udel.edu/bateman/acei

Celebrating Cultural Diversity Through Children's Literature Annotated bibliography of multicultural children's books for elementary school teachers and links to related sites. http://www.geocities.com/rfsmith21204

Child Development Associate (CDA) Child Development agency operating child care centers throughout San Diego County. http://www.cdasandiego.com

Clearinghouse on International Developments in Child, Youth and Family Policies Compares child, youth, and family policies in countries worldwide. http://www.childpolicyintl.org

IGC: Women's Net Women's Net supports women's organizations locally, nationally, and worldwide. http://www.igc.org/igc/womensnet/

Diversity Training University International Distance learning courses that teach students to become diversity trainers who are capable of cross-cultural and multicultural teaching, training, and consulting. http://www.diversityuintl.com

Early Childhood Educators Web Guide Provides sites on child development, cultural diversity, discipline, and guidance. http://www.ecewebguide.com

Family Mentor Program Aims to strengthen families and help them cope with challenges of daily life. http://www.familymentor.org

Personal Security and Terrorism Awareness A personal protection guide. http://www.odedodea.edu

University of California, Los Angeles Encompasses studies in archeology, biology, and sociocultural and linguistic theory. http://www.sscnet.ucla.edu/anthro/

Youth Indicators 1993 Trends in the well-being of American youth, from the National Center for Educational Statistics. http://www.nces.ed.gov/edstats

Psychosocial Issues for Children and Adolescents in Disasters Developed by John Bowlby. Integrates psychoanalytic concepts of child development with parts of cognitive psychology, ethnology, and human information. http://www.mentalhealth.org/cmhs/EmergencyServices/after.asp

For additional infant and toddler resources, visit our Web site at
http://www.earlychilded.delmar.com

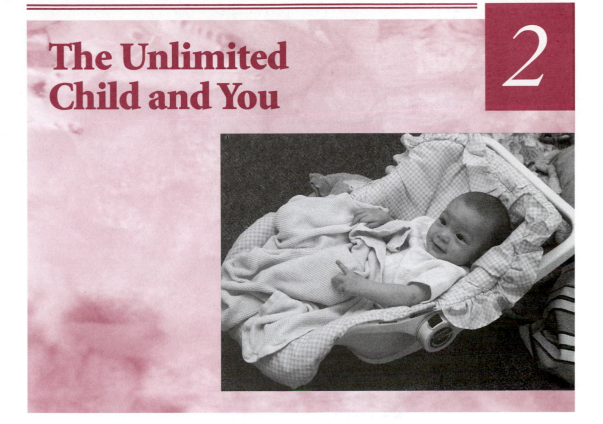

The Unlimited Child and You

2

Objectives

After reading this chapter, you should be able to:

- Identify five need levels and define each.
- Identify the five major developmental areas for assessment, and discuss how they differ from one another.
- Understand how to view the child after having done an assessment of need levels and developmental areas.
- Have a general understanding of the use of developmental profiles.
- Describe theoretical contributions for each developmental area.

Chapter Outline

Theory of the Unlimited Child
Five Need Levels
Five Major Developmental Areas
Using a Developmental Profile
Theoretical Contributions
Summary of Theoretical Contributions
Children with Special Needs
Case Study—Ideal Caregiving

THEORY OF THE UNLIMITED CHILD

The structure of this book allows for the child care philosophy that the authors believe is most helpful in child care settings. The major contributions of early childhood theorists are presented within this structure. This philosophy, which we call the *Unlimited Child*, states that every child has the capacity to develop *all* of the skills that any human being has ever developed. Unlike the tabula rasa theory of the past, which claimed that children are molded to parental or societal specifications, current research indicates that we bring to life all the potentials of our entire ancestry; all that it is possible for people to become is available in the potential of the newborn (Douville-Watson, L., 1988a).

Of course, there are environmental factors that limit the realization of our full self-potential. A child born with physical handicaps such as brain damage will not realize as much potential in certain areas as a child born neurologically intact, and a child whose ancestry dictates adult height less than 5 feet will most likely not realize the potential to play professional basketball. However, within these limiting physical and environmental factors, every child has the potential for a fulfilling and productive life, depending on how well his or her needs and abilities are fulfilled and to what extent the skills necessary to become a happy and successful adult are taught by parents and caregivers.

A brief discussion of our unlimited child theory applied to the five major developmental factors illustrates the functional value of approaching children in this way. Heredity largely dictates general physical qualities, such as height, body size, and hair color, but current research in neuropsychology and nutrition indicates that, when one physical system is weak or injured, other systems compensate by becoming stronger, sometimes even taking over the functions of the weakened system. For example, much research has been conducted on **brain plasticity**, which means that when one part of the brain is damaged, other parts take over the functions of the damaged part. However, brain plasticity is limited to critical periods of development, and after a critical period has passed, the brain is no longer able to compensate for damaged parts (Berk, 2000). What this means for the child care specialist is that infants and toddlers are in the process of forming nerve pathways, and by providing them with the proper nutrition and experiences, you can enhance physical and neurological development.

In addition to being born with certain temperament traits, children are also born with unlimited potential for loving and intimate relationships, joy, happiness, and personal fulfillment. Research clearly indicates that it is how the environment provides for children's needs and how caregivers interact with children that determine the emotional and social intelligence we exhibit as adults. There is no such thing as too much love, approval, acceptance, or positive attention for infants and toddlers. By approaching each child with unconditional regard, we help maintain the enthusiasm, curiosity, and loving nature that is present at birth and enables us to be fully human.

Approaching young children as being capable of unlimited growth establishes security, trust, confidence, and respect for the caregiver. When the caregiver does not hold high expectations but approaches children from the perspective that each individual can accomplish what he or she is motivated to do, children develop positive self-esteem and self-responsibility and avoid development of **attitude ceilings**. An attitude ceiling is a learned belief that a person is limited in what he or she can accomplish.

Everyone is raised with attitude ceilings on certain skills, abilities, and feelings. Some attitude ceilings are imposed by physical reality, such as physical size or mobility. However, many of the attitude ceilings people develop are from social beliefs that are not based in physical reality. In fact, families assign roles to each child and live out a reality based on beliefs, some of which are limiting for the individuals in the family. How much success we are allowed in areas such as personal happiness, financial success, joy, love, and academic achievement is at least partly dictated by unconscious attitude ceilings established by our early caregivers. The best antidote for attitude ceilings is to approach children from the perspective that success in all aspects of life is unlimited, and each child can succeed at whatever he or she is motivated to accomplish.

FIVE NEED LEVELS

The responsibility for helping the unlimited child reach his or her potential is a joint effort between the caregiver, the family, the community, and society. How do you know where to start or even what to attend to? Maslow's **hierarchy of needs** is a good structure to use in beginning to view the infant and toddler.

Maslow defined a hierarchy of human needs that must be met in order for a person to be happy and fulfilled (Maslow, 1954). At the most basic level are physical needs: food, air, water, shelter, and so on (Table 2–1). As a general principle, the more immediately and completely the needs of infants and toddlers are fulfilled, the more secure and happy will be their development. One frustrating experience of every infant caregiver is not being able to determine which need is not being met because infants cannot articulate need deprivation other than by crying. To help lessen this frustration, caregivers should systematically check out all needs at each of Maslow's levels, always beginning with level I, physical needs.

Once the physical needs are fulfilled, the child can operate at level II, safety needs: security, consistency, and the like. The more secure and consistent we can make the physical and psychological environment, the better for fulfilling safety needs. This is accomplished through routines, consistency, familiarity of people and surroundings, and so forth. The key to fulfilling safety needs is to reduce sudden and traumatic change as much as possible and for caregivers to remain calm during change.

When needs are minimally fulfilled at level II, children are free to operate at level III, social needs. Most people in our society spend the most energy trying to fulfill needs at this level. Even adults require the 3A's of child-rearing: attention, approval, and affection

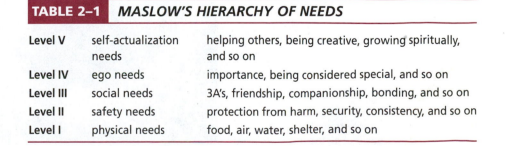

TABLE 2–1	*MASLOW'S HIERARCHY OF NEEDS*	
Level V	self-actualization needs	helping others, being creative, growing spiritually, and so on
Level IV	ego needs	importance, being considered special, and so on
Level III	social needs	3A's, friendship, companionship, bonding, and so on
Level II	safety needs	protection from harm, security, consistency, and so on
Level I	physical needs	food, air, water, shelter, and so on

(Douville-Watson, L., 1988a). Human beings are social animals, so physical bonding, hugging, companionship, and friendship are essential to our well-being. Research on development clearly shows that infants and toddlers who receive large amounts of attention, approval, and affection develop faster and are healthier than children who are deprived of these resources (Furman, 1992; Waters et al., 1995).

Once basic needs are minimally fulfilled at level III, children are free to fulfill ego needs at level IV. Early theories hypothesized that newborns do not possess an ego (a sense of self as separate from the environment). Current research indicates that even though infants are symbiotically tied to others—that is, they experience a sense of dependence on their primary caregivers—even newborns are capable of experiencing separateness or independence from others and the environment (Brazelton & Cramer, 1990). As a result, infants and toddlers need to feel special, and their individual dependence and independence needs to be respected. Despite the fact that they are dependent on adults most of the time, when their lower-level needs are fulfilled, infants can play by themselves and experience competence separate from other people.

Self-actualization needs are at the highest level, and most of us, unfortunately, don't function at this level often. These needs include helping other people, expressing creativity, and functioning on a spiritual level. Self-actualization needs are pursued only when needs at lower levels are minimally fulfilled. It is a wonderful experience indeed to see infants or toddlers so fulfilled at lower need levels that they seem to be in touch with the beauty of nature and able to give to others and explore their world creatively. Even though this level of fulfillment is difficult to achieve, it is certainly a worthwhile goal for all of us. In fact, it is impossible to give children what we do not possess ourselves, so as the caregiver, you must strive to fulfill your own lower-level needs to be free to operate at the self-actualization level (Figure 2–1).

Figure 2–1 Children and caregivers are happy when needs at all five levels are filled.

The way to determine which need is deprived in an infant or nonverbal toddler is to start with level I, physical needs, and check each one. Does the child need food, water, or relief from physical discomfort? Once physical needs are ruled out, move to the next level, safety, and check out needs at that level. Continue checking needs at each level until you find the one that is not met and then do whatever is necessary to fill the need. Keep in mind that this is a structure in which the whole child is cared for and there will be times when the child's need cannot be determined.

FIVE MAJOR DEVELOPMENTAL AREAS

Now that we have an outline to define and assess need levels, let's look at the skill areas that are important in keeping children unlimited. These skill areas can then be put together in a graphic form developed by Watson called a Developmental Profile (Watson, M. A., 1977). As previously stated, a Developmental Profile is a graphic picture of a child's development compared to age expectancies in five major developmental areas. Table 2–2 lists the five major skill areas important in human development. Assessment of each child in care compared to age norms or expectations is necessary to help the child remain as unlimited as possible (Watson, M. A., 1995).

USING A DEVELOPMENTAL PROFILE

Use the Developmental Prescription in Appendix A or another developmental hierarchy to evaluate which behaviors and skills the child can perform successfully and the point in the hierarchy at which the child can't perform higher-level behaviors (refer to Appendix B for Profile Construction). The last point at which the child performs with success is translated into an estimate of months' development in that skill area. For example, in evaluating a 12-month-old in Area I (Physical), the Developmental Prescription in Appendix A for 8 to 12 months lists six behaviors under Muscular Control, Trunk and Leg. If the child being observed can successfully perform the first three behaviors, his or her development is estimated to be 10 months (half of the age range between 8 and 12 months). Evaluate each child in all the skill behaviors of the age range in order to establish an average age level for each of the five developmental areas on the profile. Remember that these are average estimates of ages and not specific tests.

TABLE 2–2	*MAJOR DEVELOPMENTAL SKILL AREAS*
Area I	**physical:** height, weight, general motor coordination, visual and auditory acuity and so on
Area II	**emotional:** feelings, self-perception, perception of others related to self, confidence, security, and so on
Area III	**social:** interactions with peers, elders, and youngers, both one to one and in a group
Area IV	**cognitive:** reasoning, problem solving, concept formation, abstraction, imagination, creativity, and so on
Area V	**developmental learning skills:** visual, auditory, verbal, motor, and perceptual skills necessary to accurately input, remember, and express information

Figure 2–2 graphically illustrates the estimates of a 12-month-old compared to age norms on a Developmental Profile. The heavy line at 12 months indicates Juan's chronological age (C.A.) and each point indicates his development in each of the five areas. Specific skills under each area from the Developmental Prescription in Appendix A were evaluated to make up the points on the profile. By comparing relative strengths and weaknesses, programming can be done to enhance his development (refer to Appendix B for instructions on Developmental Profile Construction and Appendix A for specific age expectations). In the example, Juan is above age in responding to adult attention and below age expectancy in interacting in a group. From this profile we can see that activities should be done to help Juan feel more secure in a group setting and to help him function more independently on one-to-one interactions. Since his language skills are good, talking to Juan while in a group might help.

A word of caution is in order here. Although needs and skills must be measured to provide a structure for keeping the child unlimited, estimates of skilled development are used only to determine goals and not to label children as better or worse, or ahead or behind. Variations in development are extremely wide and fluctuating, especially for infants and toddlers, so you should assess needs and skill levels on an ongoing basis and be timely in changing your goals to keep up with the rapidly changing child. Development is a continuing process wherein people grow in the same direction at different rates.

Name: **Juan P.**   Date of Birth: **2/21/XX**
Date: **2/24/XX**   C.A.: **12 months 3 days**

MONTH AGE EXPECT.	AREA I PHYSICAL				AREA II EMOTIONAL			AREA III SOCIAL					AREA IV COGNITIVE					AREA V LEARNING SKILLS				MONTH AGE EXPECT.
	MUSCLE	SLEEP	EAT	TEETH	FEELINGS	CONTROL	TEMPERAMENT	PEERS	YOUNGER	OLDER	ONE TO ONE	GROUP	GOALS	OBJECTS	CAUSALITY	PLAY	LANGUAGE	VISUAL	AUDITORY	V-MAT	VERBAL	
18+																						18+
17																						17
16												B										16
15																						15
14																						14
13																						13
C.A. 12																						12 C.A.
11																						11
10																						10
9								A														9
8																						8
7																						7
6–																						6–

Notes: A = Juan has a little problem dealing with a group–sometimes is overwhelmed.
       B = He responds very well to one to one adult attention.

Figure 2–2 Sample Developmental Profile.

THEORETICAL CONTRIBUTIONS

Using the framework of the five developmental areas, we can now examine how the brain works, as well as some major contributions from theorists discussed in Chapter 1 toward keeping children unlimited.

Physical Development

Systematic observations of behavior by Darwin, Hall and Gesell, Watson, and Skinner have resulted in an approach called **task analysis**, which, when applied to physical development, yields a developmental hierarchy from simple to complex patterns of physical movements. For example, careful observation of the physical movements required to stand erect results in a hierarchy of behaviors, starting with the simplest arm and leg joint bending and building through a series of natural steps, such as rolling over and crawling. Contributions from behavioral pioneers have shown that any behavior can be task-analyzed and broken down into a hierarchy of steps from the simplest to the most complex behavior necessary to perform the goal.

CDA

I. 1–3

The Developmental Prescriptions presented in Appendix A are examples of general task analyses for infants and toddlers in the five major developmental areas. By carefully observing a child's behavior, the caregiver can determine the highest step on the list the child can perform, and then task-analyze the specific steps necessary to help the child move to the next level in the hierarchy. Chapter 4 provides specific tools to help children remain unlimited by mastering physical skills and behaviors using task analyses. When the caregiver uses operant conditioning by reinforcing children's successes with the 3A's, (Attention, Approval, and Affection) children grow in physical and behavioral areas at a rapid rate.

Patterns of physical development are discussed at greater length in Chapter 3. Dynamic Systems Theory (Hofsten, 1989) and Bernstein's Biodynamic Theory of Motor Development (Bernstein, 1967) are two more theories of physical development discussed in Chapter 3. These theories help the caregiver understand developmental patterns of physical and motor development.

Neuroscience Research Findings

Many scientists believe that there are a number of critical (sensitive) periods, or windows, in the first few years of childhood, when the brain demands certain types of input in order to create or stabilize certain long-lasting structures. In the first few months, the brain's higher centers explode with the aid of new synapses. By the age of two, a child's brain contains twice as many synapses and consumes twice as much energy as the brain of a normal adult.

University of Chicago pediatric neurologist, Dr. Peter Huttenlocher, indicates that the number of synapses in one layer of the visual cortex rises from around 2500 per neuron at birth to as many as 18,000 about six months later. Other regions of the cortex score similarly spectacular increases, but on slightly different schedules. Fibers continue to form throughout life, and they reach their highest average densities (15,000 synapses per neuron) at around the age of two and remain at that level until the age of 10 or 11 (Nash, 1997).

Caregivers often spend more waking time with children than parents do. What holds true for parents in the new brain research is significant for child care specialists. "Indeed, parents are the brain's first and most important teachers. They help babies learn by adapting the rhythmic, high pitched speaking style known as "Parentese" where mothers and fathers change their speech patterns in the same peculiar way. Parentese appears to hasten the process of connecting words to the objects they denote" (Nash, 1997).

Caregivers should be very aware of factors that affect attachment security in young children. Sensitive caregiving that responds quickly to the child's signals and needs is the most important factor in keeping children unlimited. The findings from many studies clearly reveal that securely attached infants have primary caregivers who respond quickly to signals, express positive feelings, and handle their babies with tenderness and sensitivity. On the other hand, insecure babies have caregivers who dislike physical contact and behave insensitively to the child's needs (Isabella, 1993). The best principle for infant and toddler social development is probably that young children cannot be given too much attention, approval, and affection; they can't be spoiled. Your sensitive caring sets the basis for all future relationships that young children will have throughout their lives.

Emotional Development

Contributions by Freud (1973/1938) and followers such as Erikson (1950) have provided an understanding of the development and motivation for emotions. Freud theorized three distinct parts of the personality, or *id*, which is present at birth and is the source of our wants and needs. The *ego* emerges during early infancy and is the *self*, including self-concept and self-esteem. The *superego* is the conscience, or the value system of right and wrong. A person's emotional states are determined by how needs and wants are fulfilled using a value system of right and wrong. Freud supposed five psychosexual stages a developing child goes through that form the foundation for personality: (1) the oral stage (birth to one year) involves sucking, eating, and exploring things with the mouth; (2) the anal stage (one to three years), when toilet training and interest in elimination become important; and (3) the phallic stage (three to six years) involves formation of sexual identity as male or female, and includes the Oedipus (male)/Electra (female) conflict, when the child tries to win the parent of the opposite sex away from the parent of the same sex. How this conflict is handled by parents and caregivers determines the amount of confidence and security the child has in his or her gender identity as an adult. The last two stages occur during middle childhood and adolescence and include (4) the latency stage, in which social values are formed from adults and peers outside the home; and (5) the genital stage, during early adolescence, when the child becomes sexually mature.

The functional value of Freud's theory for caregivers is the understanding that young children need sensitive help to fill their emotional needs at each stage, using a value system that teaches them that it is not necessary to hurt themselves or anyone else to be fulfilled and happy. When children's emotional needs are not fulfilled, frustration and anger result, and the caregiver should help children express their negative feelings in healthy ways.

Erikson's Psychosocial Theory adds to our understanding of emotional development and the qualities children need to become happy and successful adults. Erikson defined eight psychosocial stages that humans experience throughout life. The first three are extremely important in the development of infants and toddlers.

1. *Basic trust versus mistrust*—Children learn to trust or mistrust themselves and the world during infancy depending on the warmth and sensitivity they are given.

When infants are required to wait too long for comfort, or they are handled harshly and insensitively, they develop basic mistrust of themselves and others.

2. *Autonomy versus shame and doubt*—Once infants become mobile, a process of separation and individuation begins, eventually resulting in autonomy. Children need to choose and decide things for themselves, and when caregivers permit reasonable free choices and do not force or shame children, autonomy and self-confidence is fostered.

3. *Initiative versus guilt*—When caregivers support a child's sense of purpose and direction, initiative in the form of ambition and responsibility is developed. When caregivers demand too much self-control or responsibilities that are age-inappropriate, children respond by feeling overcontrolled or guilty, or both.

4. *Industry versus inferiority*—Learning to work cooperatively with others promotes industry and a sense of competence. On the other hand, caregivers who do everything for children or compete with children promote a sense of inferiority and incompetence.

5. *Identity versus identity diffusion*—Self-chosen values and goals lead to security in a child's identity. If adults control and make all decisions for the child, this leads to confusion about the meaning of his identity.

6. *Intimacy versus isolation*—Using the 3A's results in a warm and affectionate bond between caregiver and child and establishes the basis for later healthy intimate relationships. Withholding physical and emotional warmth results in children feeling isolated and rejected.

7. *Generativity versus stagnation*—Giving to and caring for others, along with productive work, foster a sense of competence in the world and in life. Being selfish and ungiving results in feeling stagnated and having no meaning of life.

8. *Ego integrity versus despair*—It is very sad to see a small child in despair. Even young children can reflect on what kind of people they feel they are and how they feel about their lives. When a child's assessment is "I did good and the world is good," ego integrity is the result. When the assessment is "I'm bad and the world is bad," despair is the result.

Erikson's stages reveal how children develop the qualities that result in a happy, meaningful life. Activities based on the first three stages should be part of the daily curriculum, and the caregiver should help promote confidence, security, and trust in each child.

Recent research on emotional development suggests that, although all emotions are present at birth, our emotional reactions are learned through stages. The development of affective reactions and self-regulation of emotions appears to be the direct result of caregiving styles.

"What wires a child's brain, or rewires it after physical trauma, is repeated experience. When the brain does not receive the right information, the result can be devastating. Emotional deprivation early in life has a similar effect" (Nash, 1997). For a more complete understanding of the development of emotions, refer to *The Organization of Emotional Life in the Early Years* (Sroufe, 1996).

Margaret Mahler's theory regarding separation-individuation and bonding and Daniel Goleman's theory of Emotional Intelligence are discussed in detail in Chapter 3. These theories help the caregiver to understand developmental patterns of the formation of **ego boundaries** (the awareness of separateness of oneself from the environment, including other people, places, and things), self-concept, self-esteem, and the skills necessary for a person to function effectively in the world.

Social Development

Contributions by numerous social learning theorists help us to understand how infants and toddlers develop relationships. The first relationships we have in the world with our parents and caregivers result in the formation of the self, which forms the basis for all future relationships.

Freud theorized that newborn infants are psychologically connected to their mother; there is no awareness of the baby being different or separate from the mother. This **symbiosis** is gradually replaced through the process of **separation and individuation** until the child develops a separate sense of self (1938).

William James (1890–1963) first identified two distinct aspects of the self: the I, or **existential self**, which is separate from the environment and other people and maintains continuous existence over time; and the **reflective self** or the "me-not me," which perceives the physical, material, and relationship qualities of experience.

The emergence of **self-recognition** has been demonstrated in infants as young as nine months and appears to be present in the majority of 15-month-olds (Bullock & Lutkenhaus, 1990). Many theorists hypothesize that the development of self lies in a **sense of agency**; for example, awareness that our actions cause other objects and people to react in predictable ways (Pipp, Easterbrooks, & Brown, 1993). By two years of age, a sense of self is well established and toddlers express possession of objects with *me* and *mine* (Levine, 1983).

The opposite side of the coin from separation-individuation is presented in the widely accepted view of infant emotional ties to the caregiver in Bowlby's Ethnological Theory of Attachment (Bowlby, 1969). According to this theory, the infant's relationship to the parent starts as a set of innate signals that keep the caregiver close to the baby and proceeds through four phases, as follows.

1. *The preattachment phase* (birth to six weeks) occurs when the baby grasps, cries, smiles, and gazes to keep the caregiver engaged.
2. *The "attachment-in-the-making" phase* (six weeks to eight months) describes when the baby responds differently to familiar caregivers than to strangers. Face-to-face interactions relieve distress, and the baby has expectations that the caregiver will respond when signaled,
3. *The clear-cut attachment phase* (eight months to two years) is when separation anxiety is exhibited, the baby protests caregiver departure, and the baby acts deliberately to maintain caregiver attention.
4. *Formation of a reciprocal relationship phase* (18 months onward) occurs when children negotiate with the caregiver and are willing to give and take in relationships.

According to Bowlby (1969), young children internalize a warm and affectionate caregiver-child bond that becomes a vital part of personality. This image, which Freud called the internalized good mother, becomes the model for all future close relationships (Bretherton, 1992).

In addition to attachment and separation-individuation, we also discuss (in Chapter 3) Freud's theory of ego boundaries, Transactional Analysis concepts of good touch and bad touch, Goleman's emotional intelligence of managing relationships, and Neuro-Linguistic Programming (NLP) theory, regarding internal dialogues and movies. These theories explain how patterns of healthy and unhealthy interactions are developed from infancy.

Cognitive Development

As mentioned in Chapter 1, the most widely used theories of higher cognition are Piaget's Cognitive-Developmental Theory (Beilin, 1992) and Vygotsky's Sociocultural Theory (Rogoff & Chavajay, 1995). Chapter 8 details several applications of Piaget's theory in child care settings, but some major principles from his theory are discussed here.

According to Piaget, children develop higher cognitive skills through four stages: (1) sensorimotor, (2) preoperational, (3) concrete operational, and (4) formal operational. Children use **schemes**, or patterns of actions, to learn at each of these stages through the intellectual functions of **adaptation** and **organization**.

Adaptation involves using schemes that have direct interactions with the environment; for example, grasping and dropping an object over and over. **Accommodation** involves changing schemes that do not work well. When children are in a familiar routine and are not required to learn new schemes, they function by means of **assimilation**, which involves refining structures to more closely fit their schemes and cognitive structures. Piaget called this internal state of assimilation **cognitive equilibrium**, which implies a consistent and comfortable condition. When children are placed into unfamiliar situations, they experience **cognitive disequilibrium** and perform more accommodation than assimilation.

The second cognitive function through which schemes are changed is called organization, which takes place internally. Organization is a process of rearranging new schemes and linking them with other schemes to form a cognitive system. For example, a baby will eventually relate schemes for sucking, dropping, and throwing with new, more complex schemes of near and far.

Although many of the hypotheses of Piaget's theory have come into question after the advent of research demonstrating that infants and toddlers have many more cognitive skills than Piaget theorized (Rast & Meltzoff, 1995), the principles and stages defined by Piaget have functional value for the caregiver in helping children remain unlimited in their cognitive development. Some additional contributions include discovery learning, awareness of readiness for learning, and acceptance of individual differences in learning rates.

Unlike Piaget, Vygotsky viewed cognitive development as an interaction between children and their social environment. Vygotsky believed that, once language is developed, children engage in **private speech**; in other words, they talk to themselves as a means of self-guidance and direction (1934/1986). Recent research supports this view with findings that children who use more private speech show more improvement on difficult tasks than children who do not use much private speech (Berk and Spuhl, 1995). In addition, children use more private speech as tasks become more difficult (Berk, 1994), and children with learning problems use more private speech than do children with normal learning skills (Diaz & Berk, 1995).

Vygotsky hypothesized that higher cognitive processes develop from verbal and nonverbal social interactions. This is accomplished when more mature individuals instruct less mature individuals within the **zone of proximal development**. This term refers to a range of tasks that a child is ready to learn with the help of more skilled peers or adults. Children make the language and actions of dialogues and demonstrations with adults part of their private speech and organize their own actions like the adults' actions. At least two aspects of this process have found research support: **intersubjectivity** and **scaffolding**.

Intersubjectivity refers to how children and adults come to understand each other by adjusting their views and perspectives to fit the other person. *Scaffolding* involves changing the support given a learner in the course of teaching a skill or concept. The instructor uses much praise and instruction in the early stages of teaching a skill and task-analyzes the steps necessary to achieve the skill. As the learner starts mastering steps, the instructor withdraws instruction and praise in direct response to the learner's ability to perform successfully. Caregivers who effectively learn to use intersubjectivity and scaffolding help children remain unlimited, because children learn to use positive private speech and succeed more easily (Behrend, Rosengran, & Perlmutter, 1992).

A final aspect of Vygotsky's theory involves the use of **make-believe play** in higher cognitive development. Vygotsky believed that children who engage in make-believe play use imagination to act out internal ideas about how the world operates, and to set rules by which play is conducted, which helps them learn to think before they act. Recent research on preschoolers supports this concept since children who engage in make-believe and pretend play are found to be more flexible and advanced in their problem-solving and thought processes (Lillard, 1993).

Nash (1997) has described some new brain research that sheds light on early childhood development.

"The electrical activity of brain cells changes the physical structure of the brain and this begins well before birth. A brain is not just a computer because the same processes that wire the brain before birth also drive the explosion of learning after birth. During the first year of life, the baby's brain produces trillions more connections than it can possibly use. Then, through competition the brain eliminates synapses that are seldom used starting around the age of 10 and leaves behind a pattern of emotion and thought."

Learning Skill Development

The most recent contributions to early childhood development are information processing theories. The most widely known computerlike model is the **store model** (Atkinson & Shiffrin, 1968). In this model, information in the form of visual, auditory, and kinesthetic images are **input** into a **sensory register** but quickly degrade unless they are stored in **short-term memory**. Short-term memory is the place where conscious operation on information occurs and where strategies are applied to make information meaningful. The length of time and the number of times we store information in short-term memory determines how likely the information is to be stored in **long-term memory**. Long-term memory is largely unconscious and holds all the meaningful experiences of our life. The final part of this model involves the **response generator**, which lets us decide to respond to stimuli at any point in the process.

A **levels of processing** model assumes that retention depends on the depth at which information is processed. In this model, we can process information on a superficial **perceptual level**, such as lowercase or uppercase letters in a word; on deeper **phonemic features**, such as the sounds associated with each letter symbol; or the deepest **semantic features**, such as the definition of the word (Craik & Lockhart, 1972).

Watson (1978), in his work with more than 4000 children, used principles from the store and levels of processing models to develop an information processing model of the essential **Developmental Learning Skills** necessary to accurately process information in preacademic skills such as letter and word recognition, spelling, and simple number combinations. The Developmental Learning Skills Model presented in Figure 2–3 has the mechanical, physical, and neurological acuity and capacity to coordinate the sensory systems necessary for learning at Level I, Sensory Coordination. The model illustrates the three major **sensory modalities** used to input most information: Visual (seeing), Auditory (hearing), and Kinesthetic (touching) input. We respond with either Motor or Verbal output. Children must possess the visual, auditory, and motor acuity and coordination necessary to accurately input stimuli, and they must develop sufficient fine motor coordination and verbal skills to output or respond accurately. It is essential when working with young children that accurate visual and auditory acuity and speech and language evaluations be performed regularly to ensure that these mechanical bases for learning are functioning normally. For example, even minor ear infections, if left untreated over time, can drastically affect a young child's development of auditory and verbal learning skills.

Figure 2–3 lists Level II, Attentional Skills, as the next process. These include **focal attention**, **prefocal attention**, and **perceptual screening** to explain how

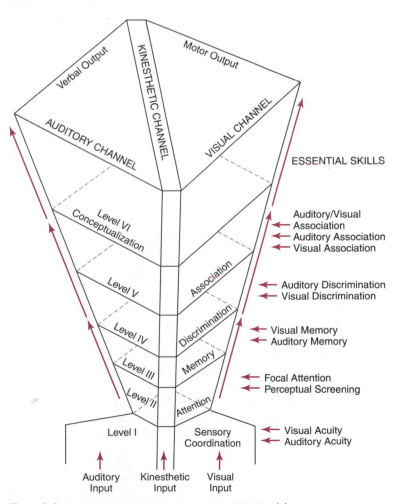

Figure 2–3 Watson's Developmental Learning Skills Model.

information from the environment is input into the brain. When we scan the environment without paying special attention to any details, or when we are so familiar with our surroundings that we don't notice specific details, we are using prefocal attention (similar to the sensory register in the store model). When we attend to specific visual, auditory, kinesthetic, olfactory, or taste stimuli, we are using focal attention. In order to focally attend successfully to an individual stimulus, it is necessary to block out all other distracting stimuli occurring at the same time. This process of screening out or eliminating irrelevant stimuli is called perceptual screening. For example, for a young child to hear your voice, he or she must focus auditory attention on the particular sounds of your voice while screening out all the other distracting visual, auditory, and other sensory stimuli occurring at the same time. Many of the problems exhibited by young children labeled as learning disabled, hyperactive, distractable, or having an attention-deficit disorder are really deficits in focal attention and perceptual screening skills. Further, the term *skills* is used here because auditory and visual focal attention and perceptual screening skills can be easily taught to young children (King, 1979).

Once sensory coordination and focal attention occur successfully, specific stimuli can be recorded in Memory (Level III). In Watson's model, information is made more meaningful and is, therefore, held longer in conscious memory when stimuli are well discriminated, associated, and categorized into a concept. Therefore, memory is aided by the use of higher cognitive skills, as well as simple repeated presentations of stimuli. Caregivers should be aware that learning improves when age-appropriate material is made more meaningful to children by helping them discriminate differences, associate similarities, and fit specific stimuli into categories.

The process of separating the important (salient) elements of a stimulus from similar stimuli surrounding it is called Discrimination, (Level IV). In Gestalt psychology, discrimination is viewed in terms of figure and ground. An object being focally attended to becomes the figure taking the forefront in perception, and similar irrelevant stimuli become the ground, therefore fading in perception. A common error in beginning discrimination is called *reversal*: lowercase letters *b* and *d*, for example, are confused with each other because the child is not focally attending to the important characteristic of the different direction of the letters.

Once stimuli are accurately discriminated and stored in short-term memory, they can be Associated, (Level V), which involves the process of connecting one stimulus with another on the basis of repeated presentation or similarities. For example, young children more often associate a picture of a chair with a picture of a table than with other choices, such as a lamp or bike, because table-chair are paired together much more often in experience. Much learning in the first three years of life is done at the association level, and early childhood experts should be aware of the associations they repeatedly present to children.

The highest level of information processing goes beyond simple perceptual skills and is called Conceptualization (Level VI). Conceptualization or concept formation is the process of placing specific stimuli into an abstract category. The term abstract in this sense means an idea not existing in the real world. For example, apples, oranges, and bananas exist in the real world because we can touch, see, taste, and smell them, but fruit is an abstract concept because it is a category name that has no single object to represent it in the world. Conceptualization is the process of placing individual stimuli in abstract categories and is the highest cognitive function necessary to perform simple academic tasks, such as letter and word recognition, spelling, and simple numeric operations.

A final important functional aspect of this model involves the sensory modalities used to process information required in learning tasks. Most adults are unaware of the information processing requirements of the tasks they require young children to perform. For example, the simple verbal request to "draw a picture of a person" requires that the child input auditory information, associate and conceptualize (what a person is), associate the auditory name with a visual image (what a person looks like), and then perform complex visual and motor skills to output the visual image. To keep the information processing requirements as simple as possible, a good rule of thumb for caregivers is to stay within the same sensory modalities for task requirements. For example, if you want a child to learn names of different fruit, require auditory input and *verbal* output by discussing what each fruit looks, smells, and tastes like; how the shapes are different; and similarities between them. If you choose to use visual input (pictures), keep verbal discussion at a minimum and require visual and motor output (pointing to pictures or drawing). By keeping tasks within the same sensory input/output modality, you reduce the complexity of the task requirements as much as possible.

Watson (1978) determined 11 Developmental Learning Skills to be essential prerequisites to learning preacademic skills. These skills are presented in Figure 2–3. Caregivers should systematically teach children over two years of age these skills as part of the daily curriculum to keep children unlimited in their learning skills.

SUMMARY OF THEORETICAL CONTRIBUTIONS

1. **Physical Development.** Major contributions to behavioral psychology, starting with Darwin and continuing through current research, provide task analysis of physical movements and behavioral skills. Breaking down goal behaviors into the natural steps, starting with the behaviors the child can perform and proceeding to the goal behavior, provides the caregiver with a powerful tool to keep children unlimited. When lots of positive attention, approval, and affection are added, the caregiver can enhance the physical development of all children in care.

   Vygotsky gave caregivers the powerful principles of private speech; the zone of proximal development, including how adults and children come to understand each other through intersubjectivity and scaffolding; and the important role of make-believe play. Use of these principles helps the caregiver keep children unlimited in their abilities to learn.

2. **Emotional Development.** Freud's psychosexual stages and the structure of personality (id, ego, and superego) provide caregivers with an understanding of the bases for feeling states. Caregivers can keep children unlimited by helping them develop a healthy ego (self-concept and self-esteem). They do this by teaching children how to identify and express their feelings and by filling their needs using a respectful value system that does not hurt the child or others.

   Erikson's Psychosocial Theory supplies stages for the development of essential personality characteristics, such as trust, autonomy, and initiative. Caregivers can plan daily activities using Erikson's stages to help children remain unlimited in their happiness and personality development.

   Teaching young children to identify and express feelings accurately in ways that help them fill their needs and not hurt others is a goal every caregiver should have to help children remain unlimited.

3. **Social Development.** To apply principles for relationships and interactions, the caregiver must first understand the development of the self. William James first defined the existential (authentic) self and the reflective self (me-not me). Bowlby's Ethnological Theory helps the caregiver understand how infants and toddlers participate in relationships through his four stages of attachment. Findings from many studies demonstrate that warm, sensitive, conscious caregiver-to-child interactions are essential to set the basis for keeping children unlimited in all their future relationships.

4. **Cognitive Development.** Piaget has provided greater understanding and more functional principles for higher cognitive development than any other theorist. The caregiver needs to be aware of the schemes that infants and toddlers use to interact with the environment through adaptation and cognitive organization (accommodation). Piaget's four stages of higher cognitive skills provide practical principles to use in keeping infants and toddlers unlimited in their higher cognitive development.

5. **Learning Skills Development.** Information processing theories help us to understand how children perceive the world and provide the caregiver with powerful tools to help children remain unlimited in their joy of learning. The store and levels-of-processing models offer understanding of how perception and memory occurs. Watson's Developmental Learning Skills model uses six levels of perceptual organization. It shows how the input and output of stimuli through sensory modalities help children remain unlimited by using the essential perceptual skills necessary to process information in preacademic tasks.

A comment on the narrowness of the information presented in this discussion is in order. There are entire bodies of research in each of the five Developmental Areas. The reader should understand that the scope of this text allows for only an overview of each area; numerous theories and research findings could not be presented in this brief review.

CHILDREN WITH SPECIAL NEEDS

All the theories, concepts, tools, and skills discussed in this book influence the care given to individual children. In no other field of child study is the theory of the unlimited child more profoundly applicable. Caregivers who use their knowledge to identify weaknesses in a child's growth areas and suggest early interventions may observe a step-by-step, positive change in the child that is a direct result of their actions.

Early interventions for at-risk infants and toddlers are currently available "in virtually every community in the United States, and in numerous other countries" (Guralnick & Bennett, 1987). Children who are considered at risk require specialized equipment, care, and curricula, and the child care specialist must learn how to care for children with special needs. Because it is impossible to cover all the special conditions and procedures necessary to care for at-risk children in one text, an overview of categories and characteristics is provided here. The child specialist should contact the appropriate associations and organizations for specific information on how to care for individual children with special needs.

The following are terms related to children with special needs.

Disability: impairment in sensory, physical, cognitive, emotional, or social areas that cause inability to perform at age level

Handicap: inability to perform up to normal expectations because of a disability

Special education: a specialized curriculum designed for a specific child or group of children with similar disabilities

Early intervention: curricula that address specific disabilities before any long-term damaging effects can occur

The following eight categories of infants and toddlers with special needs were taken from *The Effectiveness of Early Intervention for At-Risk and Handicapped Children* (Guralnick & Bennett, 1987).

1. **Environmentally At-Risk Infants and Toddlers.** Children from socially and economically disadvantaged families are included in this category. Results from several studies reveal that the most effective interventions involve attending day care and families receiving parent training on an ongoing basis. For more information, contact the local Health Department, Department of Social Services, or community charitable organizations, such as the American Red Cross.

2. **Biologically At-Risk Infants and Toddlers.** Some children experience central nervous system (CNS) damage, for example, from CNS infections, trauma, ingestion of toxins, and sustained hypoxia (lack of oxygen). Research results on interventions ranging from special nursery settings and free nursing and medical care to infant stimulation by parents yield mixed results, with very short-term positive effects. Interventions for this population appear to be more effective with parents than with children. For more information, contact the American Medical Association, County Health Department, American Association of Pediatrics, or local pediatricians.

3. **Children with Cognitive and General Developmental Disorders.** Some infants and toddlers exhibit delays in every facet of cognition, such as information processing, problem solving, and ability to apply information to new situations. Global delays in motor, language, and socioemotional areas are common with these children. They tend to reach milestones typically but at a much slower rate, with lower final levels of development, such as mental retardation, Down syndrome, and fetal alcohol syndrome. Research strongly indicates that early intervention programs prevent the decline in intellectual functioning found in mildly retarded children without intervention. Programs for moderately and profoundly retarded children are more effective with active parental participation and training, but overall they appear to be less effective than with mildly retarded infants and toddlers. For more information, contact the American Association on Mental Deficiency, the local Special Education Administration, or specific associations, such as the Down Syndrome Association.

4. **Children with Motor Handicaps.** Infants and toddlers with motor handicaps exhibit delayed motor development, retention of primitive reflexes, and abnormal muscle tone as the result of CNS damage or malformation. The three major disabilities that are accompanied by motor handicaps are cerebral palsy, myelomeningocele, and Down syndrome. Infants and toddlers with motor handicaps usually exhibit delays in other developmental areas as well because learning occurs through active exploration of the world. Research on interventions involving systematic exercise and sensory stimulation and integration indicate that early

(continued)

CHILDREN WITH SPECIAL NEEDS *(continued)*

intervention can improve motor and sensory development and encourage parent support and acceptance. For more information contact the American Medical Association, American Academy of Pediatrics, and local chapters of specific organizations such as the United Cerebral Palsy Foundation.

5. **Children with Language and Communication Disorders.** Infants and toddlers who exhibit problems with the mechanics of speech (phonation, moving air from the lungs through the mouth, and articulation) have speech disorders, and children with problems using the rules of language (labeling or forming sentences) have language disorders. Results of studies on various kinds of interventions suggest that the course of communication disorders can be modified through early intervention. For more information, contact the American Association for Speech and Language, Association for Speech and Hearing, and local chapters of associations for speech and language disorders.

6. **Children with Autism.** Infants and toddlers with autism exhibit disturbance in developmental rates and sequences, responses to sensory stimuli, communication, and capacity to relate appropriately to people, events, and objects. The incidence of autism in the general population is very low: 4 to 5 in every 10,000 births, and frequently occurs along with other handicapping conditions such as mental retardation. Research on structured early intervention programs, which include parents, have yielded highly encouraging results. For more information, contact the National Society for Children and Adults with Autism, the American Psychological Association, or your local psychological association.

7. **Children with Visual Impairments.** Infants and toddlers with severe visual impairments are found in approximately 1 out of 3000 births, with a wide variety of severity and etiology. The most important consideration is visual efficiency, which includes acuity, visual fields, ocular motility, binocular vision, adaptations to light and dark, color vision, and accommodation. Research findings indicate that early intervention helps visually impaired infants and toddlers perform closer to typical developmental expectations. Interventions using a team approach, including parents, child care specialists, and other professionals, is more effective than individual treatment approaches. For more information, contact the National Society for the Prevention of Blindness, National Council for Exceptional Children, the local Health Department, and agencies for the visually impaired.

8. **Children with Hearing Impairment.** Hearing impairments are classified by type (sensorineural, conductive, or mixed), time of onset (at birth or after), severity (mild to profound), and etiology. Research indicates that early intervention programs should include parent counseling, staff with training in audiology, staff with speech and language training, inclusion of sign language as a normal program component, the flexibility to help each family, and the inclusion of deaf adults as resources for children. For more information, contact the Council for Exceptional Children, local health department, and the Association for the Deaf and Hearing Impaired.

It is essential that child care specialists not work with special needs children in isolation. When any of the conditions described here are suspected, the child care specialist must consult professionals who are trained to evaluate, prescribe for, and treat these children. In fact, every child care program should have medical and psychological services as a regular part of the evaluation and care of children. It is also important for each child care specialist to network with other child development professionals in the area, such as psychologists, pediatricians, and speech and language therapists. The research from interventions with all types of special needs children strongly indicates that a team approach, including parents, child care staff, and specialized professionals, is necessary to keep special needs children as unlimited as possible.

Given that a team approach is necessary, several new curricula have been established for infants and toddlers with special needs. The states of California, North Carolina, and Florida are among the nation's leaders in programs for infants and toddlers with special needs. For example, *The Carolina Curriculum for Infants and Toddlers with Special Needs*, by Johnson et al. (1991), offers strategies, activities, and techniques for most categories of special needs children in all developmental areas. The child care specialist should contact the State Department of Education in these states to obtain specific information on the care of these children.

As late as 1970, most children with birth abnormalities or learning difficulties were viewed on an individual basis with no formal procedures or laws to direct their care. Educational theories and principles that would later become "Special Education" were just beginning. A landmark law was passed in 1976 called the Education of All Handicapped Children Act. This law later grew in scope and purpose and became The Individuals with Disabilities Education Act.

Because this act was passed, special needs children became entitled to appropriate public education regardless of their disability. The law provided that children should have the "least restrictive environment possible," which meant that all children would be registered in the same school district and special services would be provided as necessary.

Three- to five-year-olds were among the first to be served. Later, additional laws were passed to educate even younger children with special needs. One pediatrician, Dr. Cecilia McCarton, took exception to the accepted view that infants with special needs do not need special public assistance.

"In the 70's, the usual practice was to make a diagnosis and then send the parents of these children back to their own communities for follow-up care. There was not a single place that offered a diagnosis, prescription for care and actual appointments with those supporting professionals necessary for follow up. Parents faced extremely frustrating situations, and most often were devastated to find no available people in their community to follow through with our suggestions."

In response to the need, Dr. McCarton developed one of the first comprehensive treatment centers in the United States. She has conducted research on thousands of children with low birth weight and special anomalies. For more than 20 years, Dr. McCarton, of the McCarton Developmental Program in Manhattan, has done much to advance the areas of research in underweight preemies and children with special needs.

Functional Ability Versus Actual Age

Age appropriateness has a particular meaning in the design of curricula for special needs children. Special needs children often function at a lower level in certain areas than their actual age, so knowing the functional age of a child is essential for structuring and designing appropriate activities. Equally important is using attention, approval, and affection as a way of communicating and satisfying the child's needs.

(continued)

CHILDREN WITH SPECIAL NEEDS *(continued)*

Today, curricula for special needs children generally involve a didactic team approach. Specialists interact with each other on behalf of the child based on the type of special needs the child exhibits. A functional age is established in each area of development, and priorities for care are set using Developmental Profiles and Prescriptions.

Special Needs Children and Community Support

Caregivers must be aware of community resources for children with special needs. Many special needs children lack funding sources. Sometimes community groups or generous, qualified professionals donate their time and energy to ensure proper treatment for special groups. One example is the Nassau Cleft Palate Center and Dr. Pamela Gullagher, a plastic surgeon who volunteers her time and expertise to perform cleft palate repairs for children in need. The Nassau Cleft Palate Center has materials available for concerned parents, including *A Guide For Parents of Children with a Cleft Lip and Palate.* For more information, contact The Nassau Cleft Palate Center, Long Island Plastic Surgical Group, 999 Franklin Avenue, Garden City, Long Island, New York 11530, (516) 742-3404. Call The Cleft Palate Foundation at (412) 481-1376 for literature, resources, and parent groups nationwide.

Brain Gym

Simply described, the **Brain Gym** is a sequence of body movements and exercises that, when combined with other body movements, appears to promote new nerve networks in the brain. The human brain has three main structures: the cerebrum, the cerebellum, and the brain stem. The control center is the cerebrum, which processes all the information it receives. It is the largest part of the brain, comprising approximately 80 percent of the total area. Each of its two halves, called hemispheres, has five lobe areas. Each lobe area is responsible for specific tasks, such as recognition of images, bodily sensations, and emotions. The entire cerebrum is covered by a layer of gray matter called the cerebral cortex. This is where the higher intellectual functions originate, such as memory, receiving, and interpreting information from the five senses (vision, hearing, taste, smell, and touch).

The cerebellum is located at the back of the brain behind the cerebrum. This area helps the body maintain balance, stand upright, and coordinate muscle activity. The brain stem is the life-support system. It maintains essential functions, such as heartbeat, breathing, blood pressure, swallowing, and digestion. It is the site of the communication center in humans; it regulates additional processes, such as thirst and hunger; and it sends information to other parts of the brain.

One difference between the brain of a newborn and that of an adult is that the newborn's left and right hemisphere have not yet defined specific tasks and functions. Normally developed newborn infants have clearly defined brain anatomy waiting to be determined by stimuli processed from the environment.

By the end of 36 months, the hemispheres have defined functions with individual styles of integration. In normal children, the kind of experiences the environment offers will determine how well prepared the brain is for future learning and how well the hemispheres integrate information.

Brain Gym was developed by Drs. Paul and Gail Dennison (1995), who found that, when specific body maneuvers were done by children, their attention consistently improved. Brain Gym has successfully been used by children with autism and speech impairment, attention deficit, hyperactivity disorder, and emotional handicaps. All the maneuvers are designed to stimulate brain-center responses by working with connecting body parts that cross the body's midline. Debbie Neurnberger, a kinesthetic counselor who specializes in teaching Brain Gym techniques to children and adults, works at Mind Resources, Inc. in Honesdale, Pennsylvania. Brain Gym helps establish optimal learning readiness. Neurnberger (1994) explains, "These techniques are so easy that they are met with much skepticism. However, the results are consistently impressive. All educators should be promoting these simple techniques."

Teaching toddlers simple activities such as cross-pattern crawling, right-hand-to-left-knee exercise, Simon Says, and so forth, helps to promote focus and affects the child's focal attention. The elimination of sugar and high-carbohydrate foods is also recommended. It is also important to drink plenty of water.

Carla Hannaford, author of *Smart Moves: Why Learning Is Not All in Your Head* (1995), has this to say: "We must give learners mind/body integrative tools, such as Brain Gym, that allow them to stop the stress cycle and activate full sensory/hemisphere access."

We have defined major categories of handicapping conditions and general research findings and resources for working with infants and toddlers. This chapter has spelled out functional principles for working with children who show largely typical development.

Research in every category of special needs infants and toddlers strongly indicates that early intervention and inclusion in programs with typically developing children is helpful to the development of children with special needs. It is important to understand that children with special needs exhibit patterns and stages of development similar to those of typically developing infants and toddlers, but at a slower rate and with lower overall levels of development in certain areas.

The child care specialist should include children with special needs in programs by ensuring that the following conditions are met.

1. Infants and toddlers with special needs require more time and attention, so group size must be reduced.
2. Direct, active parent involvement in activities and procedures to assist development is necessary with these children, so parent education must be provided.
3. A team approach to including children with special needs is essential. The child specialist therefore must work closely with professionals such as psychologists, pediatricians, and speech therapists to design and implement appropriate interventions.
4. The child specialist must use specialized community resources and local and national associations to assist in the care and development of infants and toddlers with special needs.

By ensuring that these conditions are met, the child care specialist can provide effective early intervention and include special needs children in the normal child care program.

It has been estimated that the maximum amount of mental capacity used in conscious thought is only about 10 percent! This means that when we are thinking hard, 90 percent of our cognitive capacity is unused. Approaching young children with the theory that they are unlimited cognitively and perceptually encourages them to think and to learn at higher levels, giving them confidence that they are competent to understand the world. Compared to overexplaining or thinking for the child, approaching children as unlimited shows respect for their abilities to understand and participate cognitively with the adults who care for them. Children lack experience, but they do not lack to capacity to understand when given sensitive instruction and the opportunity to participate.

(continued)

CHILDREN WITH SPECIAL NEEDS *(continued)*

An example illustrates the value of applying the theory of the unlimited child to cognitive and learning skill areas. Dr. Watson once taught educable mentally handicapped children in a midwestern high school. Many of the regular students made fun of the special students, calling them stupid, retard, dummy, and the like. Since the school was proud of the chess club, Dr. Watson approached his class as being cognitively and perceptually unlimited and taught them to play chess, practicing with them daily. Within a few months, two of the mentally handicapped students were regularly winning matches with most members of the chess club and had become team players competing against other schools. This success was the result of the children being approached as capable, competent learners with the cognitive and perceptual abilities necessary to succeed when they are motivated to achieve.

The best principle for infant and toddler care is that children cannot be given too much attention, approval, and affection. They cannot be spoiled. Your sensitive caring sets the basis for all future relationships that the children in your care will have throughout their lives (Douville-Watson, L., 1988a).

Key Terms

accommodation

adaptation

assimilation

attentional skills: focal attention, prefocal attention, perceptual screening

attitude ceilings

Brain Gym

brain plasticity

cognitive disequilibrium

cognitive equilibrium

developmental learning skills

ego boundaries

existential self

hierarchy of needs

input

intersubjectivity

levels of processing

long-term memory

make-believe play

organization

output

perceptual level

phonemic features

private speech

reflective self

response generator

scaffolding

schemes

self-recognition

semantic features

sense of agency

sensory modalities

sensory register

separation and individuation

short-term memory

store model

symbiosis

task analysis

zone of proximal development

CASE STUDY   *Ideal Care*

Now that we have a framework in which to view the child, we will apply it to an ideal child care environment in which the goal is to keep a child unlimited; that is, always striving to reach his or her fullest potential.

Mary, age 30 months, enters the child care center at 7 A.M. each morning with her mother. She is greeted with a smile by the same caregiver each day. A few minutes are spent talking over what Mary's mother feels she needs today, and she receives positive attention from both her mother and the caregiver. When Mary shows she is ready for Mom to leave by willingly going to her caregiver or the other children, her mother gives Mary a hug and kiss and tells her she'll be back, and leaves. She plays happily with a little boy for a few minutes, but as soon as another child joins her, Mary stops smiling and withdraws. The caregiver, using the 3A's effectively, joins them and puts her arm around Mary while she talks and plays

 with the other children. Mary snuggles under her arm for a few minutes and then resumes playing with the children. During the morning Mary is exposed to group and individual activities that enhance large and fine muscle control and motor development. She is also involved in games for awareness and labeling of feeling states, as well as vocabulary development. Although nap time in the room is at 10:30 A.M., Mary shows signs of tiredness at 9:45, and the caregiver allows her to take her nap early. At lunch, Mary's perceptual development is aided through the provider playing a see-hear-smell-feel-and-taste game with her food. Whenever Mary exhibits a need, her caregiver sensitively and responsibly helps her fill the need right away.

Mary is helped to feel happy and fulfilled because the caregiver gives her stimulating activities in each of the five Developmental Areas each day, focusing her attention on the positives in herself and the environment. The caregiver also provides her with a lot of the 3A's of child care: Attention, Affection, and Approval.

When Mary's mother picks her up at 5:30 P.M., she is rested and happy and greets her with a hug and smile. The caregiver and the mother talk a few minutes about Mary's day and the caregiver gives the mother some follow-up activities to do with Mary during the evening.

Although this scenario is ideal and can't always be accomplished, the caregiver who has learned how to identify and meet her own needs and give herself Attention, Approval, and Affection can give the same kind of nurturing as she helps children be as unlimited as possible.

1. How can you apply the five major Developmental Areas in your daily routine?
2. What should be done when Mary starts to show signs of tiredness?
3. How does the care structure ensure consistency in Mary's need fulfillment?

Student Activities

1. Copy the Developmental Profile Form in Appendix B and assess one infant and one toddler by establishing a complete profile for each using the Developmental Prescriptions in Appendix A.
2. Observe two children and take notes on which Need Levels they appear to exhibit during the period of one hour.
3. Using the Developmental Prescriptions in Appendix A, task-analyze (write up the small steps) what you would do to help move a child's behavior from one developmental level to the next. For example, determine how you can help an infant move from "moves arms randomly" to "reaches" with arms.
4. Using the Developmental Prescriptions in Appendix A, work with one child to move him or her from one developmental level to the next for a particular behavior.

Chapter Review

1. List differences between the Unlimited Child theory and the Tabula Rasa theories of development.
2. Describe why needs at one level must be met before a person can move to the next higher level.
3. Describe a personal experience in which you were able to function at the Self-Actualization need level.
4. Compare the behavior of two children of the same age in the Social Learning Skill Area.

References

Atkinson, R. C., & Shiffrin, R. M. (1968). Human memory: A proposed system and its control processes. In K. W. Spence & J. T. Spence (Eds.), *Advances in the psychology of learning and motivation* (Vol. 2, pp. 90–195). New York: Academic Press.

Behrend, D. A., Rosengran, K. S., & Perlmutter, M. (1992). The relation between private speech and parental interactive style. In R. M. Diaz & L. E. Berk (Eds.), *Private speech: From social interaction to self-regulation* (pp. 85–100). Hillsdale, NJ: Erlbaum.

Beilin, H. (1992). Piaget's enduring contribution to developmental psychology. *Developmental Psychology, 28,* 191–204.

Berk, L. E. (1994). Why children talk to themselves. *Scientific American, 271*(5), 78–83.

Berk, L. E. (2000). *Child development* (5th ed.). Boston: Allyn and Bacon.

Berk, L. E., & Spuhl, S. T. (1995). Maternal interaction, private speech, and task performance in preschool children. *Early Childhood Research Quarterly, 10,* 145–169.

Bernstein, N. (1967). *The coordination and regulation of movements.* London: Pergamon.

Bowlby, J. (1969). *Attachment.* New York: Basic Books.

Brazelton, T. B., & Cramer, B. (1990). *The earliest relationships: Parents, infants and drama of early attachments.* New York: Delacorte Press, 25–26.

Bretherton, I. (1992). The origins of attachment theory: John Bowlby and Mary Ainsworth. *Developmental Psychology, 29,* 759–75.

Bullock, M., & Lutkenhaus, P. (1990). Who am I? The development of self-understanding in toddlers. *Merrill-Palmer Quarterly, 36,* 217–238.

Craik, F. I. M., & Lockhart, R. S. (1972). Levels of processing: A framework for memory research. *Journal of Verbal Learning and Verbal Behavior, 11,* 671–684.

Dennison, G., & Dennison, P. E. (1995). *Brain gym, teacher's edition.* Ventura, CA: Edu Kinesthetics.

Diaz, R. M., & Berk, L. E. (1995). A Vygotskian critique of self-instructional training. *Development and Psychopathology, 7,* 369–392.

Douville-Watson, L. (1988a). *The 3A's of child care: Attention, approval and affection.* Oyster Bay, NY: Lifeskills Institute.

Douville-Watson, L. (1988b). *Family actualization through research and education: F.A.R.E.* (3rd ed.). New York: Actualization, Inc.

Erikson, E. H. (1950). *Childhood and society.* New York: Norton.

Freud, S. (1973). *An outline of psychoanalysis.* London: Hogarth. (Original work published 1938).

Furman, E. (1992). *Toddlers and their mothers: A study in early personality development.* Madison, CT: International Press.

Guralnick, M. J., & Bennett, F. C. (Eds.). (1987). *The effectiveness of early intervention for at-risk and handicapped children.* San Diego: Academic Press, Inc.

Hannaford, C. (1995). Smart moves: Why learning is not all in your head. Arlington, VA: Great Ocean Publishers.

Hofsten, C. von. (1989). Motor development as the development of systems. *Developmental Psychology, 25,* 950–953.

Isabella, R. A. (1993). Origins of attachment: Maternal interactive behavior across the first year. *Child Development, 64,* 605–621.

Johnson, N. M., Jens, K. G., Attermeier, S. M., & Hacker, B. J. (1991). *The Carolina curriculum for infants and toddlers with special needs* (2nd ed.). Baltimore: Paul H. Brookes.

King, C. E. (1979). Focal attention training in kindergarten through third grade attention deficit children. Unpublished doctoral dissertation, Hofstra University, Hempstead, New York.

Levine, L. E. (1983). Mine: Self-definition in 2-year-old boys. *Developmental Psychology, 19,* 544–549.

Lillard, A. S. (1993). Pretend play skills and the child's theory of mind. *Child Development, 64,* 348–371.

Maslow, A. H. (1954). *Motivation and personality.* New York: Harper and Row.

McCarton, C. (1994). An interview with a child. Bronx, NY: Beth Israel Hospital Information Center.

Nash, J. (Feb. 24, 1997). *Fertile minds.* How a child's brain develops and what it means for child care and welfare reform. *Time.*

Neurnberger, D. (1994). *Brain gym exercises.* Honesdale, PA: Mind Resources.

Pipp. S., Easterbrooks, M. A., & Brown, S. R. (1993). Attachment status and complexity of infants' self- and other-knowledge when tested with mother and father. *Social Development, 2,* 1–14.

Rast, M., & Meltzoff, A. N. (1995). Memory and representation in young children with Down syndrome: Exploring deferred imitation and object permanence. *Development and Psychopathology, 7,* 393–407.

Rogoff, B., & Chavajay, P. (1995). What's become of research on the cultural basis of cognitive development? *American Psychologist, 50,* 859–877.

Sroufe, L. A. (1996). *The organization of emotional life in the early years.* Cambridge Studies in Social and Educational Development. New York: Cambridge University Press.

Vygotsky, L. S. (1986). *Thought and language* (A. Kozulin, trans.). Cambridge, MA: MIT Press. (Original work published 1934).

Waters, E., Vaughn, B. E., Posada, G., & Kondo-Ikemura, K. (Eds.). (1995). Caregiving, cultural, and cognitive perspectives on secure-base behavior and working models: New growing points of attachment theory and research. *Monographs of the Society for Research in Child Development*, *60*(2–3, Serial No. 244).

Watson, M. A. (1977). *Tests of group learning skills*, experimental edition. Freeport, NY: Activity Records.

Watson, M. A. (1978). Tests of group learning skills. Freeport, NY: Activity Records.

Watson, M. A. (1995). *WALDO developmental learning program*. Glen Cove, NY: Instructional Press.

Additional Resources

Craik, F. I. M., & Tulving, E. (1975). Depth of processing and the retention of words in episodic memory. *Journal of Experimental Psychology: General*, *104*, 268–294.

James, W. (1963). *Psychology*. New York: Fawcett. (Original work published 1890).

Helpful Web Sites

The American Psychological Association (APA) A wealth of information regarding psychology in all areas of inquiry. http://www.apa.org

The American Psychological Society (APS) Schedules for conventions, teaching, research, and other information. http://www.psychologicalscience.org

Psych Web Psychology-related information for students and teachers of psychology. http://www.psychwww.com

Sigmund Freud and the Freud Archives Collection of links to resources such as libraries, museums, and biographical materials. http://users.rcn.com/brill/freudarc.html

Nanny's Place for Parents Resources for parents-to-be and parents of small children and infants. http://www.moonlilly.com/parents/

For additional infant and toddler resources, visit our Web site at http://www.earlychilded.delmar.com

Birth to Preschool Developmental Patterns

3

Objectives
After reading this chapter, you should be able to:

- Define the differences between development and learning.
- Identify typical patterns of physical, emotional, social, cognitive, and learning skill development between birth and preschool ages.
- Explain the relationship between the sequence and the rate of development for individuals.
- Understand how the development of each child differs from typical patterns of development.
- Understand how children with developmental delays differ from typical patterns.

Chapter Outline
Differences between Development and Learning
The Part-Whole Relationship
Patterns of Development in Five Major Areas

DIFFERENCES BETWEEN DEVELOPMENT AND LEARNING

As with many unresolved questions in child development, entire books are written on the nature versus nurture controversy. Many authors contend that child development is the result of heredity and natural biological processes that are largely independent of learning and experience (nature), whereas many others argue that development mostly depends on learning (nurture) (Plomin, 1994). The best conclusion to date is that child development is a very complex process occurring through natural sequences and patterns that depend on learning and experience, among other processes (Berk, 2000).

For purposes of this book, **development** is operationally defined as general sequences and patterns of growth and maturity. **Learning** is only one process involved in development. Development follows a generally predictable sequence of behaviors that mark change from dependency on the environment to independence from the environment. To track development, specific behaviors common to an entire population are observed when they are first manifested or are consistently manifested. These behaviors are called **milestones**. We measure development of an individual child by comparing milestone behaviors with the large group that were used to establish what behavior is "normal" for that period of time.

Children grow in five Major Developmental Areas along the same general sequences and patterns regardless of social, cultural, or environmental influences. However, children move through these developmental sequences at largely varying rates. The rate of development for each individual is dependent on many factors, including environmental experiences, culture, heredity, metabolism, and nutrition (Berk, 2000).

A major goal of this book is to help the caregiver understand normal sequences and patterns of development and to become familiar with learning tools that enhance development in the five major developmental areas. To this end, the Developmental Prescriptions in Appendix A present general patterns of development from birth through three years of age, and construction of Developmental Profiles (Appendix B) and the CDA Goals and Objectives (Appendix C) provide the structural basis for enhancing the development of individual children.

To fully understand the learning tools presented throughout this book, the reader must have a clear understanding of what is meant by learning. For purposes of this book, the authors define *learning* as change in a response to a stimulus resulting from practice or conscious awareness. This definition takes into consideration both overt behavioral changes in responses and more internal changes in perceptions resulting from practice or conscious awareness, or both. In other words, changes in a response to a stimulus can either be observable to another person (overt) or can occur internally without obvious change in observable behavior (internal). Much of the learning that occurs during the first three years of life is this internal type. Therefore, the caregiver must consistently observe the child very carefully to understand how changes in responses create the perceptions, thoughts, beliefs, attitudes, feelings, and behaviors that comprise the young child's evolving map of the world. Since no two individuals have the same map of the world, the biggest challenge for early childhood specialists is to understand developmental patterns and determine how each child differs from expected patterns.

THE PART-WHOLE RELATIONSHIP

This chapter extends the theories, concepts, and principles presented in Chapters 1 and 2 to better understand the whole child. A necessary aspect of studying child development is to "take apart" the child into the essential skills, abilities, and factors that must be understood individually before putting the pieces back together to make a more meaningful and understandable whole. Patterns of development are discussed in each of five Major Developmental Areas in this chapter: Physical, Emotional, Social, Cognitive, and Learning (Perceptual, Language, and Academic) Skills. Then, the integration of these five factors are discussed in terms of child behaviors and the interactions between child, caregiver, and parents. Once individual parts are understood, the caregiver can apply the knowledge to competently care for the whole, living, breathing and constantly changing child.

From the moment of birth the child and the people around the child affect each other. This dynamic interaction is sometimes deliberate and controlled and sometimes unconscious behavior. Caregivers working with infants and toddlers plan many experiences for children. Simultaneous with these planned experiences are the thousands of actions that are spontaneous, that stimulate new actions and reactions and challenge both the child and the caregiver (Figure 3–1).

Magda Gerber (1998) has established an approach and structure for child care that emphasizes the interaction between child and caregiver. This approach is illustrated through her "10 principles of caregiving."

1. Involve children in activities and things that concern them.
2. Invest in quality time with each child.
3. Learn the unique ways each child communicates with you and teach him or her the way you communicate.

Figure 3–1 Children interact spontaneously with one another.

4. Invest in the time and energy necessary with each child to build a total person.
5. Respect infants and toddlers as worthy people.
6. Model specific behaviors before you teach them.
7. Always be honest with children about your feelings.
8. View problems as learning opportunities and allow children to solve their own problems where possible.
9. Build security with children by teaching trust.
10. Be concerned about the quality of development each child has at each stage.

These 10 principles fit well with the goals and objectives of the CDA certification program. A caregiver who follows all of these principles will also fulfill some major requirements for CDA certification.

PATTERNS OF DEVELOPMENT IN FIVE MAJOR AREAS

In performing psychological assessments, humans skills and abilities are separated into five major areas for evaluation. This evaluation structure provides an excellent format for understanding the development of infants and toddlers. Throughout, child development and care are discussed in terms of these five major developmental areas in order.

1. physical factors
2. emotional factors
3. social factors
4. cognitive factors
5. learning skill factors

At birth, infants are already developing and learning. They are actively involved with themselves and the world. The child constantly interacts with the world, making adjustments in actions as information is processed and organized. Understanding your role and the interaction between development, learning, and experience helps you to determine the child's present level of development, his or her potential next step, and the specific areas in which the child needs your help. This determines the child's zone of proximal development and is the basis for high-quality care.

Physical Development

Physical development includes neurological, gross physical, sensory, teething, motor, and sleep, and elimination growth. Each of these is discussed below.

Neurological Development   The nervous system is responsible for communications of all body parts and ultimately with the environment. This section defines and familiarizes the reader with the major nervous system functions. Newborns are complex beings whose growth and development is closely related to the health and integrity of the nervous system which is made up of the brain, the spinal cord, and nerve cells (neurons).

By the end of the eighth week of pregnancy the foundation for all body structures, including the brain and nervous system, are evident in the growing fetus. Nerve cells (neurons) store and transmit information. At birth the brain is packed with an estimated 100 billion neurons, many of which die due to lack of stimulation. However, each surviving neuron can make over 10,000 different connections to other cells over time (Beatty, 1995). Pathways and networks of neurons are formed that carry coded information from all body parts to the brain. The lower brain, called the brain stem, is the seat of emotion. The midbrain is responsible for regulating automatic functions, such as breathing, digestion, and alertness. Another part of the brain, called the cerebellum, regulates coordination and balance.

The cerebral cortex is what distinguishes our species as human. Considered the most important part of the brain, it is the slowest-growing and largest part of the brain. The cerebral cortex begins at around 12 months to organize and specify functions for neuron activity. Other parts of the brain continue to grow rapidly only through the second year of life, whereas the cerebral cortex continues to grow until the fourth decade of life. The nervous system is the "command center" for all the vital functions of the body.

At birth, the brain weighs 25 percent of an adult's, and by 24 months it has tripled its weight, being 75 percent of an adult's. This increased weight is due to specific brain cells, called glia, which consist of a fatty sheathing called myelin. Myelin is a substance that protects, coats and insulates neurons, helping connect impulses from one neuron to another. These impulses are coded information lines that function like insulated electrical wires, carrying vital current to where it is needed in the body and brain. The myelin coating promotes the transfer of information from one neuron to another. It is a scientific fact and the basis of much study that neurons require environmental stimulation in order to grow. This fact is also of great importance for you—the parent, grandparent, teacher, guardian, or caregiver. It has been demonstrated that physiological changes occur within the nervous system of the child as he or she processes environmental information. Your individual input controls much of the information registering within the actual nerve cells of the child. Appropriate and meaningful contact with infants by the caregiver is vital to continued overall neurological growth.

As previously stated, the cerebral cortex is the largest structure of the brain and continues to grow well into adulthood. The cerebral cortex receives stimuli in the form of sensory information. Associations are formed between the thought processes, and physical actions. Specific areas of the cerebral cortex control special functions, such as vision, hearing, and motor movement. Neurological development of these specialized areas follows a particular pattern as the development of the child progresses. Processes such as sitting, crawling, and standing are called milestones. For example, milestones for motor movement are controlled by the cortex, and the cortex develops the neurology for head and chest control before the trunk and legs.

To be a competent caregiver of infants and toddlers, it is important to recognize the impact you have on the child's neurological growth and to initiate activities that reinforce the natural sequences of behaviors that support healthy growth in all areas. You, the child's caregiver, directly affect neurological growth through the activities and interactions you provide during the first months and years of life. Caregivers have an enormously important opportunity to influence the basic structure of the child's developing neurological systems by presenting positive, appropriate activities to enhance growth and development (Douville-Watson, L., 2001).

Physical Growth   The brain grows from the inside out. The size of the head doesn't change as drastically as the weight of the head (i.e., head weight is three times heavier at age two than at birth). This weight is caused by the growing density of the brain, due to developing neuron pathways. Motor neuron pathways appear to be waiting or expecting specific stimuli at birth. These pathways are called **experience-expectant**. The environment provides expected stimuli; for example, reflex sucking during breast feeding is experience-expectant. Infant survival obviously depends on experience-expectant pathways. Another set of neuron pathways called **experience-dependent** seems to wait for new experience to activate pathways. Specific experience-dependent cells form synapses for stable motor patterns only after environmental stimuli are repeated several times. Wh'en stimulation from the environment occurs in a consistent way, a stable pathway is created and physical changes occur in the nervous system. The ability to change neurologically and behaviorally from experience is one of the human brain's greatest assets and explains our unique flexibility and adaptability to the environment.

Human babies are different from any other species because they cannot stand immediately after birth and so cannot get themselves out of harm's way. However, the gestation process results in a complete person because, if the process took any more time, the head would be too big for the birth process to safely complete. The newborn's head is the largest part of the body and is usually born first. The circumference of the head increases by about three inches during the first eight months, and by two years of age the head is 90% of adult size (Lamb & Campos, 1982). At birth, the baby's head is not fused but has "soft spots" in the front and back. The back soft spot closes after a few months, but the front spot stays soft for almost two years.

Reflexes are the beginnings of more complex behavior. As the cerebral cortex develops rapidly in the first weeks of life, reflexes quickly change from involuntary reactions to purposeful, intentional actions that support the growing child through time and experience.

Children usually gain body weight at an astounding rate during the first 12 months of life if they are physically nurtured and active, but children who are restrained from physical movement often gain weight at a slower rate. Height usually parallels weight, so children who gain weight slowly in the first three years also tend to grow in height slowly. The caregiver should be aware that there are large variations in the rate of physical growth in children under three years of age. Growth spurts and plateaus are normal for development of height, weight, activity levels, and so on, so the caregiver should keep careful records of physical milestones and consult with parents and health professionals on body development.

Newborns use all their senses: listening, seeing, tasting, touching, and smelling. Smell may be closely related to emotion because the nasal canal leads directly to the limbic system in the brain. This could explain why olfaction is the most powerful sensory anchor for evoking emotional development. Caroline Olko and Gerald Turkewitz (2001) conducted experiments suggesting that hemispheric specialization for emotion is present during early infancy. "This indicates that infant senses become physically developed as they become involved in coordinating their senses with movement and thinking" (Olko & Turkewitz, 2001).

Hearing Development Newborns respond to a range of sounds. They startle easily with sudden loud noises and become agitated with high-pitched noises. They turn their heads to locate sound and show interest in their mother's voices. Infants explore their own utterings and play with sound. A caregiver should respond to an infant's initiation of sound. This encouragement is the foundation of future language and continued learning skill development.

Infants begin babbling by around seven months, and if they are delayed in making or responding to sounds, this may be an indication of a hearing problem. Ears should regularly be checked for infections or blockage because auditory problems can drastically interfere with language development and cause later learning disabilities. One condition to be checked by a medical professional during the first 24 months is minimal ear infections. Any difficulty hearing can negatively affect the critical language development ages from birth to 36 months.

Vision Development Infants use their eyes from birth, although their vision develops relatively slowly. By the fourth month, coordination of both eyes can be observed. Before approximately five months, babies prefer contrasting colors, particularly black and white, because the contrast holds their interest longer (Walther-Lee, 1998), They focus well with both eyes at a distance of 12 inches, which is the normal distance for breast-feeding. By age two, vision is around 20/80 and full 20/20 acuity is expected by school age. Eye color is permanent by six months. **Focusing and tracking** (moving both eyes together) develops through the first three years of life, and children should be able to focus and track across a line of letters by the time they are four years old.

Teething Infants usually begin teething between four and eight months, but individuals vary widely in teething. New teeth erupt every month or so after the first one. Sometimes an emerging tooth causes an infant to be very fussy and irritable, but at other times a new tooth just seems to appear with no discomfort at all. Teething infants often like to bite things using teething rings and anything else they can put in their mouths. When an infant seems to be in pain from teething, a cold teething ring or crushed ice in a clean cloth provides both coldness and hardness for the child's gums. Never rub gums with an alcohol substance to relieve discomfort, and contact a dentist or medical consultant if pain persists. Teething infants may drool profusely, so they may need to wear a bib all day, which must be changed frequently to keep their clothes dry.

The average age for having all 20 baby teeth is around 24 months. According to Nicolas Johniditis, D.D.S., "Parents and caregivers should treat a child's first teeth with great care because the mouth is growing and first teeth create space for second teeth. Good oral hygiene and dental practice like regular brushing and check-ups from the dentist can prevent unnecessary difficulty with second teeth." In addition, young children can be introduced to the doctor, dental assistant, and office staff. This is an opportunity for them to become accustomed to the noise, lights, chair, and so forth, in a fun way rather than with a fearful association (Douville-Watson, L., 2001).

Motor Development There are a variety of theories on motor development. One theory of motor development, called the Dynamic Systems Theory, predicts that individual behaviors and skills of the growing infant combine and work together to create a more efficient and effective system. "Kicking, rocking on all fours, and reaching gradually are put together in crawling. The, crawling, standing, and stepping are united into walking alone" (Hofsten, 1989). "Each skill is learned by revising and combining earlier accomplishments to fit a new goal. Consequently, different pathways to the same outcome exist, and infants achieve motor milestones in unique ways" (Berk, 1998).

Another theory is Bernstein's Biodynamic Theory of Motor Development. Bernstein observed that when a person's body moves, it is not only responding to messages from the brain but also to outside forces, such as gravity, centripetal forces, and torque (i.e., the stress you feel at your elbow joint when you lift a weight). All these influences work together in an ever changing symphony of forces (Bernstein, 1967). In other words, according to this theory the only reason that infants do not walk at birth is that their heads are heavy and their limbs not strong enough to resist the force of gravity. Therefore, all physical functions are in preparation for walking, and gravity is used to overcome muscle weakness. According to Bernstein, larger babies are more successful at walking early because they are stronger and more able to defy gravity.

Physical development occurs in a predetermined order, starting from the head and chest and moving to trunk and lower extremities. This directional growth is readily observable as the infant gains control of head, chest, trunk, and then legs to turn over. To crawl, the infant gains control of lower back and leg muscles, and to walk, the infant gains control of neck, shoulders, back, legs, feet, and toes. Infants develop control of their arm movements from erratic waving to accurate reaching. Hand control develops from accidentally bumping and hitting to purposefully touching. Reaching occurs first, with an open hand grip. Then, the fingers develop from reflexive pinching, grasping and reflexive releasing to controlled opening and closing. Physical development progresses from large motor activity (called **gross motor control**), to small muscle activity, (called **fine motor control**). Three areas of movement that are developed over the first three years are (1) stability, (2) locomotion, and (3) manipulation. *Stability* refers to sitting and standing upright; *locomotion* refers to crawling, walking, and running; and *manipulation* includes reaching, grasping, releasing, and throwing.

Gross motor development involves large movements through milestone achievements, such as crawling, standing, walking, and throwing (Figure 3–2). Fine motor development milestones involve smaller, more refined movements, like grasping and pointing. The progression of motor development is fairly uniform, but individual children vary within and between cultures in the age at which they develop both gross

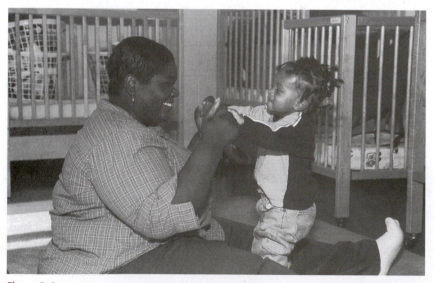

Figure 3–2 Walking is a milestone of motor development.

and fine motor skills. Milestones of development are essential for teachers to know. One of the teacher's most important tasks is to identify children who are not reaching the milestone markers within a specific range of time. The teacher becomes concerned about motor development and seeks further professional assistance only when several motor skill areas are developmentally delayed.

Appendix A provides a somewhat detailed Developmental Prescription of motor skill milestones for infants through three years of age. At around six weeks of age, children begin to hold their heads steady and erect. By two months, infants lift their upper bodies by their arms and can roll from side to back. From three to four months, babies begin grasping palm-size objects and can roll from back to side. From six to eight months, they can sit alone and begin to crawl. Between eight and ten months, babies pull up to stand and perhaps play patty cake. At this time they begin to stand alone, and then begin to walk. From 13 to 16 months, children can build a tower of two cubes, vigorously scribble with a large crayon, and begin to walk with help upstairs. At around 20 to 24 months, toddlers begin to jump in place and kick objects. By 26 to 30 months, children begin to climb, stand on one foot, and have some interest in potty training. Usually at around 36 months, the child can jump and becomes toilet trained.

As this general outline indicates, motor development is a progression from one milestone behavior to the next, based on successful integration of the previous behaviors and neurological maturity resulting from environmental experiences. Children who develop within the average range do not necessarily proceed through all of the developmental milestones or move in the exact sequence outlined in a specific Developmental Prescription. The challenge for the caregiver is to observe behavioral milestones and determine where individual children fall on the general scale of motor development. The caregiver should use a Developmental Prescription, perform careful observations of behavioral milestones, and clearly determine where individual children are compared to the normal expectations for the age range. By performing evaluations on a regular basis, caregivers can determine which areas of motor development require specific tasks and activities to enhance development and areas in which advanced development in motor skills is shown. The movements and steps involved in gross and fine motor skills can be broken down into a step-by-step format (task analysis), in which an activity is observed and measured. Children can then be taught each small step that leads to mastery of a complex task.

Sleep and Elimination Development   A *state* is an organized pattern of physical responses that relates to arousal levels. A state can last minutes, many hours, or even years. Changing a young child's state from crying or sleeping to being calm or fully alert can be difficult at times because states are relatively stable in young children. Five states of arousal have been defined and carefully studied in young children (Wolff, 1993; Zeskind & Marshall, 1991).

> **Quiet sleep.** Respirations are regular, eyes are closed and not moving, and the child is relatively motionless.
> **Active sleep.** Muscles are more tense than in quiet sleep, the eyes may be still or display rapid eye movements (REM), breathing is irregular, and there are spontaneous startles, sucks, and rhythmic bursts of movement.
> **Drowsiness.** Eyes open and close and there is increased activity, more rapid and regular breathing, and occasional smiling.

Quiet alert. Eyes open and the environment is scanned, the body is still, and respiration is more rapid than in sleep.

Active alert. The child is awake and has body and limb movements, although the child is less likely to attend to external stimulation and focuses eyes less often than in quiet alert state.

Crying. Activity and respiration rate are elevated, and there is cry vocalization and a facial expression of distress.

Newborns sleep an average of 16 to 17 hours per day. Sleep periods range from two to ten hours. By three to four months, infants regularly sleep more at night than during the day, but night awakenings are common throughout infancy and early childhood (Andes, Goodlin-Jones, & Zelinko, 1998; Kleitmar, 1963).

To help infants sleep, place the baby on his back or side on a firm mattress. *Do not* let the child sleep with a bottle. Provide dimmed light and quiet, soft voice tones. Hold and rock the child before she goes to sleep and make every effort to reduce stimulation.

Respiration is controlled by two different neural systems. One system controls the voluntary actions of breath when speaking and the other controls the autonomic breathing during different levels of sleep. The autonomic nervous system changes respiration from normal sleep, wherein breaths are slow and regular, and progresses to just before and after sound sleep, in which breathing becomes faster, more shallow, and less regular. These periods before and after deep sleep are brief dream states called REM sleep. Faster, more shallow, and less regular breathing during this state shows the activity of both neural systems being activated.

A condition in which breathing momentarily stops is called sleep apnea (Hofsten, 1989). Short periods of apnea are normal during REM sleep, but with some children these episodes are prolonged and more frequent. Infrequently, sleep apnea can become dangerous to a person's health because the period of not breathing becomes too long. Some research suggests that **Sudden Infant Death Syndrome (SIDS)** may be related to sleep apnea. SIDS is a tragic event in which a young child dies after going to sleep for a nap or at bedtime with no indication of having discomfort. Research on apnea in infants indicates that the baby's brain is not mature and therefore periods of instability occur. Since young children spend extensive periods in REM sleep, the instability of the nervous system may cause such extended apnea that the child stops breathing completely (Beatty, 1995). The incidence of SIDS is very low (two infants per 1000 births between one week and one year of age), but the American Association of Pediatrics recommends that infants who are placed on their backs to sleep have a lower incidence of SIDS (Stokes, 2001). As long as the child is awake, however, belly lying should be encouraged to develop chest muscles, which are important for normal development.

As children become more mobile and begin to crawl and walk, their sleep patterns change and they require less sleep. Children should be encouraged to rest on a daily basis, and a well-planned child care program provides morning and afternoon nap times for children under three years of age. A balance of structured physical activity and rest are essential for optimal physical and emotional development and growth.

Elimination training has been accomplished as early as six months of age with some babies, but there appears to be a moderate correlation between early forced bowel and bladder training and later emotional problems (Berk, 2000). The muscles that control bowel and bladder are called sphincter muscles and are usually not mature until after 18 months of age. Toilet training requires the child to become aware of the sensations of the sphincter muscles and to control them until the appropriate time, when he or she relaxes the muscles to eliminate. This awareness first happens with larger muscles, and control usually occurs first with bowel movements at around 24 months of age.

Bowel movements of young, nonmobile infants are generally golden in color for formula-fed babies and mushy stool is expected from breast fed babies. After about six months, when solid food is introduced, it is common to find undigested food in the stool. Children may not be toilet trained until after three years of age. In fact, a child must be over four years old to be diagnosed as having encopresis, which is lack of bowel control, and must be over five years old to be diagnosed with enuresis, which is the inability to control urination (APA, 1994).

When children are ready to be toilet trained, they practically train themselves, with a little guidance and encouragement. The best approach to toilet training is to heap a lot of positive attention on success and take as much attention away from the child as possible for toilet mistakes. The less attention brought to accidents, the better. It is important never to shame a child. The child should participate as much as possible for his or her age in cleaning up when mistakes are made. Acting as if a simple mistake was made helps the child realize that he or she can come to you for assistance during training (Douville-Watson, L., 2001).

Baby diapers should always be changed when wet. With young children, it is common to have seven or eight changes within a 12-hour period. Some children may have several bowel movements per day, while others may have only one. If a child does not have a bowel movement each day, the parents should be notified because constipation can be a problem in some cases. Diarrhea can also be a problem because of the possibility of rapid dehydration. As with other areas of physical development, accurate daily records should be kept on elimination and shared with parents. It is important to recognize that parents are your partners in toilet training, as well as in all other aspects of child care.

Emotional Development

Unlike most other warm-blooded species, human offspring cannot stand up immediately at birth and lack the ability to remove themselves from danger, hide, or go to their primary source of food. Human infants are totally dependent on the environment to supply their most basic needs. For independent physical survival, children are born nine months too soon because they require assistance for that amount of time before they can stand and move independently within the environment. Therefore, a caregiver needs to create a safe and secure space for the physical and emotional survival of the child. A child should be provided with conscious care; be kept warm, fed, and stress-free; and should have his needs fulfilled quickly. Very young children should be touched, kept close to the chest, (to hear the heart beat), talked to, played soft music, and rocked. Children should be provided with appropriate transportation to move from one place to another safely (an ideal device is a baby carrier in which the infant is carried next to the chest.).

A safe and secure environment similar to the womb creates a positive learning environment in which children feel secure to initiate responses to their environment based on interest and curiosity. Children should not be judged because they have great needs (Figure 3–3). Needs are directed energy, and directed needs become behavior. There are no bad children; there is simply forceful energy that requires redirection. When the child's

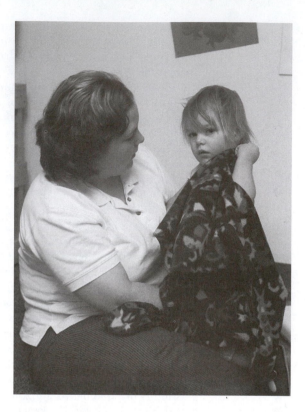

Figure 3–3 There are no bad children—only unmet needs.

needs and energy requirements are met, the child experiences a world that invites his or her participation (Douville-Watson, L., 2000).

Evolution of Feelings The most basic feelings on a physical level are pleasure and pain. It was once thought that newborns experience only these two general feeling states. However, anyone who has extensively cared for a young infant understands that infants experience and express the full range of human emotion from ecstasy to depression. Through active experience with their environment, babies quickly learn to repeat behaviors that result in pleasurable experiences and avoid, as much as they can, behaviors that result in pain. It sometimes appears that young children move through emotions rapidly. One minute a young toddler may scream, and the next moment jump into your arms and give you a hug. As the child grows older and cognitive and language skills develop, he or she is more able to use words to specify and describe many different feeling states.

During the first three years of life, the combination of traits present at birth, including physical size, health, and temperament, interact with pleasurable and painful experiences in the environment to form the growing child's personality. This section describes how temperament, security, trust, bonding versus separation-individuation, and ego development combine to help form the child's perceptions of self, others, and the world. This map of the world is the basis for the enduring reactions and patterns people have throughout life that we call personality.

Security and Trust Positive temperament traits can be enhanced by ensuring that the infant or toddler develops security and trust with caregivers.

Consistent and appropriate behavior from the caregiver is necessary to provide security for the child. Consistent but inappropriate behavior or inconsistent but appropriate behavior has been shown to be detrimental to development of security and trust.

The way to ensure consistent and appropriate caregiver behavior with children is to establish consistent routines and supply generous amounts of the 3A's of child care: Attention, Approval, and Affection. A major principle to use in shaping behavior is to reward behavior that approximates (comes closest to) the behavior you want with the 3A's, and to withdraw reward for behavior that you don't want. For example, when you ask Rose, who knows how to wash her hands, to wash up and she tries hard and does well for her level of skill development, you heap on the 3A's. If Rose doesn't try and just swishes under the water, you do not give her positive attention, approval, or affection. You don't let Rose move to the next activity until she chooses to do the task. Consistent application of this principle will help develop security and trust in the child; reward desired behavior with the 3A's and withdraw rewards when there is undesirable behavior. Security develops largely from consistent responses to specific behaviors, and trust develops largely from acceptance and appreciation of the child (Greenspan & Pollock, 1989).

Children need reasonable expectations. To have these reasonable expectations you need to know (1) normal patterns of development and (2) each child's individual pattern of development. Because the sequence of development is similar among children, you have some guidelines for your expectations. Because there is a range in the timing of development, you need to know where each child fits within that range (Figure 3–4). If you expect children to accomplish things that are below or above them developmentally, you produce undue stress. For example, you can expect 30-month-old Mark to be able to hold a spoon in his hand, fill it with food, and usually get it up to his mouth. You should not expect 9-month-old Naomi to have that level of muscular coordination. Use of Developmental Prescriptions and Profiles are important. Consistent updating of developmental steps helps children establish security and trust because they meet with success, mastery, and the 3A's rather than stress, frustration, and rejection.

Infants and toddlers depend on their caregivers for many things. Caregivers who provide comfort and assistance help children learn that the caregiver can provide a secure place and can be trusted. Children who live in a world where their needs are ignored or only occasionally met will have difficulty building security and trust. One reason that caregivers have responsibility for fewer infants and toddlers than older children is so that caregivers will be available to respond to the many needs of each dependent infant or toddler.

Young children's temperaments, feelings of self-esteem, and coping skills are important factors in their emotional development.

Temperament Temperament has been defined as "the basic style which characterizes a person's behavior" (Chess & Birch, 1965, 32). All children are born with particular temperaments. Temperament will influence what they do, what they learn, what they feel about themselves and others, and what kinds of interactions they have with people and objects.

Figure 3–4 Children who feel secure are free to explore.

Everyone is born with **temperament traits**, and until recently research has suggested that temperament is stable and not very changeable by environmental influences (Kagan, Reznick, & Gibbons, 1989; Caspi & Silva, 1995). However, a growing body of research strongly suggests that child rearing practices and other environmental factors can dramatically influence temperament during the first three years (Gunnar, 1998; Rubin et al., 1997).

Chess and Birch (1965) worked with 231 children and their parents to investigate how babies differ in their styles of behavior and their temperament. These are some of the questions they asked: How does individual temperament develop? What role does it play in personality development? What part does the environment play in shaping of personality? Is the mother's approach to the baby fixed, or does the baby's temperament affect the mother's handling? What were the specific circumstances in which the child's behavior occurred?

Their analysis of hundreds of observations and interviews revealed nine patterns of behavior. Within each pattern they found a range of behaviors. The following examples show each end of the ranges. The behavior of most people falls somewhere between these extremes. Table 3–1 lists the nine categories and extremes of behaviors observed in each category.

The following descriptions further illustrate the extremes of these patterns.

Activity Level Ryan runs into the room, yells "Hi," and goes to the blocks. He stacks them quickly, they fall down, and he stacks again and leaves them as they tumble

TABLE 3–1	*BEHAVIOR CATEGORIES OF TEMPERAMENT*	
	Extremes	
Behavioral Category	*More*	*Less*
(1) Activity Level	Hyperactive—can't sit still	Lethargic—sedate, passive
(2) Regularity	Unpredictable and inconsistent patterns	Rigid and inflexible patterns
(3) Response to New Situations	Outgoing, aggressive, approaching	Withdrawing, timid, overly cautious
(4) Adaptability	Likes surprises, fights routine, dislikes structure	Dislikes change, likes routine, needs structure
(5) Sensory Threshold	Unaware of changes in light, sound, smell; feels optimistic	Overly sensitive to changes in light, sound, smell; feels pessimistic, unrealistically negative; denies positive
(7) Response Intensity	Overly loud and animated; high energy	Overly quiet and soft; low energy
(8) Distractibility	Insensitive to visual and auditory stimuli outside self	Unable to focus attention, overly sensitive to visual and auditory stimuli
(9) Persistence	Persists until task completed; rigid and inflexible	Gives up easily, doesn't try new things

down. He walks over to stand by Melba , the caregiver, who is reading a picture book to another child. Ryan listens a few minutes and then moves on to another activity. Ryan has a high activity level. He has always been very active. He kicked and waved and rolled a lot when he was a baby. His body needs to move. He becomes very distressed when he is physically confined with a seat belt in the car or must sit quietly.

Benjamin sits quietly on the floor playing with nesting cans. He stacks the cans and then fits them inside. He accomplishes his task with few movements: his legs remain outstretched; his body is leaning forward slightly but not rocking back and forth; he has the cans close to him so his arms and hands need limited movement. Benjamin has a low activity level. He was a quiet baby, not kicking his blankets off or twisting and turning often. He becomes distressed when he has to rush around to put away toys or quickly get ready to go somewhere.

Regularity   Valeria may act like she is hungry for her first bottle at 9:00 one morning, not until 10:00 the next day, and at 8:30 the third morning. Her bowel movements occur at no regular times. Valeria's body is having difficulty establishing its biological time clock for eating, sleeping, and eliminating. She has an unpredictable body schedule.

Sarina has a bowel movement every morning at about 9:00, takes a bottle at about 9:30, and then takes a 1½-hour nap. Sarina has a well-established body schedule.

Approach or Withdrawal as a Characteristic Response to a New Situation Jamol hides behind his mother as he enters the room each morning. He hides behind the caregiver whenever someone strange walks in the door. He stands by the wall and watches others play with the new ball. He leaves food he does not recognize on his plate, refusing to take a bite. Jamol is slow to warm up. He needs time to get used to new situations. Jamol is distressed when he is pushed into new activities. Being told that a new ball will not hurt him or that the strange food is good for him does not convince him. When he feels comfortable, he will play with the new ball. He needs time and space for himself while he becomes familiar with a situation.

Carlos arrives in the morning with a big smile. He looks around the room and notices a new puzzle set out on the table. He rushes over to it, asking the caregiver about it and giggling at the picture. He takes the puzzle pieces out, puts some of the pieces back in and then seeks assistance from the caregiver. Carlos warms up quickly. He is excited about new situations and eager to try new experiences.

Adaptability to Change in Routine Llema is used to snack time at the table. She knows how to get her hands washed, seat herself, enjoy her snack with her friends, and then wash her hands and go play. Today the caregiver has planned a surprise. She takes the children out into a corner of the play yard and serves a special snack. Llema is upset because this new place for snack is different from what she is used to. Llema fusses and will not eat her snack. Llema follows routines well and finds security in their consistency. She has difficulty making adjustments when a routine is changed.

Desiree is delighted with having a surprise snack outdoors. She also adjusts quickly when the books are changed to a different shelf and the home living center is moved to a different part of the room. Desiree adapts well to changes. She takes them in stride and focuses on the experiences rather than the changes in routine.

Level of Sensory Threshold Jose is bothered by light when he is trying to go to sleep or is sleeping, so the caregiver holds a blanket to shield his eyes as she rocks him to sleep. Jose awakens when a door is quietly closed. Jose is very sensitive to noise, light, and pain. He is easily bothered by what others believe are mild sounds and light.

Ming "sleeps through anything." He can sleep in the same room with children who are playing. He does not need the room darkened. When he falls and bumps himself, he often does not even whimper. Ming has a high tolerance for sound, light, and pain. Sometimes the caregiver has to check his injuries to see if he needs help, since he may not realize his needs.

Positive or Negative Mood Angela looks at the toy shelf and says she does not like toys. She plays with a toy dog and complains about his tail. Angela's negative mood characterizes the way she views familiar experiences.

Elvira looks at the toy shelf and sees many toys she likes. She plays with a cat which has lost one eye and is limp from children's pinching fingers. Elvira loves the cat; she croons to it and cuddles it. Elvira tends to look on life positively. She is positive until something happens to hurt or anger her.

Intensity of Response   Arturo has just put a lock block together and, turning to the caregiver, he excitedly screams in her face, "Look! Look!" His response to his achievement shows up in his loud voice and his wriggling body. When Arturo cries, he cries loudly. When he talks, he talks loudly. Arturo uses a high level of energy to express himself. He puts himself fully into his response.

Carla has just put some people into her lock-blocks car and is pushing the car around. She has a smile on her face and is humming. She stops by the caregiver, points to the people, and excitedly says, "Daddy!" Carla uses a low level of energy in expressing her excitement. Her smiling, humming, and words show she is happy and excited, but her responses are quiet. She talks quietly and she cries quietly.

Distractibility   Tamela is dropping blocks into a plastic jar. She sees Sheri go by, pushing a buggy. Tamela stops putting in blocks and walks over to push another buggy. She walks by the caregiver, who is reading a book to Li. Tamela stops to listen for a few minutes and then, noticing Carolyn sliding, she goes to the slide and slides. Tamela is very distractible. She plays with something or does something she is interested in until another activity catches her attention. Then she leaves her activity to move on to the activity that has attracted her attention.

Geraldine is building a block structure. Two other children are building their own block structures. Geraldine reaches for and places the blocks she wants, occasionally looking at the others playing with blocks or glancing around the room. She notices other activities, but she concentrates her attention on her own activity with blocks. Geraldine can maintain a high level of concentration. She can continue a task even when other activities are occurring around her.

Persistence and Attention Span   Jesse takes the three puzzle pieces out of the puzzle. He successfully puts in the banana. He picks up the apple piece and tries to fit it into a space. When it does not fit, he drops the piece and leaves the table. Jesse gives up when he is not immediately successful. He does not keep trying.

Clayton takes the three puzzle pieces out of the puzzle. He then turns and pushes and turns and pushes each piece until he has returned all three pieces to their proper places. Clayton persists with an activity even when it may be challenging or frustrating or takes a long time. When he completes his task, he expresses his pleasure with smiles and words.

All people have temperament traits. Temperament behaviors can be modified but not changed drastically. Very physically active people will never become very physically quiet. As they develop, they can make adjustments and modifications to reduce and control their outer actions, but internally they still have a high need for movement.

Caregivers must identify each child's temperament as well as their own. For example, Olaf is playing with blocks. The tall stack he built falls over, one block hitting hard on his hand. He yells loudly. Ray is playing nearby and also is hit by a falling block. He looks up in surprise but does not say anything. What will you do? What will you say? What is "loud" to you? What is acceptable to you? Why is a behavior acceptable or not acceptable to you? Do you think Ray is "better" than Olaf because he did not react loudly? What you do and what you say to Olaf reflects your acceptance or rejection of him as a person, reflects whether you are able to help him adapt to his environment, and reflects your ability to adapt to the child.

Caregivers can help infants and toddlers make small adjustments in their temperament behaviors. And caregivers should consciously make some adjustments for their own temperaments. For example, since Benjamin has a low activity level, you can advise him to begin putting toys away several minutes before you expect him to complete the task. You adjust a little by giving him extra time, and he adjusts a little by working slightly faster than he might have.

Bonding and Separation-Individuation A pediatrician from Vienna named Margaret Mahler wrote extensively about the importance of bonding between parent and child and the process called separation-individuation (Greenberg & Mitchell, 1983). Personality development, security, trust, and self-concept (ego) are all related to the attachment between infant and caregivers and how separation-individuation from caregivers is conducted and experienced by the child. Mahler's phases of individuation are valuable guidelines for caregivers of infants and toddlers to understand ego development. Mahler's five phases areas follows:

Phase	*Age*
1. normal autistic phase	birth to four months
2. differentiation subphase	four months to ten months
3. practicing subphase	10 months to 15 months
4. rapprochement subphase	15 months to 36 months
5. libidinal object constancy phase	36 months throughout childhood

The normal autistic phase occurs during the first few weeks of life, when time spent asleep exceeds time the baby is awake (Mahler, Pine, & Bergman, 1975). At three to four weeks, a maturational crisis occurs, in which the infant shows increased sensitivity to the external world and has a beginning awareness that the mother is an external object. During this normal symbiotic phase, the baby organizes experiences into good (pleasurable) and bad (painful) memories, which form the basis for the ego (self).

From four to ten months, the differentiation subphase occurs, in which the baby begins to act in more self-determined ways and explores the caregiver (e.g., pulls hair, clothes). The baby also scans the world and checks back to the caregiver to discriminate "mother from other." The baby also develops skill in discriminating external from internal sensations. This discrimination forms the basis for self-awareness (self-concept) as opposed to awareness of object (anything other than self, including other people).

Once the baby becomes mobile at around 10 months, the practicing subphase begins. Because the baby can now move away from the caregiver, increased body discrimination and awareness of separateness from others manifests. The child begins using the caregiver as an emotional and physical "refueling station"—moving short distances away and then returning for refilling. Think of yourself as a recharging station, a physically and emotionally rewarding place where children feel a sense of security and return again and again for energetic nourishment.

The child becomes excited by the world, the caregiver, and his or her own body and capacities to function. During this phase, the child concentrates on his or her own abilities separate from the caregiver and becomes **omnipotent** (not aware of any physical limitations). According to Mahler and colleagues, the caregiver must be able to allow physical and psychological separation during this phase if the child is to establish good ego boundaries. The tools presented later—Circle of Safety, Shadowing,

Rueing, and Changing of the Guard, Shepherding, Positive Perception—help with this crucial separation-individuation phase of ego development.

Between 15 and 18 months, the toddler enters the rapprochement subphase where the sense of omnipotence (having no limits) is broken. What is wanted is not always immediately available, so the child experiences frustration, separation anxiety, and the realization that caregivers are separate people who don't always say yes. Often, children will alternate between clinging neediness and intense battling with caregivers at this stage because of these dependence and independence needs. Because of rapid language development during this period, the child struggles with gender identity, accepting "no," and development of beliefs, attitudes, and values that form the superego (conscience, or You voice) and the child's more complete map of the world.

Mahler's final stage of "libidinal object constancy" starts around 36 months and involves developing a stable concept of the self (one that does not change), and a stable concept of other people, places, and things. Self-constancy and object constancy are comparable to Piaget's object permanence, in which people and things continue to exist in the child's mind even when they aren't present. During this phase, it is crucial that the caregiver be available as a buffer between the child and the world while supporting and respecting the competencies of the growing child to separate and individuate without anxiety or fear. Three-year-olds truly believe that their make-believe is real. Using playthings such as toys and puppets can elicit information from them on how they are doing emotionally (Douville-Watson, 2001). In addition, the childcare tools of Mirroring, Active Listening, and Managing Relationships presented in the following chapters are helpful with the extremely difficult job of helping the child develop a stable ego with good boundaries between self and others.

Self-Concept Development Healthy personality development involves more than helping young children recognize their feelings, experience security and trust in others, enhance their positive temperament traits, and establish a healthy balance between attachment and separation-individuation. Daniel Goleman has provided the most concise and comprehensive view to date of the skills necessary for healthy personality development in his book entitled *Emotional Intelligence* (1996). In his groundbreaking work, Goleman reports that the usual way of looking at intelligence as only cognitive abilities contributes about 20 percent to the factors that determine life success (Gardner, 1995)! Eighty percent of the skills necessary for life success is determined by what he calls **emotional intelligence**.

From an extensive research review, Goleman defined five "domains" that are learned early in life and are necessary for high emotional intelligence and healthy ego development. Consistent with all five domains, parents and caregivers need to trust their basic instincts and use the 3A's (Attention, Approval, and Affection) to promote the growth of emotional intelligence. Chapter 4 spells out how these master tools help to develop emotional intelligence. Goleman's five domains are described next.

1. **Knowing one's emotions. Self-awareness**—recognizing a feeling as it happens—is the keystone of emotional intelligence. The caregiver should start helping children at birth to recognize, experience, label, and express their feelings in healthy ways.
2. **Managing emotions.** Handling feelings so they are appropriate to the situation is a skill that builds on self-awareness. Skills in soothing oneself, developing an

observing ego and maintaining a balance between thoughts, feelings, and behavior are necessary to manage emotions. Caregivers need to help children with this process of self-regulation by providing a model of balance between rational behavior and expression of emotions. As Josephs points out in *Character Structure and the Organization of the Self* (1992), "in identification with the other, one begins to treat oneself as one was treated by the other." As children acquire language (which is accomplished largely on a subconscious basis), they also acquire the value system of beliefs and attitudes which form their super-ego, conscience, or "You voice."

The conscience is formed within the first three years and becomes the **you voice** in the dialogues we all conduct in our thinking. Vygotsky's private speech (discussed in Chapter 2) refers to practicing dialogues between the You voice (the internalized caregivers who become the super-ego) and the **I voice** (the ego or self). We all consistently conduct internal dialogues between these two major parts of ourselves. For example, the I voice, which expresses our needs and desires might say, "I'm hungry." Depending on how our caregivers responded to our hunger needs in the past, our You voice will respond negatively or positively. If we had nurturing caregivers who validated and supported fulfillment of our hunger needs, our You voice might respond, "You should get something to eat." However, if our caregivers were critical or angry with our hunger needs, our You voice will respond negatively, causing us to feel guilty or wrong for being hungry. As caregivers help infants regulate their emotions, they contribute to the child's style of emotional self-regulation. For example, a parent who waits to intervene until an infant has become extremely agitated reinforces the baby's rapid rise to intense stress (Thompson, 1990a). This makes it harder for the parent to soothe the baby in the future and for the baby to learn self-soothing (Berk, 2000). Freud used a descriptive term for a You voice developed from critical and aggressive caregivers—he called it a "primitive aggressivized super-ego" (1920/1974). When caregivers validate children's wants and needs by supporting and helping the child fulfill the need expressed by a feeling, children internalize a positive You voice. This skill of internalizing a positive You voice is essential in learning how to manage feelings, develop self-esteem, and regulate emotion.

Another essential skill in managing feelings is the development of an observing ego. For our purposes, the *ego* is awareness of our own wants, needs, and desires separate from other people, places, and things (I voice). The super-ego, or conscience, is our system of beliefs and values internalized from our caregivers (You voice). Caregivers should also help young children develop the skills needed to observe their own thoughts, feelings, and behaviors. This self-observation is called the observing ego by clinical psychologists and meta-cognition by cognitive psychologists. Caregivers who give a lot of feedback and ask a lot of questions about children's thoughts, feelings, and behaviors help children develop meta-cognition and an observing ego. Tools from Neuro-Linguistic Programming are extremely helpful for children in developing an observing ego (Bodenhamer & Hall, 2000).

3. **Motivating oneself.** Channeling emotions in the service of a goal is essential for paying attention, mastery, and creativity. Goleman refers to research on getting into the **flow** to illustrate how children can learn to balance thought and feeling and to behave in extremely competent ways (Nakamura, 1988). A basic attitude

of optimism (the belief that success is possible) and self-responsibility appear to underlie the skill of getting into the flow (Csikszentmihalyi, 1990). Caregivers of young children and infants can observe flow in infants and toddlers. For example, when an infant becomes totally engrossed in exploring her hand or the caregiver's face, you can see that her cognition, perceptions, emotions, and behaviors are all intensely focused and coordinated in their joyful exploration. When a toddler is engrossed in exploring how a toy works, you can observe the coordination of thought, feeling, and behavior that reflect being in the flow.

Many researchers of motivation consider curiosity the primary human motivator. Infants and toddlers are naturally brimming with curiosity and the desire to explore. When caregivers help fulfill basic needs at physical and safety levels and respect the children as separate individuals with the ability to be somewhat responsible for their own experiences, children feel secure and are able to get into the wonderful flow of exploring both internal and external worlds.

4. **Recognizing emotions in others. Empathy** (sensitivity to what others need or want) is the fundamental relationship skill. Recent research in infant development has demonstrated that newborns exhibit empathy within the first two months of life. When an infant is in the same environment with another living being in pain, the infant will do whatever possible to "comfort" the other (Dondi, Simion, & Caltran, 1999; Zahn-Waxler, 1991). If it is true that empathy is present at birth, then insensitivity is learned from the environment. Child care styles have a profound impact on emotional self-regulation and empathy as children grow. Caring, nurturing, and encouraging children results in children who remain empathetic toward others as they grow up (Eisenberg & McNally, 1993). On the other hand, care that is critical, negative, punitive, or aggressive results in children who rarely show signs of concern for others. Instead, they respond with fear, anger, and physical attacks (Klimes-Dougan & Kistner, 1990). Creating a positive learning environment promotes stability and fosters compassion, (Douville-Watson, L., 2000).

Implications of this research for caregivers of young children should be obvious: insensitivity, negativity, or aggression directed at infants and toddlers results in children exhibiting those qualities toward themselves and others. Child care that is sensitive, positive, and nurturing results in children who exhibit those qualities as they grow up. Although empathy needs to be encouraged and modeled more than taught, the social and verbal behaviors involved in "loving thy neighbor as thyself" (not more or less than thyself) should be modeled and directly taught.

5. **Handling relationships.** The last domain of emotional intelligence involves interacting smoothly and demonstrating skills necessary to get along well with others. It may seem odd at first to suggest that infants and toddlers manage their relationships with others, but research indicates that infants as young as four weeks detect others' emotions through "emotional contagion" (Sullins, 1991), and imitate others' behaviors and expressions within the first three months. There is no question that the behavior of a baby elicits responses from caregivers. Many parents even mark their child's first smile, step, word, and so forth with great celebration. Therefore, children learn very early in life that their behavior affects others, even though the conscious awareness that "When I do A, Mommy does B" doesn't come about until between 12 and 18 months. Goleman (1996, pp.

111–112) uses an example of a 30-month-old toddler to illustrate skills used to manage emotions in another person. Specific skills in managing others are spelled out in Chapter 4 and 5, but it is important here to understand that development of these people skills occurs during the first years of life in the relationships with our primary caregivers.

Very little research has been reported on how young children develop skills to manage emotions in others. Study of the baby's contributions to their primary relationships involves the temperament research discussed previously and studies on **interactional synchrony** (Isabella & Belsky, 1991). This term is best described as a sensitively tuned "emotional dance" in which interactions are mutually rewarding to caregiver and infant. Both people match positive emotional states, and the caregiver usually "follows" and the infant "leads" in the dance. This is a good example of the **Neuro-Linguistic Programming (NLP)** approach to establishing rapport discussed in Chapter 5. One study indicated that interactional synchrony occurs only about 30 percent of the time between mothers and babies (Tronick & Cohn, 1989). The caregiver needs to learn how to establish rapport in this type of interaction with infants and toddlers to enhance their emotional development and help them learn to manage their relationships.

To summarize healthy self-concept development results from young children being helped to recognize their feelings and the feelings of other people, establishing secure and trusting attachments with their caregivers, having their positive temperament traits supported, and having a healthy balance between bonding and separation-individuation. In addition, caregivers should understand the five domains of emotional intelligence and use tools that enhance the development of a healthy I voice and You voice.

Self-Esteem Self-esteem can be defined as follows.

"the evaluation which the individual makes and customarily maintains with regard to himself: it expresses an attitude of approval or disapproval, and indicates the extent to which the individual believes himself to be capable, significant, successful, and worthy. In short, self-esteem is a personal judgment of worthiness that is expressed in the attitudes the individual holds toward himself" (Coopersmith, 1967, 4–5).

Summarizing his data on childhood experiences that contribute to the development of self-esteem, Coopersmith wrote, "The most general statement about the antecedent of self-esteem can be given in terms of three conditions: total or near total acceptance of the children by their parents; clearly defined and enforced limits; and the respect and latitude for individual actions that exist within the defined limits" (1967, 236). It is important that children think they are worthy people. Coopersmith's three conditions for fostering self-esteem—acceptance, limits, respect—provide guidelines for caregivers.

Acceptance Each child needs to feel accepted for who he or she is right now. Children need to feel worthy and appreciated. For adults to focus on what children ought to be or what they may become can give children the impression that they are not all right. What children build on for the future is their sense of being all right now. Caregivers can encourage children to demonstrate acceptance of other children.

Limits   Adults set boundaries on behavior to help infants and toddlers learn to live safely and acceptably in their world. Society has rules. Some are physical: play in the yard, not in the street (to keep from physical harm). Some are interpersonal: you play with your doll and Greta will play with hers (possession, ownership—temporary in this case).

The boundaries set for children must fit their developmental level and be observed consistently. For example, both Yolanda and Theresa have difficulty sharing, so the caregiver does not force one to share her airplane with the other. All the children have been told, however, that when someone is playing with a toy, no one else is to take it. Therefore, when Yolanda grabs the airplane Theresa is playing with, the caregiver reaches in to hold the airplane still while she reminds Yolanda about taking a toy someone else is playing with.

Respect   Ralphino is playing with a tractor. He must play with it in the space away from children building with blocks. Miss Jana watches him push his tractor around in a circle, push it under a chair and bring it out the other side, lift it to climb the side and seat of the chair and down the other side. Miss Jana allows Ralphino to explore with his tractor. He is not hurting the tractor or the chair as he moves the tractor under and over the chair. Miss Jana does not force Ralphino to be realistic, that is, to recognize that tractors don't really drive over chairs. She allows him to use his fantasies and explorations, encourages "private talk," and uses "scaffolding" to help him learn about his world.

The Association for Self-Esteem did an extensive review of the research in this area and found that people who develop good **self-esteem** have learned and exhibit three specific skills:

1. People with good self-esteem take responsibility for their own thoughts, feelings, and behaviors. **Self-responsibility** is the keystone to independence. It is accurate to state that the most important task of child care is to prepare children to function as healthy, autonomous individuals capable of providing for their needs in ways acceptable to society. This process of self-responsibility starts at birth when the infant takes over responsibility for some physical needs (e.g., breathing, digestion, elimination) and continues until the person is capable of providing for all his or her needs as an adult. Caregivers should help children take responsibility for their own wants and needs appropriate to their developmental skills while allowing dependency in areas in which they are not yet capable of providing for themselves. To enhance self-responsibility, keep in mind the next developmental step the child will take in each of the five major areas, and provide activities to move children toward the next independent developmental step. Helping a child take as much responsibility as is age appropriate provides the child with a sense of mastery and overall successful emotional development (Douville-Watson, L., 2001).

2. People with good self-esteem are sensitive and kind toward other people. As we discussed in self-concept development, sensitivity to the feelings of others is a quality present at birth, and most children who lose their capacity for being sensitive have undergone trauma or have been cared for by insensitive, critical, or aggressive caregivers (Miller & Luthar, 1989). The old idea that some people are born without any ability to sense the feelings of others has been clearly proven untrue. Although

there are individual differences at birth, the sensitivity that children exhibit toward others later in life is clearly related to the quality of sensitivity, kindness, and respect they are shown in the first few years of life. Caregivers need to interact with kindness and model empathy to help children respond to others in kind and sensitive ways. Caregivers who value kindness and empathy help children develop self-esteem later in life (Figure 3–5).

3. People with good self-esteem make conscious positive statements to themselves about their own value and self-worth. Infants and toddlers internalize the moral values, beliefs, and attitudes of the people in their environment. This internalized super-ego, conscience, or You voice becomes one of two major parts of our personality. The You voice communicates with the other major part, called the ego, self, or I voice, through consistent dialogues in our thinking. The infant and young toddler subconsciously absorb the attitudes, statements, and feelings that their caregivers direct toward them and conduct inside talk made up of these I and You voices.

When caregivers consistently direct affection, positive attention, approval, and respect toward young children, the child develops a You voice that makes positive, supportive statements about the I voice, which in turn causes the child to feel valuable, worthy, and proud. However, when caregivers are critical, angry, demanding, or judgmental toward children, the child's You voice learns to make negative statements to the I voice, which causes guilt, anxiety, shame, and self-doubt.

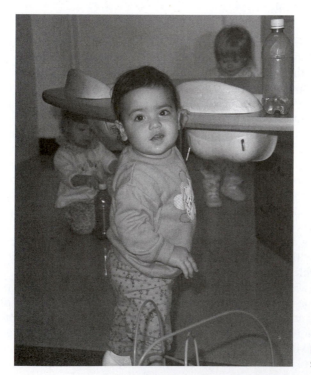

Figure 3–5 Children learn good self-esteem from specific skills.

Another important factor in the development of a healthy, supportive super-ego is that praise and approval must be *genuine* compliments that the ego can honestly evaluate as positive qualities or accomplishments. Some caregivers give too much praise and approval for behaviors that are not genuine accomplishments or positive qualities. When caregivers lavish unconditional praise and approval no matter what the child does, the child learns to value the feedback as false. This results in the child either developing expectations that he should never make mistakes or be criticized, or poor self-esteem because he is not as good as the feedback he receives. These negative reactions often become attitudes that can limit the child's later accomplishments. These children feel crushed or angry when they experience criticism from the world. Caregivers should temper praise and unconditional approval with realistic encouragement and support for the child to try again or to change the behavior when appropriate. A concept promoted by the authors is to **catch the child being good**. Giving attention to positive, appropriate behavior and withdrawing attention for unacceptable behavior increases the likelihood of repeated positive behavior and good self-esteem.

Another important factor in healthy You voice development is this child care principle: "Disapprove of behaviors; *never* disapprove of the child." When caregivers judge, blame, or criticize the child (the person) as wrong, bad, or unworthy, the child internalizes the feeling that there is something basically wrong with her as a person. Even very young children are much less likely to internalize negative feelings about themselves when it is clear that a behavior is being criticized but that their own person is still accepted and respected. For example, suppose a young child hit and hurt another child. A caregiver who responds with comments such as "What's wrong with you?" "Bad boy!" and "You are mean!" promotes guilt, a critical You voice, and the feeling that there is something basically wrong with the child as a person. On the other hand, disapproving of the behavior while respecting the child with comments such as "Hitting Sally with that toy hurt her!" or "We don't accept hitting other people!" or "Do not hit anyone!" focuses the attention on the act and is less likely to induce guilt and negative feelings about the person. When children behave in ways that are harmful to themselves, another person, or the environment, it is important to give feedback that their behavior is unacceptable and must change, but the person is not being blamed for who they are. For example, "I like you, but I don't like what you're doing right now!" separates the child from the behavior and offers an opportunity for change without threat to her ego or self-esteem.

A final factor in healthy You voice development is to always make sure children have a way to return to positive acceptance, approval, and affection. Much of the fear and anxiety we experience as adults can be traced to being physically or emotionally "cut off" as infants and toddlers. When adults treat a young child as a complete outcast and the child does not know what to do or when he or she can return to acceptance, the child experiences intense fear and anxiety because of the need for emotional attachment to the adult to feel safe and secure. Caregivers can help children develop a healthy You voice by pointing out that specific behaviors are harmful to the child, another person, or the environment and describing exactly what the child can do to regain acceptance and approval from the adult. In the example above of a child hitting another, this might take the form of saying, "Now, what you need to do is let Sally know that you didn't mean to hurt her and let me know that you will not hit her again." By asking the child to correct the mistake and make amends to the injured person, the child is provided with a way to return to approval and thus a way to feel safe and secure.

Adults who emotionally or physically cut off children without letting them know what they can do to regain approval help promote anxiety, fear, and a negative You voice.

Caregivers who (1) consistently give genuine positive attention, approval, and affection to young children for real accomplishments and qualities, (2) disapprove of behaviors that are harmful to the child, another person, or the environment but never disapprove of the child, and (3) always give the child a way of returning to approval, affection and positive attention help the child develop self-esteem and the skill of making positive conscious statements to themselves about their own value and worth.

Social Development

Normal patterns for social development are the result of our all-important relationships with our primary caregivers. The word *relationship* implies two entities: a person *relates* to another. Without discrimination of differences between me and not-me, there is a fusing of perceptions with the perceiver. The sense of complete fusion with another is a characteristic of newborn infants who have not yet established ego boundaries or awareness of their separateness from the mother. We must understand how ego boundaries are formed before we can understand more complex patterns of social development.

Me-Not Me: Development of Ego Boundaries More than a century ago, a philosopher named William James (1890/1963) defined two distinct aspects of self-awareness: the **I-self** and the **Me-self.** The I-self is separate from other people and objects (has established ego boundaries). The I-self has a private inner life that maintains existence over time, and can act on the environment.

In contrast, the Me-self is aware of being unique; possessing qualities different from other people and objects. The Me-self treats the self as an object and observes its own thoughts, feelings, behaviors, and qualities. The Me-self contains what clinical psychologists call the observing ego and cognitive psychologists call **meta-cognition** (awareness of one's own thought processes).

Development of ego boundaries and formation of the I-self occurs very rapidly within the first few months of life. It appears that moving from the symbiotic oneness with mother to evolving recognition that our own actions cause objects and people to react occurs within the first few weeks of life (Harter, 1998). For example, when a baby accidentally makes a sound and the caregiver immediately responds with affection, attention, or approval, the infant quickly associates making that sound with the caregiver's reaction and will try to repeat the sound to see if it elicits the same reaction (Figure 3–6). When an infant accidentally kicks out and the mobile above the crib moves, the baby will try to kick again to see if the mobile moves again. When the infant watches his or her foot or hand movements related to effect on the mobile, the baby associates internal desire with motor responses, which helps develop kinesthetic awareness.

These basic associations occurring within the first weeks of life form the foundation for healthy or unhealthy ego boundaries. What becomes the I-self is defined in terms of how the environment reacts to our needs and overt behaviors. When a baby cries with hunger and the caregiver immediately responds with food, secure attachment is maintained and the baby trusts that crying *causes* the caregiver to respond. However, when the baby cries and the caregiver ignores the child or responds with anger instead of food, the infant learns not to trust, experiences insecurity, and is

Figure 3–6 Healthy relationships develop from positive Attention, Approval, and Affection.

confused and frustrated because the hunger continues. Repeated ignoring or rejecting a baby's needs result in insecure attachment, confused ego boundaries, and poor I-self development (Rutter, 1998).

It should be apparent from this discussion that young infants *cannot* be spoiled, or have their needs filled too much or too often. To develop healthy ego boundaries and I-self, babies must experience secure attachments to their caregivers that consistently demonstrate that their needs and desires are important and that they have personal power to affect the environment. When caregivers are able to consistently fulfill a baby's physical and emotional needs, the infant and caregiver can engage in interactional synchrony, discussed previously.

Development of the Me-self begins between 9 and 15 months as the baby becomes more aware of the physical features of the self. Experiments using mirrors have demonstrated that some children as young as nine months become aware of their own physical features and begin experimenting with the way they look in a mirror (Bullock & Lutkenhaus, 1990). This evolving self-recognition quickly becomes the center of the child's emotional and social activity.

Mine-Yours-Ours: Relationship Development During development of the I-self and Me-self, respect for the child's physical and psychological boundaries is crucial to healthy social development. It is surprising that the field of child development has not focused more research and attention on ego boundaries, but ever since Freud defined the term (1920/1974), the idea that our physical and psychological existence needs to be respected has been studied primarily by clinical psychologists dealing with personality disorders in adults. Caregivers of young children should be aware that healthy social development requires definitions and respect for what is mine-yours-ours together.

Because infants begin life unable to care for their physical being, it is necessary for caregivers to "intrude" on their physical boundaries to provide care. *Intrude* is used here because the baby has no choice in how the caregiver handles his or her body. When the caregiver respects the baby's body and provides what Transactional Analysis researchers call **good touch**, the baby feels secure and loved. However, when the caregiver doesn't respect the baby's body and is rough or insensitive, he or she inflicts **bad touch**, which causes feelings of insecurity and physical pain (Freed, 1991).

The same principle of respect holds true for emotional boundaries. When the caregiver respects the baby's feelings and provides a positive emotional connection, the baby feels secure. In contrast, anger, criticism, or ignoring the baby is disrespectful and results in insecurity and emotional pain. In the previous section on emotional development, handling relationships was discussed as one of the five domains of emotional intelligence. The skill of handling relationships requires that the caregiver manage her own emotions, demonstrate sensitivity to the child's feelings, and communicate in a way that creates interactional synchrony (mutually satisfying interactions). To establish this finely tuned emotional dance, the caregiver must be aware of and respect the physical and emotional boundaries of the child and be aware of her own thoughts, feelings, and behaviors (Figure 3–7).

When healthy I-self, Me-self, and ego boundaries are established, the child learns to have semipermeable boundaries; allowing positive interactions to positively effect the self and not allowing negative interactions to hurt the self. Children who have their physical and psychological boundaries respected learn to respect other people's feelings as well. As a result of being able to value their own wants and needs while being sensitive to other people, these children are able to establish, manage, and maintain healthy relationships with other people.

Healthy development of the Me-self and ego boundaries are the basis for the *egocentrism* (self-interest and perspective) that toddlers exhibit, but self-interest also

Figure 3–7 Interactional synchrony is the basis for healthy relationships.

leads to efforts to appreciate the perspectives of other people. For example, research has demonstrated that newborn babies cry in response to the cry of another (Dondi, Simion, & Caltran, 1999), and infants connect emotionally with their caregivers (Zahn-Waxler, 1991).

"Mirror self-recognition precedes sustained mutual imitation and play—a partner banging an object, the partner imitating back, and the toddler copying again" (Asendorpf, Warkentin, & Baudonniere, 1996). Once a firm sense of self-awareness and language is established between 12 and 18 months, children develop a *categorical self*; that is, they categorize themselves according to the ways people differ, including age, sex, and physical characteristics (Gralinski & Kopp, 1993). This self-knowledge become the basis for comparing what is me and mine, what is you and yours, and what we share together (ours). Some studies have shown that young toddlers tend to be self-interested and possessive (Levine, 1983), but there is also much evidence that cooperation and sharing are common ways of interacting in children between 12 and 30 months (Brownell & Carriger, 1990).

Between 24 and 36 months the rapid language development of the toddler provides the basis for understanding the feelings of other people, using more words to express feelings, and active participation in managing relationships. As language rapidly increases, so does the toddler's more complete map of the world. Active **self-talk** dialogues between the I voice and the You voice, make-believe play, and beliefs about the self, the world (including other people), and the self in relation to others are exhibited during this period (Gopnik & Wellman, 1994). By the time children reach formal school age at four or five years, they have an established map of the world that includes self-concept, beliefs about the world (including other people), and a style of communication that determines how they will manage relationships with others.

Empathy Development   This heading is somewhat misleading since research discussed in the previous sections suggests that sensitivity to the feelings of other people is present at birth and infants are motivated to comfort another person who is in pain. It was also stated that, since sensitivity is present at birth, insensitivity is learned. The caregiver should understand how children learn to be insensitive to feelings so that systematic instruction can be conducted to teach children a balance of sensitivity to their own needs and desires and those of other people.

It is interesting that a review of the English language reveals no single word that describes a healthy self-interest in having one's needs and desires fulfilled. On the other hand, words are available to describe lack of self-interest (selfless), too much self-interest (selfish), and a variety of words to describe lack of interest in other people (e.g., insensitive, egocentric, narcissistic, aloof). Since the skills necessary for emotional intelligence require balance between awareness of one's own needs and the feelings of other people, a term is required that accurately depicts a healthy amount of self-interest in fulfilling one's own needs and awareness of the needs of other people.

The authors use the term **enlightened self-interest** to describe balanced awareness of one's own needs and feelings and the needs and feelings of other people. Enlightened self-interest is also the name of the philosophy on which the Constitution of the United States was founded. The makers of the Constitution accepted the philosophy that individuals are more motivated and work harder to fill their own desires than to fulfill the desires of a king, nation, or group, and it was out of this philosophy that American democracy was born (Bancroft, 1834).

For purposes of this book, enlightened self-interest means the skill of balancing one's own feelings and desires with the feelings and desires of other people. When a child learns to make other people's feelings important to the exclusion their own feelings, they become selfless victims who live a life burdened with inappropriate responsibilities for other people. On the other hand, when a child learns to make his or her own feelings important to the exclusion of other people, they become selfish manipulators who are insensitive and therefore alienated from intimacy with other people.

To understand enlightened self-interest, the caregiver must be aware of how insensitivity to the feelings of other people is learned. The basis of a person becoming insensitive to other people is physical and emotional pain created by the individual's life experiences. It is impossible to protect infants and toddlers from experiencing physical and emotional pain, no matter how sensitive and caring we are. Pain is a natural and normal life experience and is extremely valuable for our ability to stay alive and learn from experience. Just as athletes understand the saying "No pain: no gain" because muscles don't grow stronger unless they are taxed, most changes that produce growth cause some pain along with pleasure. A goal of a competent caregiver should be to help children remain "at ease" through their life experiences. Caregivers who try to protect children from all pain and keep them in a state of pleasure establish very unrealistic expectations for themselves and the children in their care.

Given that physical and emotional pain are normal life experiences, infants and toddlers learn methods to avoid as much pain as possible called **defense mechanisms**. Many defense mechanisms to avoid pain are learned consciously and work well. For example, a toddler who learns to clean a minor cut and put on a bandage reduces his pain and defends against further pain. Other defense mechanisms do not work so well and are usually learned unconsciously. For example, an infant or toddler whose caregiver yells and criticizes her much of the time may defend against the emotional pain of being rejected by detaching from her own feelings and the feelings and voice of the caregiver. This tuning out of feelings and the voice of authority could be deadly if the child is subjected to a life-threatening situation in which awareness of her feelings and listening to authority is a matter of life or death.

When a human is repeatedly subjected to emotional or physical pain over some time, or severe physical or emotional pain causes trauma, the nervous system defends against the pain by causing the individual to numb awareness of the pain-producing stimuli in the body and mind or in the environment (**detachment**). For example, people who suffer physical trauma such as a car accident or operation experience a common condition called *shock*, which is temporary detachment from painful feelings and environmental stimuli. In life-threatening situations, detachment from our feelings is temporarily helpful. A soldier in war can stay alive only by detaching from his feelings and those of the enemy, and a surgeon cannot afford to be aware of his or her feelings or those of the patient during surgery.

Infants and toddlers are very vulnerable to painful experiences because they are emotionally open (undefended) and lack experience of stimuli that produce pain and pleasure, so temporary detachment from feeling is normal at times. However, when a young child cannot escape a situation of chronic emotional pain, such as consistent abandonment, rejection, or adult anger, or a situation of consistent physical pain, such as physical or sexual abuse, detachment can become severe and long-lasting. Emotional or physical trauma can also cause pathological detachment. Under these conditions, detachment from one's own feelings or the feelings of other people, or both, can cause permanent lack of self-awareness and insensitivity to the feelings of other people.

Another factor that helps determine infant and toddler empathy involves caregiver relationship style. Watson found three problematic parenting styles from research conducted on a test of parent competency called The National Parenting Scales (Watson, 1996). Parents who exhibit a **controlling caregiver style** tend to discount and negate children's feelings and communicate in a insensitive manner, which causes emotional pain. Children often react by becoming angry and insensitive to the feelings of other people. Parents who exhibit a **detached caregiver style** often are not cognitively or emotionally involved enough with children to be aware of their feelings, so the children tend to become detached or angry with other people. Parents who exhibit a **selfless caregiver style** make the child's feelings important to the exclusion of their own, which often results in children becoming self-absorbed , guilt-ridden, and insensitive to the feelings of other people. A **healthy caregiver style** balances the feelings and needs of the child with those of the caregiver, resulting in a "win-win" rather than a "win-lose" relationship.

The development of empathy starts with the newborn being open to all stimulation from the body, mind, and the environment, in which the most immediate need or stimulus take precedence. By the age of five or six, children are capable of sophisticated, conscious discrimination of self from others in terms of thoughts, feelings, and behaviors. Infants cannot be selfish because they have not yet even formed an ego or self, so their empathy toward others is limited to how completely their own needs are fulfilled. For example, when a baby wakes up hungry in the middle of the night, she does not have the experience or awareness that her hunger is an inconvenience to her sleeping caregiver. However, when the child's basic needs are filled, she is able to be extremely curious, sensitive, and aware of other people. From this basic level, children progress to balancing their own feelings and needs with the feelings and needs of other people and become capable of intimate relationships with equal give and take.

Locus of Control Development: Self-Control and Self-Responsibility

Our culture expects individuals to behave in ways that are not harmful to themselves, other people, or the environment. These expectations are taught to infants and toddlers by their families, caregivers, and society. To live successfully with other people, children must learn to control their desires and impulses (self-control), and to take responsibility for themselves appropriate for their age and developmental abilities. The extent to which people perceive their lives as within their own control determines what is called **locus of control**. The word *locus* in this context means perceived location, so children who learn to take responsibility for themselves have an internal locus of control. Conversely, people who perceive their lives to be controlled by others have an external locus of control.

Throughout our discussions of emotional and social development, research has repeatedly indicated that healthy emotional and social development are closely related to self-control and self-responsibility. For example, two domains of emotional intelligence are self-motivation and self-control, and good self-esteem requires self-responsibility. Therefore, understanding development of a healthy internal locus of control is essential for caregivers of young children.

Much research has been conducted on how young children develop morality, which is the basis for self-control. Current thought is that children need to move beyond their parents' perspectives and internalize from their own perspective that certain behaviors are right and wrong (Grusec & Goodnow, 1994). For infants and toddlers to internalize that certain behaviors are right and others are wrong for *them*, they must feel that they have the power to choose their own behavior. Unfortunately, many adults believe that they must control children's behavior in order to care for children and keep them safe. The fact that many parents and other caregivers think that *they* control children's behavior may be largely responsible for many social problems created by people not taking responsibility for their own thoughts, feelings, and behavior. It is important to understand that it is the *perception* of control that adults have, and not actual control, that causes children to develop an external locus of control. Many parents and caregivers perceive themselves to be responsible for children's behavior when, in fact, they are neglectful in caring for and providing proper guidance for children (Figure 3–8).

The consistent emotional message communicated to children by adults who feel that they are responsible for the child's behavior is "You have no choice but to do what I tell you." Child psychologists and counselors observe external locus of control in many young children referred for behavior problems. As early as 18 months, children with "acting out" behavior typically cannot explain why they misbehave, but many express the belief that they are being controlled and made to do many things. On the other hand, the majority of children who do not act out inappropriately say that they can choose how to behave (Watson, 2001).

The question is how to respect children's choices and still provide the guidance and care they require to remain safe and healthy. Development of an internal locus of control requires that caregivers respect the right of young children to choose their behavior and to set clear and consistent positive consequences for appropriate behaviors and clear and consistent loss of positive consequences and application of negative consequences for behavior that is harmful to the child, another person, or the environment. Since children choose their behavior, they must be instructed directly in what positive consequences follow when they choose to behave positively and what negative consequences follow for choosing to behave negatively. When clear and consistent consequences are delivered to children, children quickly develop an internal locus of control (Mischel & Liebert, 1966).

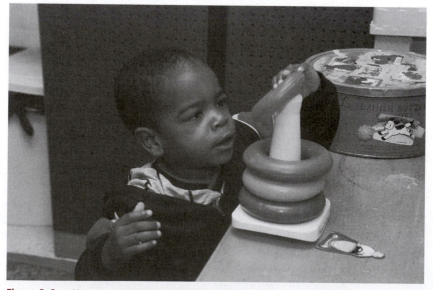

Figure 3–8 Self-responsibility is essential to an internal locus of control.

Research on the effects of punishment reveals that children of highly punitive parents are especially aggressive and defiant outside the home (Strassberg et al., 1994). Alternatives to harsh punishment that are more effective in developing an internal locus of control include time out (or time in), a warm caregiver-child relationship, and explanations of consequences, including expectations for future behavior (Larzelere et al., 1996).

Another caregiver approach that has been shown to help young children develop an internal locus of control is called **inductive discipline**. This approach involves pointing out the direct outcomes of misbehavior for the child and other people. For example, "If you hit Sam, you'll hurt him, he'll cry, and then you'll lose your special privilege. Please walk away from him now." This approach tells the child what is expected, encourages sensitivity, gives a good reason to change behavior, and empowers the child to make a positive choice (Turiel, 1998).

A final word of caution regarding self-control is important here. Many children develop an internal locus of control that is too strict and limiting of their thoughts, feelings, and behavior. Over-controlled children are likely to become obsessive-compulsive, overly anxious, fearful of making mistakes, or rigid and judgmental toward other people. To avoid development of over-control with children, keep the definition of misbehavior limited to behaviors that are clearly harmful to the child, another person, or the environment. Never define thoughts or feelings as a misbehavior. Thoughts and feelings are *never* wrong, but how we express them may be harmful. These distinctions are essential for helping infants and toddlers develop a healthy internal locus of control.

From a review of the literature, it appears that healthy social development is related to secure attachment and trust in our primary caregivers, healthy ego development, and caregiver respect and sensitivity to children's physical and ego boundaries. Healthy social development involves children being aware of their own needs and desires and those of other people, and communicating verbally and nonverbally in ways that establish interactional synchrony with others. Infants and toddlers also need help in developing an internal locus of control, self-control, and self-responsibility. Table 3–2 presents some of the major milestones for social development from birth through three years.

The Importance of Attachment

The Importance of Attachment Fourteen-month-old Louise is walking in the yard carrying a small truck in her hand. She sees Randy, the caregiver, and squeals and giggles. She walks rapidly to Randy with arms up and a big smile on her face. Attachment is the special, close relationship between the child and a caregiver. Attachment provides security for small children as they encounter new social experiences in their world and form a map of themselves, other people, and their environment.

Strong, positive attachment develops out of looking into each other's eyes, touching, stroking, and cuddling. Interational synchrony comes from rapid and consistent responses to the infant's cries and from the infant picking up on cues from the adult that the child has worth and is special. When the parent or caregiver responds quickly and appropriately to the infant's needs, such as providing food, holding, or comforting, the infant builds trust in that adult.

The relationships parents and caregivers form with little children determine what relationships children will develop later in life. Strong, sensitive attachment has a positive influence on a child's confidence, self-concept, and self-esteem for the rest of his or her life. Most research on caregiver-child relationships has examined infants with

TABLE 3–2 *MILESTONES FOR SOCIAL DEVELOPMENT: BIRTH TO 36 MONTHS*

Age	Activities
Birth to 6 months	Fusing with mother evolves into basic self-discriminations
	Basic ego boundaries established
	Feelings and tones of caregiver matched
	Empathy demonstrated
	Interactional synchrony exhibited
	Social smile observed
	Shows happiness at familiar faces
	Gains caregiver attention intentionally
	Responsible for basic physical needs (e.g., breathing, eating)
7–12 months	Me-self evolves
	Ego boundaries refined
	Self-recognition and discrimination from others exhibited
	Awareness of others' emotional signals recognized
	Social referencing and self-referencing begins
	Imitative and parallel play
12–24 months	Awareness of mine-yours-ours evolves
	Possessiveness exhibited
	Self-conscious behavior with others observed
	Stranger anxiety common
	Dramatic increase in verbal interactions
	Categorical self established; ego boundaries refined
	Beginning of cooperative play
24–36 months	Awareness that emotional reactions of others differs from self
	Increased vocabulary to express feelings
	Understand perspective of other people
	Evolving of belief structures and more complete map of self, others, and the world
	Start of active management of relationships with caregivers and peers

their mothers. The findings from this research apply equally well to infant-caregiver relationships.

1. Infants need to establish emotional attachment with their caregivers. This attachment develops through regular activities such as feeding and changing diapers, cuddling, crooning, looking, and touching.

   Caregivers should provide physical contact; learn the child's needs, schedules, likes and dislikes, and temperament; and act in ways that comfort and stimulate interactions and respond to the child's preferences.

   When more than one caregiver is responsible for a group of children, care may be shared. The primary caregiver can share her knowledge about the child's needs and preferences so that other caregivers can match their care to the child. Alternate caregivers should report observations about the child's behaviors to the primary caregiver. The primary caregiver has two main responsibilities: (1) to establish special attachment with the child and (2) to gather, coordinate, and share information about the child with other caregivers and the parents.

2. Each child needs to have a caregiver respond quickly, sensitively, and consistently to cries and cues of distress. The child then learns to trust the caregiver. When crying infants are left alone for several minutes before a caregiver responds, or when the caregiver responds quickly sometimes and leaves them alone sometimes, children are confused and have difficulty establishing a strong attachment because they cannot develop a strong sense of trust in the caregiver. Responding quickly to infant and toddler needs does not spoil the child. The most important task for an infant or toddler is to develop trust and secure attachment to the caregiver. For this to occur, the caregiver must respond quickly, consistently, and sensitively to the child's needs.

3. Each child and the primary caregiver need special time together. This "getting to know you" and "let's enjoy each other" time should be a calm, playful time to relax, look, touch, smile, giggle, cuddle, stroke, talk, whisper, sing, make faces, and establish the wonderful dance of interactional synchrony. Sometimes this can be active time, including holding an infant up in the air at arm's length while you talk and giggle and then bringing the infant up close for a hug. Other times, this can mean very quiet activities, such as rocking, cuddling, and softly stroking in a loving way (see Figure 3–7).

4. The caregiver must treat each child as a special, important person. Infants and toddlers are not objects to be controlled but individuals of worth with whom you establish a respectful, positive emotional relationship while providing for their physical, cognitive, and learning needs.

Cognitive Development

Young children think differently from adults. Adults are logical thinkers; they consider facts, analyze relationships, and draw conclusions. Young children are prelogical thinkers; their conclusions may be based on incomplete or inaccurate understanding of their experiences. For example, 2½-year-old Ivan has made a tilting stack of blocks. When he places a small car on top of the blocks, the stack tumbles down. Ivan tells Mrs. Young that the car broke the blocks. Ivan does not understand gravity, the need to stack blocks straight up rather than at a tilt, and why the car's rolling wheels may have started the car's movement downhill. The object Ivan put on the stack just before it fell was the car, so as far as Ivan is concerned, the car broke the blocks.

Jean Piaget's research contributed significantly to the knowledge of cognitive development in young children. A brilliant young scientist, Piaget began his studies as a biologist. Later, listening to children respond to questions on an intelligence test, he became intrigued by their incorrect responses and the patterns of the children's verbal reasoning. Combining his scientific orientation, his knowledge of biology, and his experiences with the children's incorrect response patterns, Piaget began to study children's cognitive development. Piaget's clinical observation method included close observations of his own three young children as well as many other children in his extensive subsequent research. He observed what children did and wrote narrative descriptions, including the date, the participants, and the actions. Later, analyzing these detailed observations, he developed his theories of cognitive development.

Stages of Cognitive Development Central to Piaget's theory is that there are stages of cognitive development; that is, four-month-olds are cognitively different from 24-month-olds. Piaget contended that the sequence of development is the same for all children. However, the age and rate at which it occurs differs from child to child.

Piaget's first two stages of cognitive development involve children between birth and three years of age. These stages, the sensorimotor stage and the beginning of the preoperational stage, are the aspects of cognitive development relevant to an infant and toddler curriculum. Part III of this book suggests experiences to match the child's level of cognitive development.

Sensorimotor Stage The sensorimotor stage of cognitive development occurs from birth to about age two. Piaget identified six substages.

Substage 1 (birth to approximately 1 month)	*Reflex* Reflex actions become more organized. Directed behavior emerges.
Substage 2 (approximately 1–4 months)	*Differentiation* Repeats own actions. Begins to coordinate actions, such as hearing and looking.
Substage 3 (approximately 4–8 months)	*Reproduction* Intentionally repeats interesting actions.
Substage 4 (approximately 8–12 months)	*Coordination* Intentionally acts as a means to an end. Develops concept of object permanence (an object exists even when the infant cannot see it).
Substage 5 (approximately 12–18 months)	*Experimentation* Experiments through trial and error. Searches for new experiences.
Substage 6 (approximately 18–24 months)	*Representation* Carries out mental trial and error. Develops symbols.

Preoperational Stage The early part of the preoperational stage is called the preconceptual stage. The preconceptual substage occurs from about two to four years of age.

The child can now mentally sort events and objects. With the development of object permanence, the child is moving toward representing objects and actions in his or her thinking without having to have actual sensorimotor experiences. The development and structuring of these mental representations are the tasks undertaken during the preoperational stage of cognitive development.

Preconceptual substage

Mentally sort objects and actions.

Mental symbols partly detached from experience.

Nonverbal classification

Graphic collections.

Focus on figurative properties.

Own interpretations.

No consistent classes of objects.
No hierarchy of classes.

Seriation
No consistent ordering of series of objects.

Verbal preconcepts
Meanings of words fluctuate, are not always the same for the child.
Meanings of words are private, based on own experience.
Word names and labels are tied to one class.
Focus on one attribute at a time—not class inclusion.

Verbal reasoning
Transductive reasoning—from particular to particular.
If one action is in some way like another action, both actions are alike in all ways.
Generalizes one situation to all situations.
Reasoning is sometimes backward—from effects to causes.
Reasoning focuses on one dimension.

Quantity
How much?
Some, more, gone, big.

Number
How many?
More, less.

Space
Where?
Use guess and visual comparison.
Up, down, behind, under, over.

Time
Remember sequence of life events.
Now, soon, before, after (Cowan, 1978)

Cognitive Functions   Piaget identified processes and functions in thinking. When you solve a problem, you feel that you understand it. Piaget calls this equilibration, a cognitive balance. This cognitive balance may be only momentary. Soon you see, hear, touch, taste, smell, or mentally think of something that presents additional information that your mind seeks to process; this is called disequilibrium. If the additional information fits something you already know, you assimilate it into your concepts. If it does not quite fit, you must make accommodations. All people use these processes and functions.

For example, Shane is looking around and notices a ball on the floor. As he crawls to it, he bumps the ball so the ball rolls. He crawls to it again, picks up the ball, looks at it, licks it, and puts it down on the floor.

Shane started out in seeming equilibrium; that is, he seemed settled and quiet. Something caused disequilibrium; that is, something stimulated him. Shane responded to seeing the ball. What he saw may match in some way what he has seen before in previous play with a ball. He may have assimilated some idea about the ball. When he bumped the ball and it rolled, he was presented with additional information about the ball that did not fit into his present concept. Therefore, through accommodation, he makes adjustments in his concept of "ball" to include the rolling movement. His disequilibrium is over, and he once again for an instant has attained equilibrium, a sense of balance, of understanding his world. These processes or functions—assimilation, accommodation, and equilibration—occur continually through life.

Cognitive Structures   Shane's actions also show one of the structures of intelligence. Shane constructs concepts or schema as his mind organizes or structures its experiences. The schema or concept of ball is constructed as Shane see, touches, holds, and tastes a ball. When he sees the ball roll, that does not fit into his schema or structure of ball-ness. He continues to construct his knowledge of ball-ness by reorganizing his schema so that now rolling is included in ball-ness. Shane's schema of ball today is different from his schema yesterday, when he had not noticed a rolling ball. Individual experiences and behavior bring about changes in schema.

Knowledge Construction   Young children construct knowledge about themselves and their world. They cannot copy knowledge. They must act on their own and construct their own meaning. Each of their actions and interpretations is unique to them. They see an object and construct thoughts about that object. Young children's thinking organizes information about their experiences so they can construct their own understanding.

Types of Knowledge   Piaget identified three types of knowledge: physical knowledge, logico-mathematical knowledge, and social-arbitrary knowledge.

Physical knowledge is knowledge children discover in the world around them. Twenty-five-month-old Tommy kicks a piece of pinestraw as he walks in the play yard. He picks up the pinestraw, throws it, and picks it up again. He drops it in the water tray, picks it up, and pulls it through the water. Tommy has discovered something about pinestraw from the pinestraw itself. Tommy uses actions and observations of the effects of his actions on the pinestraw to construct his physical knowledge of pinestraw.

Kamii and Devries have identified two kinds of activities involving physical knowledge: movement of objects and changes in objects. Actions to move objects include "pulling, pushing, rolling, kicking, jumping, blowing, sucking, throwing, swinging, twirling, balancing, and dropping" (1978, 6). The child causes the object to move and observes it rolling, bouncing, cracking, and so on. Kamii and Devries suggest four criteria for selecting activities to move objects.

1. The child must be able to produce the movement by his or her own action.
2. The child must be able to vary his or her action.
3. The reaction of the object must be observable.
4. The reaction of the object must be immediate (1978, 9).

A second kind of activity involves changes in objects. Compared to a ball, which when kicked, will move but still remain a ball, some objects change. When Kool-Aid® is put in water, it changes. Ann sees the dry Kool-Aid and observes that something happens when it is added to water. She can no longer see anything that looks like the dry Kool-Aid. She sees the water change color and can taste the difference between water without Kool-Aid and water with Kool-Aid in it. Her observation skills (seeing and tasting) are most important to provide her feedback on the changes that occur.

Logico-mathematical knowledge is invented by the child and involves relationships of objects.

Andrea is in the sandbox playing with two spoons: a teaspoon and a serving spoon. She notices the spoons are different. Although they fit into her schema of "spoon," she notices some difference in size. Thus, in relationship to size, they are different. At some time someone will label these differences for her as different or bigger or smaller than the other, but these words are not necessary for her to construct her concepts of sizes.

Social-arbitrary knowledge is knowledge a child cannot learn by him- or herself. It comes from "actions on or interactions with other people. Language, values, rules, morality, and symbol systems are examples of social-arbitrary knowledge" (Wadsworth, 1978, 52) (see Figure 3–7).

Chad is eating a banana. He bites it, sucks on it, swallows it, looks at the remaining banana, and squeezes it. All of these are concrete actions which help him construct his physical knowledge of this object. Then someone tells him this object is a banana. The name *banana* is social-arbitrary knowledge. It could have been called *ningina* or *lalisa*, but everyone using the English language uses *banana* to name that object.

In another example of social-arbitrary knowledge, Kurt follows Mrs. Wesley into the storage room. She sees him and says, "Kurt, go back into our room right now. You are not supposed to be in this room." Kurt did not make the decision that it is not permissible for him to be in the storage room; someone else decided and told him the rule.

A primary concept in Piaget's theory is adaptation, which involves changes in behavior to help children within their environment. Even small infants act in intelligent ways, not through abstract thinking, but by acting physically on the environment to meet their needs (Piaget, 1952).

Two basic principles of cognitive development are assimilation and accommodation. Assimilation refers to the process the child uses to put together separate skills in response to feedback from the environment. Accommodation is a process of changing or altering skills to better fit the requirements of a task. For Piaget, an infant who reaches or touches an object quickly develops *knowing*, an active process of coconstruction between what there is to know and the child's motivation and actions. More complex forms of knowing develop out of simple behaviors such as sucking, mouthing, and touching, according to Piaget. Assimilation, accommodation, and knowing occur, for example, during a traumatic emergency room visit, for which an infant is wrapped tightly to receive care. Later, the child may not necessarily consciously know why, but she is afraid of being confined. The experience has "taught" the child to assimilate, accommodate, and know that she fears being confined.

The **sensorimotor substage** starts at birth, when the baby explores self and the environment. Sensorimotor development involves the infant understanding his or her body and how it relates to other things in the environment (Piaget & Inhelder, 1969). The earliest form of thinking occurs during this stage, at approximately 18 months, and involves assimilation of sensorimotor cause and effect called interiorized actions. There are three key aspects of this early age: (1) infants play an assertive role in their own development, (2) their knowledge base is acquired by means of their own actions in the environment, and (3) infants need moderate challenges to master the environment. For caregivers, tasks should be provided that challenge babies are not beyond their ability to succeed. The 3A's, represent a valuable tool to help children experience challenges they can meet successfully.

Play is the child's laboratory for cognitive trial and error and rehearsal for real-life problem solving. Children begin active pretend play between 18 and 24 months. As they rapidly develop symbols and interpretations and start to reason verbally, complex sequences of play are executed. For example, two-year-olds might play "cooking," using blocks and sticks for food and utensils. From basic themes, children develop more complex strategies, perhaps using water and sand to explore measurement while learning about textures, temperatures, smells, and liquidity. Table 3–3 presents levels of exploratory and pretend play. Play develops from simple mouthing and touching objects to extremely abstract activity, in which materials are substituted and transformed to make up a complete story with beginning, middle, and end.

| **TABLE 3–3** | *LEVELS OF EXPLORATORY AND PRETEND PLAY* |

1. **Mouthing:** Indiscriminate mouthing of materials
2. **Simple manipulation:** Visually guided manipulation (excluding indiscriminate banging and shaking) at least 5 seconds in duration that cannot be coded in any other category (e.g., turn over an object, touch and look at an object)
3. **Functional:** Visually guided manipulation that is particularly appropriate for a certain object and involves the intentional extraction of some unique piece of information (e.g., turn dial on toy phone, squeeze piece of foam rubber, flip antenna of toy, spin wheels on cart, roll cart on wheels)
4. **Relational:** Bringing together and integrating two or more materials in an inappropriate manner, that is, in a manner not initially intended by the manufacturer (e.g., set cradle on phone, touch spoon to stick)
5. **Functional-relational:** Bringing together and integrating two objects in an appropriate manner, that is, in a manner intended by the manufacturer (e.g., set cup on saucer, place peg in hole of pegboard, mount spool on shaft of cart)
6. **Enactive naming:** Approximate pretense activity but without confirming evidence of actual pretense behavior (e.g., touch cup to lip without making talking sounds, touch brush to doll's hair without making combing motions)
7. **Pretend self:** Pretense behavior directed toward self in which pretense is apparent (e.g., raise cup to lip; tip cup, make drinking sounds, or tilt head; stroke own hair with miniature brush; raise phone receiver to ear and vocalize)
8. **Pretend other:** Pretense behavior directed away from child toward other (e.g., feed doll with spoon, bottle, or cup; brush doll's hair; push car on floor and make car noise)
9. **Substitution:** Using a "meaningless" object in a creative or imaginative manner (e.g., drink from seashell; feed baby with stick as "bottle") or using an object in a pretense act in a way that differs from how it has previously been used by the child (e.g., use hairbrush to brush teeth after already using it as a hairbrush on self or other)
10. **Sequence pretend:** Repetition of a single pretense act with minor variation (e.g., drink from bottle, give doll drink, pour into cup, pour into plate) or linking together different pretense schemes (e.g., stir in cup, then drink; put doll in cradle, then kiss good night)
11. **Sequence pretend substitution:** Same as sequence pretend except using an object substitution within sequence (e.g., put doll in cradle, cover with green felt piece as "blanket"; feed self with spoon, then with stick)
12. **Double substitution:** Pretense play in which two materials are transformed, within a single act, into something they are not in reality (e.g., treat peg as doll and a piece of green felt as a blanket and cover peg with felt and say "night-night"; treat stick as person and seashell as cup and give stick a drink)

Source: J. Belsky & R. K. Most. (1981). From exploration to play: A cross-sectional study of infant free play behavior. *Developmental Psychology, 17*, 630–639. Copyright © 1981 by the American Psychological Association reprinted with permission.

Learning Skill Development

Growth in learning skills requires the perceptual skills necessary to accurately process information, verbal language skills, and the pre-academic and academic skills necessary to learn effectively and efficiently. Each of these is discussed below.

Essential Perceptual Skills In our discussion of Physical Development we saw that motor movements follow a sequence from simple to more complex, and that neurological development depends largely on behavioral and environmental experiences. Motor movements require that the infant coordinate perceptual information with motor activity in order to behave consistently (Bertenthal, 1996). **Sensory grounded information** results from stimuli being processed through our sensory channels (touch, taste, smell, vision, and hearing) into our higher cortical functions, in which we attach meaning to the information. It is important for caregivers to understand how **perceptual skills** develop to enhance the growth of young children. Watson's Developmental Learning Skills Model presented in Chapter 2 is the basis for the following discussion of perceptual skills development.

Kinesthetic awareness (touch and body sensation) is present at birth. Touch is the first sensory channel that infants use to interact with the world, and sensitivity to touch is well developed at birth (Humphrey, 1978). It is well established that working on young infants' sensitivity to touch and kinesthetic awareness enhances physical, emotional, and cognitive growth (Stack & Muir, 1992). The caregiver should hold, cuddle, stroke, and provide a secure and affectionate kinesthetic environment for the young infant. Touching the baby's body parts and naming them helps develop basic associations between the kinesthetic and auditory channels. Catching the baby looking at a body part and naming it as you touch it helps develop basic associations between kinesthetic, visual, and auditory sensory channels. As soon as the infant can reach and grasp, everything is explored by putting it in the mouth. Between three and twelve months, the caregiver must keep small objects that the baby can choke on out of reach. Between nine and twelve months, exploratory mouthing gives way to improved visual-motor coordination so the baby does more holding, poking, and touching than mouthing (Lew & Butterworth, 1997).

Taste and smell perception are also present at birth. Facial expressions of newborns indicate preferences for tastes, but young babies quickly learn to like various tastes when they are paired with relief of hunger (Harris, 1997). The smell sensory channel develops similarly to taste: newborn's have smell preferences but quickly learn to like smells that are associated with pleasurable experiences, such as being held and fed. As with touch, caregivers should provide a variety of experiences and activities for babies to smell and taste. Through providing visual associations (objects or pictures) and auditory associations (naming) with tastes and smells, the caregiver enhances perceptual skill development for tasting and smelling.

Auditory (hearing) perceptual skills also develop rapidly during the first three years of life. Within the first few days after birth, infants prefer complex sounds such as voices and can discriminate a few sound patterns (Sansavini, Bertoncini, & Giovanelli, 1997). Infants prefer speech that is rather high-pitched, expressive, and ends in a rising tone (Aslin, Jusczyk, & Pisoni, 1998). Caregivers should use these qualities in speaking with infants to obtain sustained focal attention from the baby. Even mild auditory reception impairments can result in severe speech, language, and auditory perceptual skill deficits later on, so caregivers must ensure that infants and toddlers have frequent comprehensive audiological evaluations during the first three years. Additional auditory perceptual skills are discussed in the following section on Language Development.

Visual perceptual skills are probably the most important for caregivers to enhance since we use vision more than any other sensory channel to explore and learn from our world. The visual sensory channel is also the last one to mature, not becoming adult-like for several years (Hickey & Peduzzi, 1987). Newborns see objects at 20 feet about as clearly as adults do at 600 feet, so the visual acuity of infants is initially poor but rapidly improves within the first three months. Eye movements are also initially slow and inaccurate, but by two years of age toddlers have near adult visual acuity and eye movements. Therefore, enhancing visual perceptual skill development is extremely important.

Caregivers should provide a rich variety of visual stimulation and experiences for infants and toddlers. Colors, sizes, shapes, patterns, and movements should be presented in a wide variety, and caregivers should stimulate the child to focally attend to various visual stimuli (Figure 3–9). As with enhancement of skills in other sensory channels, the caregiver should pair auditory (talking about and naming), kinesthetic (touching), smell, and taste stimuli with specific visual items and pictures to help the child associate, discriminate, and remember visual stimuli. Caregivers should also help infants learn to focus and track visually. This means the baby focusing with both eyes together and following visual objects in a smooth pattern. By carefully watching the baby's eyes, the caregiver can provide rich and interesting visual experiences to enhance development of these visual perceptual skills.

Development of perceptual skills in all sensory channels follow the same sequence. Stimuli are brought into (input) the nervous system through the sensory receptors (e.g., taste buds, eyes, ears). When these receptors are healthy and coordinated (Level I, Sensory Coordination), the infants begins to focally attend to specific stimuli

Figure 3–9 Using all the senses is important to learning skill development.

and perceptually screen out distracting stimuli within the same sensory channel as well as distracting stimuli from all other sensory channels (Level II, Attention). Children who do not learn to sustain **focal attention** and **perceptual screening** with each of their sensory channels are frequently diagnosed as having attention-deficit disorder (ADD) when they reach school age. Caregivers should enhance focal attention and perceptual screening skills by providing a specific stimulus for a sustained period while they talk about, look at, and explore the specific stimulus in detail.

Additional perceptual skills are enhanced when the caregiver compares one stimulus with other stimuli to help the baby remember the stimulus (Level III, **Memory**) and perceive how it differs from other, similar stimuli (Level IV, **Discrimination**). Through touching, smelling, tasting, seeing, and hearing a stimulus, the baby quickly learns to pair (Level V, **Association**) how a stimulus looks like with how it sounds, tastes, smells, and feels. Sensory coordination, focal attention, memory, discrimination, and association are the bases for development of the essential perceptual skills that are prerequisite to the performing of higher cognitive tasks and the simplest academic tasks (Watson, 1995).

Sensory Channels and Levels of Processing Information Several general levels of information processing occur within the first three years of life. The most basic level (discussed earlier) occurs within the first few months of life, when primary neurological associations are made from sensory experiences that are the result of interacting with the world. As the baby's sensory receptors mature, basic associations between stimuli and responses within each sensory channel, and the associations between sensory channels are stored in memory and recalled more easily because of repeated presentations.

The next major level of perceptual development occurs with the evolution of basic language. Auditory-verbal associations begin within days after birth. For example, babies prefer the overall sound pattern of their native language over other languages within a few days after birth (Mehler et al., 1996). Sensory stimuli that the baby focally attends to are associated with the names and sounds representing those stimuli when the names and sounds are presented ant the same time as the stimuli in other sensory channels. The implications for caregivers are clear: naming and verbally labeling everything you catch the child focally attending to enhances associations between auditory stimuli and other sensory channels.

Another level of perceptual development involves same-modality and cross-modality processing. **Same-modality processing** involves presentation of stimuli through one modality, such as the auditory channel, and requiring a response within that same modality, such as verbalization (auditory input to verbal output). **Cross-modality processing** occurs when a stimulus in one channel, such as auditory, requires a response from a different sensory channel, such as visual-motor (auditory input to visual-motor output). Same-modality processing of visual input requires visual-motor responses (visual input to visual-motor output).

Caregivers and early childhood educators should use this rule to enhance perceptual skill development; same-modality tasks are perceptually easier than cross-modality tasks. Because many caregivers and early childhood teachers do not use this simple principle, many children reach school age with significant visual or auditory perceptual skill deficits, which quickly become learning disabilities in the school setting.

An example illustrates the importance of presenting same-modality tasks to young children. We notice 16-month-old Tisha doesn't seem to focally attend to many of the visual stimuli in her environment. We observe the caregiver presenting visual stimuli and asking Tisha to respond verbally (a cross-modality task: visual input to verbal output). We suggest that the caregiver present Tisha with a visual stimulus and require her to point to the correct match among a choice of four pictures, one of which is identical to the focused-on stimulus (a same-modality task: visual input to visual-motor output). We observe that Tisha focally attends much better and with more success because same-modality tasks are perceptually much easier than cross-modality tasks. Caregivers and early childhood educators should be very careful to consider the perceptual requirements of tasks they present to children and keep sensory input within the same modality as the required output whenever possible. In addition, caregivers should not overlook obvious physical complaints by attributing them to either learning or psychological problems. A physical checklist for health should be conducted before any psychological testing is scheduled. Sometimes a misinterpretation can be as simple as a middle ear infection that temporarily causes auditory processing difficulty.

Perceptual Skill Development and Learning Styles   Since we are born with the neurological maturity necessary to begin processing information and quickly establish preferences for using our sensory channels, and because adults generally ignore the perceptual requirements of the tasks and stimuli they present children, most children reach school age with an "imbalanced" learning style. In fact, several studies reveal that only about 10 percent of children entering formal educational programs are **balanced learners** (Watson, 1982). A balanced perceptual learning style means that the child processes information equally well through the major sensory channels necessary for higher cognitive learning (i.e., the visual, auditory, and to less extent, kinesthetic channel). Since the most basic academic tasks, such as letter and word recognition, spelling, and arithmetic operations, require effective information processing in both visual and auditory channels, most children start school with perceptual skill deficiencies.

To enhance a balanced visual and auditory learning style, caregivers must present specific tasks and activities that enhance development of the 11 essential perceptual skills. Notice in Table 3-4 that only one cross-modality skill is an essential prerequisite to the simplest academic tasks.

TABLE 3–4	*ESSENTIAL DEVELOPMENTAL LEARNING SKILLS*
Auditory Channel	*Visual Channel*
Auditory-Visual Association (cross-modality)	Visual Association
Auditory Association	Visual Discrimination
Auditory Discrimination	Visual Memory
Auditory Memory	Visual Focal Attention
Auditory Focal Attention	Visual-Motor Output
Verbal Output	

Language Development Most babies are able to screen out many sounds that are not useful in understanding their native language by the age of six months (Polka & Werker, 1994). Between six and twelve months of age, babies are usually able to recognize familiar words in spoken passages (Jusczyk & Hohne, 1997). These findings suggest that infants begin to discriminate, associate, and analyze the structure of words and sentences before nine months of age!

Adults unconsciously conduct what is called child-directed speech with babies. This means that adults automatically adjust their tone, volume, and speech patterns to capture and sustain focal attention from the baby (Moore, Spence, & Katz, 1997). Almost as soon as the baby starts to use words, caregiver speech changes to more information, directions, and questions rather than child-directed speech (Murray, Johnson, & Peters, 1990).

Communication begins with infants both verbally and nonverbally. Newborns initiate interaction by making eye contact, and by four months they gaze in the same direction as the caregiver (Tomasello, 1999). As discussed in perceptual development, it is important for caregivers to label and describe things that the baby visually attends to because this significantly enhances language development. On the other hand, caregivers who interrupt or restrict the baby's focal attention and activities impede language development (Carpenter, Nagell, & Tomasello, 1998).

The next level of language development, at around three months, involves the caregiver's copying or mimicking the baby's vocalization, which helps the child focally attend to the sounds that the caregiver makes. Then, turn-taking begins, in which the baby vocalizes, the caregiver vocalizes in return and waits for a response, and the "conversation" continues. Turn-taking games such as "patty-cake" start, at around six months, and by twelve months, babies interact actively and even initiate turn-taking interactions (Bruner, 1983).

Gestural communication begins between nine and twelve months, when the baby touches or holds objects while making sure the caregiver notices and gives attention, or the baby "directs" the caregiver to do something by pointing or gesturing (Fenson et al., 1994). When the caregiver labels and describes what the baby holds or gestures at, language development is enhanced. By the beginning of the second year, verbalization of words and phrases are associated with gestures to communicate accurately. As vocabulary increases and becomes more descriptive, gestures decrease toward the end of the second year (Namy & Waxman, 1998).

The many aspects of more complex speech development, such as grammar and semantics, are beyond the scope of this text. It must suffice to say that young children quickly learn the rules of speech governing their native language and are proficient by around six years of age. Caregivers who mold young children's language by labeling, describing, mirroring, and actively engaging the child definitely enhance the development and use of language.

Encouraging Perceptual Skills A case study may help illustrate how to enhance the development of perceptual skills. Mindy is a six-week-old who appears to have difficulty focally attending to visual stimuli. The caregiver chooses six visual objects that are very different in size, shape, color, and texture. She places herself so she can carefully observe Mindy's eyes and places all six objects within the child's visual field. The caregiver then picks up each item and hands it to Mindy to touch and feel. She discusses how each item feels, smells, and tastes; what it is called; and how it differs from the other objects. As they explore each object, making sure that all sensory channels have been used, the caregiver observes how well Mindy focuses both eyes on the object as it is moved. The activity is continued for as long as Mindy can remain interested in the visual stimuli. This type of activity enhances focal attention, perceptual screening, memory, discrimination, and association of the perceptual qualities of stimuli. Although visual perception is used in this example, the caregiver can create activities and experiences to enhance the perceptual development in all other sensory channels as well.

Key Terms

bad touch

balanced learners

catch the child being good

controlling caregiver style

cross-modality processing

defense mechanisms

detached caregiver style

detachment

development

double substitution

Emotional Intelligence

empathy

enactive naming

enlightened self-interest

experience-expectant

experience-dependent

fine motor control

flow

focal attention

focusing and tracking

functional-relational

good touch

gross motor control

healthy caregiver style

I voice

I-self

inductive discipline

interactional synchrony

learning

locus of control

Me-self

memory

meta-cognition

milestones

Neuro-Linguistic Programming (NLP)

observing ego

omnipotent

perceptual screening

perceptual skills

pretend other

pretend self

same-modality processing

self-awareness

self-esteem

self-responsibility

self-talk

selfless caregiver style

sensorimotor substage

sensory grounded information

substitution

Sudden Infant Death Syndrome (SIDS)

temperament traits

You voice

CASE STUDY

The reader should now have a working knowledge of normal patterns of development in each of the five areas for children under the age of 36 months. To test your understanding, decide if Marcus is advanced, behind, or at age level in the following evaluation summary.

Marcus, who is 24 months old, is in day care from 7:30 A.M. to 4:00 P.M. five days a week. An evaluation of his development in each of the five major areas revealed the following observations.

Physical Factors. Marcus is 36 inches tall, weights 35 pounds, has 20/20 vision, and can focus and track across a line of letters fluidly. He has all 20 baby teeth, can stand on one foot and hop, and is interested in toilet training. He can throw a ball with each hand and use a fork to eat.

Emotional Factors. Marcus clings to his caregiver much of the time and shows anxiety at the presence of strangers. He is compliant and follows direction when he feels secure, but he can become whiny when he does not receive enough individual attention. He has difficulty understanding his feelings or soothing himself. When not involved with his caregiver or other children, Marcus has difficulty being at ease.

Social Factors. Marcus has some difficulty determining what things are his, and he cooperates with other children only when he has the full attention of his caregiver. He is easily emotionally hurt by other children and cannot defend himself when other children take advantage of him. He is not often able to be sensitive to the feelings of other children. Although his language skills are sufficient, Marcus screams rather than using words when other children bother him.

Cognitive Factors. When he feels secure, Marcus is curious, explores his environment, and gains a lot of physical knowledge. Although he has some difficulty interacting with peers, he participates in active, creative pretend play and exhibits logical sequence in the stories he makes up. He uses double substitution in play and understands four- and five-direction sequences.

Learning Skill Factors. Marcus can focus and attend to both visual and auditory stimuli in distracting environments, such as a group of children. He accurately discriminates, associates, and remembers sequences of visual and auditory symbols appropriate for his age. His language development is average, and he articulates well. He appears to process information equally well both visually and auditorally. His visual-motor control appears to be at age level.

If you decided that Marcus is (1) advanced in physical development, (2) below age expectations in emotional and social development, (3) near or slightly above age level in cognitive development, and (4) average in his perceptual and language development, you have a good working understanding of normal patterns of development.

1. Determine your strengths and weaknesses in each of the five major Developmental Areas.
2. In which of the five areas is it most difficult for you to make an assessment of Marcus and of yourself?
3. How does the assessment tool used with Marcus apply to your experience working with children?

Student Activities

1. During the children's alert play time observe two children of different ages between birth and three years, focusing on one area (physical, emotional, social, cognitive). Write down everything each child does and says for five minutes. Make a chart to compare the behaviors.

Child:	*Age:*	*Child:*	*Age:*

Area:		*Area:*	

Behaviors		Behaviors	

2. Observe one child between birth and three years of age interacting with one adult. List the behaviors each uses to get the other's attention.

	Initiate	*Response*
Child		
Adult		
Child		
Adult		
Child		
Adult		

3. Define emotional intelligence.
4. Name the factors important in the development of relationships.
5. What opportunities does the growing nervous system of an infant offer a caregiver?
6. List four temperament patterns.

Chapter Review

1. How can you apply Margaret Mahler's five separation-individuation stages?
2. Review the neurological development of the brain.
3. Discuss the implications of conscious care as if you were a teacher talking to parents.
4. Temperament is an important issue. What factors influence these classifications most?
5. Discuss with a group of students the difference between specialized care and inclusion of children with special needs.
6. Name the major milestones for motor development from birth to three years of age.
7. Name 12 essential perceptual skills necessary for doing any academic task.
8. What three skills do children need to have good self-esteem?
9. Explain why caregivers should establish interactional synchrony with children.
10. Discuss Piaget's stages of cognitive development in terms of activities with two-year-olds.

References

American Psychiatric Association. (1994). *Diagnostic and statistical manual of mental disorders* (4th ed.). Washington, DC: American Psychiatric Association.

Anders, Goodlin-Jones, & Zelenko, M. (1998). Infants' regularity and sleep-wake state development. *Zero to Three, 19*(2), 5–8.

Asendorpf, J. B., Warkentin, V., & Baudonniere, P. (1996). Self-awareness and other-awareness II: Mirror self-recognition, social contingency awareness, and synchronic imitation. *Developmental Psychology, 21*, 313–321.

Aslin, R. N., Jusczyk, P. W., & Pisoni, D. B. (1998). Speech and auditory processing during infancy: Constraints on and precursors to language. In D. Kuhn & R. S. Siegler (Eds.), *Handbook of child psychology: Vol. 2. Cognition, perception, and language.* New York: Wiley.

Bancroft, G. (1834). *History of the United States.* Vol. 3, 443–450.

Beatty, J. (1995). *Principles of behavior neuroscience.* London: Brown and Benchmark.

Berk, L. E. (1998). *Child development* (4th ed.). Needham Heights, MA: Allyn and Bacon.

Berk, L. E. (2000). *Child development* (5th ed.). Needham Heights, MA: Allyn and Bacon.

Bernstein, N. (1967). *The coordination and regulation of movements.* London: Pergamon.

Bertenthal, B. I. (1996). Origins and early development of perception, action, and representation. *Annual Review of Psychology, 47*, 431–459.

Bodenhamer, B. G., & Hall, M. J. (2000). *The user's manual for the brain.* Carmarthen, Wales, England: Crown House Publishing Limited.

Brownell, C. A., & Carriger, M. S. (1990). Changes in cooperation and self-other differentiation during the second year. *Child Development, 61*, 1161–1174.

Bruner, J. S. (1983). The acquisition of pragmatic commitments. In R. M. Golinkoff (Ed.), *The transition from prelinguistic to linguistic communication* (pp. 27–42). Hillsdale, NJ: Erlbaum.

Bullock, M., & Lutkenhaus, P. (1990). Who am I? The development of self-understanding in toddlers. *Merrill-Palmer Quarterly, 36*, 217–238.

Carpenter, M., Nagell, K., & Tomasello, M. (1998). Social cognition, joint attention, and communicative competence. *Monographs of the Society for Research in Child Development, 63.*

Caspi, A., & Silva, P. A. (1995). Temperamental qualities at age three predict personality traits in young adulthood: Longitudinal evidence from a birth cohort. *Child Development, 66*, 486–498.

Coopersmith, S. (1967). *The antecedents of self-esteem.* San Francisco: W. H. Freeman.

Cowan, Philip A. (1978). Piaget: with feeling: cognitive, social, and emotional dimensions. New York: Holt, Rinehart and Winston.

Csikszentmihalyi, M. (1990). *The psychology of optimal experience* (1st ed.). New York: Harper & Row.

Dondi, M., Simion, F., & Caltran, G. (1999). Can newborns discriminate between their own cry and the cry of another newborn infant? *Developmental Psychology, 35*, 418–426.

Douville-Watson, L. (2000). Lecture #7: Child Development. Rockville Center, NY: Molloy College.

Douville-Watson, L. (2000). Lectures #2 and #3: Psychology 213. Uniondale, NY: Nassau Community College.

Douville-Watson, L. (2000). Lecture #9: Child Care, Rockville Center, NY: Molloy College.

Douville-Watson, L. (2001) Childcare Lecture #3: Neuroscience. Rockville Center, NY: Molloy College.

Eisenberg, N., & McNally, S. (1993). Socialization and mothers' and adolescents' empathy-related characteristics. *Journal of Research on Adolescence, 3*, 171–191.

Fenson, L., Dale, P. S., Reznick, J. S., Bates, E., Thal, D. J., & Pethick, S. J. (1994). Variability in early communicative development. *Monographs of the Society for Research in Child Development, 59*(5), 1–189.

Freed, A. M. (1991). T. A. (transactional analysis) for tots. Torrance, CA: Jalmar Press.

Freud, S. (1920/1974). *Beyond the pleasure principle*. From *The standard edition of the complete psychological works of Sigmund Freud*. London: Hogarth Press.

Gardner, H. (1995) Cracking open the I.Q. box. *The American Prospect*, Winter edition.

Gerber, M. (1998) Dear parent: caring for infants with respect. Edited by Joan Weaver, Los Angeles, CA: Resources for Infant Educators (RIE).

Goleman, D. (1996). *Emotional Intelligence*. New York: Bantam Books.

Gopnik, A., & Wellman, H. M. (1994). The 'theory' theory. In L. A. Hirschfeld & S. A. Gelman (Eds.), *Mapping the mind: Domain specificity in cognition and culture*. Cambridge, MA: Cambridge University Press.

Gralinski, J. H., & Kopp, C. B. (1993). Everyday rules for behavior: Mothers' requests to young children. *Developmental Psychology*, *29*, 573–584.

Greenberg, J. R., & Mitchell, S. A. (1983). *Object relations in psychoanalytic theory*. Cambridge, MA: Harvard University Press.

Greenspan, G., & Pollock, G. (1989). *The course of life*. Madison, CT: International University Press.

Grusec, J. E., & Goodnow, J. J. (1994). Impact of parental discipline methods on the child's internalization of values: A reconceptualization of current points of view. *Developmental Psychology*, *30*, 4–19.

Gunnar, M. R. (1998). Quality of early care and buffering of neuroendocrine stress reactions: Potential effects on the developing human brain. *Preventive Medicine*, *27*, 208–211.

Harris, G. (1997). Development of taste perception and appetite regulation. In G. Bremner, A. Slater, & G. Butterworth (Eds.), *Infant development: Recent advances*. East Sussex, England: Erlbaum.

Harter, S. (1998). The development of self-representations. In N. Eisenberg (Ed.), *Handbook of child psychology: Vol. 3. Social, emotional, and personality development*. New York: Wiley.

Hickey, T. L., & Peduzzi, J. D. (1987) Structure and development of the visual system. In P. Salapatek & L. Cohen (Eds.), *Handbook of infant perception: Vol. 1. From sensation to perception*. New York: Academic Press.

Hofsten, C. Von. (1989). Motor development as the development of systems. *Developmental Psychology*, *25*, 950–953.

Humphrey, T. (1978). Function of the nervous system during prenatal life. In U. Stave (Ed.), *Perinatal physiology*. New York: Plenum.

Isabella, R. A., & Belsky, J. (1991). Interactional synchrony and the origins of infant-mother attachment: A replication study. *Child Development*, *62*, 373–384.

Josephs, L. (1992). *Character structure and the organization of the self*. New York: Columbia University Press.

James, W. (1963). *Psychology*. (Original work published 1890). New York: Fawcett.

Johniditis, N. (2000). *Youth teeth* (information pamphlet). Locust Valley, NY: Nicholas.

Jusczyk, P. W., & Hohne, E. A. (1997). Infants' memory for spoken words. *Science*, *277*, 1984–1986.

Kagan, J., Reznick, J. S., & Gibbons, J. (1989). Inhibited and uninhibited types of children. *Child Development*, *60*, 838–845.

Kamii, C., & Devries, R. (1978). *Physical knowledge in preschool education: Implications of Piaget's theory*. Englewood Cliffs, NJ: Prentice-Hall.

Kleitman, N. (1963). *Sleep and wakefulness*. Chicago: University of Chicago Press.

Klimes-Dougan, B., & Kistner, J. (1990). Physically abused preschoolers' responses to peers' distress. *Developmental Psychology*, *67*, 599–602.

Lamb, M. E., & Campos, J. J. (1982). *Development in infancy*. New York: Random House.

Levine, L. E. (1983). Mine: Self-definition in 2-year-old boys. *Developmental Psychology*, *19*, 544–549.

Lew, A. R., & Butterworth, G. (1997). The development of hand-mouth coordination in 2- to 5-month-old infants: Similarities with reaching and grasping. *Infant Behavior and Development*, *20*, 59–69.

Larzelere, R. E., Schneider, W. N., Larson, D. B., & Pike, P. L. (1996). The effects of discipline responses in delaying toddler misbehavior recurrences. *Child & Family Behavior Therapy, 18*, 35–37.

Mahler, M. S. (1975). The psychological birth of the human infant. In *The selected papers of Margaret S. Mahler*, Vol. 2. New York: Basic Books.

Mahler, M. S., Pine, F., & Bergman, F. (1975). *The psychological birth of the human infant: Symbiosis and individuation*. New York: Basic Books.

Mehler, J., Dupoux, E., Nazzi, T., & Dehaene-Lambertz, G. (1996). Coping with linguistic diversity: The infant's point of view. In J. L. Morgan & K. Demuth (Eds.), *Signal to syntax*. Mahwah, NJ: Erlbaum.

Miller, J. G., & Luthar, S. (1989). Issues of interpersonal responsibility and accountability: A comparison of Indians' and Americans' moral judgements. *Social Recognition, 7*, 237–261.

Mischel, H. N., & Liebert, R. M. (1966). Effects of discrepancies between observed and imposed reward criteria on their acquisition and transmission. *Journal of Personality and Social Psychology, 3*, 45–53.

Moore, D. S., Spence, M. J., & Katz, G. S. (1997). Six-month-olds' categorization of natural infant-directed utterances. *Developmental Psychology, 33*, 980–989.

Murray, A. D., Johnson, J., & Peters, J. (1990). Fine-tuning of utterance length to preverbal infants: Effects on later language development. *Journal of Child Language, 17*, 511–525.

Nakamura, J. (1988). The study of flow and math students. In *Optimal experience and the uses of talent*. Cambridge, MA: Cambridge University Press.

Namy, L. L., & Waxman, S. R. (1998). Words and gestures: Infants' interpretations of different forms of symbolic reference. *Child Development, 69*, 295–308.

Olko, C., & Turkewitz, G. (2001). Cerebral asymmetry of emotion and its relationship to olfaction in infancy. *Laterality, 6*(1), 29–37.

Piaget, J. (1952). *The origins of intelligence in children*. (M. Cook, trans.). New York: International University Press.

Piaget, J., & Inhelder, (1969). *The psychology of the child*. London: Routledge and Kegan Paul.

Plomin, R. (1994). Nature, nurture, and social development. *Social Development, 3*, 37–53.

Polka, L., & Werker, J. F. (1994). Developmental changes in perception of non-native vowel contrasts. *Journal of Experimental Psychology: Human Perception and Performance, 20*, 421–435.

Rubin, K. H., Hastings, P. D., Stewart, S. L., Henderson, H. A., & Chen, X. (1997). The consistency and concomitants of inhibition: Some of the children, all of the time. *Child Development, 68*, 467–483.

Rutter, M. (1998). Developmental catch-up, and deficit, following adoption after severe global early deprivation. *Journal of Child Psychology and Psychiatry, 39*, 465–476.

Sansavini, A., Bertoncini, J., & Giovanelli, G. (1997). Newborns discriminate the rhythm of multisyllabic stressed words. *Developmental Psychology, 33*, 3–11.

Stack, D. M., & Muir, D. W. (1992). Adult tactile stimulation during face-to-face interactions modulates five-month-olds' affect and attention. *Child Development, 63*, 1509–1525.

Stokes, I. (2001). The role of inheritance in behavior. *Science, 248*, 183–188.

Strassberg, A., Dodge, K., Petitt, G. S., & Bates, J. E. (1994). Spanking in the home and children's subsequent aggression toward kindergarten peers. *Developmental Psychopathology, 6*, 445–461.

Sullins, E. (1991). The study of mood transfer. *Personality and Social Psychology Bulletin*, April.

Thompson, R. A. (1990). On emotion and self regulation. In R. A. Thompson (Ed.) *Nebraska symposium on motivation*.

Tomasello, M. (1999). Understanding intentions and learning words in the second year of life. In M. Bowerman & S. Levinson (Eds.), *Language acquisition and conceptual development*. Cambridge, MA: Cambridge University Press.

Tronick, E. Z., & Cohn, J. F. (1989). Infant-mother face-to-face interaction: Age and gender differences in coordination and the occurrence of miscoordination. *Child Development, 60,* 85–92.

Turiel, E. (1998). The development of morality. In N. Eisenberg (Ed.), *Handbook of child psychology, Vol. 3. Social, emotional, and personality development.* New York: Wiley.

Wadsworth, B. J. (1998). *Piaget for the classroom teacher.* New York: Longman.

Walther-Lee, D. (1998). *The changing role of grandparents: Adult children's memories of their grandparents.* Doctoral dissertation, Garden City, NY: Adelphi University, Derner Institute of Advanced Psychological Studies.

Watson, M. A. (1996). *The national parenting scales, experimental edition.* New York: Instructional Press.

Watson, M. A. (1982). *The WALDO program.* Baldwin, NY: Educational Activity.

Watson, M. A. (2001). *Mood disorders in young children.* Wheaton, MD: C.E.U. Course Lecture, American Healthcare Institute.

Watson, M. A. (1995). *The Watson Auditory-Visual Essential Skills Tests: WAVES.* Bayville, NY: Instructional Press.

Wolff, P. H. (1993). *Behavioral and emotional states in infancy: A dynamic perspective.* Cambridge, MA: MIT Press.

Zahn-Waxler, C. (1991). The case for empathy: A developmental review. *Psychological Inquiry, 2,* 155–158.

Zeskind, P. S., & Marshal, T. R. (1991). Temporal organization in neonatal arousal: Systems, oscillations, and development. In M. Weiss, & P. Zelago (Eds.), *Newborn: Attention: Biological constraints and the influence of experiences* (pp. 22–62). Norwood, NJ: Ablex Publishing Corp.

Additional Resources

Belsky, J., & Most, R. K. (1981). From exploration to play: A cross-sectional study of infant free play behavior, *Developmental Psychology, 17,* 630–639.

Douville, L. (1994). *3A's of Child Care: Attention, Approval, Affection.* Bayville, NY: Instructional Press.

Douville-Watson, L. (1994). *F.A.R.E. Family Actualization through Research and Education.* Bayville, NY: Instructional Press.

Douville-Watson, L. & Watson, M. (1998). *Child accountability programs.* Anaheim, CA: National Association for the Education of the Young Child.

Moore, G. A., Cohn, J. F., & Campbell, S. B. (1997). Mothers' affective behavior with infant siblings: Stability and change. *Developmental Psychology, 22,* 317–326.

Piaget, J. (1954). *The construction of reality in the child.* (M. Cook, trans.). New York: Basic Books.

Thompson, R. A. (1990). Vulnerability in research: A developmental perspective on research risk. *Child Development, 61,* 1–16.

Wolff, P. H. (1993). The causes, controls and organization of behavior in the neonate. *Psychological Issues, 51,* Serial No. 17.

Zahn-Wolff, P. H. (1966). The courses, controls, and organizational behavior in the neonate. Madison, CT: International Universities Press, Incorporated.

Helpful Web Sites

Association for Childhood Education International Supports child-centered whole curriculum education from infancy through early adolescence. http://www.udel.edu/bateman/acei

Child Development Associate (CDA) Child development agency operating child care centers throughout San Diego County. http://www.cdasandiego.com

Clearinghouse on International Developments in Child, Youth and Family Policies Compares child, youth and family policies in countries worldwide. http://www.childpolicyintl.org

Department of Women and Child Development Enacts and amends legislation; guides and coordinates the efforts of both governmental and nongovernment organizations. http://www.wcd.nic.in

Early Childhood Educators Web Guide Provides sites on child development, cultural diversity, discipline, and guidance. http://www.ecewebguide.com

Human Services Research Institute (HSRI) Develops policies and undertakes research, development, and evaluation projects. http://www.hsri.org

For additional infant and toddler resources, visit our Web site at http://www.earlychilded.delmar.com

The 3A's: The Master Tools for Child Care

Objectives

After reading this chapter, you should be able to:

- Use the 3A's in daily child care.
- Compare the concepts of the 3A's with your own experiences.
- Clearly define differences between the 3A's of child care and the 3A's of self-health.
- Incorporate the 3A's of child care and 3A's of self-health in your own life for one day as an experiment.
- Observe and record the process of using the 3A's with a child.

Chapter Outline

INTRODUCTION

Have you ever heard the cry of a troubled newborn that sends ripples down your spine? Ask any new parents in the first few nights of adjusting to family life what their baby's cry feels like to them. Instinctively, humans feel the distress almost as if the cry reaches the very fiber of our being. The response is almost universal: do whatever is necessary to soothe, calm, and reassure the fragile infant. Once the goal of comforting is achieved, the experience is a sense of triumph like no other. How do we respond so quickly? What lost memory motivates us to take such sudden action? Could it be that we re-experience our own sense of utter aloneness, a vibration so familiar and so foreboding that every cell wishes to quiet the call? The answer to all these questions, which can be found in these chapters, is yes.

Teaching the concepts of the 3A's—Attention, Approval, and Affection—has been a passion for the authors for more than 30 years. The life-long effects of positive, consistent, and conscious infant and toddler care has been understood by child development experts for a long time. A working premise of this book is that what you do with children matters, and that positive intention coupled with caring delivery of proven skills makes a profound difference in the lives of children.

Children give back what they are given during early childhood. They return kindness, stability, consistency, and caring as they grow up and relate to the world in the schools, workplace, and in their own families. Their interactions and caregiving become that of their own caregivers through their behavior toward other people. As previously discussed in development of the nervous system, the quality of your caring, including actions, verbal messages, voice tone and tempo, and secure handling, helps create the nerve pathways that determine each child's perceptions and map of the world. Your interactions with young children help determine how each child will eventually perceive himself or herself as worthy, unworthy, guilty, hopeful, or hopeless.

Caregivers are the engineers of the future generations. Your mission is monumental in nature. Your daily movements, efforts, and attitudes help shape and determine the destiny of the planet. You affect the very fiber of each child, and no position in society is more important. The 3A's are the master tools that ensure that your effect on children is positive and productive. In this age of mechanistic impulse redundancy, our newly awakened genetic units (our children) need to claim their human right to humane care. There is no better way available to provide this care than a wonderfully soothing dose of consciously administered 3A's.

The abilities to understand and fulfill academic requirements and to master specific skills, such as bathing and feeding babies, are necessary to your work and may even extend into your personal life. These immensely important aspects of child care, however, are not enough.

Students studying child care need to integrate their "self" into their work because no other professional field is in need of self-integration more than this most humanistic endeavor. Taking charge of tomorrow's leaders on a daily basis demands human investment since it perpetuates all future human relationships. Just how important are these future connections? Let's look at what other experts have to say.

"The child's self is constructed in the interpersonal relationships that bind her to others, she is known in the experience of connection and is defined by the responsiveness of human engagement" (Gilligan, 1988).

"It is in the context of relationships that the needs and wishes of very young children are met, or not. . . . It is in the context of relationships that infants and toddlers continue to develop expectations about how the world is, how the adults in that world behave, and their own place in the social world" (Pawl, 1990).

"When there is a sudden breakdown in the relationship between caregiver and child, whether that is natural or due to conflict, the results can profoundly effect momentarily or cumulatively the meanings children give to themselves now and in later experience" (Douville-Watson, L., 1995).

Jane Healy, in her book *Your Child's Growing Mind*, discusses the importance of warm, loving, verbal interactions between parent or caregiver and child, particularly in the first two years. She indicates that praise, prompt attention, and immediate feedback about objects in the environment develop better vocabulary and higher scores on later intelligence tests (Healy, 1988).

How important are these human connections? ". . . every experience lives on in further experiences" (Dewey, 1938, p. 28). Repeated emotional experiences are integrated into children's understandings about themselves, others, and the world they share (Denzin, 1984). In this way, "the experiences and feelings of childhood endure" (Bowman, 1989, p. 450); "they become part of children's biographies, providing the emotional foundation for future interactions and relationships" (Hatch, 1995).

How important are these connections to long-term life experiences? How do early life connections affect later years? Here is one study with remarkable conclusions. Jon Kabet-Zinn, Ph.D., in his book *Full Catastrophe Living: Using the Wisdom of Your Body and Mind to Face Stress, Pain and Illness* (1991), discusses a 40-year longitudinal health study recording illnesses and subsequent deaths. The study, done by Dr. Caroline Bell Thomas on incoming medical students at Johns Hopkins Medical School, tracked life experiences through the disease process. The study found that "the importance of emotional experiences early in life may play a strong role in shaping our health later in life."

Phillip S. Riback (1997), an assistant professor of neurology and pediatrics at Albany Medical College, stated: "Since babies are so highly dependent on their caregivers for everything, it makes some sense that their emotional state, and eventually their own emotional responses, are affected by the emotions of those who care for them."

How important are human connections? Who is responsible for these outcomes? Hatch (1995) writes, "When mother's importance is shared with others, such as fathers, preschool teachers, and day care providers, someone is still responsible for a variety of positive and negative outcomes." If we acknowledge our responsibility as caregivers, we can readily accept that "infants become partners in the give and take of human relationships" (Snow, 1989).

Why do we call people who integrate their "self" every day in their work simply caregivers, providers, teachers, or specialists? Why don't we address them respectfully in terms of the possible outcomes of their personal investment? They should really be referred to as "Most Powerful Maker of the Highly Intelligent, Serenely Compassionate, Healthy, Adaptive, Future Human Race." Although wordy, it is an accurate description of the impact your daily commitment can have on children and their future outcomes.

So, Most Powerful Outcome Maker, what can you learn for your "self" that will allow you to be available, fresh, interested, involved, and ready to take on this awesome task? Indeed, caregivers must learn to take good care of themselves, to not neglect their "self" in daily routines, and to use self-health techniques. The "master tools" for accomplishing this are the 3A's: Attention, Approval, and Affection.

THE 3A'S: ATTENTION, APPROVAL, AND AFFECTION AS TOOLS

The 3A's of child care are the master tools for promoting a positive environment and maintaining a positive emotional connection between the young child and the caregiver. The 3A's of child care—Attention, Approval, and Affection—are extremely powerful tools available to any person in just about any situation. They are not only valuable tools; their use is *essential* in the care of children. The 3A's are called master tools because they apply to everything we do all day long. Attention, Approval, and Affection are necessary to function well, have good self-esteem, remain at ease, and interact with other people in a positive and productive manner.

Examples of Attention, Approval, and Affection are meant to empower the caregiver and help facilitate an attitude change toward oneself, which emphasizes that caregiver feelings have a profound effect on children. These skills help motivate children, and when the caregiver uses these skills for personal development, he or she can enjoy the same benefit. These concepts are widely used in areas of psychology and medicine. They include techniques from the scientific study of bioenergetics and relaxation therapy that can effectively revitalize the caregiver and help him or her stay "on center." They provide that badly needed second to think and are most useful in fighting the inevitable outcome of caring for children all day, called exhaustion.

THE ATTACHMENT DEBATE AND DIMINISHED FATHER AND MOTHER ROLES

Discussion of the 3A's begins with the scientific fact that infants and toddlers require secure attachment to their caregivers for normal, healthy development. Further, a large body of research supports positive Attention, Approval, and Affection between caregivers and children as the foundation for secure attachment.

An ongoing debate in the research literature concerns whether infants exhibit less secure attachment when raised in child care as opposed to being home-reared. This debate cannot be discussed without considering the changing roles of mothers and fathers in the care of infants. As we saw in Chapter 1, one historical view was that *only* the mother could bond with the infant sufficiently to ensure healthy development. With the advent of a great number of infants and toddlers spending the majority of their day in child care, the question of how much attachment to one consistent person an infant requires in order to develop security and trust is being studied more intensely.

Researchers have identified a secure pattern of attachment and three insecure patterns (Ainsworth et al., 1978; Main & Soloman, 1990).

1. **Secure attachment.** The infant uses a parent as a secure base, strongly prefers the parent over a stranger, actively seeks contact with the parent, and is easily comforted by the parent after being absent.
2. **Avoidant attachment.** The infant is usually not distressed by parental separation and may avoid the parent or prefer a stranger when the parent returns.
3. **Resistant attachment.** The infant seeks closeness to the parent and resists exploring the environment, usually displays angry behavior after the parent returns, and is difficult to comfort.
4. **Disoriented attachment.** The infant shows inconsistent attachment and reacts to the parent returning with confused or contradictory behavior (looking away when held or showing a dazed facial expression).

A related characteristic to attachment is **separation anxiety**, which appears to be a normal developmental experience, since children from every culture exhibit it. Infants from various cultures all over the world have been found to exhibit separation anxiety starting around six months and increasing in intensity until approximately 15 months (Kagan et al., 1978). Separation anxiety is exhibited by securely attached infants, as well as different types of insecurely attached infants.

A summary of the research on infant attachment suggests that infants are actively involved in the attachment bond. Drastic changes in family circumstances, such as divorce, death, or job loss, detrimentally affect infant attachment and babies are normally capable of attaching securely to more than one adult or parent. Caregiving that is supportive and sensitive to the child's needs using the 3A's promotes secure attachment, and insensitive or inconsistent care results in insecure attachment. Finally, secure infant attachment and continuity of caregiving is related to later cognitive, emotional, and social competence.

Several important implications for caregiving and parenting and changes in father and mother roles result from these findings. The trend toward working mothers places more importance on fathers, other family members, and child care specialists to provide secure and consistent attachment and bonding with infants. Research on attachment security of infants with full-time working mothers suggests that most infants of employed mothers are securely attached, and while some studies report a difference between home-reared and child care-reared children, not all studies report a difference (Roggman et al., 1994). Since family circumstances have been shown to affect infant attachment, the stress level of the mother may partly explain differences (Owen & Cox, 1988).

The question of whether fathers are capable of bonding and establishing secure attachment with infants has been positively answered by research. In 1978, Allison Clarke-Stewart published a landmark study that observed children at 15, 20, and 30 months of age alone with their fathers, alone with their mothers, and with both parents present. Unstructured or natural observations as well as structured or limited-choice situations were arranged. The major findings showed that children were equally attached to both parents and responded more to play initiated by their fathers in structured situations and to their mothers under natural conditions. A major outcome of this study was the understanding that fathers affect their children directly and indirectly through the children's mother.

In 1981, Parke and Tinsley reported that social class made no difference in the fathers' response to their newborns, nor did attending childbirth classes. All the fathers studied looked at, touched, talked to, and kissed their newborns as much as the mother did.

In 1992, Cox and colleagues reported that, as with caregiving mothers, the more contact fathers have with their children, the more positively the relationship is affected.

Also in 1992, Laura Berk reported that, among the Aka hunters and gatherers of Central Africa, fathers devote more time to infant care than in any other known society. Husbands and wives are extremely close as they share hunting, food preparation, and social activities. The more they are together, the more the father bonds and forms attachment with the children.

In 1997, Laura Berk stated, "Fathers' affectional bonds with their babies are just as emotionally intense as mothers." When interacting with infants, mothers devote more time to physical care and expression of affection and fathers devote more time to stimulating playful interactions.

It appears that, as the economic situation has brought mothers out of the home, the need for fathers to be more involved in direct care has increased, and that fathers are capable of providing the kind of bonding and secure attachment that young children require to develop normally.

However, there are fewer fathers in American families today than there ever has been, including during World Wars I and II. Alarming statistics regarding the shrinking presence of fathers in families are presented by David Blankenhorn in *Fatherless America*: "Tonight, about 40 percent of American children will go to sleep in homes in which their fathers do not live." According to Blankenhorn (1995), the importance of the father role in child care and development has been diminished to the point where even public and political figures have no difficulty openly admitting lack of responsibility for offspring. While Blankenhorn offers 12 proposals to reverse the trend of absent fathers, nowhere in the research presented or in solutions offered is the idea that fathers must take a more direct nurturing, bonding, or hands-on approach to parenting. In fact, in Blankenhorn's definition of "The Good Family Man," which was derived from in-depth interviews with over 200 fathers, there is no direct mention of the need for fathers to nurture or directly participate in the daily hands-on care of young children.

One major outcome of the changing roles of mothers and fathers is that the primary care of infants and toddlers is becoming more the responsibility of child care specialists than parents. Yet the research clearly shows that infants need a strong and consistent bond with their parents in order to develop healthy self-concepts and the trust and security necessary to form loving relationships as adults.

The child care program, then, is often the only place in society to help parents and young children form and maintain healthy attachments. This can best be accomplished through child care programs ensuring that each infant and toddler have as few caregivers as possible, who provide consistency and predictability over time. The second half of this awesome responsibility is to provide parent and family support and training to help parents form and maintain secure attachments with their children. Parent education should include the importance of fathers and other family members providing direct nurturing and caring of the children so that mothers can work and still have loving and healthy relationships with their children.

Caregiver behaviors that ensure consistent and secure bonding and attachment with infants and toddlers are the 3A's of child care. Child care specialists who fully understand the 3A's, use them effectively with children, and systematically model and teach parents to use them with their children do more than any other present force in society to ensure emotional security for infants and toddlers.

THE 3A'S PART I: THE OUTWARD EXPRESSION

Attention

"Smile and the whole world smiles with you." We've often been put at ease when greeted by a stranger's smile or felt instant rapport with someone when he or she has returned our smile. So much is communicated without words; often the unspoken message reflects the exact meaning of how a person is feeling. When we realize that 70 percent of our total communication is nonverbal, it is easily understood why a smile says so much.

CDA

III. 8

A smile is a way to attend to yourself and to someone else. When you bring attention to a behavior in another person, the behavior increases in frequency simply because you are paying attention to it. Behaviors that are attended to, whether good or bad, desired or undesired, increase in frequency. When you tell children they have done a good job, they seem to try harder the next time. The same is true of negative behaviors. When you label a child as bad, you will likely observe more bad behaviors in that child. The power of attention is remarkable.

Of course, there are two general types of attention, falling at opposite ends of a continuum: positive and negative attention. Behavior experts know that we live in a **negative attention society**; that is, when we behave correctly we are largely ignored, and when we misbehave we receive negative attention, such as criticism, penalties, and fines. For example, several years ago the state of California attempted to implement a pilot driving program by having the police stop motorists to thank them for safe driving and give them a certificate to reduce insurance premiums. They had to discontinue the program after only a month because motorists, who are accustomed to receiving only negative attention from police, complained about being stopped even for positive attention.

Attention of any kind increases the frequency of the behavior attended to. This behavioral research finding is extremely important for caregivers because, when we attend to negative behaviors—even when the attention is negative—we actually *increase* the frequency of those negative behaviors! This simple but powerful principle is overlooked by most adults in our society. How many times have you seen posted class or group rules that focus attention on what *not* to do rather than on the behaviors we want to see? Even public signs on roads and parks break this behavioral rule by focusing attention on what *not* to do (Don't skate, spit, curse, and so on).

It has also been clearly demonstrated that focusing attention on positive behaviors results in an increase in frequency of those positive behaviors. Therefore, child care specialists must be conscious to "catch the child being good" and focus positive attention on rules and positive behaviors. Every negative behavior can be turned into the positive opposite expectation. For example, the positive counterpart of yelling is talking softly, of cursing is speaking politely, and of hitting is respecting others. Phrase all rules as general positive expectations and heap genuine positive attention on appropriate behaviors and everyone's experience will be positive.

Specific techniques for increasing positive behavior are discussed in a later chapter.

Approval

Approval from others teaches us to approve of ourselves. The best type of attention is approval. Approval of another person is a clear message that you have positive regard for that person. To children, approval says they have done something right, and it helps them feel worthwhile. Approval builds trust and self-confidence, which in turn encourages children to try new things without fear. The most important concept a caregiver must learn is always to approve of the child, even when you disapprove of his or her behavior. For example, it must be made clear to the child that I like who you are, but not what you are doing right now.

Appropriate and consistent approval develops trust in the child. Once a sense of trust is developed, children can readily approve of themselves. According to Erikson's eight stages of man, the general state of trust suggests that one has learned not only to "rely on the sameness and continuity of the other providers, but also that one may trust oneself." (Erikson, 1963).

Trust depends not only on the quantity (how many times you do a task), but also on the quality of the caregiver's relationship with the child. The caregiver's positive approval creates a sense of trust as a result of the sensitive way in which the caregiver takes time to care for the child's individual needs. Adults must convey to the child an honest concern for the child's welfare, and a deep conviction that there is meaning in what they are doing. Trust based on consistent positive caring allows the child to grow up with a sense of meaningful belonging and trust.

According to ethological theory, parental responsiveness is adaptive in that it ensures that the basic needs of the infant are met and provides protection from danger. It brings the baby into close contact to the caregiver, who can respond sensitively to a wide range of infant behaviors (Bell & Ainsworth, 1972).

As discussed in Chapter 3, the super-ego, conscience, or "you" voice is developed by the time a child is three years of age, and the most important factor in the development of a positive "you" voice is positive approval for genuine accomplishments by the primary caregivers. Children develop self-esteem from making positive statements to themselves about their own value and worth, and the child's primary caregivers are directly responsible for approving and disapproving statements that children learn to make about themselves. Caregivers should ignore behavior that is not harmful to the child, another person, or the environment, and give genuine approval for positive behaviors and accomplishments. By following this simple principle, the child care specialist can help children develop a healthy super-ego that results in good self-esteem.

Some caution should be exercised regarding when you give approval. Caregivers who approve of every little behavior and shower children with unconditional approval lose respect and authority with children. Genuine approval for real accomplishments serves to encourage children to try harder and helps them value their own efforts. Make sure the child has made genuine effort or has accomplished something of value and your approval will help children become the best that they can be.

Affection

It is hard to describe a smile and the feeling that an approving smile generates without also recognizing that affection is generally felt by the people involved. For both the sender and the receiver of the smile, an approving smile communicates warmth and affection (Figure 4–1). Gentle touching, kind words, compliments, and accepting eye contact are all ways to express affection.

When a caregiver masters the skill of giving attention to appropriate behaviors and communicating genuine approval of the child, affection is a natural outcome. There is no greater outward expression you can use than a combination of all 3A's when the child is trying to do what you expect. No clearer physical or emotional message can be given. To smile, hug, and verbally approve in a sincere way is the greatest motivator of positive behavior available to you.

Our positive focused attention toward children's behavior directs our energy and intention, the genuine approval for real success and effort is our behavior toward children, and affection is our feelings of acceptance, approval, and appreciation of children. When we, as child care specialists, combine all three of these, children cannot help but respond positively to us, their world, and themselves. That is why the 3A's are the master tools for child development and care.

In addition to creating a positive learning environment by increasing appropriate behavior in children, all 3A's used together can effectively promote self-health in the caregiver. The following discussion is taken from a lecture series entitled *Caregiver Self-Health* (Douville-Watson, 1988a).

Figure 4–1 Smiles communicate the 3A's.

DEFINITION OF CAREGIVER SELF-HEALTH

Self-health is defined as having the inner resources necessary for sustained energy. This sustained energy, as well as other skills you will learn in the chapter, will give you the tools necessary to continue to provide the high quality of child care you desire throughout each day.

The direction of attention in self-health is not outside of you but is directed inward. You "attend" to yourself. The way to do this is simple, and you already do it even though you may not have been aware of it. It is necessary to learn to be still, to be without motion, to indulge in quiet within yourself, and to create for yourself a place of peace. This special place is available to you whenever you "need a second to think," want to "get yourself together," or are trying to "be on center."

The following exercise will help you focus attention and organize your inner self. With practice, you can provide all the self-nourishment needed to support your daily routine without the plague of exhaustion. Practice this exercise at home after you have had a relaxing bath or shower.

1. Choose a quiet place where you can arrange to have no interruptions for at least a half hour.
2. Get comfortable. Many people sit on a pillow on the floor or in a chair, with their feet flat on the floor in front of them.
3. Close your eyes.
4. Breathe deeply through your nose (if possible) and try to consciously pull the air up from your lower abdomen without moving your shoulders. Take long, slow breaths that have a wave-like rhythm to them.
5. Stay in this posture. Try to avoid thinking about anything. Tell your mind to help keep your body quiet. Make your abdomen into a "balloon" as you inhale.
6. Try to imagine a quiet, peaceful place that you know, perhaps a place where you've vacationed or felt safe when you were a child. Try to recreate this place in your mind. Visualize (with your eyes closed) what it looks like. Smell the special odors associated with this place. Feel the air move around you. Hear the noises as they gently pass your ears. Listen for the familiar sounds. Be with your "self." Be with yourself in your special place. Enjoy you!

This exercise is called **self-attending**. When you attend to yourself, you visit your inner self. You can learn to do this inward attending in a very short time. You can use this technique during a hectic work day to refuel yourself. When you have practiced using this tool at work during lunch time or on your short breaks, add this self-affirming inventory before returning to work: (1) I am ready to help; (2) I have the best interests of the children in mind; and (3) I am willing to be involved with their concerns now. This will help you redirect your energy back to the children.

Child care is hard work. It is also extremely rewarding, but as in any occupation, it can sometimes be stressful. The stress you encounter, however, can largely be avoided. In fact, low stress is healthy and high stress does not add anything useful to any situation.

Dr. Phil Neurnberger is one of the top corporate trainers in the country. For years he has been a model of a person who applies self-health techniques. In his book, *The Quest for Personal Power: Transforming Stress into Strength* (1996), he states, "We are the source of our own stress. Stress never happens to us; stress is our reaction to the things that happen to us. . . . No stress is necessary . . . when the mind is disturbed, that disturbance is reflected in our environment, in our social relationships, and in our bodies. A balanced, healthy mind, in charge of its power and resources, creates a healthy body and a healthy environment. On the other hand, an unbalanced, disturbed mind creates disturbances at all levels. To create a healthy body, a healthy environment, and a healthy culture, we must become masters of the subtle thoughts and emotions of our own minds." We are also responsible for our own state of ease.

The 3A's deal with caregiver self-care and self-health. Once the caregiver understands and practices these techniques, the experience generalizes into the care of children. Only after caregivers take responsibility to care for themselves are they ready to deal with the needs of children. The fact is, you cannot give what you do not have. This is a basic premise of this book. The personal resources of the caregiver are monumentally important for successful outcomes with children.

Another basic premise of this book is that caregiving is a partnership between the adult and child. No one wants a partnership that is exhausting, draining, and without rewards. No healthy person can make a real commitment to such a relationship. That is why these techniques are essential for the caregiver. Take care of yourself so you have the resources to have your day centered on the child.

The outward expression of the 3A's uses Attention, Approval, and Affection as actual humanistic tools to help each child experience the commitment to your partnership. The most essential aspect of successful caregiving is the commitment to yourself in the care of children. By integrating yourself into your daily activities, you are able to begin to make the child in your care the primary focus of your work.

CDA
IV. 11

THE 3A'S PART II: THE INWARD EXPRESSION

Attention

The focus of attention in self-health does not go outside but stays within you; you "attend" to yourself. An accepted and proven way to bring attention to yourself is to develop the skill of meditation. Meditation can be a quiet exercise that you do by yourself in a quiet environment, or it can be an active, awake exercise that you incorporate into your daily activity as a way of focusing your positive intention on what you are doing at the time. Both forms of meditation are extremely helpful rejuvenators. Both are examples of inward expression of Attention and Self-Health.

Other wellness experts agree on the benefits of meditation. Jon Kabet-Zinn states the following: "In meditation, the breath functions as an anchor for our attention. Tuning in to it anywhere, we feel it in the body. It allows us to drop below the surface agitations of the mind into relaxation, calmness and stability . . . when we shift our attention to the breath for a moment."

"In meditation, the active mind is withdrawn to its source; just as this changing universe had to have a source beyond change, your mind, with all its restless activity, arises from a state of awareness beyond thought, sensation, emotion, desire and memory . . . in place of change or loss . . . there is a steadiness and you have a feeling of fullness" (Chopra, 1993).

Bernie Siegel, world-renowned wellness expert, writes about meditation in *Love, Medicine and Miracles* (1988): "I know of no other single activity that by itself can produce such great improvements in the quality of life."

The following is another exercise that will help you to organize your inner self. With practice you can provide all the self-nourishment needed to support your daily routine. Conscious caregiving requires you to take the opportunity to rest, breathe, and relax. A simple and restorative tool to accomplish this is to use a relaxation technique. All you need is three minutes to focus your thoughts and clear your mind.

1. Place yourself in a quiet area and focus your thoughts on yourself.
2. Clear your mind of problems.
3. Breathe deeply.
4. Use hypoallergenic hand cream and gently massage each finger, palm, and hand.
5. Continue focusing your thoughts on what you're doing and how it feels for three minutes.
6. Stay in this posture. Try to avoid thinking about anything. Tell your mind to help keep your body quiet. If your thoughts begin again, recenter yourself by concentrating on your breathing.

Approval

The inward self-expression of approval is a second tool to use for improving self-health. When you listen to yourself quietly, you may sometimes hear things you do not want to hear and phrases that make you feel bad or unworthy, such as "You should have done this or that better." These phrases that you hear when you are quiet may rob you of power to further your best interests. These outdated expressions accumulate in your brain over a lifetime. Although many people do not talk about it, self-criticism happens to most adult human beings. What we experience is simply an accumulation of old phrases that other people used to control or to protect us in the past that have become part of our "you" voice or super-ego.

These outdated messages are there for us to master. "You talk" must be replaced by language that helps you identify what you need. Self-approval begins with an honest relationship with yourself. Self-health begins with understanding what you are feeling, the relevance of your feelings, and the conscious direction of your energy. Stopping the "you talk" begins with learning to witness what your mind is chattering about. You learn to observe this chatter by visualizing it as if you are at the movies. Let it go. Don't be involved with it. Say the words "cancel" or "stop." Then consciously let go of it. When you watch this process, you become aware of how much your mind hangs on to old messages. You simply say these phrases, "Go away. I don't need you now that I am an adult."

The next step is to change your inside talk to "I messages." "I messages" begin with statements like "I want," "I feel," "I need." These are more relevant to your present needs, and are useful in your work of self-care. When you take responsibility for your own needs, you gain self-acceptance and approval. The way to gain self-approval is to install new, conscious "You messages" that completely support and agree with the "I messages." For example, if you use the I message "I want to succeed," self-approval will result when that I message is immediately followed by a conscious supportive you statement such as "You will succeed; you have the right to do well and can do well."

As discussed in Chapter 3, the dialogues between the "I" and "You" voices form the basis for self-esteem, confidence, and being at ease regardless of the environment. Attitude ceilings on success are the result of critical, limiting "You" statements, so to short-circuit these old messages, we need to install a positive, conscious "You" voice. This is accomplished by making "I" statements about what we want or need and *immediately* making a conscious "You" statement that fully supports the "I" voice. For example, let's say that Mary is a caregiver whose parents were overly critical of her weight as a child. If Mary makes the "I" statement, "I'm feeling hungry," it's very likely that her old "You" voice will make critical responses: "You shouldn't be hungry, you eat too much, you're getting fat," and so on. Mary can short-circuit these harmful messages if she states her desire ("I'm feeling hungry") and immediately makes conscious positive "You" statements that start with her name and support the "I" voice, such as "Mary, of course you're hungry, you didn't have breakfast, you should eat to stay healthy." By listening to how children speak about emotions, we can obtain some understanding of these emotional ideas (Greenspan & Greenspan, 1985).

The skill of short-circuiting old, critical "You" statements with conscious positive "You" statements in support of the "I" voice takes both self-awareness and practice. Give yourself regular quiet, undisturbed time to listen to the "I" and "You" voices and practice making supportive "You" statements that start with your name. The self-approval that evolves will be well worth the time and effort you expend to learn this essential skill.

With a little daily practice at making I statements and conscious supportive you statements, you will begin to feel the confidence and security that comes from self-approval. When you can replace old you statements with I messages and supportive you statements, you will in turn be able to help children interpret their environment from this perspective, teaching them to say "I need," "I want," "I feel," when it is relevant to do so. Your voice then becomes part of the inside talk of young children—positive inside talk. They will use this to build their own foundation of the "self," as we see in this quote: "The crying child who is comforted begins to realize that she is not alone with her private experiences. She begins to realize that they are expressed to others and can be shared with them. Here is the cornerstone of the social structuring of experience that we call the self" (Cahill, 1990, p. 2).

These exercises will help you approve of yourself more openly. It is necessary for self-esteem to recognize and state your worthwhileness out loud and congratulate yourself for a job well done. When you are able to praise yourself, you will more easily be able to praise others. "At the same time children create, differentiate, and individuate themselves, they come to understand themselves in the mirror of what others have constructed as a world" (Wartofsky, 1983).

Affection

Affection is the natural outcome of positive attention and approval. Self-affection comes from the belief that we have the right to take care of ourselves and have our needs met. Affection for yourself is a good example of self-health. It is a result of acknowledged self-attention and self-approval. It is the positive energy that comes from being able to relate affectionately to yourself and others, to have a sense of being worthy to give and receive, and to nurture and accept being nurtured by others. There is nothing wrong with taking positive energy from children as well as giving it to them.

Be aware when you give a hug to take one back, take the positive smile a child gives you when you give approval, and relish the open affection young children shower on you in return for your care. For example, affectionate touching may be more than simply a combination of touching and love; it may be an experience or effect in its own right (Dworetzky, 1996). Further, female infants tend to be more sensitive to touch than males, and this continues to be true among most adults (Pick & Pick, 1970). Touch includes many sensations; there are different neural receptors for heat, warmth, cold, dull pain, deep pressure vibrations, and light pressure (Miller, 1983). Taking as well as giving the 3A's helps maintain your emotional energy and avoids stress and burn out.

The 3A's of child care—Attention, Approval, and Affection—are powerful tools. The outward and inward expression of these skills will help you become actively aware and you will be motivated by your positive intentions to use them first with yourself and then teach them to your children.

USING THE 3A'S SUCCESSFULLY WITH INFANTS AND TODDLERS

The 3A's of child care are progressive work, a process in action. In all likelihood, you use the 3A's already without much thought about them. The 3A's are powerful and rejuvenating. They elicit responses in children that will sustain you in your vocation. When you learn to use self-health techniques with inward expression and understand your outward expression, you shape positive behaviors in children.

Observe your initial approach to unknown infants. You get down to their level (floor, blanket, or chair). You are calm, move slowly, make eye contact, enter their space, get even closer to them physically, smile, and gently begin soft speech to engage them. If you believe you have permission from them to stay close, you keep eye contact and begin slowly to inquire what they are doing, such as playing or eating. When they gesture, you follow the gesture with a similar response, this time making a sound that seems to identify their movement and keep pace with them. This usually elicits a smile or giggle. Once again you smile and make noise. You may try gently touching a shoulder or finger, and before long, you are accepted as an approving addition to the children's space. This slow progression of rapport-building is also the slow progression of the use of the 3A's. First you give Attention, then Approval, and then Affection. When this is done consciously, both child and caregiver reap the benefits. All involved feel worthy of Attention, Approval, and Affection.

One of the most positive assurances of worthiness a caregiver can receive on a daily basis is that almighty hug given unconditionally as a gift from the gleeful toddler who sweeps down upon you when you are playing on the floor. This hug, which is often accompanied by a loud and joyful sound, enters your space with such focused positive energy that each of you feels the impact. The result of this positive energy is felt by the two of you, and brings smiles to the faces of all who observe it.

Young children benefit from these important techniques. These tools help shape the child's development as it relates to mastery. Mastery is related to a child's sense of well-being, self-achievement, and eventual self-esteem. Being aware of the master tools of the 3A's helps encourage children to master their environment. Your outward expression of the 3A's helps build the child's inward development of the self, or ego.

Your patient, consistent use of these tools on a daily basis is what forms the child's inner self and places those inner voices there for their protection.

The language that is successful for you, the "I messages" and "You messages," and your use of inner approval is what will be an outward expression of your work with (and love of) children. Your interactions on a daily basis will become part of the inner voices each child hears. Therefore you must pay careful attention to the messages you send. Your help in interpreting the environment in a positive way, your encouragement and approval, and your affection and use of the "I message" becomes part of the child. The more you are able to be yourself in the child care setting and integrate yourself with your work, the more children will be able to develop positive self-concepts.

Your ability to create a positive learning environment allows children to feel safe, to gather information, and eventually to trust their senses for information about their world. All young children register their experiences through their senses. Their physical sense of hot-cold-touch-smell-hearing-and-sight is easily seen. Erikson (1963), in writing about autonomy, discusses the infant's ability to emotionally evaluate his worth as "a series of alternate basic attitudes such as trust vs. mistrust in terms of 'sense of' as in 'sense of health' or 'sense of being unwell.'" Young children rely on their senses.

Think of yourself as a recharging station—a physically and emotionally rewarding place where children feel a sense of security. The field of bioenergetics refers to these senses as part of our Human Energy Field, and states that we give off energy and in turn "sense" each other's energy. Using the exercises already discussed allows you to keep your energy centered and positive, so you can bring that positive energy to the children in your care.

Barbara Brennan, in her book *Hands of Light*, speaks of energy as measurable and existing in all of us as the Human Energy Field. She states that "the Universal Energy Field is like a Cornucopia always continuing to create more energy" (Brennan, 1989)(Figure 4–2).

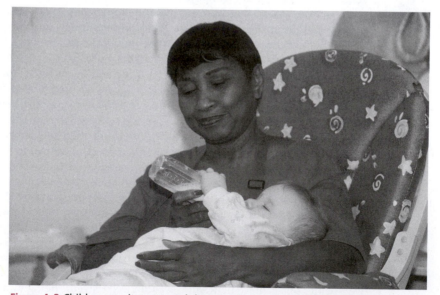

Figure 4–2 Children gravitate toward the caregiver's "Circle of Energy" to rest.

Delores Krieger talks about **prana**, the ancient name of the **Universal Energy Source**, when she teaches professionals at New York University to use energy to promote healing in hospital patients. In her book *The Therapeutic Touch*, she states: "Conceive of the healer as an individual whose health gives him access to an overabundance of prana and whose strong sense of commitment and intention to help ill people gives him or her certain control over the projection of this vital energy" (Krieger, 1992). The same energy is available to you.

The ability to help people by using the **Human Energy Field** is scientifically supported. So, as a child care specialist you can utilize these modern concepts to develop a strong sense of commitment and intention to help yourself and your children in child care settings. You can use the 3A's to create a positive learning environment and use the inward-focused skills to express appreciation of yourself and the vital impact you have on the children in your care.

In summary, the healthiest relationships result in the experience of security and happiness most of the time. The best possible connection between caregiver and infant comes from each person being actively involved in the relationship, expressing and receiving a positive exchange.

When the 3A's are focused on children, they promote appropriate behaviors and enhance a positive learning environment for children. The caregiver structures a safe place in which the young child explores and masters all of his or her growing abilities by solving problems that naturally occur within the environment. A stable, positive environment promotes trust and confidence and allows the growing infant to express all of his or her needs.

When the 3A's are focused on self, they promote self-health, personal growth, and development of the caregiver. These skills help you to be more aware of your impact on children and revitalize you, so that you can sustain a high quality of care throughout the day. The knowledge you have learned promotes trust and ultimately teaches children, by your example, to be self-confident and have trust in themselves. The challenge presented to caregivers centers on their ability to maintain their own sense of well-being while caring for children (Gilligan, 1982; Hochschild, 1983).

Using the 3A's allows children to experience the environment as a safe place to express needs and to believe that expressing all emotion is healthy. This ability to express emotion without fear promotes a healthy, happy, well-balanced individual who feels competent to handle life's challenges.

Key Terms

Affection	**prana**
Approval	**resistant attachment**
Attention	**secure attachment**
avoidant attachment	**self-attending**
disoriented attachment	**self-health**
Human Energy Field	**separation anxiety**
negative attention society	**Universal Energy Source**

CASE STUDY

Pia Eduardo was born premature, weighing 2 pounds, 10 ounces. She is now 12 days old and weighs 3 pounds, 4 ounces. She lies on her stomach sleeping in an incubator, where the temperature is mechanically controlled to duplicate the mother's womb. Pia sleeps on a slant board to help her breathe. She has intravenous lines for fluids, and heart and brain monitors are attached to evaluate her life functions continuously.

Anthony, Pia's father, comes to the hospital during his lunch hour and briefly at night because he works overtime to make enough money for Tonya, Pia's mother, to stay most of the time at the hospital with their daughter. Tonya, with the help of the hospital staff, frequently lifts Pia out of the incubator and lays her on her chest to provide skin-to-skin contact. Tonya strokes Pia's hands, feet, back, and legs, massaging them gently while she talks softly and slowly to deliberately soothe Pia. She wears no cologne so Pia can smell her natural odor and remains conscious of keeping her breathing in rhythm with Pia's breathing. This procedure of touching the skin has been shown to release brain chemicals that increase physical growth (Schanberg & Field, 1987).

The Attention, Approval, and Affection that Tonya consciously gives Pia directly affects Pia's life functions, as recorded on the monitors. When Tonya is touching, holding, bonding, soothing, and loving Pia, her heart and brain waves become stronger and more regular, her breathing becomes deeper and calmer, and she generally produces healthier patterns of physiological responses. This procedure of bonding with premature babies and providing conscious attention, approval, and affection has become standard practice in hospitals because research shows that infants who receive this bonding grow more quickly and are healthier than babies who do not receive this attention. In addition, many hospitals now conduct parenting groups to teach parents to give attention, approval, and affection to infants as a functional tool to promote health and growth.

1. From the case study, what is the most important tool a caregiver can use with a young infant?
2. What is the relationship between bonding and attachment indicated by this case study?
3. How does interactional synchrony apply to this case study?

Student Activities

1. Practice attending exercises for self-health two times this week, and take notes about your reactions.
2. Two times during the day, allow yourself five minutes to perform revitalizing exercises.
3. Apply all 3A's to two separate children, and write down their reactions.
4. List why the 3A's of self-health might affect your personal life in general.
5. Write a scenario using examples of the ways in which the 3A's might calm children and promote a positive learning environment.

Chapter Review

1. List the 3A's of child care.
2. What is the difference between giving attention to children and attending to your inner self?
3. How do you go about approving of yourself?
4. Why is using all of the 3A's together a powerful tool for motivating children?
5. Why would learning skills to revitalize yourself help you fight off exhaustion during your day?
6. Define meditation, relaxation, self-health, and self-care.
7. What is the most important aspect of this chapter for you?

References

Ainsworth, M. D. S., Blehar, M., Waters, E., & Wall, S. (1978). *Patterns of attachment.* Hillsdale, NJ: Erlbaum.

Bell, S. M., & Ainsworth, M. D. S. (1972). Infant crying and maternal responsiveness. *Child Development, 43,* 117–119.

Berk, L., & Diaz, R. M. (1992). *Private speech from social interaction to self-regulation.* Mahwah, NJ: Erlbaum Associates.

Blankenhorn, D. G. (1995). *Fatherless America.* New York: HarperCollins.

Bowman, B. 1989. Self-reflection as an element of professionalism. *Teachers College Records, 90*(3), 444–451.

Brennan, B. A. (1989). *Hands of light: A guide to healing through the human energy field.* New York: Bantam Books.

Cahill, S. E. (1990). Childhood and public life: Reaffirming biographical distractions. *Social Problems, 37,* 390–402

Chopra, D. (1993). *Ageless body, timeless mind harmony.* New York: Bantam Books.

Clarke-Stewart, K. A. (1978). Recasting the lone stranger. In J. Glick & K. A. Clarke-Stewart, (Eds.). *The development of social understanding* (pp. 109–176). New York: Gardner Press.

Cox, M. J., Owen, M. T., Henderson, V. K., & Margand, N. A. (1992). Prediction of infant-father and infant-mother attachments. *Developmental Psychology, 28:*474–483.

Denzin, N. K. (1984). *On understanding emotion.* San Francisco: Jossey Bass.

Dewey, J. (1938). *Experience and education.* New York: Macmillan.

Douville-Watson, L. (1988a). Child care lecture series, *Caregiver self-health.* Oyster Bay, NY: Lifeskills Institute.

Douville-Watson, L. (1995). Child care lecture series, *Concerned conscious care: The 3A's in action.* Bayville, NY: Instructional Press.

Dworetzky, J. P. (1996). *Introduction to child development* (6th ed.). Saint Paul, MN: West.

Erikson, E. H. (1963). The eight stages of man. In *Childhood & society.* New York: W. W. Norton.

Gilligan, C. (1982). *In a different voice: Psychological theory and works development.* Cambridge, MA: Harvard University Press.

Gilligan, C. (1988). Remapping the moral domain: New images of self in relationship. In C. Gilligan, J. Ward, J. Taylor, & B. B. Pardige (Eds.), *Mapping the moral domain,* pp. 3–19. Cambridge, MA: Harvard University Press.

Greenspan, S. I., & Greenspan, N. T. (1985). *First feelings: milestones in the emotional development of your baby and child.* New York: Viking.

Hatch, J. A. (1995). *Qualitative research in early childhood settings.* Stamford, CT: Praeger Publishers.

Healy, J. (1988). *Your child's growing mind*. New York: Doubleday.

Hochschild, A. (1989). *The second shift*. New York: Viking Penguin.

Kabet-Zinn, J., (1991). *Full catastrophe living: Using the wisdom of your body and mind to face stress, pain and illness*. New York: Bantam Doubleday.

Kagan, J., Kearsley, R. B., & Zelazo, P. R. (1978). *Infancy: Its place in human development*. Cambridge, MA: Harvard University Press.

Kreiger, D. (1992). *The therapeutic touch: How to use your hands to help or to heal*. New York: Prentice-Hall.

Owen, M. T., & Cox, M. J. (1988). Maternal employment and the transition to parenthood. In A. E. Gottfried & A. W. Gottfried (Eds.), *Maternal employment and children's development: Longitudinal research*, p. 850119. New York: Plenum.

Main, M., & Soloman, J. (1990). Procedures for identifying infants as disorganized/disoriented during the Ainsworth Strange Situation. In M. Greenberg, D. Cicchetti, & M. Cummings (Eds.), *Attachment in the preschool years: Theory, research, and intervention*, pp. 121–60. Chicago: University of Chicago Press.

Miller, J. A. (1983). Wiretap on the nervous system. *Science News*, Feb. 26, pp. 140–143.

Neurnberger, P. (1996). *The quest for personal power: Transforming stress into strength*. New York: G. P. Putnam Brothers.

Parke, R. D., & Tinsley, B. R. (1981). *The role of the father in child development*. New York: Wiley.

Pawl, J. (1990). Infants in day care: Reflections on experience, expectation and relationships. *Zero to Three, 10*(3):1–6.

Pick, H. L., & Pick, A. D. (1970). Sensory and perceptual development. In P. H. Mussen (Ed.), *Carmichael's manual of child psychology* (3rd ed.). Vol. 1. (pp. 773–847). New York: Wiley.

Riback, P. (1997). *Healthy Kids K–3*. New York: Magazine Corp.

Roggman, L. A., Langlois, J. H., Hubbs-Tait, L., & Rieser-Danner, L. A. (1994). Infant day-care, attachment, and the "file drawer problem." *Child Development, 65*, 1429–1443.

Saarni, C. (1989). Children's understanding and strategic control of emotional expression in social transactions. In C. Saarni and P. L. Harris (Eds.), *Children's understanding of emotion*, pp. 181–208. New York: Cambridge University Press.

Schanberg, S., & Field, T. M. (1987). Sensory deprivation stress and supplemental stimulation in the rat pup and preterm human neonate. *Children Development, 58*, 1431–1447.

Siegel, B. (1988). *Love, medicine and miracles*. New York: Bantam Press.

Snow, C. (1989). *Infant development*. Englewood Cliffs, NJ: Prentice-Hall.

Wartofsky, L. (1983). *Space perception and the philosophy of science*. Berkeley: University of California Press.

Additional Resources

Douville-Watson, L. (1988). Child care lecture series, *The 3A's of child care: Attention, approval and affection*. Oyster Bay, NY: Lifeskills Institute.

Douville-Watson, L., & Watson, M. (1988). *Family actualization through research & education: F.A.R.E.*, (3rd ed.). New York: Actualization, Inc.

Helpful Web Sites

10 Things Your Child Care Provider Should Expect From You Make sure your child has ongoing affection. http://www.geocities.com/Athens/6478/PRNTS.html

Divorce Wizards: Top 10 Tips to Help Your Child If one parent is disapproving of affection a child expresses toward the other parent, the child will begin to withdraw. http://www.divorcewizards.com/top10child.html

Epinions.com—Advice on How to Show Affection Showing affection for your child requires the use of many "hearts." http://www.epinions.com/kifm-Showing Affection

Declaration of the Rights of the Child—In an atmosphere of affection and moral and material security. http://www.unhcrh.ch/html/menu2/b/25.htm

Fernside Online—How to Help a Grieving Child Love each other and share hugs often. Express affection in a way your family finds most comfortable. http://www.fernside. org/grownups/how.html

Why does my child sometimes reject my affection? (Age 2) Expert: Susanne Denham discusses. http://www.parentcenter.com/expert/parenting/development/4748.html

For additional infant and toddler resources, visit our Web site at
http://www.earlychilded.delmar.com

Effective Tools for Child Care and Development

5

Objectives

After reading this chapter, you should be able to:

- Describe the characteristics necessary to become a competent caregiver, including professional preparation.
- Apply ORAOM to your work as a caregiver.
- Use the tools of Observing to Know, Circle of Safety, Catch the Child Being Good, Shadowing, Shepherding, and Behavior-Limiting Steps to enhance physical development.
- Describe and apply Changing the Guard, Ruing, Inside/Outside Self-Attention, Label and Express Feelings, Self-Soothing, and Emotion Management to enhance emotional development.
- Understand how to use Positive Perspective, Rapport Building, Respectful is Successful, Cooperation vs. Competition, Mirroring, and I Talk to enhance social development.
- Work with the tools of Naming and Labeling, Time Orientation, Cause-Effect, Baby Signing, Observe Yourself, and Concept Formation to enhance cognitive skill development.
- Train children in Focal Attention, Memory, Discrimination, Association, and Auditory-Visual Association perceptual skills to enhance learning skill development.

Chapter Outline

INTRODUCTION

The heart and soul of excellent child care are the tools used in caring for young children. This chapter provides specific, effective tools that enhance development in each of the five major areas. The child care specialist should practice using each of the tools in this chapter within the structure of a Developmental Profile (refer to Appendix A and Appendix B). The authors subscribe to the idea that objective assessment of infants and toddlers is an essential starting point for professional child care, so construction of a Developmental Profile for each child in care and then updating profiles on a regular two- to three-month basis ensures optimal growth and development.

Specific tools are presented for each major developmental area, but the principles used for each tool can be applied to all areas of care. For example, a very effective tool to enhance physical development is a task analysis, but the principles involved of careful observation, step building, successive approximation, and scaffolding are effective for all other areas of care as well.

The tools presented in this chapter, along with the master tools of the 3A's, are the functional basis for fulfilling the CDA requirements for national certification as an early childhood specialist. By learning to apply these tools with infants and toddlers based on the strengths and weaknesses indicated on a Developmental Profile, the caregiver fulfills all the CDA Goals and Objectives required for hands-on, competent care of children.

As you learned in the 3A's, it is essential for caregivers to take good care of themselves in order to provide competent care for young children. Therefore, the first tools to acquire include the skills of observing and relating to yourself and of your professional preparation as a caregiver.

CHARACTERISTICS OF A COMPETENT CHILD CARE SPECIALIST

Child Specialist Health and Awareness

Physical health is necessary to provide the high energy level needed in caregiving. Good health is also necessary to resist the variety of illnesses to which you are exposed. The importance of a healthy staff is reflected in the American Academy of Pediatrics recommendations (1996) that the health record for each employee contains

1. Evidence of freedom from active tuberculosis and an annual report of tuberculosis negative mantoux test
2. Evidence of pre-employment examination or statement from the personal physician indicating a health status permitting the employee to function in his or her assigned role
3. Evidence of recovery after specified communicable diseases
4. Reports of periodic evaluations

In addition, Hepatitis B vaccine injections are recommended, but not mandated, for employees in most states. You also need to discern whether your body is at ease. The body registers small concerns that tell you it has specific needs, and these signals can be used to help you stay in balance. Listening to the physical feelings and signals that your body gives is called body awareness.

Child Care Specialists Are Mentally Healthy In your daily relationships, you must provide physical closeness and nurture for an extended time, give emotionally more than you receive, be patient to resolve conflicts caused by someone else, and calm one child right after you have been frustrated with another. Emotionally stable child specialists have learned how to handle a variety of emotional demands in their daily experiences and how to encourage greater mental health in others (Figure 5–1).

Figure 5–1 The caregiver has warm, emotional relationships with children.

Child Care Specialists Have a Positive Self-Image   Your feelings of self-confidence and positive self-worth show that you believe in yourself. This gives you the strength to take risks, consider alternatives, and make decisions in situations where there may be no obvious correct answer.

Child Care Specialists Have a Commitment to Excellence   Striving to do your best is essential for high-quality caregiving. Read, study, visit, observe, and talk with other child specialists. Your motivation and knowledge improves excellence.

Child Care Specialists Are Caring   There is pleasure, enjoyment, and satisfaction in providing effective, high-quality care. Although some tasks may be difficult, unpleasant, or repetitious, overall caregiving should produce satisfaction every day (Figure 5–2). The child specialist reflects caring feelings to the children, parents, and to other staff members. Positive feelings help build good team rapport.

Child Care Specialists Are Professionals   Caregiving is a respected and essential profession. You provide a very important service to children, parents, and the community. The care you provide directly affects children at critical times in their lives. You have great influence and importance in the child's life and are rational and objective in your decisions and actions.

Child Care Specialists Are Open-Minded   Your perceptions, common sense, and opinions are sources of information you can use in evaluating situations and making decisions. Awareness of your expectations and those of children help you remain open. Openly listening, thinking, and learning from the ideas and opinions of others helps to increase continued growth.

Child Care Specialists Enjoy Learning   It is not possible to finish learning everything you need to know to be an effective child care specialist. New information and experiences lead to new insights, understanding, and skills. Openness to learning

Figure 5–2   The caregiver develops skill in working with children and gains satisfaction from interacting with them.

helps you seek new ideas and take advantage of new opportunities to expand your knowledge and skills.

RELATING TO INFANTS AND TODDLERS

Child Care Specialists Care About and Enjoy Infants and Toddlers
You share joy in the child's attempts and accomplishments. You show concern for the child's well-being by planning, playing, listening, comforting, and providing physical and emotional closeness.

Child Care Specialists Respect Children Each child is worthy of your respect. Your accepting behavior and considerate treatment shows that you consider each child an individual who is an important person.

Child Care Specialists Make Adjustments Good interpersonal relationships call for give and take. Close daily contact requires an attitude of giving, adjusting, and receiving.

ACQUIRING KNOWLEDGE

About Yourself

Why do you want to be a child care specialist? What are your strengths? What are your weaknesses? What is your temperament? What are your interests? What are your values? What are your expectations of yourself and others? Are you willing to put forth effort to satisfy yourself and others? How much time and effort do you think is appropriate to put into caregiving? What plans do you have to learn about yourself, others, and your program?

About Children

Child development research continues to provide new information about children. The information helps identify each child's individual characteristics and levels of development. Knowledge of patterns of physical, emotional, social, and cognitive development influence how you plan for and act with children.

About Parents

Each family situation is unique and affects your caregiving. You should continually seek information from and maintain communication with parents. Parents have special needs, desires, and expectations of themselves, their children, and you.

About Child Care Specialists' Roles

The term *caregiving* encompasses emotional interaction, instructional planning, and various types of teaching and learning techniques involving children, parents, the community, and other staff. You need to balance many roles to provide high-quality care. Understanding the responsibilities of each role will help determine your strengths and how to increase knowledge and personal growth. Utilizing all aspects of self-health ensures stamina and the ability to provide consistent high-quality care.

About Program Implementation

There are many successful ways to nurture, provide care, and teach. Knowledge of these can help you adjust and individualize caregiving procedures to meet the specific needs of the environment and the children you serve.

About Caregiving Duties

Basic knowledge about children, parents, staff, and programs are foundations for good caregiving. High-quality caregiving occurs when you have clearly defined goals and tasks. Written goals, plans, and tasks keep your duties clear.

About Materials

Child care specialists must identify which materials are appropriate for various developmental levels of children. Collect materials and information from staff and resources in the community to add value to your program.

PROFESSIONAL PREPARATION OF THE CAREGIVER

Both informal and formal educational opportunities are available to caregivers. Informal experiences may be spontaneous or planned. An article in a magazine may stimulate your thinking by providing new information and raising questions. You may take time to do further thinking and discuss your ideas with other staff, or you may think of the ideas periodically and begin changing your caregiving techniques to incorporate what you have learned.

Formal educational opportunities are those that are planned to meet specific needs. You choose experiences to help you gain desired knowledge and skill. The following types of experiences contribute to your learning either by using your experiences with children, independent study, or a combination of both.

- A mentor or a more-experienced caregiver. Having such a person available gives you opportunities to observe, participate, and discuss techniques. Mentoring is organized, supervised, and evaluated; isolated work does not count.
- Workshops, seminars. These may be sponsored by adult schools, colleges, universities, and professional organizations. They usually focus on a single topic or skill.
- Speakers. Libraries, colleges, and hospitals may sponsor speakers.
- Short courses provided by local or state groups or agencies.
- Continuing education courses sponsored by local schools and colleges.
- Technical school courses and programs in child care.
- Junior and senior college courses and programs in child care.
- Child Development Associate Certificate. "The Child Development Associate, or CDA, is a person who is able to meet the specific needs of children and who,

with parents and other adults, works to nurture children's physical, social, emotional, and intellectual growth in a child development framework. The CDA conducts herself or himself in an ethical manner" (CDA, 1992).

The Council for Early Childhood Professional Recognition has designed both training and assessment systems for persons interested in the CDA Credential. For more information, contact

Council for Early Childhood Professional Recognition
1341 G Street, NW, Suite 400
Washington, DC 20005
Telephone: (202) 265-9090 or 1-800-424-4310
Fax: (202) 265-9161

The CDA Competency Standards and assessment system for infant/toddler child specialists in center-based programs have been developed to support quality care for our youngest children by providing standards for training, evaluation, and recognition of child specialists based on their ability to meet the unique needs of these age groups.

The American Academy of Pediatrics publication, *Healthy Kids*, July 1997, contained an article entitled "Building Brainpower" (Riback 2000) which summed up the importance of child specialist preparation: "Even the earliest feelings experienced by a child can affect the brain and lay the groundwork for later emotions such as re-acting to stress, trusting others, self-esteem, and understanding one's place in the world. Since babies are so highly dependent on their child specialists for everything, it makes some sense that their emotional states, and eventually their own emotional responses, are affected by the emotions of those who care for them. Healthy, happy babies come from a loving and nurturing environment established during the early years of life."

The special developmental needs of very young children require that their care in a group setting be different from that of older children for several good reasons.

- The younger child is more dependent on the child specialist, more vulnerable to adversity, and is less able to cope with discomfort of stress from without or within;
- Physical, social, emotional, and cognitive development are more interrelated for infants than for older children, and more dependent upon a consistent relationship with an adult child care specialist; and
- The more involved and emotionally connected to the child the child specialist can be, the more secure the child feels as judged by the ease of their movements (Douville-Watson, L., 1997).

ORAOM

Before turning to specific tools for each developmental area, the caregiver must learn general skills to Observe, Record, Assess, Organize, and Manage children and the environment. We have given this essential process the acronym **ORAOM** (pronounced OROM).

Observe

Why Observe? Observations provide important information needed for decision-making. Your observations contribute details about the child, the specialist, the curriculum, the materials and facilities, and the program and policies. Observation must precede teaching. It is an ongoing process.

Who to Observe? Each child in the child care home or center needs to be observed. All program plans and implementation start with what the specialist knows about each child.

Each specialist contributes unique ideas and behaviors to the child care setting, which others can identify by observing.

Each parent participates to varying degrees in the child care program. Observing how parents interact with children and adults helps specialists.

What to Observe? Children's behavior helps us learn about the child. Infants and toddlers often cannot use words to tell about themselves. Each child is unique. Child care specialists must identify the characteristics and needs of each child, because the child is the focal point of decisions and plans regarding time, space, and curriculum. Each child is continually changing. This growth and development produces expected and sometimes unexpected changes. Living with someone every day, you may not notice some important emerging developments. Therefore, it is important to make periodic informal and formal observations on Developmental Prescriptions and Profiles and to record them so that the changes in the child can be noted and shared. This information will affect your planning for and interactions with the child.

Child care specialist behavior provides needed information. Ms. Sheila knew that she needed to improve her organization and planning. Every day she would forget some supplies she needed for snack time. She started making a checklist of snack items so she could make sure she had prepared everything. After snack time she noted whether she had all the supplies or whether she should add something else. Other specialists provided feedback also. By focusing and recording in this way, Ms. Sheila was able to improve herself. Each specialist is learning and continually developing skills. One caregiver may observe another caregiver in order to learn new strategies or to reinforce those the specialist already uses. Other people's observations can let caregivers know whether their actual practice matches the behavior intended. Continuing evaluation and planning along with feedback can help caregivers increase their effectiveness.

Ms. Josephine wanted to involve Monroe more when she shared a book with him. She selected a book she thought he would like and wrote down three questions to ask Monroe that would focus his thinking and questioning on objects from the book. She set up a small cassette tape recorder where she and Monroe would be sitting and called Monroe over to share the book with him. Later, when Ms. Josephine listened to the tape recording of her time with Monroe, she discovered that she had talked all the time and told everything to Monroe rather than allowing him to talk, share, and question. Observations of interactions provide information about the kind of responses one person has to another person or to material. Observations help you learn how you have stimulated or inhibited the desired interaction (Figure 5–3).

The child care setting, including children, equipment, materials, and arrangement of space, should be examined to determine safe and unsafe conditions. The use, misuse, and place of use of equipment and materials, traffic patterns, much-used or

Figure 5–3 Talking, listening, and playing with a child are important child care specialist behaviors.

little-used space, space where much disruptive behavior occurs, and the separation or overrunning of quiet and active space is evaluated. Make the necessary adjustments after you have evaluated how the setting works in relation to the children's needs.

How to Observe and Record Observations may be informal or formal. You may glance across the room and see Sammy roll over. You know that is the first time you have seen that happen. On the parent message board you write, "Sammy rolled from front to back this morning." Sometimes a staff member will arrange to spend a few minutes specifically observing a child, a specialist, materials, or space. These observations can provide valuable information. Writing what you observe gives you and other people access to that information later on.

Descriptions may consist of one word or be very detailed and extensive. Write down the exact behavior or situation in narrative form, using as few judgmental and evaluative words as possible.

An ethnographic report describes a total situation: the time, place, people, and how the people behave. Description of the total situation lets the specialist know about things that may not be evident in one part of a specific incident. Start with a general question such as "What is going on here?" Spradley (1980) identified nine major dimensions of every social situation.

1. space: the physical place of places
2. actor: the people involved
3. activity: a set of related acts people do
4. object: the physical things that are present
5. act: single actions that people do
6. event: a set of related activities that people carry out

7. time: the sequencing that takes place over time
8. goal: the things people are trying to accomplish
9. feeling: the emotions felt and expressed

Adults unfamiliar with infants and toddlers think that the young child does not do anything. An early education student observed the following during outdoor play in a family child care home one summer afternoon. She was to focus on one child and write down everything she saw and heard that child do and say. The purpose of this assignment was to identify and categorize the various experiences initiated by a 13-month-old child. The observer was not to interject her own interpretations into the narrative.

The play yard contained Lynn, the specialist, and six children ranging from seven months to six years of age. A portion of the report on Leslie, a 13-month-old girl, follows.

2:20   Lynn puts mat out and stands Leslie up in yard.
       Leslie looks around (slowly rocking to keep balance).
       Reaches hand to Lynn and baby-talks.
       Looks at me and reaches for me.
       Takes 2 steps, trips on mat, so remains sitting on it.
       Turns around to face me.
       Cries a little.
       Reaches for Lynn, then to me (wants to be picked up).
       Tries to stand up.
       Looks around and watches Jason.
       Reaches hand toward Lynn.
       Watches Jason and sucks middle 2 fingers on right hand.
       Looks around.
       Tries to stand periodically, then seems to change mind.
       Swings right arm.
2:45   Takes Lynn's fingers and stands.
       Walks 2 steps onto grass.
       Swings right arm and brushes lips with hand to make sound—baby
          talk.
       Turns toward Lynn and babbles.
       Lane arrives. Leslie watches and rubs left eye with left hand.
       "Do you remember Leslie?" Lynn asks Lane.
       Leslie reaches out arms to Lynn and walks to her. Hugs her.
       Listens and watches Lynn. Holds onto her for support.
       Turns around and steps on pine straw and lifts foot to see what it is.
       Watches Lynn tie Jason's shoe.
       Lynn lifts her in air, then sets her on her knee.
       She lies back in her lap and laughs.

Analysis of these descriptive statements shows that Leslie initiates a variety of interactions with people and materials. She is physically, emotionally, socially, and cognitively involving herself in her world. Specialist planning and facilitating can stimulate and build on Leslie's self-initiated behaviors.

Record

Record keeping has several purposes.

1. sharing information with parents
2. planning curriculum, strategies, and program
3. assessing children, child care specialists, and program

Message Board Some records are temporary, as is the daily message board for parents. During the time the parent is away, the infant is busily going about the business of growing up. Each new achievement, each practiced skill is an important part of the child's day. These achievements should be shared with parents. Parents want the specialist's general evaluation: How was Carlyle's day today? And they also want specific information: Phyllis drank from her cup by herself. Provide details rather than simply saying "He was good" or "She was better than yesterday."

Some records are permanent and are kept on file, for example, admission and health records, anecdotal or narrative records, and developmental profiles (see Appendix A for samples of permanent records). You and other staff will learn from experience what kinds of records are most helpful to your setting. If you never use some items of information, it is a waste of time to record them.

Taking the time to write something down seems to be the biggest obstacle to record keeping. Therefore, use records that can be written quickly and easily.

All specialists should use the same format for recording incidents. Many places use index cards and notebook entries. You can write and file the entries quickly and find and use them very easily later. Computers permit another means of storing information.

Message Board
(wall chart)

Child's Name:	Home Schedule: (stays on board)	Date: (Messages wiped off at end of every day)
E: (Eating)		
S: (Sleeping)		
T: (Toilet)		
O: (Other)		

Example:		
Dan		Feb. 16
E: 8 oz.–3 hrs.		8:30—6 oz.; 12:00—7 oz.; 3:00—8 oz.
S: 3 naps; fights sleep		8:45–11:00; 12:30–3:00
T: Doesn't like soiled diapers		BM 11:00; 3:00
O: Upset when sleep is interrupted		

Reporting Sheets Reporting sheets provide information in a form that can be filed or taken home. The Infant Welfare Society of Evanston, Inc., says this about the Care Sheets used by caregivers in its Baby Toddler Center.*

1. Care Sheets: An important source of information, both to parents and to staff. For parents they serve to answer questions and provide feedback in a reliable, concrete manner. For us, they form a detailed, day-to-day record which reflects development, health, and program.

   Each child has a file for his or her care sheets, which passes with the child from group to group. Files are kept in a specific place that is known and accessible to staff. In order to protect the confidentiality of information, staff should give the files to parents, rather than have parents seek them out themselves. Therefore, it is important for "late" staff and substitutes to know the location of files.

   Copies shall be provided to parents, upon request, at the end of the week. Care sheets shall be shown to parents at conferences.

2. Content of Care Sheets:
   a. Routines: As a minimum, some information about each of the "care routines" must be included: a) Naps: times of going to sleep and waking; b) Eating: quality of appetite; c) Elimination: number of bowel movements. In addition, it is important to make note of atypical responses; e.g., restless sleep or nightmares in a child who normally sleeps peacefully or loose stools in a child who normally has firm ones. Relative to children with specific conditions of concern, more data is required. For example, for a child with a milk intolerance, notation should be made of milk products withheld or given. For a child who has a tendency to have intestinal problems, more information should be given regarding stools. For babies, notes about food served are necessary, in order to be alert to allergies.
   b. Activities: Care sheets shall indicate the major activities of each day, as well as whether and how long the child participated. This enables the care sheets, over time, to reflect preferences and abilities of the child.
   c. Special Information: Other pertinent information which shall be recorded includes, but is not limited to, the following: a) injuries that occur at the Nursery, regardless of source; b) injuries that occur outside the Nursery, and the explanation provided by the parent; c) times the child is sent home or not accepted and the reason, including unsuccessful attempts to send a child home; d) developmental milestones reached by the child, e.g., taking a first step or saying a new word. Special instructions from parents should also be noted.

3. Style of Care Sheets: Information must be given clearly (although grammar is unimportant). Therefore, statements must be objective, rather than judgmental. For example, say "Tommy cried off and on all morning" or "Joey fought with other children over toys 8 or 10 times today" rather than "John had a terrible day." Say "Jane SEEMED restless (or tired or unhappy) today" rather than "Judy WAS sad." This is important because evaluative or judgmental statements are

*_Care Sheets_ reprinted by permission of the Infant Welfare Society of Evanston, Inc.

"emotionally loaded" and often lead to misunderstanding, whereas factual, objective statements cannot be disputed.

In order to be effective, care sheets need to be written daily. In this way information is more easily remembered, and, more importantly, is available to parents and other staff, both late in the day and early the next day.

Care sheets shall be shown to parents at parent-staff conferences.

Caregivers may use a similar care sheet or devise one which very specifically fits their program.

Assess

Assessing the Caregiver

Caregivers can assess their own behavior, using the Child Development Associate Competency Standards as criteria. As a part of the Child Development Associate training and assessment program, observations and records are made regularly. The caregiver's behavior is assessed in each of the functional areas (see Appendix C).

Honig and Lally (1981) developed checklists to assess caregivers who work with infants and toddlers. The list below shows categories of behaviors for professional child care providers of infants under 18 months.*

I. LANGUAGE FACILITATION
1. Elicits vocalization
2. Converses with child
3. Praises, encourages verbally
4. Offers help or solicitous remarks
5. Inquires of child or makes requests
6. Gives information or culture rules
7. Provides and labels sensory experience
8. Reads or shows pictures to child
9. Sings to or plays music for child

II. SOCIAL-EMOTIONAL: POSITIVE
1. Smiles at child
2. Uses raised, loving, or reassuring tones
3. Provides physical, loving contact
4. Plays social games with child
5. Eye contact to draw child's attention

III. SOCIAL-EMOTIONAL: NEGATIVE
1. Criticizes verbally; scolds; threatens
2. Forbids; negative commands
3. Frowns; restrains physically
4. Punishes physically
5. Isolates child physically—behavior modification
6. Ignores child when child shows need for attention

*Reprinted with permission from "Infant Caregiving: A Design for Training" by Alice S. Honig and J. Ronald Lally (Syracuse University Press, Syracuse, NY 1981): ABC I: Assessing the Behaviors of Caregivers (With Young Infants) and ABC II: Assessing the Behaviors of Caregivers (With Older Infants) 259–262.

IV. PIAGETIAN TASKS
   1. Object permanence
   2. Means and ends
   3. Imitation
   4. Causality
   5. Prehension: small-muscle skills
   6. Space
   7. New schemas

V. CARE-GIVING: CHILD
   1. Feeds
   2. Diapers or toilets
   3. Dresses or undresses
   4. Washes or cleans child
   5. Prepares child for sleep
   6. Physical shepherding
   7. Eye checks on child's well-being

VI. CARE-GIVING: ENVIRONMENT
   1. Prepares food
   2. Tidies up room
   3. Helps other caregiver(s)

VII. PHYSICAL DEVELOPMENT
   1. Provides kinesthetic stimulation
   2. Provides large-muscle play

VIII. DOES NOTHING

Caregivers who work with toddlers from 18 to 36 months are assessed in the categories of behaviors shown below (Honig & Lally, 1981).

I. FACILITATES LANGUAGE DEVELOPMENT
   1. Converses
   2. Models language
   3. Expands language
   4. Praises, encourages
   5. Offers help, solicitous remarks, or makes verbal promises
   6. Inquires of child or makes request
   7. Gives information
   8. Gives culture rules
   9. Labels sensory experiences
   10. Reads or identifies pictures
   11. Sings or plays music with child
   12. Role-plays with child

II. FACILITATES DEVELOPMENT OF SKILLS SOCIAL: PERSONAL
   1. Promotes child-child play (cognitive and sensorimotor)
   2. Gets social games going
   3. Promotes self-help and social responsibility
   4. Helps child recognize his own needs
   5. Helps child delay gratification
   6. Promotes persistence, attention span

SOCIAL: PHYSICAL
1. Small muscle, perceptual motor
2. Large muscle, kinesthesis

III. FACILITATES CONCEPT DEVELOPMENT
1. Arranges learning of space and time
2. Arranges learning of seriation, categorization, and polar concepts
3. Arranges learning of number
4. Arranges learning of physical causality

IV. SOCIAL-EMOTIONAL: POSITIVE
1. Smiles at child
2. Uses raised, loving, or reassuring tones
3. Provides physical loving contact
4. Uses eye contact to draw child's attention

V. SOCIAL-EMOTIONAL: NEGATIVE
1. Criticizes verbally, scolds; threatens
2. Forbids, negative commands
3. Frowns; restrains physically
4. Isolates child physically—behavior modification
5. Ignores child when child shows need for attention
6. Punishes physically
7. Gives attention to negative behavior which should be ignored

VI. CARE-GIVING: BABY
1. Diapers, toilets, dresses, washes, cleans
2. Gives physical help, helps to sleep, shepherds
3. Eye checks of child's well-being
4. Carries child

VII. CARE-GIVING: ENVIRONMENT
1. Prepares/serves food
2. Tidies up room
3. Helps other caregiver
4. Prepares activities, arranges environment to stimulate child

VIII. QUALITATIVE CATEGORIES
1. Encourages creative expression
2. Matches "tempo" and/or developmental level of child
3. Actively engages child's interest in activity or activity choice
4. Follows through on requests, promises, directions, discipline

IX. DOES NOTHING

Assessing Children In her paper "Infant Assessment: Early Intervention," presented at the 1997 Annual Conference of the National Association for the Education of the Young Child, Linda Castellanos stated, "Much controversy has emerged about the assessment of young infants. As trained observers, we (caregivers) often suspect, but are not certain of what difficulties our youngest citizens have progressing through the developmental process. Assessment pinpoints developmental difficulties and allows the caregiver to confidently plan a program of treatment.

Developmental Profiles and Developmental Prescriptions successfully diagnose current developmental lags and remediate them when possible. One can only speculate the far-reaching impact that this early intervention can have concerning the future endeavors of ones so young" (Castellanos & Douville-Watson, 1997).

Caregivers must understand infant and toddler developmental milestones. They must know each child in their care. Caregivers must utilize the 3A's of child care. They must be able to evaluate the emotional, social, physical, and cognitive aspects of the child. They must know about materials and equipment and how to arrange and manage space. They must know how to assess each child and use the Prescriptions and Developmental Profile accurately.

Caregivers should act as assessors very prudently in this age of testing and making judgments about children. They should determine before making the assessments why the assessments are necessary, which ones are appropriate, and how they will be used.

Developmental assessment is used to determine the child's level of development. It may focus on one area, such as cognition, or the whole child, for example, physical, emotional, social, and cognitive. Since children are continually developing in all areas, periodic assessment is useful.

Developmental profiles or checklists can be developed by analyzing past descriptions and selecting categories of behavior or content. You can also develop checklists by listing objectives and competencies for children or caregivers. Checklists, however, only provide information about single incidents, and the information is isolated from the situation in which it occurred.

Developmental profiles or checklists of children's behaviors can be used most effectively by noting a behavior the first time you observe it. One day you may record one new behavior for Jeff, three new behaviors for Deborah, and nothing for Sandra.

We see infants perform many tasks. However, infants cannot tell us in words what they have learned. When you assess infants or toddlers on performance by planning to observe one instance of that activity, you should take care about interpreting the results, for a child may choose not to perform. A child may have learned something but not wish to perform on that occasion.

Few caregivers have received the specialized training required to use standardized assessment techniques and tests. If your program wants to carry out specialized assessment, seek out the necessary training first.

Organize

Care Plans or Prescriptions   The caregiver organizes plans. Daily, weekly, and long-term plans are important guides to awareness and continuity of development. The child's developmental profile provides information about the child's strengths and about areas in which development may occur next. Planning specific experiences in advance for each child helps make sure you are considering the needs and development of the whole child, rather than focusing on one or two areas and forgetting other areas.

Schedule   The caregiver organizes the schedule. You decide how to use the major blocks of time and how much flexibility you need in that schedule to meet the child's needs. Consistent patterns of events help children learn order in their lives. This develops in them feelings of security and trust because they know that some parts of their world are predictable.

Materials The caregiver organizes materials. Good infant programs need a variety of learning materials every day. The caregiver will want to select some materials to set out in the room and store away the rest. The caregiver decides when to change the materials and how to arrange them for the children to get to them.

Environment The caregiver organizes the environment—the room and the play yard—to meet the developmental needs of the children. Caregivers rely on their knowledge of the individual children in their care as well as on their background in child development. Each caregiver decides how and when to change the environment.

Manage

Careful management of time, space, materials, and people is needed to provide meaningful daily experiences for children.

Time The caregiver manages and coordinates time within the guidelines of the daily schedule and plans. You give Suzy a five-minute notice before outdoor play time since Suzy takes a long time to put her toys away and start getting ready to go outside. You feed lunch to Jack at 11:00 a.m., because he falls asleep at 11:30. You allow Vanessa to get up after her half-hour sleep, because she usually takes very short naps. You encourage Joshua to stay on his cot, knowing that he usually sleeps two hours. You continue to respect the needs of each individual child (Figure 5–4).

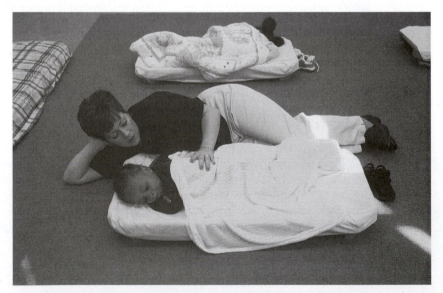

Figure 5–4 The caregiver provides nurturing attention to the waking child.

Space   The caregiver manages space. Before the children arrive, you plan and organize the space in your caregiving environment. When the children are actively using that space, you will make suggestions, decisions, and adjustments to help each child have positive experiences. Orrin is piling up blocks near the shelf. Shiwanda is trying to reach a block. For Shiwanda to get the block she wants, she will probably bump into Orrin's pile of blocks. You can walk with Shiwanda around to the other side of Orrin, where she can reach the block without getting into Orrin's space.

Materials   The caregiver manages materials. With very young children you make decisions about how many kinds of materials are needed, where they can be stored and where they can be used, what is safe or not safe, and how the materials can or cannot be used. Lois asks for a toy and begins pulling toys out of the toy box. She pulls out blocks, dolls, cars, puzzle pieces, fabric scraps, and assorted other toys. She looks back and forth between the inside of the box and the clutter of toys on the floor. She finally walks away to another part of the room, leaving all the toys behind. Too many materials can be confusing, but too few can bore a child.

People   The caregiver manages and coordinates people. When two caregivers work with a group of children, they should coordinate their plans and their actions. While the director can provide guidance, the moment-by-moment actions require dialogue and give and take between the caregivers.

Caregivers coordinate the children's use of time, space, and materials. Willard, a 15-month-old, flings toys. One of the caregivers needs to help him move to a part of the room where he can fling toys safely.

TOOLS FOR CONSCIOUS CAREGIVING

You are a child's first line of defense within the environment. You must be clear-headed and use all your senses to communicate with very young children. They depend on you for their survival, are unable to care for themselves, and try to communicate their needs. You must learn about how each child in your care is unique. You must learn to be a detective in order to solve the question, "What does this child need now?"

You may be familiar with some concepts of Changing of the Guard, The Circle of Safety, Shadowing, or Ruing, although you may have called them by other names. The reason examples are given is to associate these names with children for whom you care. The concepts help keep children safe and increase your own important role as a child care specialist. Mastery, the Outcome of Using the 3A's, applies to children of all ages. These examples will take on greater meaning as you become more experienced. The example of "Summary: Your Work" (later in this chapter) will have continued meaning as you gradually attain and develop a conscious skill base, and progress through your career.

An important premise of this text is that all children function from a need base, and there should be no judgment placed on needs. There is often a difference between what a child needs and how he or she behaves. Children behave in certain ways because their needs were met when they behaved that way in the past. Therefore, children simply behave in the way their limited experience has taught them. Needs are conveyed as information, so children give you information to help them. If children seem demanding, cry loudly, or are easily upset, their experience may have been that their needs were not fulfilled quickly, and they fear not having their needs met at all.

It is not good for anyone to feel needy. When environmental conditions remain constant, children continue to behave as they have in the past to get their needs met. You, as a child care specialist, are important because you have the power to positively affect this child's environment by providing a deliberate, kind, and purposeful response as soon as you can identify what the child needs. This promotes the child's sense of security and trust in the environment.

Child care specialists must become aware of what they do. Love of your profession is realized as you become more conscious of what you want to achieve each day with each child in care. Purposeful intent of your actions is the goal. When you purposely take action, you become consciously involved in that action. Moving slowly to gain rapport, a low hum, the vibration you provide, and your help to relax a child to sleep are all part of conscious care. Increased awareness of your nonverbal communication improves the connection between you and the children in care.

You may already use the following techniques with children. The purpose of presenting them here is to become more skillful with them in your daily routine. Research has shown these tools to be effective in enhancing development in the five major areas.

PHYSICAL DEVELOPMENT

Tool 1. Observing to Know

In at least one way, physical development is the most easily assessed and enhanced because most physical skills are directly observable. However, the caregiver must become a highly skilled, objective observer to see the subtle behavioral changes occurring in children's physical and sensory systems. When caring for children, it is common to "miss the forest for the trees" because we become too emotionally involved to objectively observe the child. Objective observation is one reason that constructing formal Developmental Profiles on a regular basis is extremely helpful.

The first step in observing to know is to emotionally remove yourself from the child and objectively observe goal behaviors. The easiest situation is when other caregivers perform care while you observe goal behaviors. However, if you are alone, you can **time-sample** goal behaviors by setting up a time schedule for observations. For example, if you want to observe Sally's precrawling behaviors, you might choose three five-minute periods during the day to focus all your attention on Sally's behaviors. The idea is to set up formal time to objectively observe the behaviors being assessed.

The next step is to know what to observe by clearly defining goal behaviors. A Developmental Prescription (Appendix A) is essential to know the important behaviors to observe in children of various ages. When you observe to know, only focus attention on a few behaviors during one observation time period. You can't watch everything at once, so limit the behaviors you observe to three or four during one observation period.

Once you have removed yourself to be objective, know exactly what behaviors to observe, and have specific times at which to make observations, the next step is to take notes on your observations. Write down exact movements the child makes, the sequence of movements, the total number of movements during the observation time (frequency), and how long the behavior or sequence lasts (duration). Familiarize yourself with the sequence of behavioral steps in physical development on the Developmental Prescription, and you will know what to record during each observation period.

Finally, compare your observation to what is expected of a child of the age being observed. Use a Developmental Prescription to compare your observations with normal expectations and record your findings on a Developmental Profile.

It is important to initially practice observing to know without interacting with the child. Before attempting time-sample observations while caring for children, observe children being cared for by others so you become familiar with these steps. Practice being an objective observer and, after you are comfortable defining goal behaviors, taking notes on the sequence, frequency, and duration of behaviors, and comparing observations with normal expectations, attempt time-sample observations while working directly with children.

Tool 2. Catch the Child Being Good

Physical development can be encouraged by using what scientists call **behavior shaping**. Behavior shaping is a specific technique: first, you "catch" a child performing a behavior and then **reward** the child at the exact moment he or she exhibits the behavior. A reward is anything that will motivate the child to attempt the same behavior again. As we learned in the 3A's, the most powerful rewards we have to give are positive attention, approval, and affection, but other things can be used as rewards, too. A toy, a favorite food, a game, or anything else that the child finds positive can be a reward. The idea is to observe the child carefully and each time he or she attempts or completes a goal behavior, immediately provide a reward and encouragement to try the behavior again.

Catching the child being good is a powerful tool to help children move from one physical developmental step to the next. The key to becoming a good "behavior shaper" is to observe carefully, define clear goal behaviors, and time your reward just as the child completes the behavior. When a child has mastered a behavior by successfully repeating it several times without error, start rewarding the next behavior in the developmental sequence. As the child becomes more proficient at a step, withhold the reward until the performance is better before asking the child to perform at the next higher level.

Caregiver enthusiasm and belief in the ability of the child to succeed is very important in catching the child being good. Demonstrate goal behaviors, physically move the child at first into the positions necessary, and encourage the child with a lot of the 3A's to become an excellent behavior shaper.

Tool 3. Circle of Safety—Safeguarding the Child

Picture a circle surrounding an infant lying on his or her back. The circle should be wide enough not to impede the developing need for movement, and should be empty except for the child. The circle is a controlled environment, and you are in control of that circle. Once movement begins, the circle must move with the child, providing a continuous safe circle for him or her to exist within. The child should be able to move, stretch, and safely explore while you constantly monitor the circle.

Protecting children involves creating a circle of safety around them that exceeds their developmental ability. This ensures a secure place for them to be safe. The child in the middle should be watched to make sure he or she is all right. Do this frequently, asking yourself, "Is the child safe?" During bath time or changing, examine the child's body. Does the skin look pink and healthy? Are there bruises? What is the condition of the child's clothes? Are there hazardous materials? Are the child's clothes clean, soft, and adequate in size?

When laying a child on his or her back, check the surrounding area in which the child will be placed. Is it clean, open, and roomy enough to move unimpeded? Are the borders of the circle strong enough to keep the child within the safety zone? Never underestimate a child's ability to reach for, or get to, an object of interest.

For toddlers, you must prepare an even larger space. Do this by pretending you are the child. Examine the environment from all angles on your hands and knees, eliminating all possible problems. Check under furniture and cushions, remove attractive articles that might break, and cover sharp edges of furniture. This expanded area is the learning environment in which the child and specialist will work. Have you removed objects of danger to minimize the "no's"?

The objective in preparing the space for a growing child is to promote a positive learning environment full of choices, so a child specialist can out-think, rather than out-run, children. The specialist's energy should be used to consciously plan for the child's well-being, exploration, and mastery.

Tool 4. Shepherding

The skill to foresee potential physical, emotional, or situational concerns and guide children safely is called **shepherding**. Assess the need for intervention, while respecting the child's ego boundaries, and encourage as much independent behavior as is safe in the situation. For example, a caregiver may assist a shy child in entering a group by coaxing and praising attempts to enter without forcing or overwhelming the child. The caregiver should gauge the amount of help necessary by allowing the child to be as responsible for him- or herself as safely possible and without the child becoming frustrated. The child should be aware of the help available and know that the caregiver is keeping the environment safe.

Lining children up, calling children in from play, and moving attention from one activity to the next while receiving cooperation and willingness is a difficult task. However, fun and happy expressions, rather than being stern or shouting, usually work. For example, begin to sing to get attention and, one by one, your promising mood will bring children to you because of the fun you are having. Think of yourself as the Pied Piper, who draws children to you based on an interesting and fun attitude. Shepherding involves keeping children organized and safe using positive attention-getting techniques rather than being harsh or demanding.

Tool 5. Shadowing

Remember seeing your shadow as a child? Your shadow was with you no matter where you went. It never seemed to get in your way. It never clouded your vision or kept you from moving ahead. Shadowing a very young child is similar. You are shadowing when you are just behind a newly mobile infant, ready to catch, but not interfering with choices or keeping him or her from exploring or mastering the environment. The child should be aware that you are there. If danger appears, or the "circle of safety" suddenly shifts, be prepared to protect the child from harm.

The words you use when shadowing children should be calm and approving to encourage mobility rather than to gain attention. Shadowing allows the child to be in control. You are there to back up the child. Your presence is known, your availability is counted on, and your permission to make choices is given. Decisions such as the direction to be taken, stops to be made, objects to be explored, and the speed of the pace are made by the child. This is the best of all worlds for the child: to be safe, encouraged, supported, and in control.

Tool 6. Behavior-Limiting Steps

Many experts on infant and toddler development avoid discussing discipline out of fear that their comments will be used inappropriately with children. While the current authors understand this, and the only discipline necessary with infants under the age of two years is to understand and fill their needs, it is essential that caregivers be able to set limits to help children learn to follow rules that keep themselves, other people, and property secure and safe. Therefore, discipline is an essential aspect of helping children develop. The following principles and procedures were taken, in part, from *Childcare Accountability Programs: CAPS* and *Establishing a Positive Learning Environment* (Douville-Watson & Watson, 1996).

The term *discipline* is used here to mean teaching appropriate behavior and setting limits on inappropriate behavior. It *does not* mean punishing children or controlling their behavior. In fact, the first principle of discipline is that adults should not control children's behavior. The most an adult can do for a child is to help the child meet his or her needs and administer consequences for the child's behavior (Douville-Watson, 1997). One of the most common errors caregivers in training make is to assume responsibility for controlling children's behavior. When you feel responsible for a child's behavior, you set up a "no win" situation, wherein you must try to control the child, which is impossible. It is essential to accept the fact that even young infants largely control their behavior, and that the caregiver is responsible to help meet needs and provide consequences. Once you accept the limits of reality regarding your control, you are in a position to help children become motivated, cooperative, and remain at ease most of the time.

The current trend in discipline is to use the concept of "time-in" rather than "time-out." **Time-in** involves keeping young children involved in enjoyable activities that are developmentally appropriate, filling their needs, and focusing attention and energy on appropriate rather than inappropriate behaviors.

We have already discussed using the 3A's to help children learn appropriate behavior. When caring for children under 30 months of age, the only discipline required is to assess the needs of the child and help fulfill them. It is *never* appropriate to completely remove attention, affection, or approval from infants, nor is shaking, hitting, or being physically or emotionally "rough" in any way acceptable. Problems usually arise when we have done everything we can think of, and the baby still screams and cries. This is the time to give responsibility to another adult, and take a break from the child to a quiet place where you can relax. Once you have regained your composure, re-enter the situation and assess all the baby's need levels again until you find what the baby requires to become at ease. Check out and observe physical needs such as teething, ear infections, stuffed sinuses, gas, and constipation. When discomfort continues for more than two hours, call the parent and consult your health professional.

Once children become mobile and enter toddlerhood, they must learn to accept "no" about certain behaviors. However, the number of behaviors they must accept "no" to is much smaller than many adults demand. The main principle to use in selecting which behaviors children must accept "no" to is to start with only those behaviors that are directly harmful to themselves, other people, or property. For example, hitting another child with a toy is *directly* harmful, but calling another child "stupid" is not *directly* harmful. While we want to teach that name-calling is not polite or respectful behavior, we do not associate the word "no" with it.

The goal is to teach children to immediately "stop and wait" when the adult firmly, but no harshly, says "no." This is most effectively accomplished through "*classical conditioning*" of the word "no" with "stopping and waiting." Responses are most easily associated when immediate and consistent consequences occur, so "no" should be consistently paired with an immediate consequence, such as removing the child. For example, it is common for toddlers to go beyond physical boundaries such as the yard, sidewalk, or street. To teach a child to stay within boundaries, the caregiver should choose a safe boundary and clearly explain and model the boundary, then stay close while the child plays, but not between the child and the boundary. When the child starts to cross the boundary, the caregiver firmly says "no," and holds the child from crossing the boundary. The caregiver then quickly diverts the child's attention to something interesting inside the boundary and heaps on the 3A's when the child moves back inside the boundary. When this procedure is *consistently* followed several times, the child will learn to "stop and wait" when you say "no," and just as important, will feel good for having displayed self-control. The caregiver must never trust that the child will honor a "no" or consistently follow directions. Instead, the caregiver should always watch to protect the child from harm.

Establishing "no" helps the young child with separation/individuation to move into another important developmental stage which is sometimes unfortunately called "the terrible twos." This important phase of personality development is mislabeled as "terrible" by controlling adults who have difficulty accepting children saying "no" to them. It is essential that children be allowed to say "no" to caregivers in order to develop a healthy sense of self and establish ego boundaries. Caregivers who do not accept "no" when it is not harmful to the child, others, or property do great harm to the child's sense of his or her right to make decisions and establish boundaries with other people. The three most effective forms of discipline with children who say "no" to practically everything are giving choices, diverting attention, and reverse psychology.

People learn to make wise choices by being able to choose. Caregivers who give children choices that they can handle for their age avoid many confrontations and teach children to choose wisely. Questions that can be answered by "yes" or "no" are often requests for problems, as is a statement that commands the child. For example, "Do you want lunch?" is likely to result in "no," as is the statement, "You're going to eat your lunch now." A much more effective approach is to give the choice: "Do you want a grilled cheese or lunchmeat sandwich for lunch? You choose."

Diverting young children's attention to safe and acceptable activities often is a way to avoid confrontations. For example, if you take a young child into a setting with many breakable objects, diverting the child's attention to objects and activities in the setting that are not breakable can avoid problems. Your attention and interest most often evokes interest on the child's part, so rather than attending to all the breakable things, pay attention and draw the child into activities that are safe and appropriate.

Sometimes, using reverse psychology is helpful in avoiding confrontations. With an oppositional two-year-old who is stuck saying "no" to everything, asking the child to do the opposite of what you really want can help. For example, if the child refuses to eat vegetables, you can ask the child to eat everything else but do not eat the vegetables. Often, children will do what is healthy for them and eat the vegetables just to demonstrate their autonomy. While this may seem somewhat manipulative, it can avert more damaging confrontations when used wisely.

With behaviors that are not directly harmful to the child, others, or property, a set of positively phrased rules and positive consequences for following rules is the single best form of discipline for children over two years of age. One of the most powerful principles of behavior shaping is "attention of *any* kind increases the frequency of a behavior" (Skinner & Belmont, 1993). Therefore, when you establish rules for children that are phrased in what *not* to do, you are actually increasing attention to those behaviors, which results in *more*, not less, of the behaviors you do not want. All rules should be phrased as the positive behavior you want to encourage. For example, the rule "talking with our inside (quiet) voice" is preferable to "no loud talking," and the positive counterpart to "No Hitting" is "Being Polite."

The number of rules should never exceed four or five and they should be general enough so the caregiver can define specific behaviors that fit under each rule. For example, a rule that states "walk quietly in the hall" is too specific because you will need other rules to cover class, lunch room, and playground walking. A better rule that fits all walking settings is "walk quietly." Table 5–1 lists a typical Rule Chart for three-year-olds. Notice that the rules are phrased as positive expectations, are general (to accommodate many behaviors), and are easily associated with positive consequences.

Once rules are defined, discussed, and modeled, a positive consequence is established for each rule, which can be provided on a daily basis. Consequences that are as

TABLE 5–1	**SAMPLE RULE CHART AND DAILY POSITIVE CONSEQUENCES: THREE-YEAR-OLDS**	
Rule	Sample Behaviors	Daily Consequence
1.	being polite and respectful *e.g., saying please, thank you, saying positive comments to others, etc.*	extra 10 minutes play time
2.	being cooperative and friendly *e.g., following directions, asking only once, smiling at others, etc.*	extra 15 minutes free time
3.	trying to do activities *e.g., following game rules, picking up after yourself, etc.*	star toward Friday Special Activity
4.	taking turns listening and talking *e.g., waiting your turn to speak, listening until the other person is finished, etc.*	telling a story during story time

naturally associated with the rules as possible should be used. For example, Table 5–1 lists extra play time as the daily consequence for being polite and respectful, and extra free time is the consequence for being cooperative and friendly.

Finally, do not expect perfection. Both Vygotsky's scaffolding and the behavior-shaping principle of successive approximation tell us to accept the child at the level at which he or she can presently perform and to sensitively help the child move toward the goal behavior. If a child is currently capable of following a rule only 20 percent of the time, provide the positive consequence at that level. As he or she learns to perform the behavior more often or better, increase the level expected to earn the consequence, but do not expect the rule to be followed 100 percent of the time because none of us are perfect.

"Catching the child being good" and heaping on the 3A's are extremely powerful in helping children behave appropriately, but when children are chronically anxious, angry, or depressed, they may not be able to follow the rules. When this occurs with children over 30 months, the caregiver must be prepared to deal with the situation by using a series of "behavior-limiting steps" to help the child follow the rules. Since drawing attention to a behavior increases it, the first limiting step is to give a child who is being disruptive a **nonverbal signal** such as making eye contact or touching the side of your nose. This signals the child that the behavior is not acceptable and provides a cue to change the behavior without drawing undue attention to the child. When the child corrects the behavior at this step, the caregiver should heap on the 3A's.

When a nonverbal signal does not help the child change a behavior, withdrawing the positive consequence for not following the rule is the next step. This gives the caregiver an opportunity to discreetly discuss what the child was feeling that caused the loss of the privilege.

Occasionally, nonverbal signals and losing positive consequences are not sufficient incentives for a child to follow the rules. In this case, the next step is for the caregiver to remove the child from the group and choose a solitary activity until the child is ready to follow the rules. When the child complies and is ready to return, he or she should verbalize (if possible) how to behave in order to re-enter normal group activity. It is *never* acceptable, and is illegal in most states, to allow a child to be unsupervised by an adult, so the quiet area should be in a place away from other children but where an adult can observe and supervise the child. The key to this working is that the 3A's are not available until the child is willing to follow the rules.

Biting Behavior

Biting, which occurs quickly and without warning, is an extremely difficult aggressive behavior to change in infants and young toddlers. Caregivers are encouraged to practice the 3A's, provide an adequate child-to-adult ratio with plenty of floor space, and provide a variety of toys to help prevent the occurrence of biting. However, when biting does occur, stating a firm "no" with a disappointed look at the child is appropriate. The child care professional should ask the toddler to apologize, if appropriate, and then say "we don't hurt, we are nice" while the hurt child is being comforted. According to the American Academy of Pediatrics, examples of appropriate positive discipline "include brief, verbal expressions of disappointment" (1996).

In addition to these procedures, information should be collected regarding what precipitated the bite. Often, this impulsive aggression consistently occurs after a set of circumstances that the biter cannot tolerate, such as feeling rejected. Therefore, getting specific information can help the caregiver change patterns to stop subsequent biting.

When all of these procedures fail, the final behavior-limiting step is to have the child removed from the setting by the parent or administrator, and provide professional help to the parent and child so the underlying reasons for the child not being able to follow the rules can be addressed and resolved.

Focusing your attention on catching the child being good, establishing positive rules and daily consequences, and being prepared with a set of behavior-limiting steps supplies the caregiver with all the disciplinary tools necessary. You can then help children develop healthy self-concepts and personality traits, and actually feel good about following the rules that keep them safe and secure.

EMOTIONAL DEVELOPMENT

Tool 1. Changing of the Guard

The first step to enhance emotional development is to provide a consistent, secure and affectionate environment for children, and Changing of the Guard helps establish this consistent and secure attachment.

Imagine you are a palace guard in charge of the Crown Jewels. You have been highly trained not to be distracted from your job and the specific duties you must perform. When it is time to leave your post, you cannot give this vital position to just anyone. The person taking your place must be recognized by you as having the same authority as yourself. You and the new guard verbally and formally exchange places. This is necessary so the Crown Jewels are always being watched with the same level of care and commitment.

The child care specialist is the child's first environmental defense against harm. No matter where children are, no matter what they are doing, a designated adult must be responsible to keep them safe. If two specialists have five children, each child is designated by name to a specific specialist. When, for any reason, one specialist must leave, even for a short time, responsibility for that child is turned over temporarily to another child specialist, who calls the child by name and says that you, Ms. Jones, will be with them until Ms. Smith gets back. The children should know the replacement's name and be told when the primary caregiver will be back. When Ms. Smith returns, she should verbalize to the children that they are once again under her supervision.

Tool 2. Ruing

Secure attachment and helping infants and toddlers become aware that they are not alone and that another person is willing to help them is essential to healthy emotional development. Ruing with infants and toddlers helps establish this essential awareness that they are not alone and that the caregiver understands and is connected with their feelings.

To rue is to mourn. Ruing is calming the mournful cry sometimes heard from a young infant. Most child care specialists have heard it. It is a sorrowful cry, pitiful in nature. Often, the specialist simply does not know what to do to soothe this child.

Ruing is an active technique used to soothe an unhappy or discontented child or emotionally connect with a happy baby. To rue is to hold an infant close to your heart and vocalize a pitch that is below the sound the child is making. Make your voice somewhat louder than the child's, and raise the pitch to match the infant's tone. Continue humming while holding the child against your chest so the baby can feel the vocalization's vibration. Continue to hum, letting the infant lead your joint sound pattern. Often, the infant becomes relaxed and will rue with you. Sometimes, you can change ruing into a song.

Tool 3. Inside Self/Outside Self Attention

Figure 5–5 illustrates the places where we can focus attention. People focus most of their attention on the visual, auditory, and tactile sensory experiences outside themselves in the world. However, becoming emotionally intelligent requires that children also learn to focus attention on the experiences inside their minds and bodies. The caregiver should begin the process of discriminating Inside Self/Outside Self Attention during infancy because the statements we make and the questions we ask direct the attention of the listener. For example, the statement "That red rose is pretty" directs attention to a visual stimulus in the outside world, and the statement "You seem happy today" directs attention to an emotion in the inside self. When the caregiver says, "Oh, Sally, your smile is so cute," Sally's attention is directed to her face and behavior, and when the caregiver smiles back at Sally, she directs attention and gives feedback from the outside world.

The caregiver should balance statements and questions between the Inside Self and Outside Self so young children develop a balance between interest in the world and interest in what is experienced inside in terms of thoughts, feelings, and behaviors. Figure 5–5 shows that our thoughts occur in the form of dialogues between the "I" and "You" voices and pictures and movies we build. Feelings are experienced through our body sensations and emotions. Behaviors are the actions we take, such as moving and speaking. The three main sources for attending to the outside world include hearing, seeing, and processing tactile stimuli through the skin. To enhance the development of emotional intelligence, the caregiver must remain conscious to keep a balance between directing the child's attention to his or her own thoughts, feelings, and behaviors and the information processed from the outside world through seeing, hearing, and physical sensations.

Tool 4. Label and Express Feelings

Along with Inside Self/Outside Self Attention, the caregiver should begin labeling feeling states from the time children are born. A good way to teach feeling states is to verbalize your own feelings and your impressions of the feelings of other people. "I'm feeling rushed today," "Jaime seems sad," and "You really look excited!" are examples of labeling feeling states. Caregivers should also model and mirror feeling states. Giving children feedback by mirroring their expressions and modeling feeling states helps to develop self-awareness and sensitivity to other people's feelings.

Feelings are inborn, but emotional reactions are learned. It is important to teach young children to accurately identify their feeling states, and express them in healthy ways. It is often easy to determine the emotions of even young infants. For example, young babies often "beam" when happy, have a "tantrum" when frustrated or angry, and "coo and smile" when happy and at ease. Caregivers should label feeling states for nonverbal infants, and as young children develop language, they should be taught to

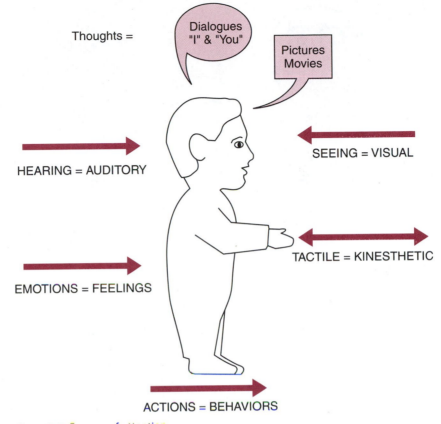

Figure 5–5 Focuses of attention.

accurately label and express their emotions. One effective tool for helping young children pay attention to and identify feelings is to use a Feelings Chart such as the one shown in Figure 5–6. This chart illustrates five primary emotions: At Ease, Happy, Sad, Angry, and Afraid, and can be used to help children accurately label their internal feelings. All human emotions are normal and are therefore healthy; no feeling state is bad or no good. The main goal for affective education is to help children be consciously aware of their feelings, and to express them in ways that are helpful to the child and not harmful to others.

Affective education starts with bringing attention to the child's internal state and labeling the child's feeling. Often the physical meter for children's feeling states are their whole bodies as they respond to different situations, especially the tummy area. The trained observer can easily identify children who are upset by their body language. "The prefrontal cortex receives a strong impulse from the great visceral nerve coming from the stomach area" (MacLean, 1990). This feeling in the gut is the physical link between body intelligence and affect associated with social behavior. Before they are able to discuss or label feelings, children must learn to recognize their at-ease state. This is most recognizable while having fun and feeling happy.

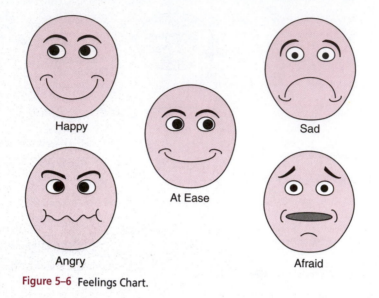

Happy

At Ease

Sad

Angry

Afraid

Figure 5–6 Feelings Chart.

Helping children to be aware of good feelings when they are in a state of ease is done after the child specialist has observed the children several times and knows when the child is at ease. Ask children how their bodies feel when at ease or while playing and having fun. Often, children will simply smile. State the feeling you sense with nonverbal children and infants. Ask them if their tummies feel good. Then show them five faces (At Ease, Happy, Sad, Angry, and Afraid). Identify Happy, and point to their stomach area, saying, "Your tummy feels happy! You're happy." If the child indicates agreement, say "Yes, that's right; you feel happy."

Show the children a picture of a happy face and say, "You look like this picture." Children begin to associate this state with the happy face picture over time. Children will then be able to point to the picture and identify this state for themselves.

Give children feedback when they appear to be in a feeling state. Tell them that they look At Ease, Happy, Sad, Angry or Afraid. Show them the pictures and ask how their tummies feel. If the child says, "I feel bad," quickly respond with "You are good. Tell me how your tummy feels" and show them the pictures. You can also say, "Your body looks like your tummy feels, like this," and point to the appropriate picture that fits your interpretation of their body language. Then ask, "Is that right?"

As children learn to identify their own body responses, discuss when they started to feel unhappy or afraid. After listening, specific information about the children's conflicts can be addressed by the child care specialist. It is important to understand that there are no judgments placed on emotional reactions because all emotions are normal. When adults do not judge or blame feeling states, children learn to identify and express emotion and develop the potential to be healthy adults.

To facilitate expression of emotions in a positive way, accept all emotions and the need to express them as normal. Toddlers are filled with energy. They are extremely curious and are very busy exploring their world. This often leads to frustration and all the unbridled emotions that go with learning how to handle new experiences. Conflicts arise from not getting what they want immediately. That is why having effective behavior-shaping techniques available and giving children an area to express feelings is essential.

Good caregiving is child-centered, meaning that children's needs are valid and important, and they need to express their feelings in positive ways.

A child care specialist who knows a child can observe how that child feels in certain situations and is emotionally available to pick up signals of frustration and alleviate a potential problem by distracting the child, involving him or her in a special project, or giving the child special attention. When you see that children need to release frustration, you can use an affective corner to help them express frustration; for example, involving them in hammering pegs or pounding pillows. When children have temper tantrums, make sure all furniture and harmful objects are out of the way. Remove undue attention from them until they are through, ask them privately to tell you what they felt if they can verbalize, and then welcome them into the group again. This is the most appropriate way to deal with tantrum behavior.

Toddler space needs to include a designated quiet and active area where the child can be observed unnoticed. You should be available to help the child release frustration. Planning a space for the release of frustration starts by understanding the developmental abilities of the specific children in care.

Ruing should be used with infants who express fear while being held. When an infant continues to cry for no apparent reason and all the measures listed in this text have been tried, the specialist is wise to allow another to help put the child at ease. Frustrations in child specialists are real feelings, too, and they need to be acknowledged. Often, primary child specialists with children who consistently cry, such as colicky babies, need to use rejuvenating techniques during breaks.

On occasion, children who bite or who are extremely aggressive cannot be directed and must be kept from hurting themselves and others. An area away from other children is useful for this purpose. No time limit is ever placed on a child, and a child may stay in the area for as long as necessary. The child is asked to stay in the area until he or she can follow the rules and rejoin the group. Biting, in particular, needs to be dealt with immediately. The child who bites needs to understand that he or she has hurt someone else, and the caregiver may want to raise the tone of voice slightly to indicate disapproval. The child must apologize to the bitten child when appropriate. The child who was bitten must be comforted and reassured first. It is the responsibility of the child care specialist to keep the children separate for a reasonable time to avoid continued conflict.

Tool 5. Self-Soothing

Teaching infants and toddlers to soothe themselves and manage their emotions may be the single most challenging task a caregiver faces. First, infants rely almost exclusively on other people for their need fulfillment, so they are not developmentally prepared at birth to soothe themselves. They must gradually learn that they can calm and soothe themselves through the feedback given by their caregivers. Caregivers who sensitively administer the 3A's and systematically teach children to use the 3A's for themselves promote and develop **self-soothing**.

Approval is self-rejuvenating when done with honest intention. When you express honest and approving intention, the positive energy that you give children is received as a motivating force. It is often called encouragement or coaxing, or in behavior modification terms, reinforcement. It works. Your approval comes from positive intention and it motivates. Your smile, eye contact, funny faces, winks, nods, verbalizations, and vocalizations are all approving behaviors and part of the approval process.

You should encourage and approve of children's actions as they progress toward set goals. For example, when a child indicates the desire to hold an object and together you have tried several times and finally succeed, the work is validated in a sense of achievement by your attention, approval, and affection. This builds a feeling of confidence and a willingness to try the next time when the child reaches for the same object. The child may attempt the task on his or her own, or he may look for your encouragement or help, but eventually the child will feel confident enough to succeed without your help.

Verbal praise and appropriate words of encouragement help children of all ages. Timing of when to give approval depends on the needs of the child. The child may start out wanting something, but becomes too tired to finish. If the child is too tired, the primary need must be cared for first (holding the child until he or she goes to sleep). After the primary needs have been met, children will once again bring their attention to other activities.

Child care specialists can help build strong self-images for the toddlers in their care. As good role models, and by using reinforcing positive self-talk, they can build language for the child to adopt. Positive self-talk is the internalization of messages children hear about themselves from others. These messages represent how they feel about themselves, and what they are capable of over time. If the messages are positive and encouraging, the child will become confident, but if they are negative, the child feels limited in the ability to succeed. These messages become the belief system of the child and the foundation for self-concept and future success or failure.

Scaffolding is a tool for promoting positive self-talk. By building sets of ideas and demonstrating how to use them, you can promote a foundation for positive self-talk. The chart below illustrates how scaffolding works when approval sustains the infant's attention. This approval validates children's mastery of their environment. Children internalize the validation they hear and make it their own as you reduce feedback.

Child Behavior	Specialist Response	Outcome
1. eyes object 2. reaches for object	observes child encourages using words like "You can do it."	specialist attention approval for mastery attempt; increased child motivation
3. looks at Specialist; tries to grasp objects again	continues to encourage softly saying "Try again; you can do it!" models success	approval for mastery attempt; increased child motivation
4. successfully grasps object	compliments effort, eye contact, gentle hug	approval and affection for mastery of task
5. smiles and shows excitement—brings object to mouth	says "Nice job! I knew you could do it!" Give 3 A's	validation of mastery observable self-approval

Older children can be encouraged to verbalize "I'm a good boy," and the child specialist can affirm this by saying, "Yes, you're a good boy," thereby supporting positive self-talk.

Tool 6. Emotion Management

Teaching young children how to manage their emotions follows the same principles as self-soothing. Starting at around 12 months of age children lose their innate abdominal breathing, therefore it is possible to teach children yoga-type breathing, systematic relaxation, and cognitive skills to balance emotions. Deep, yoga-type breathing is the single most powerful tool we know of for breaking a state of anger or anxiety. It is important for you to practice the following procedure so you can breathe deeply before demonstrating and teaching it to children.

Stick your thumbs in your "belly-button" and let your fingers relax on your tummy. Now, inhale through your nose and make a balloon out of your tummy. Do not let your chest move up when you inhale; just make a balloon in your tummy. Exhale through your mouth and make sure that you let go of all the tension in your body. Inhale through your nose, making a balloon, and exhale through your mouth, letting go of all tension. Concentrate all the power of your mind on inhaling and making a balloon and exhaling and letting go of all tension. Practice this technique for 10 breaths at a time while you remain aware of your feelings.

Once you have taught young children to breathe deeply and they begin to get angry or anxious, all you need to do is get their attention and say "Breathe!" and they will calm themselves and return to a state of being at ease within three or four breaths.

Systematic relaxation also can be taught to children beginning at around 12 months. Teach children to relax each part of their bodies, beginning with their toes and feet, by touching each part and telling the child to command that part to relax. For example, touch the child's toes and say, "Toes relax, heels relax, feet relax . . ." as you touch each part in order. Proceed from the feet to legs, back, shoulders, arms, and hands. Then, start from the back of the neck across the back, top, and front of the head to the face, neck, and chest. Finish the procedure with the tummy and whole body by having the child do deep breathing. As with deep breathing, the caregiver must practice systematic relaxation before teaching it to children.

SOCIAL DEVELOPMENT

Every interaction you have with children forms and develops their interactions with themselves and other people. Effective tools to ensure that children develop skills in managing healthy, intimate relationships include how and what we say to other people about a child (Positive Perspective), how we establish and maintain positive interactions with children (Rapport Building), how we behave toward children and expect them to behave toward others (Respectful is Successful), knowing when to compete and when to cooperate (Cooperation versus Competition), and how children verbally interact (Mirroring and "I Talk").

Tool 1. Positive Perspective

Successful relationships and social acceptance depend on developing internal controls. Children must learn to act without harming themselves, others, or the environment because they are not born with the experience for these internal controls. They need to be taught the tools to have successful, positive relationships. For the child care specialist, this includes the use of Positive Perspective. Understanding the relationship between the child care specialist and child and how you react to the child's behavior is crucial to quality child care.

One way of helping children act appropriately is to call attention to another person and the positive and cooperative things they do. By announcing positive behavior out loud, the child receives compliments and validation from the people nearby, and will continue to want to do good things. When you verbalize positives about a person around another person, you are using Positive Perspective. By combining the 3A's with Positive Perspective, the teacher strongly influences a child's behavior.

Think of Positive Perspective as another tool available to promote a positive relationship. When you use Positive Perspective, you tell a positive story about the child to others around the child. You help give a positive view of a situation than might be perceived by the children involved. For instance, say you are a teacher (or provider) in a licensed group family child care center. You wait for three-year-old Eroj to get off the bus. You have walked his two-and-a-half-year-old sister Inara to the bus stop with you. You greet Eroj with a smile and a hug. His sister is happy to see him. He has his art projects in both hands, and when he goes to hug you he drops the papers. His sister grabs them and, in the excitement of the moment she crumples one of them. Eroj becomes angry and begins to yell at his sister. She starts to cry. As you help him gather up his work, you place Inara on your hip and place your hand firmly on Eroj's shoulder. You say to him, "I'm so sorry you dropped your papers. You worked so hard on them and they are so well done (looking at papers he is showing you while walking). You should be proud of them. When we get back you can show everyone your work and then put them up on the wall if you like."

You would use Positive Perspective and continue by saying in Inara's presence, "You know, Eroj, Inara did not mean to crumple your papers. I know she would not do anything to hurt you. I know she misses you when you go to school because several times during the day she stands by the door and says your name. I know she loves you and wants to be with you. She is just too little to act as grown up as you right now. It's just what two-and-a-half-year-olds do sometimes."

This Positive Perspective has a very specific "theme." The teacher provided Eroj information he would not have had and dealt with him in a very careful way. She greeted Eroj warmly, validated his feelings of anger and worthwhileness, soothed his sister by picking her up, and discussed the situation in front of Inara. She expressed positive observations about his relationship with his sister, telling him information he would not have unless she told him. In addition, the teacher was acting as Inara's advocate.

When the teacher told Eroj how his sister acted when he wasn't there she was using Positive Perspective. The theme or message the teacher promoted in the mind of Eroj was a positive one. The message said to him: "I am important to my sister and even when I am not with her I am missed. I am secure in my position with her because she thinks of me even though I am not there. I am loved by her." The message helps to promote a positive bond between them.

The same theme can be used as a tool with very young children. Caregivers can offer similar comfort to younger children by using statements like "Oh, I know Michael didn't mean to knock down your block pile, Dori; he just lost his balance." The key to successful use of this tool is to know the child, know the facts in the situation, and frame a positive picture of the intentions and actions of the people involved.

The difference between Positive Perspective and the 3A's is that Positive Perspective influences the learning environment by telling a true story in a positive way about someone to a third party. The 3A's are used by the caregiver directly with a specific child.

The conscious use of Attention, Approval, Affection, and Positive Perspective will help foster relationships with children. The relationships with children are the core of your care. This prosocial relationship is the springboard from which children experience other relationships. The significance of many meaningful hours spent together cannot be overstated.

One of Judy Leipzig's main principles for fostering prosocial behavior is "First, develop a relationship with the child—the more loving and nurturing the better" (Leipzig, 1986). Another extremely helpful reference for promoting Positive Perspective and other tools by creating prosocial environments is Alice Honig's group games (Honig, 1988).

Miss Tara, a family child care provider, sits in a rocking chair in her den holding 5-month-old Marcus. Nearby, 27-month-old Clay, 15-month-old Kiera, 36-month-old Milinda, and 30-month-old Burton are playing. Miss Tara plays with Marcus, clapping his hands and laughing; Marcus looks at her and laughs. She lays him on his back on her lap, swings his arms, puts his hand in his mouth, and makes sounds. He reaches and puts his hands on Miss Tara's face, laughing and kicking his feet when she repeats his sounds. At the same time Miss Tara is also involved with the other children. She smiles at Clay, who is watching the other children; she smiles at Marcus. She points to Pooh Bear in response to Kiera's whimpers of "Bear" and she watches Shaun and Sarah sitting on the floor, with the lock blocks pail between them, as they construct objects.

Miss Audrey has her feet stretched out in front of her in the toddler room in a corporate child care center. Ryan is sitting on her lap and three other toddlers who are sitting around her are touching her with their hands or legs or leaning on her. Miss Audrey is holding a picture book, telling the story line by pointing to the pictures rather than by reading the words. She stops and asks Ryan to point to a tree. He puts his finger on a tree and Miss Audrey gives him a hug, turns him so he can see her smile, and says, "That's right, that is a tree."

Miss Tara and Miss Audrey are consciously aware of the power of using the 3A's of Child Care effectively. They are emotionally involved with the children, providing a warm, stable, supporting, confirming relationship which helps infants and toddlers develop a healthy foundation for life. In addition to emotional needs, caregivers anticipate physical needs and respond to the children. They select enough toys to offer the children options in their choice of playthings. They prepare the room. They interact with other staff and with parents. And they plan to actively promote the children physically, emotionally, socially, and cognitively.

Tool 2. Rapport Building (Interactional Synchrony)

Rapport is an agreement between two people that establishes a sense of harmony. This harmonious agreement with infants and toddlers has been discussed in previous chapters as interactional synchrony. Research from the field of Neuro-Linguistic Programming (NLP) has revealed how rapport is established and maintained through what is called **calibrating** and **pacing** specific behaviors. Think of rapport building as learning to dance very well with another person. When you learn to dance with an infant or toddler, it is necessary to allow the child to lead while you carefully observe their steps in the dance. *Calibrating* means carefully observing the specific steps, and *pacing* means carefully moving in harmonious synchrony with the child. There are five specific sets of behaviors that must be calibrated and paced to build rapport and dance well with a child.

1. **Posture.** Align yourself in a complementary physical posture with the infant or toddler, and change your posture to "dance" with the child face to face.
2. **Gestures.** If the child is active, calibrate and pace the movements, but if the child is passive and does not move much, then pace the inactivity.
3. **Voice tone and tempo.** With young infants, calibrating and pacing voice tone and tempo is called ruing (Tool 2, Emotional Development). With older infants and toddlers, the caregiver must listen carefully to voice tone and tempo and calibrate and pace the child.
4. **Intensity.** These behaviors include emotional intensity, as well as physical movements and vocalizations.
5. **Representational systems.** This set of behaviors is the hardest to learn to calibrate and pace because it includes all ways that the child represents his or her beliefs, perceptions, and understanding of the world. With verbal children, some representational systems include use of verb tense (past, present, future), information processing style (visual, auditory, tactile), and focus of attention (inside self; outside self; other people, places, and things).

The caregiver should practice calibrating and pacing by observing other people interact before trying it with children. Calibrate and observe the pacing of these five sets of behaviors in mothers with their children and it will quickly become obvious how good rapport is between them. Does the mother let the child lead or does she demand that the child follow her? Is she sensitive to these five sets of behaviors and does she pace the child? Once you have practice observing calibration and pacing with these five sets of behaviors in other people, try calibrating and pacing them to build rapport in your own relationships with children and adults. You'll find that the outcome is well worth the effort; you can establish interactional synchrony very quickly when you become proficient using this tool.

Tool 3. Respectful Is Successful (Ego Boundaries)

Once good rapport is established, it is possible to teach infants and toddlers to respect the boundaries of other people. A **boundary** is anything marking a limit, and people need to have their physical and emotional boundaries respected in order to feel respected and secure. Respect for a child's physical body and emotional condition is essential to managing relationships well. With young infants, respect means handling them sensitively when feeding, changing, and bathing. When an infant exhibits discomfort or displeasure, respect means to stop what you're doing and try to help the child return to a state of being at ease by assessing and addressing all their physical and emotional need levels. Respecting boundaries with toddlers means allowing them personal space at times, listening to them, and being sensitive to their needs and feelings.

When it is necessary to make your own needs or the needs of another person more important than the child's let the child know that you understand his or her desires and feelings and explain why it is necessary to cooperate with those desires and wait. Healthy relationships require *mutual* respect for boundaries, so children must learn that they need to cooperate with other people's desires as well. A good way to teach this is to let children know in advance that they will be expected to cooperate with your desire. For example, "Johnny, we will play the game you want and then you must lie down with the other children for nap time. I'm cooperating with what you want now, so it's fair that you cooperate with me later, OK?" Another way of respecting each other is to let the child know when her want or desire will be fulfilled. For example, "I must fix lunch for the group now, Sally, so I can't read you a story right now. As soon as we finish lunch and clean up, I promise to read to you."

When a child doesn't respect another person's boundaries, a good technique is to explain the consequences of the disrespect for the child and the other person. For example, "When you hit Gena you hurt her, and she is crying now because she feels hurt. You don't like to feel hurt, do you? Now, how can you help Gena?"

Healthy relationships promote respect for what is yours, what is mine, and what is ours together. Children and adults need to have times by themselves, physical and emotional space of their own, and shared time together. The caregiver who respects a child's body, mind, and feelings and expects respect in return teaches young children to interact in positive and mutually fulfilling relationships.

Tool 4. Cooperation versus Competition

One of the major concepts this book presents to caregivers is that each person has a unique map of the world, including perceptions, beliefs, and understanding, which is built from our individual experiences. One representational system of an individual's map is whether the person perceives other people as competing or cooperating with him or her. Another way of stating this is that many people perceive interactions with other people as "win-lose." Others perceive interactions as "win-win" or "lose-lose." People who are competitive tend to perceive interactions as "win-lose"; if you get what you want, then I must lose something, or vice versa. People who are pro-social and cooperative often perceive interactions as "win-win" (we both get what we want), or "lose-lose" (we both lose something because of our interaction). People who believe that all interactions should be competitive tend to be aggressive and selfish, and people who believe that all interactions should be cooperative tend to be assertive and cooperative in relationships.

Obviously, both competition and cooperation are necessary components of healthy relationships, but few parents or caregivers consciously teach children when each is appropriate to manage relationships well. As a general rule, competition is important when time and/or task mastery are involved in an activity. For example, the goal of many games is to compete in such a way that one person or group wins and the other loses. Fun competition promotes mastery and confidence with behavioral and cognitive skills. These "win-lose" interactions help children build a sense of confidence, as long as they can win sometimes. The caregiver must be careful to make sure that competitive interactions are balanced so that everyone gets the opportunity to win at times. Using Positive Perspective can help with competition between children. For example, when Mary always beats James in foot races, the caregiver might say in James's presence, "You're a really fast runner, Mary, and James is always the first one to clean up his area after play time."

Turn-taking is also important when children compete. For example, when two toddlers compete for the same toys, the caregiver can instruct the children to take turns and provide the child whose turn is second with a positive alternative until it is his turn.

Cooperative interactions should be supported and encouraged by caregivers. Generally, cooperative "win-win" relationships tend to be more pleasurable and intimate than competitive relationships. The caregiver should provide many activities that require cooperation between children for success. For example, "As soon as everyone works together to pick up the play area, we can all have ice cream!" The caregiver should also approve of cooperative interactions and catch children cooperating whenever possible, as in, "Wow, I like how Tara and Josh are playing well together. You two are really cooperating!"

Caregivers should remain aware of competitive and cooperative interactions and systematically instruct young children to accept winning, losing, and cooperating with others as normal parts of interactions. By teaching children these important relationship skills, they learn how to manage interactions that are mostly "win-win," and how the "win-lose" interactions are fun and enjoyable for both people involved.

Tool 5. Mirroring and "I Talk"

We learned in the chapter on communication to listen actively for the deeper emotional message a person sends us. We also learned to interact using "I messages" instead of "You messages." Generally, "I messages" and active listening responses are a very effective form of communication, but young children who are just beginning to use language often do not understand many words and do not have the experience necessary to actively listen. To teach effective communication to young children so they communicate well with each other and have good understanding, mirroring and "I talk" are powerful tools.

"I talk" usually starts with the word "I" and communicates a person's wants, needs, feelings, or thoughts. Young children should be taught to express their thoughts and feelings without judging or blaming other people, and "I talk" helps them learn to take responsibility. As with using I messages, children should be encouraged to talk about themselves rather than other people. When Shawna comes to you crying and says, "Burt hit me!" you can teach I talk by asking Shawna to tell you how she feels, as in, "I feel hurt and angry!"

Mirroring is repeating exactly, word for word, what another person has said. Calling Burt over and asking him to mirror what Shawna said will help him to understand her perspective and how she feels. The only word that is changed when mirroring is the word "I" is changed to "You," so Burt's accurate mirroring response would be "You feel hurt and angry." The caregiver must be actively involved in helping children make good I statements and mirroring responses by allowing communication to continue only after accurate I statements and mirroring responses are made. This is done by helping children rephrase their statements and responses. In the example, once

Burt has accurately mirrored Shawna, he is allowed to make his own I statement: "I'm sorry, I was just playing; I didn't mean to hurt." Shawna then mirrors Burt: "You're sorry; you was just playing; you didn't mean to hurt." She then is allowed to make another I statement: "That's OK, I'm better now."

Mirroring and I Talk are powerful tools the caregiver can use to help children communicate responsibly and effectively. Children who learn mirroring and I Talk become aware of other people's feelings and perspective and are able to communicate their own thoughts and feelings effectively. The caregiver should obviously use I Talk and Mirroring in his or her own communication with children to model being a sensitive, responsible, and effective communicator.

COGNITIVE DEVELOPMENT

Infants and toddlers are dynamos for cognition and information processing. As we learned in earlier chapters, neurological pathways are being formed at an amazing rate during the first three years of life as infants and toddlers develop the perceptions that form their map of themselves and the world. The stimuli that we provide children as caregivers will help determine how well they are able to function cognitively, as well as physically, emotionally, and socially.

Effective tools for enhancing cognitive development include Piaget's stages, as previously discussed, building auditory and visual language concepts through Naming and Labeling, verb use and logic through Time Orientation and Cause-Effect, sequencing and patterning individual gestures as a form of preverbal communication through Baby Signing, meta-cognition through Observe Yourself, and categorization through Concept Formation Games.

Tool 1. Naming and Labeling

One of the most complex cognitive tasks that human beings ever undertake is learning their primary language. The neurological complexities of understanding words and their meanings are still not completely understood or researched. The caregiver must begin this highly complicated instruction by understanding that language and thought occur in two major forms, auditory and visual. We literally learn to think by talking to ourselves using words (auditory), and by building pictures and movies in our minds (visual).

Because thinking occurs in the form of pictures and words, the caregiver should systematically teach infants and toddlers names, labels, and meanings of things in their environment. We use **naming** to mean use of words, and **labeling** to mean visual images or pictures. During the first nine months, the caregiver should clearly name the things in the baby's environment while pointing to and helping the child focus visual attention on the object. It is also a good idea to place word labels on the objects in the baby's environment (e.g., the label CHAIR on a chair) to aid in letter and word associations. Naming things as you point them out is called **auditory-visual association**, so the caregiver should also talk about the functions, uses, and meanings of the things in the baby's environment to help establish higher cognitive concepts.

As the child begins to pronounce his or her first words (e.g., da-da, bee-bee), the caregiver should heap on the 3A's and show the baby visual images for the words he or she is beginning to say (e.g., a picture of the father when baby says da-da). The initial naming and labeling done by the caregiver should be clear, distinct, and associate the same name and meaning with the same visual image each time: "Yes! Da-da [show picture] is your da-da; he loves you."

Even before children can articulate words by themselves, many can recognize and accurately identify objects in their environments. For example, after pairing the word *chair* with visual images and meanings of chairs (e.g., back, seat, used to sit) several times, some children as young as six months can pick out a picture of a chair from four choices when asked to point to a chair. By being very consistent and conscious of the visual and auditory stimuli that you present to children, and by taking the time to discuss the functions and meanings of things in the environment, you can enhance the language development and cognitive skills of infants and toddlers.

Tool 2. Time Orientation and Cause-Effect

It might seem odd at first to combine the orientation we have in time—past, present, and future—with cause and effect. However, since an action (cause) must occur in time before the result (effect), time and cause-effect are closely related. Listen carefully to the verb tense another person uses most frequently when he or she talks and it quickly becomes apparent that the person's time orientation is in the past, present, or future. The friend who tells you about the party she attended last week is reliving a past experience, complete with words, pictures, and movies. The co-worker who talks about his planned vacation is sharing a whole movie with sounds and sights that he has built about a future experience.

One of the many wonderful things about working with young children is that they tend to be present oriented more than past or future. The present is also where cause and effect usually occur. While it is true that an action taken today (cause) may not result in a reaction (effect) for some time, most actions result in rather immediate reactions. Even newborns make associations between cause and effect in the present. For example, when an infant moves his or her mouth in a certain way and Mommy makes a fuss, the baby quickly learns to *cause* mommy to react by smiling.

The caregiver has a powerful tool to enhance cognitive development by combining awareness of time orientation with consciously and systematically teaching young children cause and effect. The idea that "When I do A now (present), then B happens (future)" is the basis of most human learning. Teaching infants and toddlers that their present actions *always* result in some reaction helps children feel empowered and understand that they are responsible for the reactions and consequences of their behavior.

Simple games and instructions can be used to demonstrate how a child's actions cause reactions in their environment and with other people. For example, the game "Simon Says" can be used to teach children to react to instructions when "Simon" (the caregiver or a child) says to, and to not react when "Simon" doesn't say. Caregivers should systematically teach infants and toddlers the essential cognitive skills of time orientation and cause-effect during the daily activities and routine. Focusing attention on the fact that every action results in some reaction helps children to understand their power to affect the environment, including other people, and the responsibility they have for the consequences of their actions.

Tool 3. Baby Signing

Baby signing is a term used by Dr. Linda Acredolo and Dr. Susan Goodwyn (2001) in their book entitled *Baby Minds*, which helps parents and caregivers understand the cognitive processes of infants and toddlers. The term means to calibrate and pace the preverbal infant's gestures and develop nonverbal communication with the child by mirroring the child's actions. Through pacing and mirroring the baby's gestures and expressions, the caregiver can help the child function at higher cognitive levels more quickly.

Young infants should be mirrored in terms of gestures and expressions, and the caregiver should make gestures and expressions and encourage the baby to mirror. At around six months of age, the child will respond to *dialogue reading*, in which the caregiver asks questions and supplies the answers when reading picture books. At around nine months, many babies enjoy remembering things, so reading the same favorite storybook over and over helps the child remember and understand concepts. By 12 months, you can play "which hand has the penny" in which the caregiver uses a set sequence of hiding (e.g., right, right, left) to help develop sequential memory and concepts of object permanence and replacement. By 18 months, the child will respond to numbers of objects changing. The caregiver should provide stimuli that change in number and point out to the child when the number changes: "Oh look, another bird. Now there are two." By 24 months, children use their vivid imaginations, so adding happy conversations and stories at naptime or bedtime encourages creativity and the use of cognitive skills.

Baby signing is the first step in understanding the thought processes of the infant and toddler and systematically providing the child with auditory and visual stimuli that enhance the use of cognitive skills, creativity, and logic.

Tool 4. Observe Yourself (Meta-Cognition)

As discussed in the chapter on developmental patterns, self-recognition begins in some children as young as six months. Further, one of the domains of emotional intelligence is self-awareness. Infants and toddlers are involved in a very active process of defining themselves separate from their primary caregiver and the environment. A challenge for caregivers is to help young children develop a strong self-concept and awareness of self. Awareness of our thoughts and cognitive processes is called meta-cognition, and awareness of our emotions is called meta-mood.

The main tool to help older infants and toddlers develop self-awareness of their thoughts and feelings is to focus their attention on sensory grounded information. Sensory grounded information is awareness of the specific experiences occurring through our senses: seeing, hearing, smelling, tasting, and feeling (tactile). The caregiver should question young children about what they are aware of through their senses to enhance self-awareness. For example, if a caregiver asks a child how he feels and he responds "Fine," the caregiver should question further how the child knows he is fine. What does he see, hear, and feel in his body that tells him he is fine. What words does he say in his mind and what pictures does he see in his mind that help him feel he is fine. Focusing the child's attention on thoughts in terms of words and pictures in her mind, on her feelings in terms of body sensations, and on her senses helps the child develop the cognitive skills involved in self-awareness.

Using mirrors also helps develop self-recognition and self-awareness. Provide infants and toddlers with a mirror that shows the whole body when they are experiencing different feeling states. Give them feedback and direct their attention by focusing on the sensory grounded information: "See, this is how you look when you're . . . [happy, sad, and so on]. Notice your face, your lips, your eyes, your hands, and so on [pointing to each]." Do not be concerned that this tool will make children egotistical or vain because the focus of attention in the use of mirrors is the visual and auditory stimuli to become aware of their physical reactions during different emotional states. By focusing attention on sensory grounded information, you help young children develop the cognitive skills of observing their own thought processes and emotional states.

Tool 5. Concept Formation

We learned in the chapter on developmental patterns that higher cognitive processes begin with **concept formation**. A *concept* is an abstract idea in the form of a word or picture that does not exist in the real world. Some concepts are highly complex and abstract and require a great deal of reasoning and experience to understand. The basic forms of concepts are simple: we group them into categories of common things and then call them by abstract words that we learn to recognize as part of a larger group. For example, the word *chair* is learned initially through a perceptual skill called *association* because when we see a chair, we are repeatedly told that it is a chair, so we associated the auditory name *chair* with the visual image of chair. However, "chair" also becomes a concept because, after much experience seeing many different visual images of things called chair, we form the concept of "chair-ness," which includes the action of something we sit in that usually has a back and a seat. Therefore, we have a whole category of things that fit into the concept of chair. Another example of a simple concept is *fruit*. "Fruit" does not exist in the real world. You have never seen a "fruit," so it is an abstract word that represents a whole category of different-looking images that we have learned to group into a category called "fruit" because of shared characteristics.

Grouping objects into categories and assigning words to each group should be systematically taught to infants and toddlers to enhance cognitive skill development. The caregiver should supply children with groups of things (such as chairs, toys, tables, and fruit) and supply the verbal/auditory group name for each item in the group. As children start to verbalize words, the caregiver should provide children with a group of items and ask for the category name, or give the name and ask children to pick individual items that belong to the group. Older toddlers can handle more complex concepts and can more fully discuss qualities of concepts, such as the function of chair or the attributes that make something a fruit.

All activities the caregiver presents to children should be in the form of games and fun activities during the normal daily routine. Systematic instruction means starting with the simplest and most common concepts and gradually introducing more complex and abstract categories and names. Even young infants should be talked to as if they have the unlimited capacity to understand concepts, but preverbal children should always be visually presented things, along with talking. As we learn in Chapter 6, the nonverbal, emotional parts of messages are more than half of what gets communicated, so when the caregiver communicates using the 3A's, respect, and clarity, children tend to absorb the information and meanings more quickly and fully.

LEARNING SKILL DEVELOPMENT

The essential visual, auditory, and motor perceptual skills necessary to acquire language and use higher cognitive processes are learned by most children unconsciously and without direct instruction. However, because visual and auditory perceptual skills are not taught to infants and toddlers systematically, most adults are imbalanced in their information-processing preferences and many children are diagnosed as learning disabled after they enter a school setting. Most learning disabilities are the result of deficits in the essential visual and auditory perceptual skills necessary to succeed in the more complex academic skills children must learn in school. The caregiver can enhance visual and auditory developmental learning skills through systematic training during the normal daily routine, thereby averting many later learning problems.

Tool 1. Focal Attention Training

There is a growing body of research demonstrating that the perceptual skills of focal attention and perceptual screening can rather easily be taught to children and adults who have not mastered them. In fact, clinical procedures have been developed to effectively teach children and adults with Attention Deficit Disorder (ADD) to focally attend and perceptually screen within a short amount of time (Douville-Watson & Watson, 2001). Caregivers who apply the following principles of focal attention-perceptual screening training with older infants and toddlers often help those children avert later attention skill deficits.

Visual attention should be trained before auditory attention since the visual channel matures more rapidly than the auditory channel, and it is much easier to observe attentional lapses with visual-motor tasks than with auditory-verbal tasks. The caregiver should first present older toddlers with interesting visual stimuli, such as colorful pictures or slides, in a low-distraction environment, with other distracting visual stimuli removed and sound kept at a minimum. Children should be encouraged to focus visual attention on the stimuli for as long as possible without breaking focus, and they should be rewarded when they have maintained attention on the stimuli for more than a few seconds. Using visual stimuli to which the child can make motor responses, such as pointing or marking an X, helps training significantly. As the child's skill at maintaining focal attention increases, the caregiver should reward longer periods of sustained attention and encourage the child to attend longer.

Once the child is able to sustain focal attention to visual stimuli for at least 15 seconds without any lapses (e.g., looking away, fidgeting, getting up, losing interest), the caregiver should gradually introduce mildly distracting visual and auditory stimuli into the environment while encouraging the child to maintain focal attention. After the child maintains focal attention for at least 30 seconds during mildly distracting conditions, increase the visual and auditory distractions while working toward focusing visual attention without lapses for at least one minute.

When the child is able to regularly sustain visual focal attention for at least one minute without lapses in a highly distracting environment, such as a group of children in a well-lit open room, the caregiver should start the same training procedure using auditory stimuli (e.g., cassette tape, record player, or telling stories and requiring verbal responses) in a low-distraction environment. As with visual attention, as the child's focal attention skills increase, introduce more distractions until the child can listen in a normal group setting for at least one minute without being distracted.

Individual differences in learning focal attention and perceptual screening skills vary largely, so some children may require individual training for several sessions in a very quiet environment before distracting stimuli can be introduced. All children must be able to sustain visual and auditory focal attention in both low-distraction and high-distracting environments in order to learn effectively in a school setting.

Tool 2. Memory Training

Once a child is capable of some sustained visual and auditory focal attention, the caregiver can systematically perform visual and auditory memory training. There are many types of memory, based on the length of storage to recall (e.g., long term, short term), the quantity of units stored, the accuracy of recall (e.g., sequence, unit accuracy), and many other factors. For the purposes of working with infants and toddlers, we will focus on short-term recall of visual and auditory sequences, since these are the easiest to train and are essential for learning discrimination and association skills. We present one visual memory training and one auditory memory training example here, but once the caregiver understands basic visual and auditory memory training principles, she can create training activities during the normal daily routine.

The first principle to keep in mind with all perceptual skill training is to keep the stimuli presented and the responses required within the same sensory modality. What this means is that when you are training visual perceptual skills, you must present only visual stimuli and require only motor responses, such as pointing, marking, and drawing. When you train auditory perceptual skills, only auditory stimuli are presented and only verbal responses are required. Notice in the examples of visual and auditory memory games presented below that this principle is followed. This works best with 30–36-month-old children.

A good example of visual memory training is the game called "concentration." Children as young as nine months can play simple versions of this game. It is played by placing pairs of identical visual images spread out upside down on a flat surface (playing cards can be used, but pairs of simple pictures are preferable for younger children. The goal is to turn over one card and then find the duplicate on the next card turned over. When the child is correct in matching the duplicate, he or she keeps the cards and turns over two more cards until two are turned that do not match. Cards must be replaced face down in the same position when they don't match. When a child misses matching two cards, it is the next child's or caregiver's turn.

You can see that this game teaches visual memory of position, sequence, and number of units of storage, and it requires only visual stimuli and motor responses. To begin teaching a child, you can use only four cards (two matching pairs) and build up to as many pairs as the children can retain.

A good example of auditory memory training is the popular game called "telephone." The simplest version is played with two people. One person starts a list and the other person repeats the list and adds an item. For example, the caregiver might start by saying, "Jane went to the store and bought bread." The child might add, "Jane went to the store and bought bread and milk." The game continues with each person adding an item until the child cannot remember all the items in sequence (let's hope the caregiver doesn't forget first). This game becomes a lot of fun with a group of children who sit in a circle and whisper the list to the next person, adding an item. This simple game teaches auditory memory of sequence, number of units of storage, and length of storage to recall, and fulfills the training principle of requiring only auditory stimuli and verbal responses.

The caregiver should be creative in designing visual memory and auditory memory tasks and games for children during the normal daily routine. By providing memory training, the caregiver can enhance development of these essential perceptual skills.

Tool 3. Discrimination Training

Once infants and toddlers have some sustained focal attention and visual and auditory memory skills, the caregiver can undertake systematic instruction in visual discrimination and auditory discrimination. Visual discrimination is an essential perceptual skill necessary to perceive part-whole relationships, details in visual images, and fine discriminations necessary for letter and word recognition. Auditory discrimination is an essential perceptual skill to perceive subtle differences in sounds occurring in language, such as "puh" compared with "buh." Discrimination skills develop from perception of gross differences between visual and auditory stimuli to finer and more subtle differences. The caregiver should start discrimination training with young infants systematically as part of the regular daily routine.

In addition to keeping stimuli and responses within the same sensory modality (i.e., visual stimuli with motor responses and auditory stimuli with verbal responses), children must learn two basic concepts for discrimination training: same and different. Starting with young toddlers, the caregiver should present many examples of visual and auditory stimulus pairs that are the same, and other pairs that are grossly different, pointing out and verbalizing to the child the pairs that are the same and the ones that are different. For example, when feeding the baby, the caregiver might hold up two identical bottles or spoons and say, "See, these are the same," and then hold up a knife and spoon or bottle and cup and say, "See, these are different." Within a short time of making these "same-different" comparisons, the caregiver can ask the baby to point to a pair that is the same, and most children can accurately pick the same pair from the different pair. The same procedure should be used with pairs of auditory sounds that are identical and others that differ grossly.

Once same-different concepts are understood, the caregiver should systematically move from gross visual and auditory differences between stimuli, pointing out the characteristics that differ, to stimuli with less obvious differences. For example, the caregiver might point out the visual differences in outline and details between a ball and a box, saying to the baby, "See, these are different because one is round [pointing] and one is square [pointing]. The caregiver can systematically progress to harder discriminations until the child can accurately discriminate subtle differences in letter forms and sounds, such as lowercase "b" and "d" and the sounds "buh" and "duh."

Auditory discrimination training is done like visual training except that auditory sounds are used and verbal responses are required (or supplied for preverbal infants). Start with sounds that are grossly different (e.g., car horn and soft bell), and discuss the characteristics that make the sounds different. Systematically progress until the child can accurately discriminate sound differences in letter sounds and words.

Tool 4. Association Training

After some skills in sustained focal attention, visual and auditory memory, and discrimination are learned, the caregiver can undertake visual association and auditory association training. Visual association is an essential perceptual skill for combining objects, letters in words, spelling, and arithmetic computation. Auditory association is an essential perceptual skill for language development and the use of phonics in word pronunciation. Association skills develop from consistent, repeated presentation of pairs of stimuli and can be systematically taught to infants and toddlers as part of the normal daily routine.

Keep stimuli and responses within the same sensory modality (i.e., visual stimuli with motor responses and auditory stimuli with verbal responses), and teach children that "A goes with B" by repeatedly presenting pairs of visual stimuli and pairs of auditory stimuli that are naturally found together in the environment. This is accomplished by repeatedly presenting pairs of stimuli, pointing to them and saying, "See, this chair goes with this table" and the like. When performing visual association training, do not use the word labels, and only use the word labels without visual images when performing auditory association training.

After several pairings of visual stimuli, the caregiver can point to one of the objects (chair) and ask the child to point to the one that goes with it, thereby making training a game. As soon as language begins to develop, the same game can be played by associating pairs of words (e.g., "What goes with chair?").

Both visual association and auditory association training systematically proceed from associations of concrete objects in the environment to more abstract and complex associations, such as lowercase letter forms and sounds of letters. The goal of training is to help young children accurately associate uppercase and lowercase letters, letter combinations that form common words, and sounds of letters with their names (e.g., "What are the sounds for the letter A?").

Perceptual skill training should usually be done in a fun, game-like atmosphere as part of the normal daily routine, but some children require more individualized training in a one-to-one setting. When the caregiver identifies a child who has significant difficulty learning perceptual skills after individualized training has been conducted, the parents should be notified and the child should be referred to an appropriate outside professional, such as a language specialist or psychologist, for further evaluation and treatment.

Auditory-Visual Association Training (Hear-See Games)

The one essential cross-modality perceptual skill necessary for basic visual and auditory language development is auditory-visual (or visual-auditory) association. The essence of letter and word recognition, spelling, and arithmetic computation is the association of visual symbols (letter or number form) with auditory sounds (letter sound or number name). Auditory-visual association begins with naming and labeling (Tool 1, Cognitive Development). In addition to enhancing concept development with infants and toddlers, naming and labeling visual images trains auditory-visual association skills.

The caregiver should begin training with young infants by directing the child's visual focal attention to an object and saying, "See this is a . . . (chair, bottle, etc.)." Concept development is enhanced through demonstrating and discussing functions visual characteristics, and other salient qualities of the object. Repeated presentations of auditory-visual pairs should be done over time to help the child associate the auditory name with the visual image. As soon as the child begins to use words, hear-see games can be played. In these games, the caregiver supplies either the name ("chair") and the child points to the object or visual image, or the caregiver points to the visual image and the child supplies the verbal name.

Training progresses from real objects in the environment to pictures of objects, then to common forms and shapes (e.g., circle, square), to uppercase and lowercase letter forms. When associating letter forms with letter sounds, make sure repeated presentations result in consistent accuracy with one sound before introducing a second sound for the same letter form. For example, always present the same visual symbol of A and present the sound "aee" each time until the child consistently picks the correct symbol when the sound is presented or verbalizes the correct sound when the symbol is presented. All 26 letter forms should be associated with one sound before introducing a second sound for letters. For example, once the child has accurately associated correct sound-symbol pairs for all 26 letters, present the second sound for letters having more than one sound (e.g., ah = A, eh = E).

When auditory-visual association training is conducted in a systematic manner, some children become ready to combine letter sounds and symbols into simple words before the age of three years. However, the caregiver *should not* make academic skills a program goal since most children require more skill development and maturity in other areas, such as emotional and social areas. Auditory-visual association is the most important skill for language development and basic academic tasks, but the caregiver should help children obtain sufficient visual and auditory focal attention, memory, discrimination, and single-modality association skills before auditory-visual association is emphasized in the normal daily routine.

SUMMARY: YOUR WORK

Your work with children is different from custodial care. Custodial care is simply the physical maintenance of children. Your work means applying meaning to what you do. Meaning involves consciously being emotionally present with children. It is an end toward which you direct your attention and gives form to your activity.

Your work is that for which you strive (Figure 5–7). It is why you aspire to learn. You should not work independently with children until you are ready. This comes after the classes, the instruction, the theories, the papers, and the supervised training you receive. It comes with your growing desire to help, and it comes after you have changed your positive intention into a firm educational base of understanding. It continues because of the care you give yourself and your appreciation of even the

Figure 5–7 The caregivers observe when the infant is able to stand with help.

smallest successes, because, as you work with children, you see children grow and change, and how you make a difference in their world. Your work is important because it is your way of making the world a better place, one child at a time. Your work is love of your profession.

Key Terms

auditory-visual association

baby signing

behavior shaping

boundary

calibrating

Care Sheets

concept formation

discipline

labeling

naming

nonverbal signal

ORAOM

pacing

positive perspective

representational system

reward

ruing

self-soothing

shepherding

systematic relaxation

time-in

time-out

time-sample

turn-taking

CASE STUDY

Eric, a four-and-a-half-month-old, is lying on the floor when he starts to cry. His child care specialist, Audrey, picks him up. She "eats" his tummy and he laughs. She holds him up in the air and he smiles. She gets his bottle, sits in a chair, and feeds him. Eric gazes at Audrey and smiles between sips.

Grasping her finger, Eric looks around the room. Audrey stands him in her lap, holds his hands to pull him to and fro, and kisses him. He laughs. She holds him while he dances and laughs. He watches Audrey's mouth and responds as she talks to him. He leans on her shoulder and burps as he fingers the afghan on the back of the chair.

The many child care specialist responsibilities are accomplished through interactions with the people and environment in the child care setting. Several educational tools have been discussed to help develop the knowledge and strategies needed to become a good observer, recorder, assessor, organizer, manager, and facilitator to support warm, emotional relationships and enhance the physical, cognitive, and learning skill development of infants and toddlers.

Audrey has a culturally diverse group of two-year-olds that she cares for full-time on a daily basis. In order to enhance development of each child in her group, she must keep herself well organized and conduct activities in a consistent manner. She uses ORAOM with each child and her group as a whole to accomplish this difficult task. She uses different tools for various children who require help in each of the five major developmental areas.

Physical development. All children receive a lot of catch the child being good, but Cathy is a "runner" who requires circle of safety and shepherding. Tawna is very shy, so shadowing helps her feel secure. Darian has tantrums and acting-out behavior and so he often requires the use of behavior-limiting steps.

Emotional development. When Audrey gets tired she makes sure she uses changing of the guard to help the children. She does a lot of ruing with Josh, who has trouble separating from his mother; she gives inside self/outside self attention to Jane, who tends to be withdrawn; and she models self-soothing with Sammy, who does not get enough attention at home. Audrey does structured activities with her group on labeling and expressing feelings and emotion management on a daily basis.

Social development. Tawna requires that Audrey do a lot of positive perspective because her parents tend to be critical of her. Audrey also is establishing a good working relationships with Abdul, a new group member, by using rapport building. She requires Jerry and Lisa to do a lot of mirroring and I talk with each other since they are twins who fight often. She focuses the attention of the group on activities that teach respectful is successful and cooperation versus competition.

Cognitive Development. Since her group is learning language, Audrey plays many naming and labeling games with them, but Tawna and Abdul are almost nonverbal, so she uses a form of baby signing with them. She presents activities three times a week that are designed to teach children time orientation and cause-effect, and she has units of things to be grouped for concept formation activities.

(continued)

Learning skill development. Audrey's group needs help with their perceptual and language skill development, so she spends 30 minutes each day in a structured activity for memory training, discrimination training, association training, or auditory-visual association training. Tawna receives focal attention training individually twice a week since she has difficulty screening out noises during group activities.

Audrey assesses her children individually every three months using a Developmental Profile and Prescription. She is excited to see her children grow in many areas as the result of the tools she uses on a daily basis.

1. Determine which of Audrey's children have the most developmental weaknesses. Support your answer with examples.
2. How does use of the tools in this case study support the CDA Goals and Guidelines?
3. Explain why the fact that Josh is having separation issues from his mother might require Audrey to use a lot of ruing with him.

Student Activities

1. Identify your strengths and weaknesses in the caregiver roles. Write a growth plan for yourself.
2. Observe one infant and one toddler for 10 minutes each. Use narrative description to record what you see and hear. Categorize the behaviors of each.
3. Using the record of Leslie in the play yard, list her behaviors using the following categories:
   a. physical
   b. emotional
   c. social
   d. cognitive
   e. language
4. Define what conscious caregiving means to you.
5. Define affective education.
6. Observe two caregivers, each for 10 minutes. Tally a mark in the appropriate category in the following chart each time you observe the caregiver assuming that role.

	Caregiver 1	Caregiver 2
observer		
caregiver		
self		
recorder		
message board		
sheets, notes		
assessor		
caregiver		
child		
organizer		
plans		
schedules		
materials		
environment		
manager		
time		
space		
materials		
people		
behavior		
facilitator		
provider		
nurturance		
assistance		
information		
questioner		
interpreter		

7. List four available community resources and explain how each can serve your child care program.

———————————————————————————————

———————————————————————————————

———————————————————————————————

———————————————————————————————

Chapter Review

1. Review Chapter 4, The 3A's: The Master Tools of Child Care.
2. Review mastery.
3. List four personal characteristics you can use as a caregiver in the chart below. Give an example of why each is important.

Caregiver Characteristics	Why This Is Important
1	
2	
3	
4	

4. How can you teach what you have learned in this chapter to others?

5. How can you use observation in a child care program?

6. How can you become a more conscious caregiver?

References

Acredolo, L., & Goodwyn, S. (2000). *Baby minds.* Davis, CA: University of California Press.

American Academy of Pediatrics. (1996). *Recommendations for day care centers for infants and children.* Evanston, IL: Author.

Castellanos, L., & Douville-Watson. (1997). *Assessing infants.* Anaheim, CA: National Association for the Education of Young Children Conference.

Child Development Associate National Credentialing Program. (1992). *Child development associate assessment system and competency standards infant/toddler caregivers in center-based programs.* Washington, DC: Author.

Douville-Watson, L. (1997). *Conscious caregiving.* Bayville, NY: Instructional Press.

Douville-Watson, L., & Watson, M. (2001). *Focal attention training programs.* Glen Cove, NY: Instructional Press.

Douville-Watson, L., & Watson, M. (1997). *CAP: Childcare accountability programs.* Glen Cove, NY: Instructional Press.

Douville-Watson, L., & Watson, M. (1997) *Childcare accountability programs (CAPS) and establishing a positive learning environment.* Anaheim, CA: National Association for the Education of Young Children Conference.

Honig, A. S. (1988). *Baby moves: Relation to learning.* Washington, DC: International Early Childhood Conferences.

Honig, A. S., & Lally, J. R. (1981). Infant Caregiving: A Design for Training: ABC I: Assessing the Behaviors of Caregivers (With Young Infants) and ABC II: Assessing the Behaviors of Caregivers (With Older Infants). Syracuse, NY: Syracuse University Press.

Infant Welfare Society of Evanston (Illinois) Inc. Care Sheets. Not dated.

Leipzig, J. (1986). *Fostering prosocial development in infants and toddlers.* New York: Bank Street College.

MacLean, P. D. (1990). *The triune brain in evolution, role in paleacerebral functions.* New York: Plenum Press.

Riback, P. (2000). *Healthy kids online.* Albany, NY: American Academy of Pediatricians Publications.

Skinner, E., & Belmont, M. J. (1993). Motivation in the classroom: The reciprocal effect of teacher behavior and student engagement across the school year. *Journal of Educational Psychology, 85,* 571–581.

Spradley, J. P. (1980). *Participant observation.* New York: Holt, Rinehart & Winston.

Addition Resources

Council for Early Childhood Professional Recognition. (1992). *Council model for CDA assessment and training.* Washington, DC: Author.

Coopersmith, S. (1967). *The antecedents of self-esteem.* San Francisco: W. H. Freeman.

Douville-Watson, L. (1993). Lecture series II, *3A's of infant development.* New York: Instructional Press.

Nassau County Coalition on Child Abuse and Neglect. 1993. Hempstead, New York.

Helpful Web Sites

Association for the Benefit of Child Development Perceptual, cognitive, language, and social skills development. http://www.abcdonline.org/

Child Development Institute Intellectual and language development. http://www.childdevelopmentinfo.com/

Child Development Psychology Index Emotional development theories. http://psychology.about.com/cs/child

Child Development Through Time and Transition Physical, perceptual, and cognitive development. (Go to Discipline Finder, then to Psychology.) http://www.prenhall.com

KinderStart—Emotional/Social Child Development KinderStart is an indexed directory and search engine forcused on children 0 to 7. http://www.kinderstart.com/childdevelopment

National Network for Child Care (NNCC) Child Development Database http://www.nncc.org/ChildDev/childdev.page.html

ProTeacher! Child Development Research and Resources Ages and stages—physical, intellectual, and emotional development—during the first year. http://www.proteacher.com

The Whole Child ABC's of child care in physical, social, emotional, and cognitive areas. http://www.pbs.org/wholechild/abc

For additional infant and toddler resources, visit our Web site at http://www.earlychilded.delmar.com

PART *II*

Establishing a Positive Learning Environment

The four chapters in this section integrate the skills, principles, and theories learned in Part I into functional settings for care. Settings for care include communicating with and using community resources for families, understanding the variety of physical settings in which child care occurs, preparing positive indoor and outdoor environments, and designing and implementing curricula for infants and toddlers.

This section provides the caregiver with the tools necessary to assess individual children using Developmental Profiles, establish goals for growth using Developmental Prescriptions, and design and structure specific experiences and activities for each child and the group as a whole. In addition, the reader will be able to assess parent and family strengths and weaknesses so that communication with parents can enhance the growth and development of children at home.

Infants and toddlers help to develop their own curriculum by engaging energetically in activities that contribute to their growth. Through sensitivity to each child's unique needs, family strengths, cultural traditions, and community resources, a positive learning environment can be established and maintained for each child in care.

Communicating with Parents and Staff

6

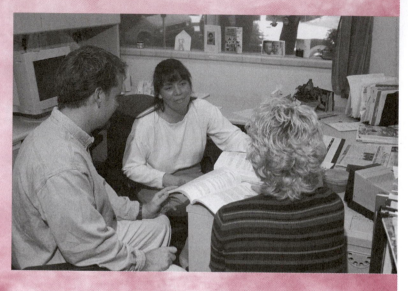

Objectives

After reading this chapter, you should be able to:

■ Develop procedures for informal and formal communication with parents.

■ Analyze the working relationships and responsibilities of the staff with whom the caregiver is working.

■ Analyze the caregiver's own performance in parent and staff relationships.

■ Understand the active listening process and how it differs from mirroring.

Chapter Outline

Introduction

Communicating Successfully with Parents, Staff, and Children

Communication Situations

Resources for Parents and Staff

INTRODUCTION

Caregivers and parents have a common goal: to provide high-quality experiences for children. In order to achieve this goal there must be communication between caregivers and parents and among the caregiving staff. Communication is a two-way process. It requires both active listening and effective expression of thoughts and feelings.

The attitudes caregivers and parents have toward each other are reflected through their communication process. The nonverbal, emotional messages that are sent in the questions asked and the statements made will either help or hinder successful communication.

In order to be an effective caregiver, it is necessary to communicate well with children, parents, staff, other professionals, and the community. You have already learned the skill of rapport building, which requires calibrating and pacing the other person's behaviors and feelings (Chapter 5). This chapter teaches skills of Active Listening, Mirroring, and the use of "I statements" in order to effectively communicate with other people in a sensitive and accepting style. Practicing these skills will help you listen to and understand others and be able to express yourself so that other people will understand and accept what you say.

COMMUNICATING SUCCESSFULLY WITH PARENTS, STAFF, AND CHILDREN

In Chapter 4 we discussed the 3A's of child care and how they affect communication between caregiver and child.

The following are excerpts from F.A.R.E. (Family Actualization through Research and Education, Actualization, Inc.; Douville-Watson & Watson, 1993) on a powerful communication technique called Active Listening.

The following communication diagram shows the general communication process. A "sender" (A) sends a message verbally and nonverbally to a "receiver" (B) who interprets the message and gives the sender feedback as to what the message means to the receiver.

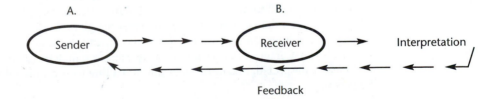

I Statements versus You Statements

As we discussed in previous sections on ego and super-ego development and self-talk, we conduct internal dialogues between the I voice or self and the You voice or super-ego. We also communicate to other people from the perspective of expressing our own thoughts and feelings through **I Statements**, or giving advice or judgments about the other person by making **You Statements**.

I Statements usually start with the word "I" and express responsibility for our own perceptions without judging the other person. For example, "I am angry" is an I Statement because it expresses a feeling without blaming another person. You Statements are often disrespectful and tell the other person how he or she is thinking, feeling, or behaving. You Statements often start with the word "you" and offer advice or an opinion about the other person. For example, "You make me angry" is a You Statement because it offers an opinion about the other person (he or she is doing or saying something wrong) and it makes the other person responsible for the speaker's feeling (anger).

When you want the other person to feel accepted and understood, make I Statements rather than You Statements. I Statements are respectful and take responsibility for the speaker's thoughts, feelings, and behaviors. You Statements, on the other hand, offer opinions, advice, and judgments about the other person and often close off further communication.

We can also make disguised I and You Statements. Active listening responses, which are discussed below, are an example of disguised I Statements. When we give feedback to a sender that clearly takes responsibility for our own perceptions and map of the world, we are making I Statements. For example, if a person sends the message, "I can't stand Mary, she is always complaining," a good active listening response might be, "It sounds like Mary's complaining is making you feel angry." Notice that, although neither I nor You were used, the feedback takes responsibility for the receiver's perception by using the words "It sounds (to me) like . . ." without blaming or criticizing the sender. Active listening and I Statements keep communication open by giving nonjudgmental feedback, which allows the sender to confirm that the message was understood ("That's right; I really get angry with her.") or correct the message ("Well, I don't really get angry; just a little annoyed.").

Disguised You Statements sometimes sound like I Statements and may even start with the word "I," but they always end up judging or giving advice to the sender. For example, "I'm angry because you did that" is a disguised You Statement because, even though it starts with "I," it blames and judges the other person.

Caregivers need to practice daily using I Statements with children, parents, and colleagues. Once you master making I Statements and giving active listening feedback, other people will respond by feeling open, relaxed, and understood in their interactions with you. Caregivers who communicate using You Statements cause other people to feel disrespected, uncomfortable, and unwilling to continue interactions with the person.

Active Listening: The "How" in Communication

Most common communication errors can be avoided by applying a technique called **Active Listening**. This technique, which was developed primarily by psychologist Carl Rogers, has been put into very practical form for teachers and parents in the parent training program, called F.A.R.E. (Douville-Watson & Watson, 1993). The most important skill in active listening is very simply to "feed back" the deeper feeling message (not the words) of the sender in the words of the receiver. This simple definition of active listening requires further explanation because, although it may sound simple, it takes practice to learn to give deeper feedback effectively.

Active listening differs from most common types of communication in the kind of feedback given to the sender. The type of feedback most commonly given is a "reaction" to the word messages of the sender. When we give reactionary feedback, we most often close off the communication process because we become emotionally involved in the words of the message. Common reactionary feedback messages are "You shouldn't say that!" "I don't agree with you!" "You're wrong!" and "I don't want to hear that kind of talk!"

Active listening, on the other hand, involves objectively listening, in a nondefensive way, for the deeper message of the sender and then giving "reiterating" rather than "reactionary" feedback. Rather than reacting to the words of the sender, the active listener interprets the entire message of the sender and gives it back to the sender.

Active listening feedback allows the sender to affirm, reject, or clarify his message. By continuing to feed back the total message of the sender, the receiver can help the sender clarify the problem and, in most cases, arrive at his own solution.

An active listener also looks for nonverbal "body language" messages. The look on a person's face, the position of the body, and what the person does with his or her hands and arms can help you to understand the full message on the deepest level. Nonverbal behavior, as well as words, feelings, and attitudes, combine to transmit the complete, deep message.

Although this technique may sound simple enough to learn, it requires active listening practice because most of us have learned to give reactionary feedback, particularly to children. With practice, however, caregivers will find the rewards of active listening worth the effort it takes to master the technique.

Here are some ways to test how well you are communicating with others.

1. Listen to the way you now respond to people. If you catch yourself reacting to the words of messages instead of the deeper meaning, you are "just talking." An active listener listens for the whole, deep message, including the words, feelings, attitudes, and behaviors.
2. An active listener never judges, criticizes, or blames another and listens for deeper feelings because feelings can never be wrong! Since the active listener looks for the deeper message, most feedback starts with words such as "It sounds like . . . ," "You seem to feel . . . ," "I hear you saying . . . ," and other phrases that reflect the sender's feelings.
3. An active listener never responds to a message with advice or personal feelings. The idea of communication is to completely understand what the other person thinks and feels. This skill may be more difficult for caregivers to learn in their relationships with children in their charge because adults have so much more experience than children and it is hard to accept the fact that children can arrive at their own solutions to problems. Adults tend to want to teach and advise children before they have completely understood the whole message that children are trying to communicate. One of the causes of the well-known "generation gap" is that children learn that adults don't understand them and don't "know where they're at." Even young children will furnish good solutions to problems if adults have

the patience to "hear them out" and give back the meaning of the messages they hear and experience without teaching or advising.

4. An active listener only adds information to a message when the other person directly asks for it and after that person has completely expressed the entire message. You will know you have received the entire message when you hear real feelings and concern about what to do. At this point, feedback such as "Have you thought about what you can do?" or "How would you solve this?" will give the child a chance to ask for advice or begin problem solving on his or her own.

Mirroring

A simple but very effective technique for establishing rapport and making sure that the other person understands your messages, and that you understand theirs, is **mirroring** (Hendrix, 1993). Mirroring simply means repeating exactly what is said without adding or interpreting any of the speaker's words. When you communicate with staff, parents, or children, it can be very helpful to ask the person to repeat exactly what you say before they give their own response. When the other person mirrors you before responding, and you mirror them before responding, a sense of trust and understanding quickly develops that is very hard to obtain any other way. By mirroring each other, mutual respect and understanding is quickly developed. Mirroring is especially effective when communicating with others from cultural and/or language backgrounds different from your own.

Try mirroring with your family or friends first so you get the idea of how it works. The only words you are allowed to change in mirroring are personal pronouns, so if the other person says "I am happy", your mirroring response is "You are happy." One final rule in mirroring is that each speaker uses "I language" rather than "You language." "I language" starts with the word "I" and results in the speaker taking responsibility for his or her own thoughts, feelings, and behaviors. "You language," on the other hand, usually blames other people and stops the speaker from taking responsibility for him- or herself. By using "I language" when speaking and mirroring each other before you respond, you can prevent most conflicts and misunderstanding.

COMMUNICATION SITUATIONS

Active Listening to Parents

Active listening helps caregivers understand parents as they express their concerns and raise questions about parenting. Parents are often isolated from other support systems and need the caregiver to listen to them and help them come up with solutions (Figure 6–1). Active listening and mirroring helps overcome language and cultural barriers as well (Lally, 1992).

Parents may want the caregiver to agree with them or reassure them, to confirm or reject ideas and pressures from family and friends. For example, Mabel rushed in one morning with her son and said, "I called my mother last night and told her I went back to work this week and she had a fit. She said it was too soon and that right now my place was at home." Listen to Mabel's words, her tone of voice; read her nonverbal cues, her facial expressions and degree of tenseness. She may be telling you that she is feeling frustrated and guilty, or she may be stating her mother's view while feeling

Figure 6–1 Parents and caregivers need to communicate to ensure the best care for the child.

fairly comfortable with her own choice of going back to work. You must listen to the whole story (words, tone, cues) to interpret accurately what Mabel is telling you.

Parents express their desires for their children. Phyllis said, "I want Velma to be happy. It bothers me to see her cry when I leave." Arlene stated, "I want Pearl to get used to babies because my baby is due next month." Listen to what the parent is saying about the child and about the parent's own needs.

Actively listen to parents so that you will fully understand what care they expect you to provide. Some parents have very definite ideas and will tell you about them. Other parents do not say anything until they disagree with something, and then they may express frustration or be angry with you. Give feedback about the parents' emotions, as well as the words they say to you.

Parents tell you much information about their children and themselves. Details about what the child does at home are needed by the caregiver each morning (Figure 6–2). Listen carefully and record the information as soon as possible (see Chapter 9, Message Board).

Sharing with Parents

Information Parents need information about the daily experiences their child has in your care. The Message Board and Care Sheets (see Chapter 9) help organize and record important things the child has done to share with the parent. Special experiences, like the child's excitement about a visiting rabbit, may go into the written record or the caregiver may tell the parent.

The child's rate and pattern of development should be shared with parents. Refer to the child's Developmental Profile (see Appendix B) to focus on recent developments and identify developmental tasks the child may soon be mastering.

Figure 6–2 Parent and caregiver assist the child in making the transition between home and the child care program.

Share ideas for stimulating the child's development, emphasizing the difference between facilitating and pushing the child. Parents are often very interested in written directions for and drawings of age-appropriate activities and homemade toys (see Chapter 9–16).

Share information relating to parental concerns about the child. Mabel may be interested in information relating to the effect of child care on her two-month-old child. Phyllis may be ready for information about separation anxiety. Arlene may need information to help her understand that Pearl's sharing Mommy with the new baby involves much more than practice in getting used to babies. Changing sleeping and eating patterns and toilet-training are also areas about which parents frequently raise questions with caregivers.

Parents need information about the child care program. Before the child is admitted, the program director shares program goals, policies, and a description of the daily program and the practical use of Developmental Prescriptions with parents. Many programs will include a developmental screening of the child as part of the initial evaluation of the incoming child. This will help guide caregivers as they make their decisions about program implementation. Many situations arise that parents need to clarify and discuss with caregivers. For example, Sal wants his 23-month-old daughter Gabriele to stop using her fingers when she eats. The caregivers can help Sal by sharing development information with him, assuring him that eating with fingers is perfectly normal at this age and use of utensils will come later when fine motor control is further developed.

Feelings Caregiving involves feelings and emotions. Parents want to know that you are concerned about their child and about them. In a variety of ways, let parents know that you like and respect their child. Parents look for caregivers who accept and like their child and who provide emotional security.

Share the excitement of the child's new developments with the parent. The first time you see children pulling themselves up on the table leg, teetering two steps, holding utensils, riding a tyke bike, turning book pages, hugging a friend, asking to go to the toilet, or catching a ball, you should be excited and pleased with their accomplishments. When you share these experiences with parents, let them know how excited you are.

Express sympathy for the child or parent in situations where there is hurt. Express empathy with the parent in some of the trying, frustrating experiences they encounter with children.

Expectations Share your goals and expectations of the child care program with parents. Your casual statements may take on more meaning than written goal statements. One caregiver described a situation in which she encouraged a child's independence: "We want to help children become as independent as they can, so when Louella resisted my helping her take off her bib, I let her try to take it off by herself. She got stuck once, and I helped her lift one arm out, and then she could do the rest by herself. Her big smile and chatter showed me how pleased she was."

Parents are interested in what you expect of yourself as a caregiver. What kinds of things do you do? How committed are you? How friendly are you? Do you think you are more important than parents? Do you extend and supplement parents or do you expect to supplant them? You communicate these expectations through your words, attitudes, mannerisms, and interactions with children and parents.

What do you expect of the children in your care? A child care program emphasizing the development of the whole child and individuality among children is supported by caregivers who facilitate that development. Assure parents that development does not follow a rigid schedule and is not identical among children. Parents often compare their child's development with another child's and gloat or fret at what they see. Caregivers who show that they believe children behave differently within a broad range of normal activity communicate to parents that adults can challenge children without putting harmful pressure on them.

Caregivers expect many things of parents. Some expectations you may express; others you should keep to yourself. You might expect parents to

- love and like their child.
- want to hear about special occurrences in their child's day.
- want to learn more about their developing child.
- be observant of the child's health or illness.
- be willing to share information about the child with the caregiver.
- respect the caregiver.

Some parents will not meet your expectations. Because caregiving occurs in the family as well as in the child care program, you will need to resolve your differences with the child's parents.

You may need to change your expectations of parents. We speak of accepting children as they are, so we need to take the same attitude toward parents. They come to the child care program because they need care for their child outside the home. They usually are not looking for situations that place additional demands and expectations on them as parents. So long as parents abide by the policies relating to health, attendance, and fee payment, they are doing their part to support the program. Information to help parents grow can be offered but not forced upon them. You may increase your awareness of the unique situation the parent faces by simply actively listening to them without judgments.

Involving Parents

In Decision-Making   Some programs involve parents in decision-making. Many not-for-profit child care centers have policy boards that include parents. These boards may make recommendations and decisions about center policy. Sometimes parents even serve on boards that make administrative decisions about hiring and firing staff and selecting curricula. However, few family child care homes and for-profit child care centers involve parents in decision-making about policy, staff, or curricula.

Parents of infants and toddlers must be involved in some decisions relating to their child's care. The parent or pediatrician selects the infant's milk or formula; the caregiver does not make that decision. Parent and caregiver must share information about the child's eating and sleeping schedules. The length of time from afternoon pick-up to mealtime to bedtime varies among families. Since late afternoon naps or snacks may improve or disrupt evening family time, parents should discuss what schedule is best for the child and family. Toilet-training must be coordinated between parent and caregiver. Both share information about the appropriateness of timing, the failures and successes of the child, and the decision to discontinue or continue toilet-training. If a parent insists that toilet-training be started or continued when you think the child is not ready, share with the parent information about the necessary development of the child before training can occur. Tell the parent about actions children take when they are showing an interest in or a readiness for toilet-training. Share with the parent the harmful effects on children of consistent failures and parental pressures. When the child is ready for toilet-training, the procedures at home and in child care must be the same so that the child does not become confused. Reassure the parent that you do not mind changing their child's diapers. Emphasize that this is another time for them to spend relating positively eye-to-eye.

With Children   Most parents of infants and toddlers in child care are employed. Therefore, parental involvement during the child care day is often limited to arrival and pick-up time. The parent can help the child take off a coat or unpack supplies when leaving the child in the morning, and can share with the caregiver information about the child's night, health, or special experiences. At pick-up time the caregiver initiates conversations about the child's experiences and projects during the day, while the parent helps the infant or toddler make the transition back to being part of the family by hugging the child or helping put on outdoor clothes.

Parent Assessment and Education

Within the past few years, there has been a growing need to quantify the skills and characteristics necessary to be a competent parent. Social and governmental interest in family values, increased laws regarding parent responsibilities, and the need for better parent education have necessitated identification, definition, and assessment of the skills that comprise competent parenting. In response to these needs, instruments to measure parent competence have been designed, most of which are checklists and survey tools with questionable theoretical and research foundation.

A set of scales called the **National Parenting Scales: NPS,** Experimental Edition (Watson, 1996) have a sound theoretical and research basis in the CDA Competency Goals and Objectives. The NPS assess parents in the essential skills included in Table 6–1 in addition to personality characteristics, environmental resources, and interactional dynamics between parent and children.

TABLE 6–1   *PARENT COMPETENCY GOALS AND FUNCTIONAL AREAS*

I. Establish and maintain a safe, healthy living environment.
1. Safe: Parent provides a safe environment to prevent injuries.
2. Healthy: Parent promotes good health and nutrition and provides an environment that contributes to the prevention of illness.
3. Learning Environment: Parent uses spatial relationships, materials, and routines as resources for constructing an interesting, secure, and enjoyable environment that encourages play and exploration.

II. Advance physical and intellectual competence.
4. Physical: Parent provides a variety of equipment, activities, and opportunities to promote the physical development of children.
5. Cognitive: Parent provides activities and opportunities that encourage curiosity, exploration, problem-solving, and responsibilities appropriate to the developmental levels and learning styles of children.
6. Communication: Parent actively communicates with children and provides opportunities and support for children to understand, acquire, and use verbal and nonverbal means of communicating thoughts and feelings.
7. Creative: Parent provides opportunities that stimulate children to play with sound, rhythm, language, materials, space, and ideas used in individual ways to express creative skills and abilities.

III. Support social and emotional development and provide positive guidance.
8. Self: Parent provides physical and emotional security and helps each child to know, accept, and take pride in himself or herself and develop a sense of independence and self-esteem.
9. Social: Parent helps each child feel accepted in groups, helps children learn to communicate and get along with others, and encourages feelings of empathy and mutual respect among children and adults.
10. Guidance: Parent provides a supportive environment in which children can learn and practice acceptable behaviors as individuals and in groups.

IV. Maintain positive and productive relationships within the family and community.
11. Relationships: Parent maintains open, friendly, honest, and cooperative interactions with each family member, encourages involvement, and supports relationships with all family members and members of the community.

V. Ensure a well-run, purposeful home, responsive to individual needs.
12. Management: The parent is a manager who uses all available resources to ensure effective home operation. Competence in organizing, planning, and cooperating with others is demonstrated.

VI. Commitment to constructive family values.
13. Family Values: Parent makes decisions based on knowledge of sound childhood principles and practices, and sets limits and values that are in the best interest of each child as a regular priority.

A general requirement of excellent child care involves a team approach between parent, the child care program, and community resources. Initial research found that a group of 80 parents entering children in child care who took the NPS worked more closely with Child Care Specialists and program goals than did parents not taking NPS (Watson, 1997). When combined with Developmental Profiles and Prescriptions for children, assessment of parent strengths and weaknesses appears to result in a cooperative team approach consistent with child care program goals.

Four Scales were developed for each of three Developmental Levels based on the ages of the children in care.

Scale I. Parenting Skills Scales: an objective multiple-choice scale measuring the essential skills in the 6 Goals and 13 Functional Areas listed in Table 6–1.

Scale II. Family Values Scale: a projective assessment measuring social and moral judgement and values applied to conflict situations with children.

Scale III. Home Environment Study: a structured study of the home environment from the perspective of children for developmentally appropriate care.

Scale IV. Parent/Child Observation and Interview: a structured observation and interview of parents with children which evaluates interaction and communication dynamics.

Quantitative results from all four scales are combined to establish a Parent Profile and a Parent Prescription detailing individual parent strengths and weaknesses and providing procedures and resources to improve caregiving skills.

Because the NPS are available in a Self Administered and a Professional Version and provide Developmental Levels from birth to 18 years, they can be used easily by the caregiver or child care program to help parents understand their parenting strengths and weaknesses and to ensure that developmentally appropriate activities and practices are continued in the home setting. Since parents can take the Scales home to complete, they are not threatened, as they might be if they were "tested."

Results from initial research using the NPS reveal four **parenting styles** that the caregiver can use to communicate effectively with parents. In the Competent Style, parents use appropriate goals and objectives. The Selfless Style of parenting involves the parents' not considering their own needs, not establishing appropriate limits, abdicating inappropriate responsibilities to the children, and lacking self-respect. In the Controlling Style, the parent is demanding or authoritarian and lacks respect and sensitivity to children's needs. In the Detached Style, the parent is not emotionally or behaviorally involved with children to an extent appropriate to the care situation.

Knowing the strengths and weaknesses of the parents in your group can help you communicate effectively and plan ways to extend the care program into the home to enhance the development of each child.

Parents need to be informed of national issues concerning child care that will affect their children, and they need to know who to write to at local, regional, and national levels to lobby for services for their children.

Parents need to be educated on how to choose a safe, developmentally correct, and growth-producing environment for their children. They need to understand the ongoing responsibilities that the caregiver has for children, what constitutes a trained or certified person, and the caregiver's level of education.

Parents should have an active relationship with their caregivers. This partnership exists in order to facilitate all the daily needs of their children.

Parents need competent parent education from someone they trust and whose experience will meaningfully affect the decisions they make. As part of that training, they need help with setting priorities to balance all areas of their lives and to help take good care of themselves and their children. They also need a designated time and place to discuss ongoing concerns with other parents of similarly aged children. They need resource materials to read, listen to, and view.

The child care facility, regardless of the type of setting, can fill all these needs. Often, a parent survey will help identify which areas should be addressed first. All the measures suggested should be practical, to help build a strong partnership between parents and caregivers.

Statistics indicate grandparents are taking care of children more than ever before. According to 1997 Children's Defense Fund, more than 1.4 million children lived with grandparents with a parent absent in the household during 1995 (Weill & Jablonski, 1997). This is a 66 percent increase since 1989.

A special invitation for grandparents who are now facing the challenge of raising grandchildren as primary caregivers should be extended, since this family situation is sometimes not evident. Some grandparents are frustrated and some are isolated. Often they try to balance the demands of working full-time and acting in the role of primary caregiver. They need encouragement and a place to confide in someone. All these factors add to grandparents' increased stress. It is understandable why these caregivers often need support.

Parent-Caregiver Conferences

It is important that **parent-caregiver conferences** have structure. Preparing an agenda and checklist, being a good listener, and keeping confidences are some of the important factors to consider (Orstein & Chapman, 1988). Consideration of differences in education, language, and cultural issues is also important (Bauette & Peterson, 1993).

Interpret each child's progress to parents within the framework of a Developmental Profile and Prescription to help parents understand and appreciate developmentally appropriate early childhood programs (Feeney & Kipinis, 1990).

Employed parents often have difficulty scheduling formal conferences. To make the most efficient use of time, plan the conference thoroughly. Identify the major purpose of the conference. If the parent requests a conference, ask what the parent's concerns are so you can prepare for the conference. If the caregiver requests the conference, tell the parent why, so the parent has time to think about it before the conference begins. Gather background information to discuss the topic. Caregiver records of observations, both formal and informal, may be helpful. Outside sources such as articles, books, pamphlets, tapes, and filmstrips may provide information for the caregiver and can be shared with the parent. You may also need to refer parents to organizations in your community or region.

Plan the conference agenda.

1. State the purpose for the conference.
2. If initiated by a parent, state your interest in listening to the parent.
   a. Actively listen to the parents.
   b. Present information that is appropriate and helpful to the discussion.

3. If the conference is initiated by the caregiver, state your information, ideas, and concerns.

   a. Actively listen to the parents' responses.

   b. Explain your points further if you think it will help the parent understand.

4. Provide additional outside information if needed.

5. Discuss the issue(s) with the parent.

6. Emphasize that both you and the parent are working together for the welfare of the child and state your future goals for the child.

Home Visits

Home visits are a regular part of Head Start programs, but few other child care programs make them. Home visits can be valuable opportunities for the parent and the caregiver to learn more about each other and the child. The caregiver can see how the parent and child relate to each other in their own home. Home visits must be planned carefully.

Identify the purpose for the visit. It is to get acquainted? Is it to gather information? Is it to work with the parent, child, or both?

Gather background information the visit requires. Do you need to take along any forms to be filled out? Will you be sharing your program goals? If so, do you have a flyer or pamphlet or will you just tell them? Are there specific problems or concerns you want to discuss? Do you have written documentation of the child's behavior to share, such as daily reports or notes, as well as resource and referral information that might be available?

When you make a home visit, you are a guest in the parent's home. You are there to listen and learn. Discuss the purpose of the conference. When you have finished talking about the issues, thank the parents for their interest, time, and hospitality, and then leave. A home visit is not a social visit.

Teenage Parents

"Kids Having Kids" is an important reality examined in a book with the same name (1996). A sufficient amount of life experience is necessary for the development of sound coping mechanisms and informed decision making, and raising children under the best of circumstances is frustrating and very difficult at times. Teenage parents have not had enough life experience to learn the valuable coping mechanisms necessary to competently deal with our extremely complex society, usually do not have family support, and almost always suffer from limited financial resources because they have not developed careers. Add the necessity to set aside childhood dreams and aspirations and place a baby's needs before their own, and it is no wonder that the large majority of teenage parents have emotional conflicts that decrease their ability to provide good parenting.

According to the Children's Defense Fund (Weill & Jablonski, 1997), "The rate of adolescent childbearing decreased in 46 states between 1991 and 1994 . . . 59.9 percent of teen births were to older teens, 37.6 percent to 15–17 year olds, and 2.5 percent to girls younger than 15." This decrease is thought to be the result of national campaigns against AIDS and the use of birth control. Even with this reduction in teenage pregnancies, nowhere is the need for a solid partnership between parents and the child care specialist more important than with teenage parents.

In order to effectively work with teen parents, the child care specialist should understand the factors that influence their parenting ability. Often mothers under 15 years of age have not received good prenatal care. A mother less than 15 years old often does not eat well or obtain regular medical care and is twice as likely to have a pre-term or low-birth-weight infant compared to a woman in her mid to late 20s. Good counseling should include a nutritional guide for teenagers, such as the following from *Food and Mood* (Somers, 1997).

Food Family	Servings/Day
Calcium-rich group	4–5
Vegetables	6–7
Fruits	4–5
Grains	8–9
Extra lean meats and legumes	4–5
Quenchers	6–8

This guide can also be recommended for young mothers using the higher servings on the scale.

Teenage parents are still not adults and need to be accepted for who they are. Whenever possible, referrals to community-based organizations that can support both the father and mother should be made. It is the responsibility of the child specialist to know what resources are available in the community.

Teenage parents need healthy concepts for parenting, including good information and role models. Information should include lessons about empty calories and good nutrition, handling finances, cleaning and organizing a home, and dealing with relationships. Good role models involve people in the community who can be of help to the new parent and increase the circle of support to the teenager. "Mothering the mother" and "parenting the parent" are increased responsibilities for the child care specialist working with teenage parents.

A role of the child care specialist is to support the positive qualities of teenage parents in their child care abilities and to highly praise their efforts. This requires setting aside time to empathize, actively listen, and mirror the young parent.

Involved teenage fathers should also be praised, encouraged, and offered options for further parent training within the community. One example is the Union Industrial Home in Trenton, New Jersey, which is a 138-year-old organization that sponsors Operation Fatherhood. Operation Fatherhood was formed in 1992 to work with 13- to 17-year-old fathers. It provides weekly support groups to talk about fathers' roles and provide support and role models for fathering. In areas with large numbers of teenage parents, the child care program can use the Operation Fatherhood model to provide supportive service to teenage fathers.

Teenage parents need good information, support, and role models that teach, through example, the daily competent care of infants and toddlers. This modeling should include the conscious application of attention, approval, and affection in addition to the mechanics of care. A competent child care professional will parent the parent by appropriately extending positive attention, approval, and affection to teenage parents.

Communicating with Staff

When more than one person works in a child care program, effective communication among staff is essential. Arranging to meet with each staff member regularly on an individual basis enhances communication. Although family child care providers often work alone in their own homes, they can contact licensing staff and other family child care providers. Group family child care arrangements employ at least two people who work with a larger group of children in the home. Child care centers usually have a staff that includes a director and one or more caregivers. The size of enrollment determines the number and kind of additional staff; these may be caregivers, cooks, custodians, bus drivers, education, social service, and health personnel.

Listening to Staff

Each caregiver needs to be a listener. Staff can exchange information and discuss program issues in a reasonable way only if all are active listeners. How you listen to one another reflects how you respect one another.

Sharing with Colleagues

Share information with colleagues. Your experiences give you information, insights, and perspectives that will help others understand issues and deal with problems.

Share your feelings and actively listen while expressing your excitement and joy about working with your colleagues. As a part of a team, you all benefit from sharing pleasurable experiences. Tactfully express frustrations, disappointments, and anger. Keeping those feelings bottled up can harm all of you. Determine what is distressing you and discuss the issue. By staying within your active listening guidelines you can focus on how staff activities are affecting program goals. You will be more likely to clear up misunderstandings and misperceptions if you focus your discussion on issues rather than on personalities.

Share feedback. Both informal and formal observations provide you with information to share with your colleagues. This kind of information is called feedback. Noting how other caregivers behave with people and materials in various settings, schedules, and routines can help the entire staff evaluate the current program and make necessary adjustments. Feedback can highlight caregiver actions that are helpful and effective, but you should use tact when commenting on a situation in which you believe your colleagues might act differently. Focus on what is best for the children and what changes can provide a better situation. Do not focus on what a caregiver did "wrong." Actions are more often "inappropriate" than "wrong." Since all caregivers are developing their skills, comments that make colleagues feel incompetent are not helpful. It is more productive to focus on appropriate alternative actions to learn and use.

Share responsibilities with your colleagues. Your colleagues will notice whether you are willing to carry your load. Even when people work under written job descriptions containing specific tasks, the total responsibilities often do not fit neatly into separate categories. Martha is responsible for getting snacks ready, but today she is rocking Natalie, who after crying and fussing has finally settled down but does not seem quite ready to be put down to play. If another caregiver volunteers to set up snacks, Natalie will not be disturbed again and so will not disturb the other children.

Share your expertise. Each person has special talents and unique insights to share with colleagues, children, and parents. Nobody appreciates know-it-alls, but we all benefit from people who are willing to share ideas that can be discussed, accepted, modified, or rejected.

Supporting Colleagues

Caregiving is physically and emotionally draining. Remembering and putting into practice the 3A's of caregiving presented in Chapter 4 will help you and your colleagues cope with stress. For example, assisting a colleague when extra help is needed reduces stress. You can provide positive emotional support by listening, using honest compliments, giving credit, and reassuring colleagues about ideas or actions of theirs that you think are appropriate (Figure 6–3). Your colleagues' knowing that you are working with them rather than against them is in itself a powerful emotional support.

Making Decisions

Caregivers need information to make intelligent staff decisions. Meet with other staff members regularly. Study and learn about issues when necessary so that you will be able to discuss subjects intelligently and make wise decisions. Identify the issue and factors that affect the decision. Raise questions with colleagues; listen, think, and take an active part in making decisions related to caregiving.

Figure 6–3 Supportive relationships are necessary among caregivers who work together in a child care program.

CASE STUDY

Amanda Hasha is a 9-month-old girl who has been in child care for the past three months. Sheila, her primary caregiver, has noticed that Amanda is not gaining weight, looks tired but does not sleep well, and cries often. Sheila met with the director and other caregivers to share her concerns and actively listened as they all confirmed her observations and suggested a parent conference. Sheila then set up a conference with Mrs. Hasha to discuss Amanda's problems.

Sheila started the conference by describing her observations using I statements. She informed Mrs. Hasha that the other caregivers had observed the same behaviors and told her the steps that have been taken to comfort Amanda. Sheila then asked Mrs. Hasha what she sees at home and actively listened to her.

MRS. HASHA: "I've had a lot of problems lately that I'm sure have affected Amanda. Her father had an accident and has been in the hospital, so I go to see him every chance I can."

SHEILA: "My! It sounds like you have been under a lot of stress and worry lately."

MRS. HASHA: "I just don't know what to do. No one else is around to help, so I sometimes have Amanda's sister watch her even though she's only eight."

SHEILA: "So, you've had no help except for your older daughter. It sounds overwhelming."

Mrs. Hasha: "Yes, it certainly is! I wish I knew how to get the kids cared for so I could be at the hospital more often."

SHEILA: "It sounds like you really need help with the children so you can help your husband more."

MRS. HASHA: "That's right. Do you have any idea who might help me?"

SHEILA: "I know there are many sources for help in the community. Have you thought to ask at the hospital, your church, or at school?"

MRS. HASHA: "That's a very good idea. Our church has a volunteer program, so I'm going to ask our minister."

SHEILA: "I'll also ask around at some of the programs the county offers. I'm sure help is available for this kind of situation."

MRS. HASHA: "Thank you so much. I know that Amanda will be better if she has an adult to care for her when I can't be there."

Within a week, Mrs. Hasha has volunteers from her church helping to care for the children. Amanda's disposition changed from stressed and insecure to calm and happy. Through the use of a parent conference, active listening, I statements, and mirroring, Sheila was able to help Mrs. Hasha share her problems and arrive at solutions to improve Amanda's health and development.

1. Describe the differences between I Statements and You Statements indicated in this case study.
2. What technique did Sheila use to elicit the source of the problem from Mrs. Hasha?
3. Discuss this case in terms of the communication tools used and their effectiveness in producing outcomes.

===== *Key Terms* =====

active listening

home visits

I Statements

mirroring

National Parenting Scales (N.P.S.)

parent-caregiver conferences

parenting styles

You statements

RESOURCES FOR PARENTS AND STAFF

Governmental

Administration for Children, Youth and
  Families
P.O. Box 1182
Washington, D.C. 20013
(202) 651-3514

Bureau of Community Health Services
Office of Maternal and Child Health
Public Health Service
U.S. Dept. of Health and Human
  Services
5600 Fishers Lane
Rockville, Maryland 20857
(301) 443-2170

Centers for Disease Control
1600 Clifton Road, N.E.
Atlanta, Georgia 30333
(404) 639-3311

National Hotline for AIDS
1-800-342-2437

Children's Bureau
Office of Human Development Services
Administration for Children, Youth and
  Families
U.S. Dept. of Health and Human
  Services
Washington, D.C. 20201

Food and Nutrition Services
U.S. Dept. of Agriculture
301 Park Center Drive
Alexandria, Virginia 22302
(202) 645-5518

Head Start Bureau
Office of Human Development Services
Administration for Children, Youth and
  Families
U.S. Dept. of Health and Human
  Services
Washington, D.C. 20201

National Caries Program
National Institute of Dental Research
9000 Rockville Pike
Bethesda, Maryland 20892
(301) 496-3571

State Departments of Health

County Health Departments

State and Regional Poison Control
  Centers

State and County Cooperative
  Extension Services

Professional

American Academy of Dermatology
930 North Meacham Road
Schaumburg, Illinois 60173-6016
(647) 330-0230

American Academy of Pediatrics
141 Northwest Point Boulevard
P.O. Box 927
Elk Grove, Illinois 60009
1-800-433-9016

American Dental Association
211 East Chicago Avenue
Chicago, Illinois 60611
(312) 440-2500

American Optometric Association
243 North Lindbergh Boulevard
St. Louis, Missouri 63141
(314) 991-4100

Health Related
American Automobile Association
100 AAA Drive
Heathrow, Florida 32746-5063
(407) 444-7000

American Red Cross
(check local listings)

Childhood Lead Poisoning
(888) 232-6789

Johnson and Johnson Consumer
  Products Information Center
199 Grandview Road
Skillman, New Jersey 08558
1-800-526-3967

Metropolitan Life
Health & Welfare Division
One Madison Avenue
New York, New York 10010
(212) 578-2211

National Center for Clinical Infant
  Programs, Zero to Three
2000 14th Street, North #380
Arlington, Virginia 22201
(800) 411-1222

Parents' Health Report
Child Health Care Newsletter
2 Taylor Drive
Glen Cove, NY 11542
E-mail: energynurse1@yahoo.com

Ross Laboratories
Columbus, Ohio 43216

U.S. Consumer Product Safety
  Commission
Office of Information and Public Affairs
Washington, D.C. 20207
1-800-638-2772

Student Activities

1. Review the four active listening steps presented in the chapter.
2. Actively listen to a parent-caregiver dialogue when the child arrives in the morning. Write down the statements and then categorize them.

	Parent	Caregiver
Information		
Questions		
Affirmation		

3. Conduct one simulated parent-caregiver conference initiated by the caregiver and another initiated by the parent.
4. Interview a caregiver who has made a home visit. Determine the purpose and procedures for the visit.
5. Role-play a child care center staff meeting about the problems of sharing play yard space.

6. Identify the responsibilities of a caregiver in a setting with which you are familiar. Categorize the activities according to whether the caregiver attends to them independently or in cooperation with other staff members, using a chart like the following.

Task	Accomplishes Independently	Needs Cooperation of Other Staff

7. What did you learn by using the Active Listening techniques?
8. List your perceived strengths in interrelationships with parents and staff. List areas where you need to set growth goals.

Chapter Review

1. What is active listening?
2. Why is effective communication with parents important?
3. Why is effective communication with staff important?
4. Write an agenda for a parent-caregiver conference initiated by the caregiver to discuss a child's toilet-training.
5. Describe two situations in which caregivers interact with each other. Identify the interpersonal skills needs.

Situation	Skills Needed: Caregiver 1	Skills Needed: Caregiver 2

6. How can you contribute to effective, positive staff relationships?

References

Bauette, G., and Peterson, E. (1993). Beginning to create a multicultural classroom. *Dimensions of Early Childhood, 21*(2), 11–12.

Douville-Watson, L. (1993). *Family actualization through research and education: F.A.R.E.* (3rd ed.). New York: Actualization, Inc.

Douville-Watson, L. (1996). *The national parenting scales: Experimental edition.* Bayville, NY: Instructional Press.

Feeney, S., & Kipinis, K. (1990). *Code of ethical conduct & statement of commitment.* Washington, DC: National Association for the Education of Young Children.

Hendrix, H. (1993). *Getting the love you want.* New York: Institute for Relationship Therapy.

Lally, J. R. (ed.). (1992). *Language development & communication: A guide, infant/toddler caregiving series.* San Francisco: Far West Lab.

Maynard, R. (1996). *Kids having kids.* New York: Robin Hood Foundation.

Orstein, A. C., & Chapman, J. K. (1988). The parent-teacher conference. *PTA Today,* V14.

Somers, E. (2000). *Food and mood.* Kansas City, KS: Owl Books.

Watson, M. A. (1997). *Giving & receiving family support through using the National Parenting Scales.* Anaheim, CA: National Association for the Education of the Young Child (NAEYC) Annual Conference.

Weill, J. D., & Jablonski, M. (eds.). (1997). *Children's Defense Fund: The state of America's children: 1997 yearbook.* Washington, DC: Children's Defense Fund.

Additional Resources

Ardell, D. B., & Tager, M. J. (1981). *Planning for wellness.* Portland, OR: Wellness Media, Ltd.

Dawley, G., & Sorger, J. (1982). *What to do . . . until the doctor calls back.* Plainfield, NJ: Bayberry Books.

Gordon, T. (1976). *Parent effectiveness training: P.E.T.* New York: Peter H. Wyden.

Greater Minneapolis Day Care Association. (1983). *Child health guidelines.* Minneapolis, MN: Author.

Hewlett, B. S. (1992). *Father-child relations.* New York: Adline DeGruyter.

Horowitz, A. M. (1981). *Prevent tooth decay: A guide for implementing self-applied fluorides in school settings.* (NIH Publication No. 82–1196). Bethesda, MD: National Institute of Dental Research.

Lally, R. J. (1995). The impact of child care policies and practices on infant/toddler identity formation. *Young Children, 51*(1), 58–67.

Lamb, M. E. (1987). *The father's role: Cross cultural perspectives.* Hillsdale, NJ: Erlbaum.

National Institute of Dental Research. (1983). *Snack facts.* (NIH Publication No. 83–1680). Bethesda, MD: Author.

National Institute of Dental Research and the National Association of Community Health Centers, Inc. (1979). *Good teeth for you and your baby.* (NIH Publication No. 79–1255). Bethesda, MD: Author.

National Institute of Dental Research and the National Association of Community Health Centers, Inc. (1979). *Una buena dentadura para usted y su bebe.* (NIH Publication No. 79–1465). Bethesda, MD: Author.

Owen, M. T., & Cox, M. J. (1988). Maternal employment and the transition to parenthood. In A. E. Gottfried & A. W. Gottfried (Eds.). *Maternal employment and children's development: Longitudinal research,* pp. 85–119. New York: Plenum.

Public Health Service. (1980). *Healthy Children.* Effective public health practices for improving children's oral health. (DHHS Publication No. [PHS] 80–50136). Washington, DC: Author.

Rogers, C. (1961). *On becoming a person.* Boston: Houghton Mifflin.

Helpful Web Sites

Choosing Child Care—A Checklist for Parents Steps in choosing child care. http://www.childcare.org/Parents/choosing-provider.htm

National Association for the Education of Young Children All caregivers should be members of this organization. http://www.naeyc.org

The Whole Child http://www.pbs.org/wholechild/index.html

For additional infant and toddler resources, visit our Web site at http://www.earlychilded.delmar.com

Effective Tools for Current Issues in Early Child Care and Development

The master tools for infant and toddler caregiving are positive attention, approval, and affection. Life energy is the force behind all human needs. Providing attention is directing our life force outward or inward, so that whatever we pay attention to grows. To commit our energy to the needs of young children, we must first give positive attention, affection, and approval to *ourselves*. Conscious care requires that we recognize the stress we create in ourselves, and learn how to create calm

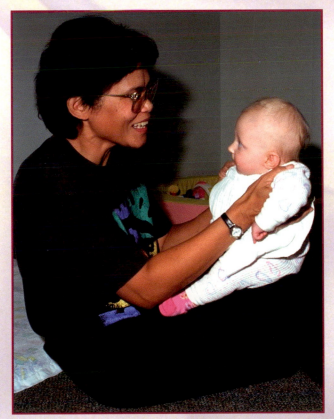

within, before we can direct our positive attention, approval, and affection toward the children in our care. First-time parents tend to direct all their attention toward their child and thus create stress, fatigue, and exhaustion for themselves. The child care specialist should model and instruct first-time parents in the conscious care of themselves, as well as their children.

Child care specialists need emotional intelligence, and the tools to communicate with parents and children in ways that teach them emotional intelligence. There are five domains or skills involved in becoming emotionally intelligent. The caregiver can develop tasks and activities that promote interactional synchrony between everyone involved, to teach parents and children the skills involved in being emotionally healthy. Current research in brain development clearly indicates that the consistency of our reactions to children actually program neural pathways to determine how children respond. Good or bad, happy or sad, feeling at ease or feeling "dis-eased"—your attitude imparts permanent changes to the nervous systems of the children in your care.

The bond between father and child is just as important for healthy child development as is the mother-child bond. In fact, recent research indicates that fathers can bond with infants just as well as mothers can. The child care specialist must actively encourage fathers to be involved in the child care program, by using communication tools such as mirroring, "I" messages, and active listening. Communicating with both parents is essential for a child care program that aims to enhance children's growth in all five developmental areas: physical, emotional, social, cognitive, and developmental learning skills.

Security issues for children and parents have recently become a major concern of child care programs. It has become necessary for child care specialists to address personal security and terrorism awareness in the child care program. A major problem, generated by catastrophe, terrorism, and times of extreme environmental insecurity, is the resulting sense of powerlessness. One tool the child care specialist can use against powerlessness is to be well informed. Many resources are available to inform caregivers about what to do in the case of disaster, and how to take action to increase personal safety and security. For example, the Department of Defense Education Activity (DoDEA) has published a *Personal Protection Guide,* which gives specific information on safety and security measures to take with children. It is imperative to establish a "circle of safety" around infants and toddlers. When leaving children in the care of another person, use the tool of the "changing of the guard."

Another important aspect of personal security and safety, is to perform a security assessment of both indoor and outdoor environments. The caregiver needs specific plans and procedures for crisis or disaster situations; these procedures should be practiced with staff, parents, and children on a regular basis. Simple tools can be used to help make children and parents feel they have some control over their own security. For example, make sure children always carry identification. At as young an age as possible, teach children how to contact police, a neighbor, a parent, or other authority, and establish a secret code word for the child's pick-up time, that only parents, caregivers, and the child know.

Probably the most important tool parents and caregivers can use to help children in situations of disaster is consistency. The child care specialist should learn how to structure the environment, and work with parents, to ensure consistent responses to children's behaviors. Child care accountability programs help caregivers and parents to be consistent in their interactions with children.

Personal crises are also a concern in the field of early child care and development. The child care specialist must be aware of tools to deal with critical issues for parents and children, such as breast-feeding issues, sudden infant death syndrome (SIDS), fetal alcohol syndrome (FAS), the sudden death of a family member, and other traumatic experiences that affect the family. Specific tools such as ruing (sharing a child's pain and mirroring his or her expressions), labeling and expressing feelings (helping children understand and express feelings), and self-soothing (deep breathing, relaxation) can be used with young children and parents who have undergone a family tragedy. By teaching parents tools such as shepherding, shadowing, and catching the child being good, the caregiver can help parents feel more able to help their children remain safe and secure.

Establishing healthy relationships with parents and children is another concern in child care. Social development is largely the result of the relationships between the child and the primary caregivers, so it is important for the child care specialist to have tools to ensure healthy relationships between children and parents. Children can be helped to feel good about themselves, and their interactions with others, through the use of "positive perspective." Specific skills in building rapport should be learned, and caregivers should apply the concepts of "respectful is successful" and "cooperation versus competition" whenever they interact with children and parents. One of the skills of emotional intelligence is managing relationships. The child care specialist should become an effective communicator to ensure healthy relationships in the child care program.

Child care specialists also need to enhance the cognitive development of children in their care. Specific tools that enhance development in several areas of cognition can be used through a daily routine of activities. Naming and labeling are the first cognitive tools to use with infants and toddlers. Once children acquire some expressive language, the tools of time orientation, cause-and-effect, concept formation, and observing oneself are effective for enhancing cognitive development. With children who exhibit language delays or speech problems, the tool of baby signing is very effective for helping them to communicate, and to increase their cognitive skills. Child care specialists must also be aware of the signs of high risk for chronic or severe developmental problems, and make referrals to professionals for further evaluation, after discussion with the parents of a child who shows such signs.

L earning disabilities and developmental delays are areas
of current concern in the field of child care and development.
By using tools that teach the perceptual skills essential for children
to accurately process visual and auditory information, the child care specialist
can instruct children through a routine of daily activities, in the skills needed to avert
learning problems and language delays. Child care specialists should systematically teach
focal attention/perceptual screening, auditory and visual memory, discrimination, and the
association skills necessary to accurately process information from the environment. By
teaching infants and toddlers basic perceptual skills, the caregiver can help children enter
formal educational settings with the development needed to acquire the basic academic
skills of word recognition, spelling, and arithmetic computation. Child care specialists
should frequently perform assessments, to establish developmental profiles and prescriptions for the children in their care. These profiles and prescriptions are then used to plan
activities that enhance the development of each child in their care.

The field of child care has become more complex and more professional within the past few years, so it is important to understand the characteristics of a good child care specialist. The Child Development Associates (CDA) guidelines for competent child care are still the standard in the United States. A caregiver must acquire formal training in child care, and developmental skills and tools, before working with infants and toddlers. Professional preparation is necessary today because caregivers must be experts at **ORAOM**—the ability to Observe, Record, Assess, Organize, and Manage a care program for infants and toddlers. Although sensitivity, caring, and love are still the most important qualities of a caregiver of young children, formal training and preparation is also necessary to deal with the intricacies of child development in our complex world.

Settings for Child Care

7

Objectives

After reading this chapter, you should be able to:

- Identify characteristics of the family child care home.
- Identify characteristics of the child care center.
- Distinguish among the regulations of child care.
- Categorize child care program emphases.
- Compare caregiver support systems.

Chapter Outline

Introduction
Choosing a Provider
Family-Based Care
Center-Based Care
Program Emphases
Program Funding
Support Groups

INTRODUCTION

Child care can be provided in-home or outside the child's residence in **family-based care** or **center-based care. In-home care** ranges from a friend, relative, or baby sitter to a live-in nanny or au pair. The obvious advantages of in-home care include consistency and familiarity of the home environment, ease of transition of care from provider to parents, and cost effectiveness in certain situations, such as more than three small children or a child with special needs. Disadvantages of in-home care include isolation of the caregiver, the caregiver's need to have her or his own physical space, and transportation costs and arrangements for the caregiver.

Care outside the child's home may be provided in a family-based child care home or a child care center. There are some similarities and differences and some advantages and disadvantages in each place of care. Family child care homes and center-based child care may be either licensed or unlicensed, depending on state regulations.

CHOOSING A PROVIDER

Many resources are available to educate parents about how to interview and select a child care provider. Please see the References and Helpful Web Sites at the end of the chapter for information sources regarding what parents look for in a caregiver. Although CDA national certification verifies that a caregiver has undergone a rigorous training and evaluation process, it is important to understand what parents look for in choosing a provider. Following is a compilation of many references for parents on how to choose a child care provider (U.S. Department of Education, 2001).

Costs

Parents must determine what they can afford before interviewing providers. If the parents' income is low, **Head Start programs** or state-subsidized programs are available, although enrollment space may be a problem. Parents often call several family-based and center-based facilities in the area to determine an average cost for the required amount of care. Depending on the average cost for care in their area, they may need to adjust their child care needs.

Ways to Find Good Child Care

Personal referrals such as friends or relatives are a reliable source. The Yellow Pages and local newspapers or even placing an ad can help to locate good caregivers. Parents can check bulletin boards in stores, churches, and other gathering places or contact community, county, state, and national agencies and associations, such as Child Development Associates (CDA) or county and state licensing agencies. Within the past few years, most states have developed referral agencies for child care. Child care resource and referral agencies such as the National Association of Child Care Resources and Referral Agencies (NACCRRA) are currently available.

Researching Prospective Providers

Parents should verify all licenses and certifications and ask in advance for phone numbers to call. A careful parent usually checks several references, talks with parents who are currently using providers, visits the site more than once at different times, and checks health and safety issues, such as electrical outlets being covered, small toys that could choke, and cleanliness.

Interviewing Prospective Providers

Parents are generally looking for a kind, responsive, and affectionate caregiver. In interviewing, they will try to determine if the person is experienced with children the age of theirs and is energetic enough to keep up with them. Providers who are calm and relaxed and who seem like someone the parents can interact with in a sharing relationship make good impressions. Parents may look for someone who shares a similar child-rearing philosophy. They will want a caregiver who treats each child as an individual who deserves respect and who accepts the family's cultural and religious values.

Observing Prospective Providers

Parents will be asking questions like these: Do their children interact well with the person? Does the caregiver encourage creative expression and promote fun and humor? How many caregivers will be involved with each child? Do they help children share, develop self-confidence, and self-esteem? Do they patiently help children solve problems?

As a prospective provider, you can fulfill all of the criteria listed above when you learn and practice the tools and techniques in this book and fulfill the requirements for CDA certification. Although these criteria may seem demanding, your education and enthusiasm for child care will result in you being the kind of caregiver that parents will respect, admire, and honor with responsibility for the care of their most precious asset—their children.

FAMILY-BASED CARE

Staffing

The family child care specialist provides care in her own home for children other than her own. The caregiver in a family child care home is usually a woman; she may be single, married, a non-parent, or a parent.

The number of children one caregiver can care for varies and usually depends on the ages of the children. Many states restrict the number of infants the caregiver can include. A family child care provider with her own three- and five-year-old might also care for four other children (Figure 7–1).

The group family child care home provides care for more children—often from 6 to 10 or 12. In some states, one caregiver may be responsible for a group of children, whereas in other states an additional caregiver is required for this number in **group family child care**.

Unique Characteristics

A family child care home provides a home-like environment for children. Familiarity with the surroundings helps the child adjust to a new setting. The physical arrangements may resemble the child's own home. There is usually a kitchen where food is prepared, a bed or cot on which to sleep, toilet facilities, and play areas. The family child care home usually allows the child to move and play within several rooms.

Figure 7–1 Several children may receive care in the familiar setting of a family child care home.

The small number of children in a family child care home allows children and caregivers time to develop close relationships. The stability and depth of this relationship contributes to the child's feelings of trust and security.

The family child care home often includes children of several ages. Two-year-old Sasha puts her arms around six-month-old Jeremy and gives him a hug. Matthew, who is three and a half, sits on the floor with one-and-a-half-year-old Michele, putting shoes on her and fastening the Velcro tapes. Year-old toddler Suzanne follows Miss Jan into the kitchen, watches four-year-old Larry get a drink of water, and then follows Larry into the den to pick up blocks. Multiaged groups of children have opportunities to learn from one another. Older and younger children provide physical, emotional, social, and cognitive support and challenges for one another.

The program in a family child care home consists of the routines of living together as a "family." Cooking and pick-up-the-room times contribute to the child's development, along with the stories, the art on the kitchen table or driveway, the tapping-pan-lid noises, the snuggles and hugs, the sitting alone under the table to watch, and the on-again/off-again interactions with other children and the provider.

The family child care home usually has a flexible schedule. The daily schedule may have a few fixed times, such as lunch for children who are awake. However, it may permit flexibility in times for eating snacks, sleeping, and playing. This flexibility minimizes the pressure on children to meet other people's schedules. The home often adjusts its schedule to the child rather than requiring the child to adjust to a schedule. For example, one child can be allowed to stay in the bedroom and sleep while other children play in other rooms of the home.

Family child care providers have autonomy. They decide what they will do, when they will do it, and how they will do it. Many states now offer mentoring programs that support the independent care of home providers.

One disadvantage for family child care providers is their heavy load of responsibilities. Caring for up to six children from eight to ten hours a day, five days a week, all alone, produces a heavy physical and emotional strain. To get time off during the day for relaxation or to attend meetings requires locating and hiring a substitute—activities demanding additional time and money.

Another disadvantage is isolation from other caregivers. Working alone in their homes, family child care providers miss the informal sharing with other caregivers of ideas, frustrations, and concerns. Many communities do not have organizations that meet the emotional and educational needs of family child care providers, thus leaving them on their own to locate the support they need or go without. Resource and referral agencies often offer organized groups.

A major difference between family child care, group family child care, and child care centers is that often infants and toddlers are overwhelmed by large, noisy centers. In contrast, young children are very relaxed in family child care settings. The advantage of group family child care is the presence of an extra provider who helps care for the six to twelve children, which allows the director and assistant to function as a team. This helps overcome feelings of isolation and fatigue often experienced by the family child care provider who solely cares for up to six children.

Regulations

For many years a state or county agency, often the welfare, health, or social services agency, has regulated family child care homes.

The regulation of family day care involves 1) the rights of children to be protected, 2) the rights of child care providers to carry on a legitimate home business without infringement of their rights, 3) the extent to which state laws can adequately regulate ALL the homes where children are in care, 4) the ability of the states to enforce their current laws, 5) the interpretation of standards to the public, parents, and potential family day care providers, and 6) the future needs of consumers of family day care who may not be able to find child care if regulations drive providers out of business. (Adams, 1982)

Three types of regulation of family child care homes are **licensing, registration,** and **certification.** To be licensed, the family child care home must meet the standards established by the local governmental agency. Standards may include the number of children to be served, physical space, equipment, and health and safety factors. In some localities zoning requirements must be met.

Many people care for children other than their own in their homes and yet remain unlicensed. It has been estimated that more than 90 percent of all family child care homes are unlicensed (Corsini, Wisensale, & Caruso, 1988). A proposed alternative to licensing is registration of family child care homes. Registration in most states is a simple process of listing the family child care home with the licensing authority.

Most states now use certification of family child care homes. Certification (sometimes called approval) is a form of regulation for purchase of care. Certification standards are, in almost every state, some modification of FIDCR (Federal Interagency Day Care Requirements) standards (Walker, 1992).

CENTER-BASED CARE

Staffing

A child care center provides care away from home for more than six children for some part of the day or night. Child care centers differ from family child care homes in several ways.

The child care center staff consists of a director and caregivers. It may also include a cook, custodians, bus drivers, education specialist, social services workers, health specialists, and others, depending on the size, goals, and financial support of the child care center.

The number of caregivers and group sizes are regulated according to the ages of children served. Adult-child ratios vary slightly among states. Typical requirements are two adults for each of the following number of children in a group.

Age of Children	Number in Group
Up to 18 months	6 to 8
18 months to 3 years	10 to 12
3 years to 6 years	14 to 20

Unique Characteristics

The child care facility may be a house, a building converted to center use, education rooms in a church, a community center, a school, or a building especially designed as a child care center. Each room, which provides for sleeping, eating, and playing in specially arranged areas, often houses one age group. The play areas may have blocks in one section, a home living section, a dress-up section, and so on. Where groups of children use rooms frequently, most states require a minimum of 30 to 35 square feet of play space per child and approximately an additional 20 square feet for children under two years old for crib space. Children may remain in that room for most of the day, with other indoor play space available in some centers and outdoor play space available at most centers (Figure 7–2).

Children in child care centers are usually grouped with those of similar age. The licensing requirements for adult-child ratios make broader multiaged grouping costly since the group must use the ratio for the youngest child in the group.

Many toys and much equipment are needed for the number and age range of children in a center. Child care centers often can purchase expensive, sturdy play equipment and a variety of toys because the number of children using them make such purchases cost effective. The equipment, other than cribs and cots, may be used by several groups of children, and the toys may be sanitized and passed back and forth among rooms to provide variety and stimulation without undue cost.

The director and caregivers plan the program in a child care center, often with input from parents. The program should put the center's philosophy and goals into practice. These philosophies and goals should cover all aspects of the child's care, of the caregiver's roles, and of parental involvement, schedules, routines, room arrangement, curriculum, assessments, and evaluations. The director determines and sets the standards of quality for the overall program. The individual caregivers are responsible for maintaining these

Figure 7–2 In a child care center, a group of children may remain in one room that is divided into playing, eating, and sleeping areas.

standards of quality in their individual rooms. It is important for caregivers not to minimize the impact they each have on the individual child placed in their care.

Since a child care center has at least two caregivers, it is more conducive to the stimulation of new ideas, release of tension and frustration, and provision of support. However, working with another adult in the same room or in the same building requires skills in getting along with others, sharing, compromising, and cooperating. Caregivers need to work constantly on maintaining and improving their working relationships with other adults. Many centers provide education and assistance through in-service education and participation in workshops and conferences, as do professional organizations such as the National Association for the Education of Young Children (NAEYC) and Child Development Associates (CDA) credentialing authorities.

Child care centers tend to have less flexible daily schedules than family child care homes. They have tended to borrow a daily schedule from schools, with 15- to 30-minute time blocks, which structure a young child's day. However, this kind of schedule is not appropriate for infants and toddlers, who need very simple schedules of large time blocks that fit their physical needs and their own interests.

Regulations

A state agency is usually responsible for child care center licensing. Each state has developed standards for child care center administration, staff, facilities, and program as a part of government's responsibility to protect its citizens. Local governmental agencies are involved with health requirements, fire codes, and zoning ordinances. Licensing identifies a set of minimum standards that a center has met; it does not guarantee quality of care.

PROGRAM EMPHASES

Holistic Care

Whether care is provided in a family child care home, group family child care home, or a child care center, it must be holistic; it must consider the whole child. Physical, emotional, social, language skills, and cognitive development are all vitally important during these early years, so balance is needed to help the child develop properly (Figure 7–3). Overemphasis in one area or limited involvement in another may create unnecessary stress or delay development.

Young children need to experience nurturance, love, consistency, touch, movement, exploration, interactions with others, comfort, challenge, and stimulation. The child care provider should be well-versed in the 3A's of childcare. These help develop the child's feelings of security and trust, self-worth and identity, curiosity, creativity, and active involvement with people and the world.

Developmental Care

The program emphasis in both home-based care and child care centers should consider the developmental needs of each child. Each child, parent, and caregiver involved in child care is developing as an individual.

Children develop naturally. It is not helpful for anyone to push, prod, or pressure them to develop. Adults can enhance, encourage, and nurture children's development in a variety of ways by taking cues from the children and providing the appropriate "match" of materials and experiences to fit the children's needs, interests, and behaviors. Under ideal conditions a variety of age-appropriate toys are made available for the child to choose from, and caretakers structure activities around the child's interests.

Each parent is developing both as a person and as a parent. How the caregiver behaves with the parent can help or hinder the parent's development.

Figure 7–3 Child care programs must be holistic, meeting the child's physical, emotional, social, and cognitive needs.

Each caregiver is developing as both a person and a caregiver. Care-givers who view themselves as learners continually discover things about themselves; they come to know more about others; and they increase both their skills as caregivers and the roles they assume as caregivers. Partnership between caregiver and parent for the benefit of the child should be an ongoing goal (Douville-Watson, 2001).

Quality Care

High-quality care is required for each child. National accreditation is being used to identify homes and centers that attain standards of quality.

The **National Association for Family Day Care (NAFDC)** began its Accreditation Program in 1988 to offer professional recognition and distinction to family child care providers whose services represent high-quality child care. The accreditation process involves the provider in an in-depth self-assessment that focuses on physical provisions in the home, child care procedures and policies, and adult-child interactions. Dimensions of the family child care home that are assessed include indoor safety, health, nutrition, play environment, interaction, and professional responsibility. The provider's self-assessment is validated by a parent and a NAFDC representative (NAFDC, 1988).

The NAEYC established the National Academy of Early Childhood Programs to administer an accreditation system for child care centers. The academy defines a high-quality early childhood program as one that meets the needs of and promotes the physical, social, emotional, and cognitive development of the children and adults—parents, staff, and administrators—who are involved in the program. Each day of a child's life is viewed as leading toward the growth and development of a healthy, intelligent, and contributing member of society.

The criteria address all aspects of an early childhood program, as follows (NAEYC, 1992).

- interactions among staff and children
- curriculum
- staff and parent interactions
- administration
- staff qualifications and development
- staffing patterns
- physical environment
- health and safety
- nutrition and food service
- program evaluation

PROGRAM FUNDING

There are a variety of sources of financial support for child care programs. Some programs utilize only one source, such as parent tuition. Other programs may receive funds from several sources: for example, Title XX, United Way, and/or parent fees. Many corporations help subsidize centers for their employees and/or set up a **Dependent Care Assistance Program (DCAP)**, which allows the employee to set aside up to $5,000 in pre-tax dollars for day care (Family Day Care Advisory Project, 1991).

Public Tax Support

Two federal programs limited to children of low-income families are Head Start and Title XX Social Services subsidized child care. Part-time and full-time care may be available for those meeting income eligibility guidelines.

Some city, state, and federal governmental units and agencies provide child care services for their employees. These are tax subsidized through use of public buildings, utilities, employees, and so on.

Public schools are opening classrooms for full-day infant and toddler child care. The space and sometimes the utilities, personnel, and equipment may be paid for with tax support.

State vocational and technical schools, community colleges, and universities may use tax monies to support child care as a part of their instructional program or as a service to their students and/or faculty and staff.

Private Support

The majority of child care in America is provided by private licensed and unlicensed family child care homes and child care centers, and it is paid for by parents through tuition and fees.

A few corporations are now providing child care alternatives. These include on-site child care centers, corporate-supported near-site child care centers and group family homes, corporate contributions to community child care, child care reimbursement, the use of pre-tax dollars to pay for care (DCAP), resource and referral services, and educational programs for parents.

Churches are "a major provider of child care in this nation" (Gormley, 1995).

As the steward of substantial resources, including real estate, capital, administrative services and health and insurance benefits, the churches are in an ideal position to make child care delivery available to families. Churches taken in the aggregate are the largest single provider of child care in the United States today. Space, location, and tax exempt status contribute to the desirability of church properties for child care programs. Of course, churches will want to consider carefully the ethical implications of their fee policies for the use of space for this ministry of child care.

United Way funds are used in many communities to provide child care services or to subsidize existing community programs.

SUPPORT GROUPS

Child Care Systems

Some public and private agencies set up child care systems. When several child care centers are administered from a central office, they often gain access to greater financial support; additional education, social, and health services; toys and equipment; caregiver training; and parent education.

A single child care center or a child care center system may make arrangements with neighboring family child care homes to serve as satellites to the center. This can benefit both home and center. The family child care provider can use center staff, toys, and materials. Since these family child care homes often care for infants and toddlers, their children often transfer to the center program when they are about three years old. The child care center is thus able to serve families with children both below and above three years of age without having to provide the more costly infant service in their center.

Child Care Networks

Many communities are establishing child care information and referral networks to serve parents, providers, and community agencies. They have several features in common, including the following (Siegel & Lawrence, 1984).

- *Matchmaking:* a commitment to parental choice in child care and respect for all parents' ability to choose the child care setting most appropriate for their own child.
- *Universality of services:* a willingness and capacity to address [the child care information and referral] needs of all parents regardless of income and family circumstance.
- *Inclusive referral system:* a capacity to work nonjudgmentally with all sectors of the provider community, including home- and center-based, public and private, profit and not-for-profit groups.
- *Community-level networking:* a cooperative relationship with community agencies and institutions that serve children and families.
- *Knowledge of child care policy and programs:* a thorough familiarity with child care regulations and public policy issues.

Some agencies have established their own information and referral networks. One hospital, in an attempt to meet the diverse needs of its staff, developed a family child care network, "a personalized child care information service—a matching of employee child care needs with the availability of spaces in family day care homes" (Torres, 1981). During the decade since then, many corporations and public and private facilities have contracted with agencies and have paid a fee to make resource and referral services available for their employees (Morgan, 1991).

Three basic types of child care information and referral services are (1) information and referral; (2) technical assistance: training; and (3) advocacy: community education (Siegel & Lawrence, 1984). Of these, technical assistance or training is directed most specifically to caregivers. Workshops, seminars, and telephone networks can provide caregivers with information about and training for the program and give directors help with administrative functions.

Family child care providers have been especially active in some areas, establishing their own networks. Meeting together, they have dealt with problems specific to their situation of caring for children in their own homes.

The mentoring program described in detail in Chapter 15 discussed the advantages of mentors to all child care settings. Child care owners and directors of programs should inquire at their nearest college for information on area mentoring programs.

The **Home Visitor** assessment and certification procedure offered by the CDA Council is a valuable certification. Information concerning this certificate is available from the CDA Council, 2460 16th Street, NW, Washington, DC 20009-3575.

The Home Visitor Certificate Program offered by the CDA Council is extremely valuable as it qualifies professionals interested in doing home advisory teaching. For more information regarding this program, contact the CDA Council.

The National Center for Early Childhood Workforce also has information regarding other mentoring programs. Contact them by telephone at (202) 737-7700.

Associations

Since the early 1980s, task forces have been established at the local, state, and national levels, and family child care associations address child care needs and solutions. The following quote still applies today (Click, 1981).

> At one end of the spectrum is the loosely organized group which meets mainly on a social level. . . . There is no set program, but providers use the time to air their grievances with the system in general and to discuss particular problems in their own day care businesses. . . . [The next level, meetings with the licensing agent] quickly becomes a way to get ideas filtered back into the bureaucratic system. [The next level involves a few dedicated caregivers plus an enthusiastic sponsor.] Meetings are held to discuss purposes, needs, expectations and even long-range plans. [County associations meet together to form state associations. Some state associations have met to form a national organization.]

Among the national organizations that provide resources for child care providers are the following.

Ecumenical Child Care Network
National Council of Churches
475 Riverside Drive, Room 572
New York, New York 10115
(212) 870-2054

The Ecumenical Child Care Network links church-housed child caregivers, early childhood educators, advocates, and church leaders nationwide.

National Association for the Education of Young Children (NAEYC)
1509 16th Street, N.W.
Washington, D.C. 20009
(202) 232-8777 or 1-800-424-2460

The NAEYC publishes a journal, *Young Children*, and various books and pamphlets that include articles and book reviews relating to many areas of infancy and caregiving. The association has regional, state, and local affiliates.

National Association for Family Day Care
1331A Pennsylvania Avenue
Suite 348
Washington, D.C. 20004
1-800-359-3817

National Child Care Association
1029 Railroad Street
Conyers, Georgia 30207
1-800-543-7161

This organization is composed of grassroots, small business entrepreneurs who seek for all children responsibly regulated, quality child care services that are provided by public, private, and sectarian programs.

National Head Start Association
201 North Union Street
Suite 320
Alexandria, Virginia 22314
(703) 739-0875

Key Terms

center-based care

certification

Dependent Care Assistance Program (DCAP)

developmental care

family-based care

group family child care

Head Start programs

holistic care

Home Visitor

in-home care

licensing

National Association for Family Day Care (NAFDC)

registration

CASE STUDY

Proud as any new parents, Marcy and Fred brought Elissa to a community group family child care. Elissa, who was three months old, was dressed in an outfit that could have been on the front page of a magazine. Everything was matching, ruffled, and coordinated, including the blanket and crib pillow. Elissa shone, with black hair and huge blue eyes. She was no ordinary child because she was the first in the area to be born from in-vitro sperm and ovum donors. The cells were matched in a test tube and then implanted. The entire community rejoiced in the blessed event as she had been long awaited. Fred and Marcy were well established, had jobs, and were liked within the community. They had been married for 12 years when Elissa was born.

Every day Elissa came in with extremely expensive, brightly colored and coordinated outfits and was handled like a fragile doll by her parents and the child care staff. All the caregivers were attracted to her radiant smile and competed to care for her. She was a joy to work with until she had to be rolled on her stomach to be changed, at which point she would begin screaming and crying until she was picked up or placed on her back. Her parents reported that she did the same thing at home, so they kept her on her back so as not to get her upset.

One day, a senior caregiver saw her discomfort at being changed. The senior caregiver and the director began an evaluation of Elissa's development using a Developmental Prescription and Profile. The first thing they did was to undress her and observe her physical development, moving her from one posture to another. It was obvious when she was placed on her stomach that the back of Elissa's head had become flat and she had a bald spot from being on her back all the time. When she was on her tummy, her head sharply hit the surface below.

(continued)

She could not raise her head without great effort and complaining. Her expression changed to being red in the face, eyes tearing, feet flaring outward, and screaming.

Further evaluation found that Elissa could not pull herself up or raise her head because she had never been placed on her stomach. Discussion with her parents revealed that they were so afraid of the possibility of sudden infant death syndrome (SIDS) that they had kept her on her back since she was born. As the result of being kept on her back and in restrictive clothing (massive ruffles and lace), she had not developed head, neck, and shoulder control to support her body when lying on her stomach.

An intervention program was designed to task-analyze the steps she needed to master to begin to raise her head, roll over, and sit upright without support. The first step was to place soft pillows under her body and head while she lay on her tummy and encourage her to stay in the position for 20 seconds. Slowly over the following three weeks, Elissa got stronger and the time spent supporting herself was increased by 10-second intervals, until she could support herself with her head raised for more than one minute.

Within six weeks of the start of this program, Elissa caught up with age expectations for the physical developmental milestones and proceeded to grow at a normal rate. Because her parents and Elissa were appealing to staff, and since it was obvious that her parents had made Elissa's comfort their first priority, the caregivers had complied with keeping Elissa in her designer clothing and on her back, therefore neglecting her physical development.

Only by performing a comprehensive assessment of her development was this benevolent neglect identified and a program to enhance her physical development implemented. In every child care setting, it is essential that assessment of development in the five major areas be performed and programs to enhance development be a part of the daily structure of care.

1. What tools of assessment were used to discover Elissa's developmental delays?
2. Describe the motivations and intentions of Elissa's parents that resulted in their neglect of her development.
3. Develop a task analysis of the steps that would be necessary to overcome Elissa's developmental delay.

Student Activities

1. Compare a family child care home and a child care center in your area using the following categories.

Staffing	Number and Ages of Children	Regulation
Family Child Care Home		
Child Care Center		

2. Interview one family child care provider and one child care center caregiver.
   a. What are the goals of the program?
   b. What are the caregiver responsibilities?
   c. What is planned for the children?

3. Make a list of local and state organizations that provide phone contacts, meetings, workshops, or conferences for caregivers.
4. How has each organization addressed cultural diversity within its setting?

Chapter Review

1. How are a family child care home and a child care center alike? How are they different?
2. Compare the responsibilities of a family child care provider and a caregiver in a child care center.
3. Describe a "holistic" child care program emphasis.
4. Describe a "developmental" child care program emphasis.

References

Adams, D. (1982). Family day care regulations: State policies in transition. *Day Care Journal, 1*(1), 9–13.

Click, M. H. (1981). The growth of family day care associations. *Day Care and Early Education, 8*(3), 39–41.

Corsini, D. A., Wisensale, S., & Caruso, G. (1988). Family day care: System issues and regulatory models. *Young Children, 4*(6), 17–23.

Douville-Watson, L. (2001). *Child care lecture, psychology 213*. Garden City, NY: Nassau Community College.

Family Day Care Advisory Project. (1991). Washington, DC: Children's Foundation.

Gormley, W. T. (1995). *Everybody's children: Child care as a public problem*. Washington, DC: Brookings Institute.

Morgan, G. (1991). Career progression in early care and education: A discussion paper. Boston: Center for Career Development, Wheelock College.

National Association for Family Day Care. (1988). *New accreditation for family day care homes*. Washington, DC: Author.

National Association for the Education of Young Children. (1992). *Accreditation by the National Academy of Early Childhood Programs*. Washington, DC: Author.

Siegel, P., & Lawrence, M. (1984). Information, referral, and resource centers. In J. T. Greenman & R. W. Fuqua (Eds.). *Making day care better*. New York: Teachers College Press.

Torres, Y. (1981). A hospital-based family day care network. *Day Care and Early Education, 9*(1), 44–45.

Walker, J. R. (1992). New evidence on the supply of childcare: A statistical portrait of family providers and an analysis of their fees. *Journal of Human Resources, 27*(1), 30–40.

Additional Resources

National Council of Churches. (1984). *Policy statement of child day care*. New York: Governing Board of the National Council of Churches.

Helpful Web Sites

The ABC's of Safe and Healthy Child Care http://www.cdc.gov/ncidod/hip/abc/abc.htm

The Arc's Q&A on Child Care Child care settings and the Americans with Disabilities Act. http://www.thearc.org/faqs/ccqa1.html

Child Care Search Engine Here are some tips on finding a child care provider. http://hometimes.com/Communities/ChildCare/

Complete Child Care Information Services Week of the Child, Provider Appreciation Day, and more. http://www.childcare.net/

CPSC Staff Study of Safety Hazards in Child Care Settings http://www.safetyalerts.com/rcls/category/child.htm

DSHS Licensed Child Care Information System How to find quality day care; read the brochure "Choosing Child Care." http://www.wa.gov/dshs/childcareinfo/

National Association of Child Care Resources and Referral Agencies (NACCRRA) Up-to-date information for parents seeking child care. http://www.naccrra.net/

NICHD Publications On-line Children are placed in a wide variety of child care settings. http://www.nichd.nih.gov/publications/publications.htm

Parenting Place Presents Childcare Finding the right child care option can be very stressful. http://www.parentingplace.com

For additional infant and toddler resources, visit our Web site at http://www.earlychilded.delmar.com

The Indoor and Outdoor Environment

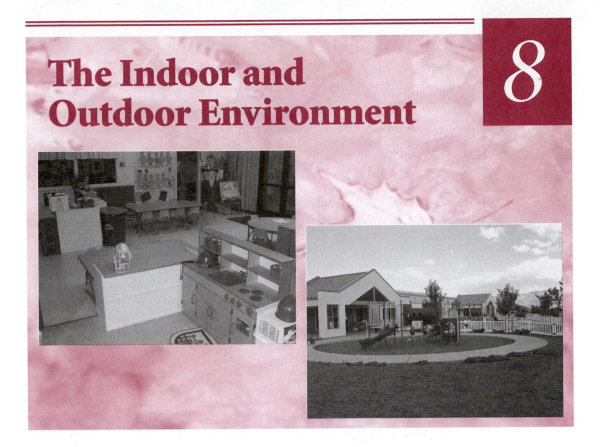

Objectives   *After reading this chapter, you should be able to:*

- ◼ Identify components of the indoor and outdoor environment.
- ◼ Analyze the appropriateness for infants and toddlers of equipment and materials used in the indoor and outdoor environment.

Chapter Outline

Room Arrangement
Play Yard Arrangement
Materials
Conditions Fostering Safety and Health

INTRODUCTION

The environment for very young children must be planned carefully. The first step is to identify your program goals. The equipment and materials you select should reflect your goals and help the children develop to their fullest potential physically, emotionally, socially, perceptually, and cognitively. This requires a variety of high-quality equipment and materials. "It is the environment, in all its manifestations, that is the curriculum" (Olds, 1983, 16). This chapter focuses on the tangible objects and space within the child care setting.

Dori Walther-Lee, President of Workplace Child Care Consultants Inc., advises using contrasting colors like black and white to help develop visual discrimination in infants, as well as to stimulate interest when planning infant space for corporate centers.

Jane Healy, a noted neuropsychologist, writes that "A variety of patterns are important: contours, horizontal and vertical lines, shapes, sizes and colors, for example. Visual feature detectors are forming which will later enable the child to discriminate such complex patterns as alphabet letters or numerals when there is a good reason for learning them" (1989).

ROOM ARRANGEMENT

Infant/Toddler Settings

The child care setting includes equipment necessary for providing basic care. Child care homes often include some special equipment or adaptations of available home furnishings (Figure 8–1).

Safety remains the highest concern when utilizing space for infants and toddlers. Structures to be avoided include rooms with angles that might be potential hazards for a mobile infant or a fast-moving, mission-bound toddler.

Figure 8–1 On cold or rainy days children enjoy the sensory table inside the child care center.

The ideal situation is to plan your space from scratch and create your blueprint based on activity centers and group sizes. In an ideal situation, you have the best possibility of avoiding hazards. Most areas, however, require conversion of space, which is a greater challenge to creative solutions because of possible safety hazards.

Whether you create new space or convert space to fit your child care needs, there are always angles, pipes, ledges, and rough surfaces that can create hazardous **drop spots**, where children could be injured. These should be turned into storage areas or made safe in some way. Products such as Ethafoam Padding® can be used around windows, corners, and rough surfaces. This padding can be laid over angled areas, reach up walls, and frame window ledges to make them safe.

By being creative and looking for every potential hazard to infants and toddlers, the child care specialist can **child-proof** any area so that it is safe.

Square footage requirements are always necessary when designing your child care setting. Infants and toddlers need a great deal of space, so whenever possible, additional footage above state and local regulations should be allowed.

Infants progress through all of the developmental phases to preschool with some of the same equipment by using it differently at various stages and ages. For example, the "Crawly Corner" by Childcraft® is convertible equipment comprised of hard foam rubber blocks. These cubes can be used in corners or can be free-standing, and are ideal for infants who are beginning to climb or for toddlers to build houses or do gymnastics safely. Using such equipment can provide safe exploration, imagination, and flexible uses for both infants and toddlers.

Equipment is needed to facilitate all areas of development and for all ages of children in the setting. One piece of equipment may aid development in more than one developmental area. For example, a child using a very low slide is moving physically and is also usually developing emotional responses such as pleasure, excitement, and pride in accomplishment. Children of various ages may enjoy the same piece of equipment. Two-year-olds may use the low slide competently, while a one-year-old may use it with caregiver assistance, and a nine-month-old may use it as a low structure to crawl on and to stand up with caregiver assistance.

Jones and Prescott emphasized that "planning space is a problem-stating as well as a problem-solving process" (1982, 18). Start with identifying the ages of the children in the program and planning your needed basic furnishings (Table 8–1). Arrange the furnishings in the room into areas based on usage (that is, a crib area for sleeping, a high chair area for eating). Jones and Prescott offered the following suggestions to child care staff for analyzing the setting.

1. Articulate program goals in a general fashion. What kinds of experiences and feelings do we wish to provide? What are the special needs of the children we serve?
2. What types of furnishings are necessary—for example, cribs for infants, climbing areas for toddlers (see Table 8-1)?
3. Look critically and closely at how well existing arrangements work.
4. Be willing to experiment with alternative arrangements. Design does not mean fixing ideas in concrete. Rather, it is a process of devising ad hoc solutions, informally monitoring how they work, and remaining open to change if the results warrant it.
5. Use large pieces of furniture such as bookcases to divide areas into different activities.

Using program goals that focus on holistic development, consider some equipment not included in Table 8–1.

Use of Playpens Playpens are used only when necessary. The purpose of a playpen is to contain the child in a small space. There may be a variety of reasons to do this. You may wish to keep the infant or toddler away from unsafe situations. You may wish to keep a child and his or her toys together. Be aware that too many toys can create a ladder for the child to climb out. Limit the amount of toys and change them frequently.

TABLE 8–1	BASIC EQUIPMENT FOR INFANTS AND TODDLERS
Child Care Center Classroom	Child Care Home
Indoor	**Indoor**
EATING	*EATING*
high chairs	high chairs
	booster seats for kitchen and dining room chairs
low chairs and tables	kitchen and dining room table
SLEEPING	*SLEEPING*
rocking chair	rocking chair
cribs	cribs
cots	family beds and sofa covered with the child's sheet and blanket for naps
TOILETING	*TOILETING*
changing table	changing table or counter space in the
supply storage	bathroom for changing diapers and
free-standing potty	storing supplies
toilet seat adapter	toilet seat adapter
steps (if needed at sink)	steps (if needed at sink)
STORAGE	*STORAGE*
coat rack	coat rack near door
cubbies	
shelves: toys, books	especially designated shelves in the family room, living room, and/or bedroom where books and toys are kept for the child care children
RECORD KEEPING	*RECORD KEEPING*
bulletin boards	wall and refrigerator door space to exhibit art treasures
record-keeping table, counter	table, counter, drawer
Outdoor	**Outdoor**
CLIMBING STRUCTURES	*CLIMBING STRUCTURES*
wood, tile, rubber tires, steps, tied ropes	rubber tires, steps, tied ropes
CONTAINERS	*CONTAINERS*
sand table or box	large plastic trays, pools for sand and water
water table or pool	

Some caregivers believe it is easier if every child has a separate playpen. Whatever the reasons, the caregiver must evaluate the use of the playpen.

Physically, infants and toddlers need gross motor movement, which includes crawling, pushing, pulling, and walking. The playpen limits the amount and types of gross motor movement. Children who spend much of their waking time in a playpen (or the crib used as a playpen) have limited opportunities for gross motor movement.

Socially and emotionally the playpen isolates rather than facilitates interactions with others. Visual and verbal exchanges must take place through the mesh of the playpen across a certain distance to the other people. Approaching others, touching, and selecting social experiences are severely limited and sometimes even eliminated when children stay in playpens. The caregiver maintains strong control, while the children have almost no control over when to get in and out of the playpen and what materials to play with. These children have little opportunity to learn to exert control over themselves and their world. For these reasons children should not be left in playpens for long periods. Wheeled walkers do not enhance upright development of the mobile infant. If their feet reach the floor only their toes bear body weight. Walkers put undo stress on back, legs, and toes before they are developed adequately. In addition there is a serious question of the safety of use and in some cases these walkers are banned by licensing regulations (American Academy of Pediatrics, 1993).

Rearranging the Setting   Arranging the room is not a one-time task. There are several reasons for change.

1. Activity areas are changed to offer new and novel areas.
2. Materials in the activity areas are changed to maintain challenge.
3. Modifications need to be made in equipment and placement when the age of the children changes.
4. Room arrangement is changed when the children's behavior shows that the room arrangement causes management problems.

Licensing regulations state minimum requirements for activity floor space per child: 35 to 55 square feet are often required, depending on whether the program serves infants and toddlers who need cribs. The arrangement of equipment, materials, activities, and people in this space is the responsibility of the child care staff. Though the arrangement of inside space may differ between child care homes and child care centers, some basic principles apply to all settings.

It is also very important not to neglect the needs of caregivers. Adult-sized chairs are more comfortable for adults and make working less physically stressful. Although the goal of a child care center is to be **child-centered**, it is important to provide for the needs of the caregivers as well.

Creating Infant/Toddler Activity Areas

The room's flexibility also reflects program goals. In describing a developmentally optimal child care center, Olds (1983) stated that "a child's successful interaction with the physical environment must satisfy three basic needs: the need to move, the need to feel comfortable, and the need to feel competent."

The Need to Move   In 1983 Olds emphasized the need for movement, stating that "Sensorial and motoric experiences are the bedrock upon which all intellectual functions are built." This is still applicable today.

The environment can be organized to provide for a variety of activities. Olds (1983) identified five categories of activity that the setting should make possible.

1. quiet, calm activities
2. structured activities
3. craft and discovery activities
4. dramatic play activities
5. large motor activities

Dalziel took the categories of wet and dry and quiet and active and related them to the arrangement of materials and space.

1. **wet-quiet area**—cooking, eating, messy media (paste, papier-mâché, etc.)
2. **wet-active area**—coats, toilet, sand, water, painting, some science materials
3. **quiet-dry area**—learning games and materials, writing, library, listening
4. **active-dry area**—large motor activities, construction (woodworking, blocks, building), dress-up, housekeeping.

To provide for these activities adequately, you must design the areas carefully to allow the child to move as much as possible from one activity area to another at will.

The Need to Feel Comfortable Olds (1983) identified the following benefits in meeting the need for comfort: "Comfortable surroundings foster playful attitudes that help lower anxiety, promote understanding, and enable children to be more open in divulging their personal responses to events and materials." Olds (1983) also suggested that variations in architecture "provide pleasing changes in sensory stimulation."

- scale—small spaces and furniture for children, larger ones for adults; areas for privacy, semiprivacy, and whole group participation; materials at child-eye level and at adult height
- floor height—raised and lowered levels, platforms, lofts, pits, climbing structures
- ceiling height—mobiles, canopies, eaves, skylights
- boundary height—walls, half-height dividers, low bookcases
- visual interest—wall murals, classical art, children's paintings, views to trees and sky
- lighting—natural, fluorescent, incandescent, local, indirect
- auditory interest—hum of voices, mechanical gadgets, music, gerbils scratching, children laughing
- olfactory interest—cookies baking, fresh flowers in a vase, plants in earth
- textural interest—wood, fabric, fur, carpeting, plastic, formica, glass
- kinesthetic interest—things to touch with different body parts; things to crawl in, under, and upon; opportunities to see the environment from different vantage points.

An activity area has five defining attributes: a physical location with visible boundaries indicating where it begins and ends, within which are placed work and sitting surfaces along with the storage and display of materials which are to be used on the surfaces in performing the activities for which the area is intended (Olds, 1983, 19) (Figure 8–2).

Figure 8–2 Children of various ages may be able to use the same piece of equipment at different paces.

The Need to Feel Competent To help the child develop feelings of competence, Olds asserted, "A teacher needs to provide a room which allows children to fulfill their own personal needs, execute tasks successfully, readily control their own tools and materials, make easy transitions, and control their own movements from place to place" (1983, 18).

PLAY YARD ARRANGEMENT

The play yard serves many functions as an integral part of a child care program. Just as caregivers evaluate and carefully design the indoor space to provide challenging and satisfying experiences, the outdoor space requires that same attention to program goals and design of space, equipment, and materials (Figure 8–3).

Designing Areas

Caregivers must know the needs and interests of their children in order to design appropriate and appealing outdoor environments. Essa recommended that "more thought should go into organizing the yard into interest areas—as indoors—to include quiet and noisy spaces, social areas, places to be alone, materials to manipulate, etc." (1981, 41).

Nature provides readily available and adaptable materials in many play yards. Grass, leaves, seeds, flowers, trees, bushes, dirt, sand, and water present intriguing exploring and manipulating opportunities. Caregivers should help children gain access to these areas and should allow and encourage their creative use of the materials.

Figure 8–3 There are many factors to consider when selecting outdoor play equipment—appropriateness, space, and cost, to name a few.

Sharing Space

The play yard needs to be able to accommodate the children in the program. If infants and toddlers share play yard space with older children, equipment and materials especially designed for the younger children should be arranged into a section in the areas of the play yard. Child care homes must utilize yards or a nearby park. With the multi-aged group of children usually present in child care homes, the caregiver must make adaptations.

Plan carefully to design shared space for use by several age groups. Establish rules identifying the way each age group can safely share the space, or have the children use the space at different times. For example, toddlers, who like to start and stop often and whose balance is sometimes unstable, may use tyke bikes on their own riding strip, and five-year-olds may have a different riding strip, where they can ride faster and ride through more complex patterns and lanes. If there is not enough space, each group may use the same strip at different times.

Safety Considerations

The play yard must be safe to get to and to use. Licensing often requires that the play yard be fenced. Many states do not allow any roadways between the day care setting and the playground areas. Grass provides the best surface covering for infants and toddlers and should cover most of the play yard. Concrete and asphalt surfaces hold the heat on hot summer days and cannot be used then by infants who are sitting and crawling. Special attention should be paid to floor or ground surfaces under climbing toys. In some cases wood chips or sand can be used, others call for impact blocks or other types of soft material rated by the height of the climbing equipment. For instance, for every 12 inches of height, 6 inches of soft ground support is needed.

As an example, most toddler slides are 22 inches high, and 6 to 10 inches of soft material is piled under the slide to offer support.

MATERIALS

Matching Goals with Materials

Materials include toys, books, paper, paint, clay, sand, glue, water, boxes, tires, and other items children use in the room and play yard. Like equipment, materials help children attain program goals relating to physical, emotional, social, and cognitive development.

Jones (1973) divided the environment into several dimensions: soft or hard, open or closed, simple or complex, intrusion or seclusion, and high mobility or low mobility. These dimensions can be applied in the child care setting to the materials, equipment, and arrangement of space as well as to the behavior of people.

Lists of materials in a child care setting help identify materials that meet children's needs (Table 8–2). Kate may need a toy that is intrusive, that puts her into contact with others. Another time she may need a toy that encourages seclusion, so she can be by herself.

Catalog age designations do not fit all children. Caregivers must determine when an item is appropriate for a particular child. Materials may have merit for some children but not for others. For example, a colorful mobile hanging above the crib may attract the attention of three-month-old Sam. It would go unnoticed by one-month-old Fred because (1) the tonic neck reflex keeps Fred's head turned to the side rather than looking up, and (2) his eyes focus best at about seven to nine inches and if the crib mattress is set low, the mobile will be beyond his focusing range.

Sand and water can be used both inside and outside. Their characteristics stimulate varied and satisfying experiences for children of all ages. Most children love sand.

Water and water play also fascinate children. Johnson offered these ideas.

"But why provide water play? The reasons are numerous. Children discover the qualities of water: water flows, things float on it, it conforms to the shape of a container, it mixes with other substances, it will evaporate. Children gain skills and concepts through water play: coordination, concepts of volume and measurement, language practice and extension, competence and mastery. Finally, children perceive water as pleasurable and satisfying, and the teacher can too if plans and precautions are made to make it a wet and wonderful experience." (1981, 14)

Age-Appropriate Materials

Selection of appropriate equipment and materials involves the caregiver's knowledge of the program goals, the children's needs and interests, the time and space for use, and the budget. Table 8–3 may help caregivers decide what to get.

With program goals emphasizing holistic development, a variety of items facilitating physical, emotional, social, and cognitive development are needed. Use Table 8–3 to help you see graphically whether there are items in each category. Some materials attract interest at particular ages. The age groupings in the guide are approxima-

TABLE 8–2   *TYPES OF EQUIPMENT AND MATERIALS*

Soft	Hard
cloth puppets	blocks
cloth and soft plastic dolls	hard plastic dolls
dress-up clothes	cars, trucks
fur	plastic curtains
pillows	sand
mats	paper
rugs	cardboard
cloth curtains	books
water	posters
clay	plastic, wood mobile
paint	wood
cloth wall hangings	linoleum
glue	baseball
ribbon	plastic bottles
cushions	catalogs
cloth mobile	magazines
rubber balls	buttons
sponge balls	metal cans
cloth scraps	sandpaper
foam scraps	
yarn	

Open	Closed
puppet	puzzle
doll	zipper
water	button/buttonhole
sand	snaps
clay	stacking rings
blocks	wind-up doll
	wind-up mobile

Simple	Complex
one-piece puzzle	four-piece puzzle
doll	doll clothes
clay	clothes fasteners

Intrusion	Seclusion
bike	large box to hide in

High Mobility	Low Mobility
bike	sit and spin
toy cars, trucks	slide
stroller, buggy	books
balls	blocks
	clay
	painting
	puzzles
	water
	sand

TABLE 8–3	*FACTORS FOR ANALYZING EQUIPMENT OR MATERIALS*
Analysis	*Items*
Facilitated Development	Telephone (example)
physical	
emotional	
social	X
cognitive	X
Age Group	
0–6 months	
6–12 months	
12–18 months	X
18–24 months	X
24–30 months	X
30–36 months	X
Senses Appealed To	
seeing	
hearing	X
touching	X
tasting	
smelling	
Number of Uses	
single	X
flexible	
Safety Factors	
nontoxic	X
sturdy	X
no sharp edges	X
Construction	
MATERIAL	
fabric	
paper	
cardboard	
rubber	
plastic	
wood	X
metal	
QUALITY	
fair	
good	
excellent	X
DURABILITY	
fair	
good	
excellent	X
Cost—$	
commercial	$15.00
homemade	
Comments	

tions; an 11-month-old and a 13-month-old may use the same item. Therefore, an item may overlap more than one age grouping. The guide will help you see which items a wide age range can use and which ones only a limited age range can use. Each age group needs a variety of items.

Infants and toddlers interact with their environment through their senses and therefore need items that stimulate these senses. At different ages children can make use of their senses in different ways. In the first few months of life infants see many things and need items to stimulate their interest in seeing. They do not have much control of their hands and fingers, so touching is limited to bumping and banging and finally grasping. A limited number and kind of items are needed to stimulate touching. However, two-year-olds actively use all their senses, and so they need a number of items to stimulate each of their senses.

Some equipment and materials can be used in only one way; others have flexible uses. Children and caregivers can adjust and adapt them in a variety of ways to facilitate development. Single-use materials are in themselves neither good nor bad, but they may be costly.

When initially purchasing equipment for all child care settings, consider buying a **choke tube,** because many states require its use. The device is a tube. Toy pieces are dropped through the opening. If the pieces go through the tube they are considered a swallowable hazard and are discarded. Only the toys with pieces larger than the opening are presented to the child.

It is important to analyze how materials and equipment are constructed. What they are made of and how they are put together will determine their durability in terms of the varied ways children will use them. This in turn will determine whether the item can serve the purposes for which it was intended in the program. Poorly constructed items that fall apart are frustrating, often unsafe for children, and costly for the program.

All child care programs must consider costs. To determine whether an item is cost effective, analyze the following factors for each item.

- the importance for program goal attainment
- the areas of development facilitated
- the durability of construction
- the number of ways it can be used
- the number of children who can use it
- the ages of children who can use it

A $45 wooden truck that is well constructed may be used for years and years by hundreds of children. In contrast, five $9 plastic trucks will probably be damaged and have to be thrown away within a year or so. Thus, for the same amount of money, the wooden truck is more cost effective.

The cost of equipment and materials can become astronomical. Therefore, most programs must decide which commercially made items they can purchase and which items they can make themselves. Some maintain that only commercially made equipment and materials have the quality young children require. Because some child care programs cannot afford to purchase all items, the quality must be built into their homemade items or they get along without the item.

Homemade Materials

Homemade items should meet high standards for construction, durability, and safety. Some things can be more individualized than commercially prepared items to stimulate the interest and development of children in the program. For example, a cardboard-mounted color photograph of each child in your room or home is an individual homemade item.

Diligent scrounging of free and inexpensive materials from parents, friends, and community businesses and industries can greatly reduce the cost of homemade items. One group that has developed a very creative and beneficial support system to child care programs for locating and using scrounged materials is the Maryland Committee for Children. In Baltimore, Maryland, it operates reSTORE, a recycling center for discarded or excess industrial materials that can be used by child care providers and parents to provide learning activities for children at a fraction of the usual cost.

Some books and articles are available that specifically identify homemade materials. Burtt and Kalkstein present "77 easy-to-make toys to stimulate your baby's mind" in their book, *Smart Toys* (1981), for babies from birth to age two. Douville-Watson identifies age-appropriate materials in seminar lectures, *Caregiver Training* (1997). Zeller and McFarland matched materials, ages, and skill development in their article, "Selecting Appropriate Materials for Very Young Children" (1981). In this text each of the chapters in Part III, Matching Caregiver Strategies and Child Development, includes ideas for homemade materials (Figure 8–4).

Figure 8–4 The refrigerator door becomes a bulletin board in a family child care home.

CONDITIONS FOSTERING SAFETY AND HEALTH

A Quiet Zone

All indoor and outdoor environments should include a **quiet zone** large enough for one caregiver and a child to sit comfortably. The space has multiple purposes. It is a place that a child may choose to go, where the child stays when ill, or when needing to release frustration. This space should be clean and comfortable, and not viewed as a place of punishment or isolation. Rather, it is a space in which the child can become organized and calm. A corner of the room or a tree away from active play can become a quiet zone.

Parent Awareness of Safety

In previous chapters, special techniques such as circle of safety, changing of the guard, and shadowing were discussed. These tools were presented to help give form to the concept of the child's environmental safety and your awareness of the impact and influences you have on children. Your ability to anticipate possible harmful situations develops more easily when you are sure that the actions you take can protect children. The most far-reaching and important issues involving children are those of health and safety.

Health and safety issues surround children in all settings and are the potential building blocks for strong caregiver-parent partnerships. Parent orientation should begin by reassuring parents that the center is a healthy and safe place to bring their child. Parents need to know that the health and safety of all the children in care is a primary directive of all center staff, and that major health and safety items are reflected in a written policy statement. This policy reflects mandates by state and federal governments. Others are health and safety recommendations established by the Department of Health and recognized professional groups such as the American Academy of Pediatrics.

The child care setting should be an ongoing example for parents to duplicate. The physical environment should be protective, well thought out, and designed from the viewpoint of the child.

Specific questions should be answered after observing the neighborhood. Is the neighborhood conducive to children walking around? How aware of safety concerns are the parents? Where have the child care customs come from? How do these customs affect the safety of all the children as a group? What should the written policy for the child care facility include? What parent health and safety classes should be included in the coming year? What is the average income of the parents? What community resources are available to help the center provide for all the necessary health and safety standards and policies? What organizations offer financial support to fulfill requirements for center children? The Health and Safety of the children in care are the highest priority; they are the base from which all else is built.

Starting from an empty outdoor space, a plan for development should be established. Centers in most states have a rigorous process to ensure that all the federal and state regulations are followed. Home care situations are generally less rigorous and depend more on the concerned, trained eye of the Child Care Specialist.

Every addition, change, piece of equipment, and all supplies must be well thought out and put through rigorous examinations for health and safety before being used in the facility. There is no time better spent. Prevention is the major rule for health and safety. If reasonable expectations for safeguarding children are understood, written down, and followed by all staff, parents, and visitors, then real work with the children and their developmental needs can follow. Managing the indoor and outdoor environments means making policies that should include the following topics.

- respectful care of children and treatment of staff
- parental partnership with all caregivers
- confidentiality of records
- proper documentation of staff and children with special needs
- control and prevention of injury
- prevention of child abuse
- staff health
- prevention and control of infectious disease
- promoting a safe environment
- individualized perspective care
- emergency care and training for staff
- ill child policy
- health training for children
- safety training for children
- transportation safety policy
- food safety policy
- community involvement
- ongoing training for staff and parents
- up-to-date medical history, immunizations, emergency numbers, and a referring pediatrician
- performance evaluations of staff at frequent intervals
- salary and benefit plans for caregivers, a way to state grievances, and a way to make suggestions for positive changes
- primary caregivers assigned to specific children, a daily log of ongoing change, and designated responsibility for each child's Developmental Prescription
- health and safety notification policy for parents of a disease to which their child was exposed, including the name of the disease, signs and symptoms, mode of transmission, period of communicability, and disease prevention measures

One staff member who is properly trained in emergency care and **cardiopulmonary resuscitation (CPR)** training must be present at all times. The nurse or designated health professional should be in contact with the parent, and when appropriate, the referring pediatrician, in the event that illness precludes a child attending care. This person is considered the health advocate for the center. He or she conducts health and safety seminars, keeps up with changing health policies, and informs the staff and parents of ongoing health recommendations.

Universal Precautions

Universal precautions must be understood and used by every person in the care setting who has contact with body fluids. Rubber gloves must be worn every time body fluids are present, such as when changing diapers and wiping up spills. Universal precautions are a set of procedures prescribed by the local Department of Health. It is the responsibility of each caregiver to receive the training and updates necessary to be aware of current policies.

Blood contaminants such as Hepatitis B pose a real health threat. Blood fluid (watery discharge from lacerations and cuts) poses a risk of the greatest concern. In addition, Hepatitis B can survive in a dried state in the environment for at least a week or even longer. Other fluids, such as saliva contaminated with blood, may contain the live virus. Procedures for handling spills of body fluids—urine, feces, blood, saliva, nasal discharge, eye discharge, and tissue discharges—*after putting on the specialist gloves*, are as follows.

1. For spills of vomitus, urine, and feces—the floors, wall, bathrooms, table tops, toys, kitchen countertops, and diaper-changing tables should be cleaned and disinfected.

2. For spills of blood or blood-containing body fluids, injury, and tissue discharges—the area should be cleaned and disinfected.

3. Persons involved in cleaning contaminated surfaces are to avoid exposure of open skin sores or mucous membranes to blood or blood-containing body fluids, injury, or tissue discharges by using gloves to protect hands. Illnesses may be spread in varying ways, such as coughing, sneezing, direct skin-to-skin contact, or touching an object or surface with germs on it. Infectious germs may be contained in human waste (urine, feces and body fluids, saliva, nasal discharge, tissue and injury discharges, eye discharges, and blood). Because many infected people carry communicable diseases without symptoms, and many are contagious before they experience symptoms, staff need to protect themselves and the children they serve by carrying out sanitation and disinfection procedures on a routine basis that prevent every potential illness-spreading condition.

   Education of staff regarding cleaning procedures can reduce the occurrence of illness in the entire group of children. Use a solution of 1/4 cup household liquid chlorine bleach to one gallon tap water when cleaning contaminated surfaces.

4. Mops should be cleaned, rinsed in sanitizing solution, wrung as dry as possible, and hung to dry.

5. Blood-contaminated material and diapers should be disposed of in a plastic bag with a secure tie, and labeled with a tag.

6. Sanitize, disinfect, and maintain toys and objects. Ensure that frequently used rooms and items are disinfected. Nondiapered children's rooms should be cleaned weekly. Thermometers, pacifiers, and the like should be disinfected between uses. Individual children's items and travel items for personal hygiene should be sent home with parents to be cleaned weekly, or after each use if more than one child uses a crib. All equipment should be cleaned and maintained by staff. Crib mattresses should be cleaned at least weekly. Each child should have his or her own bed, not to be shared with other children. Regular cleaning maintenance of the entire facility should be done weekly.

Hand-washing instructions involve modeling and assisting children in adjusting water temperature and pressure, cleaning palms and backs of hands and wrists, using liquid soap properly, cleaning nails and between fingers, drying hands properly, and disposing of paper towels.

Signs and Symptoms of Possible Severe Illness

Severe illness is indicated by the following signs and symptoms, provided by the Nassau County Department of Health (1997).

- unusual lack of movement
- uncontrolled crying
- coughing
- different breathing or wheezing
- uncontrolled diarrhea
- vomiting
- rash
- sores in the mouth
- red conjunctivitis
- head lice
- strep throat (until 24 hours after starting antibiotics)
- chickenpox (until 6 days after onset of rash or until sores are dried and crusted)
- influenza Hemophilus Pertussis (until 5 days placed on antibiotics)
- mumps (until 9 days after onset of swollen glands)
- hepatitis until one week after onset of illness or as directed by health official when immune serum globulin has been administered to all other children and staff
- measles (until 6 days after onset of rash)
- rubella (until 6 days after onset of rash)

Children who exhibit any of the above symptoms or who demonstrate unusual behavior in relation to any of the above symptoms should be removed to a predetermined place of isolation, where they should be supervised until a parent takes them home. For additional information, contact The American Red Cross, National Headquarters, Health and Safety, 18th Street NW, Washington, DC 20006.

Another publication available for health and safety is *Child Care Health Programs*, King County Dept. of Public Health, 110 Prefontaine Place South, #5r Seattle, WA 98104. You can also contact your local Health Department, or a local registered nurse (RN) or pediatrician, who will be happy to help you with additional library source information.

Immunization Schedule

The immunization schedule in Table 8–4, from the American Academy of Pediatrics, may be modified in some states that approve care of children outside the home at six weeks of age. All children must be immunized before attending day care.

TABLE 8–4 RECOMMENDED IMMUNIZATION SCHEDULE

Age in Months	Vaccine	Description
2, 4, 6, 15	*Haemophilus conjugate	Hib immunization
No regulations	Hepatitis B	3 injections shortly after birth to 18 months
2, 4 and 6 to 15 months	DPT	Diphtheria, pertussis, tetanus
4, 6, 15, 18	Polio	Poliovirus types 1, 2, and 3
2, 6, 15	MMR	Measles, mumps, and rubella viruses in combined vaccine
2, 4, 6, 15	Influenza	Type b conjugate vaccines
4	*Pneumococcal	
2	*Hepatitis A	
4	*Chickenpox	

*These are only recommendations; the child's pediatrician will help determine schedule.

Safety issues include transporting children from one area to another. Every state has seatbelt laws to protect children. The safest place for transporting children by car is the middle of the back seat in an approved car seat. Ideally, the seat should be attached to the metal frame of the car. Because of accidental eruption of air bags, all children should be seated in back seats.

First aid kits should be in the open and visible, but out of reach of children. First aid kits should include the following items (*Health, Safety, and Nutrition for the Young Child* [1997]).

- Activated charcoal
- Adhesive tape, ½-inch and 1-inch widths
- Alcohol
- Bandages, assorted sizes
- Blanket
- Cotton balls
- Flashlight
- Gauze pads, sterile, 2 × 2s, 4 × 4s
- Hot water bottle
- Instant ice pack or plastic bags
- Needle, sewing
- Roller gauze, 1- and 2-inch widths
- Latex gloves
- Safety pins
- Scissors, blunt tipped
- Soap, preferably liquid
- Spirits of ammonia

■ Splints
■ Syrup of Ipecac®
■ Thermometers, two
■ Tongue blades
■ Towels, large and small
■ Triangular bandages for slings
■ Tweezers
■ Vaseline®
■ First aid book, such as *Sigh of Relief*

First aid refers to treatment administered for injuries and illnesses that are not considered life threatening. Emergency care and first aid are based on principles that should be familiar to everyone involved in the care setting.

1. Summon emergency medical assistance (call 911 in many areas) for any injury or illness that requires more than simple first aid.
2. Stay calm and in control of the situation.
3. Always remain with the child. If necessary, send another adult or child for help.
4. Keep the child still until the extent of injuries or illness can be determined. If in doubt, have the child stay in the same position and await emergency medical help.
5. Quickly evaluate the child's condition, paying special attention to an open airway, breathing, and circulation.
6. Carefully plan and administer appropriate emergency care. Improper treatment can lead to other injuries.
7. Do not give any medications unless they are prescribed for certain lifesaving conditions.
8. Do not offer diagnosis or medical advice. Refer the child's parents to health professionals.
9. Always inform the child's parents of the injury and first aid care that has been administered.
10. Record all the facts concerning the accident and treatment administered; file in the child's permanent folder.

In most states, legal protection is granted to individuals who administer emergency care unless their actions are judged grossly negligent or harmful. This protection is commonly known as the Good Samaritan Law. Many states require a signed Emergency Care Permission form from the parent.

Animals need to be properly immunized, clean, fed, and cared for in loving ways. Permission slips for children to have access to pets should be obtained, and children with allergies should not be exposed to areas with pets.

Fire Prevention and Emergency Numbers

Fire drills should be established. A safety drill should be performed, timed, and recorded on a monthly basis. A safe place outside where everyone is to meet should be established such as a tree, building, or sign. An evacuation plan and map should be posted at all doorways.

Emergency numbers should be current and posted in a convenient place for the staff to see. New fire extinguishers should be in unlocked boxes and replaced after any use. Shatterproof safety bars or windows should be installed. All equipment must pass rigorous testing. All pools should have locked fences around them. Constant supervision is necessary whenever water play is initiated.

Regular fire drills are necessary. Determine the closest exit route and post on the wall a room diagram marked with your fire exit route. Talk with the children about times when all of you might need to get out of the building quickly; be careful, however, not to scare them. If you have nonwalkers, select one crib that will fit through doorways, put heavy-duty wheels on it, and put a special symbol on it. In case of fire, put your nonwalkers in this special crib and wheel the crib outside. Holding hands and talking calmly, walk the toddlers as quickly as possible out of the building. Continue to hold hands and talk calmly as you stand outside the building at a predesignated spot.

Materials and equipment must be selected with special care for use with infants and toddlers. Young children put everything they touch to a hard test: they bite, pinch, hit, fling, bang, pound, and tear at whatever they can. In their explorations of what they can do with the materials and equipment, young children focus on actions and do not think in terms of cause and effect so far as use is concerned. Therefore, the caregiver must take care to provide only materials and equipment that can safely withstand the child's use.

Safety is a matter to consider when analyzing the sturdiness of construction, the materials of construction, the size, the weight, the flexibility of use, and the effect the item will have on the child (Figure 8–5).

"Look for wood that doesn't splinter, wheels that won't pinch, corners and edges carefully rounded. Design, too, must be safety-conscious, stable and secure without small openings to catch fingers or limbs." (Community Playthings, 1981,10)

Figure 8–5 Scrap paper is a good recyclable resource for creative activities.

Figure 8–6 Only sterilized sand should be used in sandboxes for children.

The developmental capabilities of the child affect safety. A tyke bike may be safe for a 30-month-old but unsafe for a 9-month-old. Some equipment is safe if it is used with assistance but may be unsafe if it is used independently. For example, some children would not be able to play safely with a record player.

Aronson (1983) analyzed insurance claims for injuries in child care. She found that the following were associated with the most frequent or more severe injuries: motor vehicles, climbers, slides, hand toys, blocks, other playground equipment, doors, indoor floor surfaces, swings, pebbles or rocks, and pencils. Aronson recommended the following.*

1. Unsafe climbers, slides, and other playground equipment should be modified or eliminated. The U.S. Consumer Product Safety Commission suggests these modifications to make safer playgrounds: place climbing structures closer to the ground, mount them over 8–12 inches loose fill material such as pea gravel, pine bark, or shredded tires; space all equipment far enough away from other structures and child traffic patterns to prevent collisions; cover sharp edges and exposed bolts; limit the number of children using equipment at one time; and teach children to play safely (Figure 8–6).
2. Hazardous activities require closer adult supervision than activities with a lower injury rating.
3. Architectural features such as doors and indoor floor surfaces require special attention. Doors should have beveled edges and mechanisms which prevent slamming or rapid closure. Full-length-view vision panels

*Courtesy of Susan Aronson, Ph.D., Associate Clinical Professor Pediatrics and of Community and Preventive Medicine.

will help assure that small children are seen before the door is opened. Changes in floor surfaces and edges which might cause tripping should be modified. Long open spaces should be interrupted to discourage running in areas where running is dangerous.

4. Children must always travel in safety-approved restraints in cars, vans, and buses and follow all other safety rules.

5. Training and resources to change hazardous conditions should be made available to all staff. Injury reports should be routinely examined by trained personnel to identify and correct trouble spots. A systematic study of injury in child care centers and in home child care is needed to assist adults in making provision for the safe care of children (1983, 19–20).

Playground Safety

Guidelines for playground safety are set by the Consumer Product Safety Commission (CPSC). According to the April 2001 publication of the CPSC, 63 percent of children under two years of age are seriously injured from merry-go-rounds (Table 8–5). Consideration should be given to eliminating their installation or increasing supervision, including not allowing children under two to use the merry-go-round unaccompanied. Rules allowing only for adult accompaniment should become a standard of care.

Injuries related to playground equipment are reflected in Table 8–6, which is taken from CPSC publication number 325, National Program for Playground Safety

TABLE 8–5	INJURIES ASSOCIATED WITH PUBLIC PLAYGROUND EQUIPMENT, AGE OF VICTIM BY TYPE OF EQUIPMENT

Age of Victim (Years)	Type of Equipment						
	Total	Climbers	Swings	Slides	See-Saws	Merry-Go-Rounds	Other
Total	100%[1,2] (100%)[3]	100% (53%)	100% (19%)	100% (17%)	100% (3%)	100% (1%)	100% (7%)
< 2	3% (100%)	0% (0%)	2% (10%)	11% (64%)	4% (4%)	63% (21%)	0% (0%)
2–4	24% (100%)	21% (45%)	8% (6%)	40% (29%)	0% (0%)	25% (1%)	58% (19%)
5–9	55% (100%)	65% (60%)	53% (18%)	42% (13%)	66% (4%)	12% (<1%)	29% (4%)
10–12	15% (100%)	12% (41%)	30% (38%)	7% (8%)	31% (7%)	0% (0%)	13% (7%)
13–14	3% (100%)	3% (48%)	8% (52%)	0% (0%)	0% (0%)	0% (0%)	0% (0%)

[1]Detail may not add to total due to independent rounding.
[2]Upper percents sum vertically.
[3]Lower percents sum horizontally.

Source: National Electronic Injury Surveillance System (NEISS), 11/1/98–10/31/99, U.S. Consumer Product Safety Commission/EPHA.

TABLE 8–6	*PLAYGROUND EQUIPMENT INJURIES TREATED IN U.S. HOSPITAL EMERGENCY ROOMS, AGES OF VICTIMS BY LOCATION OF INCIDENT*

| Age of Victim (Years) | Location of Incident | | | | | |
	Total	Home	Public Park	School	Community Day Care	Other
Total	100%	100%	100%	100%	100%	100%
< 2	3%	5%	8%	0%	2%	<1%
2–4	27%	34%	23%	9%	54%	56%
5–9	56%	59%	55%	66%	42%	30%
10–12	12%	1%	12%	20%	2%	13%
13–14	2%	1%	2%	5%	0%	0%

Source: National Electronic Injury Surveillance System (NEISS), 11/1/98–10/31/99, U.S. Consumer Product Safety Commission EPHA.

(NPPS). Additional information can be obtained from CPSC Publication number 35 Mayo Clinic. Mayo Clinic Journal, May 1998.

Safety standards for all child care facilities should meet or exceed these standards. Careful selection of equipment and planning is necessary.

The Massachusetts Department of Public Health developed a Site Safety Checklist and a Playground Safety Checklist that can be used or adapted for assessing and providing safe and healthy indoor and outdoor environments for infants and toddlers (Tables 8–7 and 8–8).

TABLE 8–7	*SITE SAFETY CHECKLIST*

Item	Yes/No	Corrections/ Comments	Date Made Correction

General Environment

Floors are smooth and have a nonskid surface.

Pipes and radiators are inaccessible to children or are covered to prevent contact.

Hot tap water temperature for hand-washing is 110°–115°F or less.

Electrical cords are out of children's reach and are kept out of doorways and traffic paths.

Unused electrical outlets are covered by furniture or shock stops.

Medicines, cleansers, and aerosols are kept in a locked place, where children are unable to see and reach them.

All windows have screens that stay in place when used; expandable screens are not used.

(continued

TABLE 8–7	*SITE SAFETY CHECKLIST (continued)*

Item	Yes/No	Corrections/ Comments	Date Made Correction
Windows can be opened 6" or less from the bottom.			
Drawers are kept closed to prevent tripping or bumps.			
Trash is covered at all times.			
Walls and ceilings are free of peeling paint and cracked or falling plaster; center has been inspected for lead paint.			
There are no disease-bearing animals, such as turtles, parrots, or cats.			
Children are always supervised.			
There is no friable (crumbly) asbestos releasing into the air.			
Equipment and Toys			
Toys and play equipment are checked often for sharp edges, small parts, and sharp points.			
All toys are painted with lead-free paint.			
Toys are put away when not in use.			
Toy chests have lightweight lids or no lids.			
Art materials are non-toxic, and have either the AP or the CP label.			
Art materials are stored in their original containers in a locked place.			
Teaching aids (e.g., projectors) are put away when not in use.			
Curtains, pillows, blankets, and soft toys are made of flame-resistant material.			
Hallways and Stairs			
Stairs and stairways are free of boxes, toys, and other clutter.			
Stairways are well-lit.			
The right-hand railing on the stairs is at child height and does not wobble when held; there is a railing or wall on both sides of stairways.			
Stairway gates are in place when appropriate.			
Closed doorways to unsupervised or unsafe areas are always locked unless this prevents emergency evacuation.			
Staff are able to watch for strangers entering the building.			
Kitchen			
Trash is kept away from areas where food is prepared or stored.			
Trash is stored away from the furnace and hot water heater.			
Pest strips are NOT used; pesticides for crawling insects are applied by a certified pest control operator.			

TABLE 8–7	*SITE SAFETY CHECKLIST (continued)*

Item	Yes/No	Corrections/ Comments	Date Made Correction
Cleansers and other poisonous products are stored in their original containers, away from food and out of children's reach.			
Food preparation surfaces are clean and free of cracks and chips.			
Electrical cords are placed where people will not trip over them or pull them.			
There are no sharp or hazardous cooking utensils within children's reach (e.g., knives, glass).			
Pot handles are always turned in toward the back of the stove during cooking.			
The fire extinguisher can be reached easily in an emergency.			
All staff know how to use the fire extinguisher correctly.			
Bathrooms			
Stable step stools are available when needed.			
Electrical outlets are covered with shock stops or outlet covers.			
Cleaning products, soap, and disinfectant are stored in a locked place, out of children's reach.			
Floors are smooth and have a nonskid surface.			
The trash container is emptied daily and kept clean.			
Hot water for hand-washing is 110°–115°F.			
Emergency Preparation			
All staff understand their roles and responsibilities in case of emergency.			
At least one staff person is always present who is certified in first aid and CPR for infants and children.			
The first aid kit is checked regularly for supplies and is kept where it can be reached easily by staff in an emergency.			
Smoke detectors and other alarms are checked regularly to make sure they are working.			
Each room and hallway has a fire escape route posted in clear view.			
Emergency procedures and telephone numbers are posted near each phone in clear view.			
Children's emergency phone numbers are kept near the phone, where they can be reached quickly.			
All exits are clearly marked and are free of clutter.			
Doors open in the direction of all exit travel. Cots are placed so that walkways are clear for evacuation in an emergency.			

Source: Statewide Comprehensive Injury Prevention Program (SCIPP), Department of Public Health, 150 Tremont Street, Boston, MA 02111.

TABLE 8–8	*PLAYGROUND SAFETY CHECKLIST*

Item	Yes/No	Corrections/ Comments	Date Made Correction
All Equipment			
Nuts, bolts, or screws that stick out are covered with masking tape or sanded down.			
Metal equipment is free from rust or chipping paint.			
Wood equipment is free from splinters or rough surfaces, sharp edges, and pinch/crush parts.			
Nuts and bolts are tight.			
Anchors for equipment are stable and buried below ground level.			
Equipment is in its proper place and is not bent with use.			
Children who use equipment are of the age/development level for which the equipment was designed.			
Ground Surface			
All play equipment has 8"–12" of shock-absorbing material underneath (e.g., pea gravel or wood chips).			
Surfaces are raked weekly to prevent them from becoming packed down and to find hidden hazards (e.g., litter, sharp objects, animal feces).			
Stagnant pools of water are not present on the surface.			
There is no exposed concrete where equipment is anchored.			
Spacing			
Swing sets are at least 9 feet from other equipment.			
Swings are at least $1\frac{1}{2}$ feet from each other.			
Slides have a $2\frac{1}{2}$- to 3-yard run-off space.			
There is at least 8 feet between all equipment.			
Boundaries between equipment are visible to children (for instance, painted lines or low bushes).			
Play areas for bike-riding, games, and boxes are separate from other equipment.			
Swing sets are at least 6 feet from walls and fences, walkways, and other play areas; there is a barrier to prevent children from getting into traffic (e.g., when chasing a ball).			
Slides			
Slides are 6 feet in height or less.			
Side rims are at least $2\frac{1}{2}$ inches high.			
Slides have an enclosed platform at the top for children to rest and get into position for sliding.			

| TABLE 8–8 | *PLAYGROUND SAFETY CHECKLIST (continued)* |

Item	Yes/No	*Corrections/ Comments*	*Date Made Correction*
Slide ladders have handrails on both sides and flat steps.			
There is a flat surface at the bottom of the slide for slowing down.			
Metal slides are shaded to prevent burns.			
Wood slides are waxed, or oiled with linseed oil.			
The slide incline is equal or less than a 30-degree angle.			
Steps and rungs are 7" to 11" apart to accommodate children's leg and arm reach.			
Climbing Equipment			
Ladders of different heights are available for children of different ages and sizes.			
Bars stay in place when grasped.			
The maximum height from which a child can fall is $7\frac{1}{2}$ feet.			
Climbers have regularly spaced footholds from top to bottom.			
There is an easy, safe "way out" for children when they reach the top.			
Equipment is dry before children are allowed to use it.			
Rungs are painted in bright or contrasting colors so children will see them.			
Swings			
Chair swings are available for children under age 5.			
Canvas sling and saddle seats are available for older children.			
"S" or open-ended hooks have been removed.			
Hanging rings are less than 5" or more than 10" diameter (smaller or larger than child's head).			
The point at which seat and chain meet is exposed.			
Seesaws			
The fulcrum is enclosed or designed to prevent pinching.			
Handholds stay in place when grasped, without turning or wobbling.			
Wooden blocks or part of a rubber tire are placed below the seat to prevent feet from getting caught.			
Sandboxes			
Sandboxes are located in a shaded spot; only sterilized sand is used.			

(continued)

TABLE 8–8	*PLAYGROUND SAFETY CHECKLIST (continued)*

Item	Yes/No	Corrections/ Comments	Date Made Correction
The frame is sanded and smooth, without splinters or rough surfaces.			
The sand is raked at least every two weeks to check for debris and to provide exposure to air and sun.			
The box is covered at night to protect from moisture and animal excrement.			
The sandbox has proper drainage.			
Poisonous plants and berries are removed from play area.			
There is a source of clean drinking water available in the play area.			
There is shade.			
The entire play area can be seen easily for good supervision.			

Source: Recommendations of Statewide Comprehensive Injury Prevention Program (SCIPP), Department of Public Health, 150 Tremont Street, Boston, MA 02111.

Traffic safety involves safety near traffic and auto safety. Toddlers are excitable and change interests suddenly. Therefore, when walking with toddlers, one adult should be responsible for only a few children. You must be able to reach out and touch the children with whom you are walking. Many toddlers will not keep holding onto a rope or onto a child's hand five children away from you.

When traveling with children in a car or van be sure that each child is in U.S. safety-approved infant car seats or restraints. A crash at 30 miles per hour can produce a force on impact similar to falling from a three-story building (Transportation Hazards Commission, 1984). Check the car seats to make sure they are securely attached to the seat belt or floor. Strap the child securely into the infant car seat. Some children do not like to ride with restraints and will wriggle around until they are twisted in the straps. Be available to help settle the children and to keep their seat restraints on correctly so they will not be injured from improper use of the restraints. Check with your local or state traffic safety department or local hospital for specific details on approved infant car seats and restraints.

In the child care home or room it is essential to be able to leave and enter the room immediately. Evaluate the setting for fire safety, looking not only at what everything is made out of (will it burn?) but also at its location in the room. Children and adults need to be able to get out rapidly, and firefighters need to come in. Therefore, doors and windows should open easily, and the space in front of them should be kept free from clutter.

Equipment must be disinfected regularly. Food containers and utensils must be washed regularly and thoroughly. Since infants put toys in their mouths, these toys should be washed daily in a solution of $\frac{1}{4}$ cup chlorine bleach to 1 gallon water, or 1 tablespoon bleach per quart of water, and left to air-dry. Toys for older children should be washed regularly. Large equipment should be sprayed and cleaned. During the cold and flu season, disinfect toys and equipment more often than at other times of the year.

The floor should be cleaned daily, with spills and spots cleaned up immediately. Vinyl flooring should be swept or vacuumed and then sponge-mopped with detergent and disinfectant (never combine ammonia and bleach). Carpeting should be vacuumed daily, with periodic shampooing of the whole area. The eating area needs to be swept or vacuumed after each meal.

Sleeping equipment should be cleaned and disinfected regularly. Every caregiver must use universal precautions. Every child should have an individual sheet and blanket. These should be washed at least weekly and changed immediately if soiled. Diapers should not be changed on the sheet. The crib mattress and sides and the cots should be cleaned regularly with a disinfectant spray of 1 ounce chlorine bleach to 1 gallon water, or 1 tablespoon bleach to 1 quart water.

Toilet seats should be kept clean. Toddlers just learning to take care of their own toilet procedures often get urine and feces on the seats. Allow toddlers to be as independent as possible, and assist them when necessary with wiping, hand-washing, and clothes. Wipe the seat and spray with disinfectant afterwards. Some pediatricians recommend using an adapter seat on the toilet rather than using a potty chair. All staff should remain conscious of hand-washing procedures and wash hands after dealing directly with each individual child and help the child to wash his or her hands after toileting.

Remember that the quality of human relationships is one of your primary focuses. Your attention to cleanliness and sanitation should be an automatic procedure rather than a major obstacle to relationships. Find a balance so that the children experience a normal life. Conditions that are either dirty or overemphasize disinfecting and not touching children or materials focus undue attention on physical health while hampering emotional, social, and cognitive growth.

Human Immunodeficiency Virus (HIV) Infection

"On the basis of available data, there is no reason to believe H.I.V.-infected adults will transmit H.I.V. in the course of their normal child duties" (American Academy of Pediatrics, 1996). HIV cannot be transmitted as long as there are no open sores or other blood sources existing. HIV-positive adults may care for children. However, the HIV caregiver is at great risk due to the highly contagious environment that child care settings represent.

Parents of HIV-infected children should be alerted to exposure of such agents as measles and chickenpox. Their pediatrician will probably inject them with an immune booster such as immune globulin. Universal precautions are used on every incident of spilled blood or possible blood exposure.

If an HIV-infected child leaves the center due to exposure, the decision to return will be made by the child's pediatrician or nurse practitioner, the parents, and the director of the center. This is also a procedure for a known HIV-infected caregiver. Laws from federal, state, and local authorities are designed to protect families, and confidentiality is a legal right. All information, medical records, and personal information is set aside and kept confidential. No one shall have access to this information unless the parents give written releases. Only staff who have a need to know will be informed. They also must sign a disclosure form that is kept in the child's record.

Sudden Infant Death Syndrome and the Back To Sleep Campaign

According to the National Center for Health Statistics, 3397 deaths from SIDS occurred in 1995 (0.87 per 1000 births) compared to 1996, when 2906 deaths due to SIDS occurred (0.74 per 1000 births) after the Back To Sleep campaign was started. The Back To Sleep Campaign involves placing babies on their backs to sleep, not smoking around them, laying them on flat surfaces, washing all bedding before using it, removing all articles from cribs, not using a pillow, and regular health check-ups.

Child care professionals must take these recommendations seriously and regard them as some of the main safety procedures to use with infants. The American Academy of Pediatrics adds the warning that "It is important for caregivers to be knowledgeable about SIDS and that they take steps so they are not falsely accused of child abuse" (1996).

For additional information on SIDS, contact: The National SIDS Clearinghouse, 8201 Greensboro Drive, Suite 600, McLean, Virginia 22102, or SIDS Alliance, 10500 Little Patuxent Parkway, Suite 402, Columbia, Maryland 21044.

Key Terms

active-dry area

child-centered

child-proof

choke tube

CPR (Cardio-Pulmonary
  Resuscitation)

drop spots

HIV infections

quiet-dry area

quiet zone

universal precautions

wet-active area

wet-quiet area

CASE STUDY

Ena Robson, who was seven-and-a-half months old, had an unusual first day in the group family child care center. One of the helpers got sick in the middle of the day and another provider was called on to take her place. The first provider was ready to begin an assessment of Ena, but her replacement was not told and she did not conduct one.

Ena was small, frail, and odd looking. Her skull was box-shaped, her eyes were set far apart, and her mouth seemed to be in an unusual position when you looked straight at her. She had only a wisp of hair, she was mostly inactive, and her eyes appeared to be slow in reacting to visual changes. On her first day Ena was dressed in a tattered but clean outfit with strawberry patches and a tattered hat.

Since the regular provider was sick again the next day, the director took care of Ena and noted her odd appearance after checking her medical records. She performed a developmental assessment with the following results.

Physical, cognitive, and language skills were at the four-month level. Her social and emotional skills were at the six-month level. Since there was a significant delay in three areas (two months when she is only seven-and-a-half months old), the director decided to make referral for further evaluation to a pediatrician, language, therapist, and psychologist to follow up.

A parent conference was arranged with Ena's mother to obtain permission in writing for the referrals. Mrs. Robson arrived with Ena's grandmother, who was a trained nurse's aide, early in the morning for the conference. The director had reviewed the medical and family records in advance and found no unusual medical or family history. Della, Ena's mother, was tall but appeared to have been sick because she needed help walking, had deep circles under her eyes, and had a rather gray color to her skin. Della explained that Ena had experienced many fevers off and on but that she was well at present. The director began asking questions from an interview form, and after a short time Della became visibly stressed. Her voice changed, her arms and hands waved when she spoke, and she refused to answer questions about the pregnancy and birth of Ena. When the director rephrased the question to ask if Ena was a full-term baby, Mrs. Robson became agitated and Ena's grandmother answered in a calm voice that it would probably be best if they stopped the conference but that she would like to set up an evening appointment. A home visit was scheduled for that evening in Ena's home, and her grandmother said she would speak to Della in the meantime.

The apartment where Della and Ena lived was small and sparsely furnished. The grandmother and a registered nurse were administering an intravenous injection to Mrs. Robson when the director arrived. When Mrs. Robson saw the director, she began to cry, and Ena's grandmother sadly explained that both Della and Ena had AIDS. The director maintained a professional demeanor and actively listened to the grandmother as she discussed her sadness, anger, and disappointment. It was obvious that both Della and her mother were very fearful that the director would not allow Ena to stay in the child care setting. The director learned that Della's disease was progressing rapidly in spite of medications, and that Ena would start on medication the next day. Both Della and her mother asked the director to please keep Ena.

The director decided she would help this unfortunate family and keep Ena in the child care center as long as she was not running a fever or showing other disease complications. She assured the family that all of her staff used universal precaution techniques, and they were all aware that blood was the only transmitter of the disease. She reassured the family that her staff would hold, feed, and play with Ena in both the indoor and outdoor environments. They discussed the importance of administering the medication on a regular basis at the same time of day. As long as Ena was without disease symptoms, the director assured them that Ena was welcome to attend the setting. Both Della and her mother were relieved to hear that the staff would keep the illness confidential, since that was permitted by law.

Ena was cared for in both indoor and outdoor environments at the child care center, just like the other children. The staff provided her with more rest and activities to enhance her physical, cognitive, and language skill areas, and Ena showed improvement in her growth and development.

1. Discuss your feelings about working with a child, like Ena, who has AIDS. How do you feel you would handle such a responsibility?
2. What tools did the director use to deal with this situation? List all of them.
3. What other steps or help might the director have provided to this family?

Student Activities

1. Identify one item in your child care setting for each category of Jones and Prescott's dimensions of the environment.
2. Use Table 8–3, the Guide for Analyzing Equipment and Materials, to analyze five pieces of equipment and five materials used indoors and five pieces of equipment and five materials used outdoors in your child care setting.
3. Observe two children playing with materials. Write down the actions of each child as he or she manipulates the objects.
4. Draw a diagram of a child care room or home, showing the placement of basic equipment and activity areas.
5. Draw a detailed diagram of one activity area. Compare it to the specifications identified by Olds.
6. Draw a diagram of the play yard arrangement. Identify activity areas. List equipment and materials in each area.
7. Interview a caregiver in a child care program in which age groups share the outdoor space. Describe how that program facilitates play yard use and ensures safety.
8. In what ways does the neighborhood influence in which the child care setting is located?

Chapter Review

1. How can caregivers determine whether a piece of equipment or material is useful in the program?
2. When planning room arrangements, why do we distinguish between soft and hard, wet and dry, quiet and active?
3. What does it mean that the play yard is "an integral part of the program"?
4. List four safety factors caregivers must consider in selecting toys and equipment for infants and toddlers.
5. Describe how a toy or piece of equipment may be safe for one child and unsafe for another child.
6. List two adaptations that caregivers can make when young infants, crawlers, and toddlers share space.
7. "Go shopping" and "buy" all the fine motor equipment and materials a group of 24-month-olds will need (use supply catalogues from companies such as Child Craft and Community Playthings) and give yourself a realistic budget to work with.

References

American Academy of Pediatrics. (1996). *Caring for our children: National health and safety performance standards.* Washington, DC: American Public Health Association, pp. 92–111.

American Academy of Pediatrics. (1993). *Safety for consumers.* Glendale, IL: AAP.

Aronson, S. S. (1983). Injuries in child care. *Young Children, 38*(6), 19–20.

Burtt, K. G., & Kalkstein, K. (1981). *Smart toys.* New York: Harper & Row.

Community Playthings. (1981). *Criteria for selecting play equipment.* Rifton, NY: Author.

Consumer Product Safety Commission. (2001). Publication 35: *Playground equipment injury.*

Consumer Product Safety Commission. (1998). Publication 325: *Playground safety.*

Dalziel, S. (No date). *Spaces in open places*. Cortland, NY: SUNY, Project Change. Unpublished manuscript.

Douville-Watson, L. (1997). *Caregiver training '97. Creating boundaries using puppets*. Bayville, NY: Instructional Press.

Essa, E. L. (1981). An outdoor play area designed for learning. *Day Care and Early Education*, 9(2), 37–42.

Healy, J. (1989). *Your child's growing mind: A guide to learning and brain development from birth to adolescence*. New York: Doubleday.

Johnson, E. (1981). Water. Wet and wonderful. *Day Care and Early Education*, 8(3), 12–14.

Jones, E., & Prescott, E. (1982). Planning the physical environment in day care. *Day Care and Early Education*, 9(3), 18–25.

Marotz, L. R. et al. (2001). *Health, safety and nutrition for the young child*. Clifton Park, NY: Delmar Learning.

Massachusetts Department of Public Health. *Injury Prevention Program* (recommendations). Boston: Author.

Olds, A. R. (1983). Planning a developmentally optimal day care center. *Day Care Journal*, 1(1), 16–24.

Transportation Hazards Commission, American Academy of Pediatrics. (1984). *The perfect gift*.

Zeller, J. M., & McFarland, S. L. (1981). Selecting appropriate materials for very young children. *Day Care and Early Education*, 8(4), 7–13.

Additional Resources

Clar, P. (1981). Industrial scraps go to school. *Day Care and Early Education*, 8(3), 34–35.

Gordon, D. M. (1981). Toward a safer playground. *Day Care and Early Education*, 9(1), 46–53.

Jones, E. (1973). *Dimensions of teaching-learning environments*. Pasadena, CA: Pacific Oaks.

Salkever, M. (1980). Don't throw it away. *Day Care and Early Education*, 8(1), 55–57.

Helpful Web Sites

Babes in the Yard Make the yard a safe summer refuge for your little ones by following some simple safety guidelines. http://babyparenting.about.com/library/weekly/aa061999.htm?terms-babes+in+the+yard

Campus Child Care News. Determining overall space needs in campus child care centers. http://campuschildren.org/newsletter/nljan96/nljan96c.html

Child Care Tip of the Week, Child Care Online http://childcare.net/cctip.shtml

National Network of Child Care Children's Health and Safety. Indoor/Outdoor Safety. http://www.nncc.org/cyfernet/health.page.html

NebGuide Child Care Environment Safety Checklist, Outdoor Safety. http://ianr.unl.edu/pubs/safety/g1213.htm#list/

Outdoor Yard and Safety Arizona Child Care Resource and Referral Center. http://arizonachildcare.org/childproof/outdoorsfty.html

Sudden Infant Death Syndrome Network A world of information and support. http://sids-network.org/

The National Foundation for Infectious Diseases Fact Sheet. http://nfid.org/factsheets/Default.html

For additional infant and toddler resources, visit our Web site at http://www.earlychilded.delmar.com

Designing the Curriculum

Objectives

After reading this chapter, you should be able to:

- Identify major influences on the curriculum.
- Examine the caregiver's role in curriculum development.
- Write an integrated unit plan.
- Design an individualized curriculum for a group of children.

Chapter Outline

Infant-Toddler Curriculum
Influences on the Curriculum
Children with Special Needs
The Process of Curriculum Development
Implementing Curriculum

INFANT-TODDLER CURRICULUM

Definition and Scope of Curriculum

A curriculum is a course of study based upon a philosophy and goals. Specifically, a curriculum is the development of written goals, the definition of steps (in order of difficulty) necessary to achieve the goals, and the activities and materials necessary to accomplish the steps.

Infants and toddlers participate actively in selecting their curriculum and initiating their activities. When Jessie babbles sentence-like sounds and then pauses, Ms. Howard looks over at her, smiles, and answers, "Jessie, you sound happy today. That is a pretty ring in your hand." Jessie is playing with a large colored plastic ring that Ms. Howard has set near her. Jessie determines what she will do with the ring and what she will say. Her sounds stimulate Ms. Howard to respond to her (Figure 9–1). Daily experiences provide an integrated curriculum for children actively involved with themselves and the world around them. All are parts of the curriculum.

In the example below, the Facilitator (caregiver) offers choices to the child—child chooses—child makes decision to play with the toy the way she wants to—she

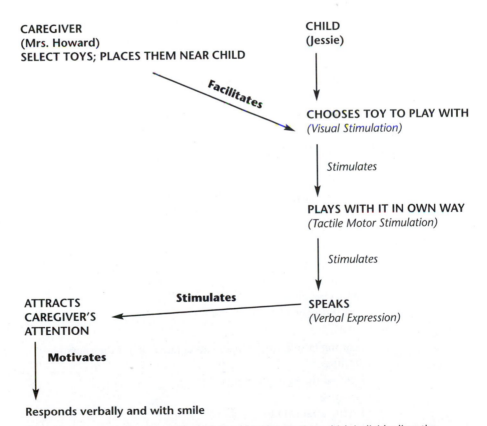

Figure 9–1 An example of caregiver-child-material interaction which individualizes the curriculum.

is self-stimulated and looks to the caregiver and vocalizes sounds. Caregiver is stimulated, takes action and is motivated to respond.

The five major Developmental Areas give an overall structure for defining goals. Each activity the child undertakes can then be broken down into these five areas. Next, activities involved in each area can be broken down into specific steps in the natural developmental hierarchy as necessary to achieve this goal. This process of breaking down tasks into their natural developmental steps is called task analysis. We task-analyze activities as specifically as necessary to ensure that the child has success at each step and attains the goal.

Example 1 The caregiver is holding four-month-old Lisa, patting her, and singing and talking to her. While the infant drinks milk from her bottle, she pats the flowers on the caregiver's blouse and looks at the flowers, the buttons, her own hand, and the caregiver's face. Lisa stops eating, talks to the caregiver, smiles, and then starts eating, patting, looking, and listening again.

Here is a task analysis of the situation described in this example using the five major Developmental Areas as a structure.

Infant Behaviors
  Motor
    Drinking milk
    Reaching
    Coordinating eye and hand to pat the flowers
  Seeing
    Focusing
    Changing focus
    Looking at attention-catching features
  Smelling
    Smelling familiar odor of caregiver
  Hearing
    Listening to caregiver's voice
    Hearing own voice
    Hearing caregiver's heartbeat
    Hearing own and caregiver's breathing
  Emotional
    Satisfying self
    Touching
    Achieving closeness
    Gratifying needs
  Social
    Gaining familiarity with and acceptance of another person
    Smiling
    Interacting with another person
  Cognitive
    Paying attention to details
    Noticing one object, then moving on to another and another

Language
  Listening
  Talking
  Responding to another's talking, singing
Caregiver Behaviors
  Observing
  Holding
  Feeding
  Rocking
  Talking
  Singing
  Listening
  Responding

Example 2 One-month-old Roger awakens from a nap and cries with intense body-jerking movements. The caregiver immediately lifts him up, holds him close, changes his diaper, prepares a bottle and feeds him, and smiles and talks quietly while doing so.

Infant Behaviors
  Physical
    Moves reflexively
    Begins to control movements
  Emotional
    Shows distress
    Calms down
  Language
    Cries
Caregiver Behaviors
  Listens
  Responds to infant's cries by physically comforting him using the ruing
    technique
  Determines cause of distress
  Responds to infant's needs for food and comforting
  Initiates and continues interacting by looking, smiling, and talking with the
    infant

Since infant and toddler curriculum involves the whole child, the child should have experiences that enhance his or her physical, emotional, social, cognitive, and perceptual skill development. The caregiver is responsible for planning and facilitating this holistic curriculum.

Each child is a distinct being, differing from others in some ways, yet sharing many of the same basic needs. *There is no single curriculum for all infants.* Caregivers have a special responsibility to design each child's curriculum by observing, thinking, planning, and putting many different skills and information together using the Developmental Areas as a structure and performing task analysis as the method.

Purposes for Curriculum

Designing curriculum serves several functions in child care.

1. The providers (caregivers) and the consumers (parents and children) contribute to the decisions on curricula.
2. The process of curriculum development helps the caregiver understand and plan so that curriculum goals and objectives are realized through daily experiences.
3. The curriculum reflects the interrelationship of the caregiver and child in determining and initiating the curriculum.
4. Task analysis of the curriculum ensures a balanced and natural progression in the experiences offered to children.
5. Awareness of need levels and task analysis of the ever-changing child supports and enhances overall growth and development.

INFLUENCES ON THE CURRICULUM

Society, the setting, the child, and the caregiver all influence the infant and toddler curriculum. Each of these influences on the child is discussed in detail in the following sections.

Influences of Society

Parents Parents place children in child care outside their own home for a variety of reasons. The majority of parents do so because they work. Their primary goal is to make sure their children are safe in a stable situation the parents can trust. Therefore, parents are concerned about the physical environment and how it is used.

Parents may share their expectations with caregivers. One aspect of curriculum is to help parents meet their needs as they relate to child-rearing and child care. Different parents have different ideas about child-rearing and parenting techniques. The following questions can stimulate varying responses from parents.

- Should a mother breast-feed or bottle-feed?
- How frequently should a parent hold and cuddle the infant?
- Should parents respond immediately to the crying infant?
- When and how should parents talk, sing, and play with the infant?
- What are appropriate mothering behaviors?
- What are appropriate fathering behaviors?

Parents also look to caregivers to reinforce and extend their own child-rearing practices. They usually convey to the caregiver their expectations for their children and their attitudes concerning parenting roles and children's behaviors.

Parents view themselves in various ways. Some parents expect to be "perfect" parents. The realities of parenting often cause them to feel guilty when they fall short of perfection or when they turn the child over to the caregiver. Their frustrations may affect their attitudes about themselves and their interactions with their children and caregivers. Sometimes jealousies develop. The child care staff can help these parents establish more realistic expectations.

Some parents seem very casual. They move in a very off-hand way from one parenting task to the next with seemingly little thought of goals or consequences. Some of these parents seem to place their children into child care with the attitude, "Do what you want to with them; just keep them out of my hair." The caregiver may need to emphasize the worth of the child and the importance of the parents' and caregivers' taste of enhancing this worth. Between these two extremes are parents who want to be good parents and who look to caregivers to assist them and their children.

Parents have ideas about what the caregiver should do. They express these positive and negative expectations verbally and nonverbally, in direct and indirect ways. Parents expect caregivers to help their children learn their values. They expect caregivers to reinforce behaviors the parents approve of. Parents expect caregivers to be competent. They place their trust in the caregiver to provide safe, healthy, reliable, affectionate, concerned, and intelligent care for their children. Parents have their own ways of judging caregiver competence. Some judgment is intuitive, based on listening to and watching the caregiver with their child. Some judgment is based on what parents think is responsible caregiver behavior.

Parents expect their children to cope with the child care setting. Working parents need to use child care and want it to be an arrangement in which the child will have satisfying as well as safe experiences. Parents expect their children to learn socially acceptable behavior. Parents define for themselves what is socially acceptable. They do not want their children to learn behaviors contrary to their own values and beliefs. Obviously, parents exert more interactive than passive influences on their children, which is explained in detail in the following section.

Corporate Child Care Advocacy

The American Institute of Physics (AIP) Childcare Center Inc. offers childcare services to AIP employees. These infants and toddlers are assessed by utilizing the developmental profiles offered in Part III of this text, allowing developmental prescriptions to be designed.

AIP employee Terri Braun recognized the need to help her associates balance family and careers. As Director of Human Resources at AIP, she was the inspiration for award-winning, state-of-the-art child care centers.

The AIP corporate sites in College Park, Maryland and Woodbury, New York are outstanding examples of child care advocacy in action. Because of Ms. Braun's direct efforts, employed parents can work with peace of mind, knowing their children are close by and are being cared for in an excellent manner. Both centers have received several awards for excellence.

As President Clinton put it, "The private sector needs to make an increasing effort to support partnerships between themselves and their employees. Child care is a national concern. . . . The welfare of tomorrow's business depends on the services offered to today's children." (Clinton, 1997).

Cultural Expectations

Parents feel pressure from family and society on their own child-rearing activities. They receive comments, praise, suggestions, scolding, and ridicule on a variety of topics. Sometimes they hear mixed opinions on the same topic. Some conflicting comments they are likely to encounter include the following.

- The parent should stay home with the newborn and very young infant/It is acceptable for the parent of a child of any age to work outside the home.
- The newborn and very young infant should stay home and not be taken visiting/The infant may be taken visiting occasionally.
- The parents are wasting their time when talking to and playing with a young baby/The parents should talk to and play with the infant.
- The infant needs lots of clothes and blankets to keep warm/The infant may need only moderate covering depending on the weather.
- The infant should start solid foods at 4 months of age/The infant should start solid food at a later age.
- The infant's solid food should be commercially prepared food/The infant should eat only mashed table food.

The behaviors of parents are a compromise between what society expects and what the parents feel comfortable with.

What one considers proper language and food are unique to one's subculture. The caregiver can draw attention positively to the similarities and uniquenesses of others. Expansion of language usage and food preference can be a part of the curriculum without negating the parent's cultural expectations.

Each caregiver brings unique cultural experiences and expectations to the caregiving role. Be aware of how these are similar to or different from those of the parents and other staff in order to plan and provide a curriculum acceptable to all.

For example, an infant will initiate visual, social, and language interactions but will stop if no one responds. If the caregiver feels uncomfortable or believes it is wrong to interact with the infant, that infant will gradually cease to initiate language or other interactions. But if the caregiver also initiates stimulation of visual, social, emotional, or language interactions, the infant will be challenged to respond and do the same.

Most caregivers have frequent physical contact with the infant because they feel comfortable doing it and because they know it is comforting to infants. When feeding a baby, most caregivers not only hold the infant and the bottle, but they also pat the infant and talk and sing. These activities meet several of the infant's needs: touching, holding, and patting help the infant feel secure and cared for; holding the bottle, talking, and singing to the infant provide a positive interaction between the caregiver and infant that stimulates the infant to look around, listen, and talk. The infant whose culture expects limited physical contact will have different experiences from the infant who has received much physical contact. Remain aware that withholding the 3A's—attention, approval, and affection—influences the child negatively just as much as providing the 3A's affects the child positively.

Cultural Diversity **Cultural diversity** means being sensitive to cultural differences in the children and families with whom you have contact. If you are embarrassed about discussing differences or prejudices, you might actually help and encourage children to form biases. You could, through omission, perpetuate oppressive beliefs and behavior (Jones & Derman-Sparks, 1992).

Child care settings offer many opportunities to experience cultural differences. Young children's beliefs and perceptions are only as limited as their interest in people, so plan activities and experiences that directly include multiculturalism (Turkovich & Mueller, 1989).

Every culture has somewhat different customs, mores, beliefs, and attitudes toward child care. While the style and form may vary from one culture to the next, all cultures have healthy child car practices. An example of different forms is the use of unleavened bread. In the Mexican culture, corn flour is made into tortillas, Sweden and Norway call it flatbrod (flat bread), and in China and India, rice is used. An example of different styles are the bright, contrasting colors of some cultures and the more subdued colors of other cultures. Each style is important and valuable to the people who practice it.

Judging the style and forms that exist in one culture is called having *bias*. To successfully integrate style and form into a curriculum, child care specialists must be aware of and examine their bias for certain styles and forms. These biases may not be obvious until they are carefully examined, and only then can they be changed.

When working with young children, it is important to be able to relate to each of them without bias or prejudice. Each infant or toddler is a unique being who develops in the same way and deserves the same positive support to remain unlimited and reach his or her full potential.

Some cultures do not talk to young children as much as other cultures. Some do not smile at them or expect a response. Some carry their babies on their backs and other cultures carry them over their hearts. Father involvement is different from one culture to another, as well as how family members interact with each other. Acceptance of these differences and the ability to perceive healthy child care practices within every culture is important for a competent child care specialist.

One way to overcome cultural bias in a child care setting is to subtly integrate music, artwork, and a variety of culturally defined materials into the curricula. Children are not born biased and they should grow up with positive memories of cultures different from their parents' that include a variety of sounds, patterns, and colors.

It is extremely important that the child care program honor individual parents' sociocultural milieus. Pacific Oaks, in Southern California, has done exemplary work in their Anti Bias Curriculum. Merril Palmer in Chicago, Bank Street College in New York, and Delmar Learning in Clifton Park, New York have developed materials that focus on cultural diversity. Other materials available for young children and adults include

Anti Bias Curriculum: Tools for Empowering Young Children, by Louise Derman-Sparks and the A.B.C. Task Force. Washington DC: N.A.E.Y.C.

Creative Resource for the Antibias Classroom (1999), by Nadia Saderman Hall. Clifton Park, NY: Delmar Learning.

Roots and Wings: Affirming Culture in Early Childhood Programs (1991), by Stacey York, Minneapolis, MN: Redleaf Press.

How to Have Intelligent and Creative Conversations with Your Kids (1994), by Jane Healy, New York: Doubleday.

Different and Wonderful: Raising Black Children in a Race-Conscious Society (1992), by Dr. Darlene Powell Hopson and Dr. Derek S. Hopson. Washington DC: Fireside.

Everyday Acts Against Racism: Raising a Child in a Multicultural World (a collection) (1996), by Marian Reddy (ed.), Seattle, WA: Seal Press.

Beyond the Whiteness of Whiteness: A White Mother of Black Sons (1996), by Jane Lazarre, Durham, NC: Duke University Press.

It is important that child care programs represent stepping stones to the formal education system and create partnerships with parents for progressive change. Some school systems have integrated into the curriculum programs with great promise for bridging the cultural gap resulting from teacher biases. The child care specialist needs to work with the local school district to ensure that antibias techniques and tools are consistent in the transition from child care to formal education.

The national SEED Project on Inclusive Curriculum (Seeking Educational Equity and Diversity) prepares teachers to lead year-long seminars in their schools reflecting on local practices. The project helps teachers welcome and respond to all children in a class and deal with student sensitivity to complex identity matters, such as race and gender.

The Celebration of Life Calendar is an effective tool to help integrate the concepts of diversity into daily activities and schedules. Tools like this help integrate multicultural concepts and practices into the program while providing a valuable vehicle for promoting positive parent input.

> "What does make a difference when you care for children from a culture different than your own is when you listen to what their parents want for them in their day-to-day care. It also means potential conflict when your beliefs and values clash with those of the parents. . . . A true multicultural infant-toddler approach in such cases would be to invite parents' input and then figure out what to do with it" (Mena & Eyer, 1997).

Nowhere is acceptance of differences more important than in the child care setting, where we grow seeds of new beginnings.

On a visit to the International Preschools in 1990, Barbara Bush stated, "The International Playgroups, as it was known during our New York days almost two decades ago, was the most special of special schools. . . . What a uniquely rich way for our children to begin to learn about the world, themselves and others!" Barbara Bush (1990). This statement encapsulates the understanding promoted by Childcare Director Nancy Brown and her staff at the International Preschools, Manhattan, New York. The International Preschools are an excellent example of child care curricula for celebrating diversity with young children and their families.

Mrs. Brown described how the goals evolved so that by 1963, the mission was to help bring quality educational programs to larger numbers of international families who came to New York City through organizations such as the United Nations and the Consular Corporation hospitals and universities. In 1968, the Creche, a popular infant-toddler program serving more than 100 children a year, was opened under the sponsorship of the New York City Commission for the United Nations. By 1972, more than 600 children were enrolled in five different programs offered by the Creche. Over the years, more than 100 countries have been represented. In 1995, the United Association for the Education of Young Children granted the International Preschools accreditation status, thereby recognizing the organization as a provider of high-quality programs that meet the developmental needs of young children.

> "The International Preschools provides young children and their families from all over the world an opportunity to share their cultures and gain a sense of international awareness through mutual understanding and respect. We recognize that all children are individuals with unique qualities and interests. Our developmentally-based program is designed to build on each individual's strengths. Through the play experience, we seek to promote the

cognitive, emotional, social and physical growth of each child within a nurturing atmosphere." (Brown, 1995)

The International Preschools' guidelines for teachers include these.

- Respect diversity.
- Avoid stereotyping.
- A girl can be strong and a boy can be gentle.
- Recognize and encourage prosocial behavior such as cooperation.
- Listen to children with attention and respect.
- Do not forget to enjoy the children!
- A relaxed and happy atmosphere makes learning fun.

Some specific curriculum suggestions to handle diversity include the following.

- Give children a flag that represents their heritage and country.
- Design the daily curriculum and the semester's outline around different countries that the children in your class represent.
- Make a calendar representing a holiday for each child.
- Involve the children in activities.
- Have the parents come and demonstrate their native costumes.
- Encourage parents to wear costumes and describe the reason for a particular celebration, and tell a story told them by their grandparents to the other parents, children, and staff.
- Have children or parents bring native food or desserts to share with others.

One holiday the entire school (all five locations) celebrates is United Nations Day. In her 2001 presentation in Anaheim at the annual NAEYC convention, Andre King, director of the Easter Seals California Child Development Center Network, discussed providing culturally consistent care.

"The 'Anti-Bias' movement asks us to acknowledge that each of us is biased toward what we have always known, and to be open to looking at other ways of doing things that might be equally valid. We are asked to consider people who are different from us and ideas that are different from ours, and find ways of living together, to tolerate each other."

In her discussion of cultural empowerment she laid out six rules.

1. Culture is learned. Children learn rules both directly by being taught ("hold your fork in your left hand and your knife in your right") and through observation. It can be a mistake to assume a person's culture from [his or her] appearance.
2. Culture is characteristic of groups. Cultural rules come from the group and are passed from generation to generation; they are not invented by the individual. Do not mistake individual differences for cultural differences. We share some characteristics with our cultural group, but we are also defined by our individual identities.
3. Culture is a set of rules for behavior. Cultural rules influence people to act similarly, in ways that help them understand each other. For instance, how we greet each other and address each other are influenced by our cultural backgrounds. Culture is not the behavior, but the rules that shape the behavior.

4. Individual members of a culture are embedded to different degrees within their culture. Because culture is learned, people learn it to different degrees. Family emphasis, individual preferences and other factors influence how deeply embedded one is in one's culture.

5. Cultures borrow and share rules. Every culture has a consistent core set of rules, but they are not necessarily unique. Two cultures may share rules about some things, but have very different rules about other things. This gets very confusing for a person operating within two cultures that have some similarities and some differences.

6. Members of [a] culture group may be proficient at cultural behavior but unable to describe the rules. Because acculturation happens gradually, as a natural process, a person may not even be aware of the consistent rules that govern his/her behavior. Just as a four-year-old who speaks very well may not know the technical rules of the language, someone who is culturally competent may not know that they are behaving according to a set of cultural rules. They have simply absorbed the rules by living with them.

The following example calendar is from *Celebrating Diversity: A Multicultural Resource* (Clegg et al., 1995).

The Celebration of Life Calendar

Month/Day	Holiday	Country
January		
1	New Year's Day; Georgian Calendar Everyone's Birthday—all add one year	China/Asia
7	Nandkusa Festival—honors seven plants that are believed to have medicinal powers	Japan
15	Martin Luther King Jr.—National Holiday remembering the African-American minister and civil rights leader	United States
February		
5	Constitution Day—present constitution was adopted in 1917	Mexico
11	National Day—commemorates the fall of the shah and the takeover of Ayatollah Khomeini (1979)	Iran
19	Independence Day—independence from the Soviet Union in 1990	Estonia
March		
(unscheduled)	Purim—Jewish Holiday commemorates Queen Esther's role in saving the Hebrews	Israel
(unscheduled)	Taiwan Al-Qudr—"the Night of Power" Muslim festival	
3	Hinamatsuri: Doll Festival—special day for girls	Japan
17	St. Patrick's Day— celebrates Christianity coming to Ireland	Ireland
22	New Year Day	India
April		
(unscheduled)	Good Friday—oldest Christian celebration commemorating the day of the crucifixion	
(unscheduled)	Easter—Christian day commemorating the resurrection of Christ	

The Celebration of Life Calendar

Month/Day	Holiday	Country
April		
(unscheduled)	Festival of Redvan-Baha'i—holiday honoring Baba Ullah, prophet founder of the Baha'i faith	
May		
1	National Holiday—commemorates the battle of Puebla in 1862 (also widely celebrated in the United States)	Mexico
22	Slavery Abolition Day	French West Indies
25	Freedom Day—commemorates the independence from foreign rule in Africa	Africa
June		
2	Republic Day	Italy
6	Memorial Day	Korea
12	Independence Day	Philippines
18	Evacuation Day	Egypt
21	Festival of Lord Gagannath, Lord of the Universe	India
July		
4	Independence Day	United States
	Tanabuta, or Star Festival	Japan
14	Bastille Day—Independence Day	France
17	World Indian Day	Eskimo
26	Independence Day	Liberia
August		
(unscheduled)	Festival of Hungry Ghosts	China
31	Independence Day	India
September		
(unscheduled)	Rosh Hashanah (Jewish New Year)	Israel
3	Independence Day	Chile
8	United Nations International Literacy Day	World
21	World Gratitude Day—to unite all people in gratitude	
29	Michaelmas—celebration of all angels in Greek and Roman Catholic Church	
October		
(unscheduled)	Grandparents Day	United States
(unscheduled)	White Sunday—American and Western Samoa, adults and children reverse roles	Samoa
(unscheduled)	National Book Day— Reading Day	United States
(unscheduled)	United Nations Day for the Elderly	World
17	Black Poetry Day	United States
24	United Nations Day—all celebrate	World
November		
(unscheduled)	World Community Day	World
(unscheduled)	Thanksgiving Day	United States
3	Sandwich Day—celebrates the birthday of John Montague, the fourth Earl of Sandwich, and creator of the sandwich	United States

(continued)

The Celebration of Life Calendar (*continued*)

Month/Day	Holiday	Country
November		
15	Schichi-Go-San—annual children's festival honoring all three-year-olds, and five- and seven-year-old girls	Japan
17	National Young Readers' Day	United States
21	World Hello Day	World
December		
6	Independence Day	Finland
13	Santa Lucia Day, the Festival of Lights	Sweden
25	Christmas—Celebration of birth of Jesus Christ	
31	New Year's Eve—Celebrates new beginning	World

Television Influences are either interactive or passive. **Interactive influences** are those in which the child directly interacts; **passive influences** affect the child without the necessity of child interaction. For example, television is a passive influence because the communication is one-way; the television does not require interaction from the child. On the other hand, the caregiver is an interactive influence because the child is required to respond to the caregiver.

Television is the largest single passive influence on families and caregivers. Because of its passive (but effective) influences on children and parents, television should be used cautiously by caregivers. Parents see role models of what parents "ought" to do. They compare their own children to those on television. Toddlers watch television and imitate repeated language and behavior they do not understand. They lack judgment to determine whether what they are doing and saying is appropriate. Caregivers see television role models and come to expect certain adult and child behavior regarding learning, achievement, and excellence. These pressures affect their selection of curriculum.

The ease with which television becomes an instant babysitter may tempt the harried caregiver at times, but hopefully the caregiver will not give in to the temptation. The caregiver needs to be aware of how television can limit infant and toddler experience. Very few television programs are appropriate for infants and toddlers. Television does not permit the child active interaction with it, and the child under three years of age cannot understand most of what is on. Special programs should be carefully selected, and the caregiver should actively view them with the toddler. The television set should *not* be left on through adult programs. Not only is the content inappropriate for toddlers, but children also need times of peace and quiet when no extra noises are intruding.

The video cassette recorder (VCR) provides a valuable tool to the caregiver when used wisely. Within the last several years, educational publishers have produced many worthwhile videos that can enhance the curriculum when used by the caregiver to help children interact with material presented.

Jane Healy, in her book *The Child's Growing Mind*, states: "It's a hard parental assignment, but try to be aware of potential anxiety-producing information to which your child is exposed, and make yourself available to help put it in perspective. TV violence and even current events are hard enough for adults to comprehend, but impossible for children. They need help and lots of reassurance in dealing with the complexities of the world."

In general, television should not be perceived as a way to keep children occupied. Only supervised programs should be allowed.

Influences from the Care Setting

Child Care Home Influences of the setting on your curriculum are varied. Physical location, financial limitations, parent work schedules, and other factors make up the child care setting. Establishing a positive learning environment is essential to quality care whatever resources and limitations you find in your particular setting. Establishing a consistent, warm, friendly environment where large doses of the 3A's (attention, approval, and affection) are administered is the way to establish the most powerful positive influence in any physical setting.

Family child care homes provide a homelike situation for the infant or toddler. Because the child must adjust to a new caregiver and a new situation, the caregiver should quickly establish the child's familiarity with a similar setting: crib, rooms, and routines of playing, eating, sleeping. A warm one-to-one relationship between the family child care provider and the child provides security in this new setting.

Child Care Center Some child care centers care for infants 6 weeks of age and older, and a few centers are even equipped to care for newborns. The very young infant must receive special care. One caregiver in each shift needs to be responsible for the same infant each day. The caregiver should adjust routines to the infant's body schedule rather than trying to make the infant eat and sleep according to the center's schedule. The caregiver will need to work closely with parents to understand the infant's behavior and changing schedule of eating and sleeping. Consistently recording and sharing information with parents is necessary to meet infant needs and involve the parents in their child's daily experiences.

Time The number and age of children in a group will affect the amount of time the caregiver has to give each child. The needs of the other children also affect how the time is allocated.

Schedules in the child care home or center are adjusted to the children and the parents' employment schedules. For instance, if three school-aged children arrive at 3 P.M., the infant feeding may be disrupted. But it can also mean there are three more people to talk and play with the infant.

If the parent works the 7 A.M. to 3 P.M. shift, the infant awakening from a nap at 2:45 P.M. may need special planning to be ready when the parent arrives. The quality of interaction can remain high even when time for interactions is limited. Caregivers should determine which earlier activities will let them spend more time with the infant on this nap schedule.

Influences from the Child

Every child has an internal need to grow, develop, and learn. During the first years of life children's energies are directed toward those purposes both consciously and unconsciously. Though children cannot tell you this, observers can see that both random and purposeful behaviors help children.

Figure 9–2 The caregiver facilitates each child's development by making the child feel secure.

The children look, touch, taste, listen, smell, reach, bite, push, kick, smile, and take any other action they can in order to actively involve themselves with the world. The fact that children are sometimes unsuccessful in what they try to do does not stop them from attempting new tasks. Sometimes they may turn away to a different task, but they will keep seeking something to do.

Infants learn from the responses they get to their actions. When the caregiver consistently "answers" cries of distress immediately, infants begin to build up feelings of security (Figure 9–2). Gradually these responses will help infants learn to exert control over their world. If caregivers let infants cry for long periods before going to them, the infants remain distressed longer. They may have difficulty developing a sense of security and trust. Remember to use the "unlimited child" principle: the more immediately and completely needs are fulfilled, the more securely and happily children will develop. You can't love or fulfill an infant or toddler too much. Add large measures of the 3A's to this principle, and you will be influencing happy and secure children.

CHILDREN WITH SPECIAL NEEDS

Because the Individuals with Disabilities Education Act was passed, children with special needs became entitled to appropriate public education regardless of their disability. The law provided that children should have the "least restrictive environment possible," which meant that all children would be registered within the same school district and special services would be provided as necessary.

Three- to five-year-olds were among the first to be served. Then, additional laws were passed to educate even younger children with special needs. One pediatrician, Dr. Cecilia McCarton, took exception to the accepted view that infants with special needs do not need special public assistance. In an interview conducted by Linda Douville-Watson in 1994, McCarton said, "In the 70's, the usual practice was to make a diagnosis and then send the parents of these children back to their own communities for follow-up care. There was not a single place that offered a diagnosis, prescription for care and actual appointments with those supporting professionals necessary for follow-up. Parents faced extremely frustrating situations, and most often were devastated to find no available people in their community to follow through with our suggestions."

In response to the need, Dr. McCarton developed one of the first comprehensive treatment centers in the United States. She has conducted research on thousands of children with low birth weight and special anomalies. Now director of the McCarton Center for Developmental Pediatrics, she has done much to advance the areas of research in underweight preemies and children with special needs.

Functional Ability versus Actual Age

Age appropriateness has a different meaning when designing curricula for children with special needs. Special needs children often function at a lower level in certain areas than their actual age, so knowing the functional age of a child is essential to structure and design appropriate activities. Equally important is using attention, approval, and affection as a way of communicating and satisfying the child's needs.

Today, curricula for special needs children generally involve a didactic team approach. Specialists interact with each other on behalf of the child based on the type of special needs the child exhibits. A functional age is established in each area of development and priorities for care are set using Developmental Profiles and Prescriptions.

Special Needs Children and Community Support

Caregivers must be aware of community resources for special children. Many children with special needs lack funding sources. Sometimes community groups or generous, qualified professionals donate their time and energy to ensure proper treatment for special groups. One example is the Nassau Cleft Palate Center and Dr. Pamela Gallagher, a plastic surgeon who volunteers her time and expertise in Long Island, New York to perform cleft palate repairs for children in need. The Nassau Cleft Palate Center has materials available for concerned parents including *A Guide For Parents of Children with A Cleft Lip and Palate*. For more information, contact The Nassau Cleft Palate Center, Long Island Plastic Surgical Group, 999 Franklin Avenue, Garden City, Long Island, New York 11530, (516) 742-3404. Call The Cleft Palate Foundation at (212) 481-1376 for literature, resources, and parent groups nationwide.

Brain Gym

The human brain has three main structures: the cerebrum, the cerebellum, and the brain stem. The control center is the cerebrum, which processes all the information it receives. It is the largest part of the brain, comprising approximately 80 percent of the total area. Each of its halves, called hemispheres, has five lobe areas. Each lobe area is responsible for specific tasks, such as recognition of visual images, bodily sensations, and emotions. The entire cerebrum is covered by a layer of gray matter called the cerebral cortex. This is where the higher intellectual functions originate, such as memory, receiving, and interpreting information from the five senses (vision, hearing, taste, smell, and touch).

The cerebellum is located at the back of the brain behind the cerebrum. This area helps maintain balance and the ability to stand upright and coordinate muscle activity. The brain stem is the life-support system. It maintains essential functions such as heartbeat, breathing, blood pressure, swallowing, and digestion. It is the site of the communication center in humans, it regulates additional processes such as thirst and hunger, and it sends information to other parts of the brain.

One difference between a newborn and an adult brain is that the newborn's left and right hemisphere have not yet defined specific tasks and functions. Normally developed newborn infants have clearly defined brain anatomy waiting to be determined by stimuli processed from the environment.

By the end of 36 months, the hemispheres have defined functions with individual styles of integration. In normal children, the kind of experiences the environment offers will determine how well prepared the brain is for future learning and how well the hemispheres integrate information.

Brain Gym was discovered and developed by Drs. Paul and Gail Dennison, who found that, when specific body maneuvers were done by children, their attention consistently improved. Brain Gym has successfully been used with autistic and speech-impaired children, attention deficit, hyperactivity disorder, and emotionally handicapped children. All the maneuvers are designed to stimulate brain-center responses by working with connecting body parts that cross the body's midline. Debbie Neurnberger, a kinesthetic counselor who specializes in teaching Brain Gym techniques to children and adults, lectures at Mind Resources, Inc. in Honesdale, Pennsylvania. Brain Gym helps establish optimal learning readiness. Ms. Neurnberger explains, "These techniques are so easy that they are met with much skepticism. However, the results are consistently impressive. All educators should be promoting these simple techniques."

Teaching toddlers simple activities, such as cross-pattern crawling, right-hand-to-left-knee exercise, and Simon Says, helps to promote focus and impacts on the focal attention of the child. The elimination of sugar and high-carbohydrate foods are also recommended. It is also important to drink plenty of water.

Carla Hannaford, author of *Smart Moves: Why Learning Is Not All in Your Head* (1995), has this to say: "We must give learners mind/body integrative tools, such as Brain Gym, that allow them to stop the stress cycle and activate full sensory/hemisphere access."

Brain Research

The child contributes to his or her own development because genetic make-up and brain potential help determine intelligence. New brain research indicates that, not only is the environment a crucial factor for brain development, but also there are specific times, called windows of learning, when the brain must be stimulated. The following is an example of how the brain is wired.

Vision	Unless exercised early on, the visual system will not develop.
Feelings	Emotions develop in layers, each more complex than the last.
Language	Language skills are sharpest early on, but grow throughout life.
Movement	Motor-skill development moves from gross to increasingly fine.

Researchers at Baylor College of Medicine, for example, have found that "children who don't play much or are rarely touched develop brains 20 percent to 30 percent smaller than normal for their age." Not only do young rats reared in toy-strewn cages exhibit more complex behavior than rats confined to sterile, uninteresting boxes, but researches at the University of Illinois at Urbana-Champaign have found the brains of these rats contain as many as 25 percent more synapses per neuron. "The data underscore the importance of hands-on parenting, of finding the time to cuddle a baby, talk with a toddler and provide infants with stimulating experiences." There is an urgent need, say child-development experts, for preschool programs designed to boost the brain power of youngsters born into impoverished rural and inner-city households. Without such programs, they warn, the current drive to curtail welfare costs by pushing mothers with infants and toddlers into the work force may well backfire. "There is a time scale to brain development, and the most important year is the first," notes Frank Newman, president of the Education Commission of the States. "By the age of three, a child who is neglected or abused bears marks that, if not indelible, are exceedingly difficult to erase" (Nash, 97).

THE PROCESS OF CURRICULUM DEVELOPMENT

Curriculum development is an ongoing process of goal setting and problem solving. As previously discussed, assessment of each child in the five major Developmental Areas provides a structure in which meaningful goals may be established. A development cycle helps ensure that the curriculum is appropriate and relevant. The process involves setting goals, selecting objectives, determining appropriate methods, using task analysis, selecting materials, evaluating the attainment of objectives, gathering feedback on the above components, and making necessary adjustments (Figure 9–3).

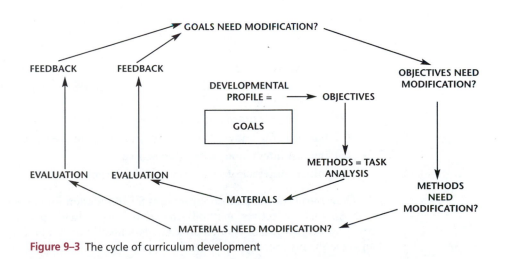

Figure 9–3 The cycle of curriculum development

Purposes and Philosophy

CDA

VI. 13

The purposes for providing child care and the philosophies of parents and caregivers need to be identified and discussed. This text reflects the following view.

1. The purposes of child care
   a. for children are to provide a positive and supportive environment with trained and experienced staff where children can develop to their fullest potential physically, emotionally, socially, perceptually, and cognitively.
   b. for parents are to provide a mutually supportive environment with a variety of materials and experiences and a staff with diverse abilities, where parents can place their children for high-quality care and where they can also receive guidance and resources for parenting.
   c. for caregivers are to provide a work environment that addresses the needs of infants, toddlers, and staff and to create a positive team to meet the needs of the families being served.

2. The philosophy of child care
   a. All people are viewed developmentally. From the moment of birth to the time of death every person is constantly growing in many ways. Focusing on the positive changes resulting from growth helps maintain a positive learning environment.
      (1) Each infant and toddler is progressing through specific sequences or stages of development.
      (2) Each parent is in a phase of parenting that contributes to the parent's knowledge and skill. Some are new parents, some are experienced, some anxious, some relaxed, some informed, some nonchalant, and some eager.
      (3) Each caregiver has his or her own level of competence. Caregivers have knowledge obtained from talking, reading, and studying and they have individual experiences with children and parents. Their views and expectations of themselves as people and caregivers all contribute to their increasing competence as caregivers.
   b. Development and growth occur through active interaction with one's environment and can be observed through the five major Developmental Areas. Each person
      (1) is an active learner.
      (2) constructs knowledge through active interactions with people and materials.
      (3) adapts previous experiences to current situations.
      (4) builds on the knowledge and skills learned from previous experiences.
      (5) initiates interactions with other people.
      (6) initiates interactions with materials in the environment.

These purposes and philosophy serve as the foundation for curriculum development. All goals, objectives, methods, materials, and evaluations are built on them, providing a consistent, integrated program. Parents, children, and caregivers all participate in the process of curriculum development.

Goals

Goals are broad generalizations about what you want a program to provide. The program's purposes and philosophy shape determination of the goals.

As an example, the Infant and Toddler Caregiver Competencies developed for the CDA credentials appear in Table 9–1. These competencies state the purpose or goal of the caregiver's behaviors. Program goals can be matched with goals for caregivers.

Mrs. Jalimek is an elementary school teacher with a two-year-old son, Leon. Her caregiver is moving, so she is looking for a new child care arrangement. She has visited several child care centers and family child care homes and interviewed the directors and caregivers. She wants a program in which a caregiver will provide strong emotional support for Leon, will learn about him and adjust to his needs, will help him have happy, satisfying experiences, will allow him to grow at his own rate, and will listen to her concerns and share information with her as a parent.

Mrs. Jalimek has seen situations where two-year-olds are seated at tables working on worksheets and struggling with numeral and alphabet flashcards. She has observed classrooms and homes in which the children play among themselves while the caregivers sit apart talking with other adults and only occasionally interacting with the children, and then mainly to reprimand them. She finally chose a program where the caregiver stated:

> I try to make this as much like a home as possible. I am available to each child. I snuggle and love them. We play and sing and laugh and sometimes cry. We cook and help with clean-up chores. When an infant is hungry, I feed him. The children know each other and watch, touch, hug, and talk with each other. They watch in the morning for each child to arrive and greet each with big smiles and waves. They recognize mommies and daddies and watch afternoon greetings and then wave and call out goodbyes in the language they use. The children act like they are comfortable here with me and with each other. I really enjoy them.

TABLE 9–1	**CDA PROGRAM AND CAREGIVER GOALS**
Program Goals	*Caregiver Competency Goals*
I. Safe, healthy learning environment	I. Establish and maintain a safe, healthy learning environment.
II. Physical and intellectual competence	II. Enhance physical and intellectual competencies.
III. Positive social and emotional development	III. Support social and emotional development of each child and provide positive guidance.
IV. Positive and productive relationships with families	IV. Establish positive and productive relationships with families.
V. Well-run, purposeful program	V. Ensure a well-run, purposeful program responsive to participant needs.
VI. Professional relationships and development	VI. Maintain a commitment to professionalism.

CDA

VI. 13

Objectives

Objectives describe specific achievements that lead to attainment of a goal. Several objectives may be directed toward the same goal.

The CDA Infant and Toddler Caregiver Competencies are organized into Competency Goals I–VI, which are subdivided into Functional Areas 1 to 13. Each of the Functional Areas lists examples of caregiver behaviors. Each behavior addresses a specific objective for the child, parent, and caregiver. (See Appendix C for the complete CDA Infant and Toddler Competency Standards.) Table 9–2 shows the interrelationships of the child's needs, parents' needs, and caregiver behaviors.

Methods

Methods are one of the means by which the curriculum occurs. The caregiver has several tasks relating to methods.

1. Knowledge
   a. of a variety of caregiver behaviors and strategies
   b. of the child's needs
   c. of how to match caregiver behaviors and strategies to the needs of the child
2. Application
   a. to assess the child in each major Developmental Area and to task-analyze developmental tasks for specific situations
   b. to select appropriate caregiver behaviors and strategies
   c. to use selected caregiver behaviors and strategies
3. Evaluation to judge whether caregiver behaviors and strategies match the child's needs appropriately

The caregiver behaviors and strategies should be consistent with the objectives, goals, and philosophy of the program. For example, one facet of the caregiver role is to act as organizer (see Chapter 5). When the caregiver views the child developmentally and as one who needs to have active interaction with materials, the care-giver may select several toys that are developmentally appropriate for the child and then allow the child to choose which toys to use. The caregiver facilitates the child's development by encouraging the child to make the choices among appropriate materials.

Materials

Materials are a vital part of the curriculum. The infant and toddler learn by interacting with materials. The child constructs knowledge by holding, tasting, shaking, hitting, throwing, looking, smelling, and listening to objects.

Some materials provide a variety of experiences: sand has texture, weight, color, and smell and can be formed, shaped, dropped, thrown, and so forth. Other objects have very limited use: a wind-up dancing doll provides little stimulation for varied and continued use.

Materials can contribute to or impede the child's development. The caregiver's selection of appropriate materials for each child facilitates that child's development (see Part III). Materials that are too easy can be boring, and those that are too difficult can be frustrating.

TABLE 9–2	RELATIONSHIP OF THE CDA OBJECTIVES TO THE CHILD, PARENT, AND CAREGIVER		
Functional Area	To Child	To Parent	To Caregiver
1. Safe	Safe environment	Reliable, safe environment for child	Provide a safe environment for the child.
2. Healthy	Good health and nutrition	Healthy and nutritious environment for child	Promote good health and nutrition.
3. Learning Environment	Access to stimulating learning environment	Appropriate, stimulating learning environment	Plan, organize, and set up appropriate stimulating learning environment.
4. Physical	Development and coordination of physical movements and senses	Opportunities for stimulating physical development	Provide equipment and interaction to stimulate physical development.
5. Cognitive	Development of thinking and problem solving	Appropriate stimulating of thinking	Provide appropriate cognitive stimulation.
6. Communication	Communicate by verbal and nonverbal means	Active involvement in communicating	Model communication through interaction with child and adult.
7. Create	Explore sights, sounds, and materials	Individualized, flexible materials and activities	Encourage child's unique explorations and creations.
8. Self	Emotional security	Trustworthy, responsive care for child	Provide love, affection, and security.
9. Social	Social interactions and social awareness	Appropriate social support and stimulation for child	Model and stimulate positive social interactions.
10. Guidance	Use acceptable behaviors	Support and reinforcing of child's appropriate behaviors	Establish and maintain management rules and routines and nurture child's self-control.
11. Families	Stability between environments at home and child care	Partnership with caregiver, exchanging information and support	Communicate with parent, sharing child's experiences and mutual concerns.
12. Program Management	Participate in consistent, appropriate quality	Predictable, appropriate, quality program	Plan, coordinate, implement quality program.
13. Professionalism	Appropriate care	Informed, learning caregiver for child	Attitude and behavior seeking continued learning.

Caregivers should select materials that contribute to the attainment of program goals and objectives. Currently popular materials or those labeled "educational" may or may not be appropriate and effective.

Evaluation

CDA V. 12

Curriculum evaluation is ongoing in an infant and toddler program. The caregiver must continually examine the daily experiences to determine whether the curriculum is individualized, is balanced (for the whole child), is relevant, is realistic, and implements the program goals and objectives.

Evaluation should always relate to the identified goals and objectives of the program. Were the goals and objectives attained? If so, what contributed to their attainment? If not, were some of them or parts of them attained? Satisfactorily or unsatisfactorily? What reasons or factors caused less than full attainment?

Statements of goals and objectives for the child care home or center serve as guidelines for evaluation. Curriculum evaluation can be informal or formal. Recorded data about children and activities may be selected to provide needed information for evaluation (see Appendix A, Developmental Prescriptions).

Feedback

Feedback is a critical step in curriculum development. Feedback comes from the parents, caregivers, and the children themselves.

Feedback uses information from each of the parts of the process of curriculum development. Are the goals and objectives still appropriate? Do new influences make it necessary to modify them? Were some methods and materials more effective than others? Do they need to be changed if the goals and objectives are modified? Was the curriculum evaluated periodically and accurately, or was it a one-time evaluation that missed several influencing factors?

Feedback from the total process is necessary to determine whether changes need to be made. Feedback also provides guidance for selecting the kinds of changes that will improve the curriculum.

IMPLEMENTING CURRICULUM

Your selection of a curriculum for an infant or toddler is based on what you know about that child's development, that is, what the child can do now and what the next step is. Your caregiver strategies should reinforce the child's present level of development and challenge the child to move toward the next level. Use of Developmental Profiles (introduced in Chapter 2) to assess the child, task analysis of the natural hierarchy of steps necessary to achieve objectives, and written Developmental Prescriptions will enhance balanced development.

Schedule

Flexibility There are two kinds of schedules.

1. The infant's schedule: each infant has an individual physical schedule.
2. The caregiver's schedule: each caregiver designs a schedule that coordinates caregiving duties with each infant's schedule.

Andrea arrives at 7:45 A.M.; Kevin is ready for a bottle and nap at 8:00 A.M.; Myron is alert and will play until about 9:00 A.M., when he takes a bottle and a nap; and

Audrey is alert and will play all morning and take a nap immediately after lunch. As caregiver, write a list of expected activities in each time block. This also will provide you with guidelines for your time.

The daily schedule must be individualized in infant and toddler care. It focuses on the basic activities: sleeping, feeding, playing. During the first months the infant is in the process of setting a personal, internal schedule. Some infants do this easily; others seem to have more difficulty.

First of all, ask parents what the infant or toddler does at home. Write this down to serve as a guideline. Next, observe the child to see whether he or she follows the home schedule or develops a different schedule.

Time Blocks The daily schedule in an infant and toddler program is organized around the child's physical schedule. As the infant spends more time awake, the schedule will change. Toddlers also differ in how much time they spend asleep or awake. Their morning and afternoon naps often do not fit into a rigid schedule of nap time from 12 to 2 P.M. The caregiver can identify blocks of time for specific types of activities but should keep in mind that no clock time fits all children.

Arrival Time During this special time the primary caregiver greets the parent and child and receives the infant or toddler. This is the time for the caregiver to listen to the parent tell about the child's night and about any joys, problems, or concerns. The parent should write down special information on the message board, for example, "exposed to measles last night."

Arrival time is also a time to help the infant or toddler make the transition from parent to caregiver. The caregiver's relationships with the child should provide a calming, comfortable, accepting situation so that the child will feel secure. Touching, holding, and talking with the child for a few minutes helps the child re-establish relations with the caregiver. When the child is settled, the caregiver may move on to whatever activity the child is ready to do.

CDA
II. 4

Sleeping Most of a newborn's time is spent sleeping, although the time awake gradually lengthens. Some infants and toddlers fall asleep easily; others need to be fed, rocked, and then held for a short time even after they are asleep. If you are responsible for several infants or toddlers, plan your time carefully so you are available to help the child fall to sleep. Provide quiet, holding, talking, singing, rubbing, and rocking. Provide toys for the other children who are awake so they will be productively occupied.

Record the child's sleeping time. Parents need to know how long and at what time their child slept. The caregiver needs to know when each infant or toddler will usually be sleeping. Each infant or toddler in your home or room may have a different nap time.

Each month infants sleep less. This affects when they will eat and when they will be alert. As each infant changes his or her sleeping schedule, the caregiver has to change the infant's feeding and playing times.

Some infants and toddlers wake up alert and happy. Others awaken groggy and crying. You can help ease the infant or toddler into wakefulness. Some you can pick up and cuddle. Talk quietly to them, and move them around so they see other things in the room that may be interesting. Usually infants and toddlers need to have their diapers changed or need to go to the bathroom when they wake up. Some infants will be hungry and need a bottle at this time.

Eating The very young infant may eat every 2 to 4 hours. Ask the parent how often the baby eats at home. Infants will tell you when they are hungry by fussing and crying. Learn their individual schedules, their physical and oral signals, so you can feed them before they have to cry. Record the time of feedings and the amount of milk or formula the baby drank.

Hold the infant when you are giving a bottle. This is not only feeding time; it is a time to nurture physical, emotional, social, cognitive, and language development.

Nutrition for Young Children

Parents are responsible for what their children eat. It is extremely important for caregivers to understand the nutritional needs of the children in their care. These nutritional needs vary with the age of the child. For example, breast milk or iron-fortified formula is all a young infant needs to sustain adequate growth until four to six months. Breast milk also helps fight infections because of the immunity factors coming from the mother. Many working mothers are unable to breast-feed for an extended a period.

It is the caregiver's responsibility to be aware of the special nutritional needs of the young infant. Parent education is an ongoing process, and it is the caregiver's responsibility to help parents make educated choices by bringing them necessary information. One way to make this information available is to have posters and written materials about the importance of nutrition for young children available for the parents.

Decisions on feeding schedules are ultimately up to the parent. According to current thinking, however, very young children should eat when they are hungry. This is called demand feeding. Demand feeding involves more flexibility for the caregiver and is one of the first steps to building a bond between that person and the children in his or her care. It is also the first step toward the child internalizing a sense of trust and security.

There are great advantages to consciously caring for the child. Holding, feeding, relating, maintaining eye contact, and ultimately building a secure foundation for the child are only possible through conscious caring. Being with the child and remaining silent and calm also allows the child to remain calm.

Parents are responsible for bringing new bottles of milk, breast milk, or formula every day. Bottles should be dated and labeled with the child's name. Do not store unopened formula for the child. Only whole, pasteurized milk should be given to children between six and 24 months. Low-fat milk does not provide enough calories or nutrients for children under the age of two years.

When preparing to feed an infant, be sure to thaw frozen breast milk under cold, running water. Never microwave it. Heating breast milk or bottled milk can also be done by placing the bottles in hot water for five or six minutes. Test the milk on the inside of your arm between the wrist and elbow to check its temperature. Do not feed an infant milk that is hot.

All bottles should be washed with hot, soapy water, rinsed, and washed in a dishwasher, or boiled for five minutes between uses. When feeding, never prop a bottle in the crib. It may cause the child to choke.

Nutritional needs vary as children develop. Solid foods are gradually introduced, and as children gain strength and are able to sit up, the skills to feed themselves develop. Foods for older infants should be cut into pieces no larger than a quarter of an inch. Older toddlers can have one-half-inch pieces. Children's eating time must be supervised.

Soft foods progress to harder foods as children sit up, become mobile, gain teeth, and have the ability to eat more without assistance. Small, bite-sized foods are introduced. Children love to feed themselves.

Meal time is a time for a few rules based on health and safety needs. Since eating is a time for communicating, it should be structured to allow a routine to develop that will promote an unhurried, relaxed atmosphere in a consistent place. All the children who are beginning to sit up should join in this community event, and all children should be seated.

Choice of foods is extremely important. Fruits, vegetables, grains, milk, and a variety of proteins should be offered at each meal. Children under age four are at high risk for choking (Marotz, Cross, & Rush, 1996). *Foods that must never be given to children in that age group include bubble gum, hard candies, peanuts, marshmallows, and hot dogs cut into rounds.* Staff must be well-versed in emergency procedures involving eating and choking. Children should eat frequently, and the content of the food being eaten evaluated. The foods should be rated and elimination of empty calories is a must.

Many nutritional choices should be offered at one time, and children should be encouraged to choose what they like to eat. Lunches and supplemental snacks should meet at least two-thirds of the Recommended Daily Allowance (RDA).

It is acceptable if children want to skip a meal or snack occasionally. Encourage community involvement, have the children stay in the area where others are eating, or allow the child to sit on your lap as you continue your routine. Toddlers in particular sometimes get too busy to take time to eat. Do not worry because they will eat at the next meal when their attention is on eating.

Food should never be used as a reward or punishment. Food classes for toddlers and older children should be held to educate and enrich older children. Food preparation can involve a group effort to fix a meal. This teaching, however, should be conducted outside the kitchen, keeping children away from potential kitchen hazards (see cooking activity in Chapter 16, Fun in the Kitchen).

Elimination Often infants need their diapers changed after eating. Check an infant's diaper after you have cleaned up from feeding. Check periodically when the child is awake. Talk and sing while you are changing the infant. Make this a pleasant time for both of you. Your positive feelings about diapering are communicated to the child. The toddler who is being toilet-trained may need special attention after meals, nap, and during play. Toilet-trained children can be helped to anticipate when they will need to go to the bathroom (for example, after a nap).

Alert Time In between sleeping and eating, infants and toddlers have times when they are very alert and attracted to the world around them. This is the time when the caregiver does special activities with them (see Part III for suggestions). The infant or toddler discovers him- or herself, plays, and talks and interacts with you and others. Children have fun at this time of day as they actively involve themselves in the world.

Determine the times when the infants and toddlers in your care are alert. Decide which times each individual child will spend alone with appropriate materials you have selected and which times you will spend with each. Each infant or toddler needs some time during each day playing with his or her primary caregiver. This play time is in addition to the time you spend changing diapers, feeding the child, and helping the child get to sleep.

As you play with the infant or toddler, you will discover how long that child remains interested. Stop before the child gets tired. The child is just learning how to interact with others and needs rest times and unpressured times in between highly attentive times. With an infant you might play a reaching-grasping game for a couple of minutes, a visual focusing activity for about a minute, a directional sound activity for about a minute, and a standing-bouncing-singing game for a minute. Watch the infant's reactions to determine when to extend to two minutes, five minutes, and so on. Alternate interactive times with playing-alone times. Infants will stay awake and alert longer if they have some times of stimulation and interaction.

Toddlers spend increasing amounts of time in play. There should be opportunities for self-directed play as well as challenge and interaction with the caregiver. Toddlers also need quiet, uninterrupted time during their day. Constant activity is emotionally and physically wearing on them.

End of the Day At the end of the child's day in your care, collect your thoughts to decide what to share with the child's parent. To help you remember, or to gather information from caregivers working earlier in the day, review the notes on the message board or on the report sheets for the parent. This sharing time puts the parent into the child's day and provides a transition for the child from you to the parent.

Routines

Purposes Routines give the infant or toddler a sense of security. The infant learns to trust repetition and lack of change. The child may not think about these routines but does feel the security of familiar activities.

Implementation Many daily routines foster physical health, particularly those related to cleaning hands, face, and teeth and to eating, sleeping, and toileting. With infants and toddlers the caregiver must care for these needs or assist with them. With washing routines, the task is to remove dirt and microorganisms as well as possible. Excellent charts and suggestions are provided in the manual, *What YOU Can Do to Stop Disease in the Child Day Care Centers* (Centers for Disease Control, 1984).

Face Washing Wet a paper towel or clean washcloth with warm water. Add soap. Liquid soap in a dispenser is more sanitary than a bar of soap because dirt and germs may remain on the soap bar. Keep dirt off the dispenser plunger. Wipe the face gently. Rinse the paper towel or washcloth thoroughly in warm water. Wipe the face gently, patting areas around the eyes.

Hand washing Hand washing is a procedure directly related to health and the occurrence of illness. Hand-washing procedures should be thorough. A quick rinse through clear water does not remove microorganisms. Frequent handwashing is a vital routine for caregivers and children to establish.

1. Caregiver
   a. Wash hands before
      (1) working with children at the beginning of the day.
      (2) handling bottles, food, or feeding utensils.
      (3) assisting child with face and handwashing.
      (4) assisting child with brushing teeth.
      (5) changing a diaper (after rubber gloves are removed).

   b. Wash hands after
      (1) feeding.
      (2) cleaning up.
      (3) diapering (rubber gloves are removed first).
      (4) assisting with toileting (rubber gloves are removed first).
      (5) wiping or assisting with a runny nose (rubber gloves are removed first).
      (6) working with wet, sticky, dirty items (rubber gloves are removed first).

2. Child
   a. Wash hands before
      (1) handling food and food utensils.
      (2) brushing teeth.
   b. Wash hands after
      (1) eating.
      (2) diapering or toileting.
      (3) playing with set, sticky, dirty items (e.g., sand, mud).

Wet the whole hand with warm water, soap it, and rub the whole hand—palm, back, between fingers, and around fingernails. Rinse with clean water, rubbing the skin to help remove the microorganisms and soap. Dry hands on a disposable paper towel which has no colored dyes in it. Throw away the towel so others do not have to handle it. You can also use small washcloths as towels, with each child using his own once and then putting it in the laundry basket.

Toddlers who can stand on a stepstool at the sink can be assisted in washing their own hands. You can turn on the water, push the soap dispenser, verbally encourage them to use their hands to wash and rinse each other, turn off the water, and if necessary hand them a towel.

Toothbrushing Help toddlers step up on the stepstool at the sink if they need assistance. Turn on the faucet so a small stream of water is running. Wash your hands. Assist in the child's handwashing.

Allow the toddlers to wet their own toothbrush. Shut off the water. Put a small amount of toothpaste on the toothbrush and then encourage toddlers to brush all their teeth (not just the front ones).

Fill a paper or plastic cup half full with water. Encourage the toddlers to rinse their mouths well. Give them more water if needed. Turn on the faucet and allow the toddlers to rinse their own toothbrush and rinse out the plastic cup. Have the children wipe off their mouths with a tissue. Return the toothbrush and plastic cup to their proper place or throw away the paper cup.

Eating Eating routines should have a positive effect on children physically, emotionally, socially, and cognitively.

Bibs protect infants' clothes when they are drooling during the first year or so of life. A little cloth bib can be changed during the day when it becomes wet and soiled. These bibs should be laundered rather than just rinsed out.

Infants and toddlers eating solid food need to wear bibs to protect their clothes and the area around them. Bibs with pockets to catch the spills are helpful. Each child needs a separate bib. The bib should be wide enough to cover the child's shoulders and reach the child's sides. It should be long enough to reach the lap; however, if it is too long, it will wrinkle the pocket and spills will not be caught. Plastic bibs should be immersed in soapy water, rinsed, and towel or air dried. Fabric bibs should be shaken, and if wet or soiled, they should be put in the laundry.

Bottle procedures are simple and need to be consistent. Infants let you know when they are hungry. Wash your hands and the infant's face and hands. Prepare a bottle (ask the parent whether it should be warm or cold). Put a bib on the infant. Hold the infant while giving the bottle. Emotionally the baby needs your closeness. Also, choking, tooth decay, and ear infection are more prevalent among babies who lie down when drinking from the bottle. Never prop up a bottle to allow a baby to drink unsupervised.

Stop periodically to burp the baby. Support the infant's head until the infant has enough neck strength to control head movements. Set the infant upright or up to your shoulder. Press firmly upward or pat on the baby's back until the burp comes. Because the baby may spit up when burping, keep a towel under the infant's mouth to keep both of you dry and to wipe off the baby's mouth. When the baby has finished drinking and burping, remove the bib if it is soiled.

An unfinished bottle should be refrigerated immediately. It may not be saved for use the next day.

After feeding infants a bottle, hold them to put them to sleep, or play with them, or put them down to play with toys and watch or play with other children.

Baby food requires one bowl and spoon per baby. If you anticipate that the baby will not eat a full jar, spoon the desired amount into a dish and put the remainder in the covered jar into the refrigerator. If the spoon is dipped into the jar during feeding, the spoon leaves saliva in the food which can contaminate the rest of the jar of food.

Wash your hands and the infant's face and hands. Put a bib on the infant.

Plan something to keep the infant's hands busy: use one of your hands to play with the baby's hands or give the child a small toy or feeding tool to grasp. Infant muscular coordination is still erratic, so waving arms and grasping hands often collide with a spoonful of food. The infant does not mind the mess, but gradually you may become frustrated, and the infant can sense your negative feelings.

When food is spilled (hit, tipped, etc.), do not spoon it up to feed to the infant. The tray and clothes surfaces are not kept as clean as the dishes and spoons; they have dirt and germs that would be spooned up with the spilled food. When infants stop eating, stop trying to feed them. *Do not force food!*

Wash the infant's face and hands while you talk and sing to the child, take off the bib, and put the child down to play. Put the dish, spoon, and bib in the kitchen to be washed. Wash off the tray with soapy water and rinse. Wash spills off surfaces.

Finger food affects space as well as eating. Prepare the area by clearing the table and clearing or covering surrounding floor space. Wash your hands and the infant's face and hands. Put a bib on the child. Wash the eating surface; finger foods often are pushed off plates and bowls onto the tray or table.

Set the finger food in front of the infant, say what it is, and encourage the baby to take the first bite. Talk with the infant, using descriptive words as the child eats. Praise the child's competence. Emphasize how special it is that the child can feed him- or herself (Figure 9–4).

Wash the infant's face and hands, take off the bib, and put the child down to play when he or she has stopped eating. Pick up any remaining food on the tray, table, and floor. Take the dish and bib to the kitchen to be washed. Wash the eating surface. Sweep or vacuum the floor. Wash your hands.

Figure 9–4 The young child soon becomes adept at eating finger foods.

Table food is prepared for the young child. Wash your hands and assist the toddler to do likewise. Put a bib on the child. Serve small portions of food. Cut up meat and firm foods into bite sizes of about a half inch.

Allow the child to pick up and use a child-size spoon with whatever hand the child chooses. Since most people are right-handed, you can place the spoon on the right side of the plate. But if the child puts the spoon in the left hand, leave it there. Provide a child-sized spoon and help the child grasp it with palm and fingers. The toddler will use both hands when eating. The hand without the spoon is sometimes used to put food in the mouth and sometimes to put food on the spoon. Do not try to keep one hand in the child's lap. When children develop the coordination needed to use utensils, they use their whole body by leaning, twisting, pushing, and grasping. Muscular control must develop before manners can be stressed.

Do not put dropped food back on the child's plate. This food should be thrown away.

Talk with children when they are eating. Name foods, tastes, and textures. Praise the children's competence in eating. Listen and enjoy their talk with you and with others.

When a child has stopped eating, wash the infant's face and hands and help the toddler to do this job.

Remove the bib and allow the child to leave the eating area and go to a play area while you complete the remaining tasks. Put the dishes, utensils, and bibs on a cart or in the kitchen to be washed. Pick up dropped food. Wash the eating surface and table and chair surfaces where sticky hands and food have touched. Sweep or vacuum under the eating area. Wash your hands.

Sleeping You control the sleeping conditions of the infant and toddler. Each child has preferences, which you must learn.

Each infant needs a separate crib with a sheet and blanket. If another infant sleeps in the crib later in the day, remove the sheet and blanket of the first child and store them or put them into the laundry. Spray the crib with disinfectant before putting on the sheet and blanket of the next child. Keep the sheet and blanket sets in cubbies or on a labeled shelf.

Licensing requirements will indicate the space needed between cribs. Many states require two feet of space between cribs.

"Cribs and playpens with slats spaced no wider than 2 3/8 inches apart must be used. Crib sides must remain up at all times and cover at least 3/4 of the child's height. The mattress must fit the crib snugly. If there is more than one inch between the crib sides or ends and mattress, the mattress is too small. Bumper pads must extend around the entire crib and tie into place with at least six ties; they need to be used until four months of age" (Greater Minneapolis Day Care Association, 1989). Check older cribs to cover slats that are too far apart.

Some infants will be sleeping while others are awake. Use sheets or blankets to hang over the crib side to create a visual barrier if you use the room for sleeping and playing.

Infants have their own schedules for sleeping. Ask parents what schedule their infants had before coming to child care. Allow children to sleep when they indicate they are sleepy.

Some infants awaken at dawn and may be ready for a morning nap by 8:30 or 9:00 A.M. As they get older, nap times change to later and later in the morning. At some point it is necessary to adjust so that nap time and lunchtime do not coincide, or you will find the infant falling asleep in his lunch. During these months either feed the infant before the nap or postpone lunch until after the child awakens. Falling asleep in the potatoes is no fun. In the process of being cleaned up the infant usually awakens and cries and fusses at the interrupted nap.

Some infants and toddlers like to be rocked to sleep; some enjoy back rubs. Some prefer to lie on their stomachs to go to sleep; some prefer to lie on their backs. Ask parents what their children prefer. Coordinate your routines with what is done at home. Share information with parents about how the infant or toddler responds with you.

Allow infants or toddlers to awaken on their own schedule and give them time to adjust to wakefulness. Change their diapers, take them to the bathroom, and talk softly to them, helping them make the transition gently. Some children are "on the move" immediately upon awakening. Provide a place and quiet activities for them.

Cribs are for sleeping; they are not play pens. When infants wake up, they should be removed from the crib to enjoy activities in other parts of the room.

Record the time the child slept. The time of day and length of time are important information for you during the day and for parents in planning activities and in noting symptoms of possible sleep problems.

If the sheet is wet or soiled, change it now so it will be ready when the child needs to sleep again.

Infants' afternoon naps depend on the time and length of their morning nap. Some infants may be awake and ready to play while the other infants and toddlers are napping. Provide space and time for these infants to be involved in meaningful activities.

Afternoon nap time may be similar for many toddlers. After lunch and diapering or toileting, toddlers can remove their shoes and lie down on a cot with their own sheets and blankets. Put the shoes in the same place under the cot each day so each toddler learns where to put them and where to look for them. If possible, reduce the light and noise level at least slightly.

Some toddlers like to have their backs rubbed or arms or legs stroked. Some like to listen to music. Hum or play quiet music without words so children can relax rather than remain alert to the words (Figure 9–5).

Toddlers will wake up at different times. Assist with diapering or toileting and putting on shoes. Designate a room or an area of the sleeping room as a quiet play area until others awaken.

Some infants and toddlers have difficulty relaxing and falling asleep. Schumann (1982) has described relaxation techniques she has used with children as young as 18 months old. After creating an environment conducive to sleep, she uses the following procedures. A quiet, steady voice along with stroking facilitate relaxation even when the child may not understand all the words being used.

"Use a quiet even voice to help the children relax each part of their bodies. Repeatedly (six to eight times) state that the body part is 'heavy.' For some children it may help to stroke firmly with two hands over the body part to be relaxed. Begin with the toes and work up the body in the following fashion: toes, feet, legs, back (or abdomen, depending on position), fingers, hands, arms, shoulders, neck, eyes, lips, and chin. After relaxing each body part, check it to see how successful each child has been. Tenseness is indicated by a raised bulging or rigid muscles or by movement of a muscle or body part. Using firm hands, strive for being able to move the body part yourself at the joint without the child's helping or keeping the area stiff. Give POSITIVE reinforcement for the way you want the body part to be. Explain to the

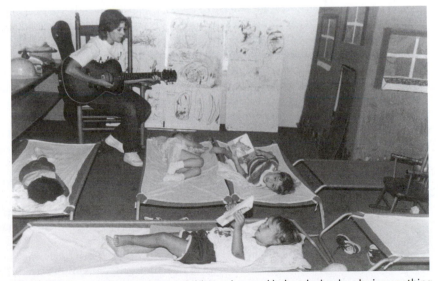

Figure 9–5 The caregiver can assist children who need help relaxing by playing soothing music.

children to let the feet stay 'heavy' while you are checking that part. As you move from talking about one body part to the next, keep your voice a continuous monotone rather than pausing. After doing two or three body parts, repeat the idea that the previous ones are still 'heavy' also."

For example, 'Your toes are heavy. Your toes are heavy. Your toes are heavy. Your toes are heavy.' (Check for relaxation, insert positive reinforcement) 'Your feet are heavy. Your feet are relaxed. Your feet are heavy. Your feet are heavy.' (Check for relaxation, insert positive reinforcement) 'Your toes are heavy. Your feet are heavy. Your legs are heavy.' By the time each child is told his eyes are heavy, it is likely that he will either already have them closed or be willing to close them at your request. . . . If a child still seems fairly alert at the end of the toe-to-head release sequence, try repeating the sequence but eliminating touch and checking of the body for relaxation. Some children might require or seek more body contact than others." (pp. 17–18).

Toileting   Diapering requires planning. If you use a changing table, have all supplies within reach. It is desirable to have the changing table next to a sink with hot and cold running water. If you do not use a changing table, use a piece of heavy plastic large enough to hold the infant's back and legs as well as the container with the supplies and a place to put the soiled diaper. Glove with latex gloves. Remove the infant's clothes or pull them up to chest level. Remove the soiled diaper. Put a disposable diaper in a covered, plastic-bag-lined container. Put a cloth diaper in a plastic bag, which will be closed with a twisty when you are finished.

    Keep one hand on the infant at all times.

    Wipe off bowel movement with toilet tissue, going from front to back. Put the tissue on the soiled diaper or drop it into the toilet stool if it is next to your changing area. Use separate toweling or tissue when turning the faucet on and off so feces will not contaminate the faucet. Use a plain paper towel or washcloth with warm water and soap to wash the infant's bottom thoroughly. Rinse the towel or cloth and rinse the baby's bottom. Throw the paper towel away, or put the washcloth in the laundry. Pretreated paper wipes are not necessary, and they sometimes irritate an infant's skin.

    Put on a clean diaper, fitting it snugly around the legs and waist. Redress the infant, wash the child's face and hands, and take the child to the next activity. Wash off the changing table or plastic sheet and spray with disinfectant. Remove gloves, and *wash your hands thoroughly* before you do anything else.

    Record the time and consistency of bowel movements. You and the parents need this information to determine patterns of normalcy and to look for causes of irregularity.

    Toilet-training may begin when the toddler is ready. Toddlers will indicate when they are ready to be toilet-trained. Their diapers may be dry for a few hours; they may tell you they have urinated or had a bowel movement after they have; they may watch other children use the big toilet—a motivation available when you have children who are already toilet-trained (Figure 9–6).

    Discuss the timing with the toddler's parents. Both the home and child care program need to begin at the same time and use the same procedures. Frequent, regular dialogue between parents and caregivers is needed to determine whether to continue toilet-training or to stop and begin again a few months later.

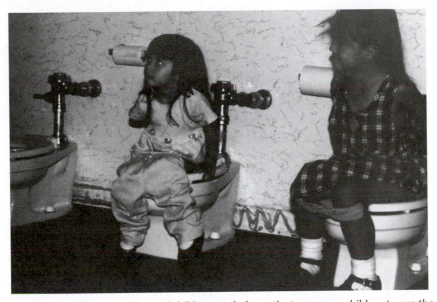

Figure 9–6 Already toilet-trained children can help motivate younger children to use the toilet.

It is often difficult for parents to resist cultural pressures for early toilet-training even when they know the toddler is not ready and is unsuccessful in attempts. The caregiver can help parents understand the needs and development of their toddler.

The toddler needs two major functions for toilet-training—biofeedback and muscular control. Toddlers learn to recognize the feelings their bodies have before they urinate or have a bowel movement. They can use this biofeedback to decide what to do. At first they seem to "observe" the feelings and afterward label what has happened. When they decide to go into the bathroom *before* elimination, they need to use muscular control until they are safely on the toilet. Timing and control must be coordinated. Toddlers may have some control but not enough to last as long as it takes to get into the bathroom, get clothes out of the way, and get seated or standing. Through trial and error, feedback and adjustments, toddlers learn what their bodies are doing and what they can control and plan.

When the child starts toilet-training, use training pants at home and at the child care program. Do *not* put diapers on the toddler during nap time. Outer clothes must be loose or easily removed to facilitate self-help.

Take the toddler to the bathroom and instruct how to pull down necessary clothes and how to get seated on the adapter seat or potty chair. For the boy who can reach standing, determine where he should stand and where he should direct his penis. Glove before proceeding. Wait until the child goes to the toilet, or wait a few minutes. Teach how to get toilet paper and how to wipe from the front to back. Then let the child try to do it alone. Check to see if assistance is needed in cleaning the child's bottom. Assist in getting clothes back up. Assist in washing the child's hands with soap and water.

Wipe off the toilet seat and spray with disinfectant if there is urine or feces on the seat or sides.

Remove gloves and wash your hands thoroughly before doing anything else.

Occasionally during play time ask children whether they need to go to the bathroom. Ask them to go after lunch and before nap time. As soon as they get up from their naps, have them go to the bathroom.

Toilet-training should be a positive developmental experience. It should take a very short time. Problems in toilet-training most often arise when adults do not pay attention to the child's lack of readiness. They pressure the child through weeks of unsuccessful experiences, during which they blame the child for the failure rather than blaming themselves for wrong timing. Help parents understand that timing for toilet-training is individual, as is learning to walk. There is no *right* age by which all children should be toilet-trained. According to many experts, children will train themselves with help when they are ready to give up diapers. Girls often are trained between 30–36 months of age and boys by 36–42 months (Carr, 1993).

Daily Activities   Routines are ready guides for caregivers so that important details of caregiving are attended to. Some routine tasks can be accomplished by the toddler alone, some can only be accomplished by the caregiver, and some tasks involve the caregiver's facilitating the toddler.

Hang outside clothes on a hook or put in the cubbie. Leave those clothes there until it is time to go back outside.

Encourage children to hold books with both clean hands and to turn the pages carefully. Help them learn to put the book back on the shelf or table when they finish looking at it.

Encourage children to take out, or off the shelf, only the toy they are going to play with. At clean-up time before lunch and before going home, have the children help put the toys where they belong.

Have the children put on a smock when painting or gluing (they should ask for help if they need it). Have them stand at the easel or table while working, and keep the supplies at the easel or table. Teach them to wash their hands while the smock is still on (in a nearby sink or in a water-filled basin or pail at the table). They should then dry their hands and throw away the towel in the nearby wastebasket. The children can then take off the smock (asking for help if they need it).

Daily Written Plans

You now have the basis to establish individualized curricula for each child in care. Appendix A presents Developmental Prescriptions that can be used to assess each child's development in the five major Developmental Areas. Additional sources that help establish age expectations can also be used, such as *The First Twelve Months of Life* (Caplan, 1978) and *The Second Twelve Months of Life* (Caplan & Caplan, 1980). Next, copy the Developmental Profile form in Appendix B. Use the sample profile to plot a profile for each child in care. Finally, task-analyze the steps necessary to help the child achieve proficiency in behaviors and skills at his or her present level. This structure can then be translated into daily and weekly plans.

Daily and Weekly Plans   Plans should be both daily and weekly. To make a daily plan, decide after your special time with the infant or toddler which of the things you did

TABLE 9–3	*PART OF A WEEKLY PLAN FOR AN INDIVIDUAL CHILD*

Example:

Child's Name:		Week:

Area of Development*	Materials	Caregiver Strategies and Comments
Physical: Vision R: Visual tracking	Red ribbon bow	Hold bow where infant can focus. Slowly move bow to side, to front, to other side. Observe eyes holding focus. Stop. Talk to infant. Repeat moving bow.
N: Changing focus	Red and blue ribbon bow	Hold red bow where infant can focus. Lift up blue bow and hold a few inches to side of red bow. Observe eyes changing focus. Continue changing positions with both bows.

*Behavior: R = Reinforced, N = New

together today you can build on tomorrow. Review and if necessary revise the plans you had made for tomorrow. Weekly plans should provide task-analyzed experiences in all five major areas of development. You can add information during the week so that you adequately reinforce the behaviors that actually occur during that week (Table 9–3).

Look at the child's Developmental Prescription (see Appendix A) to determine which behavior is new and to select one behavior to reinforce. List the appropriate materials and strategies to use with the child (see Part III).

Unit Plans Long-term planning involves your choosing appropriate themes for the next weeks and months. When you have selected your themes, you can collect materials and decide on activities long before you will need to use them. Careful long-term planning means you do not have to rush to get the information and material you need for your daily and weekly plans.

When you write down your unit plan, you can think more clearly about your ideas, add to them, revise them, and get yourself, your materials, and your room organized before you begin the unit with the children. The following outline has five major parts, which must relate to each other. The materials, preparation, procedures, and evaluation all must implement the objectives. If you have a clever idea or some cute material, but they do not fit the unit objectives, do not include them in that unit.

1. Unit objectives
2. Materials
   a. Select equipment, furniture.
   b. Select manipulatives, art, books, and toys.
3. Preparation
   a. Identify materials that need to be ordered or made.
   b. Collect and organize materials and space.
   c. Set up Learning Centers, if used.
   d. Determine caregiver's schedule for specific involvement with individual children.
4. Procedures
   a. Facilitate each child's involvement with materials and children.
   b. Facilitate the child's use of new behaviors.
   c. Interact with the child or children.
5. Evaluation
   a. Of learning
      (1) Observe each child's behaviors and compare to the unit objectives.
   b. Of the unit
      (1) Observe each child's behaviors to determine whether the unit objectives, materials, and procedures matched the child's ability to learn physically, emotionally, socially, and cognitively.
      (2) Observe each child's beginning, continuing, and failing interest in the topic.

Thematic Units Unit themes can be planned to provide new and interesting experiences for the children. You must give much thought to whether the topic is one the children can deal with physically, emotionally, socially, and cognitively.

Objectives Unit objectives for infants and toddlers differ from objectives for older children. Objectives for infants and toddlers focus on involving the child with materials and people so that the child can construct knowledge. Children of this age derive much of the information from the material itself rather than from being told something about it by or telling something about it to the adult. Therefore, the materials themselves and the child's actual use of them are more important than making and talking about something.

A thematic unit may have some objectives that are appropriate for all children and some that are appropriate for specific children. A Bumpy Unit may have the objective that the child will touch and hold bumpy and smooth objects. Both a nine-month-old and a 27-month-old can do this. An additional objective for the 27-month-old may be to say verbally which object is bumpy and to find another bumpy object.

A theme or topic may last a week or be extended as interest continues. It can be integrated into many experiences.

The Environment Room arrangement may reflect the theme. Furniture placement and tape on the floor can enrich a unit. You can arrange chairs in rows like a bus or train. A large cardboard box can be painted to look like a house when you talk about families. Use wall and hanging space for pictures, mobiles, floor-to-ceiling projects, bulletin boards, and displays.

Learning Centers **Learning centers** integrate a theme by organizing the room and materials and encouraging specific uses of a particular space. Tables, shelves, containers, floor and wall space all form part of a learning center. You can change learning centers to fit new themes.

For infants and toddlers you can organize learning centers in several ways. These children use their senses to gather information to construct knowledge, so the senses can become the focus for the learning centers—you can set up a Seeing Center, Hearing Center, Touching and Feeling Center, Smelling Center, and Tasting Center. Any or all sense centers may be used in a thematic unit. For a Bumpy Unit a Touching Center could contain bumpy objects. A Hearing Center could have bumpy and smooth objects and items which make contrasting sounds when rubbed. A Seeing Center could have clear plastic bags of gravel, corn, and flour to look at and then feel.

You can also organize centers around room-use areas. You can have a Quiet Zone, a Construction Center, a Wet Center, a Reading and Listening Center, or a Home Center. The use of themes in each learning center area for infants and toddlers is an extremely important aspect of curriculum development. Several excellent resources for learning center ideas and themes are available (Cataldo, 1983).

Materials The theme will stimulate ideas for materials. A Bumpy Unit would need all kinds of materials that are bumpy and a few materials that are smooth.

Many household items make good materials for infant and toddler units. Each chapter in Part III contains several ideas for easy-to-make materials.

Books related to the theme can be read to one or a few children at a time when they show interest in hearing a story. For toddlers most books become more meaningful when they are talked about. The caregiver may choose to tell the story in her own words rather than read the printed storyline. She can direct attention to pictures, ask questions about them, and ask the child or children to tell what they are thinking about the story. If children lose interest, put the book down; a child may choose to use the book again at a later time either with you or alone.

Strategies Most of your strategies should focus on helping the individual child become involved. Few toddlers are ready for group experiences. The young child constructs knowledge by actively using materials and engaging in a limited amount of verbal naming of the materials.

The sample thematic unit presented here shows the planning, preparation, and relationships of the unit parts. To put this unit into actual practice, you would need to match the suggested activities with the interests and needs of your children. Be sure to refer to The Celebration of Life Calendar in this Chapter.

Sample Thematic Unit on Riding Riding is physical knowledge. The child constructs this knowledge by physically experiencing riding rather than being told about riding. If your children do not ride the subway (or train, airplane, and so on), do not include those activities in your unit.

1. Objectives
   a. The child shall ride in wheeled equipment.
   b. The child shall ride on wheeled toys.

    c. The child shall show pleasure when riding.

    d. The child shall be exposed to representations of riding: toys with riders, pictures, and oral language.

    e. The child shall identify riding.

2. Webbing: Unit objectives are fostered by activities that help the child develop and use the desired concepts. Webbing is useful to help you think about the many possible concepts for a unit. Creating the webbing picture shows you the relationships of concepts to the central theme and often stimulates the development of other concepts (Figure 9–7).

3. Learning Environment

Centers	Materials	Additional Materials

a. Riding
  (1) Set
      boundaries
	(1) Tyke bike
	(2) Sit and spin
	(3) Wagon
		Pictures of children, families riding in car, city bus, etc. (Display at 2-year-old's eye level.)

b. Dramatic Play	(1) Empty card-board boxes large enough enough to seat 1–2 children (2) Toy and/or child-sized stroller (3) Pick-up truck	Floor-to-ceiling hanging: car (as is made from paper sacks cut and taped together and painted with tempera by children. The "door" opens to allow a child to enter and sit down.)
c. Language	(1) Books (about riding on or in objects familiar to the child) (2) Records (songs and sounds of riding familiar to the child) (3) Song cards (for caregiver) (4) Newsprint (5) Paper and markers (for child's "drawings" and stories)	

Other areas may contribute to the theme. A child playing with blocks may call a block a car and in sing-song fashion tell where he is "riding" as he pushes the "car" around.

4. Possible Caregiver-Initiated Activities

    a. Labeling: Use descriptive words to describe a child's actions. For example, "Maria is riding in the stroller"; "Nathan is giving his babies a ride in his wagon"; "Sasha is riding the big wheel." Name objects in pictures on the wall and in books.

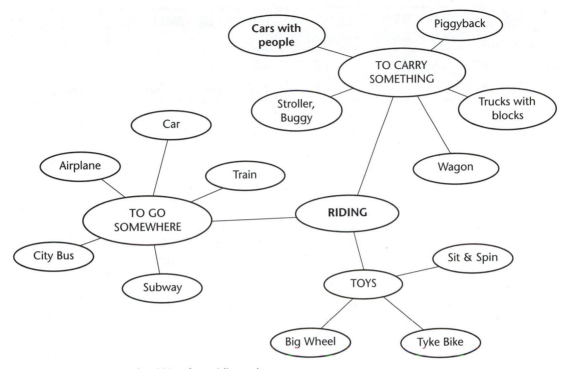

Figure 9–7 An example of webbing for a riding unit

  b. Reading: Talk about pictures from magazines or wordless picture books. Use picture books. Children can draw their own pictures to accompany their story.

  c. Listening: Listen to each child. Listen to how they make sounds and words. Respond to feelings they show. Provide verbal labels, ask questions, and listen some more.

  d. Questioning: Ask questions. For example, "Who are you giving a ride?" "Where are you going riding?" "Can that box ride in your wagon?"

  e. Singing: Make up your own songs to fit a child's actions. For example, "Li is riding, riding, riding. Li is riding her tyke bike." If you cannot make up a tune, say the words in sing-song fashion.

  Your record of each child's involvement provides assurance that the child has a balanced curriculum in the formal, planned times with you. Your informal times with each child are also important parts of the curriculum. Both the planned and informal involvement should provide a holistic, supporting, nurturing curriculum for each child in your care.

TABLE 9–4	WEEKLY GROUP RECORD OF CURRICULUM EMPHASIS IN CAREGIVER-CHILD PLANNED INTERACTIONS

DATES: **THEME:** *Riding*

	Monday	Tuesday	Wednesday	Thursday	Friday
Name	Development Area: Cognitive Recall Problem-Solving Materials: Baby Stroller Toy Truck	Development Area: Materials:	Development Area: Materials:	Development Area: Materials:	Development Area: Materials:
Name	Development Area: Physical Large motor-riding Materials: Tyke bike	Development Area: Materials:	Development Area: Materials:	Development Area: Materials:	Development Area: Materials:
Name	Development Area: Language Labeling Materials: Pictures of objects to ride in	Development Area: Materials:	Development Area: Materials:	Development Area: Materials:	Development Area: Materials:
Name	Development Area: Cognitive Creative Materials: Paper, tempera, paint	Development Area: Materials:	Development Area: Materials:	Development Area: Materials:	Development Area: Materials:
Name	Development Area: Cognitive listening, labeling Materials: Record, tape of sounds of car, train, airplane	Development Area: Materials:	Development Area: Materials:	Development Area: Materials:	Development Area: Materials:

TABLE 9–4	*WEEKLY GROUP RECORD OF CURRICULUM EMPHASIS IN CAREGIVER-CHILD PLANNED INTERACTIONS (continued)*

DATES:	THEME: *Riding*				
	Monday	*Tuesday*	*Wednesday*	*Thursday*	*Friday*
Name	Development Area: Social Independence Materials: Stroller Dolls	Development Area: Materials:	Development Area: Materials:	Development Area: Materials:	Development Area: Materials:

Key Terms

alert time

cultural diversity

Celebration of Life Calendar

daily written plans

disabilities

evaluation

facilitate

finger foods

goal setting

interactive influences

learning centers

motivate

nutrition

objectives

passive influences

problem solving

SEED Program (Seeking Educational Equity and Diversity)

Special Education

thematic units

time blocks

toileting

CASE STUDY

Merissa Golabar was born three weeks prematurely, with a low birth weight of four pounds, six ounces. The split in her lower lip at birth alerted the doctors to check her mouth carefully. Upon examination, it was apparent that the area immediately behind the top gum (called the hard palate) and the area further back (the soft palate) were split. This condition, called cleft palate, causes an unnatural airway through the roof of the mouth to the floor of the nose. As a result, Merissa needed to breathe harder to pull air into her lungs, although the condition is not life threatening. As she grows older, the condition will not be as noticeable.

The immediate concern was whether Merissa would be able to suck in order to breast-feed. A nurse gently pinched Merissa's lips while she taught her mother how to help Merissa breast-feed. However, Merissa was not able to suck and became extremely frustrated, as did her mother. To ensure nutrition and maintain her electrolyte balance, Merissa was placed in an incubator and an intravenous line was started.

(continued)

(continued)

After two days, it was time for Merissa's mother to go home, but Merissa needed to stay in the hospital. Mrs. Golabar had attempted almost hourly to help Merissa breast-feed without success and felt depressed and inadequate. Hospital staff counseled her and helped her understand that her feelings were normal and partly physically based. Often, approximately three days after delivery, some mothers experience a decrease in hormones called postpartum depression, which can last a few days. Given the problem with her daughter, it was understandable that Mrs. Golabar was very upset.

The next morning, the parents met with a plastic surgeon, who explained that Merissa's lips could be repaired later that day. The couple held and rocked their baby until time for surgery and were extremely relieved to find that the surgery was a complete success. They were told that Merissa would need several additional surgeries on her palate as she grew, but her condition could be corrected through medical and behavioral interventions. The family was referred to a local group family child care center, where staff were trained in feeding programs and cleft palate, since Mrs. Golabar had to return to work shortly.

Mr. and Mrs. Golabar were very relieved the next week to speak with Mrs. Brown, the director of At Ease Family Child Care, to find that she and her staff would design an individualized curriculum to fill Merissa's special needs. To begin, assessment of her needs in the five major areas of development on a regular basis would be performed using Developmental Profiles and Prescriptions. Then, task analysis of the steps necessary to enhance Merissa's growth would indicate the tasks and materials necessary to apply on a daily basis. Ongoing daily evaluation of the growth objectives, tasks, materials, and methods would give staff and the parents feedback so they could adjust methods and materials as necessary to fill Merissa's needs.

In addition to the individualized curriculum, specific objectives were designed for Merissa's special feeding, vocalization, and language development. The director explained how feedings would be accomplished slowly, with an up-and-down rhythm and motion at first to aid sucking and swallowing. As Merissa started more solid foods and underwent further surgeries, staff would task-analyze the steps, methods, and materials necessary to help her eat well, form clear vocalizations, and work with Mr. and Mrs. Golabar to help Merissa develop at her optimal rate. The Golabars left At Ease Child Care with optimism that they would not have believed possible just a few days before.

1. What was the major factor that allowed the Golabar family to resolve the problem and be optimistic about Merissa?
2. What must be accomplished before an individualized curriculum can be developed for any child?
3. Discuss the emotional components of every in this case study: child care staff, parents, and child.

Student Activities

1. Write down specific programs for feeding, temperament, and daily care management of a child with cleft palate. Answer the following questions.
   a. How would feedings be managed?
   b. What would be the advantage of taking a course on cleft palate?
   c. How would you deal with the child's frustrations?
   d. What conscious caregiving would you do with Merissa?

2. Obtain written goals for a group of children in child care. Evaluate them in terms of the CDA Objectives and Goals and how to design a curriculum.
3. Observe a child care program and identify specific time blocks.
4. Use one Developmental Profile and write a daily lesson plan for the child.

Chapter Review

1. Write a statement for a new caregiver that explains why flexibility in schedules is important in an infant and toddler program.
2. List three daily routines. Explain how each routine may be helpful to a child.

	Routine	Helpful
1.		
2.		
3.		

3. List two reasons for written daily plans.
4. List the five major parts of the unit plan.

   (a) _____   (d) _____

   (b) _____   (e) _____

   (c) _____

5. How can a thematic unit involve the child physically?
   emotionally?
   socially?
   cognitively?

References

Brown, N. (1995). *Guidelines for teachers.* New York: International Pre-School.

Bush, Barbara (1990). In N. Brown, Guidelines for teachers (1995). New York: International Pre-School.

Caplan, F. (1978). *The first twelve months of life.* New York: Bantam/Grosset and Dunlap, Inc.

Caplan, F., & Caplan, T. (1980). *The second twelve months of life.* New York: Bantam/Grosset and Dunlap, Inc.

Carr, L. (1993). Toilet training toddlers. Selden, NY: Lecture Series to Suffolk County "Mommy & Me Parent Trainers."

Cataldo, C. Z. (1983). *Infants and toddlers programs: A guide to very early childhood education.* Reading, MA: Addison-Wesley.

Centers for Disease Control. (1984). *What you can do to stop disease in the child day care centers.* Atlanta, GA: Author.

Clegg, L., Miller, E., & Vanderhoof, Jr., W. H. (1995). *Celebrating diversity: A multicultural resource.* Clifton Park, NY: Delmar Learning.

Clinton, W. J. (1997). NBC Broadcast, National Child Care Forum, Washington, DC.

Gonzalez-Mena, J., & Eyer, D. (1997). *Infants, toddlers, and caregivers.* Mountain View, CA: Mayfield Publishing Company.

Greater Minneapolis Day Care Association. (1989). Minneapolis, MN.

Hannaford, C. (1995). *Smart moves: Why learning is not all in your head*. Arlington, VA: Great Ocean Publishing, Inc.

Healy, J. (1989). *The child's growing mind*. New York: Doubleday.

Hopson, D. (1992). *Different and wonderful: Raising black children in a race-conscious society*. Washington DC: Fireside.

Jones, E., & Derman-Sparks, L. (1992). Meeting the challenge of diversity. *Young Children, 47*(2), 12–17.

Marotz, L. R. et al. (2001). *Health, safety and nutrition for the young child*. Clifton Park, NY: Delmar Learning.

Nash, J. (1997). Fertile minds. Special Report: How a child's brain develops and what it means for child care and welfare reform. *Time*.

Neurnberger, D. (2001). Simple mind resources techniques. Honesdale, PA: *Brain Gym Journal*.

Schumann, M. J. (1982). Children in daycare: Settling them for sleep. *Day Care and Early Education, 9*(4), 14–18.

Turkovich, M., & Mueller, P. (1989). The multicultural factor: A curriculum multiplier. *Social Studies and the Young Learner, 1*(4), 9–12.

Additional Resources

Bagnato, S. J., Kontos, S., & Neisworth, J. T. (1987). Integrated day care as special education: Profiles of programs and children. *Topics in Early Childhood Special Education, 7*(1), 28–47.

Caring for Our Children. (1996). *National health and safety performance standards: Guidelines for out-of-home child care programs*. American Academy of Pediatrics/American Public Health Association.

Castellanos, L., & Watson, L. (1997). *Infant assessment-developmental profiles, prescriptions and outcomes*. Annaheim, CA: National Conference of the Association for Education of the Young Child.

Council for Early Childhood Professional Recognition, CDA National Credentialing Program. (1987). *Child development associate assessment system and competency standards infant/ toddler caregivers in center-based programs*. Washington, DC: Author.

Helpful Web Sites

Child Care and Nutrition, Inc. Recipes for child care providers. http://www. frontiernet.net/~manage/ccni/

Child Care Choices of Boston, Children with Disabilities Choosing child care for children with disabilities. http://www.bostonabcd.org/

A Guide for Balancing Work and Families, guidelines for evaluating child care. http://depcare.chance.berkeley.edu/guide/INDEX.html

Developmentally Appropriate Care, What does it mean? National Network for Child Care. http://nncc.org/Choose.Quality.Care/qual.dap.html

Child Care Environment Safety Checklist. NebGuide. http://ianr.unl. edu/pubs/safety/g1213.html

For additional infant and toddler resources, visit our Web site at http://www.earlychilded.delmar.com

PART III

Matching Caregiver Strategies and Child Development

The chapters in Part III present how the caregiver works with infants and toddlers at specific age ranges. Each chapter refers to the developmental profiles and characteristics of children in a specific age range, lists materials, and presents examples of caregiver strategies that can be used with individual children. Refer to each chapter which contains information relevant to the children with whom you work. As your children develop, refer back to these chapters for additional information to help you meet the changes.

The *sequence* of development presented is common to all infants and toddlers. The *time* behaviors occur or the *rate* of development may differ. Two 11-month-olds may be at different levels of development. Concentrate on each child as an individual. Accept the uniqueness of each child, and compare them only to themselves. Look at their individual records to see where they are making progress; gradually developing new, more complex skills and behaviors, or where they seem to be stuck at one level. Check to see where progress of development is appropriate.

10

The Child from Birth to Four Months of Age

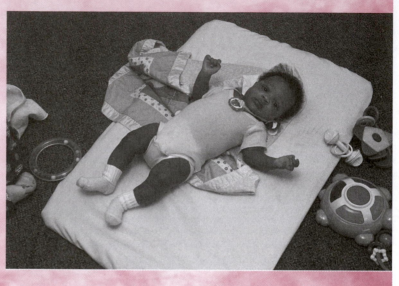

Objectives

After reading this chapter, you should be able to:

- Identify and record sequences of change in the physical, emotional, social, cognitive, and language development of infants from birth to four months of age.
- Select materials appropriate to that age-level infant's development.
- Devise strategies appropriate to that age-level infant's development.

Chapter Outline

Materials and Activities
Caregiver Strategies to Enhance Development

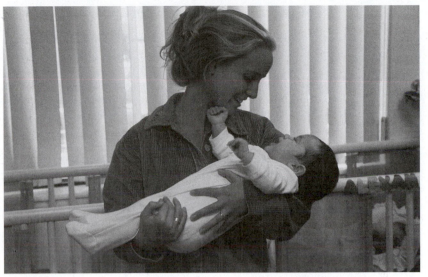

Figure 10–1 The caregiver anticipates and provides for the newborn's needs.

Kiera's Story

Kiera, 2½ months old, has just arrived at the child care home. She sits in her infant seat, which is on the floor by the sofa. Kiera's fists are closed and her arms and legs make jerky movements. As each of the other children arrive, they smile and "talk" to her, with the caregiver watching close by. Kiera looks at each child, and after a few minutes she starts to whimper, then cry. Bill, the caregiver, picks her up and says, "Are you getting sleepy? Do you want a nap?" Bill takes Kiera into the bedroom and puts her in her crib, where she promptly falls asleep (Figure 10–1).

MATERIALS AND ACTIVITIES

Materials used with infants of this age must be safe and challenging. Every object infants can grasp and lift will go into their mouths. *Before* you allow an infant to touch a toy, determine whether it is safe. Each toy should pass *all* the following criteria:

1. It is too big to swallow (use a "choke tube" to measure smaller objects).
2. It has no sharp points or edges to cut or puncture the skin or eyes.
3. It can be cleaned.
4. It has no movable parts that can pinch.
5. Painted surfaces have nontoxic paint.
6. It is sturdy enough to withstand biting, banging, and throwing.

Use Appendix A, the Developmental Prescriptions, and Appendix B, the Developmental Profile, with each infant. Children follow a *sequence* of development. There are often ranges in the *rate* of development.

To be challenging for the young infant, each material should do the following.

1. It should catch the infant's attention so the infant will want to interact with it in some way, for example, reach, push, grasp, look, taste, turn, and practice these movements over and over again.
2. It should be movable enough so the infant can use arms, legs, hands, eyes, ears, or mouth to successfully manipulate the object and respond to it.
3. It should be usable at several levels of complexity so that the infant can use it with progressively more skill.

Look for toys and materials that the infant can use in several different ways. These provide greater opportunities for the infant to practice and develop new skills. Change the toys often so they seem new and interesting. An infant seems to get bored using the same toy for months.

Types of Materials

Crib gyms	Small toys to grasp
Mobiles	Sound toys
Rattles	Pictures, designs
Yarn or texture balls	Mirrors

Examples of Homemade Materials

Materials may be homemade or commercially made. Following are suggestions for making some of your own materials.

CRIB GYM

Tie a sturdy cotton rope from one short side of the crib to the other. Tie on three different objects (these can be changed regularly) so they hang just at the end of the infant's reach. Poke a small hole in the bottom of a small colored plastic margarine tub; thread and knot it on one rope. It will swing when the infant hits it.

RATTLES

Film canister (plastic or metal): Put in one teaspoon uncooked cereal. Replace the cap and tape it on with colored tape.

Plastic measuring spoons: Tie together on a circle of strong yarn.

YARN BALLS

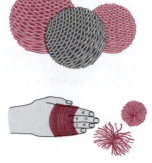

Roll up balls of washable yarn. Tuck the loose end inside. Make the balls different sizes and different colors.

Wrap yarn around the palm of your hand until you have a thick mitt. Carefully slide it off your hand and tie a short piece of yarn tightly around the middle of the "mitt." Cut the ends apart. Pull the loose ends around to shape a ball.

FABRIC TWIRLS

Cut out the center of a lid from a margarine tub. Cut carefully, leaving a clean, smooth edge. Use the remaining rim ring. Sew on three strips of printed washable fabric 3 inches long by 2 inches wide. Hang from the crib gym or put on the infant's wrist.

DESIGNS

Cut faces, wallpaper, pictures, and contrasting colored fabric to fit inside the lids of margarine tubs. Glue one piece in each lid. Hang some from the sides of the crib or give several to the infant to play with.

CAREGIVERS STRATEGIES TO ENHANCE DEVELOPMENT

Developmental Profile

Perhaps the single most difficult task of caregiving is assessing the developmental strengths and weaknesses of children. References, scales, and a step-by-step format, such as the Prescriptions in Appendix A, give only general guidelines to milestones and expectations. The caregiver still must make estimates based on observations of behavior, past experience, cultural mores, and comparisons with other children. Further, judgments of what is considered "average," "normal," and "appropriate" differ depending on the age of the child. For example, a three-month-old who is two months below age level in a skill may have a significant deficit, whereas a 30-month-old who is two months below expectations is probably within normal limits.

Because of the difficulties inherent in assessing what is expected of young children, some authorities advise caregivers not to assess children at all! This practice is not only impossible, but it results in care without any clear goals. The best approach, then, is to formally observe children often and make frequent adjustments in activities based upon their continuous growth.

Now, turn to the Developmental Profile for 10-week-old Kiera in Figure 10–2, and be cautious as you read it not to view it as a "test" or "diagnosis." Developmental Profiles are pictures of skill *estimates* and *trends* and should be used to help direct activities in major areas of skill development.

Kiera is a healthy and normal 10-week-old who was observed over a five-day period using the Child Behaviors in each of the five major areas from the Developmental Prescriptions, birth to four months. The Profile shows that her skills fall within expected ranges, with her lowest skill estimate being 8 weeks and the highest estimates being 14 weeks.

In the Physical Area (I), Kiera exhibits 100 percent of the reflexes, successfully demonstrates 75 percent of muscle control behaviors, and functions as expected in eating, sleeping, and elimination. She is estimated to be a little above age in muscle control (12 weeks) because her muscle control is more like that of a three-month-old than of a two-and-a-half-month-old.

Within the Emotional Area (II), Kiera exhibits 100 percent of "types of feelings" and 75 percent of "control of feelings" (she doesn't increase sounds with conversations yet). Displaying all types of feelings is more like a 14-week-old, and not increasing sounds with conversation is more like an eight-week-old.

Within the Social Area (III), Kiera has a little difficulty with attachment to her caregiver, but is very aware of herself and others for her age. Because she has a little trouble with attachment, Kiera is estimated to be a little below expectations in that area (8 weeks), but is above expectancy in awareness of self and others (11 and 12 weeks).

Kiera demonstrates skills in the Cognitive Area (IV) that are expected for her age. She functions in "sensory levels 1 and 2" and "permanence" as expected for her age of 10 weeks.

Finally, Kiera exhibits Learning Skills (V) at age level in visual and speech development, above average in auditory development, and slightly less than expected motor coordination; that is, she doesn't move her arms or reach her hands toward objects. Therefore, her seeing, hearing, and sounds are estimated at 11 and 12 weeks, and her motor coordination is a little below age at 8 weeks.

Using this Profile and the Materials and Caregiver Strategies listed below, child care staff should focus on those tasks and activities in less-developed areas while maintaining activities in all other skills. In this way, the caregiver encourages balanced development in all areas important to Kiera's growth.

Physical Development

Infants from birth to four months of age show a very rapid rate of physical development, which varies widely from infant to infant. One baby may turn from stomach to back early and another may reach for objects early and turn over late. Starting at birth with reflexive movements, infants rapidly gain an increasing level of muscular control over much of their bodies. In general, development moves from the simple to the more complex movements.

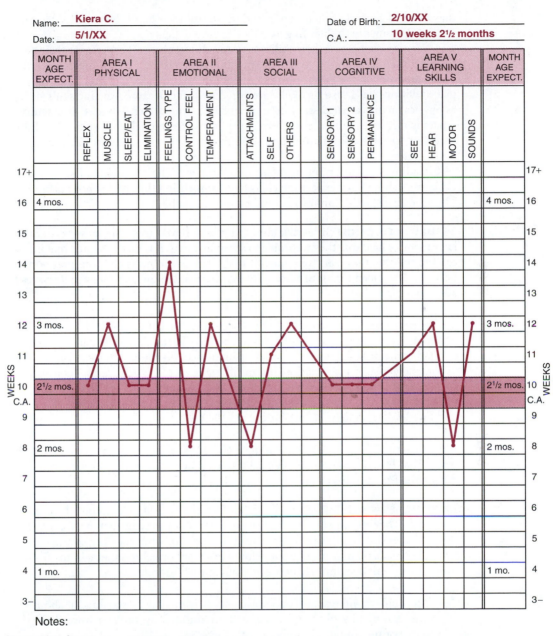

Name: **Kiera C.**   Date of Birth: **2/10/XX**
Date: **5/1/XX**   C.A.: **10 weeks 2½ months**

Figure 10–2 Developmental Profile, Kiera C.

The control moves from their heads and necks to their shoulders, backs, waists, and legs. For example, they first lift their heads up before they have the muscular control to sit and they sit before they can use their legs for standing.

Muscular control also develops from mid-body out to the hands and feet. Gradually infants are able to control to some degree their arm and leg movements before they develop control of their hands, and to control their hands before they can grasp or pick up things with their fingers.

Infants also increase their ability to notice differences and experience their world through seeing, hearing, touching, smelling, and tasting. While these perceptual senses are listed in the Prescription in Appendix A under the "Physical" area, they are placed within the "Learning Skills" area on the Profile because learning skills, as well as physical acuity, are necessary for normal development. In newborns, only acuity of senses is measured, but after the first six months, perceptual skills such as auditory, memory, visual discrimination, and so forth play an important part in learning and development.

Readiness is important in infant development. The child should set the pace. Caregivers should not expect the child to do something the child is not ready to do. The specialist should honor the uniqueness of each child.

Visual Perception In earlier times, it was believed that infants were sightless; later theories held that they were able to see only forms. It is now accepted that infants can see and that they learn very quickly to differentiate objects and interpret nonverbal cues. They spend most of their early months just looking, and they prefer faces to all other objects.

> "A newborn baby focuses best on objects that are between 8 and 14 inches away from his eyes, a range that seems to have been selected by nature . . . it being the distance at which a nursing infant sees his mother's face . . . he will spend most of his time looking to his right or to his left, rarely focusing straight ahead . . . Most young babies like to study faces . . . prefer black-and-white patterns to bright colors; complex objects to simple ones. They love looking at light." (Eisenberg et al., 1989, 97)

The basic Developmental Learning Skills of Visual/Motor Control, Visual Memory, Visual Discrimination, and Visual Association are beginning to be established during the first months of life.

Hearing Newborns can hear sounds. In fact, they could hear sounds before they were born. They respond to almost any type of sound. By moving their heads they show they can identify the direction of the sound. They do better locating sound coming from either side than from above or below, or in front or behind them. In the first few months they can discriminate between many speech sounds.

> "Most babies will react to loud noise—in early infancy by startling, at about three months by blinking, at about four months by turning toward the source of the sound." (Eisenberg et al., 1989, 96)

The basic Developmental Learning Skills of Auditory Discrimination, Auditory Memory, Auditory Association, and Auditory/Visual Association are established during the first months of life.

Taste Newborns can distinguish between water and sugar water. They prefer sugar water to plain water. They can distinguish between sweet, salty, and bitter solutions and prefer the sweet ones. Later, taste will become another sense used in exploring the world, and almost anything they come in contact with will end up in their mouths.

Smell Newborns can distinguish odors and respond positively or negatively to them. The sense of smell is another way they learn about their world.

An infant's well-developed sense of smell has implications for caregivers. Some babies may do better in adjusting to a child care setting if the mother or primary caregiver leaves an article of clothing for the baby to be wrapped up in or snuggle up with. The consistent, familiar odor can ease the transition from mother to caregiver. A child care specialist should consider not wearing cologne.

Touch The baby's most valuable tool for learning about the world is touching and being touched. The infant can feel different textures and identify elements and people through the differences in softness, roughness, and so forth.

Babies who are not touched may fail to grow normally. Further, infants have preferences for types of touching and stroking, and most babies love and need to be held and cuddled.

Movements Newborns' movements are reflexive; they occur without the infants' control or direction. Through growth and learning infants begin to control their movements.

In the first few months infants learn to use many movements well but they have not yet coordinated the movements. Bruner and his colleagues observed, recorded, and analyzed infant behavior. They found that infants learn to control their sucking in the first month of life and that sucking is used for relieving distress, holding attention, and exploration as well as for feeding. Infants may require being held more than older children, which is why it is important to hold a baby while feeding instead of simply propping up a bottle.

Reflexive hand and arm movements develop into a grasping-groping action, which can be independent of vision. Within the first four months "this slow reaching has the mouth as its inevitable terminus. There is an invariant sequence: activation, reach, capture, retrieval to the mouth, and mouthing" (Bruner, 1968, 38) (Figure 10–3). In the next year these hand and arm movements will become directed voluntary activity, which may be visually controlled.

Stability The newborn's head moves reflexively from side to side. When upright, the neck cannot yet support the head. Within the first month infants can lift their heads when lying on their stomachs. By the third month they are using their arms to push against the floor or bed to raise their heads and chests.

During these first three months infants are also busy with their legs. The legs have been kicking and pushing in the air and against anything within range. The infants roll and kick their legs from side to side. Their upper and lower back muscles are developing so that one day when they kick and roll to one side, they keep going right onto their backs or their stomachs. The baby has rolled over!

Many caregiving strategies at this time involve providing appropriate space so infants can move as they want to. The caregiver does not tell the infants to arch their backs, kick their legs, or wave their arms wildly. Infants do this naturally. The caregiver facilitates infant movement by making sure their clothes do not limit movement, by

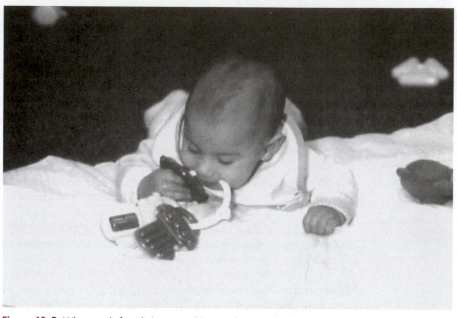

Figure 10–3 When an infant brings an object to his mouth, he is exploring the world around him.

providing a circle of safety, and by offering the infant materials and toys that are safe and appropriate.

Sleep Most newborns sleep between 14 and 17 hours a day. There will be times when they are actually awake, though their eyes are closed, and they will respond to stimulation. Newborns are relatively light sleepers, and deep sleep periods are only about 20 minutes long. The longest sleep period is usually four or five hours.

Sleep patterns will usually be consistent with a baby's other patterns. For example, a baby who is active and noisy when awake will also be active and make noises in his sleep.

Gradually the sleep patterns become more regular and shorter as the baby spends more time being alert and attentive. Eisenberg, Murkoff, and Hathaway (1989) give detailed information and tips on patterns, better sleep, sleep positions, and so forth.

Suggestions for Implementing Curriculum Physical development can be encouraged by providing opportunities for physical activity, changing the baby's position, and motivating movement without instilling "pressure to perform" (Eisenberg et al., 1989).

The caregiver can employ several strategies to enhance the infant's **muscular control**

1. Place infants in positions where they can practice developing muscular control. For example, when you lay them on their stomachs, they can keep trying to lift their heads, shoulders, and trunks. Never place infants on their stomachs to sleep.

2. Until infants can roll over, sit up, and stand by themselves, they will need to be moved into those different positions several times each day during their waking hours.

3. Interact with the infant using yourself as a stimulator. Grasp the infant's hands and slowly lift the child upright. Hold your hands in different places so the infant will look around and reach for you. Gently snap your fingers behind, beside, and in front of the infant and watch the child turn his or her head to locate the sound.

4. Use toys and materials to play with the infant; offer some for the infant to use independently.

   Place objects within the vision and reach of the infant. Select toys the infant can grasp. First there is a gross, grabbing movement. Later a more refined finger-thumb or pincer grasp is used.

Child Behavior	Materials	Examples of Caregiver Strategies
Reflex		
grasp reflex (hand closes)	finger, rattle	Lift infant's body slightly. Place object in palm of infant's hand.
startle reflex	mirror, mobile,	Touch, hold infant to calm him.
tonic neck reflex (head facing one side or other, not facing up)	toys designs	Place objects at side of crib, not above middle of crib.
Muscular Control (develops from head to feet)		
HEAD AND NECK		
Turns head	stuffed toy	Place infant on back or stomach. Place toy to one side.
holds head upright with support		Support infant's head when holding infant upright.
lifts head slightly when on stomach		Place infant on stomach.
holds head to sides and middle		Place infant on stomach.
holds up head when on back and on stomach		Place infant on stomach or back.
holds head without support		Set and hold infant upright.
TRUNK		
holds up chest		Place infant on stomach.
sits with support; may attempt to raise self; may fuss if left lying down with little chance to sit up		Place infant in sitting position. Support head and back with arm or pillow. Lengthen sitting time as infant is able.

(continued)

(continued)

Child Behavior	Materials	Examples of Caregiver Strategies
holds up chest and shoulders		Place infant on stomach.
LEG		
rolls from stomach to back		Place infant on flat surface where infant cannot roll off.
Muscular Control (develops from mid-body to limbs)		
ARM		
moves randomly	toys	Place objects within reach of infant.
reaches		
	bright toys that make noise	Place objects slightly beyond reach of infant; give to infant when child reaches for it.
HAND		
opens and closes	toys with handles, which fit in fist	Place handle in fist; help infant close fist around object.
keeps hands open		
plays with hands	colorful plastic bracelet	Place colorful objects that attract infant's attention on infant's hands, fingers (must be safe to go in mouth).
uses hand to grasp object, whole hand and fingers against thumb	toys with bumps to hold on to	Place object within reach of infant.
thumb and forefinger	Toys that can be grasped with one hand	Place object within reach of infant.
holds and moves object	Toys that can be pushed, pulled, or lifted with hands; toys that make noise	Place toy on flat surface free from obstructions.
EYE-HAND COORDINATION		
moves arm toward object; may miss it	toy, bottle	Place within reach of infant.
reaches hand to object; may grab or miss it	toy, bottle	Place within reach of infant.

The caregiver can use several strategies to enhance the infant's seeing.

1. Place the infant or objects at the correct distance so the infant can focus to see people or objects. The newborn focuses at about 8 to 14 inches. When infants are about four months old, they can adjust focal distance as adults do. The caregiver

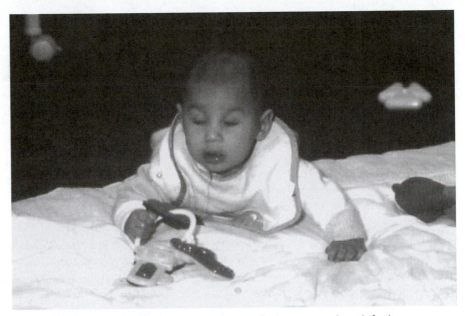

Figure 10–4 The caregiver moves a toy where the infant can see and reach for it.

can place materials at the proper focusing distance. These should attract the infant's attention (Figure 10–4).

2. Select eye-catching materials. Contrasts seem to interest infants: designs, patterns, shapes, colors. Faces also attract their attention.

Child Behavior	Materials	Examples of Caregiver Strategies
Seeing		
focuses 2 inches from eyes	Mirror, mobile, toys, pictures, designs (e.g., patterns, faces)	Place object 8 inches from infant's face.
follows with eyes	Mobile, toys, hand	Move object slowly after infant focuses on object.
stares		
sees objects beyond 8 inches	People, pictures, toys	Attract attention by shape, color, movement.
looks from object to object	Toys, mobile, designs, pictures	Provide two or more objects of interest to infant.
looks around; stops to focus on object that has caught attention; then looks at something else; continual visual searching		Provide eye-catching items in room: faces, patterned designs, contrasting colors in objects, and pictures.

The caregiver can use several strategies to enhance the infant's **hearing**.

1. Newborns respond to sound. The caregiver can produce and select sounds that help infants differentiate between voices as well as among other sounds.
2. Provide a variety of sounds. Tie a bell to the infant's wrist to catch the child's listening attention as the child moves his or her arm. Music can calm or excite infants. Clicking, clucking, snapping, humming, or singing all can provide opportunities for listening. Infants gradually learn to search for and identify the source of the sound. Later they also may try to reproduce the sound (Figure 10–5).

Child Behavior	Materials	Examples of Caregiver Strategies
Hearing		
responds to voice		Talk to infant. Answer him or her.
hears range of sounds	music, singing, caregiver movements	Talk, sing to infant. Answer him or her. Enter and leave room.
calms while hearing low-pitched sounds	humming, singing, records	Select quiet, gentle music to calm infant.
becomes agitated while hearing high-pitched sounds	singing, records	Select songs to sing to calm infant. Sing with infant; let him or her lead.
locates sound	mechanical sounds, voices, music, musical toys	Move sound around so infant searches for source.

The caregiver can use several strategies to enhance the infant's **sleep**. Anticipate when the infant probably will take a nap. Plan very calming time and activities for the infant just before nap time so the infant can get in a mood to sleep. Sitting with the infant in a rocking chair and humming a lullaby often prove very effective.

Child Behavior	Materials	Examples of Caregiver Strategies
Sleeping		
sleeps much of the day and night	flat, firm mattress	Provide restful environment and moderate temperature, free from sudden loud noises.
takes a long morning nap and a long afternoon nap		Adjust routines to fit infant's changing sleep schedule.
may have irregular sleep habits		Shorten or lengthen activities with infant to assist in establishing some pattern for sleeping.

The caregiver can use several strategies to enhance the infant's eating. Parents and pediatricians determine what and how much infants are fed during their first four months. The caregiver is responsible for making eating a happy, successful time for the infant. Organize your time so you can hold each infant when bottle feeding. Eye focusing, eye-hand coordination, as well as emotional bonding, language, and communication all occur while holding the infant for feeding.

Figure 10–5 The caregiver talks and listens to the infant.

Child Behavior	Materials	Examples of Caregiver Strategies
Eating		
takes bottle on demand	formula and bottle	Determine formula with parent. Determine schedule with parent. Hold infant when bottle feeding. Tilt bottle so milk fills the nipple to prevent infant's swallowing excess air. Burp the infant. Put infant straw in bottle.

The caregiver can use several strategies for **elimination**. Two important caregiver responsibilities are to change the infant's diaper frequently and to record the time and any abnormalities of bowel movements. Eating schedules affect the time infants have bowel movements. As they establish eating schedules, some infants develop predictable elimination patterns. Cleanliness is critical for the infant and the caregiver.

The infant's bowel movements reflect the child's health. Ask the parent what color, texture, and frequency are normal for the infant. Record the frequency daily. Record any differences in color and texture and inform the parent.

Child Behavior	Materials	Examples of Caregiver Strategies
Elimination		
begins to establish predictable eating and elimination schedules	diapers, cleansing supplies	Put on disposable gloves. Remove soiled diaper and dispose of it. Wipe infant's bottom with warm, soapy wash cloth. Rinse. Dry. Put on dry diaper. Disinfect the changing surface. Remove gloves. **Wash your hands with soap.**
establishes regular time forbowel movement		Record time of bowel movement. Note changes in times of bowel movements.
may have diarrhea or constipation (both problems call for attention)		Record type of bowel movement. Record changes in type of bowel movement. Discuss with parent. If diarrhea, notify parent immediately. Do not wait until the end of the day; the baby can dehydrate rapidly and may need medical care.

Emotional Development

Philip S. Riback, assistant professor of neurology and pediatrics at Albany Medical College in Albany, New York, has said, "Repeating tasks—sending the same messages to the brain over and over again—seems to result in certain chemical and anatomical changes that actually help a baby retain something she has learned. . . . Here's how a baby's brain develops best times to learn new skills . . . the first two years of life are considered a critical period for laying down the circuits necessary for acquiring motor skills . . . the connection between emotions and brain development is an area of considerable interest to pediatricians and child-development experts . . . feelings experienced by the child can affect the brain and lay the groundwork for later emotions." (Riback, 1997).

During the first months of life infants develop their basic feelings of security. There seems to be little "catch-up" time for emotional security. If the infant does not develop these feelings of security now, it is difficult to develop them as adequately later. Along with the parents the caregiver plays a key role in providing the kinds of relationships and experiences that enable the infant to develop this basic security.

Feelings of security and trust develop out of relations with others. Infants cannot develop these on their own. They develop these feelings from the way other people treat them. Parents and the primary caregiver are probably the most influential people in the lives of young infants in child care. Therefore, the caregiver is very directly responsible and involved in helping the infant feel secure.

Two caregiver behaviors of special importance are responding immediately to the infant's distress signals and responding constantly to the infant's signals of stress, need, or pleasure.

Temperament, the infant's basic style of behavior, gradually emerges in the first four months. Some styles are easily recognized, whereas others may be more difficult to observe.

The activity level of infants is obvious. They may kick and wriggle and squirm a great deal or they may lie quietly while either asleep or awake. Highly active infants may kick their covers off consistently and get tangled in their clothes. Their bodies get plenty of activity. They may need to be checked frequently to be sure they can move freely. A blanket may be more of a bother than it is worth, since it seldom covers the infant. Infant suits or long smocks and socks may keep the active infant just as warm. Very quiet infants may seem easy to care for. They seldom kick off their covers or need their clothes adjusted. They may, however, need to be picked up and moved around to stimulate their physical movement.

Infants' living patterns usually take on regularity in the first months of life. The infant who establishes a regular, though slowly changing, schedule for eating and sleeping creates a predictable world into which the caregiver can easily fit. Infants whose feeding and sleeping times remain erratic create stress for themselves and their caregiver.

Differing levels of sensory threshold are apparent in young infants. One infant will awaken when a light is turned on or a person steps into the room. Another infant will sleep in a brightly lit room with the record player on. When several children are in one room, special adjustments must be made for the sleeping infant who reacts negatively to light and sound.

Infants characteristically use differing levels of energy when responding to stimuli. One infant will cry loudly whenever he or she cries. Another infant will whimper and fuss and occasionally cry more loudly when very distressed. The caregiver, when responding to the infant's cries, will need to learn cues other than loudness to determine the type and severity of stress. The caregiver may need to check infants who fuss and cry quietly to make sure their needs are being met.

The caregiver can use several strategies to enhance the infant's emotional development. Whereas physical development can be enhanced by moving the infant, toys, and oneself around, emotional development demands more than manipulation.

When relating to the infant, the 3A's—Attention, Approval, and Affection—play a most crucial part in the daily emotional development of the child (Figure 10–6). The following strategies will help the caregiver to be conscious of the 3A's while performing tasks such as diapering and feeding.

Use your relationship with the child.
Focus your attention on the child's needs.
Engage the child—make eye-to-eye contact.
Move slowly and with intention.
Make meaningful physical contact.
Actively listen to his or her whole body message.
Reflect back to his or her vocal expressions and sounds.
Try to sense how the child is feeling—is the child excited, happy, frustrated?
Try to judge the amount of stimulation the child prefers.
Try to get in rhythm with the child. Let him or her lead you vocally.
Talk and sing, hum and smile.
Place the child where he or she can observe room activity.
Involve the child in activity.
When leaving the infant, tell him or her where you'll be in the room if he or she needs you.

CDA
III. 8

Figure 10–6   Gentle touching and cuddling comfort the infant.

Suggestions for Implementing Curriculum

Child Behavior	Materials	Examples of Caregiver Strategies
Types of Emotions-Feelings		
shows excitement	attention-catching objects	Use voice and facial expression to reflect back excitement.
shows stress	calming touch, talk, music singing ruing	Determine cause. Change situation to reduce stress, e.g., change diaper; change position; talk to infant (child may be bored).
shows enjoyment	Interesting, challeng-ing toys, objects	Provide pleasant experiences, e.g., give infant a bath; snuggle; converse; smile.
shows anger or frustration	ruing	Determine cause. Remove or reduce cause. Divert infant's attention, e.g., turn infant around to look at something else.

Child Behavior	Materials	Examples of Caregiver Strategies
shows fear	ruing	Hold, comfort infant. Remove fear-producing object or change situation, e.g., hold infant startled by sudden loud noise, remove source of pain.
protests		Determine what infant is protesting about. Eliminate activity or do it a different way, e.g., change how you wash infant's face. If continues, ask another caregiver to take child for you.
Control of Emotions-Feelings seems to occur automatically decreases crying	activities, toys that catch infant's attention and that infant likes	Involve infant in an activity.
increases sounds (talking)		Initiate "conversations" and respond to infant's talking.
reflects feelings in sounds (talking)		Respond to the feelings expressed, e.g., comfort a whining child; change situation.
comforted by holding		Consistently hold, caress, cuddle, and comfort when infant needs it.
Temperament activity level		Observe and identify where infant is in a range of behaviors. List adjustments you need to make to fit infant's temperament.
regularity		
approach or withdrawal as a characteristic response to a new situation		
adaptability to change in routine		
level of sensory threshold		
positive or negative mood		
intensity of response		
distractibility		
persistence and attention span		

Social Development

The caregiver must become emotionally involved with the infant. According to attachment theory, just as infants develop a unique attachment to their mothers, they can develop an additional attachment to their own primary caregivers. Many of the caregiver strategies that build this emotional relationship involve frequent use of looking and touching.

Attachment theory and research have identified phases in the development of attachment. Ainsworth (1982) identified infants' social behaviors during the first few months of life that relate to developing attachment.

Phase 1: Undiscriminating Social Responsiveness

    first two to three months

        orienting behaviors: visual fixation, visual tracking, listening, rooting, postural adjustment when held

    sucking and grasping to gain or maintain contact

    signaling behaviors: smiling, crying, and other vocalizations to bring caregiver into proximity or contact

Infants from birth to four months are egocentric; they have only their point of view. They use their senses to begin to develop a global concept of self. They need to see, hear, smell, touch, and taste themselves. People and objects are familiar insofar as they interact with the infant's sense experiences. For infants at this level people and objects do not exist as separate objects.

The caregiver can use several strategies to enhance social development. The caregiver can respond quickly to the infant's needs and can initiate interactions by looking, holding, stroking, talking, playing, carrying, and rocking the infant.

The caregiver arranges time and selects materials that help infants learn about themselves. Mirrors fascinate infants. Dots on bare feet and hands extend the infant's interest in his or her body. The caregiver arranges for the infant to interact with other people and with playthings.

Suggestions for Implementing Curriculum

Child Behavior	Materials	Examples of Caregiver Strategies
Attachment		
shows special closeness to parent; differentiates response to parent—voice, touch, presence, absence		Accept that the infant will respond differently to you than to parent. Closely observe the parent-infant interaction and then model some of the caregiving behaviors, sounds, and other characteristics of the parent.
develops familiarity with one primary caregiver (significant other)		Same caregiver provides most of infant's care, although other caregivers may share responsibility occasionally.
		Provide consistent care of infant: feed; comfort; change diapers and clothes; talk and sing and play with infant; rock and hold; put to bed; pick up when awake; respond to infant's special needs, likes, and dislikes. Touch, hold, caress, cuddle the infant.

Child Behavior	Materials	Examples of Caregiver Strategies
Self		
becomes aware of hands and feet	bright clothes, materals for hands, feet; bare feet sometimes	Provide clothes that allow freedom of movement. Occasionally put bright colors or dots on hands and feet to attract infant's attention.
smiles spontaneously, sometimes immediately at birth		
smiles at self in mirror	mirror	Smile with infant.
Others		
Establishes eye contact with another person		Hold infant so the caregiver is in infant's range of vision. Engage infant in eye contact.
recognizes voice of parent		
smiles at people (social smile)		Hold infant. Smile, talk with infant.
watches people		Place infant where you can be seen moving about. Carry infant around to see others.
talks (coos) to people		Respond and initiate talking, singing with infant.
shows longer attentiveness when involved with people		Spend time during infant's alert times interacting with infant.
recognizes parent visually		
recognizes individual people		Provide daily care, interactions with a few persons other than parent.
behaves differently with parent than with others		Accept different responses.
interacts with people		Initiate interactions, respond; place or carry infant where infant can meet people.
laughs		Play with infant; laugh with infant; respond to infant's laugh.
differentiates self from parent		
initiates talking to others		Answer infant's talk.
plays with toys	toys that attract infant's attention, challenge infant	Provide toys; change toys to renew interest.

Cognitive Development

Child caregivers are teachers and they need to know the importance of infant stimulation. Neuropsychologist Jane Healy discusses brain development of an infant in her book *Your Child's Growing Mind* (1989).

"Amazingly, although the number of cells remains almost the same, brain weight can double during the first year of life . . . as stimuli seen, heard, felt and tasted are received . . . they build new physical connections . . . During the first six months active sensory messages bombard the infant brain . . . these connections where learning begins are enriched by repeated use— Every response to sights, sounds, feelings, smells, and tastes make more connections. The weight and the thinking power of the brain increase in an elaborate geometric progression. The more work the brain does, the more it becomes capable of doing."

This means that caregivers take every opportunity to teach, knowing that to increase an infant's stimulation is to increase ultimate human intelligence.

Piaget's theory of cognitive development categorizes the first four months of life as a part of the sensorimotor stage. Infants get information in this stage through their senses and motor activity. When infants interact with their environment, they are doing something. Infants use all their senses. With experience they refine their capacities for seeing, hearing, smelling, tasting, and touching. Moving themselves, moving others, and handling objects become coordinated with their senses. For example, when hearing a sound, infants turn their heads in the direction of the sound.

Sensorimotor intelligence is primarily focused on action, not on classification and organization. . . . the knowledge that young infants have of objects is in terms of the sensorimotor impressions the objects leave on them and the sensory and motor adjustments the objects require. For young infants objects do not have an existence independent of their reactions to them (Anisfeld, 1984, 15).

The sensorimotor stage has been divided into six substages; the first two are evident in the first four months. In each stage the infant develops new behaviors.

In Stage One the newborn's behavior is reflexive. Infants quickly start to change their behavior from passive reactions to active searching. Each of the senses operates independently.

During Stage Two infants begin to coordinate their senses. They begin to develop hand-mouth coordination, eye coordination, and eye-ear coordination. One behavior can stimulate another; for example, a reflexively waving arm may attract the infant's attention so that the child visually focuses on his or her hand.

The caregiver uses several strategies to enhance cognitive development. Selecting items for and arranging an attention-catching environment stimulates the infant to respond in any way possible at his or her particular stage. Repeating and reinforcing the infant's behaviors pleases and stimulates the infant.

Suggestions for Implementing Curriculum

Child Behavior	Materials	Examples of Caregiver Strategies
Piaget's Stages of Sensorimotor Development		
STAGE 1 (*Reflex*)		
carries out reflexive actions— sucking, eye movements, hand and body movements		Provide nonrestricting clothes, uncluttered crib, which allow freedom of movement.
moves from passive to active search	visually attractive crib, walls next to crib, objects; occasional music, singing, talking, chimes	Provide environment that commands attention during infant's period of alertness.
STAGE 2 (*Differentiation*)		
makes small, gradual changes that come from repetition		Provide change for infant; carry infant around, hold infant, place infant in crib. Observe, discuss, record changes.
coordinates behaviors, e.g., a sound stimulates looking	face and voice, musical toy, musical mobile, rattle	Turn on musical toy; place where infant can see it.
puts hand, object in mouth and sucks on it	objects infant can grasp and are safe to go in mouth	Place objects in hand or within reach. Infants attempt to put *everything* in their mouths. Make sure they get only safe objects.
moves hand, object to where it is visible	objects which infant can grasp and life	Provide clothes that allow freedom of movement. Place objects in hand or within reach.
produces a pleasurable motor activity and repeats activity		Provide time, space for repetition.
Piaget's Concept of Object Permanence*		
SENSORIMOTOR STAGES 1 AND 2		
follows moving objects with eyes until object disappears; looks where object has disappeared; loses interest and turns away; does not search for it	toys and objects that attract visual attention	Place object in range of infant's vision. Allow time for infant to focus on object. Move object slowly back and forth within child's field of vision. Move object where infant cannot see it, e.g., ball which rolls behind infant.

*Object or person exists when out of sight or touch.

Learning Skills/Language Development

Language is a tool used to communicate with oneself and with others. Crying is one way infants communicate with others. Even newborns cry in different ways, depending on whether they are startled or uncomfortable.

> "Prelinguistic vocalizations contribute to the infant's developing ability to speak. In the first 8 weeks vocalizations are of two kinds: One category consists of vegetative sounds and includes burping, swallowing, spitting up, and the like. The other category consists of discomfort sounds and includes reflexive crying and fussing." (Anisfeld, 1984, 221)

Infants produce sounds as they use their mouths and throats. These sounds are the infants' "talk." At first they seem unaware of their sounds, and then gradually they begin to repeat their own sounds. Infants talk to themselves for the pleasure of making the sounds and hearing themselves talk.

Infants use several kinds of sounds as part of their language. They produce sounds as they eat and as they play with their tongues and mouths. They use their throats, saliva, tongues, mouths, and lips to produce gurgling, squealing, smacking, and spitting noises. Gradually they produce sounds that can be classified as **cooing**, which resemble vowellike sounds. A second stage of vocalization occurs between nine and 20 weeks. "It is characterized by cooing and laughter; sustained laughter occurs at 16 weeks" (Anisfeld, 1984, 222).

When infants hear someone talk to them, it stimulates them to talk. This dialogue is very important. Effective dialogue can occur when the caregiver looks at the infant while alternately listening to and answering the child's talk. The one-to-one dialogue is what stimulates the infant. Talking not directed to the infant personally is not as effective a stimulator. Adults conversing with each other in the presence of the child, or a radio or television program turned on do not involve the child in language dialogue.

Suggestions for Implementing Curriculum

The caregiver can use several strategies to enhance the infant's *language.*

1. Talk: Sounds, words, sentences, nursery rhymes, reading stories, books, and pictures with faces of many different races.
2. Sing: Humming, original songs or talking set to your own music, nursery rhymes, lullabies, songs, African drums, and bagpipe music.
3. Listen and respond: Infants will make sounds by themselves for a few months. This talk will decrease if the infants do not have someone to listen to them and to "answer" them.
4. Initiate conversation: Almost every encounter with an infant is an opportunity for conversation. Routine physical care like feeding, changing diapers, and rocking all present the necessary one-to-one situations where you and the infant are interacting. It is not necessary or helpful to talk all the time or to be quiet all the time. The infant needs times for language and conversation and times for quiet.

Child Behavior	Materials	Examples of Caregiver Strategies
Physical Components Involved in Language Communication		
back of throat		Observe and record infant's use of sound.
nose		
mouth cavity		Record repetitions, changes, and new sounds.
front of mouth		Record mood of infant when infant is making longer repetitions of sounds.
tongue		
lips		
saliva		
Actions Involved in Language Communication		
changes air flow: through nose through mouth		
uses tongue to manipulate air flow, saliva		
plays with tongue—twists, turns, sticks it out, sucks on it		
uses saliva in various places and changes sounds: gurgle in back of throat; bubbling in center of mouth; hissing, spitting with partially closed lips and tongue		
Initiating-Responding		
	rattle, objects that make sounds or noises, music box, music, talking, singing	Talk, sing to infant while feeding, changing diapers and clothes, holding, carrying around, rocking. Carry on normal conversation with infant—talking, listening, silence.
initiates making sounds		"Answer" infant with sounds or words.
responds vocally to another person		Hold infant: look at infant eye- to-eye; make sounds, talk, sing to infant; listen to infant's response; talk, sing again; listen, and so on.
makes sound, repeats sound, continues practicing sound a few minutes and lengthening to longer blocks of time		Talk with infant, show interest, look at infant.

(continued)

(continued)

Child Behavior	Materials	Examples of Caregiver Strategies
imitates sounds already known		Repeat sound infant has just made; listen to infant make sound; repeat it again; and so on.
experiments with sounds		
Crying		
cries apparently automatically in distress, frustration		Rue with the infant. Respond to infant's crying immediately and consistently.
cries differently to express hunger, discomfort, anger		Attend to the need infant expressed by crying.
cries to gain attention		Find out what infant wants.
cries less as vocalizing increases		
Cooing		
coos in vowellike sounds		Imitate, respond, and talk to infant.
adds pitch		

Key Terms

attachment theory

cooing

elimination

hearing

muscular control

sleep

smell

taste

temperament

touch

visual perception

Student Activities

1. List the child's behaviors you see in a picture of an infant under four months of age.

2. Observe one infant under four months of age. Record the infant's behavior in two five-minute sequences. Transfer the descriptions to the Developmental Profile.

3. Select toys from catalogs and newspaper ads that are said to be appropriate for an infant under four months of age. Read the toy description. Match it to the category and level of development of a specific infant.

4. Select one category of the Developmental Profiles (for example, physical development). Observe a caregiver and classify the strategies the caregiver used in that category (for example, physical support: holds hand behind infant's head and neck).

5. List five strategies which you competently use with infants from birth to four months.

6. List strategies you need to develop and list ways you intend to develop them.

CASE STUDY

Kiera is the youngest of eight children. Her closest sibling is 17 years her senior. Both of her parents are first-generation immigrants. Her mother is over 45 years old, and during her pregnancy Kiera's father, who was 15 years older than her mother, suddenly died of a heart attack. Kiera was delivered by cesarean and since her birth, her mother has cared for her only occasionally. Most of Kiera's care has been provided by her siblings, aunts, and uncles. The grief of the family is obvious to anyone observing them. The well-meaning but numerous caregivers provide a very inconsistent parenting style for Kiera. The variety of different faces and personalities who care for Kiera may help explain her inconsistent strengths and weaknesses on the Developmental Profile.

Since Kiera is presently without consistency in her environment, her child care experience should be beneficial since one primary infant specialist is assigned to her. In addition, a very consistent daily routine will be established around her needs at the center, and gentle handling and speaking to her will enhance her sense of trust and security. Home visitations at regularly scheduled times will also benefit Kiera because the home visitor will discuss consistent rules and schedules with her various caregivers at home.

1. What effect do you think a depressed family has on the development of a four-month-old? Support your thoughts with references.
2. How are the 3A's implemented with Kiera?
3. What would be your next steps if Kiera's development does *not* improve after her home life becomes more consistent?

Chapter Review

1. In each area state a purpose for using the Developmental Profiles with infants from birth to four months of age.

Area	Purpose
a. Physical	
b. Emotional	
c. Social	
d. Cognitive	
e. Language	

2. Describe how you get information about the infant's developmental levels.
3. List three toys or materials that can be used with infants from birth to four months of age. List the area(s) of development that each can enhance.

Toy/Material	Area(s) of Development
a.	
b.	
c.	

4. State two reasons why it is helpful to the infant to have the caregiver talk to him or her.

References

Ainsworth, M. D. (1982). The development of infant-mother attachment. In J. Belsky (Ed.). *In the beginning: Readings on infancy*. New York: Columbia University Press.

Anisfeld, M. (1984). *Language development from birth to three*. Hillsdale, NJ: Lawrence Erlbaum Associates.

Bruner, J. S. (1968). *Processes of cognitive growth: Infancy*. Clark University Press.

Eisenberg, A., Murkoff, H. E., & Hathaway, S. E. (1989). *What to expect the first year*. New York: Workman Publishing.

Healy, J. (1989). *Your child's growing mind: A guide to learning and brain development from birth to adolescence*. New York: Doubleday.

Riback, P. (19977). The Child. New York Times Special Report.

Helpful Web Sites

The Program Activities and Equipment—What to Look for in Quality Child Care—Amazing Baby http://www.amazingbaby.com/childcare.html

The Developing Baby—Part I A detailed description of your baby's sensory motor development, Baby Grows. http://www.parentspitara.com/babynu/grows/pg/19.htm

Study of Early Child Care National Institute of Child Health and Human Development. http://www.nichd.nin.gov/publications/pubs/early_child_care.htm

Quality Care for Infants and Toddlers National Child Care Information Center. http://www.nccic.org/

The Nature of Children's Play Sensorimotor play. http://www.kidsource.com/kidsource/content2/nature.of.childs.play.html

Toys: The Tools of Play http://www.toy-tma.org/industry/publications/fpsp/tools.html

Child Development—Capabilities timeline—First Six Months http://topcondition.com/temp/Afittot/development.htm

Entertaining Baby—activities that will enhance motor skills and cognitive development http://www.babyparenting.about.com

Skill Building Activities—Development Tracker, Baby's First Year. http://www.parentsoup.com/tracker/articles/0,12106,166461_263922,00.html

For additional infant and toddler resources, visit our Web site at http://www.earlychilded.delmar.com

11

The Child from Four to Eight Months of Age

Objectives

After reading this chapter, you should be able to:

■ Identify and record sequences of change in the physical, emotional, social, cognitive, and language development of infants from four to eight months of age.

■ Select materials appropriate to that age-level infant's development.

■ Devise strategies appropriate to that age-level infant's development.

Chapter Outline

Materials and Activities

Caregiver Strategies to Enhance Development

Theresa's Story

Theresa, six months old, is lying on her stomach on the floor, kicking her legs and waving her arms. She looks at a toy radio and drools. She fingers the toy radio. She chews and drools. She "sings" with the music. Ellie, the caregiver, winds up the toy radio. Theresa kicks her feet and smiles. She watches the radio and kicks her feet. Ellie smiles at Theresa and Theresa smiles back. She kicks her feet rapidly. Theresa looks at Wayne, another infant. Ellie speaks to Theresa. Theresa tries to lift herself by pushing on the floor with her arms. She turns herself around, still on her tummy. She kicks her feet and keeps trying to lift herself up onto her knees to a crawling position. She presses her feet against furniture. During this time she has turned about 180 degrees.

MATERIALS AND ACTIVITIES

Materials for this age group must be safe for the infants to mouth and hit and bang on themselves. These infants have developed some manual skills, but their limited control of their arm and hand muscles causes them to be rather rough on their toys and themselves. Attention-catching toys stimulate the interest of these infants and lengthen their playtime.

Types of Materials

foam toys	toys safe to bang and hit
small toys and objects to grasp	low material and equipment to climb
soft balls	on and over
sound toys	mirror
toys safe to throw	teething toys

Examples of Homemade Materials

BLOCKS

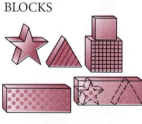

Cut foam rubber into squares, circles, rectangles, triangles, and other shapes. Cover the foam with printed fabric sewn to fit the shapes. Large shapes can be stacked as blocks.

Cut 1-inch-thick sponges into shapes. Make sure the finished pieces are a good size to handle but too big to swallow.

Cover foam ball with washable pattern fabric.

Use Appendix A, the Developmental Prescriptions, and Appendix B, the Developmental Profile, with each infant. Children follow a sequence of development. There are often ranges in the rate of development.

CRIB GYM

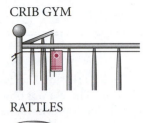

Tie a colorful 3-inch-wide strip of fabric in between the slats. Make individual cloth toys that will move when the infant pulls the ties.

RATTLES

Empty and wash childproof clear plastic medicine bottles. Put in uncooked cereal—one teaspoon white, one teaspoon red (dyed in food coloring). Use sturdy glue to fasten cap tightly.

MUSIC, SOUNDTOYS

Use empty cardboard cans with lids (oatmeal, potato chip). Put jingle bells or loose items like blocks inside. Glue the lid on securely and tape around the edges. When the infant pushes and rolls it, the bells or blocks will make a noise.

FOIL PIE PANS

Place disposable pie pans near the infant to use for a mirror, for grasping, and for banging. Check frequently. If a sharp edge or tear develops, discard.

BEANBAG

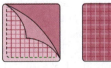

Sew together along three sides two double layers of 3-inch-square colorful terrycloth fabric. Turn right side out. Fill the pouch half-full with aquarium rocks that have been boiled to sanitize them. Sew the fourth side shut.

BRACELET

Sew a 4-inch length of elastic together to make a circle. Sew on several yarn pompoms. Place on wrist or ankle for infant to watch while waving arms and kicking feet.

SOCKDOLL

Use a child's sock. Make eyes, nose, and mouth with permanent nontoxic marker or sew features with embroidery thread. Sew on short yarn hair. Stuff with foam or nylon scraps. Sew closed at bottom (top of sock). Caution: Make sure the "hair" is secured and cannot pull out.

CAREGIVER STRATEGIES TO ENHANCE DEVELOPMENT

Developmental Profile

Please refer to the Developmental Profile in Figure 11–1 for Theresa Y., a healthy infant with a chronological age (C.A.) of six months. Theresa was observed over a two-week period and estimates were made of her skill development in the Child Behaviors from the Prescriptions in Appendix A. The profile indicates her lowest as development area "teeth" (five months) and her highest as attachment and visual-motor control (eight months).

Specifically, Theresa can perform behaviors in the Physical Area (I) under "muscular control" indicative of an eight-month-old, such as sitting unsupported for short times and pulling herself to a standing position. Because two upper and two lower teeth are not through her gums yet, she is estimated at the five-month rather than the six-month level in that area.

Theresa was estimated in the Emotional Area (II) to be a little above C.A. (seven months) in temperament because she has a very good attention span and persistence for her age.

Regarding the Social Area (III), Theresa is estimated at the eight-month level because she differentiates well between people and exhibits strong attachments to people she cares about.

The Cognitive Area (IV) was estimated to be at C.A., except that Theresa misses special toys, which suggests a little higher level of object permanence (7 months).

Within the Learning Skills Area (V), Theresa's language development is as expected, but she exhibits better eye-hand coordination (eight months) and visual skills (seeing; seven months) than many children her age. The skills of eye-hand coordination (visual-motor), seeing, and hearing are placed within the Learning Skills Area (V), although they appear within the Physical Area (I) in the Prescription. This is done because higher levels of visual and auditory perception skills and visual-motor control are essential for pre-academic skills, such as letter and number recognition.

To summarize, Theresa is a healthy six-month-old who exhibits average to above-average skills in all areas, with the exception of teeth. The caregiver should design activities for all developmental areas and focus specific tasks on teething, for example, teething ring, and chewing things. In this way, Theresa is assured of a balanced developmental program.

Physical Development

Infants develop rapidly during this four-month period. They are awake and alert longer. They are becoming more coordinated. They can sit when propped and are developing the ability to sit alone and can sit in a highchair. They can roll over and may creep. They can grasp objects intentionally and move and bang them purposefully.

The head, neck, arm, chest, and back muscles are used to maintain a sitting position. These are developing from the pushing and pulling and kicking and rolling the infant does. Even when the infant can sit when propped or sit alone, these muscles tire easily, so care must be taken to allow the infant to change positions.

By the middle of the first year infants can stand on their legs. The muscles in their heads, necks, arms, chests, backs, and legs are all functioning but are not yet coordinated. With the aid of people and furniture infants can stay standing and begin to take

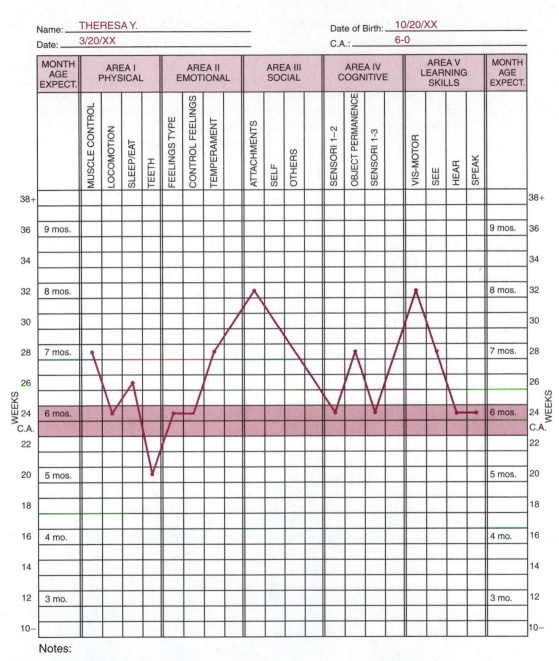

Name: THERESA Y.

Date: 3/20/XX

Date of Birth: 10/20/XX

C.A.: 6-0

Figure 11–1 Developmental Profile, Theresa Y.

steps. Their ankle, foot, and toe muscles develop strength and coordination with the rest of their bodies (Figure 11–2).

Locomotion While infants are developing some stability in relation to the force of gravity (sitting, standing), they are also attempting to move forward (**locomotion**).

Between the fourth and fifth months, the infant will roll from stomach to back and, by the sixth month, most can roll from back to stomach. Creeping is the first locomotor movement, which starts around the sixth month (refer to Physical Development in Developmental Prescriptions in Appendix A). Regan is lying on her stomach, reaching for a toy. She twists her body, pulls with her arms, and pushes with her legs. Slowly she moves forward to the toy. To accomplish this major task Regan used her head, neck, back, arm, and leg muscles to move and to lift the top part of her body up and down without tipping over. She may even get up on her hands and knees and rock. Infants can be encouraged to move at this stage by placing toys just out of reach.

By the seventh month she may actually be able to crawl about on her hands and knees and may pull herself to a standing position. By the eighth month she may put one foot in front of the other when held in a standing position.

Manipulation Manipulation involves reaching, grasping, and releasing. In the first year infants move from reflexive to voluntarily controlled manipulation. During the first six months infants develop from erratic waving to carefully controlled reaching. They use shoulder, elbow, wrist, and hand movements to coordinate with what they see in order to reach purposefully and successfully to an object. Control of reaching is necessary to accompany the task of grasping.

Newborns grasp reflexively. For the next few months their hands will close on anything that touches them. They will grasp objects with either hand. Gradually infants

Figure 11–2 The caregiver smiles, talk, and encourages the infant's movements.

begin to open their hands and use the whole hand to "palm" a toy. Around the end of the fourth month, the child will be able to move toys from one hand to the other. By the end of the first year, an infant will be able to use thumb and forefinger to assist in grasping objects (see "Hand" in Developmental Prescriptions in Appendix A).

Seeing By the fourth month, vision has pretty much matured. When visually following a moving object (**tracking**), the baby's eye and head movements are as coordinated as an adult's. The infant is visually attracted by colorful objects and will show preferences for specific colors. Infants at this age are also attracted by faces, shapes, and designs, and may reach for a favorite toy or object. By five months many infants will smile at themselves in a mirror.

To encourage visual stimulation, hang pictures and objects at eye level, near the floor or at crib level, where infants can observe them. Put up new pictures and mobiles frequently and provide a safety mirror to stimulate new interest.

Elementary skills of Visual Memory, Visual Discrimination, Visual Association, and Visual-Motor Control can be enhanced through simple "games."

Hearing Infants enjoy making sounds and playing with sounds. Imitate infants' sounds back to them. Hearing and seeing and hearing and reaching are becoming more coordinated. While more is known about vision than the other senses, it is believed that all the other senses develop at about the same time as vision. Elementary Developmental Learning Skills of Auditory Discrimination, Auditory Memory, Auditory Association, and Auditory/Visual Association can be enhanced through simple games at this age (Douville-Watson-Watson, 1995).

Eating Many pediatricians recommend that infants begin solid foods at about six months of age. Mouthing and swallowing solid foods involves a coordination of muscles different from those used for sucking. Begin solid foods when the parents request it. Use the same kind of spoon the parents use so the infants do not have to adjust to different sizes and shapes of spoons while they learn to retrieve food from a spoon and swallow the food without spitting it out or choking.

Feeding time presents an opportunity to socialize, and the infant may be distracted from eating to coo and gurgle with his caregiver between eating spurts. This social exchange is very important to later social development.

By the sixth month, the infant may insist on holding the bottle or may try drinking from a cup, even without being ready to give up the bottle. By the seventh month, even though it is too early to use a spoon, the infant will want to feed himself or herself and show resistance to being fed. It's time to let the child try it! At this time finger foods are developmentally appropriate. The experience of eating with fingers is an important one.

Teething Infants usually begin **teething** at this age. Infants react differently to teething. Sometimes an emerging tooth causes an infant to be very fussy and irritable, while other times a new tooth just seems to appear with the infant behaving no differently at all. Teething infants often like to bite on something. They use teething rings as well as anything else they can put into their mouths. If an infant seems to be hurting, a cold teething ring or crushed ice in a clean cloth provides coldness as well as hardness for the child's gums. Teething infants may drool profusely. They may need to wear a bib all day, and it may need to be changed frequently to keep their clothes dry.

Suggestions for Implementing Curriculum

Child Behavior	Materials	Examples of Caregiver Strategies
Muscular Control		
HEAD AND NECK		
holds head up independently		Allow infant to lift head. Keep hand near to provide support.
holds head in midline position	mobiles, crib gyms	Put some objects above center of crib.
holds head up when on back, stomach, and sitting		Place infant where child can safely look around.
TRUNK		
holds up chest, shoulders; arches back, hips		Provide clothes that allow freedom for pushing up, kicking, and wriggling. Check area for safety.
sits with support; may attempt to raise self; may fuss if left lying down with little chance to sit up		Provide pillows, firm items to prop infant against.
Hold infant in sitting position.		
leans back and forth	place toys within reach	Keep area around infant free of sharp objects. Infant topples over easily.
sits in a chair	chair with back	Use chair strap for safety. Let infant sit in chair, but for a short time, for the infant's muscles tire quickly.
sits unsupported for short time	safe, flat sitting space	Place in safe area where infant can sit and play or watch. Infant will tire soon and will lie down.
pushes self to sitting position	flat sitting space	Provide uncluttered space where infant can roll around and push with arms and legs to sit up alone.
LEG		
lifts legs when on back and stomach		Provide clothes that allow free kicking.
rolls from stomach to back		Place where infant can move freely and safely. Keep crib sides up. Keep hand on infant while changing diapers.
straightens legs when standing		Hold infant in standing position for short periods. Hold infant's sides firmly when child bounces.
stamps feet when standing		Firmly hold infant upright and provide flat surface for infant to push and move feet against.

Child Behavior	Materials	Examples of Caregiver Strategies
rolls from back to stomach		Place where infant can move freely and safely. Keep crib sides up. Keep hand on infant while changing diapers.
raises to hands and knees		Place on flat, firm surface
stands with support		Hold infant's sides or hands while infant is standing on flat surface.
pulls self to standing position		Hold infant's hands and allow infant to use own muscles to pull self up. Check furniture and shelving to make sure neither will tip over when infant pulls on them to stand up.

LOCOMOTION

Child Behavior	Materials	Examples of Caregiver Strategies
kicks against surface to move	floor space, sturdy furniture	Provide area where there is safe resistance, e.g., carpeting that helps traction, bare feet on vinyl, furniture to push against.
rocks on hands and knees	blanket on floor	Provide clear, safe area where infant can safely raise self up and rock, then lurch forward and fall on face. Praise infant for success in getting to hands and knees.
creeps on stomach	blanket on floor	Provide clear safe area where infant can creep. Place toy slightly out of reach to motivate creeping. Encourage and praise creeping.
uses legs to pull, push self when sitting	floor space	Sit a short distance from infant. Call child's name. Encourage infant to come to you. Show excitement and give praise.

ARM

Child Behavior	Materials	Examples of Caregiver Strategies
visually directs reaching, hitting	crib toys, movable toys	Provide toys that infant can reach and hit. Provide large toys infant can accurately hit against.
throws objects	soft, light toys; objects	Select toys that are light and will not go far and hit other children. Place infant in an area where child can safely throw objects.

HAND

Child Behavior	Materials	Examples of Caregiver Strategies
grasps objects with whole hand and fingers against thumb	clutch ball	Provide toys that allow infant to wrap hand around some part. Flat surfaces slip out of grasp.
uses thumb and forefinger	small toys of any shape	Make sure toys are too big to be swallowed. Infant will pick up anything, even mouth it.
picks up object with one hand; passes it to the other hand	small toys of any shape	Place toys around infant so child will use both hands. Ask for toy from one hand. Give toy to each hand.

(continued)

(continued)

Child Behavior	Materials	Examples of Caregiver Strategies
uses objects in both hands	banging toys	Play banging game with blocks, bells, balls.
grasps and releases objects	toys that fit in hand or have handles	Play game, "Put it here." You put one toy in a pile. Infant picks up and puts down a toy in the same place.
drops objects	unbreakable toys and objects, pail	Provide space for dropping. Play game, "Drop it." Stand up and drop toy into pail. Infant stands against chair and drops toys into pail.

Seeing

focuses on objects near and far	designs, pictures, wall space	Regularly change pictures, floor- to-ceiling projects, and bulletin boards to stimulate new looking.
distinguishes color, distance; depth perception	colorful objects	Provide colorful items. Put materials with reach so infant can succeed. Respect infant's resistance to moving where child does not feel safe.
distinguishes visually attractive objects	faces, designs, shapes, color in room's materials and space	Note preferences for faces, designs, shapes. Make frequent changes.
has visual preferences	favorite faces, pictures, objects	Observe infant's reactions to pictures, objects. Provide access to favorites by displaying them again later.

Hearing

listens to own voice		Provide quiet space where infant can enjoy hearing own voice.
listens to others' voices		Place near other infants and caregivers. Direct your talking to the infant.
looks around to locate sound	sounding toys, cans, bells	Play game: shake can beside infant. Wait for child to turn around and find you shaking the can. Shake bells beside you. Wait for infant to locate the ringing bells. Talk and sing with the infant.

Sleeping

takes a long morning nap and a long afternoon nap		Adjust routines to fit infant's changing sleep schedule.

Eating

6 months begins solid foods		
eats baby food (new tongue and swallowing technique)	mashed foods, baby spoon, heated dish, plastic-lined bib, washcloth	Clean up infant and self for feeding time. Check with parent about desired food. Feed patiently while infant learns to eat from a spoon. Talk calmly. Praise infant's accomplishments. Clean up.

Child Behavior	Materials	Examples of Caregiver Strategies
drinks from cup (new tongue and swallowing technique)	cup with special cover to control flow of milk, juice	Hold cup for infant. Tilt up and back to give infant time to swallow before next drink. Allow infant to help hold cup.
eats at "mealtimes" with solid foods, milk, juice	food grinder	Provide milk or juice in cup and solid foods at regular mealtimes to fit into the infant's sleep and play schedule.
feeds self finger foods	bite-size food	Clean up infant, self, and eating area. Provide food and time to eat it. Minimize distractions. Talk with infant, encourage infant, label food and actions. Clean up.
Teeth		
first teeth emerge: 2 middle lower, 2 middle upper	hard teething rings: firm, safe objects to bite, cold objects to bite	Provide objects safe for infant to bite on hard. May occasionally put ice in sterile cheesecloth for infant to bite on.
Elimination		
decreases number of times of urination and bowel movements	daily report form	Check diapers frequently; may be dry longer. Record bowel movements

Emotional Development

CDA III.8

Infants now express a wider range of **emotional development**. Pleasure, happiness, fear, and frustration are displayed in a variety of sounds, such as gurgles, coos, wails, cries, along with physical movements like kicking rapidly, waving arms, bouncing, rocking self, and smiling.

Fear Many infants experience what is called **stranger anxiety**, especially between five and seven months of age. People whom the infant doesn't know or does know but does not often see may find the infant afraid of them. The infant may cry, cringe, hide, or move away. This very normal infant behavior occurs at a time when the infant is beginning to construct the idea of self as separate from others. It is important that "strangers" not feel something is wrong with them. A substitute caregiver may experience this infant withdrawal because the infant has established familiarity and attachment to the primary caregiver, whereas the substitute is different.

It is also during this period that the infant may demonstrate anxiety at being separated from mother or the caregiver. The infant may become nervous or distraught if the caregiver is too far away or out of sight. Take every opportunity to tell the child that you will leave and will return. Introduce the substitute caregiver and explain that this person will take good care of him or her until you return. It is important to tell the infant when you have returned.

Temperament

Activity Level   The **high active** infant may kick and wriggle and jerk, and therefore tip over when sitting propped more often than the **low active** infant. High active infants need sitting times even though they need more caregiver assistance. On the other hand, low active children are easy to leave in a sitting position longer than may be good for their muscles because they may not fuss and move enough to tip over. These children need to be moved from sitting to lying on their stomachs, to holding, to sitting (Figure 11–3).

Approach or Withdrawal as a Characteristic Response to a New Situation   Infants from four to eight months of age are experiencing many new situations. They are introduced to solid foods and probably will be encouraged to try various vegetables, fruits, and meats. They are beginning to creep and move into room areas on their own, sometimes into areas not meant for them. Those infants who characteristically encounter newness easily may take in stride new foods and new spaces. They have food preferences, but the act of trying something new usually does not distress them. Infants who characteristically hesitate or withdraw in new situations need new experiences presented slowly. Allow time for the infant to become familiar with one kind of food before introducing a new one. Allow the infant to seek new floor spaces and gain familiarity with them; do not move the infant around from new space to new space.

Figure 11–3 The caregiver helps children sit upright to explore a confined space.

Suggestions for Implementing Curriculum

Child Behavior	Materials	Examples of Caregiver Strategies
Types of Emotional Feelings		
shows pleasure in watching others		Place infant where child can see others playing.
shows pleasure in repetitive play	favorite toys	Provide favorite toys. Share pleasure in repetitive actions e.g., clapping hands.
shows depression		Discuss possible causes with parent. Provide consistent loving, touching, holding, and playing whenever possible.
shows fear of strangers		Introduce strangers carefully. Do not let stranger hover closely. Give the infant time to become accustomed to the stranger at a distance. Use ruing.
shows fear of falling down		When infant is standing and falling, keep area safe. Comfort when needed and then encourage infant and praise infant's standing.
shows frustration with stimulation overload		Provide quiet space and time for the infant. Constant visual and auditory stimulation is nerve-racking. Comfort, hold, talk softly to frustrated infant.
shows happiness, delight, joy; humor expressed with laughs, giggles, grins		Share laughing, giggling. Play funny games, e.g., "Touch your nose"—hold your finger by your head and slowly move it to touch the infant's nose while you say excitedly, "I'm going to touch your nose."
shows rage		Allow infant to kick legs, flail arms, scream, and cry for a short time. Determine the cause of the rage. Reduce or eliminate the cause if possible. Use touching, rocking, soothing talk to help the infant calm down.
		Verbally affirm and acknowledge the infant's anger and distress. Remain calm, and present soothing support.
Control of Emotions-Feelings		
sometimes stops crying when talked to, sung to		Talk calmly, soothingly to crying infant. Use ruing.
Temperament		
activity level		

(continued)

(continued)

Child Behavior	Materials	Examples of Caregiver Strategies
regularity		List two of the infant's behaviors in each category that indicate the infant's basic style. List adjustments you need to make to help the infant cope with daily situations.
approach or withdrawal as a characteristic response to a new situation		
adaptability to change in routine		
level of sensory threshold		
positive or negative mood		Follow the strategies of applying the 3A's, make eye-to-eye contact, move deliberately, and talk consistently. Use your senses to determine how much stimulation the child requires. Hold, cuddle, and soothe.
intensity of response		
distractibility		
persistence and attention span		

Social Development

CDA III. 9

Infants are now developing definite and strong attachments to parents and the primary caregiver. The primary caregiver's presence, consistent care, and emotional involvement with the infant reinforce the attachment.

Infants are engaged in several new social experiences. Their developing physical skills of manipulating objects and moving themselves around contribute to their cognitive development of constructing a concept of self and not-self. During this time, from four to eight months of age, many infants relate more frequently to other adults and children. Their interest and mobility contribute to their initiating and responding in interactions with others (Figure 11–4).

Figure 11–4 The caregiver encourages the infant to play.

Ainsworth (1982) identified several social behaviors during this age range.

Phase 2:   Discriminating Social Responsiveness
6 months or more.
discriminates between familiar and unfamiliar persons.
Responds differently to them.
differential smiling, vocalization, crying.

Phase 3:   Active Initiative in Seeking Proximity and Contact
around 7 months.
signals intended to evoke response from mother or attachment figure.
locomotion facilitates proximity seeking.
voluntary movements of hands and arms.
following, approaching, clinging—active contact behaviors.

Suggestions for Implementing Curriculum

Child Behavior	Materials	Examples of Caregiver Strategies
Attachment		
shows strong attachment to parent		Reinforce attachment to parent.
differentiates response to parent		
shows familiarity with one specific caregiver		Assign a specific, primary caregiver to a specific infant. One caregiver can be a primary person (significant other) to several infants. Primary caregiver assumes responsibility for emotional involvement with the infant while providing care for the whole child.
shows intense pleasure and frustration with person to whom attached		Accept and share pleasure; calm, soothe, stroke, and sing during infant's frustrated periods.
Self		
recognizes self in mirror	foil, metal, or plastic shatterproof mirrors	Provide hand mirror for the infant to see self. Provide full-size mirror for infant to see self and others.
seeks independence in actions		Allow infant to accomplish tasks by self when possible, e.g., creeping to toy, pulling self up.
plays self-designed games		Allow infant to play own game. Do not distract infant or make infant change and play your game.

(continued)

(continued)

Child Behavior	Materials	Examples of Caregiver Strategies
Others		
observes others		Place the infant where child can observe others' activities.
imitates others		Play games with the infant. Imitate each other, e.g., open mouth wide, stick out tongue.
recognizes children		Allow infant to touch and "talk to" other children. Stay close so each is safe from pinching, or hitting.
plays with people		Let older children and other adults play looking, hearing, and touching games with the infant.
seeks parent's and caregiver's attention by movement, sounds, smiles, and cries		Respond immediately and consistently to happy, sad, or angry pleas for attention.
follows parent and caregiver to be in the same room		Arrange the room so the infant can see you from any place the infant is in the room.
resists pressures from others regarding feeding and eating		Encourage but do not force the infant to eat. Adjust the time to stop and start according to the infant's rhythm.
acts shy with some strangers		Hold and provide security to the infant when meeting a stranger. Allow the infant time to hear and see the stranger before the stranger touches the infant or even gets too close.

Cognitive Development

Infants in sensorimotor substage 3 are constructing the beginnings of the concept of objects separate from themselves. When an object they are watching disappears, they will visually search for it, but they will not manually search for it. When an object they are holding disappears, they will search manually for it. Their senses still strongly control their actions when found, they will usually celebrate it by mouthing it. (Figure 11–5). As Dr. Healy said in her book *Your Child's Growing Mind,*

> "Each child must build individual networks for thinking; this development comes from within, using outside stimuli as materials for growth. A baby will give explicit clues about what kind of input is needed and let you know when it isn't interesting anymore. Babies come equipped with the 'need to know'; our job is to give them love, acceptance, and the raw material or appropriate stimulation at each level of development. Your own common sense, augmented by current knowledge, is the best guide." (Healy, 1989)

Figure 11–5 The child has found the hidden object and celebrates by mouthing it.

Suggestions for Implementing Curriculum

Child Behavior	Materials	Examples of Caregiver Strategies
Piaget's Stages of Sensorimotor Development		
STAGE 3 (REPRODUCTION)		
produces a motor activity, catches interest, and intentionally repeats the activity over and over	objects that attract attention: contrasting colors, changes in sounds, variety of textures, designs	Watch movements the infant repeats. Waving arm may hit the crib gym; the infant may wave arm more to hit the crib gym again. Watch which movements the infant repeats. Provide materials that facilitate, e.g., new items on the crib gym.
repeats interesting action		The infant may pound fists on legs. Watch to see that child's actions are safe.

(continued)

(continued)

Child Behavior	Materials	Examples of Caregiver Strategies
develops hand-eye coordination further; looks for object, reaches for it, and accurately touches it	toys	Place blocks, dolls, balls, other toys near the infant where child can reach them.
imitates behavior that is seen or heard	toy, food, body	Initiate action; wait for infant to imitate it; repeat action, e.g., smile, open mouth.

Piaget's Concept of Object Permanence

SENSORIMOTOR STAGE 3

visually follows object searches visually for short time when object disappears does not search manually	toys, bottle, or objects that attract visual attention	Show infant a toy. Play with it a minute and then hide the toy. Bring it out and play with it again. (You will not "teach" the infant to look for the toy. Enjoy playing with the infant and toy.)
sees part of object; looks for whole object when object disappears	familiar toy, bottle, rattle, teething ring, ball, doll	Cover up part of object with a blanket or paper. Infant will pull object out or push off blanket, e.g., play peek-a-boo.

Learning Skills/Language Development

The crying, cooing, and babbling of the infant help develop the physical mechanisms that produce speech (Figure 11–6).

> "Following the cooing period there is an extended period in which infants engage in **babbling**. Babbling continues the diversification of sounds begun in cooing. The main difference between the two is in function. Whereas cooing seems to have the function of expressing feelings of comfort, babbling is primarily sound play." (Anisfeld, 1984, 221–22)

Infants seem to produce sounds first and then "discover" them to reproduce over and over again. They experiment with these sounds and begin to make changes in them. The difference may consist of the same sound made from a different part of the mouth. For instance, when infants play with a voiced sound and the tongue and saliva at the back of their mouths, they produce a gurgle. With the same sound, tongue, and saliva at the front of the mouth, they produce a hissing or spitting sound. Infants listen to themselves and seem to enjoy their vocal play.

Babbling is playing with speech sounds. It is spontaneously produced rather than planned. Infants in their babbling use and learn to control their physical speech mechanisms. They babble different speech sounds, combine them into two- and three-syllablelike sounds. They control air flow to produce wordlike sounds and change the intensity, volume, pitch, and rhythm of their babbling sound play.

Infants also listen to the sounds around them. When you repeat the sound infants have just made, they may imitate your sound. This stimulation and repetition encourages their practice and the result is increased control over their language. This

Figure 11–6 The caregiver talks and listens to the infant's new sounds.

stimulation also helps infants begin the two-way communication process of talking-listening-talking. They are finding that when they talk, you will listen; infants make you talk to them. Cooing and babbling sounds are used to provide pleasure as well as to convey feelings. Conversations include pitch and volume added to strings of sounds that seem like syllables or words. Infants imitate and initiate private and social talking.

Suggestions for Implementing Curriculum

Child Behavior	Materials	Examples of Caregiver Strategies
coos vowellike sounds for many minutes		Respond with talk.
babbles syllablelike sounds		Respond with talk.
responds to talking by cooing, babbling, and smiling		Talk directly to infant.
imitates sounds		Make sounds, talk, sing to infant.
initiates sounds		Listen and respond.
makes vowel sounds		
looks for person speaking		Place yourself so that the infant can see you when you converse together.
looks when name is called		Call the infant by name and talk with child.
makes consonant sounds		
babbles conversation with others		Respond with talking.

(continued)

(continued)

Child Behavior	Materials	Examples of Caregiver Strategies
reflects happiness, unhappiness in sounds made		Let your voice reflect response to mood.
babbles 2- and 3-syllable sounds		Respond with talking.
uses intensity, volume, pitch, rhythm		Use normal speaking patterns and tones when talking to the infant.

Key Terms

babbling

emotional development

high active

locomotion

low active

stranger anxiety

teething

tracking

CASE STUDY

Theresa's parents both work at home. Her mother works late evenings and her father works early mornings. Theresa is on "demand" breast-feeding except for one day a week that both parents are out of the house. During that day, she gets (thawed) frozen breast milk from a bottle.

Both parents care for Theresa. They both manage to take breaks at the same time to give quality time to "Terry Bear," as she is affectionately called. Sometimes they all take walks together, with each parent taking turns carrying her. She enjoys the movement and facing her parents in her infant backpack, but she is also curious about the sights and sounds around her.

Theresa recently started going to child care and is learning to adjust and make the transition. To help, she keeps her satin blanket with her, which she enjoys chewing on when resting. Theresa's level of stimulation and support is extraordinary. She is above average in most of her developmental areas. However, her teething development is somewhat weak, which points out the wide fluctuations in development of infants and toddlers.

1. Why is Theresa allowed to keep her blanket and chew on it?
2. What would happen to Theresa if you took away her blanket? Why do you think that would happen?
3. How old should a child be before he or she no longer needs "attachments" to favorite things?

Student Activities

1. Listen to the "talk" of one infant between four and eight months of age. Write down the sounds you hear (they may be strings of vowels or syllables, e.g., aaaa; babababa).
2. Observe a caregiver talking to an infant who is this age. Write down what the caregiver says and what the infant says.
3. Observe one infant from four to eight months of age. Record the infant's behavior in two five-minute sequences, using narrative description. Transfer the descriptions to the Developmental Profile.
4. Examine the written records of one infant from four to eight months of age. List the Wednesday nap times for eight weeks. Identify any changes in nap times.
5. Observe one infant who is creeping. Write a description of the infant's physical movements.
6. List five strategies to use with an infant from four to eight months of age.
7. List strategies you need to develop and list ways you intend to develop them.

Chapter Review

1. When an infant can roll from stomach to back and from back to stomach, what additional caregiver strategies are needed? Explain three.
2. Deborah, a five-month-old, is sitting up against a pillow on the floor. She is looking at the toy she has just thrown out of her reach. She leans forward, tips over, and cries. Describe what you would do next. Explain why you would do it.
3. List three caregiver strategies that facilitate the emotional development of the infant between four and eight months.
4. Describe the changes in eye-hand coordination of an infant between four and eight months old.

References

Ainsworth, M. D. (1982). The development of infant-mother attachment. In J. Belsky (Ed.), *In the beginning: Readings on infancy*. New York: Columbia University Press.

Anisfeld, M. (1984). *Language development from birth to three*. Hillsdale, NJ: Lawrence Erlbaum Associates.

Douville-Watson, L., Watson, M. (1995). *Improving learning development with games*. Glen Cove, NY: Instructional Press.

Healy, J. (1989). *Your child's growing mind: A guide to learning and brain development from birth to adolescence*. New York: Doubleday.

Helpful Web Sites

Baby Development. The Baby Corner. http://www.thebabycorner.com/infants/dev.html

Toddler Teething. Basic Baby Care. http://www.americanbaby.com/ab/CDA/featureList/0,1309,33,00.html

Easing the Pain of Baby Teething. The Baby Corner. http://www.childfun. com/baby/teething.shtml

Activities for Young Toddlers. About Baby Parenting. http://babyparenting.about.com/ cs/activitiesandfun/index.html

Developmental Milestones. Baby Social and Emotional Development. http://www.babycenter.com/refcap/babydevel/6576.html

Ear Infections from 8 to 12 months. Baby See Baby Do. http://www.aboutears. com/earinfections/frearinfections.htm

Caring for Infants and Toddlers in Groups: Necessary considerations for Emotional, Social, and Cognitive Development. http://www.zerotothree.org/caring.html

Health Questions and Answers: Starting Solids, GeoParent. http://GeoParent. com/experts/health/startingsolids.htm

Skill Building Activities—Development Tracker, Baby's First Year. http://www. parentsoup.com/tracker/articles/0,12106,166461_263922,00.html

Bureau for Children, Youth, and Families. Infant Toddler Services Program. http:// www.kdhe.state.ks.us/bcyf/cds/its/index.html

For additional infant and toddler resources, visit our Web site at
http://www.earlychilded.delmar.com

The Child from Eight to Twelve Months of Age

12

Leroy's Story

Leroy, eight months old, is sitting on the floor with several toys in front of him that Miss Virginia, the caregiver, has just placed there. He picks up a pink toy elephant, lifts it up and down in his right hand and says, "Ahh. Ah, Ah, Yah, Ahya." He picks up lock blocks, saying, "Eee, Ahh, Ahh." He throws down the blocks and then picks up blocks and twirls one in his left hand. He puts down the blocks and crawls away to another part of the room and sits up to watch a child run cars. He crawls to Miss Virginia, who pulls him up to his knees. He stares at her and says, "Ayy." He crawls to the toys, sits back, and then pulls to the train. He pulls up on his knees to the toys and pats the ball. He starts to stand up and goes back to his knees. He pushes the train and it goes forward; his eyes get big. Miss Virginia pulls him up. Leroy stands and goes up on his toes as he holds her hands. Miss Virginia picks him up and holds him in her lap a minute.

MATERIALS AND ACTIVITIES

Infants in this age range are mobile and will encounter an expanded world. All objects within reach must be safe to taste and touch and move. These infants need space as they continue to develop control of gross motor movements, such as crawling, standing, pulling, and throwing objects. Materials to manipulate must be small enough to grasp with the palm and fingers or with thumbs and forefingers, but not small enough for them to swallow. Attention-catching materials stimulate infants to select and use those materials (Figure 12–1). The Celebration of Life Calendar in Chapter 9 has additional ideas you can integrate to use with this age level and share with parents.

Types of Materials

very low materials to climb over	stroking, textured objects
sturdy furniture to pull self up next to and walk around	sound toys
	mirrors
balls to clutch	crayons
stacking objects	puppets
nesting objects	pictures
pail and small objects to drop into it	one-piece puzzle

Examples of Homemade Materials

CLUTCHBALL

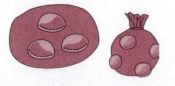

Cut a circle of colorful, washable fabric. Put polyester filling on one part of the fabric and sew around it, creating a lump. Repeat, making a second lump. Baste stitch around the edge of the circle and pull the circle almost closed. Stuff in polyester filling to pad the ball. Sew through the fabric and wind thread around the gathered end, creating a tuft of fabric.

Review Chapter 3. Use Appendix A, the Developmental Prescriptions, and Appendix B, the Developmental Profile, with each infant. Children follow a *sequence* of development. There are often ranges in the *rate* of development.

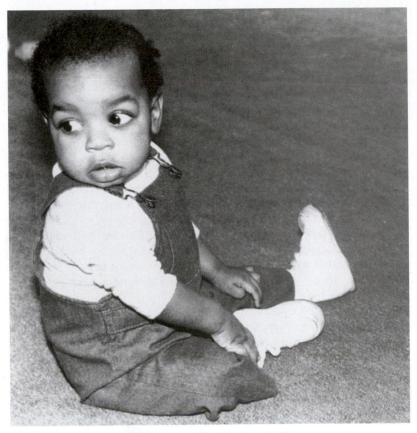

Figure 12–1 Sounds and objects attract the infant's attention.

NESTING TOYS

Select three containers of different sizes, such as plastic margarine tubs or cardboard tubes.

PUZZLE

Glue a picture of one simple object on a piece of thick cardboard (use white glue and water mixture to cover the whole picture and cardboard). Cut out the object, making a simple shape. Place the object into the matching frame.

PUPPET

On a child-sized white sock, use a nontoxic waterproof marker to draw a face on one side, hair on the other side.

CAREGIVER STRATEGIES TO ENHANCE DEVELOPMENT

Developmental Profile

Marcel, an eight-month-old, was observed over a three-day period. The Developmental Profile in Figure 12–2 was the outcome. The Child Behaviors from the Prescriptions in Appendix A were used to make estimates of Marcel's skills in each major area of development. His highest estimate is 11 months in "locomotion," and the lowest estimate is five months in "teeth." This range may suggest significant strengths and weaknesses in Marcel's development at this time.

Within the Physical Area (I), Marcel exhibits strength in his muscle control and locomotion. Estimates of 10 and 11 months are based on his skills for climbing on furniture, walking, and standing without assistance. The low score in "teeth" (five months) came about because Marcel is having pain and a hard time teething. This is also affecting his eating and sleeping patterns and his temperament (six months).

Estimates in the Emotional Area (II) are at age level in "types of feelings" (eight months) and slightly below age in "control of feelings" (seven months) and "temperament" (six months). His difficulty teething causes him to be cranky and lose control of his feelings more easily.

Marcel exhibits Social (III) and Cognitive (IV) development near his age level with no significant strengths or weaknesses being observed.

Within the Learning Skills Area (V), Marcel shows language, visual, and auditory skills at age expectancy. Because he can stack blocks and take off his clothes, the estimate for visual-motor control (eye-hand coordination) is above age at 10 months.

Marcel exhibits strengths in his Physical and Visual-Motor development and problems with sleeping, eating, emotional control, and temperament as the result of teething problems. While these problems are temporary, the caregiver should design activities and tasks to help with these problems, including discussing solutions with Marcel's parents and pediatrician.

Physical Development

Infants of this age are rapidly developing muscular control. They learn to sit alone. They crawl, stand with support, and walk with help. Creeping evolves into crawling, where the arms and legs are used in opposition. On hands and knees the infant first slowly moves one limb and then another. With increased control, crawling can become a very fast and efficient means of locomotion, providing the infant with a new world of possible experiences.

When infants have gained stability in standing upright, they can turn their efforts toward moving forward (walking). Ryan is standing next to a chair watching a bright toy on the floor sparkle in the sunshine. He leans toward it and reaches for it, but he cannot reach it. He takes one step away from the chair while still holding on to the chair. He still cannot reach it. He takes another step, and his hand slips off the chair. He is now on his own. He takes another step, stops, weaves, takes another step, and

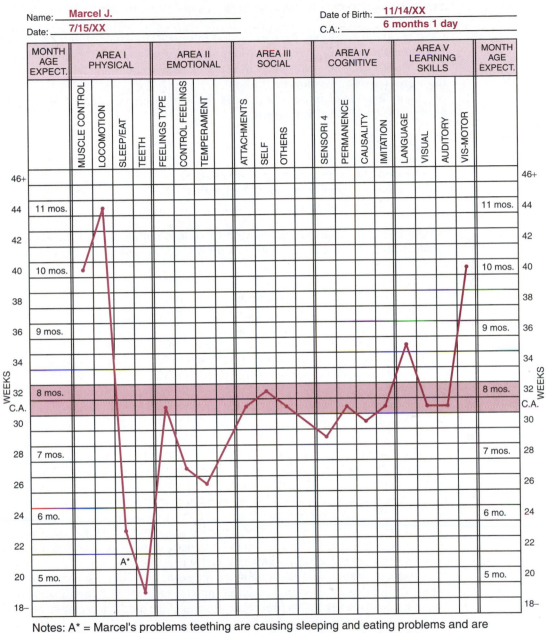

Figure 12–2 Developmental Profile, Marcel J.

Notes: A* = Marcel's problems teething are causing sleeping and eating problems and are temporarily affecting temperament.

then falls down. Ryan is beginning to walk. His first attempts at locomotion are filled with standing, stepping, weaving, sitting or falling down, pushing himself back up to standing, and trying again. Ryan will repeat this cycle thousands of times, a process that strengthens his muscles and develops his coordination. To accomplish this task Ryan needs open floor space, where he can walk without bumping into furniture or having to step on or over toys on the floor.

Many months of movement precede the actual accomplishment of walking. Shirley (1931) identified four stages.

1. an early period of stepping, in which slight forward progress is made (3–6 months)
2. a period of standing with help (6–10 months)
3. a period of walking when led (9–12 months)
4. a period of walking alone (12–15 months)

All infants proceed through these levels of locomotion, though the age varies among infants. A formerly quiet baby may show a sudden spurt of activity during this time.

"Although the baby starts practicing muscle control almost immediately, integrating reflex motor movements into controlled patterns takes a long time. The baby needs many things to see and to touch with body, mouth and hands. Initially the infant's movements seem random, but as he gets the feel of his own body in space, connections build to help the child organize his muscles around independent plans of action. Most children enjoy being stroked with a variety of pleasant textures—for example, velvet, a feather, a soft-bristled brush, or cotton—or having their limbs gently manipulated." (Healy, 1989)

The accomplishment of unassisted walking is the product of both maturation and appropriate experiences. No one can hasten a child's walking if the child is not ready. We can, however, facilitate a child's movements. Infants need adequate floor space where they can roll, crawl, climb, reach, stand, and walk. Caregivers should be cautious in the equipment they use. Playpens can very easily become prisons that restrict movement. Wheeled walkers can put undue strain on the infant's back, restricting the development and coordination of head, neck, arm, chest, back, leg, and foot muscles, while putting too much emphasis on leg movement.

Infants of this age use their thumb and fingers to grasp objects. Using this skill often, they continue to develop their finger muscles and eye-hand coordination. Because they do not have good control of the strength of the pinch, they may sometimes pinch another child hard enough to hurt.

Holding a finger straight, infants poke at themselves and objects around them. They push and pull and may keep repeating their actions.

These infants are developing control of their arms, so now they can clap and bring both hands to mid-body repeatedly. Their hands can grasp some objects, so they may bang objects together. They can hold crayons and make marks with them (refer to Appendix A, Developmental Prescription: Muscle, Hand).

These children are beginning to use each hand for different tasks. They may pick up a toy with one hand, transfer it to the other hand to hold, and then pick up another toy. They may reach out and stack one block, transfer the other toy to that hand, and stack the second block.

Infants are now beginning to be able to stroke objects, controlling their arm and hand movements so that they can touch lightly over the surface of an object. They can explore objects now by touching lightly rather than by pinching.

Infants now can hold their own bottles if they are still using them. Allow the child this independence. Help the infant grasp the cup and then allow the child to drink by him- or herself, assisting only if necessary.

An infant's soft palate is important in making sounds and later in forming words to speak. To guard against the infant's soft palate becoming misshapen, place a straw in a hard plastic bottle. This prevents the child from sucking too hard.

Infants now use both fingers and a spoon to eat and may use them at the same time. They are developing finger and arm control, which helps in using a spoon and in picking up food with their fingers. Infants want to get the food into their mouths, and they use every way they can to accomplish this task.

Infants use their new teeth to bite anything put into their mouths. Check toys, materials, and utensils a child uses to determine that they can withstand biting.

Sleep patterns continue to change gradually. At this age infants take a morning and afternoon nap but have more awake time in which to be alert to play. Each infant has a personal sleep schedule. It is affected by the child's own body needs for sleep as well as by the sleep routines at home. If the infant is awakened at 5:00 A.M. to get ready to come to child care, that child may need a morning nap earlier than an infant who was allowed to sleep until 7:00 A.M.

Suggestions for Implementing Curriculum

Child Behavior	Materials	Examples of Caregiver Strategies
Muscular Control		
TRUNK, LEG		
raises self to sitting position	flat surface	Keep area clear of objects that would hurt the infant if child falls on them.
sits alone		Provide a short time to sit. Infant may tire soon.
stands holding on to furniture or hand	sturdy chair, bench, table	Remove furniture that could tip over on infant.
stands without assistance	flat surface	Allow infant to stand alone.
sits from standing		Keep area clear of objects that could hurt infant. Infant often falls down when trying to sit down from standing.
squats and stands		Watch sharp-cornered furniture. Pad corners as needed. Infant often stands up underneath furniture (tables) and bumps head.

(continued)

(continued)

Child Behavior	Materials	Examples of Caregiver Strategies
LOCOMOTION		
crawls	obstacle-free space	Allow infant to crawl. Play with infant to stimulate crawling. Place toys slightly beyond reach to stimulate crawling.
steps forward	obstacle-free space	Hold infant's hand; provide furniture to lean on for support when stepping forward.
crawls up steps	low 2- to 4-step equipment	Allow infant to crawl up steps. Watch so you can assist infant's getting back down safely. Barricade any steps you do not want the infant to use.
steps sideways	equipment, furniture to hold on to	Allow infant to stand and step around furniture. Keep chairs, toys away from path.
walks with help	obstacle-free area	Hold infant's hand(s). Slowly walk around, allowing infant to step and balance as he or she needs to. Infant's swaying body will give you clues for stopping and starting.
climbs on furniture	low, sturdy furniture	Infant can climb but has not learned how much space his or her body takes up so may climb into areas where the child does not fit. Watch, caution, and assist when necessary.
HAND		
uses thumb and forefinger	toys, dolls	Provide objects small enough to pinch and lift.
uses thumb and two fingers	toys, dolls	Provide objects small enough to pinch and lift.
brings both hands to middle of body	banging objects, foil pie pans, blocks	Play clapping, banging games with infant. Play pat-a-cake game.
uses finger to poke	pillow, ball, small box	Provide soft objects to poke into. Watch carefully because infant may poke other children's face, eyes, and so on.
carries objects in hands	attractive objects small enough to grasp but too big to swallow	Provide objects that can be carried.
holds and uses pen, crayon	flat surface, fat felt marker, fat crayon, paper	Provide materials and space. Demonstrate where marks go (on paper, not floor or table). Remain with infant when child is using marker or crayon. Allow child to make the kind and number of marks he or she wants to. Praise child for the interest and effort. Put materials away when child decides he or she is finished.

Child Behavior	Materials	Examples of Caregiver Strategies
reaches, touches, strokes object	textured objects	Provide objects of different textures. Infants can stroke, not just grasp and pinch. Demonstrate gentle stroking. Describe the texture, e.g., "the feather is soft." Allow infant to gently stroke many objects.
uses one hand to hold object, one hand to reach and explore	objects small enough to grasp	Provide several objects at once that stimulate infant's interest.
stacks blocks with dominant hand	blocks, small objects	Allow infant to choose which hand to use in stacking objects.
takes off clothes	own clothes with big buttonholes, zippers	Infant's fingers are beginning to handle buttons, zippers. Allow infant to play with these. Infant does not understand when to undress and when to keep clothes on. Discourage undressing when you want infant to stay dressed.

Sleeping

may have trouble sleeping	calming music, musical toy	Provide adequate time to spend with infant preparing for sleep. Rock, sing, talk, stroke. Respond immediately if infant awakens during regular sleep time. Rub child's back, talk quietly as you attempt to help infant go to sleep again.
takes morning nap and afternoon nap	quiet, dim, clean sleeping space	Determine infant's preferences for going to sleep. Feed, hold and rock, rub infant's back, hum and sing to help get the infant to sleep.
seeks parent or caregiver presence		Primary caregiver should prepare infant for sleep, put infant to bed, respond if sleep is interrupted, and get infant up from nap.

Eating

holds bottle	bottle	Allow infant to hold bottle while you hold infant.
holds cup	cup with special cover	Allow infant to hold own cup. Assist when necessary, e.g., the spout is at infant's nose rather than mouth.
holds and uses spoon	child-size spoon	Provide food that can fit on spoon. Allow infant to use spoon to feed self. Assist when necessary with difficult food. Praise infant's efforts and successes. Child will hold spoon in one hand and eat with fingers of other hand.
uses fingers to eat most food	finger food	Wash hands and face *before* eating. Allow infant to use fingers to pick up food. Wash hands, face, chair, and whole area after eating time.

(continued)

(continued)

Child Behavior	Materials	Examples of Caregiver Strategies
starts establishing food preferences		Identify and record infant's food likes and dislikes. Plan a balanced diet for child, emphasizing foods child likes. Do not force foods child does not like.
may eat less		Do not force eating. Infant's body may need less. Children make adjustments in the amount they eat. Be sure children have food available they like so they can make choices about *amount* rather than *kinds* of foods.
Teeth		
begins to get teeth	teething ring; cold, hard objects to bite; bib	Provide objects safe to bite. Cold soothes the gums. Change bib as needed since drooling increases.

Emotional Development

Positive interactions with caregivers help infants develop good feelings about themselves. Infants express their happiness in many ways. They also express their anxiety and fears.

Out of fear and/or uncertainty an infant may regress temporarily to an earlier stage. Understanding this regression helps the caregiver to be aware that the child may need more reassurance than is given to a younger infant. The caregiver should be alert and notice when the child is feeling confident once more and able to function at age level again.

At this age infants are developing preferences. Providing toys they like not only adds to their pleasure in playing with the toys but also enhances their feelings of asserting some control over their world.

Developing physical skills makes infants more independent in feeding and dressing themselves. Allowing them to accomplish as many tasks as possible on their own helps them strengthen their sense of independence.

External influences like a verbal "no" or a firm look may sometimes cause infants to limit or change their behavior. Follow up your restrictive words or looks with an explanation. For example, when an infant throws food on the floor, the caregiver can say, "No. You need the carrots up here in your dish. Let's see you put a carrot in your mouth." Sometimes infants will stop their own negative action. You may see them pick up food or a toy, start to throw, and then stop their arm movement and put the object down carefully. This early self-restriction may be caused by distraction rather than self-control. Nevertheless, praise such actions to reinforce acceptable behavior.

As soon as the child has minimal verbal skills, Positive Perspective and applying the 3A's will elicit positive emotions. Remember that the most powerful way to promote positive feelings is to reward appropriate behavior and remove reward from behavior and reactions that are unwanted. Removing attention for negative behavior

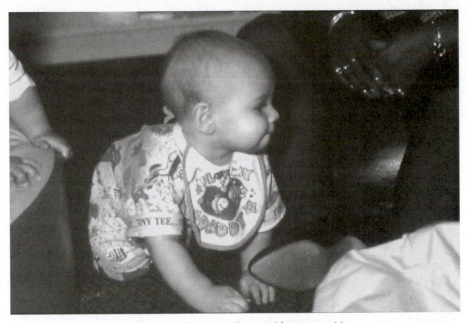

Figure 12–3 Crawling enables the infant to explore a wide new world.

works better than drawing attention to it. Be sure to trust the child's motives. Children are doing the best they can at all times.

The temperaments of infants produce varying responses to experiences. The high active infant who is crawling will spend much time and energy trying to crawl wherever you allow the child to go. His or her whole body is moving and developing physically. These children move into new areas and may keep changing their place in the environment frequently. The changing environment in turn stimulates their senses and their involvement with the world. The low active infant who is crawling will initiate crawling but move around less than a high active infant. These children may have the ability to move their whole bodies but may choose instead to use their eyes and hands and arms to search and interact in their space (Figure 12–3).

Some infants approach new situations openly. When new solid foods and finger foods are introduced, they try them. They accept and eat many of the foods, and those they reject, they reject with minimal fussing. Other infants are hesitant or resist new situations. Each new food causes these infants to pull back and at first reject the new food. With encouragement, these infants may taste the new food and then determine whether they like it or not. Sometimes they so actively resist a new food that it is difficult to get them to eat enough of it to develop an acceptance of it.

Variation in intensity of response often shows up when infants are pulling themselves up and falling down. Falling down, whether toppling forward or sitting down hard on their bottoms, always surprises infants. It is also sometimes painful. One infant will scream and cry loudly. Another may cry quietly or whimper or perhaps look surprised and upset but will not verbalize his or her discomfort.

Persistence at trying to stand upright and step forward leads toward walking. Very persistent infants will try again and again to stand or step. Falling down becomes a deterrent only after many tries. Other infants persist only a few times, then stop their efforts and change to some new task or interest.

Suggestions for Implementing Curriculum

Child Behavior	Materials	Examples of Caregiver Strategies
Types of Emotions-Feelings		
shows happiness, joy, pleasure		Share infant's feelings. Reflect back smile, positive tone of voice; hug, pat.
shows anxiety		Use calm, quiet talking, singing. Cuddle, stroke. Remove from situation if necessary.
shows fear		Determine and remove cause of fear if possible. Use calm, quiet talking, singing. Cuddle, stroke.
shows anger, frustration; has tantrums		Determine and remove cause if possible. Use calm talking, may sometimes hold and soothe infant. Help infant start a new activity. May sometimes ignore a tantrum.
rejects items, situations		Allow infant to make choices. Figure out alternative choices for situations he really needs, e.g., time or place choices.
develops preferences with toys, people		Identify and record infant's preferences. Make sure these toys are available frequently.
shows independence—helps with feeding and dressing self	cup, spoon, clothes child can manipulate	Allow infant to help feed and dress self. This takes much time and patience. Lengthen eating time to adjust to self-feeding skills.
shows affection		Accept and return affection with smile, hug, cuddle.
begins developing self-esteem		Provide positive affirmation of infant through your tone of voice, looks, touch.
Control of Emotions-Feelings		
begins to learn to obey "No"		Use "No" sparingly so infants can determine important situations when they must control their behavior. Use firm, not angry, voice. Use firm, not smiling, look on face.
sometimes inhibits own behavior		Praise infant for self-control; e.g., infant raised arm to throw book and then put it down on table.
obeys commands: No-No; Stop		Use commands sparingly. Praise infants when they obey.

Child Behavior	Materials	Examples of Caregiver Strategies
Temperament		
activity level		List two of the infant's behaviors in each category that indicate the infant's basic style.
approach or withdrawal as a characteristic response to a new situation		List adjustments you need to make to help the infant cope with daily situations.
adaptability to changed routine		
level of sensory threshold		
positive or negative mood		
intensity of response		
distractibility		
persistence and attention span		

Social Development

Interactions with others are increasing. The mobility infants now have enables them to encounter different people and to move away from them. These infants initiate interactions with others and respond to others' interactions with them (Figure 12–4).

Figure 12–4 At this age infants are often uncertain—sometimes fearful.

The infant's egocentric perspective is evident. These infants do not clearly separate others' desires and needs from their own. Therefore, they are often fearful and uncertain and occasionally clingy. They are very possessive of materials and people. Such materials and people still seem part of the infant, not completely separate, and thus they seem to belong to the infant.

The caregiver is familiar to the infant and fosters a sense of security. The infant therefore tries to keep the caregiver in sight, reinforcing his or her feelings of security.

Suggestions for Implementing Curriculum

Child Behavior	Materials	Examples of Caregiver Strategies
Others		
initiates interactions with others		Respond to infant's behavior. Talk, play with infant. Allow infant access to other children and adults.
responds		Initiate talking and playing with infant.
may fear strangers		Keep strangers from forcing themselves on infant, who may not want to be held by stranger.
keeps parent or caregiver in sight		Allow infant to follow you around. Arrange room so infant can see you from different areas of the room.
initiates play		Respond and play infant's game, e.g., pat-a-cake.
becomes assertive; initiates action to fill needs	Encourage infant's assertiveness	Observe to determine whether infant is getting aggressive and will need cautions.
wants own pleasure; may not consider others		Verbalize limits and help infant choose other activities, materials.
initiates play		Play games with infant, e.g., "Can you do this?" Wave hand, clap hands, etc.
is possessive of people		Verbally assure infant you will be here and will come back to talk, play with infant again.
is possessive of materials	many toys	Provide enough toys and materials so infant does not need to share.
may become shy, clinging		Hold, hug, pat; allow infant to remain close; verbally assure infant you are here.
may demand attention		Provide positive verbal attention even though you may be busy with another child.

Cognitive Development

Assimilation and accommodation begin to operate independently. Infants of this age are beginning to separate their thinking about what they want to accomplish from how they can accomplish it.

The establishment of **object permanence** is the major development during this age range. The infants remember events, people, and objects for increasingly longer periods. Awareness of object permanence forms the basis for rapid development of representations in play and language.

These infants are constructing a concept of self separate from all other entities. People and toys become real entities that continue to exist even when the infants cannot see them (Figure 12–5). With this concept, infants now actively search visually and manually for people or objects that are no longer visible. These infants are mentally constructing a representation of the person or object. This mental representation of

Figure 12–5 Other people and toys are beginning to be perceived as "not self" by the infant.

the real entity forms the foundation for increasingly complex forms of representation. Along with thinking about other people as separate from themselves, these infants also begin to determine that others can cause actions. They will incorporate others' actions into their own play.

At this stage infants imitate people and things that are not present. They have established sufficient auditory and visual Developmental Learning Skills to remember and reproduce things they have seen and heard: ". . . early imitation serves a learning function, that is, infants imitate to advance their comprehension and mastery of behaviors that interest them" (Anisfeld, 1984, 44).

Suggestions for Implementing Curriculum

Child Behavior	Materials	Examples of Caregiver Strategies
Piaget's Stages of Sensorimotor Development		
STAGE 4 (coordination)		
differentiates goals; can focus on reaching and focus on toy	toys, visually attractive objects	Place objects near infant.
Piaget's Concept of Object Permanence		
establishes object permanence; object exists when it is no longer visible; child seeks toy that rolls behind box		Play hiding games, e.g., hide the doll under the blanket; place the block behind you.
Causality		
learns that others cause actions		Verbalize caregiver's own actions, e.g., "I put the ball behind me."
Imitation and Play		
imitates other's actions; uses actions as play		Introduce new copy games. Allow time and space for infant to play.

Learning Skills/Language Development

Infants at this age use combinations of sounds, babbling, and words to converse with themselves and others (Wilson, 1989). "Just as the sensorimotor exploration of objects lays the groundwork for object representation, so the sensorimotor exploration of speech lays the groundwork for speech representation" (Anisfeld, 1984, 224).

"Newborns can distinguish frequency and pitch, but finer discriminations aren't possible until about 1 year. Sounds from the environment, music, and human speech are all necessary for a well-balanced auditory diet—perhaps even before birth. Soothing, pleasant and interesting sounds inspire curiosity and a receptive attitude toward language. A noisy and confusing environment can be detrimental to development." (Healy, 1989)

Anisfeld identified levels of meaning, characterizing the first level as pre-symbolic use of words. "The early words have a sign character. . . . They are **context bound**" (1984, 67). Infants learn to associate a word with a particular object or action. They respond to the word in that context but cannot identify it in other contexts. For example, each day the caregiver says "Sit in your chair" as she gets the infants ready for lunch. When told to "sit in your chair," Beverly looks at her chair. She does not look at other chairs around the room. "Chair" relates to a specific chair, not to a class of objects called "chairs." ". . . [C]hildren's early words are nonsymbolic because they function primarily as responses to specific stimulus contexts" (Anisfeld, 1984, 69). An infant says the word in association with the context in which it was learned: ". . . the context-boundness of the first level results from a conceptual limitation. The child does not automatically conceive of words as independent of the specific contexts of their use" (Anisfeld, 1984, 70).

Reading aloud to infants facilitates their language development. Linda Lamme (1985) recommends in *Growing Up Reading* that

"Pointing to things in pictures and labeling them orally is especially important in the first year when your infant, though not yet talking, is acquiring so much language. Relate what is in the book to your infant's experience. 'You have a ball just like that one!' Repetition is important also. After seeing a page several times, your infant will begin to recognize the pictures. You'll quickly come to realize your infant has distinct book preferences.

The last guideline is: The earlier you begin to read aloud, the better. If your child can become used to having stories read aloud before he or she starts walking, reading-aloud sessions can be sustained during those mobile, early walking times. Children who are learning to walk have a hard time sitting still to listen to a story if they have not previously become hooked on book reading." (1985, 51)

Scribbling is related to the language/reading/writing processes the infant is developing. In her earlier work on infants, *Growing Up Writing*, Lamme (1984) wrote the following.

"Well before his first birthday, your child is ready to make marks on paper or chalkboard. Those first marks will be random scribbles. Your child won't even be watching as he is making the mark and will not see the connection between the mark on paper and the writing tool in his hand. The first stage of development is called 'uncontrolled scribbling.'

The outstanding feature of these early writing attempts is that they are more than random marks; they represent your child's intentions to create something. Scribbling has been termed 'gesturing with a pencil.' The role of scribbling in writing development has been compared with babbling in oral language development. In each case, there is probably some random sound or scribble made but, in both cases, your child is intending to communicate." (1984, 38)

Suggestions for Implementing Curriculum

Child Behavior	Materials	Examples of Caregiver Strategies
babbles		Respond with talk.
shouts		Respond to infant's feelings.
labels object sounds	bell, rattle	Name important objects. Use one word. Then use in a sentence, e.g., "Bell" (while pointing to it). "Ramon has a bell."
uses names: Mama, Dada		Reinforce by talking about Mama and Dada.
responds to familiar sounds		Provide familiar music, routine changes. Acknowledge infant's response, e.g., "Tasha heard the spoons being put on the table."
responds to familiar words		Frequently use names or labels that infant is learning, e.g., ball, shoe, coat.
responds to own name		Use infant's name when you start talking with that child.
makes sounds that reflect emotions		Respond to the infant's message about how he or she feels. Name the emotions, e.g., "Garrett is angry."
repeats syllables, words, e.g., bye-bye		Label frequent behaviors and respond to infant's use, e.g., say "bye-bye" and wave; repeat occasionally.
makes sounds like conversation		Respond verbally to infant's "conversation," e.g., "Holly is talking to her truck."
repeats, practices word over and over		Allow infant to play with words. Respond and praise occasionally.
connects words with objects, e.g., says "kitty"—points to kitty	familiar toys, objects	Point or touch objects you verbally label. Word is representing that particular object.
chooses books	picture books of familiar objects	Point to picture of object and say name of object. Repeat often.
scribbles randomly	paper, markers	Provide writing space and materials.

Key Terms

context bound
language development
object permanence

CASE STUDY

Marcel, for being eight months, is advanced in both learning skill and motor skill development. He has learned to stand, walk, and crawl with balance and coordination. No obstacle seems to stop him. This may be related to the fact that he has a three-and-a-half-year-old brother with whom he plays and tries to imitate. Marcel's brother encourages and enjoys playing with Marcel.

In addition to a single-father household, he enjoys the support and care of two grandmothers and one grandfather. All three are home and both Marcel and his brother attend half-time child care. At the time of the assessment, Marcel had no evidence of teeth emerging, and he spent one five-day period showing signs that four teeth were about to break through the gums. His happy disposition suddenly changed. It seemed that nothing pleased him, and he refused to stay in one position for any length of time. Marcel's grandmother wanted to put whiskey on his gums, but the family pediatrician convinced her that any product with alcohol was not good for children. Instead, a cold wash cloth and a hard teething ring were recommended. Marcel's father works nights, so he takes the afternoon shift caring for Marcel. Marcel is mature enough to walk, strong enough to squirm away, and quick enough to slip out of a holding grip when a wave of pain came over him. Marcel tested the frustration limits of everyone in the household, including his brother. At one point a grandmother started to get angry, shouting at Marcel, and the other grandmother quickly declared that it was her turn to care for Marcel. With help from child care staff, the family decided to move a large bed into the corner of Marcel's room, and an adult laid down with Marcel at night so he could move about as he needed to in safety as he tried to sleep. After a week of the ordeal, all four teeth broke through his gums and Marcel quickly returned to his pleasant and active self.

1. Why would applying alcohol to his gums be bad for Marcel?
2. What would be the effects of becoming angry with a child who is as agitated as Marcel was? Why?
3. What do you think the behavior of a less physically developed child would be with a similar teething problem?

Student Activities

1. Observe one infant who is walking with support. Identify the following.
   a. what infant held onto for support
   b. where infant walked
   c. what you think caused infant to sit or fall down (lost balance, got tired, lost interest, wanted to get somewhere else fast)
2. Use narrative description to record your observations of one caregiver for five minutes. Then categorize the caregiver's behaviors that relate to social development.

Initiating Behavior		Responding Behaviors	
Caregiver's Behavior	Infant's Response	Infant's Initiating Behavior	Caregiver's Response

3. Observe one infant between 8 and 12 months of age. Record the infant's behavior in two five-minute sequences using narrative description. Transfer the descriptions to the Developmental Profile.
4. List five strategies that you use with infants between 8 and 12 months of age.
5. List strategies you need to develop and list ways you intend to develop them.

Chapter Review

1. Why is sharing difficult for the infant between 8 and 12 months of age?
2. List five strategies you can use to facilitate the physical development of an infant in this age range, using this format.

Caregiver Strategy	Specific Physical Development
1.	
2.	
3.	
4.	
5.	

3. An 11-month-old is responding to labels of objects. Describe a game you can play with this child to stimulate the child's understanding and use of language.
4. Identify four ways an infant in this age range asserts independence.

References

Anisfeld, M. (1984). *Language development from birth to three.* Hillsdale, NJ: Lawrence Erlbaum Associates.

Healy, J. (1989). *Your child's growing mind: A guide to learning and brain development from birth to adolescence.* New York: Doubleday.

Lamme, L. L. (1984). *Growing up writing.* Washington, DC: Acropolis Books Ltd.

Lamme, L. L. (1985). *Growing up reading.* Washington, DC: Acropolis Books Ltd.

Shirley, M. M. (1931). *The first two years: A study of twenty-five babies. Postural and Locomotor Development,* Volume 1. Minneapolis: University of Minnesota Press.

Wilson, L. C. (1989). Sounding off! *Pre-K Today,* 3(6), 51–53.

Helpful Web Sites

Your Amazing Baby. Physical Development, What to Expect Months 8 and 9. http://www.amazingbaby.com/physical.html

Life with Baby: Pregnancy and Beyond. Milestones—10 to 12 months. http://www.alexian.org/progserv/babies/10to12m/milestones12m.html

Eye Wonder. Helping Babies Learn to See, Age: Eight to 12 months. Things to do. http://www.sola.com/professional/techtips/tip71.html

Moms Online. Infant Attention the First Year. http://oxygen.com/family

Will I grow out of it? Milestones and Warning Signs for Speech Development. http://www.blankees.com/baby/speech/lan03.htm

Activities for Young Toddlers. About Baby Parenting. http://babyparenting.about.com/cs/activitiesandfun/index.html

Purdue News. Research looks at brain and behavior development in infants. http://www.uns.purdue.edu/uns/html4ever/0007/corbetta/babybrain.html

For additional infant and toddler resources, visit our Web site at http://www.earlychilded.delmar.com

The Child from Twelve to Eighteen Months of Age

13

Objectives

After reading this chapter, you should be able to:

- Identify and record sequences of change in the physical, emotional, social, cognitive, and language development of toddlers between 12 and 18 months of age.
- Select materials appropriate to that age-level toddler's development.
- Devise strategies appropriate to that age-level toddler's development.

Chapter Outline

Caregivers of Toddlers

Caregivers or teachers who are in charge of toddler programs strive to be

- empowered facilitators who structure environments to minimize conflicts and maximize explorations.
- practiced in the 3A's of Child Care—Attention, Approval, and Affection.
- skillful, patient observers who help with problem solving and promote positive perspective.
- organized and imaginative.
- knowledgeable in Toddler Development so that they may understand toddlers' daily struggles and enjoy their daily triumphs.
- consistent, gentle and firm natured.
- easily amused.
- genuinely fond of toddlers. (Douville-Watson, 1979)

The Toddler

Andrea, 15 months old, stands looking around. She walks over to two-year-old Jenny, who is sitting on the sofa. She stands between Jenny's legs and bounces up and down to Hokey Pokey music from the record player. Andrea and Jenny dance around. Jenny lies down on the floor and Andrea crawls on top of her. Jenny moves and Andrea follows. They both lie quietly for a minute. Andrea walks to the toys. She picks up a toy plastic milk bottle and lifts it to her mouth to drink. She sits down and puts three lock blocks in the bottle. Allen, the caregiver, says, "Shake it, Andrea." She shakes the bottle, and it makes a noise. She shakes it again. She puts a pail over her head and walks around peeking under the edge of the pail and "talking." Andrea climbs into a child's rocking chair, turns around to sit down, and starts rocking. She "talks" and rocks and then climbs out of the chair and walks around, following Allen.

Toddlers solve problems on a physical level. Watch toddlers at play for just 5 minutes and you will see them walk (which looks like wandering), climb, carry things around, drop things, and continually dump whatever they can find. These large-muscle activities are not done to irritate adults—they are the legitimate activity of toddlers. Piaget calls this the sensorimotor stage of development (1952, 1954) (Gonzalez-Mena, 1986).

MATERIALS AND ACTIVITIES

Walking is a major development for toddlers at this age. They are fascinated with toys to pull or push as they toddle around (Figure 13–1). They climb over objects. They may ride wheeled toys. They grasp and throw and drop objects again and again. They are moving into imaginative play and need materials that can facilitate their play.

Review Chapter 4. Use Appendix A, the Developmental Prescriptions, and Appendix B, the Developmental Profile, with each child. Children follow a *sequence* of development. There are often ranges in the *rate* of development.

Figure 13–1 Toddlers need toys and space that encourage walking, jumping, and other physical activities.

Types of Materials

pull toys
push toys
trucks, cars
low, riding wheel toys
low, 3-step stairs to climb
blocks
pail with objects to put in and take out
water and sand toys and area

soft objects to throw
mirrors
dolls
puppets
puzzles
picture books and cards
paper, nontoxic markers, crayons
audio records and tapes

Examples of Homemade Materials

The Celebration of Life Calendar can provide suggestions for classroom themes.

PULL TOY

Use plain or painted empty spools. Thread and knot spools on a length of clothesline rope.

SOUND/SIGHT BOTTLE

Use a clear plastic liter bottle (soft drink). Wash it thoroughly and allow to dry inside. Put inside material or objects that will make noise (sand, wooden or plastic blocks, metal bottle caps). Add confetti for color interest. Screw on bottle cap and glue securely. Tape over rough edges of cap.

TOSS BOX

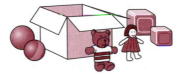

Collect several small, soft toys and place in a cardboard box. Show child how to take out objects, stand away from the box, and throw the objects into the box. Paint the inside of the box to attract the child's attention as a "target."

EXPLORING TUBS

Place one solid object in a margarine tub. Put lid on. When children shake it, they hear a noise. Encourage the children to take off lid to discover what is inside. Put lid back on. Have several tubs available with different objects inside, e.g., plastic clothes pins, large wooden thread spools.

PICTURE CARD

Use a square of 2- or 3-ply cardboard. Place a photograph of a child on the cardboard and cover the whole square (front, back, and sides) with contact paper or laminating film. Also use colorful pictures cut from magazines. Select pictures that are simple and show one object, such as a car, cat, flower, or bird. Select pictures of objects the child is familiar with.

CLOTHING FRAME BOARD

Cover wood 12″ × 12″ × 2″ with fabric. Glue one piece of fabric to each side of wooden frame, with fabric opening at center of frame. Sew buttons on one side at center, buttonholes on other side. Or put on large snaps. Or sew in large-toothed zipper.

CAREGIVER STRATEGIES TO ENHANCE DEVELOPMENT

Developmental Profile

Andrea's Developmental Profile is presented in Figure 13–2. She was observed over a two-week period on the child behaviors listed in the Developmental Prescription (Appendix A), and is three months below C.A. in Social Development, "self," and three months above expectations in "others." Overall, Andrea shows healthy, normal development.

In terms of the Physical Area (I) and the Emotional Area (II), Andrea is estimated to be within expected behavior. However, she seems to not focus attention on herself or her needs, and is much more concerned about gaining attention and the needs of others. As a result, she is estimated to be below age in "self" development (12 months), and above age in "others" (18 months).

The minor problem of her not considering her needs and being overly concerned about others might be related to a slightly higher "imitation" estimate in Cognitive Development (IV) and "language" (sounds) in Learning Skills (V) (17 months). Visual and auditory learning skills are slightly advanced.

In general, Andrea exhibits expected development except for the problems in not considering herself and needing other people to be happy for her to feel secure.

The caregiver should design tasks and activities using Materials and Caregiver Strategies to help Andrea feel special and make her needs more important than the needs of others, when appropriate. Adding these activities to ones designed for all other areas will ensure a balanced program for Andrea.

Physical Development

They toddle about their own environment not necessarily to get from one part of it to another, but because they are up on their feet and it is satisfying to practice walking. Chairs become things to push and carry because pushing and carrying are also newly obtained skills a toddler delights in practicing. Chairs can also be climbed into and later, if the chairs are an appropriate size, two-year-olds may discover they can back up to them and sit down, apparently an exciting achievement when you are just learning how to do it. (Brickmeyer, 1978)

Erikson included toddlers in his second stage of development, Autonomy (1963). Piaget's "**ages and stages**" are outlined for toddlers between 12 and 18 months: Stage 5 (Twelve to Eighteen Months). This stage marks the onset of experimentation. The child begins deliberately to invent new actions she has never tried before and to explore the novel and unique features of objects. She tries to find what will happen if she uses objects in new ways. She combines objects with other objects to create new ways of doing things and uses trial-and-error approaches to discover new solutions to problems.

Piaget labeled young children's need to gather information by shaking, grasping, listening, feeling, and tasting as "schematic." This practice of information gathering continues throughout life (Figure 13–3).

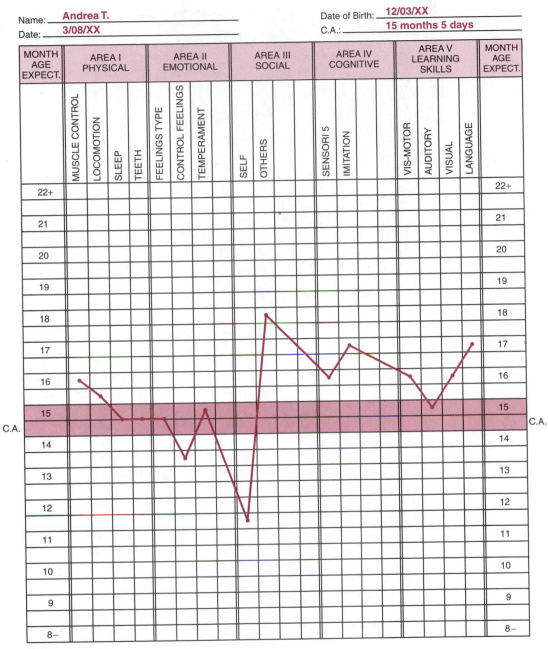

Name: **Andrea T.**
Date: **3/08/XX**

Date of Birth: **12/03/XX**
C.A.: **15 months 5 days**

MONTH AGE EXPECT.	AREA I PHYSICAL				AREA II EMOTIONAL				AREA III SOCIAL			AREA IV COGNITIVE			AREA V LEARNING SKILLS				MONTH AGE EXPECT.
	MUSCLE CONTROL	LOCOMOTION	SLEEP	TEETH	FEELINGS TYPE	CONTROL FEELINGS	TEMPERAMENT		SELF	OTHERS		SENSORI 5	IMITATION		VIS-MOTOR	AUDITORY	VISUAL	LANGUAGE	
22+																			22+
21																			21
20																			20
19																			19
18																			18
17																			17
16																			16
15																			15
14																			14
13																			13
12																			12
11																			11
10																			10
9																			9
8–																			8–

C.A. ─── C.A.

Notes:

Figure 13–2 Developmental Profile, Andrea T.

Figure 13–3 Grasping is another way to gather information.

Toddlers learn with their whole bodies—not just their heads. They learn more through their hands than they do through their ears. They learn by doing, not only by thinking. They learn by touching, mouthing, and trying out, not by being told.

Toddlers can become absorbed in discovering the world around them. If you are convinced that toddlers have short attention spans, just watch them with running water and a piece of soap. Hand washing can become the main activity of the morning! Eating is another major activity, as many toddlers switch from neat to very messy in a short time. Filling and dumping are great skills to use with food or water. Of course, toddlers do put things in as part of the process, but they are more likely to end with dumping (Gonzalez-Mena, 1986).

Ambulator fourteen-month-olds like to combine emptying with transporting things. They find favorite spots or hiding places: under the bed, in the wastebasket, or even in the sink and toilet bowl. Because emptying can be a nuisance, parents put things "off limits" or temporarily out of reach. A better way to counteract a toddler's emptying game is to provide baskets that can be filled and emptied endlessly. (Caplan & Caplan, 1980)

An expanding world opens up to toddlers as they become mobile. They walk, lurch, run, fall, bump into things, and persist in moving around in their world. They are unstable when they walk. They may topple over from stepping on an object or by leaning too far or walking too fast. They are learning to make adjustments so that they can remain upright. Their muscles are developing and coordinating gradually so that in the next months their walking will become more stable (Wilson, 1988).

Suggestions for Implementing Curriculum

Child Behavior	Materials	Examples of Caregiver Strategies
Muscular Control		
TRUNK		
Shows high energy, is active, moves from one activity to another		Provide a variety of materials and activities so the child can change activities and play objects often. These toddlers frequently do not "make" anything or complete an activity. Schedule clean-up and help put away toys at end of playtime.
Raises self to standing.	Sturdy furniture to grasp; flat surface.	Provide space where toddlers can stand up safely. Caution them about standing up under furniture.
LOCOMOTION		
May prefer crawling to walking.		Allow toddler to crawl when child wants to. It is faster than walking when the child is just beginning to walk.
Walks alone.		Allow toddler to walk alone when child wants to. Provide a hand to hold onto when child seeks help.
Climbs up stairs with help.	Stairs.	Provide handrail or your hand to assist child with balance.
Climbs down stairs with help.	Stairs.	Provide handrail *and* your hand. Balance is still poor when walking down stairs.
Climbs over objects.	Low, sturdy furniture, equipment, boxes.	Provide low climbing equipment, furniture, e.g., stuffed footstool, sturdy cardboard boxes, covered foam incline.
HAND		
Uses thumb against fingers.	Small toys, crayons, pens	Provide materials toddler can grasp.
Shows hand preference.		Allow toddler to use whichever hand he or she chooses.
Points with finger.	Pictures, books, objects.	Play pointing game, e.g., open picture book—"Point to the tree."
Carries, exchanges objects in hands.	Small toys	Ask toddler to carry toys to another part of the room. Hand toddler another toy to carry.

(continued)

(continued)

Child Behavior	Materials	Examples of Caregiver Strategies
Throws objects.	Soft, small objects.	Provide a place and target where toddler can throw objects.
Rolls and catches objects.	Large, small balls.	Sit on floor with legs open and outstretched and roll ball back and forth with toddler.
EYE-HAND COORDINATION		
Reaches and grasps accurately.	Toys, objects that hand can grasp.	Provide toys and objects in places where toddler can safely reach, grasp, lift, and move them.
Scribbles.	Paper, nontoxic markers, crayons.	Provide flat surface for toddler to use paper and marker or pen. Admire and praise the marks the toddler makes.
Helps in dressing, undressing.	Buttons, snaps, zipper cards, books, clothing frame board, large dolls with clothes.	Allow toddler to do as much as possible. Assist when toddler needs help.

Seeing

Watches people, objects, actions.	Space with few visual obstructions.	Provide space where people are visible to toddler. Allow toddler to choose what to watch.
Bends, looks from different directions.		Place toys, materials in different places. Allow toddler to move materials. Toddler may look up from the floor, look down between legs, look sideways under a table.
Visually scans area around.		Allow toddler to look around. Toddler may gaze around for periods of time. Provide interesting visual stimuli.
Visually searches.		Toddler may look for specific object, person. Assist if child nonverbally or verbally requests your help.

Sleeping

Begins to move from morning and afternoon nap to afternoon nap. May fall asleep during lunch.		Adjust eating and nap schedule so toddler does not miss lunch.

Eating

Eats three meals.		Determine mealtime. Make adjustments for individual children as necessary.
Feeds self: uses cup, spoon, and fingers.	Food, plate, cup, spoon.	Allow toddler to feed self as much as possible. Assist when necessary.
Expresses food likes and dislikes.		Record food preferences. Provide foods child likes. Introduce new foods gradually. Combine foods child does not like with ones child does like to provide needed nutrition.
May eat less food.		Do not force eating. Make food as attractive as possible.

Emotional Development

Toddlers seek both dependence and independence. Most fears at this stage are learned from adults. This is why caregivers must take an inventory of themselves and recognize what emotional messages they are conveying to an impressionable toddler. It is the continued responsibility of the caregiver to promote a positive learning environment.

For many tasks toddlers need help. The caregiver can provide toddlers with emotional strength and security, accepting toddlers' very real dependence (Wilson, 1987). Toddlers are also trying to become independent. Emotionally they need support that affirms their importance as individuals who can make some choices and accomplish some tasks all by themselves. Their growing sense of achievement enhances their developing positive feelings of self-worth and demonstrates **cause and effect** (Figure 13–4).

Toddlers' anger and frustration may come out as temper tantrums. Distinguish between kinds of tantrums. Frustration tantrums may respond to changing the conditions that caused the child's frustration. Toddlers sometimes have tantrums in order to get their own way. Toddlers' manipulation tantrums sometimes need to be ignored because they are seeking negative attention. Giving attention during the tantrum may

Figure 13–4 The caregiver lets toddlers concentrate on exploring toys by themselves.

reward the toddler and encourage future outbursts. Instead, the caregiver should provide positive attention soon after the tantrum is over.

Toddler negativism may be expressed by "No!" or in tantrums. Their pursuit of independence may carry over into doing the opposite of what was requested. Rephrase command statements and refocus attention to something of interest to the toddler. For example, you might rephrase "Put the doll away" to "Mary Jane, where can you find a place to put the doll down? She needs to go to sleep."

Children learn concepts of right and wrong from adults. Toddlers are just beginning to use words, and they respond to some labels and commands. But words alone will not control their behavior until they construct concepts of rightness and wrongness. These concepts are constantly being revised and expanded as the toddlers compare their behavior with adults' reaction to that behavior. At this age toddlers cannot separate themselves from their actions enough to understand the idea, "I like you but I do not like what you are doing." Therefore, caregivers need to find ways to help toddlers discriminate between right and wrong while still accepting each child as a worthy person no matter what his or her behavior.

Direct behavior gently, but physically. Don't depend on words alone. Prevent dangerous behavior before it occurs—hold a threatening arm before it has a chance to hit. Lead a child by the hand back to the table to finish a snack. Don't let children get in trouble and then yell at them. If you find yourself saying "I knew that was going to happen," next time don't predict; prevent it (Gonzalez-Mena, 1986).

Children's ability to adapt to change in routine during this time of negativism may create problems. The toddler who is very adaptable may change routines easily or with a little fussing. For example, putting that toddler's chair in a different place in the room may create interest for the child. A toddler who has difficulty adapting to change may react negatively, resisting the moving of the chair by fussing or crying or even having a tantrum. This child may combine resistance to change with negativism.

"A good technique to use with any toddler is to catch the child being 'good' and praise his or her behavior. Consistently using the 3A's of caregiving—Attention, Approval, and Affection—when the child has behaved correctly will help the child know what is right. Allowing the child to choose between two positive outcomes helps the child to learn to make decisions as well as to have more control over his or her environment." (Douville-Watson, 1988)

Suggestions for Implementing Curriculum

Child Behavior	Materials	Examples of Caregiver Strategies
Types of Emotions-Feelings		
Expresses emotions in behavior and language.		Determine and respond to toddler's emotions.
Recognizes emotions in others.		Be consistent in showing emotions, e.g., happiness—smile and laugh; anger—firm voice, no smile.

Child Behavior	Materials	Examples of Caregiver Strategies
May fear strangeness.		Introduce new people, new experiences to toddler. Caution others not to "rush" the child. Allow child to approach or withdraw at own rate.
Shows excitement, delight.		Respond with similar excitement, e.g., touching a pretty flower, an animal.
Expresses sense of humor.		Giggle and laugh with toddler.
Shows affection.		Accept and return physical and verbal show of affection.
Displays negativism.		Provide honest, workable choices, e.g., "Do you want to run or walk to the table?"
Has tantrums.		Determine and remove cause if possible. Sometimes ignore. Proceed calmly with involvement with other children, activities.
Uses play to express emotions, resolve conflicts.	Blocks, dolls, home living, clothes, toy animals.	Provide props for acting out fear, frustration, insecurity, joy.
Seeks dependency, security with parent and caregiver.		Provide touching, holding, stroking interactions; respond quickly and consistently to toddler's needs.
Seeks to expand independence.		Allow toddler to attempt activities by him- or herself. Do not take over if toddler can be successful without you.

Control of Emotions-Feelings

Begins to learn right and wrong.		Verbalize which behavior is right and which behavior is wrong. Give reasons. Since toddlers are only just beginning to conceptualize "right-wrong," only occasionally can they apply the concept to control their own behavior.
Reinforces desired behavior.		Praise toddler for controlling own behavior.

Temperament

Activity level. Regularity. Approach or withdrawal as a characteristic response to a new situation. Adaptability to change in routine. Level of sensory threshold. Positive or negative mood. Intensity of response. Distractibility. Persistence and attention span.		List two of the toddler's behaviors in each category that indicate the toddler's basic style. List adjustments you need to make to help the toddler cope with daily situations.

Social Development

Toddlers are **egocentric**; they see the world from their own point of view. In the first year and a half of life their bodies and the objects they play with are perceived to be part of "self." Gradually, as the concept of object permanence develops, they differentiate "self" from other objects and people, which become "not self." This major development in toddlers provides the basis for life-long expansion of their concept of self and their interactions with others and provides the child with one of his or her earliest experiences with self-image. "Caregiver acceptance is extremely important at any stage of development. This acceptance is internalized and becomes one with the child's self" (Douville-Watson, 1979).

Toddlers behave differently toward different people. They recognize differences in people and adjust their interactions with them. They may be eager and excited with a familiar caregiver and quiet and withdrawn with a substitute.

Toddlers play with toys and materials and sing and talk usually by themselves in solitary play. They may look at other children and play near them, but they do not interact with them in play. Toddlers now engage in **solitary play** (playing alone) and parallel play (playing near but not with other children); they decide what kind of interaction they want with others(Figure 13–5). At this age the toddler is more adept at dealing with older children and adults than with peers.

Figure 13–5 Toddlers decide what kind of interaction they want with others.

Suggestions for Implementing Curriculum

Child Behavior	Examples of Caregiver Strategies
Self	
Has concept of self.	Positively reinforce toddler as an individual.
Is egocentric: understands only own viewpoint.	Do not expect toddler to "feel sorry for" someone toddler has hurt. Toddler assumes everyone thinks and feels the way he or she does.
Others	
Seeks presence of parent or caregiver.	Allow toddler to follow you around. Tell child when you are going out of sight.
Plays games.	Play games with toddler. Respond and play child's games.
Occasionally shares.	Provide enough materials and equipment so sharing can be encouraged but not required.
Acts differently toward different people.	Expect different responses to different people. Accept toddler's choices.
Uses variety of behaviors to gain attention.	Identify toddler's usual behaviors to gain attention. Respond to any of those behaviors as quickly as possible.
May be shy with some people.	Do not force toddler to interact with all people. Allow child to keep a distance and watch.
Engages in parallel play.	Provide materials and space so toddlers can play with own materials but near each other.

Cognitive Development

This is a time for learning, so opportunities to learn should be provided, including learning how to learn.

> Too often adults give children answers to remember rather than problems to solve. This is a grave mistake. Unless children develop the art of problem solving . . . their brains will remain underdeveloped. (Healy, 1989)

Providing stimulation to the learning toddler influences his or her development now and in the future.

Object permanence becomes more firmly established. At this age toddlers may search for an object they have seen moved and hidden.

Toddlers of this age are interested in observing the effects of their own and other's actions. Exploration is done using trial and error. These little explorers try, probe, and

Figure 13–6 Toddlers learn about their physical world by putting themselves in different spaces.

practice activities and observe the results of their actions. Logical reasoning is not a part of trying an action a different way (Figure 13–6).

Now that toddlers are aware that others cause actions to occur, imitation of others' behaviors becomes a part of their play. They use some play behaviors repeatedly in the same pattern and develop their own ritual play. Researchers have found that stimulating playthings are more important for cognitive development after age one than in earlier months.

Availability of interesting and challenging play materials in children's environment after the first year correlates with later IQ and school achievement in reading and math (Healy, 1989).

Suggestions for Implementing Curriculum

Child Behavior	Materials	Examples of Caregiver Strategies
Piaget's Stages of Sensorimotor Development		
STAGE 5 (Experimentation)		
Object Permanence		
Watches toy hid and moved. Looks for it where it was moved.		Play game with child. Hide the object while child watches. Let the child watch you move the object to a different place under the blanket. Ask, "Where is it? Can you find it?" Observe and allow child to find the object. Praise child for good watching and thinking.

Child Behavior	Materials	Examples of Caregiver Strategies
Causality		
Investigates cause and effect.		Allow and encourage child to search, identify relationship between an action and the effect of it, e.g., "What made the ball go under the table?"
Sees self as causal agent.		Verbally identify the child as cause of the action, e.g., "Laquata kicked the ball."
Explores various ways things happen.	Water toys, water basin.	Allow the child time to play with the water and toys to discover different actions of water and of objects in the water.
Employs active trial-and-error to solve problems.	Narrow-neck milk carton, different sizes and shapes of objects.	Provide time and materials that stimulate child to think and try out ideas. Ask questions but do not tell answers or show child.
Experiments.		Provide open-ended toys and materials that encourage several uses. Encourage child to see how many ways the child can use them. Ask questions and allow time for the child to experiment; ask, "What happens?"
IMITATION AND PLAY		
Copies behaviors of others.		Encourage child to pretend: to drink from a pretend bottle like baby Gwen, to march like Pearl, to pick up toys. Think about your own behaviors; child will copy what you do. Be sure your actions are the kind of actions you feel comfortable seeing the child copy.
Turns play with imitation into rituals.		Allow child to repeat own play and develop own preferences. For an example, a child may see you hug a child who comes in the morning and imitate your hugging. The child may repeat this imitation and develop the ritual of hugging the child who has just arrived.

Learning Skills/Language Development

Language in toddlers of this age expands from less reliance on sounds and babbling to more use of recognizable words. Many word approximations are used and reinforced and become a usable part of toddlers' expressive vocabulary.

Toddlers use a word for many different things. "Wawa" may mean anything to drink. "Mama" may mean any woman. Word meaning is usually flexible. The toddler may call anything that is round a "ball."

This is the time the vocabulary of the toddler can be expanded by your use of words to label actions and objects. It is also a time to make them more aware of the world around them by pointing out sounds to listen to and naming what they are. By 18 months the toddler will be asking what things and sounds are as they categorize their world.

Eighteen months to two years of age is a period of rapid language growth. By the second birthday, vocabulary has increased to at least 50 words. At this time, we see the emergence of the ability to form sentences. This begins with two-word combinations, such as "Eat cookie" or "Go bye-bye." By age three, the child is a real conversational-ist, producing three- to four-word sentences, answering simple questions, and even relating events of the day (Soman, 1994).

Reading and books can provide enjoyable experiences for toddlers. Several different kinds of children's literature interest toddlers.

> Point-and-say books have pictures of familiar objects and little text. The object of reading this type of literature is to increase your child's vocabulary, to compare pictures in a book with known items in the environment, to familiarize the child with books, and to show your baby that books have meaning.
>
> Nursery rhymes, chants, poems, and songs are best chanted or sung throughout the day rather than just presented at read-aloud sessions. Then, at a later time, it can be thrilling to watch your infant associate the rhymes that he or she already knows with the picture representing that rhyme in a book. Nursery rhymes help your child become familiar with the sounds of language. They assist the transition from telegraphic speech, where one word represents a sentence, to mature language, where each word is pronounced. (Lamme, 1985, 57–58)

Writing can be encouraged by allowing children to watch you as you write names, labels, and notes. The interrelationships among language, reading, and writing are evident at an early age.

At what age can you begin assisting your child in becoming a writer? You can begin by reading to your child at birth. All the reading you do during the first years aids writing development by exposing your child to writing. Just before one year of age, your baby can be given (under supervision) his first writing tools—water-soluble markers and large sheets of paper. His writing experiences will have begun. (Lamme, 1984, 17–18)

Suggestions for Implementing Curriculum

Child Behavior	Examples of Caregiver Strategies
Uses intonation.	Use intonation in your talk with toddler.
Babbles sentences.	Respond to toddler's babbling.
Repeats, practices words.	Repeat toddler's word. Occasionally expand into a sentence, e.g., "gone-gone"; "The milk is all gone."

Child Behavior	Examples of Caregiver Strategies
Imitates sounds of other people, objects.	Enjoy toddler's sounds. Play sounds game—point to objects and make sound of object, e.g., dog barking.
Responds to word and gesture conversation.	Become very familiar with toddler's words and gestures. You often have to guess what the toddler is saying. Make a statement or ask a question to determine if you are interpreting correctly, e.g., "Taylor wants to go outside."
Responds to many questions and commands child cannot say.	Choose a few questions and commands you can use often and consistently. The toddler will learn what they mean through many experiences, e.g., "Go get your coat."

It is extremely important to teach basic visual and auditory perceptual skills before letter and word recognition.

Child Behavior	Materials	Examples of Caregiver Strategies
Uses word approximations for some words.		Watch the toddler's behavior to help you experience what the child is experiencing. What do you see at the point where the child is looking, pointing, reaching? Say a word or sentence to test whether you are interpreting the word correctly.
Uses words in immediate context.		Notice what the toddler is doing, saying, or needing right now. Toddler's talk is about immediate needs and desires, not past or future situations.
Identifies familiar pictures.	Pictures, picture book.	Orally label objects. Ask toddler to point to or name familiar picture.
Uses markers, chalk.	Markers, paper, chalk.	Provide table space and materials. Write labels and sentences for child.

Key Terms

ages and stages
cause and effect

egocentric
solitary play

CASE STUDY

Andrea is a 15-month-old who comes from an upper-middle-class professional family. Both of her parents have successful professions and work full time, so Andrea is in full-time child care. Her Developmental Profile indicates that she has average to above average overall development but is weak in development of self-interest. This may be because her parents are very busy and Andrea must seek their attention, but she seems to need the attention and approval of other people almost all the time in order to feel secure and happy. When child care staff pay attention to other children, Andrea appears to get upset and withdraws and pouts.

To help Andrea, a Developmental Prescription was established that task-analyzed the steps necessary to help Andrea share attention and enjoy time by herself. First, the principle of "Catch the child being good" was implemented. Then, a meeting was held with her parents to establish "special time" each day with each of her parents. The child care staff also used the tool of Positive Perspective, and within a short time, Andrea was able to spend time by herself enjoyably and share the attention of her caregivers.

1. Describe how and why each of these tools would help with Andrea's problem.
2. What other tools could be used to help a child focus on themselves more?
3. What would be the next steps to take if all the tools didn't help Andrea?

Student Activities

1. Interview one caregiver. Ask the caregiver to describe the following.
   a. behaviors of a toddler between 12 and 18 months who is angry
   b. behaviors of the caregiver who is responding to the toddler's angry behavior

   Write the caregiver's descriptions and then put an X beside the descriptions of the *physical* behaviors of the toddler and the caregiver.

Behavior of Angry Toddler	Responding Behaviors of Caregiver

2. Listen to one toddler. Make a list of the child's words and "sentences." Watch the child's body language and nonverbals. Then write down the complete sentences you think the child meant (you must think about the context in which the toddler was talking).

Words, Phrases	Meaning
Gone-gone	It is all gone; or, She went away.

3. Write one lesson plan to use with one toddler to help reinforce a word the toddler uses and to expand its use with sentences. Use the plan with the toddler. Evaluate the toddler's involvement. Evaluate the written lesson plan.

4. Observe one toddler between 12 and 18 months of age. Record the toddler's behavior in two five-minute sequences, using narrative description. Transfer the descriptions to the Developmental Profile.

5. List five strategies to use with toddlers between 12 and 18 months of age.

6. List strategies you need to develop and list ways you intend to develop them.

7. Use the Celebration of Life Calendar to set up a holiday theme for your classroom.

Chapter Review

1. If the toddler cannot say the name of an object or person, but you think the child understands the object-name match, how can you find out whether the child has connected the correct name with the correct object or person?

2. Describe something Juanita would do that shows she has developed the concept of the permanent object.

3. Describe two situations in which a toddler interacts with others. Describe two situations in which a toddler plays alone.

   With others

   a.

   b.

   Alone

   a.

   b.

4. List five safety precautions you need to take with the toddler between 12 and 18 months of age.

5. With the development of eye-hand coordination, what can toddlers do now that they could not do as well several months earlier?

6. How is the child integrating his or her experience.

References

Brickmeyer, J. (1978). *Guidelines for day care programs for migrant infants and toddlers.* New York: Bankstreet College.

Caplan, F., & Caplan, T. (1980). *The second twelve months of life.* New York: Bantam/Grosset and Dunlap, Inc.

Douville-Watson, L. (1979). Child Development Lecture Series II. Merrick, NY: Bellmore-Merrick School District II.

Douville-Watson, L. (1988). *Child care lecture series. The 3A's of child care: Attention, approval and affection.* Oyster Bay, NY: Lifeskills Institute.

Erikson, E. (1963). *Childhood and society* (2nd ed.). New York: Norton.

Gonzalez-Mena, J. (1986). *Toddlers: What to expect.* Washington, DC: NAEYC.

Healy, J. (1989). *Your child's growing mind: A guide to learning and brain development from birth to adolescence.* New York: Doubleday.

Lamme, L. L. (1984). *Growing up writing*. Washington, DC: Acropolis Books Ltd.

Lamme, L. L. (1985). *Growing up reading*. Washington, DC: Acropolis Books Ltd.

Piaget, J. (1952). *The origins of intelligence in children*. (M. Cook, trans.) New York: International Universities Press.

Piaget, J. (1954). *The construction of reality in the child*. (M. Cook, trans.) New York: Basic.

Soman, B. (1994). Lecture series. *The development of communication skills*. Garden City, NY: Adelphi University Center for Communication Disorders.

Wilson, L. C. (1987). Mommy, don't go! *Pre-K Today*, *2*(1), 38–40.

Wilson, L. C. (1988). Gross-motor activities for toddlers. *Pre-K Today*, *2*(7), 34–35.

Helpful Web Sites

Toddlers—Physical Development. Milestones, 14 to 36 months. Click Physical Development. http://www.parentsplace.com/toddlers/

Caring for Your Toddler. Basic Are, Physical Cognitive and Common Problems. http://www.zerotothree.org

Childcare Network. Toddlers: Emphasizing fine and gross motor skills. http://www.childcarenetwork.net/toddlers.htm

Simple Steps: Developmental activities for Infants, Toddlers, and Two-Year-Olds. http://npin.org/books/miller99.html

Child Development Institute. Intellectual and language development. http://www.childdevelopmentinfo.com

For additional infant and toddler resources, visit our Web site at http://www.earlychilded.delmar.com

The Child from Eighteen to Twenty-Four Months of Age

14

Objectives   *After reading this chapter, you should be able to:*

■ Identify and record sequences of change in the physical, emotional, social, cognitive, and language development of children from 18 to 24 months of age.

■ Select materials appropriate to that age-level child's development.

■ Devise strategies appropriate to that age-level child's development.

Chapter Outline

Materials and Activities

Caregiver Strategies to Enhance Development

Lennie's Story

Lennie, 23 months old, walks to a child-sized rocking chair, backs up to it and sits down. He rocks and watches the other children. He gets off the chair and sits on his legs to pick up blocks. He picks up a block wagon, stands up, and walks around. He holds the block wagon in his left hand, tries to put on another block with his right hand, and succeeds. He puts the wagon on the floor and pushes it. He takes off one block and then takes off five blocks; he puts them back on. Jasper walks past and Lennie says, "No, Jasper. That mine." Tracey takes the block wagon. Lennie reaches for it and says, "That mine." Lennie picks up the wagon and begins putting blocks in it. He picks up the block wagon and a block bag, gets up and walks around, talking to himself.

MATERIALS AND ACTIVITIES

Walking, climbing, and riding materials and activities are enjoyable for children at this age. They are practicing their gross motor skills and developing increased competence in using them. Their finger and wrist muscles are developing so they can manipulate more complex objects. Their imaginations are expanding as they construct internal representations of their world. The Celebration of Life Calendar will help you celebrate diversity with this age group.

Types of Materials

textures	tunnel
snap toys	riding toys and cycles
large stringing beads	water play equipment
blocks	sand play equipment
toy people	soap paint
caps or lids to twist off containers	finger paint
toys to throw	tempera paint
tools: hammer, broom, shovel	puzzles
cars, trucks	books
zippers	telephones
hairbrush	dolls
toothbrush	stuffed animals
low, wide balance beam	puppets
sliding board	music: records, tapes
pull and push toys	modeling dough
balls	markers, crayons, chalk, pens
low stairs	containers to fill and empty

Review Chapter 3. Use Appendix A, the Developmental Prescriptions, and Appendix B, the Developmental Profile, with each child. Children follow a *sequence* of development. There are often ranges in the *rate* of development.

Examples of Homemade Materials

TUNNEL

Use a sturdy, long rectangular cardboard box large enough for child to crawl through. Cut out ends and tape edges to prevent scraping the child and tearing the box. Place several boxes end-to-end or in a square or zigzag pattern.

PUPPET

Use a paper plate. The child tears colored paper and yarn and pastes the pieces on the paper plate. These puppets are safer without a wooden stick handle.

TARGET

Use a plastic pail (empty ice cream or peanut butter container). Place tennis balls or yarn balls in pail. Use a piece of yarn to mark where the child will stand to throw objects into the pail.

CLAY DOUGH RECIPE

2 C plain flour
2 C water
1 C salt
3 teaspoons cream of tartar
2 tablespoons oil
food coloring

Combine flour, salt, and cream of tartar. Combine oil, food coloring, and water. Pour liquids into flour-salt mixture. Stir to get pie dough consistency. Cook, stirring over medium heat until ball forms. Store in a covered container.

Shape into a ball, then dip into food coloring, rolling ball back and forth. Watch colors change. Keep manipulating dough to keep it soft. All sorts of shapes can be made, such as a vase (make paper flowers to go in it).

BOOK

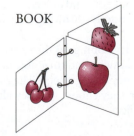

Cut three pieces of sturdy cardboard. Select three magazine pictures that make a sequence or that have something in common (e.g., they are all red). Glue one picture on each piece of cardboard. Cover the pictures and cardboard with contact paper. Connect the pieces by punching holes in the side of the cardboard and tying together with yarn.

CAREGIVER STRATEGIES TO ENHANCE DEVELOPMENT

Developmental Profile

Lennie is a 23-month-old whose Developmental Profile is presented in Figure 14–1. His C.A. was actually 22 months and 29 days, but because the days are more than 15, the C.A. is rounded to the next higher month. Inspection of the Profile reveals that Lennie exhibits problems in the Emotional and Social Areas and is within age expectations in other areas.

Specifically, Lennie is estimated at age level in the Physical Area (I), the Cognitive Area (IV), and the Learning Skills Area (V). He is estimated to be significantly below age level in the Emotional Area (II)—control of feelings and temperament (18 months)—and the Social Area (III)—self (20 months) and others (18 months). These estimates are low because Lennie exhibits an average of two temper tantrums per day and bites other children between three and four times per day. Upon closer examination, it appears that Lennie has tantrums in response to being told that he cannot do something by caregivers, and he bites when other children have toys or things he wants. For some children this age, biting is common.

In general, Lennie is a 23-month-old who exhibits normal development except for having temper tantrums and biting behavior. These aggressive and anti-social behaviors must be limited by the caregiver to ensure the safe care of Lennie and the other children. In addition to using the Caregiver Strategies described below, complete withdrawal of the 3A's, diverting attention away from the negative behavior, and attending to children who are being appropriate are all techniques that can effectively reduce tantrums and biting behaviors. Furthermore, the caregiver can "catch the child being good" and give approval when Lennie accepts "no" and shares appropriately with others. Also, role playing how to accept "not having your own way" and "how to share" can also help eliminate these inappropriate behaviors. A specific plan to reduce and eliminate tantrums and biting should be added to other Caregiver Strategies to provide Lennie with a comprehensive balanced program.

Physical Development

Children of this age are gaining much more stability and coordination. They can stand up, squat, reach over, and stand upright again without toppling. They climb on just about everything and, when they are around 18 months old, they try climbing out of their cribs. They will soon succeed. They climb up and down stairs by holding onto a rail or hand to maintain balance, but still do not alternate their feet. They move rapidly, both walking and running. They jump with both feet. They become increasingly more adept at kicking a ball and by around 22 months they can pedal a cycle such as a Big Wheel and they love to push and pull toys and objects (Figure 14–2). They can throw objects at targets rather than randomly throwing and tossing, though they seldom hit the intended target.

These children's fine motor muscles are developing, so they have increased control of their fingers and wrists. They probe and twist and turn objects (Figure 14–3). They now can more easily release the objects they have grasped. The muscles relax, allowing them to drop or throw an object when they choose to. They also are more accurate in directing the dropped or thrown object.

Name: **Leonard C.**   Date of Birth: **7/29/XX**

Date: **10/18/XX**   C.A.: **22 months 29 days**

MONTH AGE EXPECT.	AREA I PHYSICAL				AREA II EMOTIONAL				AREA III SOCIAL			AREA IV COGNITIVE				AREA V LEARNING SKILLS				MONTH AGE EXPECT.
	MUSCLE CONTROL	LOCOMOTION	SLEEP	TEETH/TOILET	FEELINGS TYPE	CONTROL FEELINGS	TEMPERAMENT		SELF	OTHERS		SENSORI 6	OBJECT	SYMBOL/PLAY	IMITATION	VIS-MOTOR	AUDITORY	VISUAL	LANGUAGE	
30+																				30+
29																				29
28																				28
27																				27
26																				26
25																				25
24																				24
23																				23
22																				22
21																				21
20																				20
19																				19
18																				18
17																				17
16–																				16–

C.A. (at row 23)

A* (below FEELINGS TYPE column near row 18)

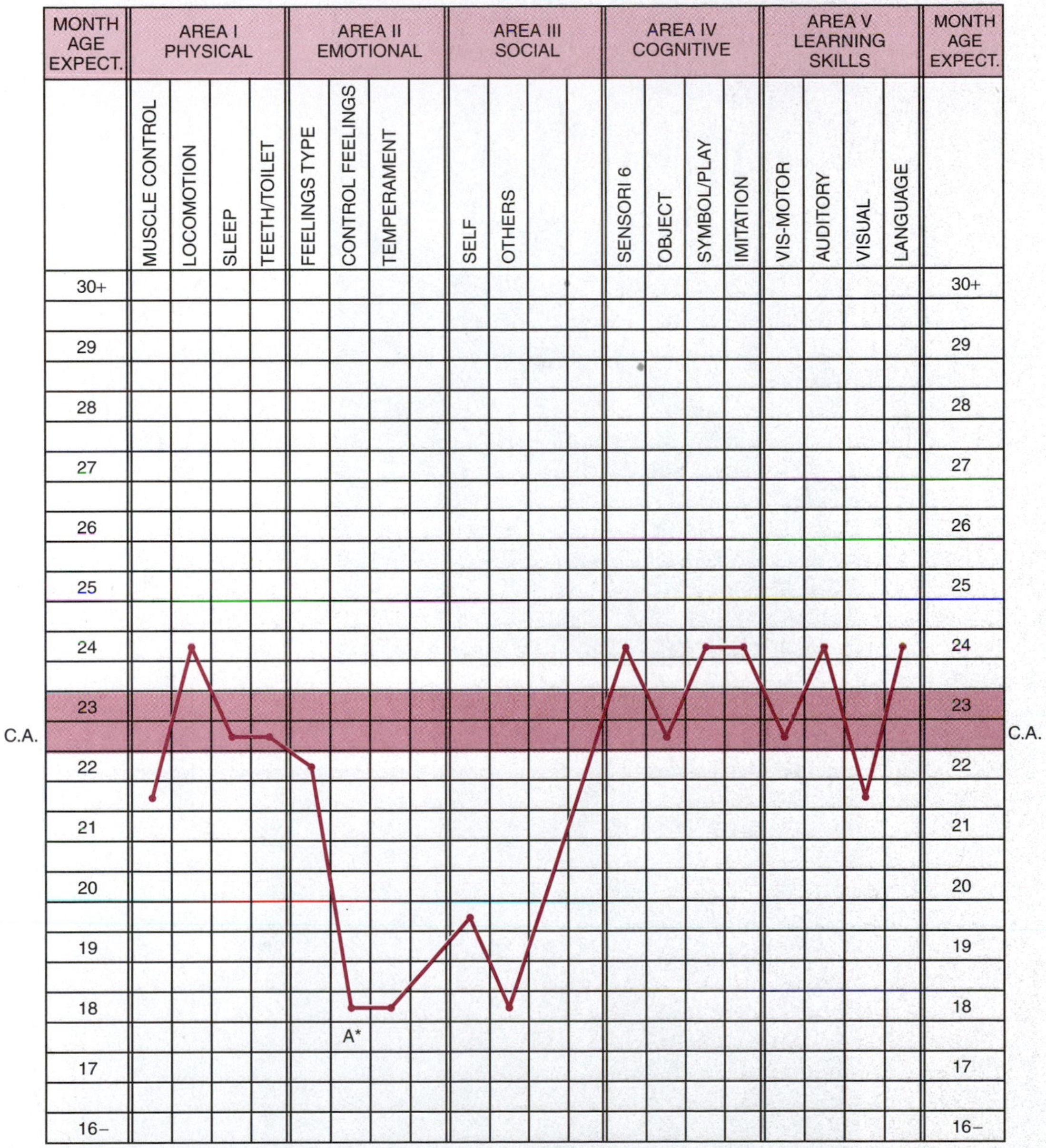

Notes: A* Lennie bites others and has tantrums each day.

Figure 14–1 Developmental Profile, Leonard C.

Figure 14–2 Toddlers can push and pull objects.

Figure 14–3 The caregiver provides a variety of toys to promote fine motor development.

At 18 months many children can turn the pages of a book several at a time, but by 24 months they will be able to turn pages one at a time.

Some children may be favoring one hand over the other at this time. Determine each child's dominant hand and allow the child to use it. The child may occasionally use the other hand when using a spoon, for example; if the child occasionally chooses to do so, this will not be harmful. The caregiver should allow the child to develop and maintain the handedness that is comfortable. Do not attempt to make a left-handed child use utensils and toys with the right hand. That child's neurological patterns have developed with his or her left-handedness. Attempting to change a child's handedness may cause both neurological and muscular stress.

Suggestions for Implementing Curriculum

Child Behavior	Materials	Examples of Caregiver Strategies
Muscular Control		
LOCOMOTION		
walks forward	flat floor, ground,	Keep area clear of toys or
walks backward	clear of toys	caution child about obstacles.
walks sideways	area clear of toys	Play with child: walk sideways, forward, backward.
runs with stops and starts	clear area	Provide *flat* running space. On incline child may run down too fast and fall on face.
jumps with both feet	low steps, box, block, plastic crate	Keep other children away from jumping spot when one child is jumping to the floor. Sometimes catch child as he or she jumps. Release and steady child so he or she can climb and jump again.
kicks object	large ball: beach ball, nerf ball, soccer ball, volleyball, rubber ball	Provide space where child can kick the ball and it will not go too far, e.g., into a big cardboard box or into a corner.
walks up stairs holding railing; walks down stairs holding railing	steps and rail	Provide equipment and time for child to safely walk up and down.
pushes and pulls objects while walking	small wagon, strollers, pull toys, push toys that make noise, attract visual attention	Provide clear space for walking where pushed and pulled toys have room to move without bumping and catching on equipment, furniture, rug.
climbs	sturdy box, cubes, footstool, low climbing gym	Provide equipment. Remain close by to assist getting down if needed.

(continued)

(continued)

Child Behavior	Materials	Examples of Caregiver Strategies
pedals cycle	low riding cycle; not high tricycle	Provide space for fast and slow riding, for turning curves and in circles. Keep away children on foot.
ARM		
throws object at target	bean bag; ball, box, cardboard or wood shape with large holes cut in it	Place target at edge of play area so object is thrown away from children.
HAND		
grasps and releases with developing finger muscles	small toys, objects, pail, box	Provide objects for game of pick- up-and-drop.
pulls zippers	zipper board, book, clothes with large zipper with tab	Provide large zipper with tab large enough for small fingers to pinch and pull. Demonstrate where to hold fabric in other hand.
helps dress and undress self		Allow child to do as much as possible. Plan ahead to provide enough time for child who dresses and undresses slowly.
scribbles	paper, pens, crayons, markers, pencils, flat hard surface	Provide space and time to scribble. Show scribbling boundaries (edges of paper, not beyond edges).
increases wrist flexibility; turns wrist to turn object	small objects to twist and turn; jars and screw-on lids	Provide toys that stimulate manipulating, e.g., attractive, textured on several sides. Demonstrate twisting jar lid on and off.
establishes right- or left-handedness		Allow child to pick up objects and use them with hand child chooses. Do not change object into other hand.
turns book pages	sturdy pages in books	Read to child, carefully turning each page by grasping the upper right-hand corner and moving hand down to middle of page to gently turn the page.
digs with tool	shovel, scoop, spoon; sand, dirt	Provide tools which are not sharp and will not bend. Provide space designated for digging. Demonstrate where sand or dirt may and may not go.
makes individual marks with crayon or pen	paper, pen, crayon, marker	Listen if child talks about his or her marks. Praise child.
Sleeping		
may move from crib to bed or cot	firm cot, mattress	Talk about the change *before* it happens. Emphasize child is getting bigger and now can use a *bigger* bed. Demonstrate where shoes go, where blanket is. Provide quiet talk, music, touch familiar to child.

Child Behavior	Materials	Examples of Caregiver Strategies
Eating		
controls cup and spoon better		Emphasize how well child is using cup, spoon. Be patient with spills.
may eat anything, then change to picky eating		Allow child to change eating behavior. Don't fuss at or push child. Child usually will get adequate nutrition if variety of foods are provided.
Teeth		
has most baby teeth; uses toothbrush	toothbrush, tooth-paste, cup of water	Assist when necessary with applying toothpaste and cleaning face afterwards.
Elimination		
may show interest in and readiness for toilet training	potty chair, training pants; slacks, leggings easy to remove	Show child where potty chair is. Encourage child to use it. Praise child when he or she does. Do not push child. Many show interest in potty chair months before they are ready for actual transition to toilet-training. See Chapter 3 for the child who is ready for consistent toilet-training.

Emotional Development

Children of this age are continuing to develop positive and negative feelings about themselves. They interpret responses from caregivers and children as reflecting their self-worth.

Children's fantasies increase at this age. They are very real and may sometimes be frightening. Brickmeyer's comments are notable today.

"Caregivers must be made aware that sudden fears occur often in toddlers and that caregivers must be prepared to deal with the child lovingly and warmly, in a fashion that does not communicate to the child that the fears are remarkable, outrageous, funny or unreasonable. Sometimes a child can be reassured by a good look at the cause of his or her fright while being held by a loved and trusted caregiver. The caregiver should encourage but not force the child to make a careful examination of the feared object, offering labels and explanations while the child examines it. Occasionally, an articulate toddler can explain his fear: . . . Occasionally, particularly if the cause of the fear is unremovable—a place in a room, for example—after experimenting with changes of furniture or of light and shadow, caregivers may have to resign themselves to offering comfort and the security of laps and arms to help the child weather it out." (Brickmeyer, 1978)

At this stage, children's feelings are hurt by criticism and they are afraid of disapproval or rejection. They become easily frustrated and are able to communicate some feelings and desires. It is important to consciously use the 3A's and Positive Perspective (see Chapter 5) at this stage of development.

Emotions are reflected in intense behaviors. These children can swing between extremes, such as smiling, laughing—screaming, crying. Their basic pattern of intensity of response is affected by their swings into even more intensive behaviors. Children who usually respond loudly may now scream and yell or laugh shrilly. Children who have a low intensity of response may use more energy and respond more loudly or actively than usual.

As toddlers approach their second birthdays, they are aware that they have a "self" and that they are separate from the world of other people and things. They now want to act like separate social beings. Becoming a separate psychological being is one of the most complicated tasks a toddler has to face. During the two years starting from birth, the child establishes a very strong attachment to the mother. When dependence on her begins to diminish, separation follows. The more enjoyable and secure the relationship with the mother has been, the easier the separation process (Caplan & Caplan, 1980). This is also true of the primary caregiver who often spends more time with the child than a parent.

Suggestions for Implementing Curriculum

Child Behavior	Examples of Caregiver Strategies
Types of Emotions-Feelings	
views internal feelings and as same	Recognize that the child does not feel angry external behavior and yet acts inappropriately.
shows one or more emotions at same time	Identify the child's emotions. Respond to the child's needs.
continues to develop feelings about self	Provide consistent behavior and feedback that helps the child feel good about self; help child know he or she is a worthy person.
changes feelings about self	Reflect to child that child is still a loved person when child reflects negative or angry feelings about self.
seeks approval	Provide verbal and nonverbal approval of child as a person and of child's behavior when it is positive.
may develop new fears	Listen to child's fears. Accept them as real. Comfort child. Reassure child of your concern and of your presence. You may demonstrate that the object is harmless, e.g., siren toy. If you cannot convince the child, remove the toy.
increases fantasy	Listen to child's fantasies. Accept them as real to the child. Enjoy funny, happy fantasies. Comfort and reassure child of his or her safety when child has scary fantasies, e.g., "There's a monster in the kitchen."
may increase aggressiveness	Remain nearby to caution, remind, and sometimes remove object or child from situation.
seeks security in routines	Provide consistent routines that child can use by him- or herself as child increases competence and seeks independence.

Child Behavior	Examples of Caregiver Strategies
may become shy again	Allow child to hold back or withdraw. Provide time for child to observe without having to enter into interactions with others.
sometimes rejects parent or caregiver	Allow child to express rejection in words and behaviors. Continue to express your affection for the child.
Control of Emotions-Feelings	
uses reactions of others as a controller of own behavior	Use words, facial expressions, gestures to indicate approval and disapproval of child's behavior.
may resist change	Explain change *before* it happens. Provide reason for the change. Motivate by emphasizing the specialness of the child who now is allowed to do something else. Remember that development is a process not a product. Give time for lessons to be learned.
moves to extremes, from lovable to demanding and stubborn	Allow child to express swings in behavior. Show acceptance of child as a person. Help child work on his or her demands and stubbornness by suggesting alternatives in behavior.
Temperament	
activity level	List two of the child's behaviors in each category that indicate the child's basic style. List adjustments you need to make to help the child cope with daily situations.
regularity	
approach or withdrawal as a characteristic response to a new situation	
adaptability to change in routine	
level of sensory threshold	
positive or negative mood	
intensity of response	
distractibility	
persistence and attention span	

Social Development

Children of this age are continuing to develop a sense of self. They use words that identify them as separate people, such as I, mine, me, you. These children are also expanding their relationships with others. They are beginning to recognize other people's feelings and they are experimenting mentally as they begin to develop an inner sense of empathy.

"One child will hit the other and produce howls of pain and rage; the child may be so intrigued by the dramatic results of hitting that he or she will hit again, just to see if the results are as interesting as those produced by the first blow. All too often adults who observe this kind of behavior are horrified and react loudly, "Naughty; that's bad; say you are sorry; you shouldn't hit people!" Confused by the intensity of the adult reaction, he or she usually

Figure 14–4 Toddlers do not share toys easily, so the caregiver should provide enough toys of a similar nature for them to use.

mumbles the magic word "sorry," getting the toddler off the hook, but offering little or no understanding of what he or she did to deserve the scolding. Because a toddler has little understanding that the feelings he or she experiences are also experienced by other people, adults should concentrate on the child who is hurt, saying briefly to the offender: "Hitting hurts. I feel sorry that _____ has been hurt." Thus, the offender is told that hitting is not allowed because it hurts the person who is hit and that the adult is sorry that someone is hurt. (Brickmeyer, 1978)

Although toddlers still have difficulty sharing toys (Figure 14–4), children imitate the behavior of others. While they demand more personal attention, they also can accept shared attention. They try to please others and may help in situations where they are praised.

The 3A's of caregiving—Attention, Approval, and Affection—used together appropriately can now be seen in one child's relationship with another.

Suggestions for Implementing Curriculum

Child Behavior	Examples of Caregiver Strategies
Self	
is egocentric, sees things from own point of view	Recognize that child thinks others think and feel the way he or she does. Help child identify own ideas and feelings.
may change identity of self from day to day	Provide feedback to child about self so child can identify consistency within self.
identifies materials as belonging to self	Recognize and allow ownership of toys.

Child Behavior	Examples of Caregiver Strategies
uses I, mine, me, you	Verbally respond to child's use of pronouns, reinforcing distinction child makes between self and others.
Others	
demands attention	Both initiate and respond to child to provide attention to child's needs. Share looks, touch, and words with child when you may be busy with another child.
begins to be aware of others' feelings	Help child identify and verbalize others' feelings, which appear in their behavior, e.g., "Allen is crying; he is sad."
believes people have changes in identity—change in role changes person	Identify yourself in your different tasks, e.g., when you sweep and clean, when you cook, when you rock a child.
expands social relationships	Encourage child to interact with others. Be present and provide your support when child encounters a new child or adult.
looks to others for help	Consistently provide assistance when needed. Praise child for seeking help with something child would not be able to do for self, e.g., putting on shoe and then seeking help for tying laces instead of fussing and crying.
imitates tasks of others	Allow and enjoy child's watching you and others. Enjoy the imitations and don't be concerned that the imitation might be incomplete or inaccurate. The child will continue to watch and imitate.
wants to help, assist with tasks, clean-up	Encourage the child to help put toys away, clean up, etc. Work along with child. Child can be a very good helper if he or she sees how you do it.
may do opposite of what is requested	Carefully word your requests. The child's negativism comes out in a frequent "no." Think of different ways to produce desired behavior without saying, "Do this."
has difficulty sharing	Provide enough toys and materials so child does not have to share. Suggest allowing another child to play with toy when child finishes. Provide alternative toys to the child who must wait for a desired toy.
engages in parallel play	Provide toys, materials, and space for children to play near each other. Allow them to talk with each other. You talk to each of them. Allow them to choose if they want to trade toys or do something else.

Cognitive Development

Children of this age are gradually using mental trial and error. This is much faster than the sensorimotor trial and error, in which children had to manipulate objects.

Object permanence is established. These children know that an object or person exists even when they cannot see it and they remember where objects belong. They know that they exist separate from other people and objects (Wilson, 1987).

Children of this age imitate past events. They remember the ideas by internal representation and reproduce them at a later time. For example, the caregiver washing the child's face is imitated later by the child as the child washes a doll's face.

Symbolic play is children's representation of objects or feelings or ideas. They will imitate housework and enjoy helping. Symbolic play serves several functions: Children can express conflicts and work them out in the pretend world. They can seek gratification of unsatisfied needs they feel they have, such as playing the baby to get the extra nurturing they desire. They can pretend to be other people or objects, thereby reflecting their understanding of other people or objects as separate from themselves and trying behaviors similar to or different from their own.

At around 22 to 24 months, a caregiver can determine what is going on with a child cognitively by role playing with puppets or dolls. Often the troubled child explains very clearly to the caregiver a situation that might have been disturbing.

This is a good way for the child to get feedback in a positive way, a good place to use the 3A's and Positive Perspective, and a good way to help them problem solve and help to continue to develop good *self-esteem* in the child.

Suggestions for Implementing Curriculum

Child Behavior	Examples of Caregiver Strategies
Piaget's Stages of Sensorimotor Development	
STAGE 6 (Representation)	
Mental trial and error	
tries out ideas mentally, based on past concrete experiences	Allow child time to figure out solutions. If child seeks assistance, help child think about the problem, e.g., "What can you use to reach that block?"
Object permanence	
sees object disappear, mentally remembers object, and figures out where it went	Allow the child to think and search for object. Give clues, ask questions only after the child has acted and still needs assistance.
Deferred imitation and symbolization	
imitates past events	Observe the child's representations. Identify the ideas that seem very important to the child.
Symbolic play	
resolves conflicts	Allow the child to act out conflict in play with toys and materials. Observe how the child works out conflict so he or she feels better.
compensates for unsatisfied needs	Observe child's play. Identify consistent themes in child's play, e.g., child's talk and actions about being a good or a naughty child.
tries roles	Provide clothes and materials that help child pretend to be someone else.

Learning Skills/Language Development

Teach basic learning skills daily, including visual memory, auditory discrimination, and other skills. Language throughout life is clearly linked with emotion, and it is important to remember that children who get enough cuddling and unconditional love have a better chance at learning language—and everything else (Healy, 1989).

Caregivers must be careful not to criticize children's speech patterns. Good grammatical structure is learned by children when adults set good examples and repeatedly use words correctly. Remember to use the 3A's when speech is used correctly as well as to encourage children when they have verbalized.

At this age children's vocabulary is expanding rapidly as they label objects that they now recognize as separate entities (Figure 14–5). Children construct the principle that

> "words are labels for socially defined classes of objects and events. This achievement is reflected in more systematic and productive extension of words and in accelerated growth of vocabulary. . . . This is the time when children may tire their caregivers by constantly asking for the names of things (e.g., what's this?). They eagerly utter the words they hear and explore their uses. (Anisfeld, 1984, 86) (Figure 14–6)

Children use their language to express needs and to direct others. They question as they seek to learn about their word (Wilson, 1988).

Children of this age use nouns, verbs, and pronouns as they combine their words into two- and three-word sentences. These children produce word sequences,

Figure 14–5 The caregiver uses familiar objects to play choosing and naming games.

Figure 14–6 Outdoor activities provide many opportunities to observe, question, label, and praise toddlers' actions.

that is, several words in sequence that convey a thought or action but are not regular sentence patterns. For example, Cameron says, "Key go car" when he sees his mother take the key ring out of her purse. She responds, "Yes, I have the key. We are going in the car."

These children follow simple one- and two-step oral directions. There are two broad classes of language functions: "the **cognitive function**—to name, indicate, describe, and comment; and the **instrumental function**—to request, reject, manipulate, and express desires. . . . [W]ords are used for cognitive purposes before they are used for instrumental purposes" (Anisfeld, 1984, 91).

Caregivers and children use words to classify objects and actions. Words help children organize what they see and hear and do. Anisfeld reported that when adults do the following things they help young children develop proper language.

- The adult speaks to children in short sentences.
- The adult articulates more clearly to young children than to others.
- The adult talks about the situation in which the child is involved.
- The adult expands what the child says ("fills in the missing words as she echoes the child's utterance").
- The adult extends what the child says ("continues a thought started by a child").
- The adult imitates what the child says ("repeats all or part of what the child had said").

Pictures, books, and storytelling stimulate language interactions among caregivers and children. Lamme (1985) relates several experiences that involved toddlers in the reading process.

> "Pointing out things in pictures and encouraging your toddler to participate in the 'reading' helps your child become more active in the reading process. Maybe you have tried to skip a page or shorten a story in an effort to speed up the bedtime ritual. Has your toddler surprised you by noticing and demanding the whole story? Even at these young ages, toddlers are actively listening to stories and remembering them word for word!
>
> Because reading sessions with your toddler are likely to be so short, it is important to read aloud frequently—several times during the day."

Choose reading materials for young children carefully. Stimulate the toddlers' interests in "reading" and hearing stories often.

> "Your toddler will enjoy the classic fairy tales read over and over again. Stories like 'The Three Little Pigs' or 'The Three Billy Goats Gruff' will encourage your child to chant the repetitive parts as he or she sings and plays around the house. You and your toddler can act out the tales. If you make a flannel board with characters of these familiar stories or have puppets for the story characters, your child can experience the stories in lots of ways other than just by hearing them. Active involvement in the story plot is a real key for toddlers.
>
> Your toddler will enjoy books that are small in size because they are easy to carry around the house. . . .
>
> Your toddler will still enjoy much of the literature that appealed to him or her as an infant—nursery rhymes especially. Some toddlers can proceed through a favorite Mother Goose collection and chant each rhyme.
>
> Your toddler will also enjoy bigger books which are "two laps wide" for lap reading. Many children's picture books are wider than they are long so that you can spread the book out and see the pictures. (Lamme, 1985, 58–59)

Toddlers experiment with markers, chalk, and crayons as their interest in scribbling continues. Encourage their scribbling by providing time and attention to their use and enjoyment of writing.

Don't ask your child what his scribbles are. The scribbles at this stage do not represent anything. Rather, comment on what is apparent—lines from top to bottom or across the page, dots, and colors. You might say, "I like your orange and brown picture" or "What beautiful blue lines!"

> "Your child may be far more interested in the process of making scribbles than in the product produced by those scribbles. You, however, may want to write your child's name in the corner of the picture, letting him watch as you write. As scribble pictures get framed, mounted or displayed, your youngster soon learns that his scribble pictures are valued. He will want to draw more, not only because scribbling is so innately pleasurable but also because his scribbling attracts your positive attention" (Lamme, 1984, 39).

Suggestions for Implementing Curriculum

Child Behavior	Materials	Examples of Caregiver Strategies
uses language to reflect own meaning; expects others to have same meaning		Recognize limited meaning of child's use of words. Be careful not to read extra meaning into what the child says.
expands vocabulary rapidly, labeling objects		Verbally label and also point, touch objects and actions in child's world. Also expand the label into a sentence, e.g., "Ball. Michael has a ball."
points to objects and pictures named by others		Play games, look at pictures, read books; say, "Point to the bird" or "Where is the car?"
learns social words—hello, please, thank you		Consistently use social words in their correct context. Say "please" and "thank you" to the child. When child requests item, repeat request and add the word "please," e.g., "Carrot please."
uses language to express needs, desires		Listen to child's expression of needs. Verbally respond so child knows that his or her words get your attention and you understand them. Use words and actions to meet child's needs or explain why you cannot meet them, e.g., "The milk is all gone."
uses language to direct others		Listen to child's commands. Respond verbally and with action following child's directions or explain why you are not, e.g., "Here is a napkin" when child asks for one.
questions; asks "What's that?"		Answer child's occasional and persistent questions. This is how the child learns labels and other information about the world. Provide simple answers, not complicated ones, e.g., "That is a flower" rather than a description of petals, leaves, stem, etc.
uses nouns, verbs, pronouns		Speak normally with the child so child can hear complete sentence patterns.
is learning prepositions		Use in natural contexts, e.g., "The ball rolled under the table," "Put the book on the shelf."
calls self by name		Use the child's name when talking directly to child.
follows one-step direction		Use simple directions and praise when the child follows them, e.g., "Please put the truck here."
follows two-step direction		Make sure child is aware that you are giving directions. Use simple directions, e.g., "Please pick up this book and put it on the shelf."
makes two- and three-word sentences		Use both short and long sentences with the child. Praise child and respond to child's sentences, e.g., Child: "Coat on?" Caregiver: "Yes, you need your coat on."

Child Behavior	Materials	Examples of Caregiver Strategies
looks at books	cloth or paper or cardboard picture books	Read books with child. Demonstrate proper care of books. Allow child to look at books alone.
listens to stories and rhymes		Tell stories that the child can understand. Use rhymes, poems.
scribbles	markers, chalk, crayons, paper	Provide writing space and materials. Show interest and approval of scribbling. Share scribbling with others.

Key Terms

cognitive function

instrumental function

symbolic play

CASE STUDY

The child care staff were very frustrated with Lennie's biting behavior. Not only had he broken the skin on several children's bodies, his daily tantrums caused damage to furniture and equipment. The director had a parent conference with Lennie's parents after the Developmental Profile was completed to discuss biting and tantrum behavior and found that Lennie's mother was very defensive and aggressive when questioned about his behavior. Being an only child, it appeared that his mother was overly defensive about his behavior, although she did not seem to be concerned about Lennie's feelings. Further, she kept referring everything back to how his behavior effected her.

Since it was determined from the conference that a prescription that directly involved the parents was not possible at the time, Lennie's biting and tantrum behavior were task-analyzed and a Developmental Prescription was established for the child care setting. This involved using the tools: labeling and expressing feelings, self-soothing, catching the child being good, emotion management, and behavior-limiting steps.

After a month of implementing the plan, Lennie's behavior had improved only slightly. It was at this time that his primary caregiver started to notice bruises on Lennie's back and legs. At first, she thought the bruises were the result of his violent tantrums, but one day he came in with a fresh bruise that looked like a hand print. When Lennie was questioned, he became sullen and quiet and withdrew from his caregiver, whom he liked.

1. What steps should the caregiver take at this point?
2. How would you react emotionally to this situation? How would you deal with and express your feelings?
3. What further steps and tools could you use to help Lennie?

Student Activities

1. Observe one caregiver for 10 minutes. Use narrative description to write down everything caregiver does and says. Then categorize the behavior using a format like the following.

Caregiver Behavior (What Caregiver Did)	Caregiver Initiated	With Whom?	Caregiver Responded	To Whom?	Area(s) of Child Development Involved

2. Identify one characteristic temperament of one child (by records, caregiver information, or your own observation). Observe to see how the caregiver makes adjustments in the routine or expectations of the child to the situation and how the caregiver helps the child make adjustments. For example, the caregiver may tell a low active child several minutes early that it is time for the child to put on outdoor clothing.

3. Make one toy and allow two children this age to use it. Observe and write down how they used it, what they said, and your judgment about whether they seemed interested, challenged, or bored using it. Also evaluate the toy's construction.

Toy	How Used?	Child's Comments	Interesting/ Challenging/ Boring?	Sturdy, Torn, Broken?

4. Observe one child between 18 and 24 months of age. Record the child's behavior in two five-minute sequences, using narrative description. Transfer the descriptions to the Developmental Profile.

5. List five strategies to use with children between 18 and 24 months of age.

6. List strategies you need to develop and list ways you intend to develop them.

7. Develop a theme for the month using the Celebration of Life Calendar.

Chapter Review

1. List three physical changes that enable the child to become more independent.

2. Chris and Marlin both pick up a car and start pulling on it. What can you do and what can you say that shows appropriate understanding of their needs and desires?

3. List three ways symbolic play helps a child.

4. Identify two possible developments in the child's language and state two strategies for each that a caregiver can use to facilitate that development.

Child's Development of Language	Caregiver Strategies
1.	1.
	2.
2.	1.
	2.

References

Anisfeld, M. (1984). *Language development from birth to three*. Hillsdale, NJ: Lawrence Erlbaum Associates.

Brickmeyer, J. (1978). *Guidelines for day care programs for migrant infants and toddlers*. New York: Bankstreet College.

Caplan, F., & Caplan, T. (1980). *The second twelve months of life*. New York: Bantam/Grosset and Dunlap, Inc.

Healy, J. (1989). *Your child's growing mind: A guide to learning and brain development from birth to adolescence*. New York: Doubleday.

Lamme, L. L. (1984). *Growing up writing*. Washington, DC: Acropolis Books Ltd.

Lamme, L. L. (1985). *Growing up reading*. Washington, DC: Acropolis Books Ltd.

Wilson, L. C. (1987). Peek-a-boo . . . I see you! *Pre-K Today, 1*(6), 32–33.

Wilson, L. C. (1988). What's in the box? *Pre-K Today, 2*(4), 38–39.

Helpful Web Sites

Talking About Me: Activities for Toddlers (18 to 36 Months Old). What Do Toddlers Do?
http://www.ed.gov/Family/RSRforCaregvr/toddlers.html

Activities for Fathers and Toddlers (18–36 Months): Activities, Teaching, Monitoring.
http://fatherwork.byu.edu/toddlerA.html

Your Toddler's Health: Illness and Injuries, Wellness and Prevention. http://www.babycenter.com/toddler/toddlerhealth

Toddler Safety Checklist: Drowning, Choking, Furniture Danger. http://www.babycenter.com/toddler/toddlerhealth

Information for Parents with Children and Toddlers. http://vm.cfsan.fda.gov/~dms/wh-infnt.html

Getting Your Toddler Back to Bed: Overcoming Nighttime Terrors in Two-Year-Olds. http://family.go.com

The Importance of Play: Structured and Unstructured Play. http://www.parenthood.com

For additional infant and toddler resources, visit our Web site at http://www.earlychilded.delmar.com

The Child from Twenty-Four to Thirty Months of Age

Objectives

After reading this chapter, you should be able to:

- Identify and record sequences of change in the physical, emotional, social, cognitive, and language development of children from 24 to 30 months of age.
- Select materials appropriate to that age-level child's development.
- Devise strategies appropriate to that age-level child's development.

Chapter Outline

Materials and Activities

Caregiver Strategies to Enhance Development

Cathy's Story

Twenty-six-month-old Cathy picks up a fire truck and walks up on the porch with it. She pushes it around on the floor, then picks it up and takes it out into the yard. Ms. Susan asks her what she has. Cathy responds, "A truck," and smiles. Ms. Susan asks what kind of truck. Cathy says, "Red," and smiles. Cathy picks up a ball and says, "Watch me throw it." She moves the fire truck and tells Ms. Susan, "Can't find ladder." Ms. Susan gives her the ladder and starts to put it on the fire truck. Cathy requests, "Let me do it." Cathy puts a toy fireman in the truck and plays with it. She says to Ms. Susan, "See the truck," and then, "See if it goes?" As Cathy plays with the fire truck, the ladder falls off again and she says, "Oh, no," and looks at Ms. Susan. She takes the truck to Ms. Susan to fix the ladder, saying "It fall off" and pointing to the ladder. She watches Ms. Susan fix the ladder and plays with it again. Another child gets the fire truck and begins to play with it. Cathy tells the child, "I want the truck, Bill." Bill gives the fire truck back to Cathy, who says, "Thank you, Bill."

MATERIALS AND ACTIVITIES

Riding toys are favorites at this age (Figure 15–1). The children also use climbing and jumping equipment frequently. Kicking and throwing are more accurate than before and are enjoyed by the children. Finger, hand, and wrist movements include grasping and releasing, but they also coordinate with vision, enabling the children to string beads and to use crayons and other drawing and writing tools. Children take pleasure in manipulating objects and materials. They focus on the process rather than on producing a product. They respond to and create music. They enjoy symbolic play. They can find meaning in pictures and books representing ideas with which they are familiar.

Figure 15–1 The caregiver provides riding toys of different sizes for young children.

Review Chapter 5. Use Appendix A, the Developmental Prescriptions, and Appendix B, the Developmental Profile, with each child. Children follow a *sequence* of development. There are often ranges in the *rate* of development.

Most adults who work with toddlers wonder when and how children begin to be able to look at situations from another person's viewpoint. Some toddlers may seem to behave in a sympathetic fashion occasionally or briefly, but such behavior is probably indicative of actions they have observed rather than an expression of understanding for what someone else is feeling. A toddler may, for example, look concerned if another child cries, may rush over to pat the unhappy one, offer a cracker or toy, or may even burst into tears. More commonly, however, toddlers pursue their own important affairs with little or no regard for what their playmates are doing or feeling. A toddler who is pushing a doll carriage around the room may push the carriage over any obstacles, including people, with little recognition that this may hurt the unfortunate person in his or her path (Brickmeyer, 1978).

Types of Materials

balance beam	large pegs and boards
climbing equipment	large beads and string
bouncing equipment	markers, crayons, pens, chalk
rocking boat	modeling dough
wagon	construction material: wood, styrofoam, glue
cycles	
wheeled toys	rhythm instruments
items to throw	records
balls	tape recordings
blocks	puppets
trucks, cars	dress-up clothes
dolls, people, animals	pictures
jars with twist lids	books
items to put together or pull apart	puzzles
knobs	matching games

Examples of Homemade Materials

Themes and ideas are available in the Celebration of Life Calendar in Chapter 9.

BALANCE BEAM

Put masking tape on the floor to indicate a line on which the child can walk.

In the yard partially bury a tree trunk so that several inches remain above ground. Place so that no branch stubs are on the top walking surface.

PEG BOARD

Cut a piece of heavy cardboard to fit in the bottom of a box (shoe, gift, hamburger). Cut holes in the cardboard. Cut ½-inch dowel rod into 1½–2-inch lengths. Paint if desired. Store cardboard and pegs in the box and put on lid.

MARACAS

Collect gourds in the fall. Allow to dry. The seeds will rattle when the gourd is shaken.

DRUM

Poke a hole through both ends of an oatmeal box. Pull a strong string through the box and both ends and extend 12–24 inches (measure on one of your children). Tape the box lid onto the box. Tie a knot or leave the ends loose and tie a bow each time you put it around a child's neck.

SOAP PAINT

Use 1 part soap flakes, 1 part water, and food coloring. Beat the mixture with a hand eggbeater. Skim off soap suds to paint on table top or shelf paper or freezer paper.

FINGER PAINT

Use liquid starch, dry tempera paint, and soap flakes. Pour out about a tablespoon of liquid starch on shelf or freezer paper. Sprinkle dry paint on starch. Sprinkle soap flakes on starch. Children mix ingredients as they paint.

TEMPERA PAINT

Mix ½ cup dry tempera paint and ½ cup dry detergent. Add water until mixture is thick but not runny. Keep in covered jar.

PUPPETS

Use paper sandwich bags. Child can use crayons or glue on paper to decorate puppet. Help child fit hand in bottom of sack.

CLOTH BOOK

Use pinking shears to cut heavy cloth to make several pieces the same size. Stack the pieces and sew down the middle by machine or by hand. Cut out colored pictures from magazines or cards. Glue one picture per page. Make a theme book, e.g., children riding, or use pictures of different objects or activities.

GROUP BOOK

Make a group book. Children can tear out magazine pictures of objects; the pictures may fit a theme. Glue to pieces of paper. Staple the pages together. Write the title page. Write what children dictate to you for the other pages. (Paper may first be cut into a shape that matches the theme, e.g., pumpkin, leaf.)

PUZZLE

Cut out one uncluttered colored picture from a magazine.

a. *Glue it to the center of the cardboard.*

b. *Cover the picture and cardboard with contact paper. Pencil the picture into three to five sections that are visually recognizable (head, legs, tail). Cut around the picture, being careful to cut only the picture and not the cardboard.*

c. *Cut the remaining hole slightly larger.*

d. *Glue the remainder of the cardboard onto a second piece of cardboard the same size. Fit the puzzle pieces into place. If necessary, trim so the pieces come out easily.*

MATCHING GAME

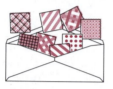

Cut two 2-inch squares from each page of a wallpaper sample book. Make about six sets, using different pages. Store the pieces in an envelope. To play, mix up the pieces and then select squares that match.

MATCHING GAME

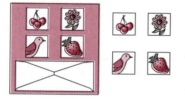

Select four picture sets of objects that are alike, e.g., two cardinals, two mice, two daisies, two German shepherds. Glue one of each set onto the bottom of a styrofoam tray. Glue the other four pictures onto cardboard and cut into small squares. Glue part of an envelope in the tray to hold the loose cardboard pieces. Randomly pick pieces that match the pictures on the tray. Ask child to point to matching object.

Activities Ideas

The following are examples of activities that help children construct knowledge.

Exploration

Cooking

recipe chart	stir	see
oral language	beat	hear
measure	smell	taste
sift	feel	

Growing Plants

carrot	bean sprouts	observations
sweet potato	food	comparisons
beans	care	charting
lettuce	rate of growth	

Representations
Oral Language

conversation	poetry	singing and rhythms
information gathering	nursery rhymes	dramatic play
story telling	fingerplays	

Objects

painting rocks, seeds, pine cones

creating prints with potatoes, carrots, celery; footprints, handprints, fingerprints

Pictures

magazines, photographs

art media: crayons, painting, tear and paste

Books

wordless picture books

naming objects books

books with a storyline to read or tell in your own words

CAREGIVER STRATEGIES TO ENHANCE DEVELOPMENT

Developmental Profile

Figure 15–2 shows Cathy's Developmental Profile, which is based on a 10-day observation of the Child Behaviors from the Developmental Prescription in Appendix A.

Cathy exhibits a generally low profile in all areas except for the Emotional Area (II), where estimates suggest near age-level expectancies.

Within the Physical Area (I), Cathy is estimated to be four months below C.A. in muscle control because she can't stand on one foot yet and tends to be physically clumsy for her age. She is also having difficulty with toilet-training and isn't ready for training pants yet, therefore achieving an estimate of 18 months.

Cathy has a quiet, accepting temperament, displays positive and negative self-worth, and therefore functions near C.A. in the Emotional Area (II).

Socially (III), Cathy does not realize her skills and abilities and does not show independence. She does whatever other children or adults tell her to do. As a result, she is estimated to be at the 16- to 18-month level socially.

Cognitively (IV), Cathy functions more like an 18-month-old than a 26-month-old. She has trouble classifying, labeling, and understanding concepts such as up, down, more, and now.

Within the Learning Skills Area (V), Cathy exhibits low visual-motor control (23 months), auditory skills (21 months), visual skills (18 months), and language skills (16 months). She appears to learn better from auditory than visual information, but her overall perceptual and language development is estimated to be almost a year below age expectations.

In summary, Cathy exhibits general developmental lags in most of the important areas. She is estimated to be almost a year below age expectancy in both cognitive and learning skills. These deficits are considered extreme for her age and are cause for

Name: **Cathy F.**

Date: **06/08/XX**

Date of Birth: **04/06/XX**

C.A.: **26 months 2 days**

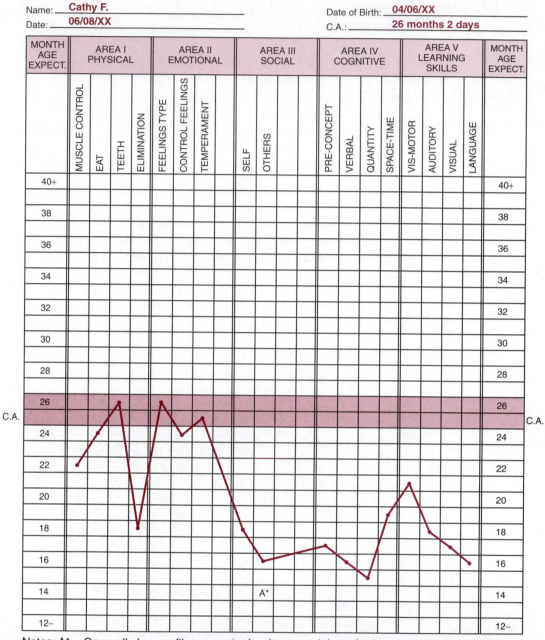

Notes: A* = Generally low profile suggests development delays–further evaluation necessary.

Figure 15–2 Developmental Profile, Cathy R.

further evaluation. The caregiver should hold a conference with Cathy's parents to explore whether formal evaluations by a psychologist and her pediatrician should be done to help determine the causes of these lags.

Physical Development

The two-year-old can stand, bend, walk, run, and jump. Riding toys are favorites at this age (see Figure 15–1). These children also use climbing and jumping equipment frequently. Kicking and throwing are more accurate than before and are enjoyed by the children. Toddlers are more flexible and stable in their movements than before (Figure 15–3). Their eye-hand coordination is more accurate, so they can reach and grasp objects, but they still have difficulty using hands and fingers independently. They are able to fit objects together and like to put them together and pull them apart. Toddlers may use either their right or left hand, but most still have not established handedness. These children are visually fascinated with some new items. They spend more time observing. They use a spoon when eating and are learning to use a fork. Some children this age have all 20 baby teeth. These children may learn to brush their teeth. Many children this age are ready for toilet-training and may even train themselves if the opportunity is provided.

Figure 15–3 The young child is becoming more coordinated and can stoop and stand easily.

Suggestions for Implementing Curriculum

Child Behavior	Materials	Examples of Caregiver Strategies
Muscular Control		
MOVEMENT		
bends at waist	dropping and picking up objects: pail and plastic rings	Play game with child. Observe appropriateness of materials, interest of child.
climbs	low objects: steps up to slide, tires	Select safe materials and safe height.
jumps	two- to three-step equipment	Keep floor or ground space clear where jumping. Block off higher levels so jump is safe distance for muscles and balance.
stands on one foot	song for lifting one foot	Make up rhyme or song about standing on one foot. Child will stand on one foot for only a few seconds. Praise child. Encourage child to try again.
ARM		
throws	target—large paper sack or plastic basin; objects—nerf ball, yarn ball	Provide space for child to throw objects at target. Decorate target so child is aiming at hoop or door.
HAND		
touches	textured objects: sandpaper, fur, corduroy, egg, carton bottom, juice can	Make feely box. Allow child to pull out objects to touch and see. Label objects for child. Label textures for child.
twists	jars and cans with lids; large plastic nuts and bolts	Provide objects that twist on and off easily.
Eating		
uses spoon	spoon that fits child's hand	Provide food that can be spooned easily.
is learning to use fork	fork that fits child's hand	Provide food that will stay on fork.
uses fingers		Cut solid food in small pieces so it can be picked up with fingers.
Teeth		
has all 20 baby teeth		
brushes teeth		
toothbrush, toothpaste		Assist with toothpaste and water.

Child Behavior	Materials	Examples of Caregiver Strategies
Elimination		
is learning to use toilet	training pants, potty chair or adapter seat	Ask whether child needs to go to toilet. Assist with clothes. Assist with hand washing. Glove hands. Clean up potty chair or toilet seat. *Wash your hands.*
has completed toilet training	training pants, potty chair or toilet	Ask whether child needs to go to toilet before and after nap, before outside play. Assist with clothes as needed. Assist with hand washing. Clean up, and *wash your hands*.

Emotional Development

Feelings about the self continue to develop: positive and negative self-image, competence, acceptance. Children this age are becoming more independent at the same time they recognize their need for help. They attempt to please and show affection. At 24 months they make less demands and have a better ability to express themselves. However, by 30 months these easier-going children suddenly fall into what has been termed the **terrible twos**. They become more demanding and more possessive about their things. They become frustrated, say no to almost everything and have **temper tantrums**. They may suddenly want help with things they previously could do and want to do things they are not able to do. They may be aggressive, then shy, then "act like a baby." They cannot handle choices and demand sameness and consistency. In fact, meeting their need for sameness may well be the best way to handle the 30-month-old. Routines provide children this age with consistency and security. They may be affectionate (Figure 15–4) at one moment and want no affection the next.

Figure 15–4 Friends show affection for each other.

Here, the caregiver's skills of being well organized, consistent, and flexible (as discussed earlier in Chapter 5) may be challenged. Be sure to use plenty of the 3A's for your own benefit, as well as directly with the children.

We have tried to point out some of the behavioral components of healthy development in toddlerhood, a stage in which a child attempts to become an autonomous being capable of competently functioning in an environment appropriately geared to his or her needs and abilities. It should be clear that children who are given sufficient opportunities to explore, to use their senses, to be physically active, to use expressive materials, and to develop language skills may often—through the very nature of these activities—be destructive, messy, noisy, impudent, and defiant.

Suggestions for Implementing Curriculum

Child Behavior	*Examples of Caregiver Strategies*
Types of Emotions-Feelings	
feels comfortable with self	Provide experiences in which child can succeed often, feel pleasure with self.
feels positive self-worth	Give the child positive feedback. Reinforce other people's reflections of the child as a worthy person.
feels negative self-worth	Be sensitive to the child's frustrations with tasks and with social encounters. Provide reassurance of the child's worth.
Control of Emotions-Feelings	
expresses emotions	Accept the child's feelings as honest rather than manipulative.
Temperament	
activity level	List two of the child's behaviors in each category that indicate the child's basic style. List adjustments you need to make to
regularity	help the child cope with daily situations.
approach or withdrawal as a characteristic response to a new situation	
adaptability to change in routine	
level of sensory threshold	
positive or negative mood	
intensity of response	
distractibility	
persistence and attention span	

Social Development

Twenty-four-month-olds enjoy the company of other children; they are beginning to interact. Because toddlers still have some difficulty sharing, they often engage in parallel play. It is possible to involve children this age in group interest centers, such as sitting at the same table and playing with play dough on an individual basis. Toddlers recognize emotions in others and may help with tasks. By 30 months these children interact with each other, but often they may quarrel over possessions rather than participate in a cooperative effort. They may help with some chores. Following a routine may allow the caregiver to gain some cooperation in tasks and cleaning up.

Suggestions for Implementing Curriculum

Child Behavior	*Examples of Caregiver Strategies*
Self	
realizes own skills	Provide materials and equipment that child can use to own satisfaction. Provide challenging materials that child can use.
Others	
shows independence	Allow child to accomplish as many tasks as possible by self. Assist when asked or when you anticipate you are needed.
acts to please adult	Provide verbal and nonverbal positive feedback to child. Recognize child's need for your attention and approval. Plan activities child can help you with (clean-up).
shows feelings to others	Show feelings to child. Show appropriate actions with feelings, e.g., happy—laugh, physical excitement; sad—hug, pat, listen. Praise child when child uses those behaviors.
recognizes emotions in others	Label children's behaviors. Verbalize about feelings of others. Provide appropriate responses to behaviors. Praise child when child identifies others' emotions. Praise when child responds to others' emotions.
understands "mine" and "yours"	Reinforce possession by child and others. It is "mine" while using it.
shares some	Provide materials and equipment so some sharing is necessary. Praise child who shares. Verbalize reasons for sharing. Recognize, however, that not all children can share yet.
helps others	Provide opportunities for purposeful helping—clean-up, passing out items, assisting with clothing. Praise and thank for helping behaviors.
engages in parallel play	Plan space and materials so children can play close to others without having to interact in play.

Cognitive Development

Many children between 24 and 30 months are entering Piaget's preoperational stage of cognitive development. The first substage of the preoperational stage is the **preconceptual**, which occurs from about two to four years of age. These children can mentally sort some objects and actions. The mental symbols are partly detached from experience. Early nonverbal classifications are called graphic collections, in which children can focus on figurative properties. These children form some verbal preconcepts, but the meaning of words may fluctuate from one time to another. Verbal reasoning is from particular to particular.

Preconceptual children are constructing and organizing knowledge about a wide range of areas in their world. They are beginning to classify objects and to develop very limited ideas of quantity, number, space, and time. Due to their preference for routines and sameness, their sense of time is based more on what happens after an event rather than on an understanding of "later" or minutes of time passage.

The development of the symbolic function occurs in the preconceptual stage. It involves the following mental representations, presented here in increasing complexity. In the child's **search for hidden objects** the object remains permanent (does not cease to exist) in the child's thinking even when the child cannot see it. These experiences form the basis for more specific representational thinking. In **deferred imitation** the child imitates another person's behavior even when that person is no longer present. A child engaged in *symbolic play* may give the caregiver a stone and tell the caregiver to eat this apple; the stone represents the real object. The child's *drawings* may be scribbles, experiments with the media, or they may begin to be representations; a child may point to a mark he or she has made on a piece of paper and say his or her own name. **Mental images** are pictures in the mind with which children can carry out action sequences internally. **Language** (words) represent objects or behaviors. As children develop language, they use their mental images, which represent thoughts (Wadsworth, 1978, 64).

Children at this age are active explorers, seeking information through manipulating and observing their world. As problem-solvers, they now move beyond trial and error to mental manipulation of ideas and physical manipulation of objects to construct their reasoning.

When there is only "one right way" to play, opportunities for experimentations and new discovery are limited. Common household objects, tools, cooking utensils, and gadgets are particularly fascinating because adults use them. Nesting and stacking objects and containers for dumping and pouring are examples of good mental stimulators. They require active handling and teach about relationships, top, middle, bottom, small, big, bigger, and biggest. Blocks of different sizes are the best toys of all (Healy, 1989).

Suggestions for Implementing Curriculum

Child Behavior	*Examples of Caregiver Strategies*
Piaget's Preoperational Stage, Preconceptual Substage	
NONVERBAL CLASSIFICATION	
makes graphic collections	Allow child to create own classifications.
VERBAL PRECONCEPTS	
uses words differently at	Listen and ask for clarification of words used differently. different times
uses words with private meanings	Listen to child's words in context; reword or question to find meaning.
begins to label classes of objects	Repeat and identify class of object. Extend child's label to include other objects.

Child Behavior	Examples of Caregiver Strategies
focuses on one attribute	Reinforce classifications. Child has not yet formed stable classes of objects.
VERBAL REASONING	
reasons from particular to particular	Understand and accept child's classification of behaviors that seem alike. Ask for clarification if needed.
QUANTITY	
understands some, more, gone, big	Use quantity words in context with objects. Respond and expand on child's use.
NUMBER	
understands more	Use objects to identify more.
SPACE	
understands up, down, behind, under, over	Use spatial-position words with actions, e.g., "I will lift you up. I am putting you down on the floor."
TIME	
understands now, soon	Label actions in terms of time, e.g., "Let's wash your hands now."

Learning Skills/Language Development

Auditory and visual learning skills are the foundation of language. Children of this age are rapidly increasing their vocabulary. Their vocabulary may include as many as two to three hundred words. This is a time for space words.

> ". . . more new space words are added to the child's vocabulary in the six-month period from Two to Two-and-a-half than in any other six-month period . . . The increase in use of two space words combined gives exactness to location: 'right home,' 'way up,' 'in here,' 'under the table.' " (Ames & Ilg, 1980, 89).

Building on their use of language to name objects with single words, they proceed to a more complex structuring of language, the sentence. Anisfeld says that they *construct* sentences; they do not reproduce sentences from memory (1984, 113). Thus, the child has to think and select words that express the child's ideas in ways others can understand.

Anisfeld has identified several types in the child's development of mental associations.

Demonstrative naming: The first word in a demonstrative-naming phrase points out an object; the second names it, e.g., "this ball" or "here spoon."

Attribution: Children give objects a specific attribute, often using an adjective-noun combination, e.g., blue shoes. The attribute "blue" distinguishes one particular pair of shoes from all other items in a class of things called "shoes."

Possession: Children make special associations between a person and an object, often using a two-word sentence, e.g., "mommy chair."

Action: Action sentences separate the action from the actor and from the object and explore the relations among these three. Children's descriptions of their own or other's actions at this age include sentences like "ride big-wheel" and "I jump."

Recurrence: A recurrence sentence tells of a thing or event that happens again. Children often use "more" to express this, for example, "more juice," "more ride."

Negation: The negative sentences of children this age usually say that something desired or expected is not there or has disappeared or that the child cannot, is not permitted to, or does not want to do something. A child may say, "no car" or "no hit."

Children use many sentences that contain specific word patterns. They hear others use word patterns and then use these same word patterns over and over in their process of constructing language (Figure 15–5). Thus they learn to use word-order patterns common to their language, but they cannot tell you the basic rule or principle of word order they are using.

Another kind of patterning children learn is rhyme patterning. They learn emphasis and rhythm of word parts, words, and sentences along with the words themselves and syntax. For example, "*MY* ball" means something different from "my *ball*." Children learn to use the appropriate stress and intonation to express their specific ideas.

Many sentences young children use are incomplete. Very young children use subject-and-verb and verb-and-object sentences but seldom use subject-verb-and-

Figure 15–5 The repetitive lyrics of a song help a child learn proper word patterns.

object sentences. They also often omit function words, such as *on*, *in*, *a*, and *the*. They do this because they have to plan and coordinate all the parts (words) of their sentences. The more words they use, the more difficult it is for them to construct a sentence.

Children also extend their construction of language to include two ways of forming new words. They begin to use the plural and the past tense forms of words. By now children understand that there is more than one hand, or eye, or foot. They listen to others talking and learn that the word changes when referring to more than one hand. They then construct their words to include plurals, for example, *hands*, *eyes*, and so forth. However, at this age they apply the same plural rule to all words, making words such as *foots*. Applying the same kind of pluralization to all words is called overregularization or overgeneralization. When children can distinguish between what is happening now and what has happened previously, they can begin to use some words that are in the past tense, such as "I jumped." They also overregularize past tense forms, constructing words like "goed" and "seed."

Books contain language patterns, which serve as examples to children who are busily constructing language; therefore, you should read to children often. Children also can read books with pictures. These experiences provide practice in putting thoughts into oral language. Books will soon be selected frequently by toddlers.

"Play, according to many American child-development experts, offers children a way to discover who they are and who they can be (for example, see the 1980 book *Who Am I in the Lives of Children?* by Feeney et al.; Bergen's 1988 book *Play as a Medium for Learning and Development*; and Vivian Paley's 1986 *Boys and Girls: Superheros in the Doll Corner*). Children given the chance to enjoy a variety of experiences of play—role-playing, make-believe play, social play with peers, individual creative and artistic play, dyadic play with an adult—not only develop cognitively and socially but also become self-actualized." (Tobin & Davidson, 1989)

Written language is becoming more a part of the children's world. They see print at home, along the highway, and in other homes or centers. They look at the print in a book as the caregiver reads the story or tells the storyline. They see their own names on each of their own papers. They are eager to make their own marks. Writing opportunities can be provided to them in several ways.

Find or make a chalkboard—the larger the better for very young children. You can make one by painting a large, very sturdy piece of cardboard with chalkboard paint. Since your youngster is standing up and using pressure to write and draw, make the board very sturdy. One that bounces will be hard to write on and may frustrate children.

Put the chalkboard in a central location where it will get lots of use. A hallway or a child's room is a good place. Buy thick, soft chalk because regular-size chalk breaks easily. Although it's messier, soft chalk makes dark marks more easily than hard chalk.

Some children may be doing controlled scribbling, which has several characteristics.

"Gradually, after much playing around with markers, chalk, and crayons, your child's scribbles become more controlled. He begins to see the relationship between the marks he is making on paper and the writing utensil in his hand. His scribbles are more systematic. . . . The lines go up and down . . . or in circles. Dots may surround the picture. . . . He systematically scribbles with each marker in the box. . . . Later, as part of the scribble pattern, circles, triangles, arrows, and squares may emerge." (Lamme, 1984, 39–40)

Suggestions for Implementing Curriculum

Child Behavior	Materials	Examples of Caregiver Strategies
uses demonstrative naming	toys, objects	Point to and label objects, e.g., "a foot," "a hand," "a nose." Extend to sentence: "Mary has a foot; Myron has a foot."
uses attribution	toys, objects	Combine labels, e.g., "red car," "big book." Extend to sentence: "Ray has the red car; Twila has the green car."
uses possession	toys, objects	Identify and label. "Roger's shoe, Jenny's shoe."
uses action	toys, objects	Identify and label own and child's actions: "Urvi sits on the floor." "Stewart is eating."
uses recurrence		Use word patterns that indicate repeating or additional, e.g., at snack ask each child if he or she wants *more* apple.
uses negation		Use "no" with action, e.g., "No hitting; no kicking." Follow up commands with reasons.
learns word order		Use proper word order, e.g., "The truck moves." Extend child's "Move truck" to "Yes, the truck moves."
learns prosodic patterning		Use expression when talking. Accent the proper syllables. The child will imitate you.
uses subject-verb pattern		Use whole sentences. Expand the child's sentences.
uses verb-object pattern		Use whole sentences. Expand the child's sentences.
omits function words		Use whole sentences. Expand the child's sentences.
selects and uses books	picture books, story books	Read aloud. Listen to the child "read."
controls scribbling	markers, crayons, chalk, chalkboard, paper	Provide materials and space. Write labels and notes to the child. Share the child's scribbling.

Key Terms

action sentences

attribution

deferred imitation

demonstrative naming

language

mental images

negation

possession

preconceptual

recurrence

search for hidden objects

temper tantrums

terrible twos

CASE STUDY

Cathy is a sweet 26-month-old who comes from a family on welfare. She is given child care through the Department of Social Services and often comes to care without having eaten, poorly dressed, and unclean. Her mother is a 16-year-old day laborer with three other small children and has not be married.

A parent conference to explain the Developmental Profile and establish a Developmental Prescription for Cathy revealed that her mother is so overwhelmed, uneducated, and limited in her understanding of English that she will not be able to follow up on further evaluations outside the child care setting.

The child care staff had a meeting to establish a Developmental Prescription that would help Cathy overcome her general developmental delays.

Assume that you are a member of the staff.

1. List possible causes for Cathy's delays in each of the five major developmental areas.
2. List the steps you would take to help determine more clearly the causes for the general delays.
3. What family support could be provided that would help Cathy receive better care at home?

Student Activities

1. Observe a child 24 to 30 months old for 15 minutes during play time. Write a narrative description.
   a. Categorize the child's social behaviors.
   b. List behaviors that indicate preconceptual classifications.
   c. Practice word ordering; feed back extended words.
   d. List the kinds of representations the child used.
2. Make a theme picture book. Use it with a child. Observe the child's emotional reactions. Observe the child's language. Involve the child in rereading the book.
3. Make a puppet with a child using the theme ideas from the Celebration of Life Calendar that best relates to the child.

Chapter Review

1. List two developing physical accomplishments of a child 24 to 30 months old.
2. Describe a situation in which the child is asserting independence.
3. Write an example of the following language patterns.
   a. demonstrative naming
   b. attribution
   c. possession
   d. action
   e. recurrence
   f. negation

References

Ames, L. B., & Ilg, F. L. (1980). *Your two-year-old: Terrible or tender?* New York: Delacorte Press.

Anisfeld, M. (1984). *Language development from birth to three.* Hillsdale, NJ: Lawrence Erlbaum Associates.

Brickmeyer, J. (1978). *Guidelines for day care programs for migrant infants and toddlers.* New York: Bankstreet College.

Healy, J. (1989). *The child's growing mind: A guide to learning and brain development from birth to adolescence.* New York: Doubleday.

Lamme, L. L. (1991). *Growing up writing.* Washington, DC: Acropolis Books Ltd.

Tobin, W., & Davidson, D. (1989). *Preschool in three cultures.* New Haven, CT: Yale University.

Wadsworth, B. J. (1978). *Piaget for the classroom teacher.* New York: Longman.

Additional Resources

Stone, L. J., & Church, J. (1973). *Childhood and adolescence* (3rd ed.). New York: Random House.

Wilson, L. C. (1988). When toddlers play. *Pre-K Today, 2*(5), 36–37.

Helpful Web Sites

The Parent's Common Sense Encyclopedia. Tantrums. http://www.sleeptight.com/EncyMaster/T/tantrums.html

Talking with Toddlers and Two-Year-Olds. General guidelines for communicating with young children. http://www.nncc.org/Guidance/dc34_talk.toddlers.html

Terrible Twos: Helpful Hints, Dr. Alvin Eden, M.D. http://www.tnpc.com/parentalk/toddlers/todd29.html

Yes, You Can Spoil a Child . . . After the Age of Two Years Part 1. http://www.shpm.com/articles/parenting/index.shtml

Are Babies Smarter Than Adults? (brain growth in infants and toddlers). http://www.findarticles.com/cf_0/m1272/2655_128/58037920/p1/

Dr. Greene. Temper Tantrums? http://www.drgreene.com/toddlers.asp

For additional infant and toddler resources, visit our Web site at http://www.earlychilded.delmar.com

The Child from Thirty to Thirty-Six Months of Age

16

Objectives

After reading this chapter, you should be able to:

■ Identify and record sequences of change in the physical, emotional, social, cognitive, and language development of children from 30 to 36 months of age.

■ Select materials appropriate to that age-level child's development.

■ Devise strategies appropriate to that age-level child's development.

Chapter Outline

Materials and Activities
Caregiver Strategies to Enhance Development
Authors' Closing Note

Juan's Story

Juan, 35 months old, is playing in the play yard. He sits on a bigwheel and rolls backward, gets off and runs around with other children, picks at the ground and finds a grub, which he takes to show the caregiver. Juan walks around showing the grub to others, sits on a small trike, takes the grub and puts it by a tree trunk, sits on the ground, climbs a tree, climbs down and runs after a soccer ball, plops on a bigwheel, and then kicks a soccer ball back and forth with another child. At another time he again plays with a grub. When asked where the grub is, he stops, puts his hands up in the air and says, "He's dead." He finds another grub and shows it to the caregiver, saying, "He might be sleeping. Wake up, grub." The bug moves and rolls up again. Juan says, "He went to sleep again."

MATERIALS AND ACTIVITIES

Children this age are active, eager learners. They practice newly acquired skills and develop new ones. They like large muscle activity and are developing their fine muscles for more controlled manipulation of objects. They enjoy imaginative play. Their play incorporates their imagination, their language, and their understanding of themselves and others. They explore their world. They represent their ideas not only in play and language, but they also recognize pictures. They construct sentences to share their ideas (Figure 16–1). They listen to stories and enjoy and participate in rhymes, fingerplays, music, and singing. This age integrates well with themes for cultural diversity. Use the Celebration of Life Calendar for ideas.

Figure 16–1 Language experience charts expose the young child to the process of writing what is spoken.

Review Chapter 5. Use Appendix A, the Developmental Prescriptions, and Appendix B, the Developmental Profile, with each child. Children follow a *sequence* of development. There are often ranges in the *rate* of development.

Types of Materials

riding toys	markers, crayons, chalk, pens
wagon	wooden beads and string
trucks for hauling	rhythm instruments
rocking boat	records
tunnel, barrel to crawl through and on	tapes
cardboard blocks	dramatic play props
wooden unit block set	puppets
wooden people	books
wooden animals	materials to explore—feel, measure, use

Examples of Homemade Materials

PROP BOXES

Gather props for a specific story or role. For example, put a stethoscope, white shirt, and small pad of paper in a shoebox for doctor props. In a larger box put a child-sized firefighter's hat, boots, and poncho.

PUPPETS

Use cardboard tubes from paper towels. Cut paper to make face. Child uses markers or crayon to make face and clothes features. Glue face on tube.

BOOK: JOURNAL

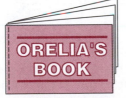

ORELIA'S BOOK

Sew or staple sheets of unlined paper together. Each morning ask child to identify one toy or activity he or she wants to play with. Write a sentence identifying what the child chose. Allow the child to scribble and draw on the page. Read the sentence to the child. Label book with the child's name. Send home each Friday.

WOODEN PEOPLE OR ANIMALS

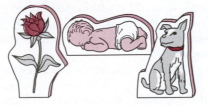

Draw or cut out of a magazine pictures of people: infants, children, adults; firefighter, police officer, doctor; or animals or other objects, such as cars or houses.

Glue pictures on a piece of 1-inch-thick white pine board. With a jigsaw, cut around the outside of the picture on three sides, cutting the bottom straight across. Sand the edges smooth. Apply two coats of nontoxic sealer. The object will stand up by itself.

Activity Ideas

Keeping records of informal observations, besides the records on the Developmental Profiles, will assist you in planning appropriate experiences for each child. Plan for a holistic curriculum. Identify your children's interests. Use these to focus your thematic units. Plan mostly individual activities. Some short small-group activities may be included, such as reading or telling a story, singing a song, saying a rhyme, or doing fingerplay. Each small-group activity is appropriate also for use with individuals.

Children construct physical knowledge by moving objects and observing changes in objects. They observe the effects of their pulling, pushing, rolling, kicking, jumping, blowing, sucking, throwing, swinging, twirling, balancing, and dropping objects. They observe changes in objects; for example, when they put a drop of blue food coloring in a clear glass of water. Offer materials and activities that help children discover the physical characteristics of objects.

Children construct logico-mathematical knowledge by inventing relationships among objects. Comparisons of quantity, number, space, and time are explorations into relating two or more objects or events in a new and abstract way. Children can seek relationships among any kinds of materials. Games and activities that use the invented relationships help stimulate and reinforce their constructions. For example, a bulletin board of all the children's handprints provides opportunities for each child to place his or her hands over other children's handprints and make comparisons.

Children learn social-arbitrary knowledge from other people. They learn language from people. They learn the names of objects, meanings of words, intonations in pronouncing words, and word order and syntax from others. They learn the rules for living from others. They learn valuing from others. The caregiver bears the major responsibility in the child care program for providing this information and helping the child construct social-arbitrary knowledge. The child's physical, emotional, social, and cognitive development are all involved in constructing social-arbitrary knowledge.

CAREGIVER STRATEGIES TO ENHANCE DEVELOPMENT

Developmental Profile

Juan was observed over a five-day period as he performed the Child Behaviors of the Developmental Prescription in Appendix A. The resulting Developmental Profile, is presented in Figure 16–2, indicates that Juan functions at or above age expectancies in all areas except Learning Skills (V), where he is estimated to function seven to eight months below age.

Specifically, Juan exhibits skills slightly above age expectancies in "muscle control" (36 months) and "sleeping" (40 months) within the Physical Area (I).

He also exhibits age-level skills in Emotional (II), Social (III), and Cognitive (IV) Areas. In fact, his Cognitive skills in "verbal responding," "classification," and "quality" are slightly above age expectancies.

However, Juan exhibits some significant perceptual and language skill delays. His "visual-motor control" is slightly below age (33 months), and "auditory skills" (26 months), "visual skills" (30 months), and "language skills" (29 months) are significantly low. Juan has difficulty expressing himself verbally, recalling what he sees and

Name: **Juan S.**

Date: **12/17/XX**

Date of Birth: **1/15/XX**

C.A.: **35 months 2 days**

MONTH AGE EXPECT.	AREA I PHYSICAL				AREA II EMOTIONAL			AREA III SOCIAL			AREA IV COGNITIVE				AREA V LEARNING SKILLS				MONTH AGE EXPECT.
	MUSCLE CONTROL	SLEEP	EAT	ELIMINATION	FEELINGS TYPE	CONTROL FEELINGS	TEMPERAMENT	SELF	OTHERS	CONTROL	VERBAL REASON	CLASSIFICATION	QUANTITY	SPACE-TIME	VIS-MOTOR	AUDITORY	VISUAL	LANGUAGE	
49+																			49+
47																			47
45																			45
43																			43
41																			41
39																			39
37																			37
35																			35
33																			33
31																			31
29																			29
27																			27
25																A*			25
23																			23
21–																			21–

C.A. (left and right margins at the 35/33 row)

Notes: A* = Better visual than auditory–language skills lower than cognitive skills.

Figure 16–2 Developmental Profile, Juan S.

hears (visual and auditory memory), discriminating differences between pictures and words (visual and auditory discrimination), and perceiving similarities in what he sees and hears (visual and auditory association). He is a somewhat better visual than auditory learner, although both channels are below age expectancies.

In summary, Juan is a healthy 35-month-old who functions at or above age level in all areas except Learning Skills (V). Juan exhibits significant enough lags in visual, auditory, and language skills to warrant further evaluation for possible learning disabilities. The caregiver should have a conference with the parents to go over the profile and discuss the need for further evaluations in learning skills and language areas.

A specific program of Caregiver Strategies to improve visual, auditory, and language skills should be combined with tasks and activities in all other areas to ensure a balanced program for Juan.

Physical Development

Children of this age are increasing their stability in both fast and slow movements. They walk evenly both quickly and slowly. They can walk backward. They run quickly and usually maintain their balance. They can alternate feet going upstairs. They can master a tricycle. They jump up and down, they jump off objects, and they jump forward. They can twist and turn to dress and undress, and they can use their small muscles to hold clothes and attempt buttoning, snapping, and zippering. They practice their physical skills. Right- or left-handedness is now established, though children use both hands in many activities (Figure 16–3).

At this age children can establish sleep routines which they can do themselves. Before nap they can go to the bathroom and wash their hands. They can sit on their cots, take their own shoes off, and put the shoes under the cot. They can lie down with their heads near their name tapes. When they awaken, they can go to the bathroom

Figure 16–3 The caregiver allows the child to use crayons in either or both hands even though handedness may be established.

and return to put on their shoes. If others are still sleeping, they can choose a quiet activity, such as looking at books or listening to a story or music with earphones.

Most children have completed toilet-training by 36 months of age. They need to wear clothes they can remove quickly and easily. They need easy access to the bathroom, and they need occasional questions and reminders to go to the bathroom.

Suggestions for Implementing Curriculum

Child Behavior	Examples of Caregiver Strategies
Muscular Control	
MOVEMENT AND COORDINATION	
walks evenly	Provide uncluttered floor space.
runs	Provide space and games for appropriate running.
jumps in place and forward	Play games, sing songs that encourage jumping.
dresses and undresses self with assistance	Allow time for child to manipulate clothes.
	Demonstrate how to hold button and buttonholes, zipper and cloth, and so on.
uses fine motor coordination	Turns one page at a time.
HAND	
has established handedness	Allow child to select hand to use.
Sleeping	
assists with preparation routines	Plan time in schedule for children to do as much of routines as possible. It takes longer for a child to wash and dry hands than if you help, but child needs to be independent and to develop skills. Help with tight snaps and so on.
Elimination	
is in process of or has completed toilet training	Provide assistance when needed. Assist with clothes and hand washing when needed. Clean up area. *Wash your hands.*

Emotional Development

Children of this age express their emotions and feelings strongly. They let you know how they feel and then may move beyond their anger or happiness and soon express a different feeling.

These children's negativism is expressed in several ways. Sometimes negative behavior is a way of asserting themselves and their independence.

These children are enthusiastic learners, enjoying themselves and their discoveries. Their developing mastery of skills enhances their feelings of competence, self-worth, and acceptance of self (Figure 16–4).

These children may become physically aggressive. Their widening world presents many new experiences. They may use aggression in their attempts to feel they have some control of their world.

Figure 16–4 When young children continually make new discoveries, they become enthusiastic learners.

At about 33 months they will begin to think in terms of their own past and may pretend to be a baby again. This regression may be a need based on their own development or the presence of a new baby in the family. Whatever the cause, these toddlers need lots of the 3A's and the time and patience to regain their proper place in their environment.

Persistence in continuing a task enables these children to discover many things. As they explore, their persistence will probably enable them to accomplish enough so that they have the feeling that "I did it" or "See what I found out." Children generally discover the love of learning when they are offered developmentally correct choices and are positively praised for their decisions by the caregiver who combines the 3A's of Child Care: Attention, Approval, and Affection. This love of learning is obvious when the child has a long attention span and displays great persistence in finishing a task. A short attention span, however, limits a child's exposure and involvement in many activities.

Suggestions for Implementing Curriculum

Child Behavior	Examples of Caregiver Strategies
Types of Emotions-Feelings	
reacts strongly	Accept child's initial response. Help child keep within bounds of appropriate behavior, e.g., let child express anger by vigorously riding a bigwheel for a while, drawing an angry picture, or punching a pillow.
acts negatively	Rephrase suggestions to child. Stimulate interest in a different activity.

Child Behavior	*Examples of Caregiver Strategies*
learns enthusiastically	Reinforce child's excitement with learning. Provide opportunities for challenging experiences.
is mastering skills	Provide toys, equipment, and materials that the child needs to use often to master skills.
Control of Emotions-Feelings	
is physically aggressive	Provide activities for child to work out feelings and need to control, such as using a puppet for imaginary play or letting the child be a leader in a structured activity. Paint, draw, use clay, dance or, if possible, be out of doors to run, jump, and yell.
Temperament	
activity level	List two of the child's behaviors in each category that indicate the child's basic style. List adjustments you need to make to help the child cope with daily situations.
regularity	
approach or withdrawal as a characteristic	
adaptability to change in routine	
level of sensory threshold	
positive or negative mood	
intensity of response	
distractibility	
persistence and attention span	

Social Development

Egocentrism continues to be present in the preconceptual substage. Even though young children can distinguish themselves from others, they are only slowly developing the ideas that follow from this. They are just beginning to understand that others have feelings. They assume that when they speak, everyone understands the exact meaning of their words; they do not realize that others may give different meanings to the same words or experiences.

Young children interpret changes in appearance to mean changes in the basic object or person. "Preconceptual children generally do not see things or people as having a core and consistent identity over time" (Cowan, 1978, 133). This fluctuation includes their concepts of self. "They seem to have little idea that their 'self' of a few days ago is relevant to what is happening now, today" (Cowan, 1978, 133).

Children continue to identify their "selfness" within their world. Their toys are a part of themselves, and they remain very possessive of the toys and materials they are using. However, their strengthening sense of self also provides a foundation for expanding interactions with others. Children this age are increasingly aware of others as individuals. They use adults as resources, seeking assistance from them when they decide they need help (Figure 16–5). They become directive with others, exerting control over people, animals, and toys as they learn ways to control their world. Children

Figure 16–5 The caregiver is available to share materials and attention.

this age sometimes recognize others' needs and may help with tasks or initiate or respond with assistance.

These children's self-control is increasing. Their desire for instant gratification is being modified, so they sometimes accept delayed gratification. They may take turns occasionally. At times they may decide to share, and they may play cooperatively for short periods of time. The research strongly suggests that it is the felt experience, over and over and over again, of being cooperated with; the experience of having an important adult put aside his or her own needs to meet the child's very real needs; the experience of that important adult showing empathy, concern, respect, and nurturance toward the baby or toddler that begins to ingrain in that child the deepest sense of these prosocial qualities (Wolf, 1986).

Suggestions for Implementing Curriculum

Child Behavior	Examples of Caregiver Strategies
Self	
acts possessive	Provide enough toys and materials so child can control use of some of them for a time.
Others	
seeks assistance	Allow child to use you as a resource. Help where needed. Do not take over.
directs others	Provide opportunities for child to exert acceptable control over others.
helps others	Praise child's spontaneous helping. Ask for assistance so child can help with routines and so forth.

Child Behavior	*Examples of Caregiver Strategies*
Control of Self	
plays cooperatively	Provide toys, materials, and time.
shares	Encourage by providing opportunities to share, e.g., when eating orange or apple slices.
takes turns	Use daily routines to help control wasiting time, e.g., taking turns to wash hands.

Cognitive Development

CDA II.5

Children at this age are curious, exploring problem-solvers. They are seeking to discover what makes things tick, what objects are made of, and how actions happen. They use observing, questioning, manipulating, classifying, and measuring to learn about their world.

In the preconceptual stage children may attempt to put objects in an order, like biggest to smallest buttons, but unless the materials present cues, such as fitting together, the children are not able to determine the logic of ordering. **Arranging objects** in a series is guesswork for young children because they do not understand the relationships in a series of objects.

These children continue to construct physical knowledge about the properties of objects (Figure 16–6). They construct logico-mathematical knowledge about relationships. And they construct social-arbitrary knowledge about language and social rules and values.

Figure 16–6 Blocks, pegs, and other manipulatives provide cues to young children for matching shapes.

Adults and children understand experiences differently. Even if both a child and an adult were present during the same experience, each would learn and experience something different.

Jane Healy, in her book *Your Child's Growing Mind* (1989), gives several ways to help "bridge the schema" (fill in) gaps.

1. As you solve problems together, talk through your own questions. "I wonder how I should start?" "Could I put them together?" "Is it working?" "What's going to happen?" "How did I do?"
2. Ask your child similar questions.
3. Phrase them simply and give the child plenty of time to think and answer.
4. Let the child repeat each solution several times to understand it.
5. Encourage understanding. Ask "Why do you think that happened?" "Why did/didn't that work?"

At around 36 months, depending upon temperament, children calm down. They become less resistant and use words like "yes" and "will" to replace the earlier "no" and "won't." The three-year-old is generally a happy, secure and somewhat conforming person, for a few months at least. Often you will hear the child repeat back to you the 3A's that you have given him or her over and over again.

Suggestions for Implementing Curriculum

Child Behavior	Examples of Caregiver Strategies
Piaget's Preoperational Stage, Preconceptual Substage	
NONVERBAL CLASSIFICATION	
makes graphic collections	Encourage child to use art media to represent. Listen to child's explanation of own classification system.
VERBAL PRECONCEPTS	
uses words differently at different times	Observe context of talk. Ask for clarification of meaning if necessary.
labels objects in one class	Remember that child's meaning may not be as inclusive as yours. Determine exactly what child meant.
VERBAL REASONING	
thinks one action is like another action	Observe the behavior that precedes a child's talking. Determine how child is drawing relationships among his or her actions.
reasons from effect to cause	Think backward from action to previous action to understand child's reasoning.
QUANTITY	
understands some, more, gone, big	Use words labeling quantity. They are a part of the daily experiences.
NUMBER	
understands more	Use words labeling number as a comparative. Use daily situations, e.g., "There are more rocks in this pail than in that pail."

Child Behavior	Examples of Caregiver Strategies
SPACE	
understands up, down, behind, under, over	Label child's actions when child is moving into different positions in space, e.g., "Merrilee is behind the box. Ashton is under the box."
TIME	
understands now, soon, before, after	Use time words in daily experiences, e.g., "We wash our hands before we eat." "We go to the bathroom after naptime."

Learning Skills/Language Development

Visual and auditory perceptual skills should be learned daily. Children this age continue to increase their vocabulary. Their daily experiences provide opportunities for them to construct meanings of new objects and to extend previously learned concepts. The labeling process is now part of children's construction of the identity of objects.

These children continue to overregularize words. However, more and more of their plural words are formed correctly. These children are very gradually constructing concepts of time, and most of their new time words come during this period. The past is still an abstraction they are attempting to understand. They still overregularize past tense verbs, saying things like, "Jim bited me" and "I bringed these out."

Sentence length increases as children increase their use and familiarity with frequently used vocabulary, word-order patterns, and stress and intonation patterns. They speak more complete sentences and are able to express several ideas in a sequence of sentences.

Dramatic play provides opportunities to combine language with imagination. These children can describe their actions and say what they think others might say. They are practicing their language and fitting it into a social context.

Books play an increasingly important role. Reading aloud provides book language patterns. Reading the pictures encourages self-expression, and talking about the story or the pictures facilitates comprehension of the language (Figure 16–7).

Scribbling continues as the child is involved in the writing process. Each child is developing scribbling at his or her own rate.

"Children are scribblers from the time they hold a writing tool until after they learn to write their names. There is a progression to their scribbles which moves from random scribbling, to controlled scribbling, to the naming of scribbling, to writing mock letters and words, to learning, finally, how to write. It is important not to underestimate the value of scribbling as a foundation for writing." (Lamme, 1984, 37)

Caroline Columbus, a nationally recognized forensic handwriting analyst, discusses the importance of encouraging children to express themselves through scribbling.

With the advent of computers the written word is being replaced by the printed word. It is important to allow children to develop their own writing

Figure 16–7 Books stimulate involvement in making and reading familiar stories.

integrity by encouraging scribbling which by its simple free nature will later develop into handwriting skills (Columbus 98).

You model many uses of writing for children. You write their names. You write a note to their parents. You write sentences on their art work papers. You write dictated sentences on their pages of scribbling. You write charts about daily experiences; for example, planting beans and writing on the chart what they look like each day. In this way, the children experience meaningful uses of writing.

Suggestions for Implementing Curriculum

Child Behavior	Materials	Examples of Caregiver Strategies
Increases vocabulary		
associates word and object		Introduce new objects to see and feel and use. Label objects and actions with single words and use in sentences.
Improves syntax		
word order		Repeat child's sentence, using proper word order.
two- and three-word sentences		Respond to child's meaning. Extend the sentence.
longer sentences		Respond to child's meaning. Commend his or her ideas.

Child Behavior	Materials	Examples of Caregiver Strategies
Improves word forms		
uses plurals		Use correct plural form. When child says "foots," restate the word, e.g., "See your feet."
uses past tense		Use correct past tense. When child says "He bited me," restate: "He bit you? Show me where he bit you."
Improves reading skills		
listens to stories, "reads" pictures and storybooks	records, pictures, picture books	Read aloud. Listen to child "read." Use expression. Tell or read story line.
uses controlled scribbling	markers, chalk, crayons, pencil, paper	Write to child. Write notes to child and others. Label objects. Write dictated sentences.

Fun in the Kitchen

Teaching about food, cooking, and kitchen safety is fun and important. Even nonverbal, very young children should be told what they are eating—why it is important and what shape, color, and category of food it is—to encourage a healthy respect for the needs of the body; the joys of taste, smell, and texture; and the ability to share and have a growth experience.

- All participants must wash their hands well before doing this food-related activity.
- No child with a cold (or disease symptoms of any kind), cuts, or abrasions may have direct contact with food.
- Children who touch their noses during the activity must stop and wash their hands again before continuing.
- All children should have a job and a place to sit or stand.
- All participants should take turns.
- No one talks when someone else is talking.
- Everyone reaps the rewards of the end product.

Making Pancakes (20 minutes) The caregiver prepares all cups, spoons, plates, and ingredients before children are invited to participate. No styrofoam products of any kind should be used.

- Each person does one thing to facilitate batter preparation.
- A low-heat electric pan is used in front of children. All children watch the demonstration. Heat, electricity, and cooking safety are discussed. Children watch at arm's distance from the hot pan.
- All help set the table.
- Everyone enjoys eating the finished pancakes.

Other Food Activities

The following two examples can be adapted to other teaching experiences, depending on the age of the children.

Hold a tea party, using real decaffeinated herb teas. Each tea has a different color, smell, and taste.

To acquaint the child with vegetables, use the tops of broccoli. Pretend they are trees and the children are giants. Dip the tree into vanilla yogurt (each child has a separate portion). Discuss the color, texture, variety, and importance of vegetables. You can use other vegetables, such as jicama or slightly steamed sweet potato.

Both food lessons should use the time to discuss how different people from different parts of the world have different vegetables, fruits, and foods. Involve one mother at a time; ask her and her child to bring in their family's favorite foods or different ethnic favorite foods and snack. Discuss this concept with the other children.

Remember that you are promoting successful future eating habits. A well-balanced diet is essential. The concept of "no garbage" in our bodies is important to help children choose the best fuel to obtain healthy bodies, calm minds, and a state of well-being.

Key Terms

arranging objects
dramatic play
scribbling

CASE STUDY

Juan exhibited average or above-average growth in all areas except Learning Skills. In his home, his parents and four siblings speak only Spanish. Rosa, a Spanish-speaking child care specialist held a parent conference to explain the Developmental Profile and help establish a Developmental Prescription for Juan. Both of his parents were very concerned about Juan's language and learning skill delays and wanted to take immediate action to help him. Rosa explained that the staff would have a meeting to set up a Developmental Prescription and she would meet with the parents to go over the steps necessary to help Juan.

A program was begun in individual focal attention training; memory, discrimination, and association training; naming and labeling; and concept formation. Rosa was assigned the task of finding appropriate Spanish-speaking professionals to conduct further assessments of Juan. After getting appropriate recommendations, Rosa met with Juan's parents, and further speech, language, and learning skill evaluations were scheduled.

1. List the professionals that Juan should be referred to for evaluation.
2. What family support should be given to help Juan?
3. Describe how you would conduct learning skill training in focal attention, memory, discrimination, and association with Juan on an individual basis.

Student Activities

1. Observe one child for 10 minutes in a play yard. Write a list of the child's activities. Identify equipment and materials used.
2. Observe one child for 10 minutes in a play yard. Tally the times the child shares a toy or equipment. Tally the times the child plays *with* another child.
3. Observe a caregiver for five minutes. Write down the dialogue the caregiver has with a child or with several children. Categorize the caregiver's statements that mirror, support, or respond to the child's statements.
4. Observe children at play. List the language and actions that indicate their developing concepts of quantity, number, space, and time.
5. Plan and use one activity with a child to facilitate the child's construction of physical knowledge.
6. Plan and use one activity with a child to facilitate the child's construction of logico-mathematical knowledge.
7. Plan and use one activity with a child to facilitate the child's construction of social-arbitrary knowledge.

Chapter Review

1. List three tasks children this age can complete by themselves.
2. List four tasks children can assist you with.
3. Describe one way to deal with an angry child.
4. Write one example of a child's statement that uses a word to which the child has given a meaning different from that which adults give the word.
5. Compare how children learn physical knowledge, logico-mathematical knowledge, and social-arbitrary knowledge.

References

Columbus, C. (1998). *Open discussion on handwriting analysis.* Raymond, NH: Self-published.
Cowan, P. A. (1978). *Piaget with feeling.* New York: Holt, Rinehart & Winston.
Healy, J. (1989). *Your child's growing mind: A guide to learning and brain development from birth to adolescence.* New York: Doubleday.
Lamme, L. L. (1984). *Growing up writing.* Washington, DC: Acropolis Books Ltd.
Wolf, D. P. (1986). *Connecting: Friendship in the lives of young children and their teachers.* Washington, DC: Exchange Press.

Additional Resources

Cohen, J. (1997). *Program for social and emotional learning.* New York: Teachers College, Columbia University.
White, B. L. (1973). *The first three years of life.* Englewood Cliffs, NJ: Prentice-Hall.

Helpful Web Sites

KidsPoint. You and Me Program, designed for toddlers ages 18–36 months.
http://www.healthpointfitness.com/kidspoint/toddlers.html

Children and Divorce. The Different Age Stages: 18 months/3 Years (Toddlers).
http://www.divorcesource.com/info/children/toddlers.shtml

KidsHealth. The Power of Play. How play helps your child's development.
http://kidshealth.org/parent/growth/learning/power_play_prt.htm

National Network for Child Care. Ages & Stages–Three-Year-Olds. http://www.
nncc.org/Child.Dev/ages.stages.3y.html

Preschool and Beyond. Learning to identify a quality preschool.
http://babyparenting.about.com/cs/preschoolbeyond/index.htm

Speech and Hearing Skills Evaluation Checklist: Age 3. Calculator for milestones.
http://www.babycenter.com/calculator/6783.html

For additional infant and toddler resources, visit our Web site at
http://www.earlychilded.delmar.com

SUMMARY: CLOSING NOTE

The beginning of the twenty-first century found the huge gap between humankind's intellectual development and emotional development even more obvious. With the advent of an operational definition and curricula for teaching emotional intelligence and research suggesting only moderate correlation with cognitive intelligence, we now have the knowledge and skills necessary to improve the humanity of the next generation. As a caregiver of infants and toddlers, you have an essential position to ensure that our offspring learn how to interact humanely and intimately with other people, develop healthy self-esteem, maintain a balance between thinking and feeling, and improve the quality of life experience.

You are in the unique position to assist education and society in changing from an exclusive emphasis on cognitive and behavioral skills to greater emphasis on a state of being at ease with ourselves, regardless of environmental circumstances. By placing importance on the emotional and social development of children, as well as the other major areas of physical, cognitive, and learning skills, you can significantly help create a social structure in which compassion, understanding, and ethical behavior is valued and practiced.

Caregivers of children from birth through the toddler age are in an ideal position to lay the foundation for emotionally and socially intelligent individuals. Your abilities to practice self-health and sensitively care for young children will determine the course of development for individuals and society in the twenty-first century. Congratulations on your choice of the most important position in society!

—Michael and Linda D. Watson

Developmental Prescriptions

APPROXIMATELY BIRTH TO FOUR MONTHS OF AGE

Child Behavior	Date First Observed	Practicing	Proficient

Physical Development

MUSCULAR CONTROL

Reflex

  Grasp reflex

  Startle reflex

  Tonic neck reflex

Head and neck

  Turns head

  Holds head upright with support

  Lifts head slightly when on stomach

  Holds head to sides and middle

  Holds up head when on back and on stomach

  Holds head without support

Trunk

  Holds up chest

  Sits with support

  May attempt to raise self

  May fuss if left lying down with little chance to sit up

  Holds up chest and shoulders

Leg

  Rolls from stomach to back

Child Behavior	Date First Observed	Practicing	Proficient

Arm

    Moves randomly

    Reaches

Hand

    Opens and closes

    Keeps hands open

    Plays with hands

    Uses hands to grasp object

        Whole hand and fingers against thumb

        Thumb and forefinger

        Holds and moves object

Eye-hand coordination

    Moves arm toward object; may miss it

    Reaches hand to object; may grab or miss it

SEEING

    Focuses 8 inches from eyes

    Follows with eyes

    Stares

    See objects beyond 8 inches

    Looks from object to object

    Looks around; stops to focus on object which has caught attention; then looks at something else; continual visual searching

HEARING

    Responds to voice

    Hears range of sounds

    Calms while hearing low-pitched sounds

    Becomes agitated while hearing high-pitched sounds

    Locates sound

SLEEPING

    Sleeps much of the day and night

    Takes a long morning nap and a long afternoon nap

    May have irregular sleep habits

EATING

    Takes bottle on demand

ELIMINATION

    Begins to establish predictable eating and elimination pattern

    Establishes regular time for bowel movements

Child Behavior	Date First Observed	Practicing	Proficient

Emotional Development

TYPES OF EMOTIONS-FEELINGS

    Shows excitement

    Shows stress

    Shows enjoyment

    Shows anger

    Shows fear

    Protests

CONTROL OF EMOTIONS-FEELINGS

    Seems to occur automatically

    Decreases crying

    Increases sounds (talking)

    Reflects sounds (talking)

    Comforted by holding

TEMPERAMENT (List two behaviors that indicate basic style.)

    Activity level

    Regularity

    Approach or withdrawal as a characteristic response to a new situation

    Adaptability to change in routine

    Level of sensory threshold

    Positive or negative mood

    Intensity of response

    Distractibility

    Persistence and attention span

Social Development

ATTACHMENT

    Shows special closeness to parent

    Develops familiarity with one primary caregiver

SELF

    Becomes aware of hands and feet

    Smiles spontaneously

    Smiles at self in mirror

OTHERS

    Establishes eye contact with another person

    Recognizes voice of parent

    Smiles at people (social smile)

    Watches people

    Talks (cooing) to people

Child Behavior	Date First Observed	Practicing	Proficient

Shows longer attentiveness when involved with people

Recognizes parent visually

Recognizes individual people

Behaves differently with parent than with others

Interacts with people

Laughs

Differentiates self from parent

Initiates talking to others

Plays with toys

Cognitive Development

SENSORIMOTOR STAGE 1

Reflexive actions

Passive to active search

SENSORIMOTOR STAGE 2

Small, gradual changes come from repetition

Coordination of behaviors, e.g., sound-looking

Puts hand, object in mouth and sucks on it

Moves hand, object where can see it

Produces a pleasurable motor activity and repeats activity

OBJECT PERMANENCE

Follows moving object with eyes until object disappears.
Looks where object disappeared

Loses interest and turns away

Does not search for it

Language Development

PHYSICAL COMPONENTS INVOLVED IN LANGUAGE COMMUNICATION

Back of throat

Nose

Mouth cavity

Front of mouth

Tongue

Lips

Saliva

ACTIONS INVOLVED IN LANGUAGE COMMUNICATION

Changes air flow: through nose; through mouth

Uses tongue to manipulate air flow, saliva

Plays with tongue—twists, turns, sticks it out, sucks on it

Child Behavior	Date First Observed	Practicing	Proficient

Uses saliva in various places and changes sounds: gurgle in back of throat; bubbling in center of mouth; hissing, spitting with partially closed lips and tongue

INITIATION–RESPONDING

Initiates making sounds

Responds vocally to another person

Makes sound, repeats sound, continues practicing sound and lengthening to longer amounts of time

Imitates a few sounds he or she already knows

Experiments with sounds

CRYING

Cries apparently automatically in distress, frustration

Cries differently to express hunger, discomfort, anger

Cries to gain attention

Cries less as vocalizing increases

COOING

Coos in vowel-like sounds

Adds pitch

APPROXIMATELY FOUR TO EIGHT MONTHS OF AGE

Child Behavior	Date First Observed	Practicing	Proficient

Physical Development

MUSCULAR CONTROL

Head and neck

Holds head up independently

Holds head in midline position

Holds head up when on back, stomach, and sitting

Trunk

Holds up chest, shoulders; arches back, hips

Sits with support

May attempt to raise self

May fuss if left lying down with little chance to sit up

Leans back and forth

Sits in a chair

Sits unsupported for short time

Pushes self to sitting position

Child Behavior	Date First Observed	Practicing	Proficient

Leg

    Lifts legs when on back and stomach

    Rolls from stomach to back

    Straightens legs when standing

    Stamps feet when standing

    Rolls from back to stomach

    Raises self to hands and knees

    Stands with support

    Pulls self to standing

Locomotion

    Kicks against surface to move

    Rocks on hands and knees

    Creeps on stomach

    Uses legs to pull, push self when sitting

Arm

    Visually directs reaching, hitting

    Throws objects

Hand

    Grasps objects with whole hand and fingers against thumb

    Uses thumb and forefinger

    Picks up object with one hand; passes it to the other hand

    Uses objects in both hands

    Grasps and releases objects

    Drops objects

SEEING

    Focuses on objects near and far

    Distinguishes color, distance; depth perception

    Distinguishes visually attractive objects

    Has visual preferences

HEARING

    Listens to own voice

    Listens to others' voices

    Looks around to locate sound

SLEEPING

    Takes a long morning nap and a long afternoon nap

EATING

    Begins solid foods (new tongue and swallowing technique)

    Drinks from cup (new tongue and swallowing technique)

Child Behavior	Date First Observed	Practicing	Proficient

  Eats at "mealtimes"—solid foods, milk, juice

  Feeds self finger foods

TEETH

  First teeth emerge: 2 middle lower, 2 middle upper

ELIMINATION

  Decreases number of times of urination and bowel movements

Emotional Development

TYPES OF EMOTIONS-FEELINGS

  Shows pleasure in watching others

  Shows pleasure in repetitive play

  Shows depression

  Shows fear: of strangers; of falling down

  Shows frustration with stimulation overload

  Shows happiness, delight, joy, humor

  Shows rage

CONTROL OF EMOTIONS-FEELINGS

  Sometimes stops crying when talked to, sung to

TEMPERAMENT (List two behaviors that indicate basic style.)

  Activity level

  Regularity

  Approach or withdrawal as a characteristic response to a new situation

  Adaptability to change in routine

  Level of sensory threshold

  Positive or negative mood

  Intensity of response

  Distractibility

  Persistence and attention span

Social Development

ATTACHMENT

  Shows strong attachment to parent

  Differentiates response to parent

  Shows familiarity with one specific caregiver

  Shows intense pleasure and frustration to person with whom attached

SELF

  Recognizes self in mirror

  Seeks independence in actions

  Plays self-designed games

Child Behavior	Date First Observed	Practicing	Proficient

OTHERS

  Observes others

  Imitates others

  Recognizes children

  Plays with people

  Seeks parent's and caregiver's attention by movement, sounds, smiles, cries

    Follows parent and caregiver to be in same room

    Resists pressures from others regarding feeding and eating

    Acts shy with some strangers

Cognitive Development

SENSORIMOTOR STAGE 3

  Produces a motor activity, catches interest, and intentionally repeats the activity over and over

  Repeats interesting action

  Develops hand-eye coordination further

  Looks for object, reaches for it, and accurately touches it

  Imitates behavior the child can see or hear

OBJECT PERMANENCE: STAGE 3

  Visually follows object

  Searches visually for short time when object disappears

  Does not search manually

  Sees part of object; looks for whole object

Language Development

Coos vowel-like sounds for many minutes

Babbles syllable-like sounds

Responds to talking by cooing, babbling, smiling

Imitates sounds

Initiates sounds

Makes vowel sounds. Looks for person speaking

Looks when name is called

Makes consonant sounds

Babbles conversation with others

Reflects happiness, unhappiness in sounds made

Babbles two- and three-syllable sounds

Uses intensity, volume, pitch, and rhythm

APPROXIMATELY EIGHT TO TWELVE MONTHS OF AGE

Child Behavior	Date First Observed	Practicing	Proficient

Physical Development

MUSCULAR CONTROL

Trunk and leg

Raises self to sitting position

Sits alone

Stands holding onto furniture or hand

Stands without assistance

Sits from standing

Squats and stands

Locomotion

Crawls

Steps forward

Crawls up steps

Steps sideways

Walks with help

Climbs on furniture

Hand

Uses thumb and forefinger

Uses thumb and two fingers

Brings both hands to middle of body

Uses finger to poke

Carries objects in hands

Holds and uses pen and crayon

Reaches, touches, strokes object

Uses one hand to hold object, one hand to reach and explore

Stacks blocks with dominant hand

Takes off clothes

SLEEPING

May have trouble sleeping

Takes morning nap and afternoon nap

Seeks parent or caregiver presence

EATING

Holds bottle

Holds cup

Child Behavior	Date First Observed	Practicing	Proficient

Holds and uses spoon

Uses fingers to eat most food

Starts establishing food preferences

May eat less

TEETH

Begins to get teeth

Emotional Development

TYPES OF EMOTIONS-FEELINGS

Shows happiness, joy, pleasure

Shows anxiety

Shows fear

Shows anger, frustration

May have tantrums

Rejects items, situations

Develops preferences with toys, people

Shows independence—helps with feeding and dressing self

Shows affection

Begins developing self-esteem

CONTROL

Learning to obey "No."

Sometimes inhibits own behavior

Obeys commands: No-No, Stop

TEMPERAMENT (List two behaviors that indicate basic style.)

Activity level

Regularity

Approach or withdrawal as a characteristic response to a new situation

Adaptability to change in routine

Level of sensory threshold

Positive or negative mood

Intensity of response

Distractibility

Persistence and attention span

Social Development

OTHERS

Initiates interactions with others

Responds

Child Behavior	Date First Observed	Practicing	Proficient

May fear strangers

Keeps parent or caregiver in sight

Initiates play

Begins to identify with children of own sex

Becomes assertive

Wants own pleasure; may not consider others

Imitates play

Is possessive of people

Is possessive of materials

May become shy, clinging

May demand attention

Cognitive Development

SENSORIMOTOR STAGE 4

Differentiates goals

Can focus on reaching and focus on toy

Object permanence

Object permanence established; object exists when it is no longer visible; child seeks toy that rolls behind object

Causality

Understands that others cause actions

Imitation and play

Imitates other's actions; uses actions as play

Language Development

Babbles

Shouts

Labels object sounds

Uses names: mama, dada

Responds to familiar sounds

Responds to familiar words

Responds to own name

Makes sounds which reflect emotions

Repeats syllables, words, e.g., bye-bye

Makes sounds like conversation

Repeats, practices word over and over

Connects word with objects: says word and points to object

APPROXIMATELY TWELVE TO EIGHTEEN MONTHS OF AGE

Child Behavior	Date First Observed	Practicing	Proficient

Physical Development

MUSCULAR CONTROL

Trunk

Shows high energy, is active, moves from one activity to another

Raises self to standing

Locomotion

May prefer crawling to walking

Walks alone

Climbs up stairs with help

Climbs down stairs with help

Climbs over objects

Hand

Uses thumb against fingers

Shows hand preference

Points with finger

Carries, exchanges objects in hands

Flings objects

Throws objects

Rolls and catches objects

Eye-hand coordination

Reaches and grasps accurately

Scribbles

Helps in dressing, undressing

SEEING

Watches people, objects, actions

Bends, looks from different directions

Visually scans surrounding area

Visually searches

SLEEPING

Begins to move from morning and afternoon nap to afternoon nap

EATING

Eats three meals

Feeds self; uses cup, spoon, and fingers

Expresses food likes and dislikes

May eat less food

Child Behavior	Date First Observed	Practicing	Proficient

Emotional Development

TYPES OF EMOTIONS-FEELINGS

Expresses emotions in behavior and language

Recognizes emotions in others

May fear strangeness

Shows excitement, delight

Expresses sense of humor

Shows affection

Displays negativism

May have tantrums

Uses play to express emotions, resolve conflicts

Seeks dependency, security with parent and caregiver

Seeks to expand independence

CONTROL OF EMOTIONS-FEELINGS

Begins to understand right and wrong

Reinforces desired behavior

TEMPERAMENT (List two behaviors that indicate basic style.)

Activity level

Regularity

Approach or withdrawal as a characteristic response to a new situation

Adaptability to change in routine

Level of sensory threshold

Positive or negative mood

Intensity of response

Distractibility

Persistence and attention span

Social Development

SELF

Has concept of self

Is egocentric: understands only own viewpoint

OTHERS

Seeks presence of parent or caregiver

Plays games

Occasionally shares

Acts differently toward different people

Uses variety of behaviors to gain attention

May be shy with some people

Engages in parallel play

Child Behavior	Date First Observed	Practicing	Proficient

Cognitive Development

SENSORIMOTOR DEVELOPMENT: STAGE 5

   Object permanence

      Watches toy hidden and moved

      Looks for it where moved

   Causality

      Investigates cause and effect

      Sees self as causal agent

      Explores various ways things happen

      Employs active trial-and-error to solve problems

      Experiments

   Imitation and play

      Copies behaviors of others

      Turns play with imitation into rituals

Language Development

   Uses intonation

   Babbles sentences

   Repeats, practices words

   Imitates sounds of other people, objects

   Responds to word and gesture conversation

   Responds to many questions and commands child cannot say

   Uses word approximation for some words

   Uses words in immediate context

   Identifies familiar pictures

   Uses markers

APPROXIMATELY EIGHTEEN TO TWENTY-FOUR MONTHS OF AGE

Child Behavior	Date First Observed	Practicing	Proficient

Physical Development

MUSCULAR CONTROL

   Locomotion

      Walks forward

      Walks backward

      Walks sideways

Child Behavior	Date First Observed	Practicing	Proficient

Runs with stops and starts

Jumps with both feet

Kicks object

Walks up stairs holding railing; walks down stairs holding railing

Pushes and pulls objects while walking

Climbs

Pedals cycle

Arm

Throws object at target

Hand

Grasps and releases with developing finger muscles

Pulls zippers

Helps dress and undress self

Scribbles

Increases wrist flexibility, turns wrist to turn object

Establishing right- or left-handedness

Turns book pages

Digs with tool

Makes individual marks with crayon or pen

SLEEPING

May move from crib to bed or cot

EATING

Controls cup and spoon better

May eat anything, then change to picky eating

TEETH

Has most baby teeth

Uses toothbrush

ELIMINATION

May show interest in and readiness for toilet training

Emotional Development

TYPES OF EMOTIONS-FEELINGS

Views internal feelings and external behavior as same

Shows one or more emotions at same time

Continues to develop feelings about self

Changes feelings about self

Seeks approval

May develop new fears

Child Behavior	Date First Observed	Practicing	Proficient

Increases fantasy

May increase aggressiveness

Seeks security in routines

May become shy again

Sometimes rejects parent or caregiver

CONTROL OF EMOTIONS-FEELINGS

Uses reactions of others as a controller of own behavior

May resist change

Moves to extremes, from lovable to demanding and stubborn

TEMPERAMENT (List two behaviors that indicate basic style.)

Activity level

Regularity

Approach or withdrawal as a characteristic response to a new situation

Adaptability to change in routine

Level of sensory threshold

Positive or negative mood

Intensity of response

Distractibility

Persistence and attention span

Social Development

SELF

Is egocentric, sees things from own point of view

May change identity of self from day to day

Identifies materials as belonging to self

Uses I, mine, me, you

OTHERS

Demands attention

Begins to be aware of others' feelings

Believes people have changes in identity

Expands social relationships

Looks to others for help

Imitates tasks of others

Wants to help, assists with tasks

Child Behavior	Date First Observed	Practicing	Proficient

May do opposite of what is requested

Difficulty sharing

Engages in parallel play

Cognitive Development

SENSORIMOTOR DEVELOPMENT: STAGE 6

Mental trial and error

Tries out ideas mentally, based on past concrete experiences

Object permanence

Sees object disappear, remembers object, and figures out where it went

Deferred imitation and symbolization

Imitates past events

Engages in symbolic play

Resolves conflict

Compensates for unsatisfied needs

Tries roles

Language Development

Uses language to reflect own meaning; expects others to have same meaning

Expands vocabulary rapidly, labeling objects

Points to objects and pictures named by others

Learns social words—hello, please, thank you

Uses language to express needs, desires

Uses language to direct others

Questions

Uses nouns, verbs, pronouns

Is learning prepositions

Calls self by name

Follows directions of one-step or two-steps

Uses two-word sentences; three-word sentences

Looks at books

Listens to stories and rhymes

Scribbles

APPROXIMATELY TWENTY-FOUR TO THIRTY MONTHS OF AGE

Child Behavior	Date First Observed	Practicing	Proficient

Physical Development

MUSCULAR CONTROL

  Movement

    Bends at waist

    Climbs

    Jumps

    Stands on one foot

  Arm

    Throws

  Hand

    Touches

    Twists

EATING

  Uses spoon

  Is learning to use fork

  Uses fingers

TEETH

  Has all 20 baby teeth

  Brushes teeth

ELIMINATION

  Is learning to use toilet

  Has completed toilet training

Emotional Development

TYPES OF EMOTIONS-FEELINGS

  Self-esteem

    Feels comfortable with self

    Feels positive self-worth

    Feels negative self-worth

CONTROL OF EMOTIONS-FEELINGS

  Expresses emotions

TEMPERAMENT (List two behaviors that indicate basic style.)

  Activity level

  Regularity

  Approach or withdrawal as a characteristic response to a new situation

  Adaptability to change in routine

Child Behavior	Date First Observed	Practicing	Proficient
Level of sensory threshold			
Positive or negative mood			
Intensity of response			
Distractibility			
Persistence and attention span			

Social Development

SELF

Realizes own skills

OTHERS

Shows independence

Acts to please adult

Shows feelings to others

Recognizes emotions in others

Recognizes the difference between "mine" and "yours."

Shares

Helps others

Engages in parallel play

Cognitive Development

PREOPERATIONAL STAGE: PRECONCEPTUAL

Nonverbal classification

Makes graphic collections

Verbal preconcepts

Uses words differently at different times

Uses words with private meanings

Labels objects in one class

Focuses on one attribute

Verbal reasoning

Reasons from particular to particular

Quantity

Understands some, more, gone, big

Number

Understands more

Space

Understands up, down, behind, under, over

Time

Understands now, soon

Child Behavior	Date First Observed	Practicing	Proficient
Language Development			
Uses demonstrative naming			
Uses attribution			
Uses possession			
Uses action			
Uses recurrence			
Uses negation			
Learns word order			
Learns prosodic patterning			
Uses subject–verb			
Uses verb–object			
Omits function words			
Selects and uses books			
Uses controlled scribbling			

APPROXIMATELY THIRTY TO THIRTY-SIX MONTHS OF AGE

Child Behavior	Date First Observed	Practicing	Proficient
Physical Development			
MOVEMENT AND COORDINATION			
Walks evenly			
Runs			
Jumps in place and forward			
Dresses and undresses self with assistance			
Has established handedness			
SLEEPING			
Assists with preparation of routines			
ELIMINATION			
Is in process of or has completed toilet training			
Emotional Development			
TYPES OF EMOTIONS-FEELINGS			
Reacts strongly			
Acts negatively			
Learns enthusiastically			
Is mastering skills			
CONTROL OF EMOTIONS-FEELINGS			
Is physically aggressive			
TEMPERAMENT (List two behaviors that indicate basic style.)			
Activity level			

Child Behavior	Date First Observed	Practicing	Proficient

Regularity
Approach or withdrawal as a characteristic response to a
new situation
Adaptability to change in routine
Level of sensory threshold
Positive or negative mood
Intensity of response
Distractibility
Persistence and attention span

Social Development
SELF
Acts possessive
OTHERS
Seeks assistance
Directs others
Helps others
CONTROL OF SELF
Plays cooperatively
Shares
Takes turns

Cognitive Development
PREOPERATIONAL STAGE: PRECONCEPTUAL
Nonverbal classification
Makes graphic collections
Verbal preconcepts
Uses words differently at different times
Labels objects in one class
Verbal reasoning
Thinks one action is like another action
Reasons from effect to cause
Quantity
Understands some, more, gone, big
Number
Understands more
Space
Understands up, down, behind, under, over
Time
Understands now, soon, before, after

Language Development
INCREASES VOCABULARY
IMPROVES SYNTAX
Word order
Two- and three-word sentences
Longer sentences

Child Behavior	Date First Observed	Practicing	Proficient
IMPROVES WORD FORMS			
Plurals			
Past tense			
IMPROVES READING SKILLS			
Listens to stories, "reads" pictures, storybooks			
USES CONTROLLED SCRIBBLING			

Developmental Profile and Instructions

INSTRUCTIONS

Copy the Developmental Profile form. Create a profile for each child in care by following these instructions.

1. Write the child's name, date(s) of assessment(s), and date of birth (D.O.B.) on the profile. (Use the Sample Profile in Figure 3-2 as an example.)
2. Calculate Chronological Age (C.A.) by using the following method:

		Year	Month	Day
Assessment	=	2003	2	24
D.O.B.	=	2002	2	21
C.A.	=	1(12 mo)	0	3

3. Place the C.A. in months in the middle shaded C.A. row on the profile and put one-month intervals at each row for children with C.A.s from 1–17 months and two-month intervals for C.A.s from 18 months up (see Figure B-1 for example).
4. Write the child behaviors assessed from the Developmental Prescription (Appendix A) under each major Developmental Area on the Profile (see Sample Profile in Figure B-2).
5. Observe how the child performs on each skill and place an X on the row representing the monthly development for each listed Child Behavior.
6. Connect the Xs to graphically illustrate the child's Developmental Profile.
7. Write notes on strengths and weaknesses shown by the Profile.

Name: _____

Date: _____

Date of Birth: _____

C.A.: _____

MONTH AGE EXPECT.	AREA I PHYSICAL				AREA II EMOTIONAL			AREA III SOCIAL				AREA IV COGNITIVE				AREA V LEARNING SKILLS				MONTH AGE EXPECT.

C.A.

Notes

Figure B–1 Blank Developmental Profile

Name: **Juan P.**

Date: **2/24/XX**

Date of Birth: **2/21/XX**

C.A.: **12 months 3 days**

MONTH AGE EXPECT.	AREA V LEARNING SKILLS				AREA IV COGNITIVE					AREA III SOCIAL					AREA II EMOTIONAL			AREA I PHYSICAL				MONTH AGE EXPECT.
	VERBAL	V-MAT	AUDITORY	VISUAL	LANGUAGE	PLAY	CAUSALITY	OBJECTS	GOALS	GROUP	ONE TO ONE	OLDER	YOUNGER	PEERS	TEMPERAMENT	CONTROL	FEELINGS	TEETH	EAT	SLEEP	MUSCLE	
18+																						18+
17																						17
16																						16
15											B											15
14																						14
13																						13
C.A. 12																						C.A. 12
11																						11
10																						10
9														A								9
8																						8
7																						7
6–																						6–

C.A.

Notes: A = Juan has a little problem dealing with a group–sometimes is overwhelmed.

B = He responds very well to one to one adult attention.

Figure B–2 Sample of completed Developmental Profile

CDA Competency Standards for Infant/ Toddler Caregivers in Center-Based Programs

The CDA Competency Standards are the national standards used to evaluate a caregiver's performance with children and families during the CDA assessment process. The Competency Standards are divided into six **competency goals**, which are statements of a general purpose or goal for caregiver behavior. The competency goals are common to all child care settings. The six goals are defined in more detail in 13 **functional areas**, which describe the major tasks or functions that a caregiver must complete in order to carry out the competency goal.

Each functional area is explained by a **developmental context**, which presents a brief overview of child development from birth to 3 years and provides a rationale for the functional area definition and examples of competent caregiver behavior that follow. Three different developmental levels are identified—young infants (birth–8 months), mobile infants (9–17 months), and toddlers (18–36 months). Children develop at different rates, and descriptions of these levels emphasize the unique characteristics and needs of children at each stage of development.

Each functional area is further explained by a list of sample caregiver behaviors. These examples describe behavior that demonstrates that a caregiver is acting in a competent way or exhibiting a skill in a particular functional area. During the assessment process, most Candidates will exhibit other competent behavior, and a competent Candidate might not demonstrate all the examples listed under a functional area. The examples are organized according to developmental stages of children from birth to 3 years, in order to emphasize the importance of the special skills needed to work with young infants, mobile infants, and toddlers. Special bilingual specialization examples are presented for several functional areas.

The samples of caregiver competency included in the standards should serve as a basis for recognizing other, more specific behaviors that are important to the individual Candidate. A competent Candidate might not demonstrate all the examples listed in the following pages. CDA Candidates and individuals conducting or participating in CDA training will be able to think of many different ways to demonstrate skill in the six competency goals and 13 functional areas.

Competent caregivers integrate their work and constantly adapt their skills—always thinking of the development of the whole child. In all functional areas, it is important for competent caregivers to individualize their work with each child while meeting the needs of the group. In every area, too, caregivers must promote multiculturalism, support families with different languages, and meet the needs of children with handicapping conditions and special needs. And, while demonstrating skills and knowledge, competent caregivers must also demonstrate personal qualities, such as flexibility and a positive style of communicating with young children and working with families.

COMPETENCY GOAL I

To establish and maintain a safe, healthy, learning environment

1. FUNCTIONAL AREA: SAFE

Candidate provides a safe environment to prevent and reduce injuries.

Developmental Context One of the most essential services for children is to ensure their safety and well-being. Indoor and outdoor areas should be free of dangerous conditions and materials. Adults should teach children about safety and comfort children when hurt. Adults should be attentive and have the skills and knowledge to prevent injuries and to handle emergencies, accidents, and injuries appropriately when they occur. In a safe environment, children will learn gradually to protect themselves and look out for others.

Young infants (birth–8 months) must be attended to carefully. A safe and secure environment is essential to their development. Because of infants' vulnerability and relative helplessness, adults must attend to each infant at all times in order to ensure his/her continued safety.

Mobile infants (9–17 months) are changing each day. As their rapidly increasing motor skills lead them into new areas, adults must anticipate new hazards that may arise.

Toddlers (18–36 months) are increasingly curious about their world. They stretch boundaries and test everything in their surroundings. Adults must be attentive to their activities and ensure their safety while giving them simple explanations for safety precautions.

Examples For example, the competent Candidate working with infants and toddlers:

- Keeps both the inside of the center and the outdoor play areas free of debris, structural hazards, unguarded space heaters, tools, and dangerous substances (e.g., medicine, cleaning products, matches, chipping paint, toxic plants, small objects that could be swallowed, balloons, and plastic bags).
- Ensures that safety equipment (e.g., fire extinguishers and smoke detectors) are in place and operable and knows how to use them.
- Maintains an easily accessible and current list of phone numbers for contacting parents and emergency services, including poison control, fire company, and medical help.
- Uses diagrams, pictures, and words understood by children and adults to post instructions and practice procedures for fires and other emergencies, including safety procedures for children with handicapping conditions.
- Plans and practices monthly fire drills for moving all children in care to safety as quickly as possible.

- Ensures that outdoor play equipment is safe for small children and in good repair.
- Responds immediately and sympathetically to a child's injury or fear of injury and encourages the same response by the children.
- Takes safety precautions in a reassuring manner without overprotecting or making children fearful.
- Anticipates and makes plans to prevent potentially dangerous situations (e.g., children left unattended while sleeping or separated while on a field trip).
- Maintains first aid supplies—gauze, tape, syrup of ipecac, tweezers, scissors, and soap—and knows basic first aid procedures appropriate for young children (e.g., how to handle choking, treating cuts, etc.).
- Uses safe auto and bus travel procedures, including use of appropriate car seats for children.
- Discusses safety information with parents and tells them about resources (e.g., poison control centers) that provide services to families in their own language.
- Makes areas safe for children at different developmental stages; for example, putting safety gates on stairways; covering electrical outlets with safety plugs; inspecting children's equipment (e.g., cribs and car seats) at least weekly; securing, rearranging, or removing furniture that could fall or be pulled over, and securing carpeting and rugs.
- Supervises all children's indoor and outdoor activities.
- Keeps informed about safety standards for toys and equipment and shares this information with parents.
- Adapts the indoor and outdoor environment so that children with handicapping conditions can maximize their independence (e.g., safe use of mechanical aids or equipment).
- Requires parents to authorize in writing all persons allowed to pick children up from the program.

Young Infants The competent Candidate working with young infants also, for example:

- Locks side rails on cribs in "up" position when children are napping.
- Places infants in a comfortable and safe position for sleeping.
- Stays with infants on changing table or when bathing.

Mobile Infants The competent Candidate working with mobile infants, for example:

- Holds child's hand when near dangerous areas (e.g., roads, deep water, or steps).
- Knows children's individual differences in their tendency to bite, climb, and escape. Watches or stays close to children to anticipate and respond to these actions.

Toddlers The competent Candidate working with toddlers also, for example:

- Helps toddlers stop dangerous actions toward themselves and others.
- Explains cause and effect in dangerous situations in simple language, demonstrating as much as possible.
- Teaches safe use of playground equipment.

Bilingual Specialization In addition, the competent Candidate working towards the bilingual specialization:

- Explains and practices safety procedures (e.g., fire drills) using the language best understood by the children.
- Utilizes cultural values and practices in providing safety education.

2. FUNCTIONAL AREA: HEALTHY

Candidate promotes good health and nutrition and provides an environment that contributes to the prevention of illness.

Developmental Context Good health involves sound medical and dental practices and good nutrition. Adults should model and encourage good health and nutrition habits with children. Food should be nutritious, prepared carefully, and served in a relaxed atmosphere. Prompt care should be given to children who are or become ill or hurt. Children need a clean environment that is properly lighted, ventilated, and heated or cooled. Indoor and outdoor areas should be free of materials or conditions that endanger children's health. Care of the child's physical needs communicates positive feelings about his/her value and influences the child's developing identity and feelings of self-worth. Parents and caregivers should exchange information about children's physical health frequently.

Young and mobile infants (birth–17 months) need affectionate and competent physical care geared to their individual needs and rhythms. Adults can help infants regulate their eating, sleeping, and other activities gradually, while continuing to balance the infant's and the group's needs.

Toddlers (18–36 months) imitate and learn from the activities of those around them. Good health habits can be established through modeling and encouraging tooth brushing, hand washing, nutritious eating, etc.

Examples For example, the competent Candidate working with infants and toddlers.

- Learns about good nutrition for children from birth to 3 years old and helps plan age-appropriate, nutritious meals and snacks. While respecting family customs and habits, the caregiver shares nutrition information with parents and encourages them to provide healthy foods when they contribute food to the center.
- Conducts activities in a positive, relaxed, and pleasant atmosphere to reduce tension and stress.
- Washes hands before and after toileting a child, helping child blow nose, and food preparation and eating.
- Attends to each child's physical needs (e.g., toileting, eating, exercising, and napping).
- Provides affection for all children.
- Provides adequate ventilation and lighting, comfortable room temperatures, and good sanitation.
- Makes sure play areas and materials are cleaned daily.
- Establishes procedures for care of sick children; for example, isolating a child with a contagious illness from well children, contacting parents and medical providers, and administering medicine.
- Helps children develop basic health habits.
- Keeps handy current emergency telephone numbers for each child's parent(s), nearest relative, and medical providers.
- Communicates frequently with parents about children's health, nutrition, communicable diseases, and medications and cooperates with parents and health specialists.
- Follows center procedures for maintaining health records, administering medications, first aid, and cooperates with health and nutrition staff.
- Establishes a relaxed mealtime routine that makes eating pleasant for each child.
- Limits sugar, salt, processed foods, unnecessary chemical additives, and artificial

coloring and flavoring in meals and snacks and encourages parents to do the same.

■ Informs parents about health resources (e.g., physicians or community clinics) that provide services to families in their primary language.

■ Recognizes unusual behavior and physical symptoms in children and encourages parents to obtain appropriate treatment.

■ Works cooperatively with health professionals and parents to meet the needs of children with handicapping conditions.

■ Recognizes symptoms of possible abuse and neglect and is alert to play or behavior that indicates physical or sexual abuse. If physical or sexual abuse is suspected, the competent Candidate seeks out resources for information and support, follows state law in response, responds sensitively to child's and family's needs and cooperates in carrying out treatment plans.

■ Recognizes the signs of a health crisis that children with special needs may have and responds appropriately (e.g., seizures).

Infants The competent Candidate working with **young and mobile infants** also, for example:

■ Cleans with sanitizing solution, at least daily, all toys and objects used and "mouthed" by infants.

■ Makes provisions for sanitary diaper changing and disposal.

■ Washes hands thoroughly before and after each diaper change and before each feeding.

■ Supports mothers who wish to continue breast feeding infants.

■ Follows a sanitary procedure for preparing, storing, and labeling baby bottles.

■ Responds to infant's individual rhythms, while working towards regularity in feeding, sleeping and toileting.

■ Manages group so as to be able to concentrate on the individual feeding of infants and to hold infants for bottle feeding.

■ Recognizes rashes and skin irritations and works with parents to prevent and treat them.

■ Recognizes conditions that cause tooth decay in infants and takes measures to prevent them.

■ Works cooperatively with parents and shares information frequently concerning nutrition, weaning, and introducing solid foods, while showing respect for different practices and values.

■ Offers children opportunities to gradually feed themselves by providing finger foods and allowing adequate time for pleasurable feeding.

■ Does not put children to bed with a bottle unless it contains water.

Toddlers The competent Candidate working with toddlers also, for example:

■ Uses role playing, modeling, visual material, and real objects to teach healthy physical, mental, dental, and nutritional practices.

■ Plans health care and educational activities that integrate health and nutrition information from the children's cultures with medically accepted health and nutritional practices.

■ Has age-appropriate expectations of toddlers' abilities and helps them to develop self-help skills in eating, toileting, washing hands, tooth brushing, etc.

■ Works with parents in planning for toilet learning, respects different family practices and expectations, and is sensitive to each child's readiness.

■ Understands toddlers' explorations, concerns, and curiosities about their own and others' bodies and responds with information at their level; for example, explaining the physical differences between boys and girls matter-of-factly in simple terms.

Bilingual Specialization The competent Candidate working towards the **bilingual specialization**, for example:

■ Provides written health information for parents (e.g., notices about immunizations) in both languages.

■ Utilizes cultural values and practices in providing health and nutrition education.

3. FUNCTIONAL AREA: LEARNING ENVIRONMENT

Candidate uses space, relationships, materials, and routines as resources for constructing an interesting, secure, and enjoyable environment that encourages play, exploration, and learning.

Developmental Context Children of all ages learn from their own experience and by imitation. Adults can guide and encourage children's learning by ensuring that the environment is emotionally supportive; invites active exploration, play, and movement by children; and supports a broad array of experiences. A reliable routine together with a stimulating choice of materials, activities, and relationships enhances children's learning and development.

Young infants (birth–8 months) begin to learn from their immediate surroundings and daily experiences. The sense of well-being and emotional security conveyed by a loving and skilled caregiver creates a readiness for other experiences. Before infants can creep and crawl, adults should provide a variety of sensory experiences and encourage movement and playfulness.

Mobile infants (9–17 months) are active, independent, and curious. They are increasingly persistent and purposeful in doing things. They need many opportunities to practice new skills and explore the environment within safe boundaries. Adults can share children's delight in themselves, their skills, and discoveries, and gradually add variety to the learning environment.

Toddlers (18–36 months) are developing new language skills, physical control, and awareness of themselves and others each day. They enjoy participating in planned and group activities, but they are not yet ready to sit still or work in a group for a very long time. Adults can support their learning in all areas by maintaining an environment that is dependable but flexible enough to provide opportunities for them to extend their skills, understanding, and judgment in individualized ways.

Examples For example, the competent Candidate working with infants and toddlers:

■ Uses materials, books, and equipment that are stimulating to each child and suitable to individual learning styles, including those of children with handicapping conditions.

■ Uses materials that demonstrate acceptance of each child's sex, family, race, language, and culture.

■ Provides easily accessible learning materials (e.g., puzzles, books, stacking toys) that children can explore by themselves as well as putting some materials away for special times or for use at later stages of development.

■ Organizes space into identifiable areas that encourage appropriate and independent use of materials.

■ Balances active and quiet, free and structured, individual and group, indoor and outdoor activities.

- Provides many opportunities for children to develop their senses and ability to concentrate.
- Provides a variety of natural and pleasurable sounds such as music, normal conversation, outdoor sounds, etc.
- Observes individual children and the group frequently and modifies the environment to meet their changing abilities, needs, and interests.
- Varies routines spontaneously to take advantage of unusual opportunities (e.g., goes outside in the snow, invites a visiting grandmother to share stories or songs with children, lets the children watch workers and machinery on the street, or plays with one child for an extra period of time when additional adults are available to care for group).
- Supports relationships between adults and children, as well as between children in care, as an important aspect of the learning environment.
- Schedules day so there is time for individual attention to each child.
- Encourages children to become involved in activities that extend their attention spans.
- Provides simple and consistent routines for mealtimes, naps, preparing to go out, changing activities, clean up, etc.; supports children's learning through these routines.
- Makes and helps parents make toys and equipment from easily available materials for use in the home and center.
- Adapts the daily schedule to accommodate children with special needs rather than requiring them to fit the schedule.

Young Infants The competent Candidate working with young infants also, for example:

- Changes an infant's position and location often during the day and responds to the child's developing skills (e.g., sitting up, rolling over, reaching for objects, and making noises).
- Provides a learning environment for nonmobile infants that encourages mouthing, reaching, batting, grasping, babbling, and social interaction.
- Understands and respects the individual eating and sleeping needs of healthy infants.
- Frequently carries the child about in arms, on a hip, or in a sling.
- Takes the infant out of doors to experience various temperatures, light variations, breezes, etc.
- Provides the infant with the sights and sounds of other living things—humans, animals, and plants—including caregiver's own face.
- Recognizes the importance of a consistent relationship between a caregiver and infant and makes caregiver-child interaction the base of the infant's learning environment.

Mobile Infants The competent Candidate working with mobile infants also, for example:

- Arranges room so that mobile infants have an area for free movement protected from older children.
- Provides space indoors and outside for exploration initiated by the child.
- "Baby-proofs" the environment so that there are many opportunities for child-initiated learning and limit-setting is minimized.
- Understands that intense feelings and rapid changes in mood and energy influ-

ence the child's response to the environment and adjusts routines, activities, and materials supportively.

Toddlers The competent Candidate working with toddlers also, for example:

■ Expands the learning environment to include the community when possible; for example, short trips to the local shops, walks around the block, community events.

■ Introduces a variety of materials and opportunities for learning based on an understanding of toddlers' developmental level, abilities, and interests; for example, provides water play in an area that can get wet, covers children's clothes with plastic smocks or removes clothing in warm weather, and limits such play to few children so each has plenty of room and free use of utensils.

■ Provides a step stool when necessary so that children can use toilet and wash hands independently as soon as possible.

Bilingual Specialization
In addition, the competent Candidate working towards the bilingual specialization, for example:

■ Uses objects, music activities, and celebrations that are meaningful to young children to encourage development of both languages and cultures.

■ Helps parents identify resources in their homes, families, and community that will support the development of both languages.

COMPETENCY GOAL II

To advance physical and intellectual competence.

4. FUNCTIONAL AREA: PHYSICAL

Candidate provides a variety of equipment, activities, and opportunities to promote the physical development of children.

Developmental Context Physical development is an essential part of the total development of children. Developing physically includes using large and small muscles, coordinating movements, and using the senses. Large-motor development includes strengthening and coordinating the muscles and nervous system, controlling large motions using the arms, legs, torso, or whole body. Small-motor development involves the ability to control and coordinate small, specialized motions using the eyes, mouth, hands and feet. Adults should provide materials, equipment, and opportunities for indoor and outdoor activities that encourage this development and recognize and respect the wide differences in individual rates of physical development.

Establishes and maintains a routine for use of the second language in daily activities.

Young infants (birth–8 months) begin all learning through physical movement, taste, touch, smell, sight, and sound. By moving their arms, hands, legs, and other body parts, by touching and being touched, infants develop an awareness of their bodies and their ability to move and interact with the environment. By using their mouths to explore, hands to reach and grasp, whole bodies to roll over and sit up, they master the necessary skills needed for developmental stages that follow.

Mobile infants (9–17 months) delight in practicing and achieving new physical skills—crawling, standing, sitting down, cruising, and walking. They interact with their environment in a practical way, using all senses to examine and manipulate objects, and begin to understand cause and effect, space, and distance in this way.

Toddlers (18–36 months) continue to master physical skills at their own individual rates. Their learning and interaction with the environment continue to be active. Although they are gaining greater control and satisfaction through use of their small muscles (e.g., painting, drawing, or working with puzzles), they need opportunities to exercise their large muscles often each day.

Examples For example, the competent Candidate working with infants and toddlers:

- Arranges and encourages physical activities, knowing how children's physical development affects their cognitive, social, and emotional development.
- Observes and evaluates children's developmental levels in order to provide activities for physical skills and development of the senses at the appropriate level for each child.
- Plans and participates daily in appropriate large-muscle activities (e.g., playing ball, running, jumping, climbing with children both indoors and outdoors).
- Provides a variety of activities from children's culture(s) (e.g., dances, music, fingerplays, and active games).
- Provides opportunities for children to develop their senses by noticing colors, smelling odors, distinguishing sounds, feeling and touching a variety of objects, and tasting different foods.
- Communicates to children and their parents the importance of outdoor play and physical activity for healthy growth and development.
- Plans for and supports children's changing needs for active play, quiet activity, and rest.
- Supports and encourages, but never forces, children who are fearful of physical activity because of illness, accidents, abuse, limited opportunity, or overprotective caregivers and parents.
- Observes and evaluates children's physical development, recognizes signs of possible physical handicaps and developmental delays, refers parents to appropriate services, and follows up on referrals or individual development plans.
- Adapts the program to meet the special needs of children with handicapping conditions, taking into account the importance of physical development to self-concept and social development.
- Avoids overprotecting children with handicaps, supports their independence, includes them in physical activities with other children (making modifications only when necessary), and encourages parents to do the same.

Young Infants The competent Candidate working with young infants also, for example:

- Gives infants freedom and opportunities to move and explore in a variety of safe spaces (e.g., bare floor, carpet, mattress, grass).
- Maximizes warm and loving physical contact with infants by providing a variety of physical contact from soothing to stimulating, depending on the infant's readiness and need.
- Provides appropriate activities and materials to help infants develop small muscles by grasping, dropping, pulling, pushing, throwing, fingering, and mouthing.

Mobile Infants The competent Candidate working with mobile infants also, for example:

- Encourages active manipulation of a variety of objects and the use of tools; for example, strings to pull toys, a pail to carry objects, a shovel to scoop sand.
- Shares children's pleasure in and provides them safe opportunities to practice repeatedly creeping, crawling, cruising, walking, climbing, descending stairs, and other physical movements.
- Provides opportunities for the development of eye-hand coordination in ways that are challenging and satisfying for the child; for example, fitting objects into a hole in a box, self-feeding.

Toddlers The competent Candidate working with toddlers also, for example:

- Increases variety of opportunities for large- and small-muscle activities and sensory development as children are ready (e.g., introducing ride-on toys, play dough, puzzles, listening games, fingerplays, boxes for climbing).
- Cooperates with parents in toilet learning when toddlers appear to be ready.
- Provides extended opportunities for children to repeatedly practice their physical skills.

5. FUNCTIONAL AREA: COGNITIVE

Candidate provides activities and opportunities that encourage curiosity, exploration, and problem solving appropriate to the developmental levels and learning styles of children.

Developmental Context Exploring and trying to understand the world is natural and necessary for children's cognitive or intellectual development. As children learn and grow, their thinking capacities expand and become more flexible. Adults should support and guide this process by responding to children's interests with new learning opportunities and to their questions, with information and enthusiasm. Cognitive growth also requires healthy development in other areas: consistent physical growth, secure emotional behavior, and positive social interaction.

Young infants (birth–8 months) begin cognitive or intellectual learning through their interactions with caring adults in a secure environment. Some of their early learning includes becoming familiar with distance and space relationships, sounds, similarity and differences among things, and visual perspectives from various positions—front, back, under, and over.

Mobile infants (9–17 months) actively learn through trying things out; using objects as tools; comparing, imitating, looking for lost objects; and naming familiar objects, places, and people. By giving them opportunities to explore space, objects, and people and by sharing children's pleasure in discovery, adults can build children's confidence in their ability to learn and understand.

Toddlers (18–36 months) enter into a new and expansive phase of mental activity. They are beginning to think in words and symbols, remember, and imagine. Their curiosity leads them to try out materials in many ways, and adults can encourage this natural interest by providing a variety of new materials for experimentation. Adults can create a supportive social environment for learning by showing enthusiasm for children's individual discoveries and by helping them use words to describe and understand their experiences.

Examples For example, the competent Candidate working with infants and toddlers:

- Observes children's play frequently to assess their cognitive development and readiness for new learning opportunities.

- Uses techniques and activities that stimulate children's curiosity, inventiveness, and problem-solving and communication skills.
- Gives children time and space for extended concentrated play and adjusts routines and schedules for this purpose.
- Provides opportunities for children to try out and begin to understand the relationships between cause and effect and means and ends.
- Understands the importance of play and often joins children's play as a partner and facilitator.
- Uses the center environment, everyday activities, and homemade materials to encourage children's intellectual development.
- Helps children discover ways to solve problems that arise in daily activities.
- Supports children's repetitions of the familiar and introduces new experiences, activities, and materials when children are interested and ready.
- Recognizes differences in individual learning styles and finds ways to work effectively with each child.
- Encourages active learning, rather than emphasizing adult talking and children's passive listening.
- Obtains (or makes) and uses special learning materials and equipment for children whose handicaps affect their ability to learn.
- Provides equipment and materials that children can explore and master by themselves.
- Is alert to the task a child is attempting and provides appropriate support.
- Recognizes learning problems and makes referrals according to center's policy.

Young Infants   The competent Candidate working with young infants also, for example:

- Talks to infants, describing what they feel, hear, touch, and see.
- Encourages manipulation and inspection of a variety of objects.
- Provides opportunities for infants to interact with adults and children and watch interactions of adults and children.
- Encourages infants in imitating others.
- Frequently plays with infants.

Mobile Infants   The competent Candidate working with mobile infants also, for example:

- Talks, sings, plays with, and reads to mobile infants.
- Gives children more space to explore as they become more mobile.
- Gives children many opportunities to figure out cause and effect, how things work.
- Provides many experiences with moving, hiding, and changing objects.

Toddlers   The competent Candidate working with toddlers also, for example:

- Encourages children to ask questions and seek help and responds to them in ways that extend their thinking; for example, "That's a good question; let's see if we can find out."
- Asks questions that have more than one answer, encouraging children to wonder, guess, and talk about their ideas; for example, "What do you think might happen... ?" or "How do you feel when... ?"
- Encourages children to name objects and talk about their experiences and observations.

- Provides opportunities to organize and group, compare and contrast thoughts, words, objects, and sensations.
- Involves toddlers in projects (e.g., cooking, gardening, and repairing) when possible.
- Reduces distractions and interruptions so that toddlers have opportunities to extend their attention span and work on one activity (e.g., block building or water play) for a long period of time.

Bilingual Specialization In addition, the competent Candidate working towards the bilingual specialization, for example:

- Provides learning experiences that lead to the understanding of basic concepts in the language most familiar to each child.
- Encourages learning of both languages through everyday experiences and activities.

6. FUNCTIONAL AREA: COMMUNICATION

Candidate actively communicates with children and provides opportunities and support for children to understand, acquire, and use verbal and nonverbal means of communicating thoughts and feelings.

Developmental Context Communication between people can take many forms, including spoken words or sounds, gestures, eye and body movements, and touch. Children need to understand verbal and nonverbal means of communicating thoughts, feelings, and ideas. Adults can help children develop their communication skills by encouraging communication and providing ample opportunity for children to listen, interact, and express themselves freely with other children and adults.

Young infants (birth–8 months) need adults who are attentive to their nonverbal and pre-verbal communication. Adults can provide better care when they respond sensitively to the individual signals of each infant. Infants' early babblings and cooings are important practice for later word expression. Infants' speech development is facilitated by an encouraging partner who responds to their beginning communications and who talks with them about themselves and their world.

Mobile infants (9–17 months) begin to jabber expressively, name familiar objects and people, and understand many words and phrases. Adults can build on this communication by showing an active interest in children's expressions, interpreting their first attempts at words, repeating and expanding on what they say, talking to them clearly, and telling simple stories.

Toddlers (18–36 months) increase their vocabularies and use of sentences daily. There is a wide range of normal language development during this time; some children are early, and some are late talkers. Adults should communicate actively with all toddlers—modeling good speech, listening to them carefully, and helping them with new words and phrases. Language should be used in a variety of pleasurable ways each day, including songs, stories, directions, comfort, conversations, information, and play.

For example, the competent Candidate working with infants and toddlers:

- Has realistic expectations for each child's understanding and use of speech based on knowledge of language development and the individual child.
- Talks often with individual children and stimulates conversation among children and with adults in the room.

- Provides activities that encourage children to develop listening and comprehension skills.
- Helps children connect word meaning(s) to experiences and real objects.
- Recognizes, understands, and respects local speech patterns and idioms.
- Respects the language of non-English-speaking families, encourages them to communicate freely with their children in the language parents prefer, and helps them find opportunities to learn English.
- Is aware of the caregiver's role as a language model for children and uses affectionate and playful tones, clear speech, and responsive conversation.
- Listens attentively to children, tries to understand what they want to communicate, and helps them to express themselves.
- Shares children's communication/language achievements with parents.
- Uses a variety of songs, stories, books, and games—including those from the children's cultures—for language development.
- Talks with children about special experiences and relationships in their families and home lives.
- Recognizes possible impairments or delays that affect hearing and speech, helps families find resources, cooperates with treatment plans, and finds ways to communicate positively with these children.

Young Infants The competent Candidate working with young infants also, for example:

- Responds to the infant's cooing sounds and imitates them, encouraging a "conversation" in which the infant can often take the lead.
- Talks to infants about what they can see while giving physical care (e.g., diapering and feeding).
- Talks with parents about the meaning of an infant's beginning communications (e.g., different kinds of crying).
- Responds to infant's body signs and nonverbal cues that signal discomfort, excitement, pleasure, etc., and verbally describes the infant's feeling.
- Sings to infants or uses voice in interesting ways that encourage infants to listen.

Mobile Infants The competent Candidate working with mobile infants also, for example:

- Responds enthusiastically to an infant's first words.
- Uses gestures to demonstrate the meaning of words to infants.
- Names and talks about infants' feelings, behaviors, activities, clothing, body parts, etc., to help expand their vocabularies.
- Elaborates on children's short phrases to help them express intended meaning.

Toddlers The competent Candidate working with toddlers also, for example:

- Uses everyday conversations with children to enrich and expand their vocabulary.
- Provides opportunities for children to represent their ideas nonverbally through activities (e.g., painting, music making, and creative movement).
- Helps children learn, understand, and use words to express thoughts, ideas, questions, feelings, and physical needs.
- Writes toddlers' "stories" and labels their drawings, showing the relationship between spoken and printed words.
- Looks at picture books and magazines with children to stimulate talking.

■ Listens to taped stories using a variety of voices reflecting gender and culture differences.

Bilingual Specialization In addition, the competent Candidate working towards a bilingual specialization, for example:

■ Demonstrates ability to understand, speak, read, and write in both languages.
■ Understands the principles and characteristics of bilingual language development in children and explains these to parents.
■ Assesses each child's language abilities and uses activities that are appropriate to the child's level of development in each language.
■ Helps children associate word meanings in both languages with familiar objects and experiences.
■ Encourages older toddlers who are fluent in either language to help less fluent children.
■ Helps parents understand the importance of children's learning the home language and culture and their role in providing experiences to meet this goal.
■ Helps parents understand the child's attempts at communication in a second language.
■ Allows children opportunities to express themselves in the language of their choice.
■ Encourages English-speaking children and families to learn a second language.
■ Uses lullabies, songs, games, stories, books, and fingerplays from both languages, asking parents for examples from their childhood.
■ Makes sure there are consistent language models for both languages used in the program, through selection and use of materials and personnel.
■ Takes an active role in labeling children's actions and surroundings in their home language and encourages children to use these words.

7. FUNCTIONAL AREA: CREATIVE

Candidate provides opportunities that stimulate children to play with sound, rhythm, language, materials, space, and ideas in individual ways and to express their creative abilities.

Developmental Context All children are imaginative and have creative potential. They need opportunities to develop and express these capacities. Creative play serves many purposes for children in their cognitive, social, physical, and emotional development. Adults should support the development of children's creative impulses by respecting creative play and by providing a wide variety of activities and materials that encourage spontaneous expression and expand children's imagination.

Young and mobile infants (birth–17 months) are creative in their unique and individual ways of interacting with the world. Adults can support their creativity by respecting and enjoying the variety of ways very young children express themselves and act on their environment.

Toddlers (18–36 months) are interested in using materials to create their own product—sometimes to destroy and create it again or to move on. For example, they become absorbed in dipping a brush in paint and watching their stroke of color on paper. They use their voices and bodies creatively—swaying, chanting, and singing. They enjoy making up their own words and rhythms as well as learning traditional songs and rhymes. Adults can provide water, sand and other raw materials and opportunities for toddlers' creativity, and can show respect for what they do. Make-believe and pretend appear gradually, and adults can join in imaginative play, while helping toddlers distinguish between what is real and what is not.

Examples For example, the competent Candidate working with infants and toddlers:

- Recognizes that the process of creating is as important—and sometimes more important—than the product.
- Understands that each child's creative expression is unique and does not encourage uniformity.
- Allows time for spontaneous and extended play within the daily routine.
- Includes a variety of music, art, literature, dance, role playing, celebrations, and other creative activities from the children's culture(s) in program activities.
- Participates in make-believe games with children.
- Models and encourages children's creativity in language; for example, through rhymes, imaginative stories, and nonsense words.
- Provides unstructured materials (e.g., blocks, paint, clay, or musical instruments) that are appropriate for children at different ages.
- Encourages thorough, repeated exploration of creative materials whenever possible; for example, by letting a block structure stand so that building can continue the next day or by letting one child play with soap suds for an extended period of time.
- Models creativity by using homemade materials and found objects.
- Helps parents understand the importance of creative expression in children's development and the need to provide children with opportunities for creative activities (e.g., storytelling, playing make-believe, using art materials).
- Encourages children to try new and different activities.
- Provides for "messy" activities with children (e.g., water and sand play, finger painting, and drawing with markers).

Young and Mobile Infants The competent Candidate working with young and mobile infants also, for example:

- Recognizes that exploration and discovery by infants through their movements, voice, and expression are creative acts.
- Is alert and responsive to infants' initiatives to play, move, and use materials, gradually introducing new things to be combined and used in ways that infants can invent; for example, pieces of fabric of different colors and textures, rhythm instruments or objects that make different noises, assorted empty food containers.
- Provides a variety of music and rhythm experiences for infants.
- Shares infants' joy in a variety of ways—clapping, smiling, hugging—in order to encourage their spontaneity and creativity.

Toddlers The competent Candidate working with toddlers also, for example:

- Gradually introduces a variety of art materials, allows toddlers time to explore in their own ways, and shows interest in what they do.
- Provides and rotates a variety of male and female dress-up clothes and other "props," including those from the children's culture(s).
- Plays make-believe with each toddler, following the child's lead and taking care not to overstimulate or frighten the child.
- Keeps informed about cultural resources in the community and uses them with children when possible.

Bilingual Specialization In addition, the competent Candidate working towards a bilingual specialization, for example:

- Helps children develop creative abilities through activities and discussion in both languages.
- Helps children identify and imitate creative forms found in the art, music, and dance of both cultures.

COMPETENCY GOAL III

To support social and emotional development and provide positive guidance

8. FUNCTIONAL AREA: SELF

Candidate provides physical and emotional security for each child and helps each child to know, accept, and take pride in himself or herself and to develop a sense of independence.

Developmental Context All children need a physically and emotionally secure environment that supports their developing self-knowledge, self-control, and self-esteem and, at the same time, encourages respect for the feelings and rights of others. Knowing one's self includes knowing about one's body, feelings, and abilities. It also means identifying one's self as a girl or boy and a member of a family and a larger cultural community. Accepting and taking pride in one's self comes from experiencing success and being accepted by others as a unique individual. Self-esteem develops as children master new abilities, experience success as well as failure, and realize their effectiveness in handling increasingly challenging demands in their own ways.

Young infants (birth–8 months), during the first few weeks and months, begin to build a sense of self-confidence and security in an environment where they can trust that an adult will lovingly care for their needs. The adult is someone who is consistently available and feeds the child when hungry; keeps the child warm and comfortable; soothes the child when distressed; and provides interesting things to look at, taste, smell, feel, hear, and touch.

For **mobile infants** (9–17 months), a loving caregiver is a resource or "home base" who is readily available and provides warm physical comfort and a safe environment to explore and master. This emotional stability is essential for the development of self-confidence as well as language, physical, cognitive, and social growth.

Toddlers (18–36 months) become aware of many things about themselves, including their separateness from others. A sense of self and growing feelings of independence develop at the same time that toddlers realize the importance of parents and other caregivers. The healthy toddler's inner world is filled with conflicting feelings and ideas—independence and dependence, confidence and doubt, fear and power, hostility and love, anger and tenderness, aggression and passivity. The wide range of toddlers' feelings and actions challenge the resourcefulness and knowledge of adults who provide them emotional security.

Examples For example, the competent Candidate working with infants and toddlers:

- Treats each child as an individual with his or her own strengths and needs and unique characteristics.
- Is sensitive to differing cultural values and expectations concerning independence and expression of feelings.

■ Addresses each child by name, talks with each child every day, and encourages each child to call other children and adults by name.

■ Has affectionate and appropriate physical contact with each child daily in ways that convey love, affection, and security.

■ Helps children through periods of stress, separation, transition, and other crises.

■ Offers children, when possible, choices in activities, materials, and foods and respects their choices.

■ Encourages and helps children practice skills when eating, getting dressed, using toys and equipment, cleaning up, and helping others.

■ Gives one-to-one attention to each child as much as possible.

■ Enjoys children and directly expresses the enjoyment to them.

■ Delights in each child's success, expresses kindness and support when a child is having trouble, and helps him/her learn from mistakes.

■ Helps children recognize, label, and accept their feelings (e.g., joy, affection, anger, jealousy, sadness, and fear) and express feelings in culturally appropriate ways.

■ Models the recognition and expression of feelings by naming his/her own feelings while expressing them.

■ Provides many opportunities for all children, including those with handicaps, to feel effective, experience success, and gain the positive recognition of others.

■ Understands the effect of abuse and neglect on children's self-concept and works sensitively with such children.

Young Infants The competent Candidate working with young infants also, for example:

■ Listens carefully to an infant's cry and makes decisions quickly and appropriately: allows an infant to cry briefly when settling into sleep, comforts an infant who is distressed, or feeds an infant who is hungry.

■ Provides appropriate affection using personal attention rather than food or "things."

■ Gently and pleasantly provides basic physical care—feeding, bathing, dressing, diapering—respecting the tempo and sensitivities of the baby.

■ Holds the infant close, allowing him/her to feel the caregiver's body warmth and heartbeat and to feel comfortable in the adult's arms.

■ Creates a personal relationship with each infant and knows the kind of cuddling, stroking, talking, and playing that brings comfort and good feelings to each individual infant.

Mobile Infants The competent Candidate with mobile infants also, for example:

■ Removes the exploring infant from an obstacle that is too frustrating, comforts the child, and provides an alternative activity.

■ Recognizes periods when the child has difficulty separating from parents or is fearful of new adults and is supportive of the child.

■ Talks to child frequently about his/her family—where they are, when they will come back, and what they do together.

■ Communicates, with eyes and voice, attention and interest to an exploring child at a distance from the caregiver.

■ Welcomes a child who comes for nurturing with a loving voice, hugging, or stroking.

Toddlers The competent Candidate working with toddlers also, for example:

■ Responds to toddler's intense feelings of love, joy, loneliness, anger, and disappointment with sympathetic attention.

■ Provides opportunities for toddlers to learn to help themselves (e.g., taking off jackets or pouring juice) and shares children's pleasure in new skills.

■ Helps the toddler understand his/her own feelings and express feelings in acceptable ways.

■ Supports child's developing awareness of him/ herself as a member of a family and of an ethnic or social group by talking about families (using photographs, mirrors, or other appropriate objects) and by celebrating cultural events with children.

■ Uses simple books, pictures, stories, and discussion to help children identify positively with the events and experiences of their lives; for example, single-parent families, extended families, divorce, moving, or birth of siblings.

Bilingual Specialization In addition, the competent Candidate working towards a bilingual specialization, for example:

■ Helps children feel good about themselves as speakers of each language.
■ Supports the child's attempt to use a second language.
■ Helps each child deal with the stress of separation, using the child's home language and a tone and style compatible with the family's heritage.

9. FUNCTIONAL AREA: SOCIAL

Candidate helps each child feel accepted in the group, helps children learn to communicate and get along with others, and encourages feelings of empathy and mutual respect among children and adults.

Developmental Context Children need to develop social skills that help them work and play cooperatively and productively with other children and adults. To do this, children need to feel secure about themselves, appreciate other people, and enjoy positive social interaction.

Young infants (birth–8 months) enter the world with a capacity and a need for social contact. Yet each one is unique in styles of interacting and readiness for different kinds of interactions. Infants need both protective and stimulating social interactions with a few consistent, caring adults who get to know them as individuals. The adults' understanding responses to their signals increase infants' participation in social interactions and their ability to "read" the signals of others.

Mobile infants (9–17 months) are curious about others but need assistance and supervision in interacting with other children. They continue to need one or a few consistent adults as their most important social partner(s).

Toddlers (18–36 months) social awareness is much more complex than that of younger children. Toddlers can begin to understand that others have feelings too—sometimes similar to and sometimes different from their own. They imitate many of the social behaviors of other children and adults. As toddlers become increasingly interested in other children, adults should guide and support their interactions, recognizing that they continue to rely upon familiar adults for emotional stability.

Examples For example, the competent Candidate working with infants and toddlers:

■ Learns about children's stages of social development and helps children and parents deal with such typical issues as separation anxiety, negative behavior, shyness, sexual identity, and making friends.

- Has realistic expectations for young children's social behavior based on their level of development.
- Serves as a social model by building a positive relationship with each child and parent and by maintaining positive relationships with other adults in the center.
- Responds quickly and calmly to prevent children from hurting each other.
- Helps children learn to respect the rights and possessions of others, in light of local expectations regarding sharing.
- Encourages children to ask for, accept, and give help to one another.
- Encourages children to make friends.
- Helps the children become aware of their feelings and those of others by talking about feelings with each child.
- Encourages children to express their feelings and assert their rights in socially acceptable ways.
- Encourages play and relationships among all children across racial, language, ethnic, age, and gender groupings, including children with handicaps.

Young Infants The competent Candidate working with young infants also, for example:

- Recognizes that infants need a consistent social partner (caregiver) who is dependable, warm, and loving.
- Responds to social gestures and noises of infants and elaborates appropriately, playing responsive social games.
- Takes advantage of opportunities for social play during feeding, bathing, dressing, and other aspects of physical care.
- Makes eye contact often.

Mobile Infants The competent Candidate working with mobile infants also, for example:

- Structures periods of time for social interaction with other children, remains available to protect, comfort, or facilitate, but does not interfere unless necessary.
- Provides infants with opportunities to observe social interactions among older children and among adults.
- Provides more than one attractive toy to minimize conflicts and waiting.
- Engages in social play with children that supports their developing social skills (e.g., taking turns with a ball, conversing at mealtime, sharing a snack, putting toys away).
- Encourages children to comfort and help each other.

Toddlers The competent Candidate working with toddlers also, for example:

- Encourages children to interact with each other in playful and caring ways.
- Understands that sharing, taking turns, and playing with others is difficult for toddlers and encourages their attempts to use words to resolve conflicts.
- Encourages cooperation rather than competition.
- Helps toddlers understand that sometimes they must wait for attention because of other children's needs.

Bilingual Specialization In addition, the competent Candidate working towards a bilingual specialization, for example:

- Recognizes when social roles and expectations for children in their family setting are different from those of the child care program, and helps children behave appropriately in each.

■ Recognizes when culture conflicts arise and works jointly with parents to resolve them.

10. FUNCTIONAL AREA: GUIDANCE

Candidate provides a supportive environment in which children can begin to learn and practice appropriate and acceptable behaviors as individuals and as a group.

Developmental Context Knowing what behavior is appropriate or acceptable in a situation is an important skill. Children develop this understanding when consistent limits and realistic expectations of their behavior are clearly and positively defined. Understanding and following simple rules can help children develop self-control. Children feel more secure when they know what is expected of them and when adult expectations realistically take into account each child's development and needs.

Young infants (birth–8 months) begin to adapt their rhythms of eating and sleeping to the expectations of their social environment through the gentle guidance of sensitive caregivers who meet their needs. The basic trust in adults and the environment that is established at this time directly affects the child's responsiveness to positive guidance later and promotes the development of self-discipline.

Mobile infants (9–17 months) want to do everything but they have little understanding about what is permissible and cannot remember rules. Adults can organize the environment in ways that clearly define limits and minimize conflicts. While respecting the child's experiments with saying "no," they can reinforce positive social interaction (e.g., hugging) and discourage negative behaviors (e.g., biting).

Toddlers (18–36 months) move through recurring phases of extreme dependence and independence as they gain new skills and awareness. They require an understanding caregiver who remains calm and supportive during their struggle to become independent. Adults must be resourceful in recognizing and encouraging self-reliant behavior while setting clear limits.

Examples For example, the competent Candidate working with infants and toddlers:

■ Knows a variety of techniques for positive guidance (e.g., listening, reinforcement, and redirection) and uses each appropriately.

■ Relates guidance practices to knowledge of each child's personality and level of development.

■ Avoids negative methods (e.g., spanking, threatening, shouting, isolating, or shaming children).

■ Establishes guidelines for children's behavior that are simple, reasonable, and consistent to encourage self-control.

■ Establishes routines that are consistent and reliable, yet flexible to children's needs.

■ Alerts children to changes in activities or routines well in advance and handles transitions from one activity to another with clear directions and patience.

■ Is able to modify play when it becomes overstimulating for any of the children, including children with handicapping conditions.

■ Builds a trusting relationship with children as a foundation for positive guidance and self-discipline.

■ Anticipates confrontations between children and defuses provocative behavior.

■ Addresses the problem behavior or situation rather than labeling the child involved.

■ Accepts children's sad or angry feelings, provides acceptable outlets for children to express them, and teaches words for feelings.

■ Helps parents develop realistic expectations for children's behavior in ways that help avoid disciplinary problems (e.g., discussing how long children can sit still).

■ Encourages parents to talk about childrearing, guidance, and self-discipline and refers them to classes, books, and other resources, as appropriate.

■ Knows parents' disciplinary methods and expectations and selects those appropriate for use in the center.

■ Recognizes that sometimes serious behavior problems are related to developmental or emotional problems and works cooperatively with parents towards solutions.

■ Is aware of each child's limitations and abilities, uses guidance techniques accordingly, and explains rules at child's level of understanding.

Young Infants The competent Candidate working with young infants also, for example:

■ Creates an environment of love and trust through warmth and responsive caring.

■ Guides infants gradually into regular sleeping and eating patterns while remaining responsive to individual needs.

■ Responds to infants' needs for comfort and protection.

Mobile Infants The competent Candidate working with mobile infants also, for example:

■ Provides children with a variety of positive options, focusing on what children can do.

■ Uses firm "no" only when necessary to maintain children's safety; moves the child or dangerous object, and gives a simple explanation.

■ Has realistic expectations about children's attention spans, interests, social abilities, and physical needs, including those of children with handicapping conditions.

■ Redirects children gently while explaining limits.

■ Gives children realistic choices and accepts the choices made; for example, "Do you want to read a book with me or play on the climber?" or "Shall we have the apples or bananas for snack today?"

Toddlers The competent Candidate working with toddlers also, for example:

■ Lets toddlers solve some of their own problems.

■ Limits inappropriate behavior in ways that show respect and support for the toddler's sense of dignity.

■ Avoids power struggles with toddlers who say "no" or refuse to cooperate, by using redirection, distraction, acceptance, or active listening.

■ Explains the reasons for limits in simple words, demonstrating whenever possible.

■ Uses firm and friendly techniques (e.g., reminding and persuading) when rules are forgotten or disobeyed.

■ Uses positive language with children, for example, "walk" rather than "don't run."

Bilingual Specialization In addition, the competent Candidate working towards a bilingual specialization, for example:

■ Uses the language in which each child understands expectations, limits, and guidance.

COMPETENCY GOAL IV

To establish positive and productive relationships with families

11. FUNCTIONAL AREA: FAMILIES

Candidate maintains an open, friendly, and cooperative relationship with each child's family, encourages their involvement in the program, and supports the child's relationship with his or her family.

Developmental Context Today's families take many different forms. Each family has primary responsibility for its own children, and parents may share this responsibility for their children with others. The parents and the caregiver become partners who communicate respectfully and openly for the mutual benefit of the children, the family, and the caregiver. Caregivers also recognize that parenthood, too, is a developmental process and that they can support parents in their role.

Young infants (birth–8 months) are establishing patterns of sleeping, waking, eating, playing, and social activity. They can be supported in developing some stability in these routines by the sensitive and consistent response of adults. Parents and caregivers can respond more appropriately to the infant's signals when they share details with each other about the baby's day—sleeping, eating, diapering, playing activities, and moods.

Mobile infants (9–17 months) may have difficulty separating from the parents even when the caregiver is a familiar and trusted person. Caregivers and parents need to discuss ways of handling this, recognizing that it may be upsetting both for the adults and the child. Caregivers should recognize the potential for competition between themselves and parents and work to avoid it. Caregivers and parents also need to agree on reasonable and safe limits as children begin to explore and wander.

Toddlers (18–36 months) develop their own special routines and rituals in order to feel more organized and secure. It is essential that parents and caregivers share common understanding of the child's patterns and provide constant, dependable support for the toddler's growth towards self-definition.

Examples For example, the competent Candidate working with infants and toddlers:

- Recognizes that children's primary caregivers may be single mothers or fathers, both parents, stepparents, grandparents, uncles, aunts, sisters, brothers, foster parents, or guardians.
- Helps parents understand the development of their child and understand the child's point of view.
- Provides opportunities for parents and other family members to share their skills and talents in the program.
- Recognizes that caregivers can support parents in their role.
- Offers parents information about health and social services and other resources in the community.
- Respects each family's cultural background, religious beliefs, and childrearing practices.
- Observes strict confidentiality regarding children and families and makes parents aware of this policy.
- Suggests activities and materials that parents can share with their children at home.

- Encourages parents to talk about important family events and their children's special interests and behavior at home and shares information frequently with parents about the child's experiences in the center.
- Is able to discuss problem behavior with parents in a constructive, supportive manner.
- Supports parents in making arrangements for school or an alternative child care program when necessary.
- Develops attachment towards children without competing with parents.
- Encourages parents to visit the center, participate in activities, and make suggestion for the daily program.
- Respects and tries to understand the parents' views when they differ from the program's goals or policies and attempts to resolve the differences.
- Tells parents about children's achievements and shares their pleasure in new abilities.
- Helps parents with separations from child, recognizing parents' possible concerns about leaving their child.
- Supports children and families under stress, working cooperatively with other professionals, as appropriate.
- Helps parents recognize their feelings and attitudes about handicapping conditions.
- Helps parents identify resources to diagnose and treat children with handicapping conditions.
- Helps parents obtain clear and understandable information about their children's special needs and information about the family's legal right to services.
- Encourages and assists parents to communicate confidently about their children with government and other community agencies.

Young Infants The competent Candidate working with young infants also, for example:

- Supports parents in becoming involved observers of their infant.
- Exchanges information regularly with parents about the child's life at home and in the center, including routines and changes in care, favorite activities, etc.
- Responds with interest and information to concerns of parents about sleep, waking, feeding, or particulars related to infant's needs and development.
- Shares parents' desire to understand meaning of baby's cries and to respond sensitively.
- Makes suggestions to parents about how to stimulate infants' vision, touch, and hearing at home.

Mobile Infants The competent Candidate working with mobile infants also, for example:

- Recognizes the recurring stress of separation for child and parents and attempts to ease it for them.
- Helps parents understand child's possible fear of strangers.
- Helps parents to provide safe home environment for mobile infant.
- Talks with parents of mobile infants about the beginning of independence and the child's use of the word "no."
- Decides with parents what limits to set.
- Suggests use of household items to provide a stimulating environment and to encourage the curiosity of mobile infants.

Toddlers The competent Candidate working with toddlers also, for example:

- Discusses child's rituals and routines with parents.
- Discusses with parents the reasons for toddlers' emotional outbursts and negative behaviors and possible ways of handling them.
- Explains the toddler's pride and interest in imitating adults and learning to use tools to make things.
- Sends home projects made by the children.
- Helps parents find ways to enjoy time with their toddlers and to help toddlers after time in group setting.
- Coordinates toilet learning plans with parents and frequently communicates on child's progress.
- Supports toddler's sense of belonging to his/her family.

Bilingual Specialization In addition, the competent Candidate working towards a bilingual specialization, for example:

- Regularly communicates, orally and in writing, with parents and children in their preferred language.
- Helps parents understand the program goals for bilingual development.
- Knows parents' views on such issues as the use of the home language within the program, childrearing, and biculturalism and incorporates their views into program planning.
- Regularly communicates with parents about child's bilingual development and helps them find ways to support this within the family.
- Supports families' desires to communicate their language and cultural heritage to their children through cultural practices.

COMPETENCY GOAL V

To ensure a well-run, purposeful program responsive to participant needs

12. FUNCTIONAL AREA: PROGRAM MANAGEMENT

Candidate is a manager who uses all available resources to ensure an effective program operation. The Candidate is a competent organizer, planner, recordkeeper, communicator, and a cooperative co-worker.

Developmental Context Running an effective program requires a systematic approach. A systematic approach means that the Candidate can determine the needs of her/his operation, families, and children; can make plans based on those needs; and can keep accurate records of needs, plans, and practices. Such a systematic approach should be applied to keeping records of attendance, fees, health status, and home visits. It should include specific plans for meeting the needs of children and their families and coordinating communication among involved adults through written information, meetings with parents and resources persons, and frequent informal discussion.

Examples For example, the competent Candidate working with infants and toddlers:

- Works with parents to identify the strengths and needs of each child.
- Develops skills in observing and recording information about children and their families in a nonjudgmental manner; uses the information in the planning and implementation of the daily program.

- Maintains up-to-date records concerning the growth, health, behavior, and progress of each child and the group, and shares the information with parents and appropriate center personnel.
- Considers goals and objectives for each child and for the group as a whole and develops realistic plans responsive to the needs of all, including children with handicapping conditions.
- Implements plans for each child by identifying developmentally and culturally appropriate activities and materials for each day.
- Has a clear understanding of her/his responsibilities within the program.
- Discusses issues that affect the program with appropriate staff and follows up on their resolution.
- Works as a member of a team with others in the classroom and the program, including substitutes, parents, and volunteers.
- Supports other staff by offering assistance and supervision when needed.
- Makes or obtains materials and equipment appropriate to the developmental needs of the children.
- Coordinates program plans (including guidance and discipline techniques) with parents, specialists, and program personnel, when appropriate.
- Knows the language resources of each family and uses these in the program.
- Works with appropriate staff to choose substitutes carefully, requiring experience with children of the same ages whenever possible.
- Orients new or substitute caregivers and volunteers to routines and special needs and abilities of each child.
- Implements procedures that help children make a smooth transition from one group to another.
- Knows the social service, health, and education resources of the community and uses them when appropriate.
- Recognizes possible developmental programs, works with parents and specialists to develop plans specific to the needs of each child, and implements recommended treatment by following up on referrals, and working with the family to meet goals for the child.
- Establishes liaison with community services that respond to family violence (e.g., Parents Anonymous, Child Protective Services, and local shelter programs).

Bilingual Specialization In addition, the competent Candidate working towards a bilingual specialization, for example:

- Uses knowledge of language development and bilingualism to plan for each child and group.
- Recognizes and helps others recognize the needs of children and families who speak a different language and operate in a different cultural context.
- Makes use of available evaluation instruments in the non-English language.
- Takes account of families' concerns about such issues as language usage and culturally different styles of relating.
- Works with appropriate staff in choosing substitutes who meet the language needs of the children and program whenever possible.

COMPETENCY GOAL VI

To maintain a commitment to professionalism

13. FUNCTIONAL AREA: PROFESSIONALISM

Candidate makes decisions based on knowledge of early childhood theories and practices; promotes quality in child care services; and takes advantage of opportunities to improve competence, both for personal and professional growth and for the benefit of children and families.

Developmental Context Professionals working with young children and their families make decisions based on knowledge of early childhood education and family life and demonstrate a commitment towards quality care for young children. The professional caregiver continues to set new goals and take advantage of training or educational experiences that will help her/him to grow more competent. Recognizing that the way they relate to one another directly affects the quality of child care and sets an example for children, adults in a child care setting work to resolve issues and problems among themselves cooperatively and respectfully. They also work together to educate the community at large about the needs of young children. The child care provider should develop relationships with other child care professionals and establish a network for information and support.

Examples For example, the competent Candidate working with infants and toddlers:

- Enjoys working with young children in a group setting and demonstrates a positive attitude in her/his role.
- Understands the philosophy of the program and can describe its goals and objectives to others.
- Continues to gain knowledge of physical, cognitive, language, emotional and social development as a basis for planning program goals.
- Keeps all personal information about children and families confidential.
- Continually evaluates own performance to identify needs for professional growth.
- Participates in peer evaluation and is able to accept comments and criticism from colleagues, supervisors, and parents in a constructive way.
- Takes advantage of opportunities for professional and personal development by joining appropriate professional organizations and attending meetings, training courses, and conferences.
- Keeps informed about child care practices, research, legislation, and other developments in early childhood education.
- Seeks information relevant to the needs of the children s/he is serving (e.g., information on infant development, bilingual development, children with handicapping conditions) from professional magazines, community colleges, community services, other caregivers, and community members.
- Recognizes that caregiver fatigue, low morale, and lack of work satisfaction decrease effectiveness, and finds ways to meet her/his own needs and maintain energy and enthusiasm.

- Works cooperatively with other staff members, accepts supervision, and helps promote a positive atmosphere in the center.
- Learns about new laws and regulations affecting center care, children, and families.
- Advocates quality services and rights for children and families.
- Keeps abreast of current regulatory legislative and workforce issues that affect young children and families.
- Works with other professionals and parents to develop effective strategies to communicate to decisionmakers the needs of children and families.
- Develops the ability to state needs for additional resources for individual children or some aspect of the program.
- Recognizes that special skills are necessary for working with children at different ages and developmental stages and seeks appropriate information and training.
- Is aware that some of the normal developmental characteristics of children (e.g., crying, messiness, dependency, willfulness, negative behavior, curiosity about genital differences, etc.) often make adults uncomfortable. The caregiver can acknowledge these feelings in her/himself, co-workers, and parents while minimizing negative reactions toward children.
- Seeks information about sexual abuse and child abuse and neglect, keeps up-to-date on laws and policies concerning reporting and treatment of abuse, and learns effective ways of working with affected children and families.

Bilingual Specialization In addition, the competent Candidate working towards a bilingual specialization, for example:

- Demonstrates ability to understand, speak, read, and write in both languages and uses these skills in all aspects of the program.
- Increases knowledge about bilingual education by reading, attending workshops, and consulting professionals.
- Maintains and works to increase fluency in her/ his second language.
- Consistently provides opportunities for all children to acquire a second language.
- Promotes the effective functioning of the bilingual program by attempting to clarify issues relating to bilingualism and multiculturalism.
- Advocates for children's and families' rights to use and develop their own language and culture.

The Celebration of Life Calendar

The celebration of Life Calendar can be used as a cornerstone for cultural diversity in your curriculum. Please feel free to copy it and fill in special days for children in care, share copies with parents, enlarge it on a copier and hang it on the wall, or use it as a basis for activities during the day.

Having each parent fill in their own cultural celebrations is a good way to get families involved because you can ask parents to come in on their celebration days or send in special activities so that all children in care experience various ethnic foods, activities, and customs. Also, if your group is homogeneous, you can use the special days listed at the bottom of each month to help children broaden their experiences of other cultures.

January

1, New Year's Day
7, Nandkusa Festival—Japan
15, Martin Luther King, Jr. National
     Holiday—United States

February

5, Constitution Day—Mexico
11, National Day—Iran
19, Independence Day—Estonia

March

3, Hinamatsuri—Japan
17, St. Patrick's Day—Ireland
22, New Year Day—India

Unscheduled, Purim—Israel
Unscheduled, Taiwan Al-Qudr—Muslim countries

April

Unscheduled, Good Friday—Christian countries
Easter—Christian countries
Festival of Redvan-Baha'i

May

1, National Holiday—Mexico
22, Slavery Abolition Day—French West Indies
25, Independence from Foreign Rule—Africa

June

2, Republic Day—Italy
6, Memorial Day—Korea
12, Independence Day—Philippines
18, Evacuation Day—Egypt

21, Festival of Lord Gagannath—India

July

4, Independence Day—United States
14, Bastille Day—France
17, World Indian Day—Eskimo
26, Independence Day—Liberia

Unscheduled, Tanabuta (Star Festival)—Japan

August

31, Independence Day—India
Unscheduled, Festival of Hungry Ghosts—China

September

3, Independence Day—Chile
8, United Nation's International
   Literacy Day—World
21, World Gratitude Day—World

29, Michaelmas—Greek Orthodox and Roman Catholic
   Celebration
Unscheduled, Rosh Hashanah—Israel

October

17, Black Poetry Day—United States
24, United Nations Day—World
Unscheduled, Grandparents' Day
   —United States

Unscheduled, White Sunday—Samoa
Unscheduled, National Book Day—United States
Unscheduled, United Nations Day for the
   Elderly—World

November

3, Sandwich Day—United States
15, Schichi-Go-San—Japan
17, National Young Readers Day
   —United States

21, World Hello Day—World
Unscheduled, World Community Day—World
Unscheduled, Thanksgiving Day—United States

December

6, Independence Day—Finland
13, Santa Lucia Day—Sweden
25, Christmas—Christian countries
31, New Year's Eve—World

Glossary

A

abstract —an idea not existing in the real world; the basis of a concept.

accommodation —Piaget's process of changing or altering skills to better fit the requirements of a task.

action sentence —in language development, action sentences separate the action from the actor and object and explore the relations among these three.

active listening —the skill required to simply "feed back" the deeper feeling message (not words) of the sender in the words of the receiver.

active-dry area —an area in the child care center suitable for activities such as large motor activities, construction, and housekeeping.

activity area —a designated space designed for a specific function and a specific age group of children. Size shape and utility of space may include apparatus and equipment necessary to promote the safety and enhance the maturation of children.

adaptation —a change in behavior that helps the child survive in his or her environment, described by Piaget as a cognitive skill.

affection —one of the 3A's; a feeling of warmth, acceptance, and respect.

ages and stages —a use of chronological age as it relates to functional behavior or a level of development clearly distinguishable from the previous level of development.

approval —one of the 3A's of child care; feedback that a person is accepted as he or she is.

arranging objects —the task of arranging objects in a series is guesswork for young children because they do not understand the relationships within a series of objects.

assimilation —Piaget's way of explaining how children refine cognitive structures into schemes.

association —information processing Level IV, wherein two stimuli are connected on the basis of repeated presentation together.

attachment theory —a theory that infants are born needing an emotional attachment to their primary caregiver.

attention —one of the 3A's of child care; focusing sensory modalities (e.g., visual, auditory) on a person or object.

attentional skills —focal attention, prefocal attention, and perceptual screening are perceptual skills necessary to focus visual and auditory attention on stimuli.

attitude ceiling —a belief that a person develops from environmental feedback that he or she is limited in what he or she can accomplish in any area of life, real or unreal.

attribution —children give objects a symbol with meaning.

auditory-visual association —the highest level and cross-modality perceptual skill essential for basic academic tasks, such as letter and word recognition.

avoidant attachment —one of the types of attachment between infants and primary caregiver that results in inconsistent and insensitive caregiver attention.

B

babbling —prelanguage speech wherein the baby explores diversification of sounds.

bad touch —a term used in transactional analysis for touching that does not respect the person's body or boundaries and is inappropriate, rough, or insensitive.

balanced learner —one who processes information equally well through both major sensory channels necessary for higher cognitive learning, that is, both visual and auditory channels.

baby signing —nonverbal language using gestures and expressions in infants.

behaviorism —school of psychology wherein stimuli, responses, and rewards that influence behavior are studied.

behavior shaping—use of observation and positive and negative rewards to elicit behaviors.

boundary—anything marking a limit, specifically, physical and emotional limits relating to safety and security in toddlers.

brain gym—sequences of body movements that appear to promote nerve networks, resulting in clearer processing of information and cognition.

brain plasticity—when one part of the brain is damaged, other parts take over the functions of the damaged parts.

C

calibrating—term used for careful observations of sets of behaviors to establish rapport.

cardiopulmonary resuscitation (CPR)—artificial external means of manually starting and maintaining a human heartbeat.

caregiver—a person who gives care to another; a person responsible for helping another meet his or her wants and needs.

care sheets—record forms for observations, activities, and routines during daily care.

catch the child being good—conscious attention to positive, appropriate behavior and withdrawing attention for unacceptable behavior.

cause and effect—in sensorimotor development, allows a child to identify the relationship between an action and its effect.

center-based care—child care provided away from home for more than six children for some part of the day or night.

certification—a form of regulation for professional child care; standards vary by state.

child-centered—the overall goal in the design of the child care center.

child-proof—to ensure a safe environment by removing potential hazards.

choke tube—plastic tube used to determine safe sizes of objects for child play.

classical conditioning—association of an unconditioned stimulus with a conditioned stimulus that evokes specific conditioned or unconditioned responses.

cognitive-developmental theory—Piaget's theory that children construct knowledge and awareness through manipulation and exploration of their environment.

cognitive disequilibrium—Piaget's term for children's cognitive reaction when placed in new and unfamiliar situations in which old schemes no longer work well.

cognitive equilibrium—Piaget's term for a cognitive state in which a child's schemes work to explain the child's environment.

cognitive functions—refers to one of two broad classes of functions to name, indicate, describe, and/or comment.

competent caregiver style—a style of caregiving that uses appropriate goals and objectives.

conceptualization or concept formation—higher cognitive skill wherein specific stimuli are associated with an abstract category name or symbol.

controlling caregiver style—a style of caregiving that tends to discount and negate children's feelings and communicate in an insensitive manner, which causes emotional pain.

cooing—the second stage of vocalization in infants from birth to four months old, which resembles vowel-like sounds.

cross-modality processing—it occurs when a stimulus in one channel (e.g., auditory) requires a response from a different sensory channel, such as visual.

culture—values and beliefs held in common by a group of people.

cultural diversity—cultural differences within a group.

curricula—planned goals, objectives, methods, and techniques to teach something to someone.

D

defense mechanisms—methods learned to avoid pain from life experiences.

deferred imitation—imitation of another person's behavior even when that person is no longer present.

demonstrative naming—in language development, a process in which the first word points out an object and the second names it (e.g. "this ball").

dependent care assistance program—a program that allows an employee to set aside up to $5000 in pre-tax dollars for child care.

detached caregiver style—a style that often is not cognitively or emotionally involved enough with children to be aware of their feelings, in that the children tend to become detached or angry with other people.

detachment—a condition that occurs when the nervous system defends against pain by causing the individual to numb awareness of the pain in body and mind and/or in the environment.

development—operationally defined as general sequences and patterns of growth and maturity.

developmental care—program emphasis, in both home-based care and child care centers, on the developmental needs of children.

developmental learning skills—perceptual skills necessary to accurately input, store, and output information, including attention, memory, discrimination, and association.

discipline—behavior-limiting steps to reduce harmful behaviors.

discrimination —information processing skill wherein differences between two stimuli in the same sensory modality, such as visual and auditory, are perceived.

disoriented attachment —a form of attachment between infant and primary caregiver in which the infant has usually been traumatized by severe or prolonged abandonment.

double substitution —pretend play in which two materials are transformed, within a single act, into something they are not in reality.

dramatic play —a form of play that provides opportunities to combine language with imagination.

drop spots —angles, pipes, ledges, and rough surfaces on which children could be injured.

E

early childhood educator —a professional who has been trained to educate young children.

eating —pediatricians recommend introducing solid foods at approximately six months of age.

ecological systems theory —Bronfenbrenner's theory of psycho-social structures that influence the development and behavior of people.

ego —Freud's term for the self, self-concept, and self-esteem.

egocentric —toddlers see the world from their own point of view; in the first year and a half of life their bodies and the objects they play with are perceived to be part of "self."

ego boundaries —the awareness of separateness of oneself from the environment, including other people, places, and things.

elimination —the process of excreting urine and feces from the body. Two important caregiver responsibilities are changing diapers frequently and recording the time of and any abnormalities of bowel movements.

emotional development —the ability in infants to express pleasure, happiness, fear, and frustration.

emotional intelligence —five "domains" learned early in life that are necessary for healthy ego development, good relationships, and fulfillment in life experiences.

empathy —sensitivity to what others feel, need, or want; it is the fundamental relationship skill present at birth.

enactive naming —an approximate pretense activity that does not confirm evidence of actual pretense behavior.

enlightened self-interest —balanced awareness of one's own needs and feelings and the needs and feelings of other people; the philosophical basis of democracy.

equilibrium —a state of homeostasis or balance.

ethnology —the study of behavior patterns that promote survival of the species.

evolutionary theory —the theory that child development is genetically determined and happens automatically.

existential self —William James' term for the sense of self that exists separate from the environment or other people; the "authentic" self.

exosystem —bronfenbrenner's term for the influences that are not a direct part of a child's experience but influence development, such as parent education.

experience-expectant —a term describing preprogrammed activity of the species.

experience-dependent —a term describing neuron pathways that require new experience to activate new pathways and form stable motor patterns after environmental stimuli are repeated several times.

F

faciliate —to help with an activity that someone cannot do by his- or herself at the time.

family-based care —child care provided outside the child's residence.

fear —physical and psychological reaction to threat.

fine motor control —a developmental learning skill in which small muscle control is learned.

flow —a term used for highly productive activity in which thought, feeling, and behavior are extremely competent and appear almost effortless.

focal attention —perceptual process by which individual stimuli are separated from all surrounding stimuli and are consciously processed in awareness.

focusing and tracking —moving both eyes together in fluid pattern; develops through the first three years of life.

functional-relational —bringing together and integrating the use of an object in an appropriate manner with its intended purpose.

G

genital stage —Freud's psychosexual stage occurring in early adolescence when children become consciously aware of their sexuality.

good touch —transactional analysis term for respectful, sensitive, and pleasurable touch.

gratification —satisfaction of a need.

gross motor control —a developmental learning skill in which large muscle activity and control is integrated.

group family child care —child care provided for 6 to 12 children.

guide —to direct toward a desirable goal.

H

Head Start programs—state-subsidized child care programs for low-income families.

healthy caregiver style—a style of caregiving that balances the feelings and needs of the child with those of the caregiver, resulting in a "win-win" rather than a "win-lose" relationship.

hearing—physical and neurological process of bringing sound into the nervous system.

hierarchy of needs—in which lower needs are satisfied before higher needs

high active—infant temperament type in which infant may kick, wriggle, and jerk, requiring the caregiver to provide more assistance while the infant learns to sit up.

holistic care—a type of care that considers the whole child, including physical, emotional, social, language skills, and cognitive development.

home visit—a meeting in the child's home providing an opportunity for the professional caregiver to see how the parent and child relate to each other in the home setting.

home visitor—a person who performs an assessment and certification procedure offered by the CDA council.

human energy field—the psychological, spiritual, and life energy that is thought to surround human beings.

Human Immunodeficiency Virus (HIV) infection—disease that is transmitted through open sores or other blood sources.

I

I statements—expressions of thoughts and feelings.

I voice—a major personality part that represents the ego or self in inner dialogue.

I-self—awareness of being separate from other people and objects; the basis for establishing ego boundaries.

imprinting—term from ethnology to explain early critical period for imitating and attaching to a "mother figure."

imitation—to mimic or copy; in development, a normal stage of play.

in-home care—child care that takes place in the child's home.

inductive discipline—an approach that involves pointing out the direct outcomes of misbehavior for the child and other people.

infant—a child from birth to 18 months of age.

information processing theory—theory of perception and cognition from learning research and computer technology that explains how information is input, associated, memorized, and output.

input—information processing term to explain the process of moving stimuli from the environment into the higher cortical areas of the brain.

instrumental function—in language development for 18- to 24-month-olds, the second of two broad classes of function, meaning to request, reject, manipulate, and comment.

interactive influences—influences in which the child directly interacts.

interactional synchrony—a sensitively tuned "emotional dance," in which interactions are mutually rewarding to caregiver and infant.

intersubjectivity—Vygotsky's term to explain how children and adults come to understand each other by adjusting perceptions to fit the other person's map of the world.

L

labeling—providing visual labels for association and language development.

language—visual and auditory symbols representing objects and ideas.

language development—during 8 to 12 months of age, an infant's use of combinations of sounds, babbling, and words to converse with self and others.

latency stage—Freud's psychosexual stage occurring between 6 and 11 years of age when social values and contacts outside the home become important.

learning—processing information in such a way that internal and external behavior is changed and a new response is elicited.

learning center—an environment that is organized to promote and encourage learning.

levels of processing—a concept drawn from information processing theory that explains how retention occurs.

licensing—granting of official documentatioon of standards met by an individual or organization.

locomotion—in infants ages four to seven months, the attempt to gain stability when moving forward against the force of gravity.

locus of control—the extent to which a person perceives his or her life as within his or her own control.

long-term memory—skill in recalling stimuli presented more than 24 hours in the past.

low active—infant temperament style of little movement; caregivers may leave the baby in one position longer than infants who are high active.

M

macrosystem—bronfenbrenner's term for influences on development from the general culture, including laws and customs.

make-believe play —Vygotsky's term for using imagination to act out internal concepts of how the world functions and how rules are formed.

manipulation —includes reaching, grasping, and releasing objects; in the first year of development the control of objects moves from reflexive to voluntary.

maturation —naturally unfolding course of growth and development.

me-self —the self as an object; the self observes its own thoughts, feelings, behaviors, and qualities.

memory —the process of storing and recalling stimuli at a later time.

mental images —pictures in the mind with which children can carry out action sequences internally.

mesosystem —bronfenbrenner's term for the second level of influence for the child, such as child care and school.

meta-cognition —awareness of one's own thought processes.

microsystem —Bronfenbrenner's term for the innermost level of influence found in the immediate surrounding of the child, such as parents and child development specialists.

milestones —specific behaviors common to an entire population that are used to track development and are observed when they are first or consistently manifested.

mirroring —a technique used in communication of repeating exactly what is said without adding or interpreting any of the speaker's words.

mobile infant —child between 9 and 17 months of age.

modeling —in development, one way a child learns how to act like an adult.

motivate —to stimulate someone to action.

movements —in newborns from birth to four months, movements are reflexive; they occur without the infant's control.

muscular control —physical development in infants from birth to four months.

N

naming —presentation of auditory names to teach association and concept formation.

National Association for Family Day Care (NAFDC) —an association offering professional recognition and distinction to family child care providers whose services represent high-quality child care.

National Parenting Scales (NPS) —assesses essential parenting skills based on CDA competencies.

natural selection —darwin's concept to explain how species adapt to survive over time.

needs hierarchy —Maslow's theory of motivation predicts that needs at one level of a hierarchy must be filled before needs at the next higher level are attended to.

negation —ignoring; acting in such a way as not pay attention to the importance of what a person says or their authority.

negative attention society —a term describing the social reinforcement structure of ignoring positive, appropriate behavior and punishing inappropriate behavior.

negative reinforcers —consequences for a behavior that have the effect of decreasing the frequency or duration of the behavior.

neuro-linguistic programming (NLP) —psychological approach to understanding another's map of the world, including perceptions, beliefs, feelings, behaviors, and thoughts.

noble savage —Rousseau's term for a young child, who is born without a moral sense of right and wrong.

nonverbal signal —any feedback given visually without the use of auditory stimuli.

normative approach —observing large numbers of children to establish average or normal expectations.

O

object permanence —starting at 8 to 12 months, infants remember events, people, and objects for increasingly longer periods.

observational learning —in child development, one of the major ways in which children learn is to observe the behaviors of others.

observing ego —describes skills in observing ones thoughts, feelings, and behaviors.

omnipotent —the sense of being unaware of any physical limitations and feeling above physical laws.

operant conditioning theory —a theory about the process of increasing or decreasing the frequency or duration of behaviors through association with positive and negative reinforcing stimuli.

oral stage —Freud's first stage, wherein the child is preoccupied with oral gratification, birth to 30 months.

ORAOM —acronym for Observe, Record, Assess, Organize, and Manage child care.

organization —a process of rearranging new sets of information (schemes) and linking them to other established schemes to reform a cognitive system.

output —information processing term for the process of getting information from the higher cortical areas to expression in the world through verbal or motor responses.

P

pacing —matching complementary behavior to another person to build rapport.

parent-caregiver conferences —periodic meetings between parents and caregiver to review documentation and interpretation of each child's developmental progress.

parenting styles —the caregiving style of a child's parents.

passive influences —influences that affect a person without the necessity of interaction, such as television.

passive influences —influences that affect a person without the necessity of interaction, such as television.

perceptual level — information is taken in through the five senses and integrated. Feedback is established and monitored to rate how competently the brain functions. This is referred to as a sensory level.

phallic stage —Freud's stage between 3 and 6 years of age in which the child wants to win the mother, Oedipal (boys) or father, Electra (girls) away from the parent of the same sex.

phonemic features —sounds usually associated with letter symbols.

physical development —when infants ages 8 to 12 months rapidly learn to crawl, stand with support, and walk with help.

positive reinforcer —consequences for behavior that have the effect of increasing the frequency or duration of the behavior.

positive perspective —caregiver tool in which child is talked about to third person in positive terms while child is present.

possession —children make special associations between a person and an object, often using a two-word sentence; e.g., "mommy chair" to indicate possession.

prana —a name given by the ancient people of India that represents the life force (energy).

preconceptual —the first substage of Piaget's preoperational stage of cognitive development in which children can mentally sort some objects and actions.

prescriptive level —the highest behavior in a task analysis that a child can successfully perform to begin instruction.

pretend other —a child's make-believe other person or object.

pretend self —pretend play directed toward self in which pretense is apparent.

private speech —Vygotsky's term for internal dialogue that children use for self-guidance and understanding.

psychoanalytic theory —Freud's theory of personality development, including psychosexual stages.

psychosocial theory —Erikson's stage theory of development, including trust, autonomy, identity, and intimacy.

psychosexual stages —crucial experiences in Freud's theory that form the foundation for personality development.

Q

quiet-dry area —a place where activities such as games, library, and listening can take place.

quiet zone —a place to which a child can go to get away from the group.

R

recurrence —the repetition of an activity.

reflective self —William James' term for the self that discriminates itself from others and the environment and is defined by being different from the "other."

registration —in most states, this is a simple process of listing the family child care home with a licensing authority.

representational system —Neuro-Linguistic Programming term for any system a person uses to represent his or her unique map of the world.

relational —bringing together and associating two or more materials in a manner that may not initially be intended by the manufacturer.

resistant attachment —a form of connection between infant and primary caregiver in which the infant resists emotionally and physically connecting with the caregiver.

reward —anything that is used to increase the frequency or duration of a behavior.

ruing —caregiver tool in which the child's voice and tones are calibrated and paced by caregiver.

S

same-modality processing —a processing form in which tasks presenting visual input require visual-motor output and tasks presenting auditory input require verbal output responses.

scaffolding —a term describing incremental steps in learning and development from simple to complex.

schemes —Piaget's concept to explain cognitive patterns of actions used to learn new information.

scribbling —nonsense writing marks.

search for hidden objects —the object remains permanent (does not cease to exist) in the child's thinking even when the child cannot see it.

secure attachment —a connection between infant and primary caregiver in which the infant feels safe and responds warmly to the caregiver.

self-awareness —sensory grounded information regarding one's existence; what a person sees, hears, and feels in the body related to self.

self-attending —an exercise to help organize the inner self.

self-esteem —respect for one's own abilities.

self-health —focus on the physical, social, emotional, cognitive, and learning skill factors within oneself; taking good care of oneself.

self-recognition —conscious awareness of self as different from others and the environment; occurs first usually between 9 and 15 months of age.

self-responsibility —taking over responsibility for fulfilling some of one's own needs.

self-soothing —comforting and making oneself at ease.

self-talk —dialogues between the I voice and the You voice; verbalizations to self.

selfless caregiver style —a style in which the caregiver makes the child's feelings important to the exclusion of the caregiver's own, which often results in children becoming self-absorbed, guilt ridden, and insensitive to the feelings of other people.

semantic features —language features, including concepts.

sense of agency —in development of self, the awareness that the child can affect other people, places, and things.

sensorimotor substage —Piaget's first stage of cognitive development, which is focused on motor activity and coordination of movements.

sensory grounded information —awareness of experience through sensory stimuli: visual, auditory, tactile, smell, and taste.

sensory input —stimuli (information) processed through the 5 senses to the high brain.

sensory modalities —information processing term to explain the sensory structures of visual, auditory, and motor channels used to input, store, and output information.

sensory register —reaction (experience) to sensory input.

separation anxiety —fear exhibited at the loss of physical or emotional connection with the primary caregiver.

separation and individuation —the process of defining self as separate from others, which starts in infancy and continues throughout childhood.

sequence pretend —the repetition of a single pretense act with minor variation or linking together different pretense schemes.

sequence pretend substitution —the same as sequence pretend except using an object substitution within sequence.

shepherding —a caregiver tool with which a child is "guided" in a safe and respectful way.

short-term memory —storage and recall within a short amount of time, usually less than 24 hours.

simple manipulation —visually guided manipulation excluding indiscriminate banging and shaking.

sleep —most newborns sleep between 11 and 21 hours a day. Infant sleep is not a continuous activity.

smell —perception of odor (newborns can distinguish odors and respond positively or negatively).

social learning theory —a theory that added social influences to behaviorism to explain development.

sociocultural theory —Vygotsky's theory on development, which predicts how cultural values, beliefs, and concepts are passed from one generation to the next.

solitary play —playing alone; a child may look at other children and play near them, but children do not yet interact.

stability —within the first month, infants can lift their heads, by the third month they are using their arms to push against the floor to raise their heads and chests.

stages —normal patterns of development that most people go through in maturation, first described by Jean-Jacques Rousseau.

stimuli —initial energy behind a need that creates an action.

substitution —using a "meaningless" object in a creative or imaginative manner or using an object in a pretense act in a way that differs from how the child has previously used the object.

sudden infant death syndrome (SIDS) —a tragic event in which a young child dies after going to sleep for a nap or at bedtime with no indication of discomfort.

super ego —freud's term for the conscience, value system of right and wrong, or "You voice" which was thought to be taught to children by adults.

survival of the fittest —Darwin's theory that only the best-adapted members of a species are able to continue to thrive.

symbolic play —children's symbolic representations of objects, feelings, or ideas.

systematic relaxation —a technique of managing one's own emotions; includes yoga-type breathing to break states of anger or anxiety.

T

tabula rasa —Locke's term, meaning blank slate, which implied that infants are a "blank screen" at birth and are completely molded by the influences of the environment.

task analysis —analysis of a behavioral goal in which movements are broken down into a step-by-step format and each small step leading to mastering a complex task is taught in sequence.

taste —newborns can distinguish between sweet, salty, and bitter solutions.

teaching —a process of active instruction that provides information to others.

teething —begins in infants from approximately four to eight months old and refers to teeth breaking through the gums.

temper tantrums —angry emotional outburst and frustrated behavior when the toddler suddenly wants to do things he or she can no longer do and does not want to do things he or she can do.

temperament —physical, emotional, and social personality traits and characteristics.

temperament traits —personality and behavioral qualities thought to be inherently present at birth and which can be influenced by environment.

terrible twos —the age from 24 to 30 months, when children become more demanding and more possessive of their things and say no to almost everything.

time-in —keeping children involved in an enjoyable activity that is developmentally appropriate; filling the energy and need for activity positively.

time-out —a behavior-limiting step in which a child is excluded from normal activity until he or she can behave appropriately.

time-sample —a type of observation in which goal behaviors are observed during specific times in a normal routine.

toddler —a child between 10 and 36 months of age.

touch —a baby's most valuable tool for learning to identify textures (e.g., softness, roughness) through tactile and kinesthetic awareness.

tracking —visually following a moving object with both eyes.

U

Universal Energy Source —an ancient belief in a life force that every living thing possesses.

universal precautions —medical term for a series of standard procedures used to keep the patient and staff as healthy and safe as possible during physical care.

V

visual perception —the process of inputting, storing, recalling and reproducing visual stimuli.

W

walking —a child's movements for walking are executed with support from an adult or furniture; walking starts in the latter part of infancy.

wet-active area —a place for activities involving painting, water, sand, science, and so on.

wet-quiet area —a place for activities such as cooking, eating, and pasting.

Y

you statements —giving advice or judgment to another person.

you voice —the conscience, super ego, and value system formed within the first three years.

young infant —a child between birth and eight months of age.

Z

zone of proximal development —Vygotsky's term for a range of tasks that a child is developmentally ready to learn.

Index